Privacy, Security and Information Management:
an Overview

Andrew B. Serwin *with*
Peter F. McLaughlin and John P. Tomaszewski

AMERICAN BAR ASSOCIATION
Business Law Section

Cover design by ABA Publishing.

Page layout by Quadrum Solutions.

Printed in the United States of America.

15 14 13 12 11   5 4 3 2 1

Library of Congress Cataloging-in-Publication Data

Serwin, Andrew B.

   Privacy, security and information management : an overview / by Andrew B. Serwin with Peter F. McLaughlin and John P. Tomaszewski.

     p. cm.

   ISBN 978-1-61632-977-8 (alk. paper)

   1. Computer security—Law and legislation—United States. 2. Data protection—Law and legislation—United States. 3. Privacy, Right of—United States. I. McLaughlin, Peter F. II. Tomaszewski, John. III. Title.

   KF1263.C65S47 2011

   342.7308'58--dc23

                       2011024607

Table of Contents

Preface

This book is the culmination of a significant effort by the authors to distill a broad and complex set of legal concepts into a book that provides an overview of an emerging area of the law. It does not purport to offer guidance on every law that exists on a particular topic, but rather to provide key insights and outlines of thought from some of the leading practitioners in the space. For a more detailed treatment of privacy, *Information Security & Privacy: A Guide to Federal and State Law and Compliance*, by Andrew Serwin, is available from Thomson-Reuters.

The statements of opinion in this book do not necessarily represent those of Foley & Lardner LLP, TRUSTe, or the companies mentioned in this book, and may not be consistent with the authors' personally espoused views or beliefs.

Acknowledgements

Writing acknowledgments is always the hardest part of any book for me, as it requires some reflection on the process, your co-authors, maybe even as in this case, a co-author that got away. Perhaps it is the hardest part because it is the final piece of a completed book and the sheer weight of the process finally wears you down.

I always start acknowledgments by thanking my family for tolerating all of the work that goes into a book, but in this case I really want to thank my co-authors—Peter McLaughlin, who I am also lucky enough to call a colleague, and John Tomaszewski, for their work on this book. It would not have happened without them, and I would do another book with them any time, though I am not sure the feeling is mutual.

Moving from colleagues, to former colleagues, I have to thank TGS once again for bringing me to his playground, and then departing with extreme prejudice. Maybe he ran out of rhymes, maybe he ran out of luck, or maybe he just decided to "choose wisely," but the new playgrounds didn't quite have the same luster as the old one apparently. That said, TGS knows how to enter, and more importantly exit, in a way that gets everyone's attention.

Other former colleagues didn't have the same rhyming skills but managed to make their transitions a bit less prejudicial. To Will—I miss having you here, but am really happy you ended up where you did. They are lucky to have you. Our favorite animal rights activist—I hope the pigeons were issued body armor in your new haunt. I will have to join you, The Show, and the Master of Horse for a night that ends with your hoodie pulled over your head.

This acknowledgment would not be complete without thanking Susana Darwin and the ABA Business Law Section Publications Board. I had the honor of serving on that Board, and was pleased that they chose to support this project. Due to reasons on the author side of the divide, this book wasn't a model for publication process, and I really want to thank Susana and the Board for sticking with it and getting this book out.

Finally, an acknowledgment wouldn't be complete without a shout out to my favorite former privacy lawyer, who should have been a co-author on this book. I will simply say, "Based on the findings of the report, my conclusion was that this idea was not a practical deterrent for reasons which at this moment must be all too obvious."

Andrew B. Serwin
May 2011

CHAPTER 1.

Introduction

1:1.   The rise of information security and privacy

Information security and privacy issues are not new, but mass attention and compliance efforts are at an all time high, and appear only to be increasing, particularly as litigation and high-profile security breaches continue to draw attention to these issues. That privacy and information security concerns have been a societal problem for a long time is demonstrated by the fact that many wiretapping laws are called "eavesdropping" laws, referring to people standing in the so-called eavesdrop of a house listening to conversations before telephones were invented.

Current hot issues in information security and privacy include the following:

- pretexting;
- financial privacy;
- privacy litigation;
- outsourcing to foreign countries;
- electronic health records and personal health records; and
- social networking.

Issues that have arrived, but without complete impact on the privacy landscape, include interoperability of medical records, non-HIPAA covered medical information, genetic privacy, and increased concerns over computer crimes and control of one's identity. Just a few years ago, there were a limited number of privacy and security laws in the United States, and they generally applied only to companies in certain industries (such as health care and financial institutions). Now, the number of laws is staggering. Many new laws apply, or will apply, to companies in *all* industries, not just certain industries. Moreover, though there is no federal law that generally requires information security, certain Federal Trade Commission ("FTC") actions indicate that the FTC is imposing a generalized duty to impose information security via the Federal Trade Commission Act. As this trend continues, many companies may face a situation where data security issues must be directly and quickly addressed, or they will incur extensive FTC-mandated administrative costs and burdens.

Compliance with these laws is not only a legal reality, but it is also a business reality, as frequent and well-publicized data security incidents demonstrate. These days the newspapers are full of stories about high-profile data security incidents that usually involve numerous consumers. This, in large part, results from the 46 states, plus Puerto Rico, New York City, and Washington D.C., that have enacted laws that require notice of security breach incidents. These laws have increased the publicity that is received when these incidents occur, heightening consumer awareness of the incidents. Security breach is now a concern under HIPAA due to the recent changes to HIPAA that should be finalized in 2011, and now many foreign countries are beginning to enact security breach laws as well.

Notice of security breach laws is just one of the categories of laws that are being enacted. Identity theft is also an area of great legislative concern. Numerous states have enacted privacy and security laws that cover a variety of information categories, including the following:

- internet privacy restrictions;
- financial privacy;
- unauthorized access to networks and information;
- wiretapping and privacy in electronic communications;
- identity theft;
- data security and data destruction;
- notice of data security breaches;
- spyware and phishing;
- restrictions upon the use of Social Security numbers;
- video and cable privacy;
- genetic privacy;
- pretexting;
- telecom privacy; and
- restrictions upon government entities.

As this book will demonstrate, these general categories represent just the tip of the regulatory and administrative iceberg. Within these and other categories, there are an extensive number of laws and regulations and myriad issues a company must consider if it intends to comply with these requirements. Moreover, there are laws, including laws regarding wiretapping, that are becoming more important as electronic communication becomes the preferred mechanism for business communication. Also, contrary to popular belief, many of these privacy and security laws apply to all companies, not just companies in the health or financial industries or those that collect data regarding children.

Now, with more and more companies exploring international markets, the laws of the European Union ("EU") and other countries are becoming more relevant. These laws differ in many ways from the laws in the United States and compliance with one standard, even the generally higher EU standard, will not guarantee U.S. compliance. Moreover, other nations, including Japan and Argentina, have also enacted broad privacy laws. The laws of these jurisdictions are the subject of *Information Security and Privacy: A Guide to International Law and Compliance* (West 2010).

The cost of failing to comply with these requirements is high. In addition to the regulatory fines and penalties, companies face litigation costs defending suits by individuals, as well as, in some cases, class action suits alleging violations of these laws. The direct costs of remedying non-compliance after an incident can be staggering—some companies have disclosed costs that reach into the millions of dollars. And these costs do not include the potential loss of business that can result from consumer trepidation created by a company permitting the wrongful acquisition of a consumer's data.

1:2.   General privacy principles

Laws that regulate privacy and security typically involve restrictions on the collection of data (usually information that identifies a person, particularly if coupled with other sensitive information), the transfer or dissemination of information, and the security of the information, as well as the accuracy of the information that is collected and stored. As the discussion below demonstrates, certain organizations have expressed these principles in different ways, but all of these laws involve the application of these principles.

1:3.   Organisation for Economic Co-operation and Development Guidelines: a beginning

The Organisation for Economic Co-operation and Development ("OECD") is a group of 34 member countries, including the United States, that wish to foster democratic government and the market economy.[1] The OECD was one of the first organizations to recognize the issues that privacy could create in a global economy and to generate what was, in essence, a model for member countries to follow regarding privacy practices. This occurred on September 23, 1980, when the OECD Guidelines on the Protection of Privacy and Transborder Flows of Personal Data ("OECD Guidelines" or "Guidelines") were adopted.[2] If there is one document that serves as the basis of the privacy laws that are in existence today, particularly the EU Data Protection Directive, it is the OECD

---

1.   See, generally, http://www.oecd.org/document/58/0,2340,en_2649_201185_1889402_1_1_1_1,00.html (last visited February 4, 2011).

2.   Guidelines Governing the Protection of Privacy and Transborder Flows of Personal Data http://www.oecd. org/document/18/0,3343,en_2649_34255_1815186_1_1_1_1,00.html (last visited February 4, 2011).

Guidelines. While these guidelines are not binding, even on the member countries, they are useful in providing a framework for later privacy legislation.

The OECD Guidelines contain the following principles:

- collection limitation principle;
- data quality principle;
- purpose specification principle;
- security safeguards principle;
- openness principle;
- individual participation principle;
- accountability principle; and
- international application principle.

1:4.   Scope of OECD Guidelines

The Guidelines apply to personal data, in both the public and private sectors, which, because of the manner in which it is processed or because of the nature or the context in which it is used, poses a danger to privacy and individual liberties.[3] The Guidelines do not prevent the application of different protective measures to different categories of personal data depending upon the nature and the context in which the data was collected, stored, processed, or disseminated; the exclusion from the application of the Guidelines of personal data that obviously does not contain any risk to privacy and individual liberties; or the application of the Guidelines only to automatic processing of personal data.[4]

Exceptions to the Guidelines, set forth in Sections 2 and 3 of the Guidelines, including those that are related to national sovereignty, national security, and public policy, are intended to be as few as possible and made known to the public.[5] Ultimately, these Guidelines are considered minimum standards, which are supplemented by additional measures for the protection of privacy and individual liberties.[6]

1:5.   Collection limitation principle

The OECD Guidelines call for limits to the collection of personal data and requires that any such data should be obtained by lawful and fair means and, where appropriate, with the knowledge or consent of the data subject.[7]

---

3.   Guidelines Governing the Protection of Privacy and Transborder Flows of Personal Data, Part 1, Section 2.

4.   Guidelines Governing the Protection of Privacy and Transborder Flows of Personal Data, Part 1, Section (3) (a) to (c).

5.   Guidelines Governing the Protection of Privacy and Transborder Flows of Personal Data, Part 1, Section 4(a) to (b).

6.   Guidelines Governing the Protection of Privacy and Transborder Flows of Personal Data, Part 1, Section 6.

7.   Guidelines Governing the Protection of Privacy and Transborder Flows of Personal Data, Part 2, Section 7.

1:6. Data quality principle

Personal data should also be relevant to the purposes for which it is to be used, and to the extent necessary for those purposes, should be accurate, complete and up-to-date.[8]

1:7. Purpose specification principle

The purpose for which personal data is collected should be specified not later than at the time of data collection. Subsequent use should be limited to the fulfillment of these purposes or others that are not incompatible with these purposes. New purposes must be specified on each occasion of change of purpose.[9] Personal data should not be disclosed, made available, or otherwise used for purposes other than those specified in accordance with this requirement except with the consent of the data subject, or by the authority of law.[10]

1:8. Security safeguards principle

Personal data should be protected by reasonable security safeguards against risks such as loss or unauthorized access, destruction, use, modification, or disclosure of data.[11]

1:9. Openness principle

The Guidelines suggest that there should be a general policy of openness about developments, practices, and policies with respect to personal data. Readily available means should exist to establish the existence and nature of personal data and the main purposes of its use, as well as the identity and usual residence of the data controller.[12]

1:10. Individual participation principle

The Guidelines suggest that individuals should have the right to obtain from a data controller, or otherwise, confirmation of whether or not the data controller has data relating to the individual; to have communicated to him data relating to him within a reasonable time, at a charge, if any, that is not excessive, in a reasonable manner, and in a form that is readily intelligible to him; to be given reasons if a request is denied,

---

8. Guidelines Governing the Protection of Privacy and Transborder Flows of Personal Data, Part 2, Section 8.

9. Guidelines Governing the Protection of Privacy and Transborder Flows of Personal Data, Part 2, Section 9.

10. Guidelines Governing the Protection of Privacy and Transborder Flows of Personal Data, Part 2, Section 10(a) to (b).

11. Guidelines Governing the Protection of Privacy and Transborder Flows of Personal Data, Part 2, Section 11.

12. "Data controller" means a party who, according to domestic law, is competent to decide about the contents and use of personal data regardless of whether or not such data are collected, stored, processed or disseminated by that party or by an agent on its behalf. Guidelines Governing the Protection of Privacy and Transborder Flows of Personal Data, Part 1, Section 1(a).

and to be able to challenge a denial; and to challenge data relating to him and, if the challenge is successful, to have the data erased, rectified, completed, or amended.[13]

1:11. Accountability principle

A data controller should be accountable for complying with measures that give effect to these principles.[14]

1:12. International application: free flow and legitimate restrictions

The Guidelines encourage member countries to consider the implications for other member countries of domestic processing and re-export of personal data.[15] Member countries are also encouraged to take all reasonable and appropriate steps to ensure that transborder flows of personal data,[16] including transit through a member country, are uninterrupted and secure.[17] Member countries are cautioned to refrain from restricting transborder flows of personal data between themselves and other member countries except where another country does not substantially observe these Guidelines or where the re-export of such data would circumvent a country's domestic privacy legislation.[18] A member country may also impose restrictions regarding certain categories of personal data for which its domestic privacy legislation includes specific regulations in view of the nature of the data and for which the other member country provides no equivalent protection.[19]

Member countries are also encouraged to avoid developing laws, policies, and practices in the name of the protection of privacy and individual liberties that would create obstacles to transborder flows of personal data that would exceed requirements for these protections.[20]

1:13. National implementation

In implementing the principles set forth above, member countries are encouraged to establish legal, administrative or other procedures or institutions for the protection of

---

13. Guidelines Governing the Protection of Privacy and Transborder Flows of Personal Data, Part 2, Section 13(a) to (d).
14. Guidelines Governing the Protection of Privacy and Transborder Flows of Personal Data, Part 2, Section 14.
15. Guidelines Governing the Protection of Privacy and Transborder Flows of Persona Data, Part 3, Section 15.
16. "Transborder flows of personal data" means movements of personal data across national borders. Guidelines Governing the Protection of Privacy and Transborder Flows of Personal Data, Part 1, Section 1(c).
17. Guidelines Governing the Protection of Privacy and Transborder Flows of Personal Data, Part 3, Section 16.
18. Guidelines Governing the Protection of Privacy and Transborder Flows of Personal Data, Part 3, Section 17.
19. *Id.*
20. Guidelines Governing the Protection of Privacy and Transborder Flows of Personal Data, Part 3, Section 18.

privacy and individual liberties in respect of personal data.[21] Member countries are particularly encouraged to adopt appropriate domestic legislation; to encourage and support self-regulation, whether in the form of codes of conduct or otherwise; to provide for reasonable means for individuals to exercise their rights; to provide for adequate sanctions and remedies in case of failure to comply with measures that implement these principles; and to ensure that there is no unfair discrimination against data subjects.[22]

1:14.   International cooperation

Member countries are also encouraged, where requested, to make known to other Member countries details of the observance of the principles set forth in these Guidelines.[23] Member countries should also ensure that procedures for transborder flows of personal data and for the protection of privacy and individual liberties are simple and compatible with those of other member countries which comply with these Guidelines.[24] Member countries are also encouraged to establish procedures to facilitate information exchange related to these Guidelines and mutual assistance in the procedural and investigative matters involved.[25]

Member countries are also encouraged to work toward the development of principles, domestic and international, to govern the applicable law in the case of transborder flows of personal data.[26]

1:15.   Principles adopted by the Asia-Pacific Economic Cooperation

The Asia-Pacific Economic Cooperation ("APEC") is an organization similar to the OECD, but for the Pacific Rim.[27] It too has adopted privacy principles that are supposed to serve as the basis for legislation for member countries: the APEC Privacy Framework 2004 ("Framework").[28] As with the OECD guidelines, the Framework provides high-level principles that do not provide significant detail regarding legislation, but do provide a direction for member countries.

As a general matter, exceptions to the principles contained in the Framework, including those relating to national sovereignty, national security, public safety, and public policy, should be limited and proportional to meeting the objectives to which the exceptions relate, and should be made known to the public to the extent permitted by local law.

---

21. Guidelines Governing the Protection of Privacy and Transborder Flows of Personal Data, Part 4, Section 19.

22. *Id.* (a) to (e).

23. Guidelines Governing the Protection of Privacy and Transborder Flows of Personal Data, Part 5, Section 20.

24. *Id.*

25. Guidelines Governing the Protection of Privacy and Transborder Flows of Personal Data, Part 5, Section 21.

26. Guidelines Governing the Protection of Privacy and Transborder Flows of Personal Data, Part 5, Section 22.

27. See generally, http://www.apec.org (last visited February 7, 2011).

28. http://publications.apec.org/publication-detail.php?pub_id=390 (last visited March 28, 2011).

1:16.   APEC information privacy principles

Preventing Harm

Personal information protection should be designed to prevent the misuse of information, in light of the interests of the individual to legitimate expectations of privacy.[29] Specific obligations should factor in this risk, and remedial measures should be proportionate to the likelihood and severity of the harm threatened by the collection, use, and transfer of personal information.[30]

Notice

Personal information controllers should provide clear and easily accessible statements about their practices and policies with respect to personal information that should include the fact that personal information is being collected; the purposes for which personal information is collected; the types of persons or organizations to whom personal information might be disclosed; the identity and location of the personal information controller, including information on how to contact them about their practices and handling of personal information; and the choices and means the personal information controller offers individuals for limiting the use and disclosure of, and for accessing and correcting, their personal information.[31]

Additionally, all reasonably practicable steps should be taken to ensure that notice is provided either before or at the time of collection of personal information.[32] Otherwise, notice should be provided as soon after as is practicable.[33] It should be noted that under the Framework, it may not be appropriate for personal information controllers to provide notice regarding the collection and use of publicly available information.[34]

Collection Limitation

The collection of personal information should be limited to information that is relevant to the purpose for which it is collected.[35] The information should be proportional and collected through lawful and fair means, and, if appropriate, with notice given to the individual.[36]

---

29.   APEC Privacy Framework 2004, Part III, Principle I, Section 14.

30.   APEC Privacy Framework 2004, Principle I, Section 14.

31.   APEC Privacy Framework 2004, Principle II, Section 15(a) to (e).

32.   APEC Privacy Framework 2004, Principle II, Section 16.

33.   *Id.*

34.   APEC Privacy Framework 2004, Principle II, Section 17.

35.   APEC Privacy Framework 2004, Principle III, Section 18.

36.   *Id.*

Uses of Personal Information

Personal information collected should be used only to fulfill the purposes of collection and other compatible or related purposes except with the consent of the individual whose personal information is collected; when necessary to provide a service or product requested by the individual; or by the authority of law and other legal instruments, proclamations, and pronouncements of legal effect.[37]

Choice

Where appropriate, individuals should be provided with clear, prominent, easily understandable, accessible, and affordable mechanisms to exercise choice in relation to the collection, use, and disclosure of their personal information.[38] It may not be appropriate for personal information controllers to provide choice when collecting publicly available information.[39]

Integrity of Personal Information

Personal information should be accurate, complete, and up-to-date to the extent necessary for the purposes of use.[40]

Security Safeguards

Personal information controllers are to protect personal information that they hold with appropriate safeguards against risks, such as loss or unauthorized access to personal information, or unauthorized destruction, use, modification, or disclosure of information or other misuses.[41] The safeguards should be proportional to the likelihood and severity of the harm threatened, the sensitivity of the information and the context in which it is held, and should be subject to periodic review and reassessment.[42]

Access and Correction

The APEC Framework suggests that individuals should be able to obtain from the personal information controller confirmation of whether or not the personal information controller holds personal information about them; have communicated to them, after having provided sufficient proof of their identity, personal information about them within a reasonable time, at a charge, if any, that is not excessive, in a reasonable manner, in a form that is generally understandable; and challenge the accuracy of information relating to them and, if possible and as appropriate, have the information rectified, completed, amended, or deleted.[43] Access and opportunity for correction should be provided except where the burden or expense of doing so would be unreasonable or disproportionate

---

37. APEC Privacy Framework 2004, Principle IV, Section 19.
38. APEC Privacy Framework 2004, Principle V, Section 20.
39. *Id.*
40. APEC Privacy Framework 2004, Principle VI, Section 21.
41. APEC Privacy Framework 2004, Principle VII, Section 22.
42. *Id.*
43. APEC Privacy Framework 2004, Principle VIII, Section 23(a) to (c).

to the risks to the individual's privacy in the case in question; the information should not be disclosed due to legal or security reasons or to protect confidential commercial information;[44] or the information privacy of persons other than the individual would be violated.[45] If a request or a challenge is denied, the individual should be provided with reasons why and be able to challenge the denial.[46]

Accountability

A personal information controller should be accountable for complying with measures that give effect to these principles.[47] When personal information is to be transferred to another person or organization, whether domestically or internationally, the personal information controller should obtain the consent of the individual or exercise due diligence and take reasonable steps to ensure that the recipient person or organization will protect the information consistently with these principles.[48]

1:17.   Privacy and security: the seven U.S. privacy principles

In the United States, the principles are expressed slightly differently, but also in a form that is non-binding on many companies. There are a variety of state and federal privacy statutes that identify different duties and obligations regarding the level of privacy afforded to consumers' information. As a general principle, the differences relate to the type of information in question and the type of business involved, as well as what jurisdiction the consumer resides in. U.S. laws reflect these privacy principles in different ways.[49]

Following are the seven U.S. privacy principles:

Notice. Companies can be required to give individuals notice about the purpose for which private information was gathered, as well as how information collected by a company will be used. A company can also be required to provide users with information regarding how they can register complaints and inquire regarding privacy issues, whether a company discloses information to third parties, and what the methods and standards are for limiting and using information.

Choice. Companies can be required to give users the option of not disclosing their personal information to a third party and requesting that their information not be utilized for purposes other than those originally disclosed at the time of collection. For certain sensitive information, companies must receive explicit permission from the user before the information is disclosed to third parties or used for purposes other than that for which it was originally collected.

---

44. "Confidential commercial information" is information that an organization has taken steps to protect from disclosure, where such disclosure would facilitate a competitor in the market to use or exploit the information against the business interest of the organization causing significant financial loss.

45. APEC Privacy Framework 2004, Principle VIII, Section 24.

46. *Id.*

47. APEC Privacy Framework 2004, Principle IX, Section 25.

48. *Id.*

49. These principles have been expressed in the EU Safe Harbor principles, which are not applicable to many U.S.-based businesses. They represent general principles regarding privacy that are reflected to varying degrees in different federal and state laws.

Onward Transfer. Before a company discloses any information to a third party, it can be required to apply the above-referenced notice and choice principles. If a third party is acting as an agent for a company, the third party in some circumstances can be required to comply with the privacy principles as well.

Access. Companies typically are required to permit users to have access to their personal information. A company can also be required to afford users the opportunity to amend, delete, or alter personal information when it is inaccurate, with the caveat that access need not be provided when the cost of providing access would be disproportionate compared to the risk of violation of the individual's privacy or when providing access would violate another's privacy.

Security. A bedrock principle of many privacy laws is information security. While absolute security is not required, a company can be required to take reasonable precautions to protect private information from misuse, disclosure, unauthorized access or alteration, particularly if affirmative representations regarding data security are made.

Data Integrity. Ensuring the accuracy and completeness of the data can also be required. One of the main principles is that private information collected by a company must be relevant to the purposes for which it was collected.

Enforcement. Companies can also be required to provide some enforcement mechanism to protect an individual's privacy rights, including a reasonably affordable and accessible dispute-resolution system. They can also be obligated to self-remedy problems arising out of their failure to meet the requirements of the principles.

CHAPTER 2.

Internet Privacy

I. Overview

2:1. Introduction to Internet privacy

The Internet was one of the first areas in which the federal government regulated privacy in a structured way. The Children's Online Privacy Protection Act ("COPPA") is an Internet-specific privacy law that can directly or indirectly impact many businesses. COPPA, while one of the first Internet-based laws, is specific to particular individuals: children 12 or under. COPPA is covered in chapter 3.

Most Internet privacy laws are tied to the collection or dissemination of personally identifiable information. California has, as it has in many other areas, led the way with broad Internet privacy legislation, though other states, such as Utah, have also enacted regulations. Moreover, some states, such as Minnesota, also regulate Internet privacy through their unfair competition and consumer protection laws. Either way, given the extensive reach of the Internet, businesses must be careful to ensure they are compliant with all relevant laws. In many ways, the issue of anonymous subpoenas, covered in the privacy litigation chapter, is exclusively an Internet issue, and this raises a number of privacy issues.

At the federal level, the Federal Trade Commission (the "FTC") regulates Internet privacy issues, particularly those arising from false or misleading statements in an online privacy policy. State attorneys general, including in New York, have also been active on Internet privacy issues.

2:2.   Role of FTC in privacy and security enforcement

As the main privacy watchdog at the federal level, the FTC is the agency that is empowered to investigate and enforce the violation of federal laws related to privacy and security, such as Gramm-Leach-Bliley, COPPA, and others. Additionally, the FTC also has enforcement power under the FTC Act, which prohibits unfair and deceptive trade practices, as well as false advertising. As is more fully discussed elsewhere, the enforcement theory of the FTC has expanded to include more than false statements regarding privacy and security under the false advertising prong and now can include claims of unfair practices, even in the absence of a misrepresentation. The FTC's role in information security and privacy is discussed in chapter 15.

2:3.   Analyzing ISPs obligations

Internet service providers ("ISP"s) face a number of regulations. In addition to potential regulation under telephone-based laws, certain broadband providers can be regulated under cable privacy laws. Additionally, Internet-based privacy laws frequently impact ISPs, as do certain state laws that are specific to ISPs, including Arkansas, Minnesota, and Utah. Certain states, such as Georgia, place disclosure obligations on ISPs. While there has been talk at the federal level of imposing a record retention obligation on ISPs, only Colorado has done so.

2:4.   Reporting requirements of an ECS or RCS

Anyone, while engaged in providing an electronic communication service or a remote computing service to the public through a facility or means of interstate or foreign commerce, who obtains actual knowledge of any facts or circumstances from which there is an apparent violation of laws that prohibit child pornography, must as soon as reasonably possible provide to the CyberTipline of the National Center for Missing and Exploited Children, the mailing address, telephone number, facsimile number, electronic mail address of, and individual point of contact for, such electronic communication service provider or remote computing service provider.[1]

To the extent the information is within the custody or control of an electronic communication service provider or a remote computing service provider, the facts and circumstances included in each report may include the following information: information relating to the identity of any individual who appears to have violated a federal law described in 18 U.S.C. § 2258A(a)(2), which may, to the extent reasonably practicable, include the electronic mail address, Internet protocol address, uniform resource locator, or any other identifying information, including self-reported identifying information; information relating to when and how a customer or subscriber of an electronic

---

1.   18 U.S.C. §§ 2258A(a)(1)–(2).

communication service or a remote computing service uploaded, transmitted, or received apparent child pornography or when and how apparent child pornography was reported to or discovered by the electronic communication service provider or remote computing service provider, including a date and time stamp and time zone; information relating to the geographic location of the involved individual or website, which may include the Internet Protocol address or verified billing address, or, if not reasonably available, at least one form of geographic identifying information, including area code or zip code; the information described in subparagraph (A) may also include any geographic information provided to the electronic communication service or remote computing service by the customer or subscriber; any image of apparent child pornography relating to the incident such report is regarding; and the complete communication containing any image of apparent child pornography, including any data or information regarding the transmission of the communication, and any images, data, or other digital files contained in, or attached to, the communication.[2]

2:5. Forwarding of report

The National Center for Missing and Exploited Children shall forward each report made under subsection (a)(1) to any appropriate law enforcement agency designated by the Attorney General.[3] The National Center for Missing and Exploited Children may forward any report made under this law to an appropriate law enforcement official of a state or political subdivision of a state for the purpose of enforcing state criminal law.[4] The National Center for Missing and Exploited Children may forward any report made under this law to any appropriate foreign law enforcement agency designated by the Attorney General, subject to the conditions established by the Attorney General.[5] If the National Center for Missing and Exploited Children forwards a report to a foreign law enforcement agency, the National Center for Missing and Exploited Children shall concurrently provide a copy of the report and the identity of the foreign law enforcement agency to the Attorney General or the federal law enforcement agency or agencies designated by the Attorney General.[6]

The Attorney General shall enforce this section.[7] The Attorney General shall designate promptly the federal law enforcement agency or agencies to which a report shall be forwarded under subsection (c)(1).[8] The Attorney General shall promptly in consultation with the secretary of state, designate the foreign law enforcement agencies to which a report may be forwarded under subsection (c)(3); establish the conditions under which such a report may be forwarded to such agencies; and develop a process for foreign law enforcement agencies to request assistance from federal law enforcement agencies in obtaining evidence related to a report referred under subsection (c)(3).[9]

---

2.   18 U.S.C. §§ 2258A(b)(1)–(5).

3.   18 U.S.C. § 2258A(c)(1).

4.   18 U.S.C. § 2258A(c)(2).

5.   18 U.S.C. § 2258A(c)(3).

6.   18 U.S.C. §§ 2258A(c)(3)(B)(i)–(ii).

7.   18 U.S.C. § 2258A(d)(1).

8.   18 U.S.C. § 2258A(d)(2).

9.   18 U.S.C. §§ 2258A(d)(3)(A)–(C).

The Attorney General shall maintain and make available to the Department of State, the National Center for Missing and Exploited Children, electronic communication service providers, remote computing service providers, the Committee on the Judiciary of the Senate, and the Committee on the Judiciary of the House of Representatives a list of the foreign law enforcement agencies designated in the statute.[10] If an electronic communication service provider or remote computing service provider notifies the National Center for Missing and Exploited Children that the electronic communication service provider or remote computing service provider is making a report under this section as the result of a request by a foreign law enforcement agency, the National Center for Missing and Exploited Children shall, if the Center forwards the report to the requesting foreign law enforcement agency or another agency in the same country designated by the Attorney General, notify the electronic communication service provider or remote computing service provider of the identity of the foreign law enforcement agency to which the report was forwarded, and the date on which the report was forwarded; or notify the electronic communication service provider or remote computing service provider if the Center declines to forward the report because the Center, in consultation with the Attorney General, determines that no law enforcement agency in the foreign country has been designated by the Attorney General.[11]

An electronic communication service provider or remote computing service provider that knowingly and willfully fails to make a report required under 18 U.S.C. § 2258A(a) (1) shall be fined according to the following: in the case of an initial knowing and willful failure to make a report, not more than $150,000; and in the case of any second or subsequent knowing and willful failure to make a report, not more than $300,000.[12] Nothing in this section shall be construed to require an electronic communication service provider or a remote computing service provider to monitor any user, subscriber, or customer of that provider; monitor the content of any communication of any person described in paragraph (1); or affirmatively seek facts or circumstances described in sections (a) and (b).[13]

Subject to certain exceptions, a law enforcement agency that receives a report shall not disclose any information contained in that report.[14] A law enforcement agency may disclose information in a report to an attorney for the government for use in the performance of the official duties of that attorney; to such officers and employees of that law enforcement agency, as may be necessary in the performance of their investigative and recordkeeping functions; to such other government personnel (including personnel of a state or subdivision of a state) as are determined to be necessary by an attorney for the government to assist the attorney in the performance of the official duties of the attorney in enforcing federal criminal law; if the report discloses a violation of state criminal law, to an appropriate official of a state or subdivision of a state for the purpose of enforcing such state law; to a defendant in a criminal case or the attorney for that defendant, to the extent the information relates to a criminal charge pending

---

10.   18 U.S.C. § 2258A(d)(4).

11.   18 U.S.C. §§ 2258A(d)(6)(A)–(B).

12.   18 U.S.C. §§ 2258A(e)(1)–(2).

13.   18 U.S.C. §§ 2258A(f)(1)–(3).

14.   18 U.S.C. § 2258A(g)(1).

against that defendant; to an electronic communication service provider or remote computing provider if necessary to facilitate a response to a legal process issued in connection to a criminal investigation, prosecution, or post-conviction remedy relating to that report; and as ordered by a court upon a showing of good cause and pursuant to any protective orders or other conditions that the court may impose.[15]

The electronic communication service provider or remote computing service provider shall be prohibited from disclosing the contents of a report to any person, except as necessary to respond to the legal process.[16] Nothing in the preceding sentence authorizes a law enforcement agency to provide child pornography images to an electronic communications service provider or a remote computing service.[17]

2:6.   Permitted disclosures by the National Center for Missing and Exploited Children

The National Center for Missing and Exploited Children may disclose information received in a report under subsection (a) only to any federal law enforcement agency designated by the Attorney General; to any state, local, or tribal law enforcement agency involved in the investigation of child pornography, child exploitation, kidnapping, or enticement crimes; to any foreign law enforcement agency designated by the Attorney General; and to an electronic communication service provider or remote computing service provider.[18] The notification to an electronic communication service provider or a remote computing service provider by the CyberTipline of receipt of a report shall typically be treated as a request to preserve.[19] Pursuant to this requirement, an electronic communication service provider or a remote computing service shall preserve the contents of the report provided for 90 days after such notification by the CyberTipline.[20] Pursuant to the requirement above, an electronic communication service provider or a remote computing service shall preserve any images, data, or other digital files that are commingled or interspersed among the images of apparent child pornography within a particular communication or user-created folder or directory.[21] An electronic communications service or remote computing service preserving materials under this section shall maintain the materials in a secure location and take appropriate steps to limit access by agents or employees of the service to the materials to that access necessary to comply with the requirements of this subsection.[22] Nothing in these provisions shall be construed as replacing, amending, or otherwise interfering with the authorities and duties under 18 U.S.C. § 2703.[23]

---

15.   18 U.S.C. §§ 2258A(g)(2)(a)(i)–(vii).
16.   18 U.S.C. § 2258A(g)(2)(B)(i).
17.   18 U.S.C. § 2258A(g)(2)(B)(ii).
18.   18 U.S.C. §§ 2258A(g)(3)(A)–(D).
19.   18 U.S.C. § 2258A(h)(1).
20.   18 U.S.C. § 2258A(h)(2).
21.   18 U.S.C. § 2258A(h)(3).
22.   18 U.S.C. § 2258A(h)(4).
23.   18 U.S.C. § 2258A(h)(5).

2:7.   Limited liability for electronic communication service providers, remote computing service providers, or domain name registrar

Except as provided below, a civil claim or criminal charge against an electronic communication service provider, a remote computing service provider, or domain name registrar, including any director, officer, employee, or agent of such electronic communication service provider, remote computing service provider, or domain name registrar arising from the performance of the reporting or preservation responsibilities of such electronic communication service provider, remote computing service provider, or domain name registrar may not be brought in any federal or state court.[24] This does not apply to a claim if the electronic communication service provider, remote computing service provider, or domain name registrar, or a director, officer, employee, or agent of that electronic communication service provider, remote computing service provider, or domain name registrar engaged in intentional misconduct, or acted, or failed to act with actual malice or with reckless disregard to a substantial risk of causing physical injury without legal justification.[25] An electronic communication service provider, a remote computing service provider, and domain name registrar shall minimize the number of employees that are provided access to any image provided under these rules and must honor a request from a law enforcement agency to destroy the image.[26]

2:8.   Use of technical elements relating to images reported to the CyberTipline

The National Center for Missing and Exploited Children may provide elements relating to any apparent child pornography image of an identified child to an electronic communication service provider or a remote computing service provider for the sole and exclusive purpose of permitting that electronic communication service provider or remote computing service provider to stop the further transmission of images.[27]

The elements authorized may include hash values or other unique identifiers associated with a specific image, Internet location of images, and other technological elements that can be used to identify and stop the transmission of child pornography.[28]

2:9.   Use by electronic communication service providers and remote computing service providers

Any electronic communication service provider or remote computing service provider that receives elements relating to any apparent child pornography image of an identified child from the National Center for Missing and Exploited Children under this section may use such information only for the purposes described in this section, provided

---

24.   18 U.S.C. § 2258B(a).
25.   18 U.S.C. §§ 2258B(b)(1)–(2).
26.   18 U.S.C. §§ 2258B(c)(1)–(2).
27.   18 U.S.C. § 2258C(a)(1).
28.   18 U.S.C. § 2258C(a)(2).

that such use shall not relieve that electronic communication service provider or remote computing service provider from its reporting obligations.[29] Nothing in this law requires electronic communication service providers or remote computing service providers receiving elements relating to any apparent child pornography image of an identified child from the National Center for Missing and Exploited Children to use the elements to stop the further transmission of the images.[30] The National Center for Missing and Exploited Children shall make available to federal, state, and local law enforcement involved in the investigation of child pornography crimes elements, including hash values, relating to any apparent child pornography image of an identified child reported to the National Center for Missing and Exploited Children.[31] Any federal, state, or local law enforcement agency that receives elements relating to any apparent child pornography image of an identified child from the National Center for Missing and Exploited Children may use such elements only in the performance of the official duties of that agency to investigate child pornography crimes.[32]

2:10. Posting of information on social networking cites operating as a waiver of privacy

In *Beye v. Horizon Blue Cross Blue Shield of New Jersey*, the district court addressed an issue that will likely recur—the impact on a person's privacy of their voluntary disclosure of sensitive information on a social networking site.[33] In this case, the court ordered the plaintiffs to produce evidence that was posted on social networking sites, even if it reflected sensitive medical conditions (allegedly eating disorders in this matter), because of the diminished expectation of privacy due to the posting and sharing of the information.

This principle was recently reaffirmed by a court in California in a case involving MySpace. In *Moreno v. Hanford Sentinel, Inc.*, the court of appeal affirmed a demurrer to an invasion of privacy claim because the plaintiff in the case had posted the material that served as the basis of the invasion of privacy claim on MySpace (though it was subsequently removed).[34]

2:11. Logging of IP addresses

One of the issues many companies raise is whether there is a legal obligation to log users' actions on a website, including by keeping log files of users' activities. One court, while not directly holding that logging was not required, did address the issue in the context of a party's document production and retention issues. In *Columbia Pictures Industries v. Bunnell* the district court addressed whether the new federal rules required disclosure and retention of server log files that were only temporarily resident

---

29. 18 U.S.C. § 2258C(b).

30. 18 U.S.C. § 2258C(c).

31. 18 U.S.C. § 2258C(d).

32. 18 U.S.C. § 2258C(e).

33. Beye v. Horizon Blue Cross Blue Shield of New Jersey, 2:06-cv-05337-FSH-PS (D. N.J. December 14, 2007).

34. Moreno v. Hanford Sentinel, Inc., 172 Cal. App. 4th 1125, 91 Cal. Rptr. 3d 858 (2009).

in RAM.[35] The court noted that while server logging was helpful in many cases, it was not "essential to the functionality of the website" and, absent a preservation order, the court seemed to indicate that logging was not legally required.

2:12.   Internet gambling

Preventing online gambling in the United States has been a priority for the U.S. government for a significant period of time. There is now a new tool to prevent online gambling due to the recent passage of the Unlawful Internet Gambling Enforcement Act,[36] which legislators have aimed at cutting off the money supply of the Internet gambling industry. While many commentators have discussed the financial aspects of this law, which are extremely important to understand, equally important are the law's restrictions that affect websites and other providers on the Internet as well, including a notice and takedown system that is similar in certain ways to that of the Digital Millennium Copyright Act. Additionally, though it attempts to recognize the protections of the Communications Decency Act ("CDA"), which provides immunity to certain online acts by "service providers," the interaction of this law and the CDA could present challenges for service providers, even those that are not directly providing gambling related services.

2:13.   Defining prohibited conduct

The statute attempts to walk a legal tightrope and not affect the numerous state and federal laws that currently govern gambling. This is accomplished through a narrowed definition of "Unlawful Internet Gambling." This term means, in essence, placing, receiving, or otherwise knowingly transmitting a bet or wager[37] by any means that

---

35.   Columbia Pictures Industries v. Bunnell, 2007 WL 2080419 (C.D. Cal. 2006).

36.   Title VIII of the SAFE Port Act, Pub. Law 109-347. The UIGEA has been supplemented by regulations finalized in 2008 that are available at http://edocket.access.gpo.gov/2008/pdf/E8-27181.pdf (last visited March 28, 2011).

37.   The term "bet or wager" (A) means the staking or risking by any person of something of value upon the outcome of a contest of others, a sporting event, or a game subject to chance, upon an agreement or under-standing that the person or another person will receive something of value in the event of a certain outcome; (B) includes the purchase of a chance or opportunity to win a lottery or other prize (which opportunity to win is predominantly subject to chance); (C) includes any scheme of a type described in section 3702 of title 28; (D) includes any instructions or information pertaining to the establishment or movement of funds by the bettor or customer in, to, or from an account with the business of betting or wagering; and (E) does not include (i) any activity governed by the securities laws (as that term is defined in section 3(a)(47) of the Securities Exchange Act of 1934 for the purchase or sale of securities (as that term is defined in section 3(a) (10) of that Act); (ii) any transaction conducted on or subject to the rules of a registered entity or exempt board of trade under the Commodity Exchange Act; (iii) any over-the-counter derivative instrument; (iv) any other transaction that (I) is excluded or exempt from regulation under the Commodity Exchange Act; or (II) is exempt from State gaming or bucket shop laws under section 12(e) of the Commodity Exchange Act or section 28(a) of the Securities Exchange Act of 1934; (v) any contract of indemnity or guarantee; (vi) any contract for insurance; (vii) any deposit or other transaction with an insured depository institution; (viii) participation in any game or contest in which participants do not stake or risk anything of value other than (I) personal efforts of the participants in playing the game or contest or obtaining access to the Internet or (II) points or credits that the sponsor of the game or contest provides to participants free of charge and that can be used or redeemed only for participation in games or contests offered by the sponsor; or (ix) participation in any fantasy or simulation sports game or educational game or contest in which (if the game or contest involves a team or teams) no fantasy or simulation sports team is based on the current membership of an

involve the use, at least in part, of the Internet[38] if the bet or wager is unlawful under any applicable federal or state[39] law where the bet or wager is initiated, received, or otherwise made.[40]

Unlawful Internet Gambling does not, however, include intrastate transactions,[41] intra-tribal transactions,[42] or interstate horseracing.[43] This narrowness of the definition is a recognition that there are many forms of gambling that are permitted under state and federal law. Thus, the statute does not regulate any use of the Internet that falls within these exclusionary definitions. It also should be noted that Congress attempted to address the issue of otherwise legal conduct becoming illegal merely because the

---

actual team that is a member of an amateur or professional sports organization (as those terms are defined in section 3701 of title 28) and that meets the following conditions: (I) All prizes and awards offered to winning participants are established and made known to the participants in advance of the game or contest and their value is not determined by the number of participants or the amount of any fees paid by those participants. (II) All winning outcomes reflect the relative knowledge and skill of the participants and are determined predominantly by accumulated statistical results of the performance of individuals (athletes in the case of sports events) in multiple real world sporting or other events. (III) No winning outcome is based (aa) on the score, point-spread, or any performance or performances of any single real-world team or any combination of such teams; or (bb) solely on any single performance of an individual athlete in any single real-world sporting or other event. 31 U.S.C. § 5362(1).

38. The term "Internet" means the international computer network of interoperable packet switched data networks. 31 U.S.C. § 5362(5).

39. The term "State" means any State of the United States, the District of Columbia, or any commonwealth, territory, or other possession of the United States. 31 U.S.C. § 5362(9).

40. 31 U.S.C. § 5362(10)(A).

41. The term "unlawful Internet gambling" does not include placing, receiving, or otherwise transmitting a bet or wager where (i) the bet or wager is initiated and received or otherwise made exclusively within a single State; (ii) the bet or wager and the method by which the bet or wager is initiated and received or otherwise made is expressly authorized by and placed in accordance with the laws of such State, and the State law or regulations include (I) age and location verification requirements reasonably designed to block access to minors and persons located out of such State and (II) appropriate data security standards to prevent unauthorized access by any person whose age and current location has not been verified in accordance with such State's law or regulations; and (iii) the bet or wager does not violate any provision of (I) the Interstate Horseracing Act of 1978 (15 U.S.C. §§ 3001 *et seq.*), (II) chapter 178 of title 28 (commonly known as the "Professional and Amateur Sports Protection Act"), (III) the Gambling Devices Transportation Act (15 U.S.C. §§ 1171 *et seq.*), or (IV) the Indian Gaming Regulatory Act (25 U.S.C. §§ 2701 *et seq.*). 31 U.S.C. § 5362(10)(B).

42. The term "unlawful Internet gambling" does not include placing, receiving, or otherwise transmitting a bet or wager where (i) the bet or wager is initiated and received or otherwise made exclusively (I) within the Indian lands of a single Indian tribe (as such terms are defined under the Indian Gaming Regulatory Act) or (II) between the Indian lands of 2 or more Indian tribes to the extent that intertribal gaming is authorized by the Indian Gaming Regulatory Act; (ii) the bet or wager and the method by which the bet or wager is initiated and received or otherwise made is expressly authorized by and complies with the requirements of (I) the applicable tribal ordinance or resolution approved by the Chairman of the National Indian Gaming Commission and (II) with respect to class III gaming, the applicable Tribal-State Compact; (iii) the applicable tribal ordinance or resolution or Tribal-State Compact includes (I) age and location verification requirements reasonably designed to block access to minors and persons located out of the applicable Tribal lands and (II) appropriate data security standards to prevent unauthorized access by any person whose age and current location has not been verified in accordance with the applicable tribal ordinance or resolution or Tribal-State Compact; and (iv) the bet or wager does not violate any provision of (I) the Interstate Horseracing Act of 1978 (15 U.S.C. §§ 3001 *et seq.*), (II) chapter 178 of title 28 (commonly known as the "Professional and Amateur Sports Protection Act"), (III) the Gambling Devices Transportation Act (15 U.S.C. §§ 1171 *et seq.*), or (IV) the Indian Gaming Regulatory Act (25 U.S.C. §§ 2701 *et seq.*). 31 U.S.C. § 5362(10)(C).

43. The term "unlawful Internet gambling" shall not include any activity that is allowed under the Interstate Horseracing Act of 1978 (15 U.S.C. §§ 3001 *et seq.*). 31 U.S.C. § 5362(10)(D)(i).

communication is routed to a state where the conduct may be illegal, though it is legal where the bet was placed. The concept of "intermediate routing" was therefore inserted into the statute and any intermediate stops a communication makes are ignored for purposes of considering whether an illegal bet or wager was made.[44]

The law, like certain federal privacy statutes, places different burdens on businesses that provide different services. As discussed below, businesses that are "in the business of betting or wagering," "designated payment systems," as well as participants in them, and "financial transaction providers" all have related but distinct burdens placed upon them. As such, it is important to assess the nature of the business at issue when analyzing regulatory compliance.

2:14.   Preemption of other laws

This law is not intended to preempt any state law prohibiting gambling, or to impact the Interstate Horseracing Act.[45] Congress also explicitly stated that no portion of this law was to be construed as altering, limiting, or extending any federal or state law or tribal-state compact prohibiting, permitting, or regulating gambling within the United States.[46]

2:15.   Use of financial instruments for unlawful Internet gambling

The main purpose of the law is to regulate the use of certain financial instruments in online gaming. Thus, it is illegal for any person in the business of betting or wagering[47] to knowingly accept the following, in connection with the participation of another person in unlawful Internet gambling:

- credit, or the proceeds of credit, extended to or on behalf of such other person (including credit extended through the use of a credit card)
- an electronic fund transfer,[48] or funds transmitted by or through a money transmitting business,[49] or the proceeds of an electronic fund transfer or money transmitting service, from or on behalf of such other person

---

44. The intermediate routing of electronic data shall not determine the location or locations in which a bet or wager is initiated, received, or otherwise made. 31 U.S.C. § 5362(10)(E).

45. 31 U.S.C. § 5362(10)(D)(ii). Congress was explicit regarding its intent on horseracing. "It is the sense of Congress that this subchapter shall not change which activities related to horse racing may or may not be allowed under Federal law. This subparagraph is intended to address concerns that this subchapter could have the effect of changing the existing relationship between the Interstate Horseracing Act and other Federal statutes in effect on the date of the enactment of this subchapter. This subchapter is not intended to change that relationship. This subchapter is not intended to resolve any existing disagreements over how to interpret the relationship between the Interstate Horseracing Act and other Federal statutes." 31 U.S.C. § 5362(10)(D)(iii).

46. 31 U.S.C. § 5361(b).

47. The term "business of betting or wagering" does not include the activities of a financial transaction provider, or any interactive computer service or telecommunications service. 31 U.S.C. § 5362(2).

48. The term "electronic fund transfer" (i) has the meaning given the term in section 903 of the Electronic Fund Transfer Act (15 U.S.C. § 1693a), except that the term includes transfers that would otherwise be excluded under section 903(6)(E) of that Act; and (ii) includes any fund transfer covered by Article 4A of the Uniform Commercial Code, as in effect in any State. 31 U.S.C. § 5362(11)(B).

49. The terms "money transmitting business" and "money transmitting service" have the meanings given the

- any check, draft, or similar instrument which is drawn by or on behalf of such other person and is drawn on or payable at or through any financial institution[50]
- the proceeds of any other form of financial transaction, as the Secretary[51] and the Board of Governors of the Federal Reserve System may jointly prescribe by regulation, which involves a financial institution as a payor or financial intermediary on behalf of or for the benefit of such other person.[52]

2:16. Regulations on payment systems

The Secretary of the Treasury and the Board of Governors of the Federal Reserve System, in consultation with the Attorney General, issued regulations[53] (which the Secretary and the Board jointly determined to be appropriate) requiring each designated payment system[54] and all participants in these systems to identify and block or otherwise prevent or prohibit restricted transactions[55] through the establishment of policies and procedures reasonably designed to identify and block or otherwise prevent or prohibit the acceptance of restricted transactions in one of several ways.[56] These policies must allow the payment system and any person involved in the payment system to identify restricted transactions via codes in authorization messages, or by other means, and to block restricted transactions identified as a result of the policies and procedures, or to prevent or prohibit the acceptance of the products or services of the payment system in connection with a restricted transaction.[57]

In setting these regulations, the relevant officials must identify types of policies and procedures, including nonexclusive examples, which will be deemed to be reasonably designed to identify and block or otherwise prevent or prohibit the acceptance of the products or services with respect to each type of restricted transaction. Participants must also, to the extent practical, be permitted to choose among alternative means of identifying and blocking, or otherwise preventing or prohibiting the acceptance of the products or services of the payment system in connection with, restricted transactions. Certain restricted transactions or designated payment systems from any requirement

---

terms in section 5330(d) (determined without regard to any regulations prescribed by the Treasury Secretary there under). 31 U.S.C. § 5362(11)(E).

50. The term "financial institution" has the meaning given the term in section 903 of the Electronic Fund Transfer Act, except that such term does not include a casino, sports book, or other business at or through which bets or wagers may be placed or received. 31 U.S.C. § 5362(10)(C).

51. The term "Secretary" means the Secretary of the Treasury. 31 U.S.C. § 5362(8).

52. 31 U.S.C. § 5363(1) to (4).

53. Prohibition on Funding of Unlawful Internet Gambling; Final Rules, 73 Fed. Reg. 69382 (Nov. 18, 2008) http://edocket.access.gpo.gov/2008/pdf/E8-27181.pdf (last visited March 28, 2011), codified at 12 CFR Part 233 (Federal Reserve) and 31 CFR Part 132 (Treasury).

54. The term "designated payment system" means any system utilized by a financial transaction provider that the Secretary and the Board of Governors of the Federal Reserve System, in consultation with the Attorney General, jointly determine, by regulation or order, could be utilized in connection with, or to facilitate, any restricted transaction. 31 U.S.C. § 5362(3).

55. The term "restricted transaction" means any transaction or transmittal involving any credit, funds, instrument, or proceeds described in any paragraph of section 5363 which the recipient is prohibited from accepting under section 5363. 31 U.S.C. § 5362(7).

56. 31 U.S.C. § 5364(a).

57. 31 U.S.C. § 5364(a)(1) to (2).

imposed under such regulations may be exempted if the Treasury Secretary and the Federal Reserve Board jointly find that it is not reasonably practical to identify and block, or otherwise prevent or prohibit the acceptance of, the transactions. The regulations must also provide guidance regarding ensuring that transactions in connection with any activity excluded from the definition of unlawful Internet gambling are not blocked or otherwise prevented or prohibited by the prescribed regulations.[58]

A financial transaction provider[59] is considered to be in compliance with these regulations if it relies on and complies with the policies and procedures of a designated payment system of which it is a member or participant to identify and block restricted transactions, or otherwise prevent or prohibit the acceptance of the products or services of the payment system, member, or participant in connection with restricted transactions, and the policies and procedures of the designated payment system comply with the requirements of the regulations.[60]

A person has no liability if he identifies and blocks a transaction, prevents or prohibits the acceptance of its products or services in connection with a transaction, or otherwise refuses to honor a transaction that is a restricted transaction, or one that the person reasonably believes to be a restricted transaction.[61] In the case of a designated payment system or a member of a designated payment system, there is no liability if it relies upon the policies and procedures of the payment system, in an effort to comply with the regulations.

These requirements are to be enforced exclusively by the federal functional regulators, in connection with designated payment systems and financial transaction providers, subject to the respective jurisdiction of such regulators under the relevant sections of Gramm-Leach-Bliley and the Commodities Exchange Act. The FTC has jurisdiction for any designated payment systems and financial transaction providers not otherwise subject to the jurisdiction of any federal functional regulators.[62]

2:17.   Civil remedies

In addition to other available remedies, the district courts have exclusive jurisdiction to prevent and restrain violations of this law via actions brought by certain entities and individuals.[63] The United States government, via the Attorney General, can bring an action to retrain or prevent a restricted transaction.[64] A temporary restraining order, a preliminary injunction, or an injunction against any person to prevent or restrain a restricted transaction in accordance with rule 65 of the Federal Rules of Civil Procedure

---

58. 31 U.S.C. § 5364(b)(1) to (4).

59. The term "financial transaction provider" means a creditor, credit card issuer, financial institution, operator of a terminal at which an electronic fund transfer may be initiated, money transmitting business, or international, national, regional, or local payment network utilized to effect a credit transaction, electronic fund transfer, stored value product transaction, or money transmitting service, or a participant in such network, or other participant in a designated payment system. 31 U.S.C. § 5362(4).

60. 31 U.S.C. § 5364(c)(1) to (2).

61. 31 U.S.C. § 5364(d).

62. 31 U.S.C. § 5364(e).

63. 31 U.S.C. § 5365(a).

64. 31 U.S.C. § 5365(b)(1)(A).

can be entered.[65] State attorneys general (or other comparable state officials) of a state in which a restricted transaction has, or will be, initiated, received, or otherwise made may bring a proceeding to restrain an actual or threatened violation.[66] As with actions brought by the United States, the district court may grant a temporary restraining order, a preliminary injunction, or an injunction against any person to prevent or restrain a restricted transaction in accordance with rule 65 of the Federal Rules of Civil Procedure.[67]

For a restricted transaction that allegedly has been or will be initiated, received, or otherwise made on Indian lands[68] the United States has enforcement authority and the enforcement authorities specified in an applicable tribal-state compact negotiated under IGRA[69] will be carried out in accordance with that compact.[70]

It should be noted that this law in no way permits any authorized person to initiate proceedings against any financial transaction provider, to the extent that the person is acting as a financial transaction provider, to prevent or restrain a restricted transaction.[71]

2:18.   Limitations regarding interactive computer services

The Communications Decency Act of 1996 has a broad impact on the liability of interactive computer services,[72] and UIGEA recognizes the CDA's reach. Subject to the circumvention restrictions, the only relief that can be granted against an interactive computer service is removal of, or disabling of access to, an online site that violates the financial restrictions. The same relief can be granted against an interactive computer service that has a hypertext link to an online site that resides on a computer server that such service controls or operates. The only exception is if the service provider that commits a violation of these restrictions has liability under the circumvention requirements.[73]

This relief can only be granted after notice and an opportunity for the service to appear are provided.[74] Relief granted must specify the interactive computer service to which it applies, specifically identify the location of the online site or hyperlink to be removed or disabled, and not impose any obligation on an interactive computer service

---

65. 31 U.S.C. § 5365(b)(1)(B).

66. 31 U.S.C. § 5365(b)(2)(A).

67. 31 U.S.C. § 5365(b)(2)(B).

68. The definition of this term is the same as used in section 4 of the Indian Gaming Regulatory Act. 31 U.S.C. § 5365(b)(3).

69. Section 11 of the Indian Gaming Regulatory Act. 25 U.S.C. § 2710.

70. 31 U.S.C. § 5365(b)(3)(A). It should be noted that no portion of this section is to be construed as altering, superseding, or otherwise affecting the application of the Indian Gaming Regulatory Act. 31 U.S.C. § 5365(b)(3)(B).

71. 31 U.S.C. § 5365(d).

72. The term "interactive computer service" has the meaning given the term in section 230(f) of the Communications Act of 1934 (47 U.S.C. 230(f)). 31 U.S.C. § 5362(6).

73. 31 U.S.C. § 5365(c)(1)(A).

74. 31 U.S.C. § 5365(c)(1)(B).

to monitor its service or to affirmatively seek facts indicating activity violating this law.[75]

Interactive computer services can only be liable under other laws[76] if the service has actual knowledge and control of bets and wagers and it operates, manages, supervises, or directs an Internet website at which unlawful bets or wagers may be placed, received, or otherwise made or at which unlawful bets or wagers are offered to be placed, received, or otherwise made; or it owns or controls, or is owned or controlled by, any person who operates, manages, supervises, or directs an Internet website at which unlawful bets or wagers may be placed, received, or otherwise made, or at which unlawful bets or wagers are offered to be placed, received, or otherwise made.[77]

2:19. Criminal penalties

Any violation of this law can give rise to a prison term of not more than five years, a fine as permitted under Title 18, or both.[78] Upon conviction, a court may also enter a permanent injunction enjoining such person from placing, receiving, or otherwise making bets or wagers or sending, receiving, or inviting information assisting in the placing of bets or wagers.[79]

2:20. Circumventions

It should be noted that a financial transaction provider, or any interactive computer service or telecommunications service, may be liable under this law if the entity has actual knowledge and control of bets and wagers, and it operates, manages, supervises, or directs an Internet website at which unlawful bets or wagers may be placed, received, or otherwise made, or at which unlawful bets or wagers are offered to be placed, received, or otherwise made; or owns or controls, or is owned or controlled by, any person who operates, manages, supervises, or directs an Internet website at which unlawful bets or wagers may be placed, received, or otherwise made, or at which unlawful bets or wagers are offered to be placed, received, or otherwise made.[80]

While other restrictions on gaming, particularly Internet-based gambling, may be passed in the future, this law presents a large hurdle to offshore gaming sites since the flow of money is now greatly restricted. The true impact of this law, however, will not be seen until an enforcement pattern is established for the final Treasury Department regulations, which were published in 31 CFR Part 132 and became effective June 1, 2010. P. Either way, given the prominence of gaming sites, the fabric of cyberspace will be permanently altered by this law.

---

75. 31 U.S.C. § 5365(c)(1)(C) to (E).
76. 18 U.S.C. § 1084(d).
77. 31 U.S.C. § 5365(c)(2).
78. 31 U.S.C. § 5366(a).
79. 53 U.S.C. § 5366(b).
80. 31 U.S.C. § 5367.

2:21.   Digital Millennium Copyright Act and privacy

The Digital Millennium Copyright Act (DMCA) provides immunity for four different types of conduct by ISPs, if the prerequisites are met: transitory digital connections; system caching; information residing on systems or networks at the direction of users; and information location tools.[81] While much has been made over the use of DMCA subpoenas, the subpoena power is not so broad that it covers all forms of conduct under the DMCA.

The DMCA has privacy implications because it provides a simplified subpoena mechanism that can result in disclosure of Internet users' information. A copyright owner or a person authorized to act on the owner's behalf, even before a case is commenced, may request the clerk of any U.S. district court to issue a subpoena to a service provider for identification of an alleged infringer.[82] This differs from normal civil subpoenas because typically a case must first be filed before subpoenas can be issued. The request must contain a copy of the notification to the designated agent that was previously sent, the proposed subpoena, and a sworn declaration stating that the purpose of the subpoena is to obtain the identity of an alleged infringer and that the requested information will only be used for the purpose of protecting copyrights.[83] If the subpoena is issued, it requires the service provider to expeditiously disclose to the subpoenaing party information sufficient to identify the alleged infringer of the material described in the notification to the extent the service provider has this information.[84]

However, it should be noted that this simplified procedure is not available for every form of conduct covered by the DMCA. Indeed, where an ISP is acting as a mere conduit for information, and not storing information, the simplified DMCA subpoena power is not available.[85] One of the issues that has been left open by courts is what is required for a service provider to be found to have "reasonably implemented" a policy that requires termination in appropriate circumstances for repeat infringers. One court has held that a service provider implements a policy if there is a functioning notification system and a procedure for dealing with DMCA-compliant notifications and if it does not actively prevent copyright owners from collecting information needed to issue these notifications.[86]

One of the issues copyright holders have raised with the DMCA is whether a service provider has an obligation to investigate for infringement. The Ninth Circuit has held that a service provider does not have such an investigative duty.[87]

---

81.   17 U.S.C. § 512.

82.   17 U.S.C. § 512(h)(1).

83.   17 U.S.C. § 512(h)(2).

84.   17 U.S.C. § 512(h)(4) to (5).

85.   *See*, Recording Industry Ass'n of America, Inc. v. Verizon Internet Services, Inc., 351 F.3d 1229 (D.C. Cir. 2003).

86.   Perfect 10, Inc. v. CCBill LLC, 488 F.3d 1102 (9th Cir. 2007), *cert. denied* 128 S. Ct. 709, 2007 WL 2455134 (U.S.).

87.   *Id.*

2:22.   Bankruptcy Reform Act of 2005

Amendments to the Bankruptcy Reform Act of 2005, 11 U.S.C. § 363, have attempted to address the privacy concerns created by companies filing bankruptcy. The FTC and state attorneys general previously dealt with these concerns when eToys went through the bankruptcy process, as well as during other bankruptcy cases. The issue that courts have struggled with is whether a bankruptcy trustee can sell a customer's personally identifiable information[88] as an asset of the bankrupt company (the "debtor") if the debtor's privacy policy does not address the issue of whether a customer's personal information will be sold in a bankruptcy. Trustees are now precluded from selling personal information unless the sale is consistent with the privacy policy existing at the time of the bankruptcy filing or, after appointment of a consumer privacy ombudsman and after notice and a hearing, the court approves such sale or such lease after giving "due consideration" to the facts, circumstances, and conditions of such sale or such lease and finding that any sale or lease would not violate other applicable laws.[89]

If a court is required to appoint a consumer privacy ombudsman under the Act, then the trustee must appoint a disinterested person to serve at least five days before any related hearing.[90] Notice of the hearing must be given to the consumer privacy ombudsman, who must be a person other than the trustee.[91] The consumer privacy ombudsman's role is to appear at the hearing and provide information to the court to assist it in the consideration of the facts, circumstances, and conditions of the proposed sale or lease of personally identifiable information under Section 363(b)(1)(B).[92]

This information may include the following:

(1) the debtor's privacy policy;

(2) the potential losses or gains of privacy to consumers if such sale or such lease is approved by the court;

(3) the potential costs or benefits to consumers if such sale or such lease is approved by the court; and

(4) the potential alternatives that would mitigate potential privacy losses or potential costs to consumers.[93]

A related privacy issue is addressing the transfer of information in the merger or acquisition context. When a merger or other acquisition is happening care must be taken

---

88. "Personally identifiable information" means (A) if provided by an individual to the debtor in connection with obtaining a product or a service from the debtor primarily for personal, family, or household purposes (i) the first name (or initial) and last name of such individual, whether given at birth or time of adoption, or resulting from a lawful change of name; (ii) the geographical address of a physical place of residence of such individual; (iii) an electronic address (including an e-mail address) of such individual; (iv) a telephone number dedicated to contacting such individual at such physical place of residence; (v) a social security account number issued to such individual; or (vi) the account number of a credit card issued to such individual; or (B) if identified in connection with 1 or more of the items of information specified in (A), (i) a birth date, the number of a certificate of birth or adoption, or a place of birth; or (ii) any other information concerning an identified individual that, if disclosed, will result in contacting or identifying such individual physically or electronically. 11 U.S.C. § 101(41A).

89.   11 U.S.C. § 363(b).

90.   11 U.S.C. § 332(a).

91.   *Id.*

92.   11 U.S.C. § 332(b).

93.   *Id.*

to ensure that privacy issues are not ignored. As with bankruptcy issues, there can be restrictions on the transfer of personally identifiable information, depending upon the policy under which the information was collected. For example, if the information was collected under an opt-in policy that requires user consent before a change is made, then transferring the information can be problematic, particularly if the privacy policy greatly restricts the possibility of transfer and does not address the issue of transfer if there is a merger or acquisition of assets.

2:23.   Practice Pointer—Complying with Bankruptcy Reform Act

The key to complying with the Bankruptcy Reform Act is to have a privacy policy in place that informs consumers, presumably at the time they provide you information, that their information may be treated as an asset of the company and sold in a bankruptcy or other sale of all, or substantially all, of the company's assets. Certain companies will take the added step of stating that the privacy policy in effect at the time of information collection will not apply in the bankruptcy context.

2:24.   Opt-in versus opt-out issues

An issue that many companies have to address is under what circumstances they will share customer information with third parties. Some companies will not share information unless a consumer specifically consents to the disclosure. This is commonly called an "opt-in" policy because the consumer has expressly permitted the disclosure. There are also companies that take a different approach and share information unless a consumer objects to his or her information being shared. This type of policy is also known as an "opt-out" policy, because unless the consumer objects, the information will be shared.

A common issue faced by companies is what happens when a company changes its policy and has data that it has collected under a prior version of a privacy policy. There is no federal or state statute that prohibits a change in a privacy policy, though there are issues with the FTC that companies must be aware of. The FTC has brought enforcement actions against companies that change policies and share information when consumers were previously informed that their information would not be shared without their express consent. While this raises issues if a company has elected to use an opt-in policy, it is notable that in recent cases the FTC has not based its allegations on the change of policy alone and instead focused on the opt-in nature of the policy. An important example of this enforcement is the FTC's consent degree (proposed at the time of this books publication) against Google, which would require opt-in for subsequent charges to Google's privacy policy (76 Fed. Reg. 18762; May 20, 2011.)

This is important to businesses that utilize an opt-out scheme because in many situations businesses may, over time, want to change how and with whom they share information. Since there is no express restriction upon changes in privacy policies (and changes are expressly contemplated in many laws) a common question is whether a company that gathers information under a prior version of an opt-out privacy policy can change that policy and share previously collected information in new ways.

There is no law prohibiting this practice and, prior to the Google case, the FTC had not publicly taken the position that such an act is a deceptive trade practice. Whether such a change would be permitted would likely depend upon the language of the policy and whether consumers were aware that the policy was subject to change and if the policy informed them how changes to the policy will be communicated (which would presumably include advising them to check the policy that is posted for amendments) and when these changes will be effective.

2:25.   Double opt-ins

One thing that companies are beginning to consider is whether, though it is in no way legally required, double opt-ins should be used. This process involves using a second step after a person signs up to receive commercial e-mails. Instead of just sending commercial e-mails after receiving opt-in consent, an e-mail is sent to the recipient (usually with a Web link) and the recipient must click on the link and confirm their consent to receive e-mails. While this is not the norm, or even accepted to the point to be considered a best practice, it is being utilized more as companies become more concerned about the costs associated with e-mail litigation.

2:26.   Blogging

Blogging has become one of the more popular methods of posting information and communicating on the web. Indeed, some companies are now using blogs for internal communication, as well as to receive customer feedback. Blogs are in large part very similar to the message boards of old, but offer an easier user interface and more immediate activity. Privacy issues abound, including general Internet-based issues, as well as concerns regarding public posting and defamation liability. The CDA is of note, as are the subpoena issues identified in chapter 4, including regarding the anonymity issues that plaintiffs often face. Finally, to the extent blogs are used by companies for internal purposes, or if they contain information relevant to litigation, there may be retention requirements even for these forms of communication.

2:27.   ADA and websites

There are a number of cases, discussed below, that in certain circumstances apply the ADA to websites. While there are no binding guidelines, companies may want to consider the federal access regulations for the government. In *National Federation of the Blind v. Target Corp.*, the Northern District of California court addressed the application of the ADA to websites that allegedly discriminated against the blind.[94] Target operates Internet sales via its website, as well as brick-and-mortar stores. It permits the use of its website to facilitate sales in its brick-and-mortar in the brick-and-mortar arena, as well as offering unique web offerings. Target had not attempted to accommodate blind users of its website, though there were allegedly protocols available to design an Internet site that was accessible to such users, including the use of "alternative text" which is invisible code embedded beneath graphics.

---

94.   National Federation of the Blind v. Target Corp., 452 F. Supp. 2d 946 (N.D. Cal. 2006).

The plaintiffs in this matter alleged that because they could not use the Target. com website they were denied full and equal access to the Target stores. The action was based upon alleged violations of the Americans with Disabilities Act, the Unruh Civil Rights Act, and the California Disabled Persons Act. The court concluded that the allegations should survive a motion to dismiss, including because the services on the website were services of a place of public accommodation.[95] The court stated that the website operated as a gateway to some of the services for the brick-and-mortar stores, and therefore liability could exist as a result. The court also noted that to the extent that the website offered information services that are not connected to the stores and which do not affect the enjoyment of goods and services offered in the stores, the plaintiffs could not state a claim for violation of the ADA.[96]

The court also examined the application of the dormant commerce clause, concluding that the dormant commerce clause did not preclude application of California law, and thus the plaintiffs also stated a claim for violation of California's unique laws. The court noted that Target could generate a web page specific to California, as other websites had done for foreign users.[97] The court also noted that it was possible for Target to determine the geographic location of its users and target content based upon the location of the user.[98]

While websites can be tied to a place of public accommodation, and thus subject to the ADA, the connection that is used to connect to the Internet would not be subject to the ADA and hence ISPs should not be bound by the ADA's requirements.[99]

One issue to note is that there are federal requirements that address accessibility of websites. While generally they are not applicable to private websites, there are certain times where the government regulations apply—in particular where there is a website provided under contract to the federal government.[100]

2:28.   Understanding internet service provider compliance

Internet service providers face a number of privacy issues. In addition to the laws discussed in this chapter, they also face heightened burdens under the Electronic Communications Privacy Act[101] and state wiretap laws,[102] as well as telecom and cable privacy laws, in certain circumstances.

---

95.   *Id.* at 955.

96.   *Id.* at 956.

97.   *Id.* at 962.

98.   National Federation, 452 F. Supp. 2d at 962.

99.   *See* Belton v. Comcast Cable Holdings, LLC, 151 Cal. App. 4th 1224 (2007) (cable provider not subject to Unruh Act claim); *see also*, Torres v. AT&T Broadband, LLC, 158 F. Supp. 2d 1035, 1037 (N.D. Cal. 2001) ("[t]he ADA includes an exhaustive list of private entities that constitute a public accommodation, and a digital cable system is not one of them.").

100. http://www.access-board.gov/sec508/overview.htm.

101. See Chapter 6.

102. See Chapter 8.

2:29.   Amendments to privacy policies

One court, in the context of assessing a party's obligation to disclose server logs addressed the issue of amendments to privacy policies. While it did not address directly the issue of retroactive amendments, the court noted that the defendant's privacy policy was not a reason to preclude disclosure of IP addresses and other information that could lead to the identification of users because the defendant's website reserved the right "at any time to modify, alter or update the policy." The court concluded that because the defendant reserved the right to make these changes it could make those changes to comply with the obligations of the order.[103]

The Ninth Circuit addressed the effect of a retroactive modification to a contract, finding it unenforceable, and there has been speculation about the impact of this case on the issue of retroactive modifications to privacy policies.[104] The *Douglas* case involved changes to an online agreement related to telecom services, not privacy, though it did examine when modifications to an online agreement were effective. In sum, the court held that the changes (including changes to pricing and an arbitration clause) were not enforceable because they were posted without notice and because they were likely unconscionable under California law.[105] While this case could be read to impact the retroactive modification analysis, given the differences in privacy policies, particularly where the customer agrees to notice via posting on the website, a factor not present in the *Douglas* case, modifying a privacy policy by posting notice on a site would still appear to be proper.

2:30.   Are IP addresses "personally identifiable information"?

A court in California has addressed whether IP addresses are "personally identifiable information."[106] In this case, the court, based upon the terms of the defendant's privacy policy, indicated that IP addresses, and associated server logs, were not personally identifiable information.[107]

2:31.   Subscriber information and privacy

There are a number of cases that have held that there is no expectation of privacy in customer information that is provided to ISPs.[108] However, courts have been somewhat inconsistent in their interpretation of federal privacy law regarding ISPs. While the federal courts have typically held there is no constitutional right of privacy in customer

---

103. Columbia Pictures Industries v. Bunnell, 2007 WL 2080419 (C.D. Cal. 2006).

104. Douglas v. U.S. Dist. Court for Cent. Dist. of California, 495 F.3d 1062 (9th Cir. 2007).

105. Douglas, 495 F.3d at 1066 ("Indeed, a party can't unilaterally change the terms of a contract; it must obtain the other party's consent before doing so. This is because a revised contract is merely an offer and does not bind the parties until it is accepted. And generally 'an offeree cannot actually assent to an offer unless he knows of its existence.'").

106. Columbia Pictures Industries v. Bunnell, 2007 WL 2080419 (C.D. Cal. 2006).

107. *Id. See also* Johnson v. Microsoft Corp. (W.D. Wash. 2009); VPR v. Docs 1-1017 (2:``-CV-02068j; C.D. Ill. Apr. 29, 2011).

108. United States v. Hambrick, 55 F. Supp. 504 (W.D. Va. 1999), aff'd 225 F.3d 656 (4th Cir. 2000), cert. denied, 531 U.S. 1099, 121 (2001); United States v. Kennedy, 81 F. Supp. 2d 1103 (D. Kan. 2000); *see also* Guest v. Simon, 255 F.3d 325, 336 (6th Cir. 2001); Freedman v. AOL, Inc., 2005 WL 2982234 (D. Conn. 2005).

identifying information stored by ISPs, state courts have not consistently followed this.[109] The New Jersey courts have found that their state constitution implicitly creates a right of privacy that protects, in certain circumstances, the disclosure of this type of information, particularly where the subpoena requesting the information was improperly issued or defective.[110]

2:32.   Online offers

One court recently addressed when an online advertisement is, or is not, an offer. In *Trell*, the defendants had a website that solicited individuals to submit a story and other ideas to them. The plaintiff submitted a story, and it was rejected by the defendants. The plaintiff argued that the statements on the website constituted an offer, which he accepted by submitting a response to them. The court drew a distinction between an advertisement, which is seen as an offer for a third party to make an offer, and an actual offer made to a third party. The court stated:

> Statements that urge members of the general public to take some action in response thereto, as is clearly depicted in the Amended Complaint herein, are commonly characterized as advertisements. Advertisements are not offers—they invite offers. Likewise, responses to advertisements are not acceptances—they are offers.[111]

This ruling is consistent with a number of other non-online advertising cases.[112]

---

109. *See* Guest v. Leis, 255 F.3d 325 (6th Cir. 2001); United States v. Kennedy, 81 F. Supp. 2d 1103 (D. Kan. 2000); United States v. Hambrick, 55 F. Supp. 2d 504 (W.D. Va. 1999); United States v. Cox, 190 F. Supp. 2d 330 (N.D. N.Y. 2002).

110. *See* State of New Jersey v. Reid, 389 N.J. Super. 563 (2007).

111. Trell v. American Association of the Advancement of Science, 2007 WL 1500497 (W.D. N.Y. 2007), citing Mesaros v. United States, 845 F.2d 1576, 1580-81 (Fed. Cir. 1988); Leonard v. Pepsico, Inc., 88 F. Supp. 2d 116, 122 (S.D. N.Y. 1999).

112. Rhenalu v. Alcoa, Inc., 224 F. Supp. 2d 773 (D. Del. 2002); MLMC, Ltd. V. Airtouch Communications, Inc., 215 F. Supp. 2d 464, 478 (D. Del. 2002); Hartle v. United States, 18 Cl. Ct. 479, 483 (Ct. Cl. 1989); Hoon v. Pate Construction Co., 607 So.2d 423 (Fla. App. 1992), *cert. denied*, 618 So.2d 210 (Fla. 1993); Chang v. First Colonial Sav. Bank, 242 Va. 388 (Va. 1991); Kane v. League of Oregon Cities, 66 Or. App. 836 (1984); Anderson v. Board, etc., of Public Schools, 122 Mo. 61 (Mo. 1894); Osage v. Homestead Inc. v. Sutphin, 657 S.W.2d 346 (Mo. Ct. App. 1983); Group One, Ltd. v. Hallmark Cards, Inc., 254 F.3d 1041 (Fed. Cir. 2001).

Chapter 3

The Children's Online Privacy Protection Act

3:1. Children's Online Privacy Protection Act (COPPA)

The Children's Online Privacy Protection Act (COPPA)[1] is a law that is directed to protecting the personally identifiable information of children 12 and under.[2] COPPA is enforced by the FTC, and COPPA has been one of the statutes that the FTC has utilized as the basis of a number of enforcement actions.

COPPA applies to owners of the following:

(1) commercial websites that are directed to children 12 and under that collect personal information from children;

(2) general websites that knowingly collect personal information from children 12 and under; and

(3) general websites that have a separate children's area and that collect personal information from children 12 and under.[3]

---

1. Many get this law confused with the Children's Online Protection Act, an unrelated and now overturned law, the revival of which ironically has served as the basis for the Department of Justice's spate of subpoenas to Internet Service Providers. Indeed, after a trial on the merits, the Eastern District of Pennsylvania ultimately concluded the COPA was unconstitutional. ACLU v. Gonzales, 478 F. Supp. 2d 775 (E.D. Pa. 2007), order aff'd, 534 F.3d 181 (3d Cir. 2008), cert. denied, 129 S. Ct. 1032 (2009).

2. 15 U.S.C. § 6501(1).

3. 15 U.S.C. §§ 6501(9), 6502(a)(1).

If a website is subject to COPPA, it must post a privacy policy on the homepage of the website and link to the privacy policy on every page where personal information is collected.[4] The website must also provide notice about the site's information collection practices to parents and obtain verifiable parental consent before collecting personal information from children.[5]

COPPA also precludes websites from conditioning a child's participation in a game, contest, or other activity on the child disclosing more personal information than is reasonably necessary to participate in that activity.[6] The website must also maintain the confidentiality, security, and integrity of personal information collected from children.

Parents have certain choices regarding the use of their children's information. Websites are required to provide parents a choice as to whether their child's personal information will be disclosed to third parties. Parents must also be given access to their child's personal information and the opportunity to delete the child's personal information and opt out of future collection or use of the information.[7]

While COPPA appears only to apply to information that is gathered from children, there is some indication that the FTC may view COPPA as applying much more broadly. While COPPA would not facially appear to apply to information regarding children 12 and under if that information is not received directly from the child, the FTC's view may be that COPPA restricts certain marketing related activities involving children, irrespective of how the information is obtained. Thus, if your business collects information regarding children 12 and under from someone other than the child himself, some thought should be given before any marketing activities are undertaken. If personally identifiable information regarding children 12 and under is simply included in databases that are used for marketing purposes, and not otherwise segregated so that marketing activities do not take place, your company may run afoul of the FTC's interpretation of COPPA.

On March 15, 2006, despite calls for reforms, the FTC decided to retain the COPPA regulations found at 16 C.F.R. §§ 312, *et seq*. and 15 U.S.C. §§ 6501 to 6508.

3:2.   Age representations and click-wrap agreements

While the FTC does not view these blanket age representations as necessarily sufficient under COPPA, one federal court in Ohio found that an Internet website could not be sued for relying upon a blanket statement in a clickwrap agreement that all users were over 18, and that it had no obligation to assess the truth of these representations, particularly where the website had specifically disclaimed any obligation to do so.[8]

---

4.   16 C.F.R. § 312.4(b)(1).

5.   16 C.F.R. §§ 312.4(c)(1)(a)(B), 312.5.

6.   16 C.F.R. § 312.7.

7.   16 C.F.R. § 312.8.

8.   Doe v. SexSearch.com, 502 F. Supp. 2d 719 (N.D. Ohio 2007), judgment aff'd, 551 F.3d 412 (6th Cir. 2008).

3:3.   Recent COPPA enforcement actions

After announcing the retention of the COPPA Rule, the FTC has brought several cases, three of which had seven-figure fines as part of the resolution of the cases. As more fully discussed below, these cases appear to demonstrate that the FTC is quite focused on COPPA compliance, despite the questions that had been raised concerning whether the COPPA Rule would be retained.

3:4.   COPPA FAQ

The FTC has published a FAQ regarding COPPA that it recently revised.[9] The FAQ provides guidance on the deletion of children's information, the use of session cookies, disclosure of information to third parties, and issues regarding the collection of children's information.

Practice Pointer—Complying with COPPA

Determining whether a company collects information from or about children 12 and under is the first step to determining whether COPPA is applicable. This is true even if the company does not believe that it is subject to COPPA, because merely adding a data field that collects age may subject the company to COPPA for certain users. Thus, eliminating the collection of age, if at all possible, is likely the best method for sites that are not targeted to children to avoid COPPA's reach.

If age information must be collected, and the site does not want to be subject to COPPA, it is important to utilize session cookies, or some other mechanism, that will restrict children's attempts to access the website if an inappropriate age is identified.

The FTC has also expressed concern about conduct that encourages children to falsify their age, so care should be taken regarding the message that is posted if a child enters an ineligible age.

3:5.   FTC enforcement actions—Pre-COPPA enforcement— In the Matter of Geocities

The first case the FTC brought in the children's online Space was against Geocities—also its first Internet case. The case pre-dated COPPA, involved the collection of children's information, and is more fully discussed in chapter _.

3:6.   FTC enforcement actions—Pre-COPPA enforcement— In the Matter of Liberty Financial Companies, Inc.

In another case that pre-dated COPPA, the FTC brought an enforcement action against Liberty Financial Companies for allegedly falsely representing that information collected from children would be maintained anonymously. The FTC alleged that in fact the information that was collected was not anonymous and was maintained in an identifiable manner. The FTC also believed that while the site generally wasn't applicable to children, there were several portions of the site that made it appealing to children, including

---

9.   *See* http://www.ftc.gov/privacy/coppafaqs.shtm, revised October 7, 2008 (Last visited February 7, 2011).

the use of contests and prizes. In one of these areas, Liberty Financial was alleged to have asked for financial information from children, as well as personally identifiable information such as name, address, age, and e-mail address.

The matter was resolved via a consent decree, which included reporting requirements and precluded Liberty Financial from collecting personal information if the company had actual knowledge that the child did not have parental consent to provide the information. Liberty Financial was also required to post a clear and prominent privacy statement on its websites directed to children under 13 that explained the company's privacy practices regarding the use and collection of personal information. Finally, Liberty Financial was required to obtain verifiable parental consent, consistent with COPPA, for children under 13.

3:7. FTC enforcement actions—COPPA enforcement matters—In the Matter of Toysmart.com

The first enforcement case brought after the effective date of COPPA was against Toysmart.com in its bankruptcy proceeding. This case involved the sale of children's personal information in violation of the website's privacy policy, according to the FTC. The privacy policy at issue stated that information collected from customers would never be shared with third parties. When the company ran into financial difficulties and filed for bankruptcy, it attempted to sell the information. On July 10, 2000, the FTC filed a lawsuit against Toysmart.com to block the sale of the information.

The case was ultimately resolved by settlement. Among the terms of the settlement was the requirement that Toysmart.com not sell the customers' information as a standalone asset and that only a "qualified buyer," defined as an entity that is in a related market and that expressly agreed to be Toysmart.com's successor in interest as to the customer information, could buy the information. Additionally, the qualified buyer was required to follow the terms of the existing privacy statement and could not change the information practices unless it obtained opt-in consent from the prior customers.

3:8. FTC enforcement actions—COPPA enforcement matters—In The Matter Of BigMailbox.com, Inc., Monarch Services, Inc., et al., and Booksmart, Ltd., Noan Quan

In this matter, BigMailbox.com and Quan were alleged to have improperly collected personal information from children under 13 years of age without parental consent. These defendants operated a number of different Web sites and jointly agreed to pay $100,000 in civil penalties. The Girlslife.com Web site targeted girls age 9–14 and offered content that was targeted to this demographic. Girlslife.com partnered with BigMailbox. com and Booksmart, Ltd. in offering free e-mail accounts and online message boards for children. The FTC alleged that the defendants collected person information from children, including full name, home address, e-mail address and telephone numbers, and did not post privacy policies that complied with COPPA. Moreover, the defendants did not obtain verifiable parental consent from parents prior to collecting information. This was particularly problematic to the FTC because the privacy policy allegedly stated that information would not be collected without verifiable parental consent. The FTC also alleged that the defendants collected more personal information from children than was required for participation in the sites' activities.

In addition to civil penalties, the FTC required the deletion of all information collected from children since COPPA became effective. Certain other defendants were also barred from making deceptive claims in their privacy policies.

3:9. FTC enforcement actions—COPPA enforcement matters—In the Matter of Lisa Frank, Inc.

In this case the FTC alleged that Lisa Frank, Inc., a manufacturer of popular toys and school supplies for girls, which also operated a website that advertised those products, violated COPPA in a number of ways. The FTC alleged that the website was directed toward children and that the defendant had actual knowledge of the fact that it was collecting information from children. Lisa Frank, Inc. was alleged to have failed to obtain verifiable parental consent before any collection or use of personal information; to have failed to provide direct notice to parents about its intent to collect personal information from children, that parental consent was required for the collection, and other requisite disclosures; and to have failed to make the requisite disclosures on its website. The FTC also alleged that the company violated the provision that a website operator cannot condition participation in an online activity on a child providing more information than is reasonably necessary for the activity.

The settlement permanently barred Lisa Frank, Inc. from future violations of COPPA and required certain representations regarding children's privacy online. It also required the company, if it operates a child-directed site after the settlement, to place a hyperlink to the FTC's website pages regarding the COPPA rule. The settlement also called for the payment of a civil penalty of $30,000.

3:10. FTC enforcement actions—COPPA enforcement matters—In the Matter of American Popcorn Company (Jolly Time)

In this enforcement matter, the FTC alleged that American Popcorn Company maintained a website with a "Kid's Club" section that contained information and material, including contests, directed toward children 12 or under. The company was alleged to have collected information, including personal information such as name, e-mail address, and home address, from children 12 or under who used the Kid's Club, without obtaining parental consent. The FTC also alleged that the company conditioned participation in certain online activities based upon children disclosing more information than was needed to participate in those activities. Additionally, the FTC alleged that certain of the statements regarding parental consent in the online privacy policy were inaccurate.

This matter resolved for a civil penalty of $10,000, as well as requirements that the company meet the terms of the COPPA rule and not make further misrepresentations regarding policies about collecting, disclosing, or using children's person information. There were also additional reporting requirements and document retention requirements.

3:11.   FTC enforcement actions—COPPA enforcement matters—In the Matter of The Ohio Art company (Etch-A-Sketch)

In this case, the FTC alleged that the manufacturer of the Etch-A-Sketch collected person information from children who used a particular portion of the website—when they registered for a service known as "Etchy's Birthday Club." The site allegedly collected names, addresses, e-mail addresses, dates of birth, and ages from children as part of an online prize give-away. The FTC alleged that rather than getting verifiable parental consent, the company merely asked children to get their parent's permission before providing information. The FTC also alleged the company collected more information than was reasonably necessary to participate in the online activity and that the internet privacy policy did not properly or accurately disclose the information collection practices of the website and did not make certain disclosures required by COPPA. Finally, the FTC alleged that the site failed to provide parents the opportunity to review the personal information that was collected from the children or to inform parents of their right to prevent further collection and use of the information.

The settlement with the FTC called for the payment of a $35,000 civil penalty, as well as the requirement that the company meet the requirements of COPPA.

3:12.   FTC enforcement actions—COPPA enforcement matters—Mrs. Field's Famous Brands, Inc.

In its seventh COPPA enforcement case, the FTC alleged that Mrs. Field's Cookies collected personal information from children 12 or under via websites that were directed to children 12 and under. These websites offered birthday clubs and provided coupons for free products. While the information was not provided to third parties by the company, the company was alleged to have collected personal information from more than 84,000 children, including their full name, address, birth date, and e-mail address, without first obtaining verifiable parental consent.

Mrs. Field's paid civil penalties of $100,000 and agreed not to violate COPPA in the future. At the time, this settlement represented the largest COPPA civil penalty.

3:13.   FTC enforcement actions—COPPA enforcement matters—In the matter of Hershey Foods Corporation

Hershey Foods Corporation operated more than 30 websites, many of which the FTC believed were directed toward children. While the company attempted to get parental consent via an online form, the FTC alleged that this form did not meet the COPPA standards because, in the FTC's view, this method was not reasonably calculated to ensure that the person providing consent was the child's parent. This was because the company allegedly took no steps to ensure that a parent or guardian saw or filled out consent forms. Moreover, the FTC alleged that even if the form was not filled out, the company still collected personal information from children.

This case represented the first COPPA case to challenge a company's method of obtaining parental consent. The resolution involved the payment of a civil penalty of

$85,000, as well as the company's agreement not to violate COPPA in the future. It also included typical record retention and disclosure requirements to monitor compliance with the settlement agreement.

3:14.   FTC enforcement actions—COPPA enforcement matters—Bonzi Software, Inc.

Bonzi Software marketed software that displayed only briefly an interactive icon on users' computers. The registration form required users to provide personal information when users obtained the software, including a date of birth. As a result, the FTC alleged that Bonzi Software had actual knowledge that children were registering to obtain its software. The FTC alleged that Bonzi software failed to provide direct notice to parents concerning the information that it was collecting from children and did not obtain verifiable parental consent before collecting this information. The FTC also alleged that Bonzi Software did not provide adequate privacy disclosures online or a reasonable means for parents to review the personal information collected from their children.

The settlement required the deletion of all information collected in violation of COPPA, prohibited future COPPA violations, and imposed civil penalties of $75,000 among the defendants.

The case was notable at the time because it was the first so-called actual knowledge case brought by the FTC.

3:15.   FTC enforcement actions—COPPA enforcement matters—In the Matter of UMG

The FTC alleged that UMG operated a number of general audience websites, as well as websites that were appealing to children. The websites offered a number of online resources and activities including newsletters, fan clubs, bulletin boards, and other similar information. The websites' registration forms allegedly collected personal information including name, birthday, home address, e-mail address, gender, and phone number, as well as information regarding buying preferences and music preferences. Because it collected the date of birth, the FTC alleged that UMG had actual knowledge it was collecting information from children 12 and under. The FTC also alleged that certain websites were directed to children under COPPA. The FTC alleged that UMG violated COPPA because it sent notices to parents after collecting the children's person information.

UMG was ordered to pay a $400,000 civil penalty, in addition to having records retention and other requirements placed on it.

3:16.   FTC enforcement actions—COPPA enforcement matters—In the Matter of Xanga.com, Inc.

Xanga.com was a social networking site that permitted users to create pages and blogs that contained extensive personal information, as well as other content. In this case, the FTC alleged that Xanga and certain individuals violated COPPA by failing to "provide notice to parents of their information practices," failing to obtain verifiable parental consent before collecting information from children, and using and disclosing personal information from children online.

Ultimately the matter was resolved via a consent decree, which imposed additional reporting and disclosure requirements, as well as the payment of a $1 million fine. This was the largest fine at the time for a COPPA violation. It is likely that such a large fine was assessed, in part, because there were over 1,700,000 Xanga accounts alleged to have been created in five years for children who were 12 or under.

3:17. FTC enforcement actions—COPPA enforcement matters—In the Matter of Imbee.com

In its second consecutive online social networking case under COPPA, the FTC alleged that the operators of Imbee.com operated a social networking site specifically targeting kids and "tweens." The website was promoted as a "free, secure, social networking and blogging destination specifically designed for kids ages 8 to 14." It claimed to have a "purposely designed level of safety and satisfaction for young members" and was promoted as being "safer than other social networking sites." Despite these representations, the FTC alleged that Imbee.com collected and maintained personal information from children 12 and under without notifying their parents and obtaining verifiable parental consent. Imbee.com was alleged to have permitted over 10,000 children to create accounts. The account creation process included the collection of person information such as name, date of birth, parent's e-mail address, other e-mail addresses, gender, user names, and passwords. The FTC also alleged that children who had registered were permitted to create and post text, photographs, and other content on their personal pages, which could not be viewed by others until the parent had completed the registration process. However, if the parent did not respond to Imbee.com's e-mail notification or complete the registration process, the site maintained the information.

The FTC alleged that these actions were a violation of COPPA because information was collected before verifiable parental consent was given, because there was a failure to provide sufficient notice of what information was collected online, as well as the site's use and disclosure practices for the information, and also because the site failed to provide notice of the types of information that was collected from children prior to obtaining verifiable parental consent. The FTC also alleged that the e-mail notice to parents was insufficient because while it provided general information about the site, it did not disclose that the site had already collected personal information regarding the child and failed to inform parents of the right to review or have their children's personal information deleted.

The resolution of the matter required the payment of a $130,000 civil penalty, prohibited the defendants from further violating COPPA, and required the deletion of all information collected and maintained in violation of COPPA. There were also record-keeping and disclosure requirements, as well as internal training requirements.

3:18.   FTC enforcement actions—COPPA enforcement matters—In the Matter of Sony BMG Entertainment

In this action under COPPA, Sony BMG was alleged to have knowingly collected personal information from 30,000 under-age children on almost 200 websites without first obtaining verifiable parental consent. These sites were alleged to have permitted children to create personal fan pages, review albums, upload content including photos and videos, engage in private messaging, and post comments on message boards and other online forums. The FTC alleged that this permitted children to interact with other individuals of all ages, including adults. The FTC also alleged that Sony Music violated section 5 of the FTC Act by stating that users that were 12 or under would be restricted from participating in certain activities on the Web. The settlement required a payment of a civil penalty of $1 million, the deletion of information that was collected or maintained in violation of COPPA, and compliance reporting and recordkeeping obligations, as well as the distribution of certain FTC information regarding COPPA.

The case and FTC's assessment of a significant fine for the alleged violations show the FTC's continuing interest and desire to enforce COPPA. The case also demonstrates that the FTC intends to enforce COPPA against general websites that may be attractive to and therefore be directed to children.

3:19.   FTC enforcement actions—COPPA enforcement matters—United States v. Playdom, Inc., a subsidiary of Disney Enterprises, Inc.

On May 12, 2011, the FTC released a proposed consent order against Playdom, Inc., an operator of "virtual worlds" that had recently been acquired by The Walt Disney Company. The FTC alleged that Playdom improperly collected personal information from hundreds of thousands of children under 13. Beyond the record $3 million settlement figure, the case also represented a stop by the FTC into the operations of "cloud computing."

CHAPTER 4.

The Communications Decency Act

4:1.   Communications Decency Act

The goals of the Communications Decency Act ("CDA") were to promote the growth of the Internet, to encourage restrictions on improper content, and at the same time, to limit the liability of ISPs for publishing statements that were authored by third parties. One of the underlying themes of laws regarding the Internet, as well as the cases interpreting them, is that the Internet is so delicate that it can be destroyed by the heavy-handed regulation of legislatures and courts. This thinking underlies the CDA and the Internet tax debate, as well as many other issues. In 2008, a Ninth Circuit decision questioned for the first time this underlying theory, and instead posited a theory that online commerce should not gain certain benefits over offline activity.[1]

---

1.   Fair Housing Council of San Fernando Valley v. Roommates.Com, LLC, 521 F.3d 1157, fn. 13 (9th Cir. 2008), ("The dissent stresses the importance of the Internet to modern life and commerce, Dissent at 1176, and we, of course, agree: The Internet is no longer a fragile new means of communication that could easily be smothered in the cradle by overzealous enforcement of laws and regulations applicable to brick-and-mortar businesses. Rather, it has become a dominant—perhaps the preeminent—means through which commerce is conducted. And its vast reach into the lives of millions is exactly why we must be careful not to exceed the scope of the immunity provided by Congress and thus give online businesses an unfair advantage over their real-world counterparts, which must comply with laws of general applicability.").

The CDA was passed by Congress in response to a particular case, *Stratton Oakmont, Inc. v. Prodigy Services Co.*, which held an Internet service provider liable for defamation due to a message placed upon a message board it ran.[2] The basis of that court's ruling was that Prodigy exercised editorial control over the messages because it selectively deleted certain messages and not others. The Ninth Circuit recently summarized the purpose of the CDA as follows:

> In passing section 230, Congress sought to spare interactive computer services this grim choice by allowing them to perform some editing on user-generated content without thereby becoming liable for all defamatory or otherwise unlawful messages that they didn't edit or delete. In other words, Congress sought to immunize the *removal* of user-generated content, not the *creation* of content: "[S]ection [230] provides 'Good Samaritan' protections from civil liability for providers ... of an interactive computer service for actions to *restrict* ... access to objectionable online material. One of the specific purposes of this section is to overrule *Stratton-Oakmont* [sic] *v. Prodigy* and any other similar decisions which have treated such providers ... as publishers or speakers of content that is not their own *because they have restricted access* to objectionable material." H.R.Rep. No. 104-458 (1996) (Conf.Rep.), as reprinted in 1996 U.S.C.C.A.N. 10 (internal citations omitted) (emphasis in original).[3]

The CDA impacts Internet privacy and security issues in two ways.[4] First, it can impact the liability of an ISP related to postings of information and statements regarding other persons or entities. Second, given its restrictions upon liability, as well as the anonymous status of many posters on blogs, chat rooms, or bulletin boards, many companies or individuals that are defamed or otherwise harmed will typically sue the anonymous posters and subpoena their identity from the ISP.

It is also frequently addressed in spyware and phishing cases where software companies gather information and block programs. Indeed, a software company that gathered a list of sites that appeared to be phishing sites was immune under the CDA because it gathered the information from a third party.[5]

4:2.   Communications Decency Act—Restrictions upon liability

In defamation actions one of the key issues is whether a person is a publisher or speaker of information. The CDA provides that neither providers nor users of an

---

2.   Stratton Oakmont, Inc. v. Prodigy Services Co., 23 Media L. Rep. (BNA) 1794, 1995. WL 323710 (N.Y. Sup 1995).

3.   Fair Housing Council of San Fernando Valley v. Roommates.Com, LLC, 521 F.3d 1157 (9th Cir. 2008).

4.   47 U.S.C. § 230.

5.   Associated Bank-Corp. v. Earthlink, Inc., 2005 WL 2240952 (W.D.Wis. 2005).

interactive computer service[6] will be treated as a publisher or speaker of information that is provided by another information content provider, which therefore eliminates liability.[7] The CDA also eliminates liability for any provider or user of an interactive computer service related to:

(1) any action voluntarily taken in good faith to restrict access to or availability of material that the provider or user considers to be obscene, lewd, lascivious, filthy, excessively violent, harassing, or otherwise objectionable, whether or not such material is constitutionally protected; or

(2) any action taken to enable or make available to information content providers or others the technical means to restrict access to material described above.[8]

The CDA appears to apply immunity beyond the mere publication of information. Certain courts have held that the CDA also gives immunity for service providers even where they have taken on "a publisher's traditional editorial functions—such as deciding whether to publish, withdraw, postpone or alter content ..."[9] The CDA does not, however, provide immunity for a service provider where the service provider contributes to the content. The First Circuit addressed the scope of CDA immunity and held, as have other Circuit Courts, that the immunity will apply to sites, even where the construction and operation of the site have some influence on the content that is posted.[10] Indeed, in one case a website that provided multiple-choice questions and a series of essay questions that shaped the eventual content was found to fall within the CDA's grant of immunity, even for claims of invasion of privacy.[11]

One Ohio federal court recently addressed the scope of CDA immunity with state law claims and found that it applied broadly and barred a number of common law claims.[12] However, another court recently held that allegations by the FTC that the sale of pretexted phone records violated the FTC Act were not barred by the CDA because these claims did not seek to treat the defendant as a publisher under the CDA.[13]

---

6. "Interactive computer service" means any information service, system, or access software provider that provides or enables computer access by multiple users to a computer server, including specifically a service or system that provides access to the Internet and such systems operated or services offered by libraries or educational institutions. 47 U.S.C. § 230(f)(2).

7. 47 U.S.C. § 230(c)(1). "Information content provider" means any person or entity that is responsible, in whole or in part, for the creation or development of information provided through the Internet or any other interactive computer service. 47 U.S.C. § 230(f)(3).

8. 47 U.S.C. § 230(c)(2).

9. Carafano v. Metrosplash.com Inc., 207 F. Supp. 2d 1055, 1064 (C.D. Cal. 2002), aff'd on other grounds, 339 F.3d 1119 (9th Cir. 2003), holding modified by, Fair Housing Council of San Fernando Valley v. Room-mates.Com, LLC, 521 F.3d 1157 (9th Cir. 2008); see also Blumenthal v. Drudge, 992 F. Supp. 44 (D.D.C. 1998) (service provider's retention of editorial right, even if not exercised, did not preclude CDA immunity); Batzel v. Smith, 333 F.3d 1018 (9th Cir. 2003), rejected by, Chicago Lawyers' Committee for Civil Rights Under Law, Inc. v. Craigslist, Inc., 519 F.3d 666 (7th Cir. 2008).

10. Universal Communication Systems, Inc. v. Lycos, Inc., 478 F.3d 413 (1st Cir. 2007), rejected by, Chicago Lawyers' Committee for Civil Rights Under Law, Inc. v. Craigslist, Inc., 519 F.3d 666 (7th Cir. 2008).

11. Carafano, 207 F. Supp. 2d at 1066.

12. These included: breach of contract; fraud; negligent infliction of emotional distress; negligent misrepresentation; breach of warranty; violation of the Ohio Consumer Sales Practices Act; and failure to warn. Doe v. SexSearch.com, 502 F. Supp. 2d 719 (N.D. Ohio 2007).

13. FTC v. Accusearch, Inc., 2007 WL 4356786 (D. Wyo. 2007).

The CDA has also been applied to the online dating service context, and the Court addressed whether there was immunity for a website that allegedly sent false dating profiles and continued to send profiles of members that were no longer part of the website.[14]

4:3.   CDA and defining who is an interactive service provider

The Tenth Circuit recently construed who was an interactive service provider in the context of a company that paid to gather and then publish confidential telephone records. In this case the court of appeal stated "We therefore conclude that a service provider is 'responsible' for the development of offensive content only if it in some way specifically encourages development of what is offensive about the content."[15] In this case, the Defendant had paid researchers to gather information that was later disclosed on the Internet, so the CDA was found not to apply.

4:4.   Immunity for the conduct of affiliates

Courts have also applied the CDA immunity to service providers that merely provide Internet connections to the web where the ISP's service is used to send e-mails, even where the e-mails are offensive or illegal, even where they are sent by affiliates.[16] In *Beyond Systems*, the plaintiff alleged it received a number of unsolicited and deceptive e-mails regarding certain websites that were allegedly affiliates of the defendants. Notably, the content itself was not created by the defendants.[17] The Court examined the conduct of Rackspace, a defendant that provided hosting and web services, and concluded that, as an "interactive computer service provider," Rackspace could not be held liable under Maryland's anti-spam law, due to the CDA.[18]

Roommates.com is a website that attempts to match potential roommates up in an online forum based upon certain preferences. Roommates.com did two key things as part of the registration process to use its site, in addition to asking general background questions: (1) it provided a structure through a series of mandatory questions regarding sex, sexual orientation, and whether users would bring children; and (2) it provided an open-ended "Additional Comments" section. A variety of Fair Housing Councils in California brought a lawsuit seeking to hold Roommates.com liable for asking these questions and thereby inducing its users to violate Fair Housing laws. Roommates.com believed it was immune from liability due to the CDA because it did not create the content, but instead only displayed the responses of its users.

The *Roommates.com* case addressed an important issue—what is the level of online conduct by a website owner that will defeat immunity.[19] While there have been other cases that have indirectly addressed the issue, *Roommates.com* is the first case to

---

14.   Anthony v. Yahoo!, 421 F. Supp. 2d 1257 (N.D. Cal. 2006).

15.   FTC v. Accusearch, 570 F.3d 1187, 1199 (10th Cir. 2009).

16.   Beyond Systems, Inc. v. Keynetics, Inc., 422 F. Supp. 2d 523 (D. Md. 2006).

17.   Beyond Systems, 422 F. Supp. 2d at 529.

18.   Beyond Systems, 422 F. Supp. 2d. at 536.

19.   Fair Housing Council of San Fernando Valley v. Roommates.com, LLC, 521 F.3d 1157 (9th Cir. 2008).

directly confront it. The issue was raised in this case because, as noted above, unlike message boards, blogs, or other forms of online communication, as part of the sign up process Roommates.com asked questions regarding sex, sexual orientation, and whether the person has children.[20] According to the plaintiffs, these questions, if asked offline, allegedly violated Fair Housing laws. Additionally, Roommates.com also had a search engine that permitted users to search for potential roommates based upon allegedly discriminatory categories.[21]

The Ninth Circuit concluded that the CDA did not provide immunity for certain portions of the Roommates.com website. Regarding the mandatory, posted questions, the Ninth Circuit concluded that Rommates.com did not have immunity under the CDA.

> Roommate created the questions and choice of answers, and designed its website registration process around them. Therefore, Roommate is undoubtedly the "information content provider" as to the questions and can claim no immunity for posting them on its website, or for forcing subscribers to answer them as a condition of using its services.

***

> The CDA does not grant immunity for inducing third parties to express illegal preferences. Roommate's own acts—posting the questionnaire and requiring answers to it—are entirely its doing and thus section 230 of the CDA does not apply to them. Roommate is entitled to no immunity.[22]

This was because by posting the mandatory questionnaire Roommates.com helped develop, at least in part, the content.[23] The Ninth Circuit also addressed whether Roommates.com had immunity for the allegedly discriminatory comments made by users in the "Additional Comments" section. The Court concluded that Roommates.com had immunity for these statements since, unlike in the other portions of the site, it did not "develop" the content.[24]

---

20. Roommates, 521 F.3d at 1164.

21. Roommates, 521 F.3d at 1167.

22. Roommates.com, 521 F.3d at 1165. ("The salient fact in Carafano was that the website's classifications of user characteristics did absolutely nothing to enhance the defamatory sting of the message, to encourage defamation or to make defamation easier: The site provided neutral tools specifically designed to match romantic partners depending on their voluntary inputs. By sharp contrast, Roommate's website is designed to force subscribers to divulge protected characteristics and discriminatory preferences, and to match those who have rooms with those who are looking for rooms based on criteria that appear to be prohibited by the FHA." 521 F.3d at 1172.).

23. The Ninth Circuit noted that this portion of its holding was consistent with its prior holding in Batzel v. Smith, 333 F.3d 1018 (9th Cir. 2003); *see also* Anthony v. Yahoo Inc., 421 F. Supp. 2d 1257 (N.D. Cal. 2006).

24. Roommates.com, 521 F.3d at 1173-74 ("Roommate publishes these comments as written. It does not provide any specific guidance as to what the essay should contain, nor does it urge subscribers to input discriminatory preferences. Roommate is not responsible, in whole or in part, for the development of this content, which comes entirely from subscribers and is passively displayed by Roommate. Without reviewing every

The Ninth Circuit then addressed the search engine and e-mail notification system created by Roommates.com that permitted users to search for roommates based upon allegedly discriminatory categories. This search engine was not a generic search engine that could be used to search upon discriminatory categories, but rather one that was explicitly based upon allegedly discriminatory categories.

> Roommate's search function is similarly designed to steer users based on discriminatory criteria. Roommate's search engine thus differs materially from generic search engines such as Google, Yahoo! and MSN Live Search, in that Roommate designed its system to use allegedly unlawful criteria so as to limit the results of each search, and to force users to participate in its discriminatory process.[25]

The Ninth Circuit also concluded that immunity under the CDA did not exist for placing the same allegedly discriminatory categories in search fields in a search engine.[26]

Two other prior Ninth Circuit decisions were then discussed and clarified by the Court. The conclusion that minor editorial changes under *Batzel* were subject to immunity was affirmed, though the Court, without directly addressing the issue, appeared to question whether the editor in that case actually fell within the CDA.[27] The Court also recognized the distinction between choosing what material is placed in an online posting from an editorial perspective versus making the choice to publish material online in the first place. While the former falls within CDA immunity, the latter does not.[28]

The Court also clarified its holding in *Carafano v. Metrosplash.com. Inc.*,[29] limiting its prior conclusion: "We correctly held that the website was immune, but incorrectly suggested that it could never be liable because 'no [dating] profile has any content until

---

essay, Roommate would have no way to distinguish unlawful discriminatory preferences from perfectly legitimate statements. Nor can there be any doubt that this information was tendered to Roommate for publication online. This is precisely the kind of situation for which section 230 was designed to provide immunity.") (internal citations omitted).

25.   Roommates.com, 521 F.3d at 1167.

26.   *Id.* ("Roommate designed its search system so it would steer users based on the preferences and personal characteristics that Roommate itself forces subscribers to disclose. If Roommate has no immunity for asking the discriminatory questions, as we concluded above, see pp. 1163–65, it can certainly have no immunity for using the answers to the unlawful questions to limit who has access to housing.").

27.   Roommates.com, 521 F.3d at 1170 ("Our opinion is entirely consistent with that part of Batzel which holds that an editor's minor changes to the spelling, grammar and length of third-party content do not strip him of section 230 immunity. None of those changes contributed to the libelousness of the message, so they do not add up to 'development' as we interpret the term.").

28.   Roommates.com, 521 F.3d at 1170-71. ("The distinction drawn by Batzel anticipated the approach we take today. As Batzel explained, if the tipster tendered the material for posting online, then the editor's job was, essentially, to determine whether or not to prevent its posting—precisely the kind of activity for which section 230 was meant to provide immunity. And any activity that can be boiled down to deciding whether to exclude material that third parties seek to post online is perforce immune under section 230. But if the editor publishes material that he does not believe was tendered to him for posting online, then he is the one making the affirmative decision to publish, and so he contributes materially to its allegedly unlawful dissemination. He is thus properly deemed a developer and not entitled to CDA immunity.") (internal citations and foot-notes omitted).

29.   Carafano v. Metrosplash.com. Inc., 339 F.3d 1119 (9th Cir. 2003).

a user actively creates it.'"[30] Going further in a footnote, the Court stated, "We disavow any suggestion that *Carafano* holds an information content provider *automatically* immune so long as the content originated with another information content provider."[31] Instead, the Court concluded that *Carafano* was correctly decided because the content at issue was created and developed entirely by the user, using neutral tools without prompting or help from the website operator.[32] Other courts have reached different conclusions regarding these issues under the CDA.[33]

4:5.   The CDA and gripe sites

Certain "gripe sites"—in particular, consumer complaint forums—have been disqualified from CDA immunity if they exercised organizational control, added descriptive headings, and gave instructions to specific users about what type of content to include.[34] This issue has also been addressed in the case of companies that characterize certain Internet conduct, including where a service provider allegedly sent so-called spam complaints. If the company does not contribute to the content, the CDA appears to preclude liability.[35] Ultimately, the distinction that seems to be drawn by the cases is whether the service provider has developed, at least in part, the content.

It should also be noted, as shown by *Beyond Systems*, that the immunity afforded ISPs is not limited to defamation. It includes negligence, state law unfair competition, tortuous interference with prospective economic advantage, claims under Title II of the Civil Rights Act of 1964, and breach of contract claims.[36]

Thus, the CDA has been held to provide complete immunity to a claim against a party that it acted as a publisher.[37] Moreover, merely exercising editorial or other self-regulatory functions is not enough to impose liability.[38]

4:6.   The CDA and social networking

Social networking is a large part of web activity, and one issue that has arisen is the scope of CDA immunity in situations where the service provider has played a role as an intermediary for improper conduct, including issues with minors and other forms of

---

30. Roommates.com, 521 F.3d at 1171, quoting Carafano at 1124.

31. Roommates.com, 521 F.3d at 1170.

32. *Id.*

33. Chicago Lawyers' Committee for Civil Rights Under Law, Inc. v. Craigslist, Inc., 519 F.3d 666 (7th Cir. 2008).

34. MCW, Inc. v. Badbusinessbureau.com, L.L.C., 2004-1 Trade Cas. (CCH) P 74391, 2004 WL 833595 (N.D. Tex. 2004).

35. Optinrealbig.com, LLC v. Ironport Systems, Inc., 323 F. Supp. 2d 1037 (N.D. Cal. 2004).

36. Ben Ezra, Weinstein, and Company, Inc. v. America Online Inc., 206 F.3d 980, 986, 46 Fed. R. Serv. 3d 35 (10th Cir. 2000); Perfect 10, Inc. v. CCBill, LLC, 340 F. Supp. 2d 1077 (C.D. Cal. 2004), aff'd in part, rev'd in part and remanded, 481 F.3d 751 (9th Cir. 2007), opinion amended and superseded on denial of reh'g, 488 F.3d 1102 (9th Cir. 2007), cert. denied, 128 S. Ct. 709, 169 L. Ed. 2d 553 (2007) and aff'd in part, rev'd in part and remanded, 488 F.3d 1102 (9th Cir. 2007); Novak v. Overture Services, Inc., 309 F. Supp. 2d 446 (E.D. N.Y. 2004); Noah v. AOL Time Warner, Inc., 261 F. Supp. 2d 532, 538 (E.D. Va. 2003), aff'd, 2004 WL 602711 (4th Cir. 2004); Schneider v. Amazon.com, Inc., 108 Wash. App. 454, 464 (Div. 1 2001).

37. *See, e.g.,* Universal Communications Systems, Inc. v. Lycos, Inc., 478 F.3d 413, 418-19 (1st Cir. 2007).

38. Zeran v. American Online, Inc., 129 F.3d 327, 330-31 (4th Cir. 1997).

alleged sexual misconduct. Certain plaintiffs have alleged that social networking sites know sexual predators are using their services, and therefore CDA immunity does not exist.[39] This argument was recently rejected by the Fifth Circuit when it found that MySpace was immune from claims that it had allegedly failed to implement safety procedures to prevent sexual predators from allegedly misusing MySpace. The Court did not consider the plaintiffs' argument that MySpace lacked immunity under the CDA due to its alleged role in creating the content due to an online questionnaire. However, it should be noted that the Ninth Circuit recently addressed this issue in *Roommates. com,*[40] and given the questionnaire as described in the *Doe v. MySpace, Inc.* case, it would appear to fall within the "neutral" category that would still support immunity.

4:7.   Communications Decency Act— immunity v. defense

While certain courts have referred to the CDA as providing immunity, other courts have characterized the CDA's protections as not immunity from suit, but rather a defense to liability.[41]

4:8.   Communications Decency Act—Disclosures by interactive computer services

Providers of interactive computer services must, at the time of entering an agreement with a customer, notify the customer in an appropriate manner that parental control protections are commercially available and that these protections may assist in limiting access to material that is harmful to minors. The notice must identify, or provide the customer with access to information identifying, current providers of such protections.[42]

4:9.   Takeaways from the Ninth Circuit for the CDA

The Court also offered guidance for other businesses on the Internet as to what it means to "develop" content, and in sum it appears that the case can be read to say that it is not necessarily the use of categories that defeats immunity, but rather the mandatory use of categories that defeat immunity. Thus, if the categories, even if discriminatory, are created by the users, they may not defeat immunity.

It should be noted that the Court was not seeking to impose liability upon "neutral" search engines that can be used to run discriminatory searches:[43]

> If an individual uses an ordinary search engine to query for a "white roommate," the search engine has not contributed to any alleged unlawfulness in the individual's conduct; providing *neutral* tools to

---

39. Doe v. MySpace, Inc., 528 F.3d 413 (5th Cir. 2008), cert. denied, 129 S. Ct. 600, 172 L. Ed. 2d 456 (2008).

40. Fair Housing Council of San Fernando Valley v. Roommates.Com, LLC, 521 F.3d 1157 (9th Cir. 2008).

41. Energy Automation Systems v. Xcentric Ventures, LLC, 2007 WL 1557202 (M.D. Tenn. 2007).

42. 47 U.S.C. § 230(d).

43. Roommates.com, 521 F.3d at 1169.

carry out what may be unlawful or illicit searches does not amount to "development" for purposes of the immunity exception.[44]

The Court also provided guidance for dating and housing websites, as well as other sites that would offer similar services, in essence stating that the use of drop-down menus might solve some of the issues:

> A dating website that requires users to enter their sex, race, religion and marital status through drop-down menus, and that provides means for users to search along the same lines, retains its CDA immunity insofar as it does not contribute to any alleged illegality; this immunity is retained even if the website is sued for libel based on these characteristics because the website would not have contributed materially to any alleged defamation. Similarly, a housing website that allows users to specify whether they will or will not receive emails by means of *user-defined* criteria might help some users exclude email from other users of a particular race or sex. However, that website would be immune, so long as it does not require the use of discriminatory criteria.[45]

Thus, having user input on the criteria that are used in general and having these criteria become searchable, but non-mandatory categories, may be one path to avoid liability.[46]

The Ninth Circuit also offered guidance on when a website lost immunity due to edits that it makes to user-generated content:

> A website operator who edits user-created content—such as by correcting spelling, removing obscenity or trimming for length—retains his immunity for any illegality in the user-created content, provided that the edits are unrelated to the illegality. However, a website operator who edits in a manner that contributes to the alleged illegality—such as by removing the word "not" from a user's message reading "[Name] did *not* steal the artwork" in order to transform an innocent message into a libelous one—is directly involved in the alleged illegality and thus not immune.[47]

---

44. *Id.*

45. *Id.*

46. *Id.* at 1172 ("The mere fact that an interactive computer service 'classifies user characteristics ... does not transform [it] into a 'developer' of the 'underlying misinformation.'").

47. Roommates.Com, 521 F.3d at 1169.

4:10.   Prior rulings regarding categories and the CDA

In a case that predated the opinion in *Roommates.com*, a court in Florida held that merely providing categories for a website was insufficient to defeat CDA immunity.[48] In *Whitney Information Network, Inc. v. Xcentric Ventures, LLC*, the Court addressed whether a website's creation of categories that were used to describe a third party would defeat CDA immunity. The Court concluded that the mere creation of categories, even those that were derogatory, absent other facts, was not sufficient to defeat CDA immunity.

> Nevertheless, the Court finds that Defendants cannot be considered to be information content providers of the reports about WIN that include these categories. WIN has not presented any evidence demonstrating that Defendants participated in any way in the selection of these categories to describe WIN. Indeed, WIN simply contends that Defendants supplied a list of categories from which some users selected the phrases "con artists", "corrupt companies", and "false TV advertisements" to categorize their reports. *See* Response at 5-6. However, the Court finds that the mere fact that Xcentric provides categories from which a poster must make a selection in order to submit a report on the ROR website is not sufficient to treat Defendants as information content providers of the reports about WIN that contain the "con artists", "corrupt companies", and "false TV advertisements" categories.[49]

4:11.   CDA and employers

In one case an employer attempted to argue that it was immune from suit under the CDA for an employee's claim that there were sexually-explicit materials on a computer that was used by numerous employees, since the materials were provided by another service provider.[50] Noting that the defendant failed to provide any authority to support this claim, the Court summarily rejected the application of the CDA in this context.

However, California courts have concluded that an employer can be an interactive service provider, and hence immune under the CDA, for the acts of an employee if the employee uses the employer's computer system to make threats to others.[51] In *Delfino*, an employee of the defendant used the defendant's computer system to make threats against the plaintiff. The plaintiff sued the employer, claiming it was liable for the employee's acts. The court of appeal concluded that the CDA applied and that the

---

48. Whitney Information Network v. Xcentric Ventures, LLC, 2008 WL 450095 (M.D.Fla. February 15, 2008).

49. *Id.* at *10.

50. Avery v. Idleaire Technologies Corp., 2007 WL 1574269 (E.D. Tenn. 2007).

51. Delfino v. Agilent Technologies, Inc., 145 Cal. App. 4th 790 (2006), 30 A.L.R.6th 639 (6th Dist. 2006), review denied, (Feb. 28, 2007) and cert. denied, 128 S. Ct. 98, 169 L. Ed. 2d 22 (2007).

employer was immune from suit, even though the claim was not one for defamation, the tort that is traditionally associated with CDA immunity.[52]

4:12.   CDA and Criminal liability

In what appears to be a case of first impression, the District Court for the Eastern District of Pennsylvania addressed whether the CDA provided immunity for criminal liability.[53] In *VoiceNet*, a news reader and Internet service provider sued certain government officials for violation of 42 U.S.C. § 1983, based upon the immunity afforded them under the CDA and other laws. Plaintiffs' servers were seized by law enforcement based upon the allegation that child pornography was contained on the servers. The plaintiffs argued they were immune from prosecution and thus the seizure was improper. The Court first held that the CDA did provide immunity from criminal liability for service providers.[54] The plaintiffs attempted to argue that § 1983 had been violated due to the violation of the CDA, but given the fact that this case was one of first impression, the court declined to give the plaintiffs the right to sue under § 1983 because the right was not clearly established at the time of the alleged violation.[55] The Court also rejected an attempt to borrow a violation of the ECPA to give rise to a § 1983 claim because the ECPA had its own remedial scheme.[56]

4:13.   The CDA and injunctive relief

One open question is whether the CDA would bar injunctive relief against a website. Given that most injunctions require a showing of probable success on the merits for injunctive relief to issue, the CDA likely will impact requests for injunctive relief as well.

Practice Pointer—CDA

The CDA impacts privacy because of the immunity it creates for service providers. Since there is generally no liability for the "publisher" of a defamatory statement, the effected person will likely want to sue the person that posted the comment. As such, the service provider will frequently receive a subpoena for records related to the identity of the person that posted the comments. Service providers react in different ways to these subpoenas. Some will turn over information, with or without notice, and some may try and oppose the subpoenas. The individual that posted the defamatory comments may also attempt to prevent their identity from being disclosed.

4:14.   The CDA and state securities laws

The First Circuit has held that an entity running financial message boards that contain information regarding companies is immune from liability under state securities laws

---

52.   *Delfino*, 145 Cal. App. 4th at 805.
53.   VoiceNet Medications Inc. v. Corbett, 2006 WL 2506318 (E.D. Pa. 2006).
54.   *VoiceNet*, 2006 WL 2506318 at 8.
55.   *VoiceNet*, 2006 WL 2506318 at 13.
56.   *VoiceNet*, 2006 WL 2506318 at 15.

because such liability attaches due to the publication of materials posted by another person, and therefore CDA immunity applies.[57] It also held that message board postings will not be treated any differently even where the construction and operation of the website has some influence on the content of the postings. It also concluded that neither the existence of notice of the false nature of the postings, nor the ability for users to create multiple user accounts changed this conclusion.

4:15.   Statements in Form U-5 and immunity for online defamation

The Second Circuit, based upon a decision by the New York Court of Appeals, found that statements made on a U-5 form, one Broker-Dealers are required to fill out, are privileged and cannot serve as the basis of a defamation claim, though this holding was not based upon the CDA.[58]

4:16.   E-mails and the CDA

One court recently held that allegedly defamatory or actionable statements in email were not protected by the CDA's grant of immunity. In this case a person forwarded certain information found on the Internet, and in some cases added allegedly actionable commentary. The Court rejected CDA immunity because commentary was added by the sender. It also appears that the court concluded, independent of the commentary issue, that this type of conduct was not within the CDA's grant of immunity.[59]

4:17.   CDA held not a basis for a motion to dismiss

One federal court held, in light of its conclusion that the CDA was an affirmative defense, that it could only be raised via a 12(c) motion or a motion for summary judgment, at least where the defendant's status as an interactive service provider was not disputed.[60]

---

57. Universal Communication Systems, Inc. v. Lycos, Inc., 478 F.3d 413 (1st Cir. 2007).

58. Rosenberg v. Metlife, Inc., 493 F.3d 290 (2d Cir. 2007) (citing Rosenberg v. Metlife, Inc., 8 N.Y.3d 359 (2007)).

59. John Doe Anti-Terrorism Officer v. The City of New York, 06-CV-13738(BSJ) (S.D.N.Y. 2008).

60. Curran v. Amazon.com, Inc., 2008 WL 472433 (S.D. W.Va. 2008).

CHAPTER 5

Unauthorized Access to Networks/ Computer Crimes

I. Computer Fraud and Abuse Act

5:1. Introduction

Certain portions of the Controlling The Assault of Non-Solicited Pornography and Marketing Act of 2003 (CAN-SPAM)[1] impacted the Computer Fraud and Abuse Act (CFAA). However, the CFAA regulates Internet-related activities in contexts beyond CAN-SPAM. The CFAA was enacted to address the increasing number of computer crimes that were not covered under existing law. Until 1994, the CFAA only provided criminal penalties, but statutory amendments to the CFAA added civil remedies, which can be used by companies to protect their networks and recover damages for unauthorized access. The CFAA also initially applied almost exclusively to government computers. Now, the statute has much broader coverage, as it applies to any computer used in interstate commerce.

---

1.   *See* chapter 8.

The CFAA can apply in a variety of contexts. It can be relevant in cases where business competitors improperly engage in certain conduct, including "scraping" websites. It comes into play when employees depart and use their companies' networks to send or obtain trade secret information. It also, of course, applies in the more traditional settings, including those involving hacking and the release of worms, Trojan horses, or other malicious programs. It also has new applications, including the digital rights management debate, as well as some overlap with state identity theft laws when information is obtained improperly from computer networks.

Many states have enacted laws that are broader than the CFAA. Certain of these laws, as well as the CFAA, offer civil remedies in addition to criminal penalties. In cases involving e-mails, both the CFAA and the ECPA, discussed in this chapter, may be implicated, as will state wiretap laws.

The CFAA has been used extensively in employer-versus-employee litigation, particularly where an employee attempts to take confidential or other sensitive information and use it to compete with his former employer. A split in the circuit courts appears to be occurring over the scope of the CFAA and whether the CFAA is implicated in these situations, given the subsequent amendments to this law.

The CFAA has both civil and criminal remedies, so it is a powerful tool that can be used to stop illegal activities on computer networks or involving computers.

5:2.   Defining a "computer" under the CFAA

Since the theft of information does not always relate to direct access to a computer system, one question that has been litigated under the Computer Fraud and Abuse Act is whether a CD is a "computer" under the Act.[2] The importance of this question relates to the fact that if a computer is not implicated, then the CFAA is not violated by improper access to information. In *GRW Medical*, the defendant refused to return a CD at the termination of his employment, in order to gain leverage over his former employer. The CD allegedly contained proprietary and trade secret information regarding the plaintiff. Ultimately the court concluded that a CD does not in and of itself process information and that it therefore was not a computer covered by the CFAA.[3]

The district court in Connecticut addressed whether transmitting confidential information that was not obtained via a computer violated the CFAA, holding that mere transmission, if the information wasn't obtained from a computer as defined by the CFAA, would not support a claim.[4]

Some courts have held that the government need not show that any information was misused, but rather that the violation is the abuse of a computer to obtain the information.[5]

---

2.   GWR Medical, Inc. v. Baez, 2008 WL 698995 (E.D. Penn. 2008).

3.   *Id.*

4.   Cenveo, Inc. v. Rao, 659 F.Supp.2d 312 (D.Conn. Sep. 30, 2009) (NO. 3:08 CV 1831 (JBA)).

5.   United States v. Willis, 476 F.3d 1121, 1125 (10th Cir. 2007); *see also*, S.Rep. No. 104-357, at 7–8 ("[T]he crux of the offense under subsection 1030(a)(2)(C) . . . is abuse of a computer to obtain the information."

5:3.   Defining a protected computer

One argument defendants have made is that the CFAA does not apply to conduct that is exclusively conducted in one state and does not cross state lines. As long as the computer is connected to the Internet, this argument will likely be rejected by courts.[6]

5:4.   Preemption of state trespass law on unauthorized access

The CFAA is not intended to preempt state law claims based on unauthorized access to a computer, including trespass to chattels or other claims.[7]

5:5.   Acts that constitute crimes under the CFAA

It is a criminal act for anyone to intentionally access a computer without authorization or beyond the scope of any authority that has been granted, whether the computer is owned by the government or not, if the conduct involved an interstate or foreign communication.[8] It is also a criminal act to knowingly, and with the intent to defraud, access a protected computer[9] (i) without authorization or (ii) beyond the scope of any authorization, if the person furthers a fraud and an item of any value is obtained, if the value obtained is over $5,000 in any one-year period.[10] The wages of employees used to repair damage[11] can be considered when a court considers the $5,000 requirement.[12]

---

6.   United States v. Trotter, 478 F.3d 918 (8th Cir. 2007) (upholding conviction based upon in-state conduct because computer was connected to the Internet); citing United States v. Mitra, 405 F.3d 492 (7th Cir. 2005); *see also* Charles Schwab & Co v. Carter, 2005 WL 351929, at *3 (N.D. Ill. 2005); Patrick Patterson Custom Homes, Inc. v. Bach, 586 F.Supp.2d 1026, 1033-34 (N.D.Ill.2008) ("[I]t suffices to state the computer was used for the business and the business operated in two different states.") (citing Modis, Inc. v. Bardelli, 531 F.Supp.2d 314, 319 (D.Conn.2008)); Charles Schwab & co. Inc. v. Carter, 2005 U.S.Dist. LEXIS 21348 at *26 (N.D.Ill. 2005); Continental Group, Inc. v. KW Property Management, LLC, 622 F.Supp.2d 1357, 1370 (S.D.Fla.2009); Paradigm Alliance, Inc. v. Celeritas Techs., LLC, 248 F.R.D. 598, 602 n. 5 (D.Kan.2008) (citing Reno v. ACLU, 521 U.S. 844, 850 (1997), in concluding that a "computer that provides access to worldwide communications would satisfy the element of interstate communications"); Nordstrom Consulting, Inc. v. M & S Techs., Inc., No. 06 C 3234, 2008 WI, 623660, at *12 (N.D.Ill. Mar. 4, 2008).

7.   Hecht v. Components Intern., Inc., 22 Misc. 3d 360, 867 N.Y.S.2d 889 (N.Y. Sup. 2008), citing Pacific Aerospace and Electronics v. Taylor, 295 F. Supp. 2d 1188, 1194 (E.D. Wash. 2003).

8.   18 U.S.C. § 1030(a)(3).

9.   The term "computer" means an electronic, magnetic, optical, electrochemical, or other high speed data processing device performing logical, arithmetic, or storage functions, and includes any data storage facility or communications facility directly related to or operating in conjunction with such device, but such term does not include an automated typewriter or typesetter, a portable hand held calculator, or other similar device. 18 U.S.C. § 1030(e)(1). The term "protected computer" means a computer (A) exclusively for the use of a financial institution or the United States Government, or, in the case of a computer not exclusively for such use, used by or for a financial institution or the United States Government and the conduct constituting the offense affects that use by or for the financial institution or the Government; or (B) which is used in or affecting interstate or foreign commerce or communication, including a computer located outside the United States that is used in a manner that affects interstate or foreign commerce or communication of the United States. 18 U.S.C. § 1030(e)(2).

10.   18 U.S.C. § 1030(a)(4); America Online, Inc. v. LCGM, Inc., 46 F. Supp. 2d 444 (E.D. Va. 1998); YourNet-Dating, Inc. v. Mitchell, 88 F. Supp. 2d 870 (N.D. Ill. 2000).

11.   The term "damage" means any impairment to the integrity or availability of data, a program, a system, or information. 18 U.S.C. § 1030(e)(8).

12.   U.S. v. Middleton, 231 F.3d 1207 (9th Cir. 2000).

It is also unlawful for a person to knowingly cause the transmission of a program, code, or command that intentionally (1) damages a protected computer; (2) accesses a protected computer and recklessly causes damage; or (3) accesses a protected computer without authorization and causes resulting damage.[13]

5:6.   Requirement of intent

There are certain portions of the CFAA, including under predecessor versions of the statute, that do not require intent to cause damage in order to establish a violation.[14] However, in order to establish a violation of § 1030(a)(5)(a), relating to the transmission of codes, programs, or information, intent to damage must also be shown.[15] Thus, simply transmitting a software program that does not create damage will likely not be a violation of § 1030(a)(5)(a).

5:7.   Intent for unauthorized access and fraud under the CFAA

Certain defendants in CFAA cases, when caught, claim that they were acting in the interest of the plaintiff—simply to point out a security hole—and not to commit a crime. In most cases these arguments are rejected, because the intent required is not to commit another crime, but rather to access a computer system for an unauthorized purpose.[16] Defendants have attempted to argue that there is a requirement that an intent to defraud exists before a crime is committed under § 1030(a)(2)(C). This argument has been rejected by Courts, including because the statute itself only requires the intent to access the computer and, unlike other sections of the CFAA, including § 1030(a)(4), does not require knowledge or fraudulent intent.[17] This is also true in the context of those charged with aiding and abetting such a violation.[18]

5:8.   Definition of fraud

"Fraud" as used in the CFAA does not equate to common law fraud, but rather it refers to damage to property rights through dishonesty, schemes, or other artifices.[19]

5:9.   Knowledge of value not required

The CFAA delineates a number of different offenses, which can be charged as a misdemeanor, or a felony, depending upon the value involved. In one case, a defendant argued that the CFAA required knowledge of the value of the information or things obtained. The Tenth Circuit rejected this argument when it found that there was no

---

13.   18 U.S.C. § 1030(a)(5)(A)(i) to (iii).

14.   U.S. v. Morris, 928 F.2d 504 (2d Cir. 1991); U.S. v. Sablan, 92 F.3d 865 (9th Cir. 1996).

15.   See 18 U.S.C. § 1030(a)(5)(A); In re America Online, Inc., 168 F. Supp. 2d 1359 (S.D. Fla. 2001).

16.   Sawyer v. Department of Air Force, 31 M.S.P.R. 193 (M.S.P.B. 1986).

17.   United States v. Willis, 476 F.3d 1121 (10th Cir. 2007).

18.   *Id.*

19.   Shurgard Storage Centers, Inc. v. Safeguard Self Storage, Inc., 119 F. Supp. 2d 1121, 174 A.L.R. Fed. 655 (W.D. Wash. 2000).

knowledge or intent requirement that required knowledge of the value of the information obtained during a violation of the CFAA.[20]

5:10. What constitutes damages under CFAA

The type of damage shown to establish a violation of this portion of the CFAA must be one of the following types: aggregated damage that exceeds $5,000; potential modification or impairment of a medical diagnosis, examination, treatment, or care of one or more persons; physical injury; a threat to public health or safety; or damage to a government computer that is used in furtherance of the administration of justice, national defense, or national security.[21] There is no requirement that the damaged party have an ownership interest in the computers that were accessed. In one case, the Ninth Circuit rejected the defendant's argument that there must be a showing that the computer that was accessed belonged to the plaintiff.[22] Instead, it must just be shown that there was an act that violated the CFAA and that the plaintiff suffered damage. This could be shown by damage that results from the unauthorized access of data that is owned by the plaintiff but stored on another's computer.

In many cases, a business's data is one of its most valuable assets. The CFAA recognizes this, and cases have held that intangible property, including confidential data, can constitute a thing of value under the CFAA, thus supporting a violation of § 1030(a)(4).[23] Notably, courts have held that a party that obtains complete control of a network that contains data "possesses" that data at that time, whether a copy is downloaded or not.[24] This point is of import under the CFAA, as well as potentially under California's Identity Theft Statute.

In determining whether the requisite level of damage exists, a court can consider the hourly wage of any employees who repair any damage, even if the employees performed the repairs in the scope of their normal duties and were not paid any additional amounts.[25] However, lost revenue, security checks, and other similar expenditures will not count toward the damage requirement if there is no showing that there was an actual compromise of the network, data, or programs on the network.[26] However, other courts have held that lost wages and payment of consulting costs may count toward the damage requirement, even if there is no physical damage.[27] While other costs may

---

20. United States v. Willis, 476 F.3d 1121 (10th Cir 2007).

21. 18 U.S.C. § 1030(a).

22. Theofel v. Farey-Jones, 359 F.3d 1066 (9th Cir. 2004).

23. U.S. v. Ivanov, 175 F. Supp. 2d 367 (D. Conn. 2001); *see also* Carpenter v. U.S., 484 U.S. 19, 108 S. Ct. 316, 98 L. Ed. 2d 275 (1987) (confidential business data is protected under mail and wire fraud statutes).

24. U.S. v. Ivanov, 175 F. Supp. 2d 367 (D. Conn. 2001).

25. U.S. v. Middleton, 231 F.3d 1207 (9th Cir. 2000).

26. Moulton v. VC3, 2001-1 Trade Cas. (CCH) P 73202, 2000 WL 33310901 (N.D. Ga. 2000); *see also* Nexans Wires S.A. v. Sark-USA, Inc., 319 F. Supp. 2d 468 (S.D. N.Y. 2004), judgment aff'd, 166 Fed. Appx. 559 (2d Cir. 2006) (lost revenue and remedial costs did not constitute loss under CFAA).

27. EF Cultural Travel BV v. Explorica, Inc., 274 F.3d 577 (1st Cir. 2001); Creative Computing v. Getloaded. com LLC, 386 F.3d 930 (9th Cir. 2004).

count toward the $5,000 requirement, attorneys' fees for bringing an action under the CFAA do not count toward the loss[28] requirement.[29]

The Ninth Circuit has also held that any "natural and foreseeable" expenses are part of the damages amounts that can be considered. This includes impairments to the system, loss or re-creation of data, or creation of a more secure network.[30] However, numerous courts have held that economic damages, and not emotional distress or punitive damages, are recoverable.[31] The Northern District of California recently addressed whether forensic costs related to identifying an anonymous user who misappropriated information constituted "loss," ultimately concluding that the costs were indeed loss.[32]

The district court in the Northern District of Indiana also recently assessed the damage element for a § 1030(a)(5) claim in the context of alleged misconduct by an attorney as she departed her former employer.[33] In *Spangler*, the defendant was a partner in a law firm and was alleged to have taken proprietary information, including client lists and e-data files, before her departure from the firm, but as part of her plan to set up a competing law firm. The plaintiff moved for summary judgment on its CFAA claim. The Court ultimately denied the request, noting that while the plaintiff had alleged that it incurred costs to investigate the alleged improper access, it did not show that there was any impairment of data or the system that supported a finding that the losses qualified as damage under § 1030(a)(5).[34] Other courts recently examined this line of cases and concluded that since damages under the CFAA require impact to the integrity of the computer system in connection with damage, *ResDev* requires some diminution in completeness or usability of data or information on a computer system, and the allegations in this case did not meet this standard.[35]

---

28. The term "loss" means any reasonable cost to any victim, including the cost of responding to an offense, conducting a damage assessment, and restoring the data, program, system, or information to its condition prior to the offense, and any revenue lost, cost incurred, or other consequential damages incurred because of interruption of service. 18 U.S.C. § 1030(e)(11).

29. Wilson v. Moreau, 440 F. Supp. 2d 81 (D.R.I. 2006).

30. Middleton, 231 F.3d 1207.

31. Garland-Sash v. Lewis, 2007 WL 935013, (S.D. N.Y. 2007); citing In re DoubleClick Inc. Privacy Litigation, 154 F. Supp. 2d 497, 524 n.33 (S.D. N.Y. 2001); Letscher v. Swiss Bank Corp., 1996 WL 183019, at *3 (S.D. N.Y. 1996).

32. Successfactors, Inc. v. Softscape, Inc., 544 F. Supp. 2d 975, 981 (N.D. Cal. 2008) ("In such cases courts have considered the cost of discovering the identity of the offender or the method by which the offender accessed the protected information to be part of the loss for the purpose of the CFAA."); citing Shamrock Foods Co. v. Gast, 535 F. Supp. 2d 962 (D. Ariz. 2008); c.f. Tyco Intern. (US) Inc. v. John Does 1–3, 2003 WL 21638205 (S.D. N.Y. 2003); *see also*, Telequest International, Corp. v. Dedicated Business Systems, Inc., 2:06-cv-05359-PGS-ES (D.N.J. September 30, 2009) (holding that allegations regarding hiring of a forensic expert must be tied to remedying a matter that falls within the CFAA).

33. Spangler, Jennings & Dougherty, P.C. v. Mysliwy, 2:05-cv-00108-JTM-APR (N.D. Ind. March 31, 2006).

34. *Spangler*, at 13; *see also*, Resdev, LLC v. Lot Builders Ass'n, Inc., 2005 WL 192426 (M.D. Fla. 2005) (damage under CFAA requires some finding of "diminution in the completeness or usability of data or information on a computer system."); Moulton v. VC3, 2001-1 Trade Cas. (CCH) 73202, 2000 WL 33310901 (N.D. Ga. 2000) (investigative costs disallowed as damage under the CFAA where alleged incident did not result in "structural" damage to the network.).

35. Sam's Wines & Liquors v. Sean Hartig, 2008 WL 4394962, at *5 (N.D.Ill. 2008) (holding that allegations of damage that do not include an impairment of data do not adequately plead damage).

However, courts in the Ninth Circuit continue to liberally permit claims under the CFAA where there is no clear allegation of system interruption, and therefore loss, as other courts have held.[36] Other courts continue to reject this line of cases.[37]

5:11.　Must a plaintiff allege damage and loss

Certain courts have addressed whether both damage and loss must be pled to state a CFAA claim, and have concluded that both damage and loss must be pled. Damage, to certain courts must be related to the "impairment" of the system.[38] However, a number of other courts have concluded that a plaintiff need not prove damage (as referenced in § 1030(a)(5)(A)) to a protected computer to show a violation of § 1030(g), as some courts have thought is required under § 1030(a)(5)(B).[39]

5:12.　Inconsistent ruling regarding "loss"

The loss requirement under the CFAA for a civil action continues to befuddle courts. Indeed, two federal courts issued opinions on the issue within two days of each other, and reached opposite conclusions even though they relied upon the same cases to reach their conclusion.

In *P.C. of Yonkers, Inc. v. Celebrations! The Party and Seasonal Superstore*,[40] some former employees allegedly took trade secrets and confidential information regarding the plaintiffs' business and used it to open up competing businesses.[41] The defendants brought a motion to dismiss the CFAA claim, asserting that the plaintiffs failed to state a claim under the CFAA, including because they had not demonstrated any "loss" under § 1030(a)(5)(B)(1), as required by § 1030(g). The *P.C. Yonkers* court

---

36.　*See* Therapeutic Research Faculty v. NBTY, 488 F. Supp. 2d 991 (E.D. Cal. 2007) (holding that a claim could be stated under the CFAA against party that exceeded authorized use of password and thereby obtained additional access to licensed materials); citing Shurgard Storage Centers, Inc. v. Safeguard Self Storage, Inc., 119 F. Supp. 2d 1121, 1126 (W.D. Wash. 2000); *see also* Sw. Airlines Co. v. Farechase, Inc., 318 F. Supp. 2d 435, 439 (N.D. Tex. 2004); H&R Block E. Enter., Inc. v. J&M Secs., LLC, 2006 WL 1128744, at *4 (W.D. Mo. 2006); PharMerica, Inc. v. Arledge, 2007 WL 865510 (M.D. Fla. 2007) (holding that employer had demonstrated likelihood of success on CFAA claim where an employee that downloaded confidential information to use with a competitor and deleted files and records related to the downloading); Pacific Aerospace & Electronics, Inc. v. Taylor, 295 F. Supp. 2d 1188 (E.D. Wash. 2003), citing Shurgard and EF v. Explorica, Inc., 274 F.3d 577 (1st Cir. 2001).

37.　Cenveo v. CelumSolutions Software GMBH & Co KG, 504 F. Supp. 2d 574 (D. Minn. 2007) (dismissing CFAA claim based upon improper access to an employer's confidential information because the complaint did not allege an interruption of service, and therefore failed to allege loss); *see also* Spangler, Jennings & Dougherty, P.C. v. Mysilwy, 2:05-cv-00108-JTM-APR (N.D. Ind. March 21, 2006) (allegations of downloading of firm information by attorney who was leaving her employer failed to demonstrate a CFAA because there was no allegation of system impairment, and therefore no loss).

38.　Garelli Wong & Associates, Inc. v. Nichols, 551 F. Supp. 2d 704 (N.D.Ill. 2008); *see also*, Del Monte Fresh Produce, N.A., Inc. v. Chiquita Brands International Inc., _ F. Supp. 2d _, 2009 WL 743215 (N.D.Ill. 2009).

39.　Motorola, Inc. v. Lemko Corp., 609 F.Supp.2d 760, 766-67 (N.D.Ill., 2009); Steinbach v. Village of Forest Park, 2009 WL 2605283, 29 IER Cases 1080 (N.D.Ill. Aug 25, 2009) (NO. 06 C 4215); Bloomington-Normal Seating Company, Inc. v. Albritton, Case No. 09-1073 (C.D.Ill. May 13, 2009) (holding that a plaintiff is only required to show damage or loss).

40.　P.C. of Yonkers, Inc. v. Celebrations! The Party and Seasonal Superstore, L.L.C., 2007 WL 708978 (D.N.J. 2007).

41.　*Id.*

examined the *Nexans Wires* case, as well as the *Resdev* case, and concluded that these cases made a distinction between costs incurred as a result of an incident and lost revenue or other consequential damages.[42] The court noted that loss is defined by the CFAA as "any reasonable cost to any victim, including the cost of responding to an offense, conducting a damage assessment, and restoring the data, program, system, or information to its condition prior to the offense, and any revenue lost, cost incurred, or other consequential damages incurred because of interruption of service."[43] The distinction the court made is that it concluded that the "interruption of service" requirement applied only to the portion of the definition that addresses "any revenue lost, cost incurred, or other consequential damages," but not to any allegation that related to "the cost of responding to an offense, conducting a damage assessment, and restoring the data, program, system, or information to its condition prior to the offense..."[44] Thus, the court read the definition of loss to have two different components, one of which does not require an interruption of service, if the loss relates to the costs of responding to an offense conducting a damage assessment, and restoring the data, program, system, or information to its condition prior to the offense, and a second component that includes lost revenue, incurred costs, or other consequential damages that result from an interruption of service.[45] Under this definition, the Court concluded that the plaintiffs had stated a claim under the CFAA. What is notable is that the plaintiff in this matter alleged neither damage nor an interruption of service, but rather that they had suffered "substantial losses in excess of $5,000, including but not limited to losses sustained in responding to defendants' actions, investigating defendants' actions and taking remedial steps to prevent defendants' further actions."[46] Nowhere, however, did the plaintiff articulate how it suffered damage to a computer or an interruption of service.

A different conclusion was reached in *L-3 Communications Westwood Corp. v. Robicharux*,[47] In this case, former employees were alleged to have taken proprietary and trade secret information from their employer, L-3, including via a number of e-mails that were sent, as well as on an external drive that was used to copy an extensive number of confidential files. This information was allegedly used to compete with L-3 in an effort to obtain government contracts that L-3 was allegedly entitled to. The court relied upon the same cases that the *P.C. Yonkers* court did, but reached a different conclusion.[48] This court concluded, based upon the *Nexans* case, that a plaintiff must

---

42. The Court stated, "As the Second Circuit found 'the plain language of the [CFAA] treats lost revenue as a different concept from incurred costs, and permits recovery of the former only where connected to an 'interruption in service.'" Nexans Wires S.A. v. Sark-USA, Inc., 166 Fed. Appx. 559, 562 (2d Cir. 2006) (citing Civic Ctr. Motors, Ltd. v. Mason Street Import Cars, Ltd., 387 F. Supp. 2d 378, 382 (S.D. N.Y. 2005) (ruling that loss of "competitive edge" claim not caused by computer impairment or computer damage was not cognizable under the CFAA); Resdev, LLC v. Lot Builders Ass'n, 2005 WL 192426, at *5 (M.D. Fla. 2005) (similar)).

43. 18 U.S.C. § 1030(e)(11).

44. P.C. of Yonkers.

45. *Id.*

46. *Id.* at 9.

47. L-3 Communications Westwood Corp. v. Robicharux, 2007 WL 756528 *2–3 (E.D. La. 2007).

48. Citing Civil Center Motors, Ltd. v. Mason Street Import Cars, Ltd., 387 F. Supp. 2d 378, 381 (S.D. N.Y. 2005) Nexans, 319 F. Supp. 2d at 382 ("[C]osts not related to computer impairment or computer damages are not compensable under the CFAA.").

allege either damage to a computer, or an interruption of service, to show loss under § 1030(g).[49] In other words, the court also created a two-pronged definition of loss, of which one portion requires damage to a computer and the other, an interruption of service. However, the Court concluded that where the only allegation was theft of trade secrets and confidential information, and the resulting harm was misuse of the information to compete, without a showing of damage to a computer or an interruption of service, a CFAA claim could not be stated.[50]

While issues remain regarding CFAA liability and receipt of e-mails, one court concluded that the receipt of e-mails, in certain circumstances, could qualify as a CFAA violation as it could be construed as "access" of a computer. This is particularly true where a recipient directs or encourages the sender to mail the information, in which case the sender acts as the recipient's agent.[51] This holding is consistent with the *Sureguard* decision, particularly where the recipient has done more than passively receive e-mails.

In an unpublished decision, the Second Circuit Court of Appeals addressed whether the loss requirement of the CFAA could be met by loss of competitive advantage due to the alleged disclosure of trade secrets that were allegedly gathered in violation of the CFAA.[52] In *Nexans*, the plaintiff alleged that former employees had gathered confidential information from the plaintiff's computers while in the plaintiff's employ, before resigning and beginning working for a competitor.[53] While the plaintiff did not allege costs as a result of this conduct, it did allege that it had lost profits in excess of $10 million.[54] The court of appeals rejected this claim and affirmed the lower court's dismissal of the action, because the alleged losses did not result from an "interruption in service" as required by the CFAA. Thus, under this theory, loss of a "competitive edge" in business is not compensable under the CFAA if the business loss does not result from an interruption in service, in particular a loss of service or data.[55]

Other courts have questioned whether unsolicited e-mail that violates a website's terms of service would necessarily violate the CFAA, though this largely depends upon the language of the terms of service.[56] Courts have also raised questions regarding

---

49. L-3 Communications Westwood Corp. v. Robicharux, 2007 WL 756528 *8 (E.D. La. 2007).

50. *Id.*

51. MPC Containment Systems, Ltd. vs. Moreland, 2008 WL 2875007 (N.D. Ill. 2008), citing Roll Models AM. Inc. vs. Jones, 305 F. Supp. 2d 564, 567 (D. Md. 2004); *see also* Sureguard Storage Ctrs., Inc. vs. Safeguard Storage, Inc., 119 F. Supp. 2d 1121, 1123–25 (W.D. Wash. 2000).

52. *See also* AM. On-line, Inc. vs. National Healthcare Discount, Inc., 121 F.Supp. 2d 1255, 1272-73 (N.D. Iowa 2000).

53. Nexans Wires S.A. v. Sark-USA, Inc., 166 Fed. Appx. 559, 2006 WL 328292 (2d Cir. 2006).

54. *Nexans*, 166 Fed. Appx. 559.

55. *Id.*

56. *Nexans*, at 4; *see also*, Nexans Wires S.A. v. Sark-USA, Inc., 319 F. Supp. 2d 468, 471 (S.D. N.Y. 2004), judgment aff'd, 166 Fed. Appx. 559 (2d Cir. 2006); Civic Center Motors, Ltd. v. Mason Street Import Cars, Ltd., 387 F. Supp. 2d 378, 382 (S.D. N.Y. 2005); Resdev, LLC v. Lot Builders Ass'n, 2005 WL 192426 at *4–5; accord, Register.com, Inc. v. Verio, Inc., 126 F. Supp. 2d 238, 252 (S.D. N.Y. 2000), aff'd as modified, 356 F.3d 393 (2d Cir. 2004); *Telequest International, Corp. v. Dedicated Business Systems, Inc.*, 2:06-cv-05359-PGS-ES (D.N.J. September 30, 2009) (holding that lost profits are not recoverable as loss unless there is an interruption in service).

whether the larger ISPs can show the requisite impairment to the system to demonstrate loss in a CFAA claim arising out of spam.[57]

However, "interruptions in service" are not a defined term, and one court recently held that, at least under § 1030(a)(5)(a)(i), the deletion of files from a laptop was an interruption in service.[58]

5:13.   The CFAA and deletions

A District Court in Wisconsin addressed whether the use of a wiping program after the magistrate judge issued a computer inspection order was conclusive evidence of a violation of the CFAA. One of the defendants claimed that the boot up time on his computer was slow, and that was why he used a wiping program on his laptop (after the magistrate's order), which scrubbed many files from the computer, although it left certain file names that the forensic expert was able to recover.[59] The plaintiffs in this case sought an injunction and were unable to obtain one because they were not able to establish many elements of its claim, including protection beyond simple passwords; they also produced no evidence that confidentiality agreements were signed, so the deletions themselves were not sufficient evidence of improper access, though the court seemed to indicate that the deletions could be evidence of improper access at trial.

The plaintiffs also sought sanctions, but the court felt that the evidence, as presented, did not support a sanctions finding, though it did not specifically examine the recent spoliation cases. It appears the apparent lack of evidence of confidentiality and evidence of access defeated the motion.

While *Citrin* noted that hitting the delete button on a computer might not constitute a transmission and therefore be actionable under the CFAA, courts continue to find that deletions that go beyond this low standard meet the definition of an actionable event under the CFAA.[60] Some courts have held that in order for allegations of deletion to fall within the CFAA there must be more than an attempt to delete the information.[61] One court noted that the deletion without consent of information from a computer was sufficient to establish a CFAA claim.[62] The owner of the information must show that

---

57.   AOL v. NHCD, Inc., 121 F. Supp. 2d 1255 (N.D. Iowa 2000).

58.   *Id.* at 1275.

59.   B&B Microscopes v. Armogida, 532 F. Supp. 2d 744 (W.D. Penn. 2007) ("Additionally, B&B sustained a loss of $10,000 relating to lost revenue because of an 'interruption of service.' As stated above, B&B was deprived of the opportunity to sell the KPICS System when the data related to the KPICS System was deleted from Armogida's laptop. B&B had no other access to the underlying algorithm necessary to reproduce the KPICS System. Its attempts to secure the information from the OHBCI were rebuffed. Accordingly, the loss of the data from Armogida's laptop constituted an interruption of service within the meaning of 18 U.S.C. § 1030(e)(11) and 18 U.S.C. § 1030(a)(5)(B)(i)").

60.   Maxpower Corp. v. Abraham, 557 F. Supp. 2d 955 (W.D. Wis. 2008). There did not appear to be conclusive evidence that the files that were scrubbed came from the plaintiffs.

61.   Arience Builders, Inc. vs. Baltes, 563 F. Supp. 2d 883, (N.D. Ill. 2008); The Dedalus Foundation v. Banach, 2009 WL 3398595 (S.D.N.Y. 2009) (holding that the use of a secure erasure program to delete information involves a transmission of information and is therefore a violation of the CFAA in appropriate circumstances); Statera v. Henrickson, 1:09-cv-01684-JLK (D.Colo. July 17, 2009).

62.   Condux v. Haugum, 2008 WL 5244818 (D. Minn. 2008).

there has been some impairment or dispossession of the information caused by the deletion. This is consistent with holdings from other courts.[63]

In one recent case, the court concluded that the deletion, via the use of commercial software erasure programs, of over 2,000 files from a work computer violated the CFAA.[64] The information in question included business and contact lists for potential and former recruitment candidates, employers, and potential leads of both the defendant and current and former employees, all of which was obtained in the course of the defendant's employment.

5:14.   Copying of data held to be insufficient

The Northern District of Illinois Court has held that, despite the *Citrin* case, mere copying of data is insufficient to support a CFAA claim.[65]

5:15.   Aggregation of damages under CFAA

While an interest in a computer is not required to state a CFAA claim, several courts have concluded that the $5,000 in damage must be to one computer.[66]

5:16.   CFAA violations and circumstantial evidence

The government need not exclude every possible explanation for computer conduct when proving a CFAA violation. Indeed, circumstantial evidence, even where a defendant argues others might have had access to his computer or password, will not automatically defeat a prosecution.[67]

5:17.   Unsolicited e-mails creating damage

Whether unsolicited e-mails create the requisite level of damage is also an issue that has been litigated under the CFAA.[68] Indeed, in the *AOL* case the court concluded that AOL had demonstrated that the volume of unsolicited e-mail from the defendantcaused

---

63. Hecht v. Components International, Inc., 600 F. Supp. 2d 1045(N.Y. Sup. 2008), citing Dabinaw v. Dabinaw, 58 FDIDOFF, 12 Mich. 3d 1162(A) *11 (Sup. Ct. NY Co. 2006); Electra Entertainment Group, Inc. v. Santangelo, 2008 WL 4452393 at *6 (S.D. NY 2008); School of Visual Arts v. Kuprewicz, 3 Misc. 3d 278, 281 (N.Y. Sup. 2003).

64. *See* VI Chip Corp. vs. Lee, 438 F. Supp. 2d 1087, 1092 (N.D. Cal. 2006) (granting summary judgment on the CFAA where a former employee admitted to accessing the employer's file server and deleting the contents of computer files that the defendant had generated as an employee, as well as deleting the contents of a company-issued laptop).

65. Alliance International, Inc. vs. Todd, 2008 WL 2859095 (E.D. N.C. 2008).

66. Garelli Wong & Associates, Inc. v. Nichols, 551 F. Supp. 2d 704 (N.D.Ill. 2008); Cassetica Software, Inc. v. Computer Sciences Corp., 1:09-cv-00003, (N.D.Ill. June 18, 2009) (holding that mere copying of information did not violate the CFAA where there is no allegation of damage).

67. Hayes v. Packard Bell, Nec., 193 F. Supp. 2d 910, 912 (E.D. Tex. 2001); Thurmond v. Compaq Computer Corp., 171 F. Supp. 2d 667 (E.D. Tex. 2001).

68. United States v. Shea, 493 F.3d 1110 (9th Cir. 2007). ("To prosecute crimes involving the element of "transmission," the government must offer sufficient proof that the person charged is the same person who sent the transmission. Circumstantial evidence is sufficient to prove that the transmission has occurred. We confronted a wire fraud conviction based on facts similar to those presented here in United States v. Mullins, 992 F.2d 1472 (9th Cir.1993)").

damage in excess of $5,000 per year, and thus the sending of bulk unsolicited e-mail violated the CFAA.[69]

5:18. The CFAA and employee breaches of loyalty and data destruction

One of the unique aspects of the CFAA is its use of different phrases regarding authority, each giving rise to different potential liabilities. Taking certain actions "without" authority is improper, as is taking certain actions beyond the scope of authorized access. This becomes an issue when employees determine they are leaving and are therefore no longer considered to be agents of the current employer and thus may be acting beyond the scope of authorized access.[70] Examples can also include current or former employees or users of websites who go beyond the areas they are permitted to access or obtain information to which they are not entitled.[71] In one case a violation was found based upon an employee who accessed an employer's computer network to obtain trade secrets for a competitor because the employee's actions on behalf of a competitor rendered the employee an agent of the competitor and no longer an agent of the current employer. Thus, the access was not authorized.[72]

In *Citrin*, an employee determined that he was going to leave his former employer. Prior to joining his new employer, Citrin allegedly improperly used and accessed confidential information and then deleted all files on his hard drive using commercially available software.[73] Interestingly, there was a data destruction requirement in Citrin's employment contract, and he argued that his actions were therefore proper. The Seventh Circuit rejected this argument, finding that because of his breach of the duty of loyalty he was not acting with authority to destroy the data and actually terminated his agency relationship with his employer. The court also focused on the transmission of the data deletion program (via CD or the Internet) as an actionable transmission under the CFAA.[74] The Court also rejected the argument based upon the deletion requirement, finding that the purpose of the clause was not to permit someone to hide his misconduct.[75]

---

69. America Online, Inc. v. National Health Care Discount, Inc., 174 F. Supp. 2d 890 (N.D. Iowa 2001).

70. *America Online*, 174 F. Supp. 2d at 899.

71. International Airport Centers, L.L.C. v. Citrin, 440 F.3d 418 (7th Cir. 2006).

72. *See* YourNetDating v. Mitchell, 88 F. Supp. 2d 870 (N.D. Ill. 2000); Shurgard Storage Centers, Inc. v. Safeguard Self Storage, Inc., 119 F. Supp. 2d 1121, 174 A.L.R. Fed. 655 (W.D. Wash. 2000).

73. *Shurgard*, 119 F. Supp. 2d 870; *see also* United States v. Morris, 928 F.2d 504, 510 (2d Cir. 1991) (holding that an authorized computer user, acted without authorization when he used computer programs in an unauthorized way).

74. *Citrin*, 440 F.3d at 419; *see also* Lasco Foods, Inc. v. Hall and Shaw Sales, Marketing, & Consulting, LLC, 4:08-cv-01683-JCH (E.D.Miss. October 26, 2009) (applying Citrin, and holding that employee misappropriation is actionable under the CFAA); Ervin & Smith Adver. & Pub. Rels., Inc. v. Ervin, No. 8:08cv459, 2009 U.S. Dist. LEXIS 8096, at * 22-23 (D. Neb. Feb. 3, 2009) ("The Court concludes that while the Defendants ordinarily may have been authorized to access the information they appropriated from Plaintiff, that authorization was terminated when Defendants destroyed the agency relationship by accessing and appropriating the protected information for their own personal gain and against the interest of their employer.").

75. *Citrin*, 440 F.3d at 420–21. The Citrin court also examined the distinctions between "without authorization" and "exceeding authorized access." ("The difference between 'without authorization' and 'exceeding authorized access' is paper thin, but not quite invisible. In EF Cultural Travel BV v. Explorica, Inc., 274 F.3d 577, 58384 (1st Cir. 2001), for example, the former employee of a travel agent, in violation of his confidentiality agreement with his former employer, used confidential information that he had obtained as an employee to

Citrin was recently applied by the district court in the Northern District of Illinois.[76] In *Forge*, the court held that the deletion of files, and other conduct that violated an employee's duty of loyalty, constituted a violation of the CFAA because it was an act that was without authorization.[77] However, the *Citrin* and *Shurgard* cases have not been uniformly followed.[78] In *Lockheed*, the district court rejected the holding that a breach of an employee's duty of loyalty renders his actions on a system a violation of the CFAA. The court noted that despite the alleged improper nature of their actions, which included allegedly downloading confidential information for a competitor, at the time the defendants committed these acts, they had authority to access the systems that contained the confidential information.[79] These holdings are consistent with the California Supreme Court's holding that a claim for trespass to chattels due to mass e-mailing required a finding of system impairment before a claim could be stated.[80] Other courts have rejected the analysis of *Citrin* and held that employees, even where they are breaching their duty of loyalty, will not exceed their authorized access if they are otherwise permitted access to the materials in question.[81]

These cases have created issues for courts regarding the scope of the civil remedy under the CFAA.[82] In *Fiber Systems*, the defendants were alleged to have downloaded confidential and trade secret information from the plaintiff's computer system. One of the issues the court addressed was the existence of a civil remedy for violations of § 1030(a)(4). The court, as have other courts, concluded that civil claims under

---

create a program that enabled his new travel company to obtain information from his former employer's website that he could not have obtained as efficiently without the use of that confidential information. The website was open to the public, so he was authorized to use it, but he exceeded his authorization by using confidential information to obtain better access than other members of the public. Our case is different. Citrin's breach of his duty of loyalty terminated his agency relationship (more precisely, terminated any rights he might have claimed as IAC's agent-he could not by unilaterally terminating any duties he owed his principal gain an advantage!) and with it his authority to access the laptop, because the only basis of his authority had been that relationship.").

76. *Citrin*, 440 F.3d at 421.

77. Forge Indus. Staffing, Inc. v. De La Fuente, 2006 WL 2982139, at *6 (N.D. Ill. 2006) ("De La Fuente, who was a director of the company and who allegedly had started a competing business in 2001, accessed prohibited sexually explicit websites, downloaded software destruction programs onto Forge's computer, and intentionally destroyed files, records, and other information and data kept on his computer when Forge asked De La Fuente to turn the computer over to the company. As in IAC, and assuming the truth of the complaint's allegations, any authorization De La Fuente had to delete or erase information from the computer ended when he engaged in misconduct in violation of his duty of loyalty to the company.").

78. *See also* Sam's Wines & Liquors v. Sean Hartig, 2008 WL 4394962 (N.D.Ill. 2008) (applying *Citrin* and finding that an employee exceeded authorized access when he accessed information that was given to a competitor); May v. Hostetler, 2004 WL 1197395 (N.D.Ill. 2004) (holding that employee who removed copyrighted materials from employer's system for the benefit of a competitor exceeded authorized access); Models America, Inc. v. Jones, 305 F. Supp. 2d 564 (D.Md. 2004).

79. *See* Lockheed Martin Corp. v. Speed, 2007 WL 2209250 (M.D. Fla. 2007).

80. *Lockheed*, at 9; *see also*, Shamrock Foods Company vs. Gast, 535 F. Supp. 2d 962 (D. Ariz. 2008) (Accepting an interpretation of the CFAA that limits employee liability, including under the Rule of Leniency, and stating its agreement with the non-Citrin cases); Condux v. Haugum, 08-cv-04824 (D.Minn. December 15, 2008).

81. Intel Corp. v. Hamidi, 30 Cal. 4th 1342, 1347 (2003).

82. Lockheed Martin Corp. v. L-3 Communications Corp., 2007 WL 2209250 (M.D. Fla. 2007).

§ 1030(a)(4) can exist if the claim implicates one of the tests of the five factors under (a)(5)(B).[83]

A similar result was reached in *Nilfis-Advance, Inc. v. Mitchell*.[84] In *Nilfis*, the defendant was alleged to have transmitted confidential information from his employer's system to his home computer with the intent of conveying this information to the plaintiff's competitors.[85] The plaintiff alleged that this conduct constituted a violation of § 1030(a)(4) and relied upon the *Shurgard* case for the proposition that an employee with authorization exceeds his authority when he accesses files for the purpose of sending information to a competitor.[86]

One court in Pennsylvania recently rejected the *Shurgard* and *Citrin* holdings and held that an employee who deleted files on his laptop while still employed did not act "without authority," though it concluded that the acts violated § 1030(a)(5)(a)(i), which prohibits unauthorized damage to a computer.[87] *Citrin* and *Shurguard* have been rejected by other courts on the rule of lenity, among other reasons.[88]

Another court[89] recently rejected the *Citrin* line of cases and held that "Defining 'authorization' based upon the use of computer information, rather than upon the presence or absence of initial permission to access the computer, is in tension with both a plain reading of the Act and the manner in which the term 'authorization' is used in other parts of the Act. Most prominently, it is inconsistent with the Act's use of the term 'authorization' in its definition of "exceeds authorized access.""[90] Thus the court concluded that exceeding authorized access could only occur when initial access is permitted but the access of certain information is not permitted.[91]

In *Modis, Inc. v. Bardelli* the court addressed the split in cases involving whether a former employee that breaches a duty of loyalty exceeds authorized access or acts

---

83. Fiber Systems Intern., Inc. v. Roehrs, 470 F.3d 1150 (5th Cir. 2006).

84. *Fiber Systems*, 470 F.3d. at 1156; *see also*, P.C. Yonkers, Inc. v. Celebrations the Party and Seasonal Super-store, LLC., 428 F.3d 504 (3d Cir. 2005) (CFAA claim must only meet one of the tests, and are not exclusive to (a)(5) claims); Theofel v. Farey-Jones, 359 F.3d 1066, 1078 n.5 (9th Cir. 2004).

85. Nilfis-Advance, Inc. v. Mitchell, 2006 WL 827073 (W.D. Ark. 2006).

86. *Nilfis-Advance, Inc.*, at 1.

87. *Nilfis-Advance, Inc.*, at 6 (holding that allegation that employee e-mailed documents with intent to misappropriate them was sufficient to allege a CFAA claim even though the employer did not dispute that the employee was authorized to access the documents.); *see also* Personalized Brokerage Services, LLC v. Lucius, 2006 WL 208781 (D. Minn. 2006) (use of computer by an employee to set up competing companies, e-mail competitors, negotiate to sell products to competitors, and dissemination of proprietary information to competitors violated CFAA).

88. B&B Microscopes v. Armogida, 2007 WL 2814595 (W.D. Pa. 2007) ("I find that Armogida took such actions [deleting data] intentionally and for the purpose of depriving B&B of vital information relating to the KPICS System. Armogida knew that his laptop computer contained the only copy of the algorithm for the KPICS System to which B&B had access. By deleting that information, Armogida ensured that B&B could not market, sell and/or distribute the KPICS System.").

89. Brett Senior & Associates, P.C., v. Fitzgerald, 2007 WL 2043377 (E.D. Pa. 2007) (holding that employee who downloaded trade secrets, including a customer list, did not violate the CFAA because he was employed by the plaintiff at the time of the act, and therefore had authority).

90. Diamond Power International, Inc. v. Davidson, 2007 WL 2904119, *14 (N.D.Ga. 2007).

91. The term "exceeds authorized access" means to access a computer with authorization and to use such access to obtain or alter information in the computer that the accesser is not entitled so to obtain or alter. 18 U.S.C. § 1030(e)(6).

without authority.[92] The court here found, at the motion to dismiss stage, that the employee who allegedly gave trade secret information to a competitor had potentially violated the CFAA as there was a specific policy regarding use and disclosure of trade secret information that was allegedly violated.

Courts continue to reach different conclusions regarding the interpretation of the phrase "exceeds authorized access." One court rejecting a broad reading of the CFAA finding that an employee did not exceed authorized access when accessing confidential information that was allegedly later given to a competitor. This court relied upon the language of the statute and the legislative history as interpreted by the *Werner-Masuda* case, as well as the rule of leniency since the CFAA is a criminal statute.[93]

In *LVRC Holdings LLC v. Brekka* the Ninth Circuit addressed the meaning of "without authorization" and "exceeding authorized access" in the CFAA.[94] The defendant in this case emailed confidential documents to himself and his wife while still employed by the plaintiff. The plaintiff asserted that this violated the CFAA. Notably, the plaintiff did not have written employment guidelines in place that would prohibit employees from emailing LVRC documents to personal computers. Examining the dictionary definition of "authorized," the Ninth Circuit concluded that there was no support for the position that an employee's authority ends when he or she resolves to use a computer in violation of his or her duty of loyalty. Thus, the Ninth Circuit rejected the reasoning of *Citrin* in finding that the CFAA was not violated by Brekka. Two points are worth noting regarding the decision: First, the issue of "exceeding authorized access" was not before the court on appeal, though the court addressed the issue in footnote 7. Second, the Ninth Circuit fails to address the issue that the *Citrin* case is based upon a Ninth Circuit case, *United States v. Galindo*,[95] and this failure raises questions that must be resolved. Either way, the lesson of *LVRC* is that the failure to have a policy can remove the CFAA as a potential claim in this context, at least in the Ninth Circuit.

5:19. The CFAA and sovereign immunity

Certain courts have held that since there is no waiver of sovereign immunity, federal government agencies and officials are immune from suit.[96]

---

92. Diamond Power International, at *14.

93. *Modis, Inc. v. Bardelli*, 531 F. Supp. 2d 314 (D. Conn. 2008).

94. Shamrock Foods Co. v. Gast, 535 F. Supp. 2d 962, (D.Ariz. 2008).

95. LVRC Holdings LLC v. Brekka, 581 F.3d 1127 (9th Cir. 2009).

96. United States v. Galindo, 871 F.2d 99, 101 (9th Cir.1989).

5:20.   Applying the CFAA

For employers, it is important that access to confidential information is limited, through policies as well as technical means, if appropriate, to employees who actually have reason to access the information. Such restrictions will limit the employees' ability to gather confidential information at times when they may have ulterior motives to access the information, such as gathering it to give to a competitor. Policies that clearly limit employees' rights of access, as well as policies that address the issues raised under the ECPA related to the employees' lack of privacy in any communication on the network, are also typically a good idea.

Owners or operators of networks, websites, or ISPs should appropriately limit access via policies that should be available on the website as part of the terms of service or as part of the user agreement for the network or ISP.

5:21.   The CFAA and non-protectable information

One of the key uses of the CFAA is to protect employers and other holders of confidential information from improper disclosure. In many cases, employees will e-mail confidential information to themselves or others at the time they know they are leaving a company. In many cases, pricing data can be extremely important, and confidential, information. However, at least one court has found that pricing data that is subject to variances due to fluctuating costs may not be protectable, and thus its copying is not actionable under the CFAA.[97] In *HUB*, the plaintiff had proprietary pricing information that changed regularly due to changes in certain costs, including fuel. A former employee took pricing information to assist him in competing with HUB, but never actually utilized the information. In finding that the CFAA claim was not likely to succeed on the merits, the court noted that the evidence in the record demonstrated that the pricing information was likely obsolete because of the fluctuating costs.[98] The court also noted that this type of information was exactly the type of information that the defendant would gain through his years of experience.[99]

5:22.   Employer's vicarious liability under CFAA

Another recent issue that has arisen under the CFAA is the scope of an employer's vicarious liability for acts of employees.[100] In *Butera*, IBM was sued because one of its employees allegedly improperly accessed the plaintiff's network from an IBM-owned IP address. Relying upon the law of the District of Colombia, as well as other CFAA cases, the court rejected employer liability for the act of an employee, unless there were allegations that the employer's interests were furthered by the conduct.[101] Other courts

---

97.   Garland-Sash v. Lewis, 2007 WL 935013 (S.D. N.Y. 2007).
98.   HUB Group, Inc. v. Clancy, 2006 WL 208684 (E.D. Pa. 2006).
99.   *HUB*, at *11.
100. *HUB*, at *11.
101. Butera & Andrews v. International Business Machines Corp., 456 F. Supp. 2d 104 (D.D.C. 2006).

have held that absent direction by an entity, the entity is not liable for the individuals' violations of the CFAA.[102]

5:23.   Examples of violations of the CFAA—Unauthorized access

The First Circuit upheld the granting of an injunction under the CFAA against a defendant that had used a "scraper" program to obtain confidential information from the plaintiff's website. The information included pricing information that was obtained and used to undercut the plaintiff's prices. The defendant had hired a former executive from the plaintiff who had allegedly used knowledge of the plaintiff's confidential information to assist in the development of the "scraper" program in violation of a confidentiality agreement.[103]

5:24.   Examples of violations of the CFAA—Gathering of e-mail addresses

In a case that predated the enactment of CAN-SPAM, a Virginia district court held that the defendants' harvesting of e-mail addresses from other AOL customers, violated the CFAA because the sending of large numbers of unsolicited commercial e-mails damaged AOL.[104]

5:25.   Examples of violations of the CFAA—Diversion of customers/harvesting of customer lists

Diversion of customers can constitute a violation of the CFAA. In one case, a former programmer for a dating service allegedly used his knowledge of his former employer's software, as well as access codes, to route customers from the dating service to an adult oriented website. The Court concluded that these allegations, if true, constituted a violation of the CFAA.[105]

The improper gathering of customer lists can also constitute a violation of the CFAA. One court has held that the use of "bots" to obtain customer lists from the

---

102. *Butera*, 456 F. Supp. 2d. at 112; *see also* Role Models America, Inc. v. Jones, 305 F. Supp. 2d 564, 186 Ed. Law Rep. 227 (D. Md. 2004); Doe v. Dartmouth-Hitchcock Medical Center, 2001 DNH 132, 2001 WL 873063 (D.N.H. 2001).

103. Calence, LLC, v. Dimension Data Holdings, 2007 WL 1549491 (W.D. Wash. 2007).

104. EF Cultural Travel BV v. Explorica, Inc., 274 F.3d 577 (1st Cir. 2001).

105. America Online, Inc. v. LCGM, Inc., 46 F. Supp. 2d 444, 451 (E.D. Va. 1998) ("The facts before the Court establish that defendants violated 18 U.S.C. 1030(a)(2)(C) of the Computer Fraud and Abuse Act, which prohibits individuals from 'intentionally access[ing] a computer without authorization or exceed[ing] authorized access, and thereby obtain[ing] information from any protected computer if the conduct involved an interstate or foreign communication.' Defendants' own admissions satisfy the Act's requirements. Defendants have admitted to maintaining an AOL membership and using that membership to harvest the e-mail addresses of AOL members. Defendants have stated that they acquired these e-mail addresses by using extractor software programs. Defendants' actions violated AOL's Terms of Service, and as such was unauthorized. Plaintiff contends that the addresses of AOL members are 'information' within the meaning of the Act because they are proprietary in nature. Plaintiff asserts that as a result of defendants' actions, it suffered damages exceeding $5,000, the statutory threshold requirement.")

WHOIS database violated the CFAA.[106] One district court recently applied *Verio*, at the pleading stage, finding on the allegations made in the case that the use of a web crawler to collect data from other websites could potentially bind a company to an online agreement.[107]

The use of robots to gather information, including pricing information, in violation of the terms of use of a website can also violate the CFAA. Thus, where a company created a software program that allowed customers to search for airline fares online, and the data was obtained through the use of bots, in violation of a user agreement, a court concluded that these facts were sufficient to allege a violation of the CFAA.[108]

5:26.   Examples of violations of the CFAA—Defective software/time bombs

In certain cases courts have held that defective software, in particular microcode, that causes damage to data on computers can constitute a "transmission" of programs under § 1030(a)(5)(A), and therefore violate the CFAA.[109] Thus, the placement of defective disk controller software that allegedly caused damage to data on computers could violate the CFAA. "Time bomb" codes in certain cases can also violate the CFAA, though time bomb or other disabling codes that are part of a disclosed licensing arrangement would not likely fall within the CFAA.[110]

In *Roller Bearing Company of America v. American Software, Inc.*, the district court addressed whether the placement of a logic bomb in software could give rise to a CFAA violation, as well as a violation of Connecticut's computer crime law, holding that it could, because the plaintiff had alleged loss in the form of fees paid to a consultant. The district court also rejected the defendant's argument that the logic bomb had not yet caused damage.[111]

5:27.   Examples of violations of the CFAA—Setting of cookies

The intentional placement of cookies on users' computers has been sufficient to establish intent under the CFAA, even though courts have concluded that the plaintiffs could not demonstrate any damage that resulted from the placement of cookies.[112] Other courts have reached similar results regarding cookies, "action tags," and rerouting of

---

106. YourNetDating, Inc. v. Mitchell, 88 F. Supp. 2d 870 (N.D. Ill. 2000).

107. Register.com, Inc. v. Verio, Inc., 126 F. Supp. 2d 238 (S.D. N.Y. 2000), aff'd as modified, 356 F.3d 393 (2d Cir. 2004).

108. Internet Archive v. Shell, 505 F. Supp. 2d 755 (D. Colo. 2007).

109. Southwest Airlines Co. v. Farechase, Inc., 318 F. Supp. 2d 435 (N.D. Tex. 2004).

110. *See* Shaw v. Toshiba America Information Systems, Inc., 91 F. Supp. 2d 926 (E.D. Tex. 1999).

111. North Texas Preventive Imaging L.L.C. v. Eisenberg, 1996 WL 1359212 (C.D. Cal. 1996); Kalow & Springnut, LLP v. Commence Corporation, 2009 WL 44748 (D.N.J. 2009).

112. Roller Bearing Company of America v. American Software, Inc., 3:07-cv-01516-DJV (D.Conn. March 23, 2010) (assuming the allegations of the complaint as true, "....ASI wrongfully installed the Logic Bomb into the ASI Software, upon which RBC is dependent, in an effort to prevent RBC from using the ASI software on the Replacement Mainframe without paying a Deactivation Fee, all in violation of the ASI Software License.").

users through other servers, all of which allegedly breached the users' web privacy.[113] Similarly, a pharmaceutical company's use of technology to obtain personal information from users' computers that were used to access websites did not constitute a violation of the CFAA because the users could not establish damage.[114]

5:28. Examples of violations of the CFAA—Authorized users exceeding scope of authority

This claim is made primarily in connection with employees who exceed the scope of their authority, which is discussed in Section 5:18, above. In one case, the release of a computer "worm" on the Internet also violated the CFAA because, though the author had limited authority to access public Internet sites for communication purposes, his actions exceeded the scope of his authority.[115]

5:29. Examples of violations of the CFAA—Illegal subpoenas

The CFAA has been applied to litigants who have issued improper requests for information from ISPs.[116] In *Theofel*, a party requested all e-mails, without any limitation upon time or subject matter, from the opposing party's ISP. The ISP provided a sample of e-mails to the requesting party, many of which were privileged. The court held that an overbroad subpoena can constitute a violation of the CFAA, in certain cases, because it exceeds the authorized access of the requesting party.[117]

5:30. Examples of violations of the CFAA—Mere review of information

The mere review of information, even if not authorized, will not give rise to liability under the CFAA if the individual receives nothing of value.[118] In *Czubinski*, the defendant was an employee of the IRS that reviewed a number of individuals' personal tax data. Though the court acknowledged that Czubinski had exceeded his authority when he reviewed taxpayer's files, it was done not to gain anything of value, but rather to fulfill his curiosity to see information about people he knew.[119]

---

113. In re Intuit Privacy Litigation, 138 F. Supp. 2d 1272 (C.D. Cal. 2001); In re DoubleClick Inc. Privacy Litigation, 154 F. Supp. 2d 497 (S.D. N.Y. 2001) (holding that "damages" may be aggregated across all alleged victims, but only for each discrete act and each act must meet the statutory damage requirements).

114. Chance v. Avenue A, Inc., 165 F. Supp. 2d 1153 (W.D. Wash. 2001).

115. In re Pharmatrak, Inc. Privacy Litigation, 220 F. Supp. 2d 4 (D. Mass. 2002), judgment rev'd, 329 F.3d 9 (1st Cir. 2003).

116. U.S. v. Morris, 928 F.2d 504 (2d Cir. 1991).

117. Theofel v. Farey-Jones, 359 F.3d 1066 (9th Cir. 2004).

118. *Theofel*, 359 F.3d at 1078.

119. U.S. v. Czubinski, 106 F.3d 1069 (1st Cir. 1997).

5:31. Examples of violations of the CFAA— Internet advertising

Internet advertising has also served as the basis of a CFAA claim. Cases have been brought against a company that improperly accessed and copied data storage forms for Internet advertising services. This conduct, because it allegedly resulted in the advertiser being forced to incur over $5,000 in assessment costs and corrective actions, was sufficient to allege a CFAA violation.[120]

5:32. Examples of violations of the CFAA—Login pages

One issue that defendants have raised in CFAA prosecutions, as well as under their state law analogues, is that accessing a page that is public on the Internet cannot exceed authorized access or be without authority. While there are cases that have held that accessing such a page, and even attempting to enter a password is not "without authority," courts have held that once a password that grants access is entered without authority, a crime is then committed.[121]

5:33. Examples of violations of the CFAA—Misuse of passwords

One issue that has arisen is when an authorized user gives a third-party access to a website that has limited access rights. In *The Paradigm Alliance, Inc. v. Celeritas Technologies, LLC*, the district court addressed this issue when a customer of the plaintiff gave the defendant access rights via a user name and password. In this case, the defendant repeatedly attempted to use a variety of user names, passwords, and URLs to access the plaintiff's web application. Ultimately it gained access by obtaining and using a customer's username and password. While the defendant argued that the plaintiff could not show damage as a result of the access of the system, the district court rejected this argument and held that the investigative costs proved by the plaintiff were sufficient loss and damage was not required.[122]

5:34. Examples of violations of the CFAA—"Throttling"

In one case in New York a plaintiff argued that an ISP's restrictions on peer-to-peer file-sharing, known as "throttling," violated the CFAA. The district court rejected this argument finding that the plaintiff had failed to allege damage.[123]

---

120. *Id.*

121. I.M.S. Inquiry Management Systems, Ltd. v. Berkshire Information Systems, Inc., 307 F. Supp. 2d 521 (S.D. N.Y. 2004).

122. State v. Allen, 917 P.2d 848 (Kan. 1996); State v. Riley, 846 P.2d 1365 (Wash. 1993).

123. The Paradigm Alliance, Inc. v. Celeritas Technologies, LLC, 659 F.Supp.2d 1167 (D.Kan. Sep. 22, 2009) (NO. 07-1121-EFM).

5:35.   Mere violation of license under the CFAA

Certain cases have addressed whether the download of information in violation of a EULA or other license agreements creates liability under the CFAA.[124] In *Secureinfo*, the defendant hired a consultant to perform an analysis of a competitor's software.[125] The software was sent to the defendants by the consultant, who allegedly authorized the use, and the software was downloaded from the consultant's server.[126] The court concluded that because the consultant had authorized access, though the defendants' access was not a licensed one, the CFAA claim failed.[127]

5:36.   The CFAA and terms of service

In one of the better-publicized cases involving social media, a defendant was prosecuted for making misrepresentations on MySpace that were allegedly precluded by the MySpace terms of service. In this case, the alleged misrepresentations were asserted to have played a part in a teenage girl's suicide.

The misrepresentations related to an adult who claimed to be a teenage boy, "Josh Evans," complete with a false picture, and who then friended a 13-year-old girl who was a classmate of the adult's child. At the time, MySpace made users click a checkbox to agree to the privacy policy and terms of service, but did not force readers to review all of the provisions by scrolling through the terms.[128]

Despite this, the court enforced the terms to the extent that it applied them in this context, but overturned the conviction finding, in the criminal context, the terms of service ran afoul of the "void-for-vagueness doctrine," though the court recognized the inherent power of providers to police their own websites.[129]

According to other courts, a conscious violation of a website's terms of service will render the access unauthorized or cause it to exceed authorization.[130]   However, other cases have reached different results, depending on what the terms provide:

> [It] is at least arguable here that BoardFirst's access of the Southwest website is not at odds with the site's intended function; after all, the site is designed to allow users to obtain boarding passes for Southwest flights via the computer. In no sense can BoardFirst be considered an "outside hacker[ ] who break[s] into a computer" given that southwest. com is a publicly available website that anyone can access and use. True, the Terms posted on southwest.com do not give sanction to the particular *manner* in which BoardFirst uses the site—to check in Southwest customers for financial gain. But then again § 1030(a)(2) (C) does not forbid the *use* of a protected computer for any prohibited

---

124. Fink v. Time Warner Cable, 1:08-cv-09628-LTS (S.D.N.Y. July 23, 2009).

125. 1 SecureInfo Corp. v. Telos Corp., 387 F. Supp. 2d 593 (E.D. Va. 2005).

126. *Secureinfo*, 387 F. Supp. 2d at 600.

127. *Id.*

128. *Id.*

129. United States v. Drew, 259 F.R.D. 449 (C.D.Cal. 2009).

130. *Id.*

purpose; instead it prohibits one from intentionally *accessing* a computer "without authorization." As previously explained, the term "access," while not defined by the CFAA, ordinarily means the "freedom or ability to ... make use of" something. Here BoardFirst or any other computer user obviously has the *ability* to make use of southwest.com given the fact that it is a publicly available website the access to which is not protected by any sort of code or password. *Cf. Am. Online,* 121 F.Supp.2d at 1273 (remarking that it is unclear whether an AOL member's violation of the AOL membership agreement results in "unauthorized access").[131]

5:37. Enforcement provisions

Prison terms for violation of the CFAA can range from 1 to 20 years.[132] Moreover, any effected person can also bring a civil action seeking compensatory damages, as well as injunctive and other forms of equitable relief.[133] However, if the conduct that serves as the basis of the civil action arises as a result of purely economic injury, and not other forms of harm, the available damages are limited to economic damages.[134]

In many cases, equitable relief can be the most immediate and effective relief in a civil action under the CFAA. Companies can seek injunctions, including TROs, in order to limit the damages that arise from violations of the CFAA by former employees or competitors.

5:38. Injunctive relief under the CFAA

The language of the CFAA has created questions regarding whether injunctive relief is permitted under the CFAA.[135] Most courts have concluded that the civil remedies available under the CFAA include injunctive relief.[136] There have also been issues related to the scope of economic relief under the CFAA. Damages for certain violations of the CFAA, specifically violations of § (a)(5)(B)(i), are limited to compensatory damages, while others are not simply limited to compensatory damages.[137]

---

131. *See, e.g.*, Southwest Airlines Co. v. Farechase, Inc., 318 F.Supp.2d 435, 439-40 (N.D.Tex.2004); Nat'l Health Care Disc., Inc., 174 F.Supp.2d at 899; Register.com, Inc. v. Verio, Inc., 126 F.Supp.2d 238, 247-51 (S.D.N.Y.2000), aff'd, 356 F.3d 393 (2d Cir.2004); Am. Online, Inc. v. LCGM, Inc., 46 F.Supp.2d 444, 450 (E.D.Va.1998); *see also* EF Cultural Travel BV v. Zefer Corp., 318 F.3d 58, 62-63 (1st Cir.2003) ("A lack of authorization could be established by an explicit statement on the website restricting access.... [W]e think that the public website provider can easily spell out explicitly what is forbidden....").

132. Southwest Airlines Co v. BoardFirst, LLC, 2007 WL 4823761 at *14–15, (N.D.Tex. 2007).

133. 18 U.S.C. § 1030(c).

134. 18 U.S.C. § 1030(g).

135. *Id.*

136. P.C. Yonkers, Inc. v. Celebrations The Party and Seasonal Superstore, LLC, 428 F.3d. 504 (3rd Cir. 2006).

137. *P.C. Yonkers*, 428 F.3d. at 508-509; *see also* I.M.S. Inquiry Management Systems, Ltd. v. Berkshire Information Systems, Inc., 307 F. Supp. 2d 521, 526 (S.D. N.Y. 2004).

5:39. Obtaining customer information and loss under the CFAA

Certain cases have found that improper access of protected computers, which obtains proprietary information, including customer information, can give rise to a sufficient showing of damage.[138] It should be noted that these cases were decided under the version of the CFAA before recent amendments to the definition of "loss" under § 1030(e)(11), which now ties loss to an interruption of service.[139]

5:40. Misappropriation of trade secrets via e-mail forwarding

One court recently concluded whether an employee who forwarded trade secret information to a competitor while still employed engaged in an actionable trade secret misappropriation. This court concluded that this conduct demonstrated the likelihood of a high degree of success on the merits.[140]

5:41. No civil liability under § 10(b) and Rule 10b-5 for "hacking and trading" or "stealing and trading"

In one recent case the Southern District of New York held that the defendant's hacking of a computer system to obtain confidential information that he used to trade securities did not give rise to § 10(b) or Rule 10b-5 liability.[141] The basis of the court's ruling was that, though the defendant may have violated the law, he did not owe a fiduciary duty to the company about which he obtained the information. In this case an individual allegedly hacked into a secure server of Thomson Financial Inc. and obtained information about the earnings of a publicly traded company before it was announced to the public.[142] The individual allegedly used this information to trade the stock of the company. The court found there was no civil liability here because the alleged conduct was not "deceptive," which typically requires a breach of fiduciary duty or a breach of a similar duty.[143]

---

138. *P.C. Yonkers*, 428 F.3d. at 508-509; In re Intuit Privacy Litigation, 138 F. Supp. 2d 1272, 1281 (C.D. Cal. 2001); In re DoubleClick Inc. Privacy Litigation, 154 F. Supp. 2d 497, 519-526 (S.D. N.Y. 2001).

139. Four Seasons Hotels and Resorts B.V. v. Consorcio Barr, S.A., 267 F. Supp. 2d 1268, 1323 (S.D. Fla. 2003), aff'd in part, rev'd in part, 138 Fed. Appx. 297 (11th Cir. 2005) ("The value of the information [confidential customer and financial information] obtained by these acts, which Four Seasons' hotel industry expert credibly established as $2,090,000, is clearly in excess of the statutory threshold."); *see also* In re America Online, Inc., 168 F. Supp. 2d 1359, 1380 (S.D. Fla. 2001).

140. Andritz v. Southern Maintenance Contractor LLC, 2009 WL 48187, (M.D. Ga. 2009) (holding lost revenue from alleged access of trade secrets by employee on his laptop after the end of his employment is not loss under CFAA); US Bioservices Corp v. Lugo, 2:08-595 F. Supp. 2d 1189 (D. Kan. 2009) (applying the Shamrock line of cases and holding that an employee who accessed trade secrets, emailed them to their personal account and then disclosed them to a new employer did not violate the CFAA); Bridal Expo, Inc. v. Florenstein, 4:08-cv-03777 (S.D. Tex. February 3, 2009) (rejecting the *Citrin* line of cases); Resource Center for Independent Living, Inc. v. Ability Resources, Inc., 534 F. Supp. 2d 1204 (D.Kan. 2008) (CFAA claim properly pled where loss consists of the loss of confidential and proprietary information for the benefit of defendants' competing enterprise.); Resource Center for Independent Living, Inc. vs. Ability Resources, Inc., 534 F. Supp. 2d 1204 (D. Kan. 2008).

141. Verigy U.S., Inc., vs. Mayder, 2008 WL 564634 (N.D. Cal. 2008).

142. S.E.C. v. Dorozhko, 2008 WL 126612 (S.D. N.Y. 2008).

143. *Id.*

5:42. Conspiracy to violate the CFAA

The court in *Alliance International, Inc. vs. Todd* concluded that there could be conspiracy liability to violate the CFAA.[144]

II. The Economic Espionage Act

5:43. Theft of trade secrets

It is a criminal violation of the Economic Espionage Act for a person, with intent to convert a trade secret[145] that is related to or included in a product that is produced for or placed in interstate or foreign commerce, to take certain actions that inure to the economic benefit of anyone other than the owner[146] if the person intends or knows that the offense will injure the owner. Specifically, a person is precluded from knowingly stealing; without authorization appropriating, taking, carrying away, or concealing; by fraud, artifice, or deception obtaining information; without authorization copying, duplicating, sketching, drawing, photographing, downloading, uploading, altering, destroying, photocopying, replicating, transmitting, delivering, sending, mailing, communicating, or conveying information; or receiving, buying or possessing information, knowing the information to have been stolen or appropriated, obtained, or converted without authorization.[147] It is also a crime to attempt or conspire to commit any of these acts.[148]

The crime is punishable by a fine, a prison term of not more than 10 years, or both.[149] An organization that violates this law can be fined not more than $5 million.[150]

5:44. Economic espionage involving foreign states

It is also a crime if a person knowingly steals; without authorization appropriates, takes, carries away, or conceals; by fraud, artifice, or deception obtains a trade secret;

---

144. *Id.* at *8 ("While we are mindful that the antifraud provisions of the Exchange Act should be 'construed not technically and restrictively, but flexibly to effectuate its remedial purposes,' we agree with the Fifth Circuit that the Supreme Court has thus far only used the term 'deceptive' in conjunction with the breach of a fiduciary or similar duty of disclosure.") (internal citations omitted).

145. Alliance International, Inc. vs. Todd, 2008 WL 2859095 (E.D. N.C. 2008).

146. "Trade secret" means all forms and types of financial, business, scientific, technical, economic, or engineering information, including patterns, plans, compilations, program devices, formulas, designs, prototypes, methods, techniques, processes, procedures, programs, or codes, whether tangible or intangible, and whether or how stored, compiled, or memorialized physically, electronically, graphically, photographically, or in writing if: (A) the owner thereof has taken reasonable measures to keep such information secret; and (B) the information derives independent economic value, actual or potential, from not being generally known to, and not being readily ascertainable through proper means by, the public. 18 U.S.C. § 1839(3).

147. "Owner," with respect to a trade secret, means the person or entity in whom or in which rightful legal or equitable title to, or license in, the trade secret is reposed. 18 U.S.C. § 1839(4).

148. 18 U.S.C. §§ 1832(a)(1)–(3).

149. 18 U.S.C. §§ 1832(a)(4)–(5).

150. 18 U.S.C. § 1832(a).

without authorization copies, duplicates, sketches, draws, photographs, downloads, uploads, alters, destroys, photocopies, replicates, transmits, delivers, sends, mails, communicates, or conveys a trade secret; or receives, buys, or possesses a trade secret, knowing the information to have been stolen or appropriated, obtained, or converted without authorization if the act is taken with the intent or knowledge that it will benefit a foreign government, foreign instrumentality,[151] or foreign agent.[152] Any attempt or conspiracy to commit these acts is also a crime.[153]

Individuals face fines of not more than $500,000, a prison term of not more than 15 years, or both, for a violation of the Economic Espionage Act.[154] Organizations that violate this law can be fined up to $10 million.[155]

5:45.   Exceptions to liability

The act does not prohibit any otherwise lawful activity conducted by a governmental entity of the United States, a state, or a political subdivision of a state, or the reporting of a suspected violation of law to any governmental entity of the United States, a state, or a political subdivision of a state, if the entity has lawful authority with respect to that violation.[156]

5:46.   Forfeiture

In addition to the other criminal penalties, the court must order forfeiture to the U.S. government of any property constituting, or derived from, any proceeds a person obtained, directly or indirectly, as the result of a violation of the act, and any of the person's property used, or intended to be used, in any manner or part, to commit or facilitate the commission of such violation, if the court in its discretion so determines, taking into consideration the nature, scope, and proportionality of the use of the property in the offense.[157]

5:47.   Confidentiality issues

If a prosecution is commenced under the Economic Espionage Act, the court must enter such orders and take such other action as may be necessary and appropriate to preserve the confidentiality of trade secrets, consistent with the requirements of other federal laws.[158]

---

151. 18 U.S.C. § 1832(b).

152. "Foreign instrumentality" means any agency, bureau, ministry, component, institution, association, or any legal, commercial, or business organization, corporation, firm, or entity that is substantially owned, controlled, sponsored, commanded, managed, or dominated by a foreign government. 18 U.S.C. § 1839(1).

153. "Foreign agent" means any officer, employee, proxy, servant, delegate, or representative of a foreign government. 18 U.S.C. § 1839(2), 18 U.S.C. §§ 1831(a)(1)–(3).

154. 18 U.S.C. § 1831(a)(5).

155. 18 U.S.C. § 1831(a).

156. 18 U.S.C. § 1831(b).

157. 18 U.S.C. § 1833.

158. 18 U.S.C. § 1834(a).

In order to preserve trade secret protection required by this law, companies must take steps to preserve the confidentiality of the information. In many cases this means not disclosing the information to third parties. However, in certain cases disclosure is needed, or desired. In these cases a non-disclosure agreement, or NDA, is used to preserve confidentiality, but permit information sharing.

5:48. Civil proceedings

The Attorney General is also authorized to seek injunctive relief for violations of the EEA.[159]

III. Fraud and Access Devices

5:49. Fraud and access devices—Generally

It is a federal crime to knowingly and with intent to defraud produce,[160] use, or traffic[161] in one or more counterfeit access devices;[162] traffic in or use one or more unauthorized access devices[163] during any one-year period, and by this conduct obtain anything of value aggregating $1,000 or more during that period; possess fifteen or more devices which are counterfeit or unauthorized access devices; produce, traffic in, have control or custody of, or possess device-making equipment;[164] or effect transactions, with one or more access devices issued to another person or persons, to receive payment or any other thing of value during any one-year period the aggregate value of which is equal to or greater than $1,000.[165] It is also a crime, without the authorization of the issuer of the access device, knowingly and with intent to defraud, to solicit a person for the purpose of offering an access device or selling information regarding or an application to obtain an access device.[166]

---

159. 18 U.S.C. § 1835.

160. 18 U.S.C. § 1836(a).

161. The term "produce" includes design, alter, authenticate, duplicate, or assemble. 18 U.S.C. § 1029(e)(4).

162. The term "traffic" means transfer, or otherwise dispose of, to another, or obtain control of with intent to transfer or dispose of. 18 U.S.C. § 1029(e)(5).

163. The term "access device" means any card, plate, code, account number, electronic serial number, mobile identification number, personal identification number, or other telecommunications service, equipment, or instrument identifier, or other means of account access that can be used, alone or in conjunction with another access device, to obtain money, goods, services, or any other thing of value, or that can be used to initiate a transfer of funds (other than a transfer originated solely by paper instrument). 18 U.S.C. § 1029(e)(1). The term "counterfeit access device" means any access device that is counterfeit, fictitious, altered, or forged, or an identifiable component of an access device or a counterfeit access device. 18 U.S.C. § 1029(e)(2).

164. The term "unauthorized access device" means any access device that is lost, stolen, expired, revoked, canceled, or obtained with intent to defraud. 18 U.S.C. § 1029(e)(3).

165. The term "device-making equipment" means any equipment, mechanism, or impression designed or primarily used for making an access device or a counterfeit access device. 18 U.S.C. § 1029(e)(6).

166. 18 U.S.C. §§ 1029(a)(1)–(5).

This statute also prohibits any person from knowingly and with intent to defraud use, produce, traffic in, have control or custody of, or possess a telecommunications instrument that has been modified or altered to obtain unauthorized use of telecommunications services;[167] or produce, traffic in, have control or custody of, or possess a scanning receiver.[168] It is also illegal to knowingly use, produce, traffic in, have control or custody of, or possess hardware or software, knowing it has been configured to insert or modify telecommunication identifying information[169] associated with or contained in a telecommunications instrument so that the instrument may be used to obtain telecommunications service without authorization; or without the authorization of the credit card system member or its agent, knowingly and with intent to defraud cause or arrange for another person to present to the member or its agent, for payment, one or more evidences or records of transactions made by an access device.[170]

This law applies to more than just simply possessing counterfeit credit cards. Indeed, merely possessing out-of-state credit card account numbers has been held to be a violation of the restriction upon possessing counterfeit credit cards.[171] Fraudulently obtaining credit cards, through the submission of false information, constitutes a "counterfeit access device" under this law.[172] Even restaurant receipts with credit card numbers printed on them have been held to be access devices.[173] Improper possession of cellular account numbers has also been held to be a violation of this law.[174]

5:50. Criminal enforcement

These acts subject an individual to a variety of penalties if the conduct affects interstate or foreign commerce, and an attempt to commit one of these acts is punishable in the same manner as if the act were completed.[175] The interstate commerce requirement is usually quite easily met, because merely using the banking system, including making telephone calls to verify authorization by a bank employee, will satisfy this requirement.[176]

However, if there is a conspiracy to commit these acts between two or more persons, fines are available, as set forth below, along with prison terms of one-half of the terms described below.[177]

---

167. 18 U.S.C. §§ 1029(a)(6)(A)–(B).

168. The term "telecommunications service" has the meaning given such term in section 3 of title I of the Communications Act of 1934 (47 U.S.C. § 153). 18 U.S.C. § 1029(e)(9).

169. The term "scanning receiver" means a device or apparatus that can be used to intercept a wire or electronic communication in violation of chapter 119 or to intercept an electronic serial number, mobile identification number, or other identifier of any telecommunications service, equipment, or instrument. 18 U.S.C. § 1029(e)(8).

170. The term "telecommunication identifying information" means electronic serial number or any other number or signal that identifies a specific telecommunications instrument or account, or a specific communication transmitted from a telecommunications instrument. 18 U.S.C. § 1029(e)(11).

171. 18 U.S.C. §§ 1029(a)(9)–(10).

172. U.S. v. Rushdan, 870 F.2d 1509 (9th Cir. 1989).

173. U.S. v. Soape, 169 F.3d 257 (5th Cir. 1999).

174. U.S. v. Caputo, 808 F.2d 963 (2d Cir. 1987).

175. U.S. v. Edmonson, 175 F. Supp. 2d 889 (S.D. Miss 2001).

176. 18 U.S.C. §§ 1029(a)–(b)(1).

177. U.S. v. Scartz, 838 F.2d 876, 24 Fed. R. Evid. Serv. 995 (6th Cir. 1988).

Violations are generally punishable by a fine, a prison term of up to 10 years, or both,[178] while certain provisions are punishable by a fine, a prison term of not more than 15 years, or both.[179] If the violation is a repeat violation, then the crime is punishable by a fine, a prison term of not more than 20 years, or both.[180] Forfeiture of personal property used or intended to be used to commit an offense is also authorized as a remedy for any violation of this law.[181]

5:51.   Exceptions to liability

This law does not prohibit any lawfully authorized investigative, protective, or intelligence activity of a law enforcement agency of the United States, a state,[182] or a political subdivision of a state, or of an intelligence agency of the United States, or any activity authorized under chapter 224 of Title 18.[183]

It is also not a violation of the restriction upon obtaining telecommunications services for an officer, employee, or agent of, or a person engaged in business with, a facilities-based carrier,[184] to engage in conduct (other than trafficking) for the purpose of protecting the property or legal rights of that carrier, unless the conduct is for the purpose of obtaining telecommunications service provided by another facilities-based carrier without the authorization of the carrier.[185] It is also an affirmative defense in prosecutions for this specific section (other than a violation consisting of producing or trafficking) that the conduct charged was engaged in for research or development in connection with a lawful purpose.[186]

5:52.   Extraterritorial violations

Any person outside the jurisdiction of the United States that engages in an act that if committed within the jurisdiction of the United States would constitute an offense under this law is subject to the fines, penalties, imprisonment, and forfeiture provided in this law if the offense involves an access device issued, owned, managed, or controlled by a financial institution,[187] account issuer, credit card system member,[188] or other entity

---

178. 18 U.S.C. § 1029(b)(2).

179. 18 U.S.C. § 1029(c)(1)(A)(i).

180. 18 U.S.C. § 1029(c)(1)(A)(ii).

181. 18 U.S.C. § 1029(c)(1)(B).

182. 18 U.S.C. § 1029(c)(1)(C).

183. For purposes of this subsection, the term "State" includes a state of the United States, the District of Columbia, and any commonwealth, territory, or possession of the United States. 18 U.S.C. § 1029(f).

184. 18 U.S.C. § 1029(f).

185. The term "facilities-based carrier" means an entity that owns communications transmission facilities, is responsible for the operation and maintenance of those facilities, and holds an operating license issued by the Federal Communications Commission under the authority of title III of the Communications Act of 1934. 18 U.S.C. § 1029(e)(10).

186. 18 U.S.C. § 1029(g)(1).

187. 18 U.S.C. § 1029(g)(2).

188. The term "financial institution" means—(A) an institution, with deposits insured by the Federal Deposit Insurance Corporation; (B) the Federal Reserve or a member of the Federal Reserve including any Federal Reserve Bank; (C) a credit union with accounts insured by the National Credit Union Administration; (D) a member of the Federal home loan bank system and any home loan bank; (E) any institution of the Farm

within the jurisdiction of the United States, and the person transports, delivers, conveys, transfers to or through, or otherwise stores, secrets, or holds within the jurisdiction of the United States, any article used to assist in the commission of the offense or the proceeds of such offense or property derived from the crime.[189]

Credit System under the Farm Credit Act of 1971; (F) a broker-dealer registered with the Securities and Exchange Commission pursuant to section 15 of the Securities Exchange Act of 1934; (G) the Securities Investor Protection Corporation; (H) a branch or agency of a foreign bank (as such terms are defined in paragraphs (1) and (3) of section 1(b) of the International Banking Act of 1978); and (I) an organization operating under section 25 or section 25(a) of the Federal Reserve Act. 18 U.S.C. § 1030(e)(4).

189. The term "credit card system member" means a financial institution or other entity that is a member of a credit card system, including an entity, whether affiliated with or identical to the credit card issuer, that is the sole member of a credit card system. 18 U.S.C. § 1029(e)(7).

CHAPTER 6

Privacy in Electronic and Wire Communications

I.   Overview

6:1.   In general

Privacy in electronic and wire communications has been an issue that has perplexed courts for almost a century. Initially, there was little privacy protection afforded to wire communications by the Supreme Court, but that trend shifted due to a later Supreme Court decision, as well as the enactment of certain legislation at the federal level, including the Electronic Communications Privacy Act.

Privacy in electronic and wire communications began as a Fourth Amendment issue and later progressed into a statutory and constitutional issue as these new laws were enacted. However, legislative developments were not limited to increasing privacy protections. The Foreign Intelligence Surveillance Act (FISA) was enacted in the 1970s in order to regulate the quite common practice of warrantless wiretapping. FISA also covers other, more traditional information gathering, including searches. Finally, pen registers and trap and trace devices also relate to law enforcement gathering of electronic records and these laws must also be considered when assessing the restrictions upon gathering of communication information, particularly by law enforcement.

State law also plays an important role in this area, as many states exceed the federal protections on wire and electronic communications.

6:2. History of wiretapping

There has been an extensive history of warrantless wiretapping in the United States. The first decision that held that this conduct was improper was *Katz v. U.S.*,[1] in which the Supreme Court held that warrantless wiretaps violated the Fourth Amendment.[2]

Congress then stepped into the breach and enacted Title III of the Omnibus Crime Control and Safe Streets Act, which ultimately became the Electronic Communications Privacy Act (ECPA).[3] This law controlled the interception of wire and electronic communications in connection with certain crimes.[4]

Apart from the domestic crime uses for wiretaps, numerous presidents used wiretapping in connection with national security matters, leading to political abuses, according to the report of the Church Committee, a congressional committee that studied intelligence activities.[5] These concerns led to FISA, which restricts wiretapping, physical searches, and the use of pen registers in connection with the gathering of foreign intelligence.

6:3. Fourth Amendment and wiretapping

While protection of papers was never disputed, and this protection extended to unopened mail, wiretapping received different treatment. Indeed, the Supreme Court had ruled, prior to the enactment of the ECPA, that warrantless wiretapping did not implicate, or violate, the Fourth Amendment, because the wires that were tapped were not located in the individual's house.[6] The *Olmstead* case gave us Justice Brandeis's famous dissent, which reaffirmed his belief in the right to be let alone.[7]

In *Katz*, the Court considered whether it was proper for the FBI to install a listening and recording device outside a public payphone to gather evidence of alleged misconduct.[8] The Court noted at the outset that the Fourth Amendment protects people, not places,

---

1. Katz v. U.S., 389 U.S. 347, 88 S. Ct. 507, 19 L. Ed. 2d 576 (1967).

2. Katz v. U.S., 389 U.S. at 357; ACLU v. National Sec. Agency, 438 F. Supp. 2d 754, 16 A.L.R. Fed. 2d 749 (E.D. Mich. 2006), reversed on other grounds, ACLU v. NSA, 493 F.3d 644 (6th Cir. 2007).

3. ACLU v. NSA, 438 F. Supp. 2d 754, reversed on other grounds, 493 F.3d 644 (6th Cir. 2007).

4. Pub. L. 90-351, 82 Stat. 211; American Civil Liberties Union v. National Sec. Agency, 438 F. Supp. 2d 754, 16 A.L.R. Fed. 2d 749 (E.D. Mich. 2006), reversed on other grounds 493 F.3d 644 (6th Cir. 2007).

5. ACLU v. National Sec. Agency, 438 F. Supp. 2d 754, 16 A.L.R. Fed. 2d 749 (E.D. Mich. 2006) reversed on other grounds 493 F.3d 644 (6th Cir. 2007).

6. Olmstead v. U.S., 277 U.S. 438 (1928).

7. "[The makers of our Constitution] conferred, as against the government, the right to be let alone-the most comprehensive of rights and the right most valued by civilized men ... Subtler and more far-reaching means of invading privacy have become available to the government. Discovery and invention have made it possible for the government, by means far more effective than stretching upon the rack, to obtain disclosure in court of what is whispered in the closet." (Brandeis dissenting) Olmstead v. U.S., 277 U.S. 438, 48 S. Ct. 564 (1928).

8. Katz v. U.S., 389 U.S. 347, 88 S. Ct. 507, 19 L. Ed. 2d 576 (1967).

and thus the propriety of this conduct rests on an analysis of an individual's privacy expectation. Thus, what a person exposes to the public will not be protected, even if in a traditionally protected environment, such as a home, but what a person seeks to preserve as private, even in a public area, will be protected.[9]

While not directly overruling *Olmstead*, the Court concluded that the doctrine that served as the basis for the *Olmstead* decision had been eroded by subsequent decisions, and that the FBI's installation of a listening device outside a public telephone, without a warrant, violated the Fourth Amendment.[10] The Court invalidated the search, finding that it did not fall within one of the recognized exceptions to warrantless searches.[11]

Ironically, this case, particularly the concurrence filed by Justice White, foreshadowed the debate that would occur in connection with the FISA Court and the Patriot Act. In footnote 23, the Court expressly noted that *Katz* did not address whether a warrant was required for searches involving national security.[12] Justice White went further, noting that wiretapping to protect national security has been done by a number of presidents.[13] Justice White also noted his agreement with these actions, stating that "We should not require the warrant procedure and the magistrate's judgment if the President of the United States or his chief legal officer, the Attorney General, has considered the requirements of national security and authorized electronic surveillance as reasonable."[14]

6:4. Overview of the Electronic Communications Privacy Act (ECPA)

Title III of the Omnibus Crime Control and Safe Streets Act of 1968, as amended (Title III), and portions of the Electronic Communications Privacy Act (ECPA), are the main statutes that address these issues. Many times these requests are referred to as Title III requests, though many courts refer to the requests, and the governing laws, as named in the ECPA.

The ECPA consists of the Wiretap Act and the Stored Communications Act. The individual portions of the ECPA are sometimes referred to as Title I of the Act, The Wiretap Act, which exclusively applies to the interception of communications, and Title II, the Stored Communications Act, which applies to the dissemination or review of stored communications.[15]

These acts regulate when electronic communications can be monitored or reviewed by third parties, including ISPs. Generally, it is a crime for persons to intercept or

---

9. Katz v. U.S., 389 U.S. at 351.

10. Katz v. U.S., 389 U.S. at 353.

11. Citing Carroll v. U.S., 267 U.S. 132, 153, 156, 45 S. Ct. 280, 285, 286, 69 L. Ed. 543, 39 A.L.R. 790 (1925); McDonald v. U.S., 335 U.S. 451, 454-456, 69 S. Ct. 191, 192-194, 93 L. Ed. 153 (1948); Brinegar v. U.S., 338 U.S. 160, 174-177, 69 S. Ct. 1302, 1310-1312, 93 L. Ed. 1879 (1949); Cooper v. State of Cal., 386 U.S. 58, 87 S. Ct. 788, 17 L. Ed. 2d 730 (1967); Warden, Md. Penitentiary v. Hayden, 387 U.S. 294, 298–300, 87 S. Ct. 1642, 1645-1647, 18 L. Ed. 2d 782 (1967).

12. Katz v. U.S., 389 U.S. at 358, fn 23.

13. *Id.* at 363.

14. *Id.* at 364.

15. Hall v. EarthLink Network, Inc., 396 F.3d 500 (2d Cir. 2005); Organizacion Jd Ltda. v. U.S. Dept. of Justice, 124 F.3d 354, 356 (2d Cir. 1997).

procure electronic communications,[16] which include e-mail and other electronic messages and transmissions, unless certain exceptions apply[17] including the following: (1) the communication is made through a system that is readily accessible to the general public;[18] (2) the interception or procurement is made to protect the rights or property of the provider, although random monitoring cannot be done;[19] (3) a provider of electronic communication service reviews a communication to record the fact that a wire or electronic communication was initiated or completed if the purpose is to protect the provider, another provider, or a user, from fraudulent, unlawful or abusive use of the service;[20] (4) the interception or procurement is made by court order;[21] (5) the originator or addressee of any communication consents to the disclosure;[22] (6) the communication is divulged to a person employed or authorized, or whose facilities are used, to forward such communication to its destination (including employers);[23] or (7) the communication is inadvertently obtained and the communication appears to pertain to the commission of a crime, if the communication is divulged to law enforcement.[24]

6:5.   Temporal distinctions—An introduction

Title I only applies to conduct that occurs at the precise time of transmission.[25] This is in contrast to conduct that violates Title II, which relates to the improper acquisition of the contents of stored communications—i.e., after their transmission.[26] Thus, the difference between the two titles is a temporal one. Title I applies only to the interception or accessing of information while in transmission, while Title II applies to the unauthorized access of storage communications.[27] This has lead to some inconsistent results, as is discussed later in the chapter.

6:6.   Public versus private service providers

An important distinction created by the ECPA is its differing treatment of service providers that provide communications service to the "public" and those that do not. As discussed below, there are additional hurdles for "public" service providers when

---

16. "Electronic communication" is defined as any transfer of signs, signals, writing, images, sounds, data, or intelligence of any nature transmitted in whole or in part by a wire, radio, electromagnetic, photoelectronic or photooptical system that affects interstate or foreign commerce. 18 U.S.C. § 2510(11).

17. 18 U.S.C. § 2511(1)(a).

18. 18 U.S.C. § 2511(2)(g)(1).

19. 18 U.S.C. § 2511(2)(a)(1).

20. 18 U.S.C. § 2511(2)(h)(ii).

21. 18 U.S.C. § 2511(2)(a)(ii)(A).

22. 18 U.S.C. § 2511(3)(b)(ii).

23. 18 U.S.C. § 2511(3)(b)(iii).

24. 18 U.S.C. § 2511(3)(b)(iv).

25. Steve Jackson Games, Inc. v. U.S. Secret Service, 36 F.3d 457 (5th Cir. 1994); U.S. v. Moriarty, 962 F. Supp. 217, 221 (D. Mass. 1997) (drawing temporal distinction between acquisition of communications during transmission under Title I and acquisition of contents of communications in a non-contemporaneous manner under Title II.).

26. Bohach v. City of Reno, 932 F. Supp. 1232, 1236-37 (D. Nev. 1996) (Electronic communications are not intercepted when they are in electronic storage.).

27. U.S. v. Moriarty, 962 F. Supp. 217 (D. Mass. 1997).

they monitor or disclose communications. This is important for businesses because an employer who simply provides e-mail or other Internet service to its employees is not a service provider to the "public" and therefore is under lesser restrictions.

6:7.   Defining an electronic communication service

One issue that impacts ECPA liability and exceptions to liability is what entities qualify as an electronic communication service. A provider of an electronic communication service is permitted to review communications in certain circumstances under § 2511(2) (a)(i). However, in the *In re Jet Blue Airways Corp. Privacy Litigation* case, it was held that an e-commerce site was not in the business of selling Internet access and therefore was not providing an electronic communication service.[28]   The Northern District of Illinois applied this reasoning and held that an entity that merely provides an e-mail address but purchases Internet access from a third-party is not a provider of an electronic communication service.[29]

6:8.   The ECPA and its lack of clarity

One issue to be aware of when interpreting the ECPA is that courts have not found its provisions to be easy to interpret. One court noted that the act is "famous (if not infamous) for its lack of clarity."[30]

6:9.   Constitutionality of the ECPA

One of the issues raised early on was whether the lower proof standards for a warrant under the ECPA violated the Fourth Amendment. This argument has been rejected.[31]

6:10.   ECPA as baseline—a conflict in holdings

The ECPA does not set a ceiling of protection, but rather a floor, a common national standard.[32] Thus, it has typically been held that states are free to adopt additional restrictions, or no restrictions at all, but lower state requirements are viewed with some suspicion.[33] As such, lower state standards are typically found not to apply, but heightened state standards will be applied by courts.[34]

However, some courts recently have held that the Stored Communications Act preempts any other state law claim for conduct that would violate the Stored

---

28.   In re Jet Blue Airways Corp. Privacy Litigation, 379 F.Supp.2d 299, 307-08 (E.D.N.Y. 2005).

29.   Steinbach v. Village of Forest Park, 2009 WL 2605283, 29 IER Cases 1080 (N.D.Ill. Aug 25, 2009) (NO. 06 C 4215).

30.   Steve Jackson Games, 36 F.3d at 462.

31.   U.S. v. Bailey, 607 F.2d 237 (9th Cir. 1979); U.S. v. Frederickson, 581 F.2d 711 (8th Cir. 1978); *see also* U.S. v. Feldman, 535 F.2d 1175 (9th Cir. 1976).

32.   U.S. v. Capra, 501 F.2d 267 (2d Cir. 1974).

33.   Capra, 501 F.2d 267.

34.   U.S. v. Marion, 535 F.2d 697 (2d Cir. 1976); *see also* U.S. v. Feiste, 792 F. Supp. 1153 (D. Neb. 1991), judgment aff'd, 961 F.2d 1349 (8th Cir. 1992); U.S. v. McKinnon, 721 F.2d 19 (1st Cir. 1983).

Communications Act.[35] This decision appears to be in conflict with the text of the ECPA, as well as other decisions interpreting the ECPA. While the ECPA does, as noted by the Court, state that it is the exclusive statute setting remedies for violations of its provisions, higher burdens imposed by state laws should not, as found by this Court, be preempted by the ECPA.

Courts continue to struggle with whether the Stored Communications Act preempts state law. One court concluded that the Stored Communications Act did not generally preempt state law, though it did so because it concluded that the Act only applied to public service providers, as well as disclosure to the government in certain defined circumstances.[36]

6:11. Purpose of ECPA

The purpose of this law is largely twofold. It is to protect the privacy of individuals and to provide remedies for the violations of this law.[37]

II. Title I: The Wiretap Act

A. *Restrictions on Interceptions and Disclosures*

6:12. Prohibited interceptions and disclosures of communications

The Wiretap Act is Title I of the ECPA. There are a number of different types of conduct that violate the ECPA. However, it should be noted that there are in essence two different violations, explained in greater detail below—intercepting communications, as well as disclosing communications if the person making the disclosure knows or has reason to know that the communication was intercepted in violation of the ECPA. Thus, it is not required that the person who uses the communication actually intercept it, if the other criteria are met.

Except as otherwise specifically provided under the ECPA, it is illegal for any person[38] to intentionally intercept,[39] endeavor to intercept, or procure any other person

---

35. Quon v. Arch Wireless Operating Co., 445 F. Supp. 2d 1116 (C.D. Cal. 2006); citing Muskovich v. Crowwell, 1995 WL 905403 at *1 (S.D. Iowa March 21, 2005); *see also* Bunnell v. MPAA, 2:06-cv-03206-FMC-JC (C.D. Cal. 2007).

36. Ideal Aerosmith, Inc. v. Acutronic USA, Inc., 2008 WL 1859811 (W.D.Pa. 2008).

37. U.S. v. Kalustian, 529 F.2d 585 (9th Cir. 1975); Lam Lek Chong v. U.S. Drug Enforcement Admin., 929 F.2d 729 (D.C. Cir. 1991).

38. "Person" means any employee, or agent of the United States or any state or political subdivision thereof, and any individual, partnership, association, joint stock company, trust, or corporation. 18 U.S.C. § 2510(6).

39. "Intercept" means the aural or other acquisition of the contents of any wire, electronic, or oral communication through the use of any electronic, mechanical, or other device. 18 U.S.C. § 2510(4).

to intercept or endeavor to intercept, any wire, oral,[40] or electronic communication[41] or intentionally use, endeavor to use, or procure any other person to use or endeavor to use any electronic, mechanical, or other device[42] to intercept any oral communication under the following conditions:

- the device is affixed to, or transmits a signal through a wire, cable, or other like connection used in wire communication;[43]
- the device transmits communications by radio, or interferes with the transmission of the communication;
- the person knows, or has reason to know, that such device or any component thereof has been sent through the mail or transported in interstate or foreign commerce;
- the use takes place on the premises of any business or other commercial establishment the operations of which affect interstate or foreign commerce;
- the purpose is to obtain information relating to the operations of any business or other commercial establishment the operations of which affect interstate or foreign commerce; or
- the person acts in the District of Columbia, the Commonwealth of Puerto Rico, or any territory or possession of the United States.[44]

---

40. "Oral communication" means any oral communication uttered by a person exhibiting an expectation that such communication is not subject to interception under circumstances justifying such expectation, but such term does not include any electronic communication. 18 U.S.C. § 2510(2).

41. "Electronic communication" means any transfer of signs, signals, writing, images, sounds, data, or intelligence of any nature transmitted in whole or in part by a wire, radio, electromagnetic, photoelectronic or photooptical system that affects interstate or foreign commerce, but does not include:

    (A) any wire or oral communication;

    (B) any communication made through a tone-only paging device;

    (C) any communication from a tracking device; or

    (D) electronic funds transfer information stored by a financial institution in a communications system used for the electronic storage and transfer of funds.

    18 U.S.C. § 2510(12).

42. "Electronic, mechanical, or other device" means any device or apparatus which can be used to intercept a wire, oral, or electronic communication other than

    (a) any telephone or telegraph instrument, equipment or facility, or any component thereof,

       (i) furnished to the subscriber or user by a provider of wire or electronic communication service in the ordinary course of its business and being used by the subscriber or user in the ordinary course of its business or furnished by such subscriber or user for connection to the facilities of such service and used in the ordinary course of its business; or

       (ii) being used by a provider of wire or electronic communication service in the ordinary course of its business, or by an investigative or law enforcement officer in the ordinary course of his duties;

    (b) a hearing aid or similar device being used to correct subnormal hearing to not better than normal.

    18 U.S.C. § 2510(5).

43. "Wire communication" means any aural transfer made in whole or in part through the use of facilities for the transmission of communications by the aid of wire, cable, or other like connection between the point of origin and the point of reception (including the use of such connection in a switching station) furnished or operated by any person engaged in providing or operating such facilities for the transmission of interstate or foreign communications or communications affecting interstate or foreign commerce. 18 U.S.C. § 2510(1).

44. 18 U.S.C. § 2511(1).

It is also illegal to intentionally disclose, or endeavor to disclose, the contents[45] of any wire, oral, or electronic communication, if the person knows, or has reason to know, that the information was obtained through the interception of a wire, oral, or electronic communication in violation of this law. It is also a violation to intentionally use, or endeavor to use, the contents of any wire, oral, or electronic communication, if the person knows or has reason to know that the information was obtained through the interception of a wire, oral, or electronic communication in violation of this law. Finally, it is a crime to intercept communications in order to interfere or impede a criminal investigation if certain specified conditions are met.[46]

6:13. Oral communications and reasonable expectation of privacy

In order for a communication to be protected by the ECPA the communication must, at some level, be private. Thus, oral communications, as defined by the ECPA, do not include conversations where there is no reasonable expectation of privacy.[47]

6:14. Review of emails on a laptop may not violate the ECPA

One court recently held that the review of emails on a laptop did not violate the ECPA because it was "questionable" whether the laptop was a "facility through which an electronic communication service is provided," and the emails were neither "temporary, intermediate storage" nor "electronic storage".[48]

6:15. Definition of intent for ECPA

The term intentional under the ECPA is narrower than the dictionary definition of "intentional." One court examined the legislative history of the ECPA and noted:

> "Intentional" means more than that one voluntarily engaged in conduct or caused a result. *Such conduct or the causing of the result must have been the person's conscious objective* ... The "intentional" state of mind is applicable only to conduct and results. Since one has

---

45. "Contents," when used with respect to any wire, oral, or electronic communication, includes any information concerning the substance, purport, or meaning of that communication. 18 U.S.C.A § 2510(8).

46. 18 U.S.C. § 2511(1).

47. *See, e.g.,* Angel v. Williams, 12 F.3d 786, 27 Fed. R. Serv. 3d 1402 (8th Cir. 1993); Matter of John Doe Trader Number One, 894 F.2d 240 (7th Cir. 1990) (government agents' surveillance of oral communications in a trading pit were not an interception of "oral communications" because the trader had no reasonable expectation of privacy); U.S. v. Pui Kan Lam, 483 F.2d 1202 (2d Cir. 1973); U.S. v. Harrelson, 766 F.2d 186 (5th Cir. 1985) (oral communications in a prison are not private, and therefore not "oral communications" under the ECPA).

48. Hilderman v. Enea TekSci, Inc., 551 F.Supp.2d 1183 (S.D.Cal. 2008).

no control over the existence of circumstances, one cannot "intend" them.[49]

In certain cases, employees' continuing to access emails on a network, unless some barrier is put up or other notice is given, is not actionable under the SCA because of a lack of intent.[50]

Practice pointer — Consent under the ECPA

While there is a consent exception to the ECPA's restrictions on disclosures, it need not be explicit and can be implied consent, but it still must be consent in fact.[51] Some courts in the context of telephone monitoring have held that monitoring policies that provide for monitoring business calls do not permit monitoring of personal calls beyond the time that is required to determine the call is a personal call.[52] Thus, consent is not routinely implied and the mere knowledge that monitoring is occurring will not give rise to a finding of implied consent in all cases.[53] However, where the employer has a no personal use policy, such policy may permit interception of personal communications in order to enforce the policy.[54]

Another court recently addressed the method of obtaining consent in an ECPA claim. It should be noted that, while not raised in the case, it is questionable whether the communications at issue fell within the ECPA.[55] That said, the court in this case held that a clause in a contract presented after the monitoring occurred was insufficient consent, though it did also hold, consistent with the ECPA, that consent of one party was sufficient.[56]

6:16.   Exceptions to consent

While one party consent can be sufficient under the ECPA, it is not sufficient if the purpose of the interception is committing a criminal or tortuous act in violation of the Constitution or laws of the United States or of any state. Certain plaintiffs have attempted to argue that the violation of state wiretap law is sufficient to meet this standard. This

---

49. Butera & Andrews v. International Business Machines Corp., 456 F. Supp. 2d 104 (D.D.C. 2006); citing S.Rep. No. 99-541, at 23 (1986); In re Pharmatrak, Inc., 329 F.3d 9, 23 (1st Cir. 2003); see also Wyatt Tec. H. Corp. v. Smithson, 2006 WL 5668246 **9-10 (C.D. Cal. 2006) (Intent is present where an individual logs into another's email account without permission and reviews materials).

50. Lasco Foods, Inc. v. Hall and Shaw Sales, 600 F. Supp. 2d 1045 (E.D. Miss. 2009) (holding that because employee still was permitted access to the network misuse of trade secret information was not actionable under the SCA), citing Sherman & Co. v. Salton Maxim Housewares, Inc., 94 F.Supp.2d 817 (E.D.Mich. 2000).

51. United States v. Lanoue, 71 F.3d 966, 981 (1st Cir. 1995).

52. Watkins v. L.M. Berry & Co., 704 F.2d 557 (11th Cir. 1983).

53. *Id.* Campiti v. Walonis, 611 F.2d 387, 394 (1979); Crooker v. United States Department of Justice, 497 F.Supp. 500, 503 (D.Conn. 1980).

54. *See, e.g.*, Briggs v. American Filter Co., 630 F.2d 414, 420 n. 8, (5th Cir. 1980).

55. Smith v. NWM-Oklahoma, LLC, 2008 WL 2705047 (July 8, 2008).

56. *Id.*

argument has typically been rejected because the courts consider the purpose of the interception, not whether it in fact might violate another state or other law.[57]

6:17.   When is a communication aurally acquired under the ECPA

Certain courts have held that a communication is not aurally acquired under the ECPA until it is listened to.[58] However, other courts have rejected this argument.[59]

6:18.   Requirement that communication be intercepted in transit for Title I violation

Another issue courts have faced is whether Title I applies to the review of communications that are stored—that is, communications that are reviewed or taken after they are sent. The most common example of this is the review of e-mails after they have been sent and delivered and are being stored on a server. Unless the e-mail or other communication is intercepted at the precise time of transmission, the conduct will not violate Title I.[60] This is because the definition of electronic communications under Title I explicitly does not embrace stored communications.[61] Similarly, in order to state a claim for violation of the ECPA, the plaintiff must show that a "device" was used to intercept a communication. Courts have consistently held that a drive or server used to receive e-mail is not an interception.[62]

While most courts have concluded that an interception must be contemporaneous with the transmission of a communication, other courts have reached different conclusions.[63] In *United States v. Councilman*, the First Circuit addressed this issue and whether communications stored in RAM were a wire communication or a stored communication, as well as when an e-mail was still regulated by Title I.[64] Councilman ran a business that provided ISP services for book dealers. He also ran an online rare and out-of-print book business that was a competitor of Amazon.com. As such, he

---

57.   Smith v. NWM-Oklahoma, LLC, 2008 WL 270547 (July 8, 2008), citing Sussman v. American Broadcasting Companies, Inc., 186 F.3d 1200, 1202 (9th Cir. 1999); Payne v. Norwest Corp., 911 F.Supp. 1299, 1304 (D.Mont. 1995), aff'd in part and rev'd in part, 113 F.3d 1079 (9th Cir. 1997); By-Prod. Corp. v. Armen-Berry Co., 668 F.2d 956, 960 (7th Cir. 1982); U.S. v. Phillips, 540 F.2d 319, 327, fn. 5 (8th Cir. 1976); Roberts v. Americable Intern. Inc., 883 F.Supp. 499, 503 (E.D.Cal. 1995).

58.   Arias v. Mut. Cent. Alarm Serv., Inc., 202 F.3d 553 (2d Cir. 2000); Greenfield v. Kootenai County, 752 F.2d 1387 (9th Cir. 1985).

59.   United States v. Lewis, 406 F.3d 11 (1st Cir. 2002); Ali v. Douglas Cable Communications, 929 F. Supp. 1362 (D. Kan. 1996); Walden v. City of Providence, 495 F. Supp. 2d 245 (D. R.I. 2007).

60.   Steve Jackson Games, 36 F.3d at 461-62.

61.   Wesley College v. Pitts, 974 F. Supp. 385 (D. Del. 1997).

62.   Ideal Aerosmith, Inc. v. Acutronic, 2007 WL 4394447 (W.D. Pa. 2007); *see also* Commonwealth v. Proetto, 771 A.2d 823 (2001); Crowley v. Cybersource Corp., 166 F.Supp.2d 1263 (N.D. Cal. 2001); Hall v. Earth-Link Network, Inc., 396 F.3d 500 (2d Cir. 2005).

63.   Potter v. Havlicek, 2007 WL 539534 (S.D. Ohio 2007), c.f. Fraser v. Nationwide Mut. Ins. Co., 352 F.3d 107, 113 (3rd Cir. 2003); Konop v. Hawaiian Airlines, Inc., 302 F.3d 868 (9th Cir. 2002); Steve Jackson Games, Inc. v. United States Secret Serv., 36 F.3d 457 (5th Cir. 1994); Wesley College v. Pitts, 974 F. Supp. 375 (D. Del. 1997).

64.   United States v. Councilman, 418 F.3d 67 (1st Cir. 2005).

routinely reviewed e-mails that his customers received from Amazon.com to try and gain competitive intelligence.[65]

Councilman argued that this conduct did not violate Title I because the interception occurred while the e-mails were still in RAM and not in transit or on the wire. Councilman primarily relied upon the fact that the definition of a "wire communication" under the ECPA expressly included a communication that was in "electronic storage," while the corresponding definition for an electronic communication did not contain the "electronic storage" concept as part of its definition. Thus, Councilman argued that an e-mail that was in electronic storage was not regulated by Title I, and his conduct was legal under the Stored Communications Act (a fact which was not disputed), so the indictment should be dismissed.[66]

The court examined the text of the ECPA, as well as the legislative history in great detail, ultimately concluding that an "electronic communication" under the ECPA would include a communication that was in transit, though stopped in RAM on its way to its ultimate destination.[67] What appeared to be the most important factor for the First Circuit was that an "electronic communication" as defined by the ECPA excluded four specified categories, and none related to a communication in electronic storage. Thus, the court believed that had Congress intended to exclude communications in storage, it would have done so directly as part of these exclusions. Moreover, the Court of Appeal noted that most of the recent changes to the ECPA, including the addition of the definition at issue, were intended to expand privacy, not restrict it. As such, the court refused to dismiss the indictment.[68]

The temporal distinction was recently reaffirmed, albeit in a way that is inconsistent with Councilman, in connection with a court order requiring disclosure of transactional records. A court in the Central District of California held that the Wiretap Act was irrelevant to the disclosure of these types of electronic records since the records were not disclosed in real time.[69] Moreover, this same court later concluded that review of communications that are stored in RAM did not give rise to a Wiretap Act violation because the communications were, at least momentarily, in storage.[70] This was based, at least in part, on a prior, unrelated, holding. In *Quon*, relying upon a Ninth Circuit decision, the *Konop v. Hawaiian Airlines* matter, the court appears to have found that the Wiretap Act is inapplicable to any communication when it is stored in RAM, even if it is transitory storage.[71]

This issue recently was addressed in the context of the use of a key stroke logger. Given that the software did not directly access electronic communications, its use was not held to be contemporaneous under the Wiretap Act.[72]

---

65. *Id.*

66. Councilman, 418 F.3d at 74.

67. United States v. Councilman, 418 F.3d 67, 75 (1st Cir. 2005).

68. *Id.* at 76-77.

69. Columbia Pictures Industries v. Bunnell, 2007 WL 2080419 (C.D. Cal. 2007).

70. Bunnell v. MPAA, 567 F. Supp. 1148 (C.D. Cal. 2007).

71. Quon v. Arch Wireless Operating Co., 445 F. Supp. 2d 1116, 1135-36 (C.D. Cal. 2006) citing Konop v. Hawaiian Airlines, 302 F.3d 868, 878 n.6 (9th Cir. 2002). The Ninth Circuit later issued an opinion in this case that is discussed in chapter 9 and was not addressed in the later decision.

72. Bailey v. Bailey, 2008 WL 324156 (E.D.Mich. 2008).

At this point the Third, Fifth, Ninth and Eleventh circuits are considered to be of the view that for a communication to be intercepted under the Wiretap Act, it must be acquired during the "flight" of the communication, though courts continue to be somewhat confused by these isues.[73] However, it should be noted that even among these courts there is debate about what "in flight" means, as can be seen by the *Quon* and *Konop* cases. The *Daily* case rejected a finding that the use of a key logger to obtain a spouse's password that was ultimately used to access emails did not violate the Wiretap Act because the emails were not obtained contemporaneously. Other cases, such as *O'Brien*, *Councilman* and *Potter v. Havlicek*,[74] reject this view and interpret the Wiretap Act in a broader way that abandons any distinction between "in transit" and "in storage."

6:19. Exceptions to liability

It is not improper under the ECPA for an operator of a switchboard or an officer, employee, or agent of a provider of wire or electronic communication service,[75] whose facilities are used in the transmission of a wire or electronic communication, to intercept, disclose, or use communications in the normal course of employment, while engaged in any activity that is a necessary incident to the rendition of the service, or to the protection of the rights or property of the provider of that service. However, providers of wire communication service to the public may not utilize service observing or random monitoring except for mechanical or service quality control checks.[76]

6:20. Exceptions to liability—Disclosure to government entities

Providers of wire or electronic communication service, their officers, employees, and agents, landlords, custodians, or other persons, are authorized to provide information, facilities, or technical assistance to persons authorized by law to intercept wire, oral, or electronic communications or to conduct electronic surveillance, as defined in § 101 of the Foreign Intelligence Surveillance Act of 1978,[77] if the provider, its officers, employees, agents, landlord, custodian, or other specified person has been provided with a court order directing such assistance signed by the authorizing judge,[78] or a

---

73. *See, e.g.*, Fraser v. Nationwide Mutual Insurance Co., 352 F.3d 107, 113 (3rd Cir. 2003); U.S. v. Steiger, 318 F.3d 1039, 1047 (11th Cir. 2003); Knop v. Hawaiian Airlines, Inc., 302 F.3d 868, 878 (9th Cir. 2002); Steve Jackson Games, Inc. v. U.S. Secret Service, 36 F.3d 457, 463 (5th Cir. 1994). For other cases that reach other conclusions, see Bansal v. Russ, 513 F.Supp.2d 264, 276 (E.D. Pa. 2007); Bailey v. Bailey, 2008 WL 324156, *6 (E.D. Mich. 2008).

74. Potter v. Havlicek, 2007 WL 539534, *7 (W.D. Ohio February 14, 2007).

75. "Electronic communication service" means any service which provides to users thereof the ability to send or receive wire or electronic communications. 18 U.S.C. § 2510(15).

76. 18 U.S.C. § 2511(2)(a)(i).

77. 50 U.S.C. § 1801.

78. "Judge of competent jurisdiction" means a judge of a United States district court or a United States court of appeals; and a judge of any court of general criminal jurisdiction of a State who is authorized by a statute of that State to enter orders authorizing interceptions of wire, oral, or electronic communications. 18 U.S.C. § 2510(9).

certification in writing by specified government actors that a warrant is not needed and all other requirements are met.[79]

These documents must set forth the period of time of the information request. Providers of wire or electronic communication services cannot disclose the existence of any interception or surveillance or the device used to accomplish the interception or surveillance to the person whose communications are being monitored.[80] While providers of wire or electronic communications services have immunity for cooperating with the government in these circumstances, they are liable for damages if they disclose the existence of the intercept to the individual.[81]

6:21. Exceptions to liability—Other exceptions— Acting under color of authority and participants in communications

Other exceptions include interceptions by individuals who are acting under the color of state authority and are either themselves participants or have consent of a participant, and by individuals who are participants in the communications (and not acting under color of state authority).[82]

6:22. Exceptions to liability—Other exceptions—Systems that transmit public communications

There are a number of exceptions to Title I for public communication systems. It is not illegal for a person to intercept or access an electronic communication made through an electronic communication system[83] that is configured in a way that the electronic communication is readily accessible to the general public.[84] People are also permitted to intercept radio communications that are transmitted by any station for the use of the general public; communications related to ships, aircraft, vehicles, or persons in distress;

---

79. 18 U.S.C. § 2511(2)(a)(ii).

80. *Id.*

81. *Id.*

82. 18 U.S.C. § 2511(2)(c) and (d).

83. "Electronic communications system" means any wire, radio, electromagnetic, photooptical or photoelectronic facilities for the transmission of wire or electronic communications, and any computer facilities or related electronic equipment for the electronic storage of such communications. 18 U.S.C. § 2510(14).

84. "Readily accessible to the general public" means, with respect to a radio communication, that such communication is not—

   (A) scrambled or encrypted;

   (B) transmitted using modulation techniques whose essential parameters have been withheld from the public with the intention of preserving the privacy of such communication;

   (C) carried on a subcarrier or other signal subsidiary to a radio transmission;

   (D) transmitted over a communication system provided by a common carrier, unless the communication is a tone only paging system communication; or

   (E) transmitted on frequencies allocated under part 25, subpart D, E, or F of part 74, or part 94 of the Rules of the Federal Communications Commission, unless, in the case of a communication transmitted on a frequency allocated under part 74 that is not exclusively allocated to broadcast auxiliary services, the communication is a two-way voice communication by radio.

   18 U.S.C. § 2510(16).

and communications made on any governmental, law enforcement, civil defense, private land mobile, or public safety communications system, including police and fire, if they are readily accessible to the general public. Interception of communications by a station operating on an authorized frequency within the bands allocated to the amateur, citizens band, or general mobile radio services, or by any marine or aeronautical communications system are also permitted.

Practice Pointer—Public Systems

This exception to liability really exists to permit the monitoring and use of non-encrypted public, emergency, or other government networks. It also permits individuals to monitor and use citizen band and other amateur radio systems. Without this exception, many normal monitoring activities, including journalists listening to police radio reports, would be illegal.

6:23.   Exceptions to liability—Other exceptions—Interception due to interference

It is also not illegal to intercept any wire or electronic communication if the transmission is causing harmful interference to any lawfully operating station or consumer electronic equipment, but only to the extent necessary to identify the source of the interference. Other users[85] of the same frequency can intercept any radio communication made through a system that utilizes frequencies monitored by individuals providing or using the system, if the communication is not scrambled or encrypted, or can engage in any conduct which is not prohibited by § 633 of the Communications Act of 1934;[86] or is excepted from the application of § 705(a) of the Communications Act of 1934 by § 705(b) of that Act.[87]

6:24.   Exceptions to liability—Other exceptions—Fraudulent, unlawful or abusive acts

Providers of electronic communication service are permitted to record the fact that a wire or electronic communication was initiated or completed in order to protect the provider, another provider furnishing service toward the completion of the wire or electronic communication, or a user of that service, from fraudulent, unlawful or abusive use of such service.[88]

---

85. "User" means any person or entity who—
     (A) uses an electronic communication service; and
     (B) is duly authorized by the provider of such service to engage in such use.
     18 U.S.C. § 2510(13).
86. 47 U.S.C. §§ 151 *et seq.*
87. 18 U.S.C. § 2511(g).
88. 18 U.S.C. § 2511(h)(ii).

6:25. Interception of communications by computer trespassers

Individuals acting under the color of state law are permitted to intercept the wire or electronic communications of a computer trespasser[89] transmitted to, through, or from a protected computer,[90] if the owner or operator of the protected computer authorizes the interception of the computer trespasser's communications on the protected computer, the person is lawfully engaged in an investigation and has reasonable grounds to believe that the contents of the computer trespasser's communications will be relevant to the investigation, and the interception does not acquire communications other than those transmitted to or from the computer trespasser.[91]

6:26. Restrictions upon interception of transmissions service providers that provide service to the public

Except as otherwise permitted, any person providing electronic communication service to the public cannot intentionally divulge the contents of any communication while in transmission to any person or entity other than an addressee or intended recipient of such communication or an agent of such addressee or intended recipient.[92] However, a person or entity providing electronic communication service to the public may divulge the contents of any such communication as authorized in § 2511(2)(a) or § 2517, with the lawful consent of the originator or any addressee or intended recipient of such communication, to a person employed or authorized, or whose facilities are used, to forward such communication to its destination, or if the communications were inadvertently obtained by the service provider and appear to pertain to the commission of a crime, if such divulgence is made to a law enforcement agency.[93]

6:27. Recipient issues and consent to interception

In cases where the recipient of a communication, in many cases a website, determines that it wants to intercept communications, or permit others to, this is likely not a violation of Title I, because the receiving website would be a party to the communication and

---

89. "Computer trespasser"—

    (A) means a person who accesses a protected computer without authorization and thus has no reasonable expectation of privacy in any communication transmitted to, through, or from the protected computer; and

    (B) does not include a person known by the owner or operator of the protected computer to have an existing contractual relationship with the owner or operator of the protected computer for access to all or part of the protected computer.

    18 U.S.C. § 2510(21).

90. " 'Protected computer' has the meaning set forth in 18 U.S.C. § 1030." 18 U.S.C. § 2510(20).

91. 18 U.S.C. § 2511(2)(i).

92. 18 U.S.C. § 2511(3)(a).

93. 18 U.S.C. § 2511(3)(b).

would be able to grant consent for the interception, with certain limited exceptions. It should also be noted that consent in this context is generally broadly construed.[94]

One court recently addressed whether a violation of the ECPA could exist where the plaintiff was the intended recipient, not the sender, of a communication. The district court held that an intended recipient could not bring a claim for violation of the ECPA.[95]

6:28.   Interceptions by party to communication

The ECPA, unlike California law, permits one of the parties to a communication to intercept or record a communication.[96] This includes interceptions even when a third party acts pursuant to the consent of a party to the communication.[97]

6:29.   EPCA and access to servers

In the *Cardinal* case, a former employee had used a password to access Cardinal's servers and review emails that contained information regarding Cardinal and its business plans.[98] These acts allegedly cost Cardinal more than $1 million in damage because one of the defendants in the case used the information to set up a competing business. Cardinal sued, claiming there was a violation of Tennessee law, as well as the ECPA. When assessing whether this conduct violated the ECPA, the court first stated that unauthorized access under the SCA has been considered to be similar to the determination as to whether there was a trespass to property.[99] The court also noted that, in addition to a mere trespass, intentional conduct must be shown to violate the SCA.[100]

The court also noted that while the SCA punished the improper access of information, it did not punish disclosing and using information obtained from an improper access.[101]

The allegation that an employee has improperly accessed information for competitive purposes has also been found to support a claim under the Stored Communications Act, where the activities were a breach of loyalty to benefit people other than the

94. Indeed, courts have emphasized that "consent" must be construed broadly under the Wiretap Act. See U.S. v. Amen, 831 F.2d 373, 378 (2d Cir. 1987) ("Congress intended the consent requirement to be construed broadly."); Griggs-Ryan v. Smith, 904 F.2d 112, 116 (1st Cir. 1990) (citing U.S. v. Willoughby, 860 F.2d 15, 19, 26 Fed. R. Evid. Serv. 1129 (2d Cir. 1988)); In re DoubleClick Inc. Privacy Litigation, 154 F. Supp. 2d 497 (S.D. N.Y. 2001).

95. Ideal Aerosmith, Inc. v. Acutronic, 2007 WL 4394447 (W.D. Pa. 2007); *see also* Klump v. Nazareth Area Sch. Dist., 425 F. Supp. 2d 622, 633 (E.D. Pa. 2006).

96. *See* U.S. v. Turk, 526 F.2d 654 (5th Cir. 1976).

97. Smith v. Cincinnati Post and Times-Star, 475 F.2d 740, 25 A.L.R. Fed. 755 (6th Cir. 1973).

98. Cardinal Health 414, Inc. v. Adams, 582 F. Supp. 2d 967 (N.D. Tenn. 2008).

99. *Id.*, citing Eofel v. Farey-Jones, 359 F.3d 1066, 1072-73 (9th Cir. 2004).

100. Cardinal Health 414, Inc. v. Adams, 582 F. Supp. 2d 967 (N.D. Tenn. 2008), citing Butera & Andrews v. IBM Corp., 456 F. Supp. 2d 104-109 (D.D.C. 2006); Wyatt Tec. H. Corp. v. Smithson, 2006 WL 5668246, **9-10 (C.D. Cal. 2006) (Intent is present where an individual logs into another's email account without permission and reviews materials).

101. Cardinal Health 414, Inc. v. Adams, 582 F. Supp. 2d 967 (N.D. Tenn. 2008), citing Sherman & Co. v. Salton Maxim Housewares, Inc., 94 F.Supp.2d 817, 820 (E.D. Mich. 2000); In re Am. Airlines, Inc., Privacy Litig., 370 F.Supp.2d 552, 558-59 (N.D. Tex. 2005).

plaintiff.[102] This is based upon § 2701(a), which makes it illegal to "intentionally [access] without authorization a facility through which an electronic communication service is provided…"

6:30. Accessing co-worker's email accounts

Accessing a co-worker's email account has been held to be a violation of the SCA.[103]

6:31. Listening to a wrongfully acquired tape of a phone call is not an acquisition

The Ninth Circuit examined what an "interception" was under ECPA and found that the act of reviewing tape recordings of telephone calls that had already been intercepted or redirected was not an interception.[104]

6:32. Use of another's login information

In *Cardinal Health 414, Inc. v. Adams*, a former employee who accessed the Cardinal account even after he left the employ of Cardinal, was found to have violated the SCA.[105] While the former employee attempted to argue that the *Sherman* case authorized his conduct, in this case that argument was rejected because the employee here continued to use the access code of another employee.

6:33. Enforcement

The violation of the disclosure restrictions can result in a fine, or imprisonment for not more than five years, or both.[106] The Attorney General is also permitted, when it appears that any person is engaged or is about to engage in any act that constitutes or will constitute a felony violation, to bring a civil action in a district court of the United States to enjoin such violation.[107]

---

102. Lasco Foods, Inc. v. Hall and Shaw Sales, Marketing, & Consulting, LLC, 4:08-cv-01683-JCH (E.D.Miss. October 26, 2009).

103. Bloomington-Normal Seating Company, Inc. v. Albritton, Case No. 09-1073 (C.D.Ill. May 13, 2009) (holding that improperly accessing a co-worker's email account is a violation of the SCA.).

104. Noel v. Hall, 568 F.3d 743 (9th Cir. 2009); *see also* United States v. Hammond, 286 F.3d 189, 193 (4th Cir. 2002), cert. denied, 537 U.S. 900 (2002); Reynolds v. Spears, 93 F.3d 428, 432-33 (8th Cir. 1996); United States v. Shields, 675 F.2d 1152, 1156 (11th Cir.), cert. denied, 459 U.S. 858 (1982); United States v. Turk, 526 F.2d 654, 658 (5th Cir.1976), cert. denied, 429 U.S. 823 (1976).

105. Cardinal Health 414, Inc. v. Adams, 582 F. Supp. 2d 967 (N.D. Tenn. 2008).

106. 18 U.S.C. § 2511(4)(a).

107. 18 U.S.C. § 2521.

6:34. Availability of civil liability for aiding and abetting violation of Wiretap Act

Unlike certain other federal statutes, there is no civil liability for a person that aids or abets a violation of the Wiretap Act.[108] Other courts continue to reject findings of vicarious liability, even finding the ultimate recipient of the emails, even if it is a competitor of the plaintiff, not liable under the SCA unless they actually directly accessed a computer and obtained the emails at issue.[109]

6:35. Requirement of commercial gain for certain violations

It should be noted that commercial advantage or private financial gain must be shown to establish certain violations that relate to the interception of a satellite transmission. If a satellite transmission, not including data transmissions or telephone calls, is not encrypted or scrambled and is transmitted (i) to a broadcasting station for purposes of retransmission to the general public, or (ii) as an audio subcarrier intended for redistribution to facilities open to the public, it is a violation of the ECPA only if the conduct is for the purposes of direct or indirect commercial advantage or private financial gain.[110]

Commercial gain must also be shown if the violation relates to the interception of a private satellite video communication that is not scrambled or encrypted and the conduct is merely the private viewing of that communication and is not for a tortious or illegal purpose. This is also true for violations related to radio communications that are transmitted on frequencies allocated under subpart D of part 74 of the rules of the Federal Communications Commission, if they are not scrambled or encrypted, and the conduct is not for a tortious or illegal purpose.

The only remedy in this situation is a lawsuit by the federal government.[111] Potential remedies include injunctive relief and civil penalties.[112]

6:36. Civil damages

Any person whose wire, oral, or electronic communication is improperly intercepted, disclosed, or intentionally used in violation of this law may recover from the person or entity, other than the United States, that violated Title I any relief that may be appropriate. The relief includes preliminary and other equitable or declaratory relief, damages, as set forth below, punitive damages in appropriate cases and reasonable attorneys' fee and other litigation costs reasonably incurred.[113] Agents of the United States, and the states, are exempt from liability.

Actual damages, or statutory damages are recoverable and range from $50 to $1,000 for certain violations (those that relate to viewing of select satellite or radio

---

108. Peavy v. WFAA-TV, Inc., 221 F.3d 158, 169 (5th Cir. 2000).
109. Cardinal Health 414, Inc. v. Adams, 582 F. Supp. 2d 967 (N.D. Tenn. 2008).
110. 18 U.S.C. § 2511(b).
111. 18 U.S.C. § 2511(5)(a)(i).
112. 18 U.S.C. §§ 2511(5)(a)(ii)(A) and (B).
113. 18 U.S.C. §§ 2520(b)(1) to (3).

broadcasts).[114] For other violations the court can award actual damages and any profits made by the violator, or statutory damages in the amount of $100 per day or $10,000, whichever is greater.[115]

6:37. Lack of civil remedy for violation of § 2512

A court recently addressed whether § 2512 gave rise to civil remedies under § 2520, concluding that it did not support a civil remedy in light of the clear language of § 2520.[116]

6:38. Defense for good faith reliance upon a warrant

Good faith reliance upon a warrant, order, certain other authorizations or a good faith determination that the conduct was permitted by 18 U.S.C. § 2511(3) or § 2511(2)(i), is a complete defense to any civil or criminal action.[117]

6:39. Governmental liability under the ECPA

One of the questions under the ECPA was whether government entities could be criminally prosecuted for violations of the ECPA. This question has generally been answered in the negative, because courts have concluded that government entities are not a "person" as defined by the ECPA.[118] However, as noted below, courts have held that government entities can be civilly liable under the ECPA.[119]

6:40. ECPA Liability and Municipalities

The Seventh Circuit has held that municipalities cannot be liable under the ECPA.[120] This decision has been rejected by the Sixth Circuit because of amendments to the ECPA that the court perceives alter the Seventh Circuit's analysis.[121]

6:41. Requirement of actual damages under the ECPA

Given the availability of statutory damages, plaintiffs need not prove actual damages in an ECPA case, even as a prerequisite to obtaining statutory penalties.[122]

---

114. 18 U.S.C. § 2520(c)(1).

115. 18 U.S.C. § 2520(c)(2).

116. Bailey v. Bailey, 2008 WL 324156 (E.D.Mich. 2008).

117. 18 U.S.C. § 2520(d).

118. Conner v. Tate, 130 F. Supp. 2d 1370 (N.D. Ga. 2001).

119. *Id.*

120. Abbott v. Village of Winthrop Harbor, 205 F.3d 976, 980 (7th Cir. 2000); Steinbach v. Village of Forest Park, 2009 WL 2605283, 29 IER Cases 1080 (N.D.Ill. Aug 25, 2009) (NO. 06 C 4215).

121. Adams v. City of Battle Creek, 250 F.3d 980, 985 (6th Cir. 2001) (holding that the amendment to add the word "entity" to § 2520 results in liability for municipalities and rejecting Amati v. City of Woodstock, 176 F.3d 952, 956 (7th Cir. 1999), cert. denied, 528 U.S. 985 (1999)).

122. In re Hawaiian Airlines, Inc., 355 B.R. 225 (D.C. Haw. 2006); distinguishing Doe v. Chao, 540 U.S. 614, 124 S. Ct. 1204, 157 L. Ed. 2d 1122 (2004).

However, the Fourth Circuit ruled that while a plaintiff must establish actual damages to obtain the statutory award under the SCA, a plaintiff need not prove actual damages in order to obtain either punitive damages or attorneys' fees.[123] The plaintiff, Van Alstyne, was employed by Electronic Scriptorium Limited ("ESL") as its Vice President of Marketing. While employed by ESL, Van Alstyne was assigned a company email account but occasionally used her personal AOL password-protected email account to conduct business. During the course of her employment, Van Alstyne claimed to have been sexually harassed by one of the owners of ESL and was ultimately terminated. Multiple lawsuits resulted and during discovery, ESL produced some of Van Alstyne's emails from her AOL account. Van Alstyne filed a second action against the principal and ESL seeking recovery under the SCA.

Van Alstyne's claim for relief was limited to punitive damages and "statutory minimum damages" under the SCA. The case went to trial and the jury rendered a verdict in favor of Van Alstyne, awarding statutory damages of $1,000 per violation of the SCA, punitive damages, and attorneys' fees. Thus, despite the lack of actual damages, Van Alstyne was awarded a significant sum by the jury. The Fourth Circuit rejected the jury's finding that statutory damages could be recovered, finding that a plaintiff must prove actual damage as a prerequisite to obtaining statutory damages under the SCA because like the Privacy Act, the SCA limits the award of damages to "actual damages suffered," as well as "any profits." The *Van Alstyne* court applied the Supreme Court's statutory analysis in *Doe* regarding language that was "in all important respects identical to that already interpreted by the Supreme Court."[124]

Despite requiring "actual damages" to be proven as a threshold matter for the recovery of statutory damages under the SCA, the *Van Alstyne* court noted that the same was not true for claims of punitive damages or attorneys' fees. This result is again based upon the language of § 2707(c) since this section lacks any language requiring actual damage. The *Van Alstyne* court reached a similar conclusion regarding § 2707(b)(3) of the SCA, which provides for "a reasonable attorney's fee and other litigation costs reasonably incurred." Again, the court believed there was no limiting language requiring actual damage to be proven prior to an award of attorneys' fees.

6:42. Governmental civil liability

There is a minor conflict in the statutory language as to whether government entities can be held liable for violations of the Wiretap Act because the definition of a "person" under the act does not include governmental entities.[125] There is a split among these courts as to whether damages are permitted against governmental entities that violate

---

123. Van Alstyne v. Electronic Scriptorium, Ltd., 560 F.3d 199 (4th Cir. 2009).

124. The *Van Alstyne* Court referenced The Wiretap Act, which is also found in the ECPA, and deals with unauthorized access to electronic communications while they are in transit (as opposed to when they are being stored). The Wiretap Act provides for "… the greater of (A) the sum of the actual damages suffered by the plaintiff and any profits made by the violator …; or (B) statutory damages of whichever is the greater of $100 a day for each day of violation or $10,000." 18 U.S.C. § 2520(c)(2).

125. Amati v. City of Woodstock, Ill., 829 F. Supp. 998, 1002-03 (N.D. Ill. 1993); Abbott v. Village of Winthrop Harbor, 205 F.3d 976, 980 (7th Cir. 2000); cf. Conner v. Tate, 130 F. Supp. 2d 1370 (N.D. Ga. 2001).

the act because certain courts have held that government entities are liable for violations of the Stored Communications Act.[126]

Other courts have held that government entities are not liable under the ECPA, though government officials can be.[127]

6:43. Exclusion of evidence due to violation of the ECPA and e-mails

There is, at best, a muddled picture on suppression under the ECPA. The statute provides that if a wire or oral communication is intercepted in violation of the ECPA, neither the communication, nor any evidence derived from it, can be received in evidence in any trial, hearing, or other proceeding in or before any court, grand jury, department, officer, agency, regulatory body, legislative committee, or other authority of the United States, a state, or a political subdivision.[128] In criminal cases, the suppression remedy frequently is dealt with under the Fourth Amendment in certain cases, but civil cases are more problematic.

However, certain courts have held that suppression is not an available remedy under the ECPA, even if there is a violation of the ECPA in gathering communications.[129] The Tenth Circuit also recently rejected a *Terry* stop analogy and held that suppression was not a remedy in a criminal case for the government's alleged violation of the ECPA.[130] This conclusion was recently reaffirmed by the Southern District of California Court.[131]

The suppression remedy under the ECPA also has created a circuit conflict on another issue. Certain courts, including the Sixth Circuit, have held that the suppression remedy under the ECPA does not apply to e-mails, because the statute only references wire and oral communications.[132] This holding is still being applied by courts, though many note that the lack of a suppression remedy does not preclude a civil or criminal

---

126. Adams v. City of Battle Creek, 250 F.3d 980, 985 (6th Cir. 2001).

127. PBA Local No. 38 v. Woodbridge Police Dept., 832 F. Supp. 808 (D.N.J. 1993); Amati v. City of Woodstock, Ill., 829 F. Supp. 998 (N.D. Ill. 1993).

128. 18 U.S.C. § 2515.

129. U.S. v. Warshak, 2007 WL 4410237 (S.D. Ohio 2007).

130. U.S. v. Perrine, 518 F.3d 1196, 1202 (10th Cir. 2008) ("Thus, violations of the ECPA do not warrant exclusion of evidence."), citing, United States v. Steiger, 318 F.3d 1039, 1049 (11th Cir. 2003); United States v. Smith, 155 F.3d 1051, 1056 (9th Cir. 1998); Bansal v. Russ, 513 F.Supp.2d 264, 282-83 (E.D.Pa. 2007); United States v. Sherr, 400 F.Supp.2d 843, 848 (D.Md. 2005); United States v. Kennedy, 81 F.Supp.2d 1103, 1110 (D.Kan. 2000).

131. United States v. Li, 2008 WL 789899 (S.D.Cal. March 20, 2008), citing United States v. Smith, 155 F.3d 1051 (9th Cir. 1998).

132. See 18 U.S.C. § 2515; United States v. Meriwether, 917 F.2d 955, 960 (6th Cir. 1990) ("[W]e cannot under the ECPA grant appellant's requested remedy-suppression. The ECPA does not provide an independent statutory remedy of suppression for interceptions of electronic communications."), citing 18 U.S.C. § 2518(10) (c) and S. Rep. No. 99-541, 99th Cong., 2d Sess. 23, reprinted in 1986 U.S. Code Cong. & Admin. News 3555, 3577; see also, United States v. Steiger, 318 F.3d 1039, 1050 (11th Cir. 2003) ("The Act's plain text ... is unambiguous, leaving little room for argument. In 1986, Title I of the ECPA amended the federal Wiretap Act to include electronic communications. However, as the Eleventh Circuit has noted, '[d]espite the fact that the ECPA amended numerous sections of the Wiretap Act to include 'electronic communications', the ECPA did not amend § 2515."); United States v. Jones, 364 F. Supp. 2d 1303, 1306 (D. Utah 2005) (quoting Steiger); Potter v. Havlicek, 2007 WL 539534 (S.D. Ohio 2007).

claim against the person who obtains or discloses the electronic communications.[133] This complicates, if not eliminates, a civil litigant's ability to obtain some form of equitable relief to prevent disclosure in the context of litigation, though an injunction still may be appropriate if the disclosure is going to be made to third-parties outside the litigation context.

6:44.   Authorization of interception of communications

The ECPA permits law enforcement in many cases to apply for warrants or orders allowing them to intercept communications and sets certain procedures for the process.[134] There are certain circumstances that permit select law enforcement officials to monitor communications for limited periods of time without a warrant or order.[135] If an interception is authorized, then law enforcement officers are permitted to use the contents in the course of their duties and can disclose it to other agencies in certain circumstances.[136]

6:45.   Enforcement of the Communications Assistance for Law Enforcement Act

If a telecommunications carrier fails to comply with an order or warrant authorizing the use of a pen register or a trap and trace device or fails to comply with the provisions of the Communications Assistance for Law Enforcement Act, the court can direct compliance with the order or warrant, including through orders to the carrier's provider of support services or the manufacturer of the carrier's equipment.[137]

Civil penalties are also permitted if an order is entered directing a telecommunications carrier, a manufacturer of certain equipment, or a support services provider to comply with an order or warrant.[138] The penalty can be up to $10,000 per day.[139]

6:46.   Videotaping of employees under the ECPA

One of the issues courts have struggled with is whether video monitoring in the workplace requires compliance with the Wiretap Act because videotaping can be an unauthorized aural interception of communications. Certain circuits have found the Wiretap Act to be inapplicable but have still required the government to meet the heightened warrant requirements of the ECPA.[140] For public employers this may require a warrant before employee videotaping is done, at least in areas where the employees have a reasonable

---

133. Potter v. Havlicek, 2007 WL 539534 (S.D. Ohio 2007).

134. 18 U.S.C. § 2516; 18 U.S.C. § 2518.

135. 18 U.S.C. § 2518.

136. 18 U.S.C. § 2517.

137. 18 U.S.C. §§ 2522(a) to (b).

138. 18 U.S.C. § 2522(c)(1).

139. 18 U.S.C. § 2522(c)(1).

140. U.S. v. Biasucci, 786 F.2d 504, 510 (2d Cir. 1986) (rejected by, State v. Haddix, 93 Ohio App. 3d 470, 638 N.E.2d 1096 (12th Dist. Preble County 1994)); U.S. v. Cuevas-Sanchez, 821 F.2d 248, 251-52 (5th Cir. 1987); U.S. v. Torres, 751 F.2d 875, 884-85 (7th Cir. 1984).

expectation of privacy.[141] The warrant requirement is obviously not applicable to non-governmental employers. Videotaping of employees is more generally covered in chapter 7, and a discussion of the constitutional requirements of videotaping generally and warrants is covered in chapter 13.

6:47. Private right of action under the ECPA for interception of encrypted signals

There has been some confusion expressed by certain courts regarding whether a private right of action exists for a violation of Section 2511, which makes the intentional interception of electronic communications illegal.[142] Section 2520 is the main remedial portion of Title I, and some courts have expressed the belief that, while there are criminal remedies for all violations, civil remedies may not exist.

However, this view has consistently been rejected by the courts of appeal.[143] For example, in *Pepe*, the district court concluded that a civil remedy did not exist for a violation of 18 U.S.C. §§ 2511 and 2512.[144] The court of appeal began its analysis of the issue by noting that DirecTV signals qualify as "electronic communications" under the ECPA, a prerequisite for a violation.[145] The court of appeal noted that while there were certain exceptions from liability for the interception of *unencrypted* satellite signals, there was no similar exception for interception of encrypted signals under § 2511(1).[146] Thus, the court of appeal concluded that a civil remedy for interception of encrypted satellite television signals did exist.

6:48. Good faith reliance on invalid warrant as an ECPA defense

The ECPA clearly establishes an exception to liability for good faith reliance upon a warrant.[147] One interesting issue is whether reliance on an invalid warrant can give rise to immunity. Courts have generally found that an invalid warrant can give rise to immunity if the ISP reasonably relied upon the invalid warrant.[148] This generally requires an examination of a two-pronged test: (1) that there was a subjective good faith

---

141. Taketa, 923 F.2d at 675.

142. 18 U.S.C. § 2511.

143. *See*, DIRECTV, Inc. v. Pepe, 431 F.3d 162 (3d Cir. 2005); DIRECTV Inc. v. Nicholas, 403 F.3d 223 (4th Cir. 2005); DIRECTV Inc. v. Bennett, 470 F.3d. 565 (5th Cir. 2006); accord, DIRECTV Inc. v. Robson, 420 F.3d 532 (5th Cir. 2005); DIRECTV, Inc. v. Minor, 420 F.3d 546 (5th Cir. 2005).

144. Pepe, 431 F. 3d.

145. Pepe, 431 F. 3d; citing DIRECTV Inc. v. Nicholas, 403 F.3d 223, 225-26 (4th Cir. 2005); U.S. v. One Macom Video Cipher II, SN A6J050073, 985 F.2d 258, 261 (6th Cir. 1993); U.S. v. Herring, 993 F.2d 784, 787 (11th Cir. 1993); U.S. v. Lande, 968 F.2d 907, 909-910 (9th Cir. 1992); U.S. v. Davis, 978 F.2d 415, 417-18 (8th Cir. 1992); U.S. v. Splawn, 982 F.2d 414, 415-16 (10th Cir. 1992) (en banc).

146. Pepe, 431 F. 3d; see also, Lande, 968 F.3d at 909-10.

147. 18 U.S.C. § 2707(e).

148. *See* Freedman v. America Online, Inc., 325 F. Supp. 2d 638, 645 (E.D. Va. 2004); citing United States v. Leon, 468 U.S. 897 (1984).

belief that there was a valid warrant; and (2) this belief was objectively reasonable.[149] Reliance upon an unsigned warrant can, in certain circumstances, be reasonable, and therefore act as a defense to an ECPA action.[150]

6:49.   Aiding and abetting liability for ECPA violations

One issue for which the ECPA has been read strictly is whether there is secondary liability for conspiracy or aiding and abetting violations of others. Secondary liability was soundly rejected by the Ninth Circuit, in a case of first impression.[151] The court focused on the language of §§ 2702(a)(1) and 2707(a) and found that the statutory language did not support liability against a person that did not directly engage in a violation.

6:50.   Consent under the ECPA

Consent can be actual or implied, but direct consent requires actual notice to the person who is alleged to have consented.[152] Implied consent can exist as well and beeps on the line or other such devices could meet the implied consent requirements.[153]

6:51.   Participation in e-mail investigations

In many cases employers will want employees to participate in investigations to determine how certain information was disseminated, as well as to determine the source of the disclosure of facts or documents. While private employees do not enjoy the same protections under the First Amendment that public employees do, even in the public employee context, the failure to participate in an investigation has been grounds for discipline, including termination.

> Bowers was questioned about the source of the compensation and benefits information the attachments described as being in place at the University. Bowers points to no authority, nor are we able to find any, that would prevent such an inquiry. On its face, the information must have *originated* from the school—not the NAACP—and the medical center worker from whom Bowers claimed to have obtained the information denied having provided it to her. On these facts, the University did not violate Bowers's First Amendment rights in seeking to ascertain the internal source of what it reasonably believed to be false and potentially harmful data about its own compensation structure.[154]

---

149. Freedman, 325 F. Supp. 2d at 648; Jacobson v. Rose, 592 F.2d 515, 523, 26 Fed. R. Serv. 2d 693 (9th Cir. 1978) (rejected by, Citron v. Citron, 539 F. Supp. 621 (S.D. N.Y. 1982)).

150. Freedman, 325 F. Supp. 2d at 650.

151. Freeman v. DirecTV, 457 F.3d 1001 (9th Cir. 2006).

152. Walden v. City of Providence, 495 F. Supp. 2d 245 (D.R.I. 2007).

153. *Id.*

154. Bowers v. Scurry, 276 Fed. Appx. 278, 2008 WL 1931263, at *3 (4th Cir. 2008).

6:52.   Purchasers of assets or businesses can monitor prior e-mail addresses

Purchasers of businesses or assets can monitor e-mail addresses that are acquired even if those e-mail addresses were previously used by a competing business.[155]

B.   *Restrictions on Devices*

6:53.   Manufacture, distribution, possession, and advertising of wire, oral or electronic communication interception devices

It is illegal for a person to intentionally send through the mail, or in interstate or foreign commerce, any electronic, mechanical, or other device, if they know, or have reason to know, that the design of such device renders it primarily useful for the purpose of the surreptitious interception of wire, oral, or electronic communications.[156] It is also improper to manufacture, assemble, possess, or sell any electronic, mechanical, or other device, if you know, or have reason to know, that the design of the device renders it primarily useful for the purpose of the surreptitious interception of wire, oral, or electronic communications. Both acts are violations if the device or any component thereof has been or will be sent through the mail or transported in interstate or foreign commerce.[157]

It is also illegal to place, with intent,[158] in any newspaper, magazine, handbill, or other publication, or to disseminate by electronic means, an advertisement of any electronic, mechanical, or other device knowing the content of the advertisement and knowing, or having reason to know, that the design of such device renders it primarily useful for the purpose of the surreptitious interception of wire, oral, or electronic communications.[159] It is also a violation of the ECPA to advertise any other electronic, mechanical, or other device, where such advertisement promotes the use of such device for the purpose of the surreptitious interception of wire, oral, or electronic communications.[160]

6:54.   Exceptions to liability

It should be noted that it is not illegal for a provider of wire or electronic communication services,[161] in the normal course of providing wire or electronic communication services,

---

155. Ideal Aerosmith, Inc. v. Acutronic, 2007 WL 4394447 (W.D. Pa. 2007).

156. 18 U.S.C. § 2512.

157. *Id.*

158. Intent in this subsection means knowing the content of the advertisement and knowing or having reason to know that such advertisement will be sent through the mail or transported in interstate or foreign commerce.

159. 18 U.S.C. § 2512.

160. *Id.* (1)(a) to (c.).

161. The ECPA also includes a service provider's officers, agents, or employees of, or a person under contract with, a provider.

to send through the mail, send or carry in interstate or foreign commerce, or manufacture, assemble, possess, or sell any electronic, mechanical, or other device knowing or having reason to know that the design of the device renders it primarily useful for the purpose of the surreptitious interception of wire, oral, or electronic communications.[162]

It is also not unlawful to advertise for sale one of the devices described above if the advertisement is mailed, sent, or carried in interstate or foreign commerce solely to a domestic provider of wire or electronic communication services or to an agency of the United States, a state, or a political subdivision thereof that is duly authorized to use the device.[163]

6:55. Enforcement

A violation of this section is punishable by a fine, or imprisonment not more than five years, or both.[164] Moreover, any communication interception devices that violate the ECPA can be confiscated.[165]

III. Title II: Stored Wire and Electronic Communications and Transactional Records Access Act

6:56. Intent of Act

The Stored Wire and Electronic Communications and Transactional Records Access Act is Title II of the ECPA. It is important to note that the purpose of Title II is to prevent hackers from obtaining, altering or destroying certain stored electronic communications,[166] as well as to create a cause of action against computer hackers—that is, computer trespassers.[167]

---

162. 18 U.S.C. §§ 2512(2)(a) to (b).

163. 18 U.S.C. § 2512(2)(c).

164. 18 U.S.C. §§ 2512(1)(a) to (c).

165. 18 U.S.C. § 2513.

166. In re DoubleClick Inc. Privacy Litigation, 154 F. Supp. 2d 497 (S.D. N.Y. 2001); *see* Sherman & Co. v. Salton Maxim Housewares, Inc., 94 F. Supp. 2d 817, 820 (E.D. Mich. 2000) ("the ECPA was primarily designed to provide a cause of action against computer hackers") (quoting State Wide Photocopy, Corp. v. Tokai Financial Services, Inc., 909 F. Supp. 137, 145 (S.D. N.Y. 1995)).

167. Kaufman v. Nest Seekers, LLC, 2006 WL 2807177 (S.D. N.Y. 2006); State Wide Photocopy, Corp. v. Tokai Financial Services, Inc., 909 F. Supp. 137, 145 (S.D. N.Y. 1995); Sherman & Co. v. Salton Maxim Housewares, Inc., 94 F. Supp. 2d 817, 820 (E.D. Mich. 2000); In re America Online, Inc., 168 F. Supp. 2d 1359, 1370 (S.D. Fla. 2001).

6:57. Distribution of stored communications

One important distinction between the Wiretap Act and the Stored Communications Act is that there is no liability for distributing a communication obtained in violation of the Stored Communications Act, unlike the Wiretap Act.[168]

6:58. Restrictions

Except as set forth below, it is illegal to obtain, alter, or prevent authorized access to a wire or electronic communication while it is in electronic storage in a system if a person intentionally accesses without authorization a facility through which an electronic communication service is provided. It is also illegal to intentionally exceed an authorization to access that facility.[169]

6:59. Exceptions permitting disclosure

The Stored Communications Act does not apply to conduct authorized by the person or entity providing a wire or electronic communications service, or by a user of that service with respect to a communication of or intended for that user.[170]

A provider of electronic communication service must disclose the contents of a wire or electronic communication that is in electronic storage pursuant to a validly issued warrant if it is in storage for 180 days or less.[171]

If the communication is more than 180 days old, is sent by electronic transmission[172] by a subscriber or customer of a remote computing service,[173] and was retained solely for the purpose of providing storage or computer processing services to the subscriber or customer, then the provider is not authorized to access the contents of the communications for purposes of providing any services other than storage or computer processing. A government entity can require disclosure without notice to the subscriber or customer, if the governmental entity obtains a warrant issued using the procedures described in the Federal Rules of Criminal Procedure, or with notice if the government proceeds via a subpoena or grand jury subpoena, or under court order.[174]

6:60. Remote computing services and *Warshak*—No clear answers for now

The Sixth Circuit previously addressed whether one of the disclosure exceptions to the ECPA, related to "remote computing services," was constitutional, ultimately concluding that 18 U.S.C. § 2703(b) was unconstitutional because it violated the Fourth

---

168. Conner v. Tate, 130 F. Supp. 2d 1370 (N.D. Ga. 2001).
169. 18 U.S.C. § 2701(a).
170. 18 U.S.C. § 2701(c)(1) to (2).
171. 18 U.S.C. § 2703(a).
172. The communication can also be created by means of computer processing of communications received by means of electronic transmission.
173. "'Remote computing service' means the provision to the public of computer storage or processing services by means of an electronic communications system." 18 U.S.C. § 2711(2).
174. 18 U.S.C. § 2703(b)(1); 18 U.S.C. § 2703(b)(2).

Amendment.[175] This case has been reversed on the basis of standing, but a discussion is included because this case was the first case to address these issues.

Warshak appeared to be limited to "remote computing services" under the ECPA, though the case relied upon other non-ISP cases and, as such, could have implications for employers and others that provide Internet-related services.

In *Warshak*, the government attempted to obtain e-mails from a remote computing service under the ECPA, (in this case Yahoo!) without a warrant. Since the communications were in storage for more than 180 days, the government obtained a court order under § 2703(b) permitting disclosure. Warshak objected to the government's attempts to get his e-mails and sought an injunction, arguing that this portion of the ECPA violated his Fourth Amendment rights. The government argued that it did not need to meet the probable cause standard in order to obtain e-mails via a court order, because the request for e-mails was not a search under the Fourth Amendment. Instead, the government's position was that it needed only to show that the e-mails were "reasonably relevant."[176]

The court of appeal ultimately felt that this issue could only be resolved by deciding whether an e-mail user has a reasonable expectation of privacy in his e-mails, considering the issue from the perspective of the party receiving the court order—in this case Yahoo!.[177] In analyzing this question, the court acknowledged that, at least under the ECPA's formulation,[178] a communication that is sent to another could be *disclosed by the recipient* because there is no reasonable expectation of privacy in a communication that is sent to most third-parties.

However, the court felt that it must look at the privacy issue from the perspective of what the ISP is permitted to do and whether there was a reasonable expectation of privacy that resulted from a person's expectations of an ISP.[179] The court identified several decisions that it believed supported its conclusion that generally an e-mail sender has an expectation of privacy in electronic communications, at least as to electronic communications that had not yet reached the intended recipient. It then concluded, based upon decisions that relate to employers' policies regarding use of electronic systems, that a sender of e-mail could have a reasonable expectation of privacy, at least as it relates to the intermediary, in the e-mails that are stored by a remote computing service. This was particularly true if the policy of the ISP only identified limited monitoring activities.[180]

The court also felt this expectation of privacy was particularly true with e-mails that were stored with or sent via a "commercial ISP."[181] Based upon this reasoning, the

---

175. *Warshak v. United States*, 490 F.3d 455 (6th Cir. 2007), rehearing en banc granted, opinion vacated (Oct 09, 2007).

176. *Warshak*, 490 F.3d at 469.

177. *Warshak*, 490 F.3d at 473.

178. State laws in many cases provide higher protections than the ECPA and would not necessarily permit disclosure of a confidential communication. See, e.g., Cal Penal Code §§ 631 *et seq.*

179. *Warshak*, 490 F.3d at 473.

180. *Warshak*, 490 F.3d at 474; see also, *Guest v. Leis*, 255 F.3d 325, 333 (6th Cir. 2007); *United States v. Heckenkamp*, 482 F.3d 1142, (9th Cir. April 5, 2007); c.f., *United States v. Simmons*, 206 F.3d 392, 398 (4th Cir. 2000).

181. *Warshak*, 490 F.3d at 473.

court concluded that the portion of the ECPA that permitted disclosure based upon a court order was unconstitutional, and it invalidated the district court's order.

The case appeared to be a departure from prior case law in several respects. This appeared to be the first time a court has made the identity of a recipient of a court order, not the identity of the recipient of the e-mails, a factor in determining whether a reasonable expectation of privacy exists. One of the main problems with considering the identity of the party that received the court order is the likelihood of inconsistent results. In this case, had the government simply subpoenaed the recipient, Warshak would not have been successful in his challenge to the ECPA. This conclusion was recognized by the court when it noted that a Fourth Amendment challenge to an order authorizing the disclosure of e-mails by the recipient of the e-mails would fail.[182] More importantly, under the court's analysis, the federal government could not obtain communications from a defendant that were sent to a state law enforcement official if the order was sent to an ISP, even though under no circumstances could one conclude a reasonable expectation of privacy exists for these communications.[183]

The prior result also does not appear to recognize the distinction between service providers that provide services to the "public," and those that do not. This case also appears to blur the lines between Title I and II of the ECPA. The court found the cases involving the interception of telephone communications to be of import, as were cases involving the *interception* of mail, stating that a letter-writer had an expectation of privacy while the communication was in the hands of an intermediary, including the post office or an ISP.[184] However, these cases would appear to be of little relevance, because of the temporal distinction created by the ECPA. The interception of communications, telephone or electronic, is governed by Title I of the ECPA.[185] As noted in this chapter, this distinction has been recognized by a number of courts, including in *United States v. Councilman*.[186]

It should be noted that in addition to the *Warshak* court, other courts are now examining these distinctions in the ECPA quite closely. One distinction courts have now drawn, at least in the Ninth Circuit, is between a remote computing service and an electronic communication service, both of which are defined terms under the ECPA. This distinction was the focus of extensive discussion in *Quon v. Arch Wireless Operating*, when the court assessed the scope of proper disclosure by a text messaging provider.[187] The employee privacy aspects of this case are discussed in chapter 7, but it is important to note in this context that one of the key issues examined in the case was whether Arch Wireless was an ECS or an RCS.

In the continuing saga that is the *Warshak* case, the district court has now addressed whether good faith reliance upon a statute later held to be unconstitutional would

---

182. Warshak, 490 F.3d at 479.

183. "Similarly, under both Miller and Katz, if the government in this case had received the content of Warshak's e-mails by subpoenaing the person with whom Warshak was e-mailing, a Fourth Amendment challenge brought by Warshak would fail, because he would not have maintained a reasonable expectation of privacy vis-a-vis his e-mailing partners." Warshak, 490 F.3d at 471.

184. Warshak, 490 F.3d at 474.

185. U.S. v. Moriarty, 962 F. Supp. 217 (D. Mass 1997).

186. United States v. Councilman, 418 F.3d 67 (1st Cir. 2005).

187. Quon v. Arch Wireless Operating Co., 529 F.3d 892 (9th Cir. 2008).

permit illegally seized information to be used in a criminal case.[188] The *Warshak* court determined that the good faith exception under *Illinois v. Krull*[189] applied to improper seizure of stored communications in this circumstance.[190]

6:61.   Disclosures of customer records

A governmental entity can require a provider of electronic communications services to disclose the contents of a wire or electronic communication, that is in electronic storage in an electronic communications system for 180 days or less, pursuant only to a warrant issued using the procedures described in the Federal Rules of Criminal Procedure by a court with jurisdiction over the offense under investigation or equivalent state warrant.[191] A governmental entity may require the disclosure by a provider of electronic communications services of the contents of a wire or electronic communication that has been in electronic storage in an electronic communications system for more than 180 days by certain means in certain circumstances.[192]

A governmental entity may require a provider of remote computing services to disclose the contents of any subscriber's or customer's wire or electronic communication that is held or maintained on that service for the subscriber or customer for more than 180 days. The government requirement applies if the provider is not authorized to access the contents of any such communications for purposes of providing any services other than storage or computer processing: without required notice to the subscriber or customer, if the governmental entity obtains a warrant issued using the procedures described in the Federal Rules of Criminal Procedure by a court with jurisdiction over the offense under investigation or equivalent State warrant; or with prior notice from the governmental entity to the subscriber or customer if the governmental entity uses an administrative subpoena authorized by a federal or state statute or a federal or state grand jury or trial subpoena, or obtains a court order for such disclosure under § 2703(d).[193] This section permits notice to be given under the terms of § 2705.[194]

6:62.   Disclosure of information regarding a subscriber

A governmental entity may require a provider of electronic communication service or remote computing service to disclose a record or other information pertaining to a subscriber to or customer of such service (not including the contents of communications) only when the governmental entity obtains a warrant issued using the procedures described in the Federal Rules of Criminal Procedure by a court with jurisdiction over the offense under investigation or equivalent state warrant; obtains a court order for such disclosure;

---

188. U.S. v. Warshak, 2007 WL 4410237 (S.D. Ohio 2007).

189. Illinois v. Krull, 480 U.S. 340 (1987).

190. U.S. v. Warshak, 2007 WL 4410237, *6 (S.D. Ohio 2007) ("Consistent with the government's request, (doc. 223), the Court holds the good-faith exception to the exclusionary rule applies, without ruling on the constitutionality of the SCA. The alleged violations of the SCA do not amount to unreasonable actions in violation of the Fourth Amendment.").

191. 18 U.S.C. § 2703(a).

192. *Id.*

193. 18 U.S.C. § 2703(a) to (b)(1) to (2).

194. 18 U.S.C. § 2703(b).

has the consent of the subscriber or customer to such disclosure; or submits a formal written request relevant to a law enforcement investigation concerning telemarketing fraud for the name, address, and place of business of a subscriber or customer of such provider, which subscriber or customer is engaged in telemarketing.[195]

However, a provider of electronic communication service or remote computing service must disclose to a governmental entity the name; address; local and long distance telephone connection records, or records of session times and durations; length of service (including start date) and types of service utilized; telephone or instrument number or other subscriber number or identity, including any temporarily assigned network address; and means and source of payment for such service (including any credit card or bank account number) of a subscriber to or customer of such service when the governmental entity uses an administrative subpoena authorized by a federal or state statute or a federal or state grand jury or trial subpoena.[196]

It should be noted that notice to the subscriber is not required for these disclosures.[197]

6:63. Requirements of a court order

A court order for disclosure of the contents of communications or subscriber information can only be issued if the governmental entity offers specific and articulable facts showing that there are reasonable grounds to believe that the contents of a wire or electronic communication, or the records or other information sought, are relevant and material to an ongoing criminal investigation.[198] In the case of a state governmental authority, such a court order cannot issue if prohibited by the law of the state.[199] A court issuing an order pursuant to this section, on a motion made promptly by the service provider, may quash or modify such order, if the information or records requested are unusually voluminous in nature or compliance with such order otherwise would cause an undue burden on the provider.[200]

While this section could be read to apply to a governmental entity in any role when it seeks this type of information, this section could also be read to only apply when a government entity seeks this information in the criminal context and not in another litigation context.

---

195. 18 U.S.C. § 2703(c)(1)(A) to (D).

196. 18 U.S.C. § 2703(c)(2)(A) to (F).

197. 18 U.S.C. § 2703(c)(3).

198. 18 U.S.C. § 2703(d).

199. *Id.*

200. *Id.*

6:64.   Recent rulings regarding subscriber privacy

The Tenth Circuit recently followed other courts when it ruled that there was no right of privacy in subscriber information maintained by an ISP.[201]

6:65.   Intent under ECPA for disclosures by ISPs

One of the issues raised in civil litigation under the ECPA is what level of intent is required for a violation. While intent is a prerequisite to a violation, certain parties have argued that this requires intent to violate the ECPA, not just intent to disclose. Most courts have rejected this, finding that the intent requirement merely requires that a party acted intentionally, and not inadvertently.[202] The knowledge element of the ECPA has also been litigated as well, and the knowledge required is simply knowledge of the factual circumstances that constitute the alleged offense, and not an understanding of the legal significance of the factual circumstances, or that there be specific intent to violate the ECPA.[203]

6:66.   Access to stored communications when sought by an intended recipient

There are several important things to note when certain information is sought after the completion of a communication. First, a website that was the recipient of the communication should, without question, be able to obtain information regarding the person originating the communication.[204] This also extends to parties authorized by the

---

201. U.S. v. Perrine, 518 F.3d 1196 (10th Cir. 2008) ("Every federal court to address this issue has held that subscriber information provided to an internet provider is not protected by the Fourth Amendment's privacy expectation.") citing, United States v. Hambrick, 225 F.3d 656 (4th Cir. 2000) (unpublished), affirming United States v. Hambrick, 55 F.Supp.2d 504, 508-09 (W.D.Va. 1999); United States v. D'Andrea, 497 F.Supp.2d 117, 120 (D.Mass. 2007); Freedman v. America Online, Inc., 412 F.Supp.2d 174, 181 (D.Conn. 2005) ("In the cases in which the issue has been considered, courts have universally found that, for purposes of the Fourth Amendment, a subscriber does not maintain a reasonable expectation of privacy with respect to his subscriber information."); United States v. Sherr, 400 F.Supp.2d 843, 848 (D.Md. 2005) ("The courts that have already addressed this issue ... uniformly have found that individuals have no Fourth Amendment privacy interest in subscriber information given to an ISP."); United States v. Cox, 190 F.Supp.2d 330, 332 (N.D.N.Y. 2002) (same); United States v. Kennedy, 81 F.Supp.2d 1103, 1110 (D.Kan. 2000) ("Defendant's constitutional rights were not violated when [internet provider] divulged his subscriber information to the government. Defendant has not demonstrated an objectively reasonable legitimate expectation of privacy in his subscriber information."); *see also*, U.S. v. Lifshitz, 369 F.3d 173, 190 (2d Cir. 2004) ("Individuals generally possess a reasonable expectation of privacy in their home computers ... They may not, however, enjoy such an expectation of privacy in transmissions over the Internet or e-mail that have already arrived at the recipient.").

202. See Freedman v. America Online, Inc., 325 F. Supp. 2d 638, 645 (E.D. Va. 2004).

203. Freedman, 325 F. Supp. 2d at 647.

204. "To summarize, plaintiffs' GET, POST and GIF submissions are excepted from 2701(c)(2) because they are 'intended for' the DoubleClick-affiliated Web sites who have authorized DoubleClick's access." In re DoubleClick Privacy Litigation, 154 F. Supp. 2d 497, 503 (S.D. N.Y. 2001).

intended recipient.[205] Second, it should be noted that in many cases records that are sought after the fact, even where the content itself is sought, would not be restricted by Title II because courts have concluded that the protection of Title II only applies "for a limited time" in the "middle" of a transmission.[206] This principle was recently affirmed in a case arising in the Central District of California.[207]

6:67.   Restrictions upon disclosures by public service providers

A person providing electronic communication service to the public can not knowingly divulge the contents of a communication while the communication is in electronic storage by that service.[208] Moreover, a public remote computing service cannot knowingly disclose the contents of any communication that is carried or maintained on that service if it is received by means of electronic transmission,[209] by or on behalf of a subscriber or customer, if it was carried or maintained solely for the purpose of providing storage or computer processing services to the subscriber or customer, if the provider is not authorized to access the contents of any such communications for purposes of providing any services other than storage or computer processing.[210]

Notwithstanding the above, a provider that provides service to the public may disclose the contents of a communication:

- to an addressee or intended recipient of such communication or an agent of such addressee or intended recipient;

- as otherwise authorized in 18 U.S.C. §§ 2517, 2511(2)(a) or 2703;

- with the lawful consent of the originator or an addressee or intended recipient of such communication, or the subscriber in the case of remote computing service;

- to a person employed or authorized or whose facilities are used to forward such communication to its destination;

- as may be incident to the rendition of the service or to the protection of the rights or property of the provider of that service;

---

205. DoubleClick, 154 F. Supp. 2d at 503; In re American Airlines, Inc., Privacy Litigation, 370 F. Supp. 2d 552 (N.D. Tex. 2005); Sherman & Co. v. Salton Maxim Housewares, Inc., 94 F. Supp. 2d 817, 821 (E.D. Mich. 2000); Educational Testing Service v. Stanley H. Kaplan, Educational Center, Ltd., 965 F. Supp. 731, 740, 119 Ed. Law Rep. 119 (D. Md. 1997); State Wide Photocopy, Corp. v. Tokai Financial Services, Inc., 909 F. Supp. 137, 145 (S.D. N.Y. 1995).

206. Doubleclick, 154 F. Supp. 2d at 503. ("In other words, Title II only protects electronic communications stored 'for a limited time' in the 'middle' of a transmission, i.e. when an electronic communication service temporarily stores a communication while waiting to deliver it. The legislative history reveals that Congress intended precisely this limited definition.").

207. Columbia Pictures Industries v. Bunnell, 2007 WL 2080419 (C.D. Cal., May 29, 2006).

208. 18 U.S.C. § 2702(a).

209. This also includes communications created by means of computer processing of communications received by means of electronic transmission.

210. 18 U.S.C. § 2702(a)(2).

- to the National Center for Missing and Exploited Children, in connection with a report submitted thereto under § 227 of the Victims of Child Abuse Act of 1990;[211] or
- to a federal, state, or local governmental entity, if the provider, in good faith, believes that an emergency involving danger of death or serious physical injury to any person requires disclosure without delay of communications relating to the emergency.[212]

Disclosure to a law enforcement agency is permitted if the contents were inadvertently obtained by the service provider and appear to pertain to the commission of a crime.[213]

A provider that provides service to the public may also divulge a record or other information pertaining to a subscriber to or customer of such service (but not the contents of communications):

- as otherwise authorized in § 2703; with the lawful consent of the customer or subscriber;
- as may be necessarily incident to the rendition of the service or to the protection of the rights or property of the provider of that service;
- to a governmental entity, if the provider reasonably believes that an emergency involving immediate danger of death or serious physical injury to any person justifies disclosure of the information;
- to the National Center for Missing and Exploited Children, in connection with a report submitted thereto under § 227 of the Victims of Child Abuse Act of 1990;[214] or
- to any person other than a governmental entity.[215]

6:68.   Out of district subpoenas under the ECPA

The District Court of Arizona recently addressed the impact of recent amendments to the ECPA and the ability of district courts to issue out-of-district warrants for the contents of electronically stored communications. This was held to be proper.[216]

6:69.   Civil subpoenas for stored communications and the ECPA

The Fourth District Court of Appeal in California addressed whether a state civil subpoena could seek to compel an e-mail service provider to disclose the content of stored communications. In this case, Apple sought to compel disclosure of certain communications to determine who had disclosed certain information regarding pending

---

211. 42 U.S.C. § 13032.

212. 18 U.S.C. § 2702(b).

213. *Id.*

214. 42 U.S.C. § 13032.

215. 18 U.S.C. § 2702(c).

216. In the Matter of the Search of Yahoo, Inc, 2007 WL 1539971 (D. Ariz. 2007).

products.[217] The court held that the ECPA did not permit Apple to subpoena these records because they did not fall within a recognized exception to the SCA.

> Here there is no pertinent ambiguity in the language of the statute. It clearly prohibits any disclosure of stored e-mail, other than as authorized by enumerated exceptions. Apple would apparently have us declare an implicit exception for civil discovery subpoenas. But by enacting a number of quite particular exceptions to the rule of non-disclosure, Congress demonstrated that it knew quite well how to make exceptions to that rule.[218]

This conclusion was also reached for the first time in federal court in a case involving a subpoena to AOL, as well as in the recent case involving YouTube.[219]

In *Flagg v. City of Detroit*,[220] the Plaintiff subpoenaed the content of text messages from a wireless provider, SkyTel. The Michigan Eastern District Court initially permitted the disclosure of the text messages from SkyTel, but the defendants moved to quash the subpoena, claiming that the Stored Communications Act precluded a provider from disclosing the content of electronic communications. The district court ultimately did not permit the subpoenas to proceed in their original form, but rather made the plaintiff reformulate the request as a Rule 34 request to the parties, finding that they had "control" of the messages.

6:70. Violation of terms not actionable under the SCA for "public websites"

Certain websites attempt to restrict access to certain classes of people, including by excluding employees or agents of certain companies. This usually occurs when there is a website that is dedicated to making negative statements or tracking litigation by or against a company. One way these sites attempt to limit access is to place a statement in the terms of use stating that by entering the site you are verifying you are not an employee or agent of a certain company. A case involving DirecTV presented such an issue.[221] In *Snow*, the plaintiff established a website that tracked corporate litigation. The site was, at some level, critical of DirecTV and contained information about the litigation it was bringing in connection with alleged piracy of its signal.[222] The plaintiff's website contained a clickwrap agreement, which stated that by agreeing to the clickwrap and selecting a username and password, the user was verifying that he

---

217. O'Grady v. Superior Court, 139 Cal. App. 4th 1423 (2006).

218. O'Grady, 139 Cal. App. 4th 1423.

219. In re Subpoena Duces Tecum to AOL, LLC, 550 F. Supp. 2d 606, (E.D.Va.,2008); Viacom International, Inc. v. YouTube, Inc., 253 F.R.D. 256 (S.D.N.Y. 2008).

220. Flagg v. City of Detroit, 252 F.R.D. 346 (E.D. Mich. 2008).

221. Snow v. DirecTV, Inc., 450 F.3d 1314 (11th Cir. 2006).

222. Ironically much of that litigation would be brought under a different portion of the ECPA.

was not associated with DirecTV.[223] Individuals affiliated with DirecTV, including some of its attorneys, accessed the site.[224]

The court noted at the outset of its discussion of the ECPA that the law provided "several clear exceptions to the bar on interception so as to leave unaffected electronic communications made through an electronic communication system designed so that such communication is readily available to the public."[225] The Eleventh Circuit disagreed with other cases interpreting the ECPA, including cases from the Ninth Circuit, and concluded that given the nature of the Internet, permitting someone to have access if they ignore an express warning by clicking on a hyperlink was insufficient to establish that the electronic communications system was private.[226] The court distinguished the *Hawaiian Airlines* case, concluding that in that case the operator of the website maintained a list of employees that he screened users against in order to only permit employees access.[227] Moreover, this court also noted that had the plaintiff merely pled that he screened the registrants before permitting access, his complaint might have survived the motion to dismiss. Since this allegation was not made, the court dismissed his complaint.[228]

The only potential way to reconcile this case with the other cases interpreting the Stored Communications Act is to conclude that the act of prescreening is critical to proving unauthorized access to an electronic communications system that is not publicly available. However, this does not account for other cases from other circuit courts that have not required such an act.

6:71.   Public display and discovery

This line of cases has also impacted discovery because as courts examine the scope of the SCA and its impact on electronic discovery, one court has found that the SCA permits disclosure of electronic communications that are publicly posted.[229]

6:72.   Procedural requirements of a court order

A court order for disclosure as set forth above may be issued by any court if the governmental entity offers specific and articulable facts demonstrating reasonable grounds for a belief that the information sought is relevant and material to an ongoing criminal investigation. In the case of a state governmental authority, a court order will

---

223. *Snow*, 450 F.3d at 1316.

224. *Id.*

225. *Snow*, 450 F.3d at 1320; 131 Cong. Rec. S11790-03 (1985); 131 Cong. Rec. E4128 (1985); see also 18 U.S.C. § 2511(2)(g).

226. *Snow*, 450 F.3d at 1321.

227. *Id.*

228. *Snow*, 450 F.3d at 1321-22.

229. Louis Vuitton Malletier S.A. vs. Akanoc Solutions Inc., 2008 WL 3200822 (N.D. Cal. 2008) ("Defendants are not required to disclose private information stored in the computer; they are only required to disclose information that the third-parties have made available to the public. Accordingly, the court finds that the Order to Compel does not violate the SCA.), citing Snow vs. Direct TV, Inc., 450 F.3d 1314, 1320-21 (11th Cir. 2006) (SCA does not create liability for individuals who "intercept" or "access" communications that are otherwise readily accessible by the general public.).

not issue if prohibited by the law of the state. The order can be quashed or modified upon a motion promptly made by a service provider if compliance with such order otherwise would cause an undue burden on such provider.[230]

6:73.   Requirement to preserve evidence

A provider or remote computing service, upon the request of a governmental entity, must take all necessary steps to preserve records and other evidence in its possession pending the issuance of a court order or other process.[231] Records (not containing the communications) must be retained for 90 days, which must be extended for an additional 90 days upon request by a governmental entity.[232]

6:74.   Backup preservation

A governmental entity may also request that a service provider create a backup copy of the contents of the electronic communications sought in order to preserve those communications. Without notifying the subscriber or customer of the subpoena or court order, the service provider must create a backup copy as soon as practicable, consistent with its regular business practices, and confirm to the governmental entity that the backup copy has been made. The backup copy must be created within two business days after receipt by the service provider of the subpoena or court order.[233] Notice to the subscriber or customer shall be made by the governmental entity within three days after receipt of the confirmation, unless the notice is delayed pursuant 18 U.S.C. § 2705.[234]

The backup must be retained until the later of the delivery of the information, or the resolution of any proceedings (including appeals of any proceeding) concerning the government's subpoena or court order.[235]

The tape must be released to the governmental entity no sooner than 14 days after notice to the subscriber or consumer if the service provider has not received notice from the subscriber or customer that the subscriber or customer has challenged the request, and the subscriber has not initiated proceedings to challenge the request of the governmental entity.[236]

It should be noted that a governmental entity can require the creation of a backup copy if, in its sole discretion it determines that there is reason to believe that notification under 18 U.S.C. § 2703 of the existence of the subpoena or court order may result in destruction of or tampering with evidence. This determination is not subject to challenge by the subscriber, customer, or service provider.[237]

---

230. 18 U.S.C. § 2702(d).
231. 18 U.S.C. § 2703(f)(1).
232. 18 U.S.C. § 2703(f)(2).
233. 18 U.S.C. § 2704(a)(1).
234. 18 U.S.C. § 2704(a)(2).
235. 18 U.S.C. § 2704(a)(3).
236. 18 U.S.C. § 2704(a)(4).
237. 18 U.S.C. § 2704(a)(5).

A customer can challenge the request to create a backup copy if within 14 days after notice by the governmental entity to the subscriber or customer, the subscriber or customer files a motion to quash such subpoena or vacate such court order, with copies served upon the governmental entity and with written notice of such challenge to the service provider. The motion or application must contain an affidavit or sworn statement stating that the applicant is a customer or subscriber to the service from which the contents of electronic communications maintained for him have been sought; and stating the applicant's reasons for believing that the records sought are not relevant to a legitimate law enforcement inquiry or that there has not been substantial compliance with the requirements of the Stored Communications Act.[238]

If a motion or application is filed then the government is permitted to file a sworn response, which may be filed in camera if the governmental entity includes in its response the reasons that make in camera review appropriate. The issue will be decided upon the papers unless the court is unable to do so.[239]

6:75. Delays in notice

A governmental entity can request that the court delay any notice required to a customer under 18 U.S.C. § 2703(b) for a period not to exceed 90 days if giving notice of the court's order granting access would have an adverse result.[240] Notice can also be delayed for 90 days if the request is through an administrative subpoena or a grand jury if a written certification is executed by a supervisory official[241] that states that providing notice might have an adverse result.[242] Extensions of up to 90 days may also be granted.[243]

When the time period ends the government entity must provide to the customer or subscriber a copy of the request along with notice that states with reasonable specificity the nature of the law enforcement inquiry and informs such customer or subscriber of the following:

- that information maintained for such customer or subscriber by the service provider was supplied to or requested by that governmental authority and the date on which the supplying or request took place;
- that notification of such customer or subscriber was delayed;
- what governmental entity or court made the certification or determination pursuant to which that delay was made; and

---

238. 18 U.S.C. § 2704(b)(1).

239. 18 U.S.C. § 2704(b)(3).

240. An "adverse result" means (A) endangering the life or physical safety of an individual; (B) flight from prosecution; (C) destruction of or tampering with evidence; (D) intimidation of potential witnesses; or (E) otherwise seriously jeopardizing an investigation or unduly delaying a trial. 18 U.S.C. § 2705(a)(2). *See also* 18 U.S.C. § 2705(a)(1)(a).

241. "'Supervisory official' means the investigative agent in charge or assistant investigative agent in charge or an equivalent of an investigating agency's headquarters or regional office, or the chief prosecuting attorney or the first assistant prosecuting attorney or an equivalent of a prosecuting attorney's headquarters or regional office." 18 U.S.C. § 2705(a)(6).

242. 18 U.S.C. § 2705(a)(1)(B).

243. 18 U.S.C. § 2705(a)(4).

- which provision of this law allowed such delay.[244]

If notice to the subscriber or customer is not required, or is delayed, the government can apply to the court for an order directing the service provider not to provide notice of the request to any other person. The court must grant the request if disclosure of the warrant, subpoena, or court order would result in the following:

- endangering the life or physical safety of an individual;
- flight from prosecution;
- destruction of or tampering with evidence;
- intimidation of potential witnesses; or
- otherwise seriously jeopardizing an investigation or unduly delaying a trial.[245]

6:76. Cost reimbursement

Government entities are required to reimburse parties that produce information in response to a government request.[246] Any costs that are reasonably necessary and directly incurred for assembling, reproducing or providing information must be reimbursed. This includes costs due to the interruption of normal business operations.[247] The fee is to be mutually agreed upon by the government and the service provider and, if agreement cannot be reached, then the court is permitted to determine the amount of the fee.[248]

However, it should be noted that the reimbursement requirement does not apply to records or information maintained by a communications common carrier that relates to telephone toll records and listings. In these cases, courts can order a payment as described above if the court determines the information required is unusually voluminous in nature or otherwise caused an undue burden on the provider.[249]

6:77. Disclosures of stored communications by non-service providers

If a communication is obtained after it is stored it is important to note that it may not be a violation of certain portions of the Stored Communications Act if it is disclosed by a person or entity that does not provide electronic communication services to the public.[250] Thus, if a person obtains stored electronic communications and that person is not an electronic communication service provider, there is likely no violation of the Stored Communications Act, though the improper acquisition may violate other state and federal statutes, including the CFAA.

---

244. 18 U.S.C. § 2705(a)(5).
245. 18 U.S.C. § 2705(b).
246. 18 U.S.C. § 2706.
247. 18 U.S.C. § 2706(a).
248. 18 U.S.C. § 2706(b).
249. 18 U.S.C. § 2706(c).
250. Wesley College v. Pitts, 974 F. Supp. 375, 389 (D. Del. 1997).

6:78.   Enforcement

If the violation of the Stored Communications Act is committed for purposes of commercial advantage, malicious destruction or damage, or private commercial gain, or in furtherance of any criminal or tortious act in violation of the Constitution, the laws of the United States or any state, the potential penalty is a fine, or imprisonment for not more than five years, or both, in the case of a first offense under 18 U.S.C. § 2701(a), and a fine, or imprisonment for not more than ten years, or both, for any subsequent offense under 18 U.S.C. § 2701(a).[251]

In all other cases the punishment is a fine under this title, or imprisonment for not more than one year, or both, in the case of a first offense under 18 U.S.C. § 2701(a) and a fine under this title, or imprisonment for not more than 5 years, or both, in the case of a person who has a prior conviction for an offense under 18 U.S.C. § 2701(a).[252]

6:79.   Disclosure of intercepted communications in response to a subpoena

A party that is in possession of improperly intercepted communications cannot turn these communications over in response to a subpoena or use them in a pending matter.[253]

6:80.   Civil actions and remedies

While there are certain immunities in the Stored Communications Act, there are civil remedies available for certain violations of the Act. Any provider of electronic communication service, subscriber, or other person aggrieved by any violation of this law is permitted to bring a civil action if it can be shown that the violation of the Stored Communications Act was a knowing or intentional violation.[254]

Available relief against any person or entity, other than the United States, includes preliminary and other equitable or declaratory relief, damages, punitive damages, reasonable attorneys' fees, and other litigation costs reasonably incurred.[255] Damages under the Stored Communications Act are the greater of actual damages and profits made by the violator or $1,000.[256]

Administrative discipline is also a potential remedy if it is determined that the United States or any of its departments or agencies violated the Stored Communications Act.[257]

A complete defense to any action exists if the defendant establishes good faith reliance upon one of the following:

---

251. 18 U.S.C. §§ 2701(b)(1)(a)–(b).

252. 18 U.S.C. §§ 2701(b)(2)(A)–(B).

253. In re Grand Jury, 111 F.3d 1066, 1077 (3d Cir. 1997); Bess v. Bess, 929 F.2d 1332, 1334 (8th Cir. 1991) (disclosure of intercepted communications in a divorce proceeding violates the Wiretap Act).

254. 18 U.S.C. § 2706(a).

255. 18 U.S.C. §§ 2706(b)(1)–(3)(c).

256. 18 U.S.C. § 2706(c).

257. 18 U.S.C. § 2706(d).

- a court warrant or order, a grand jury subpoena, a legislative authorization, or a statutory authorization;
- a request of an investigative or law enforcement officer under 18 U.S.C. § 2518(7); or
- a good faith determination that 18 U.S.C. § 2511(3) permitted the conduct.[258]

6:81. Limits on statutory damages

Since there are statutory damages available for violations of the ECPA, one of the issues for courts is whether the $1,000 statutory damage is per access, or it applies to all improper accesses by a defendant.[259] Most courts have concluded that the $1,000 penalty applies on a per access basis, so multiple accesses give rise to multiple $1,000 penalties.[260]

6:82. Actions against the United States

A person that can demonstrate a willful violation of the Stored Communications Act can bring an action in district court and recover actual damages, but not less than $10,000, whichever is greater, and reasonable litigation costs against the United States.[261] Before an action against the United States is commenced, the plaintiff must comply with the Federal Tort Claims Act and give written notice to the appropriate federal agency within two years after the claim accrues or within six months of the final denial of the claim by the agency.[262] There is no right to a jury trial in an action brought against the United States.[263] Administrative discipline is also an available remedy.[264] Relying upon the provisions of § 2707(a) as an interpretive guide, one court recently concluded that government entities are liable for wiretap violations.[265]

The United States can request a stay of any proceeding if it is determined that civil discovery will adversely affect the ability of the government to conduct a related investigation or prosecution of a related criminal case. The statute of limitations is tolled during any stay.[266]

6:83. Preclusion of civil action

The Stored Communication Act grants immunity to providers and their officers, employees, agents, and other individuals for providing information, facilities, or

---

258. 18 U.S.C. § 2706(e)(1) to (3).

259. In re Hawaiian Airlines, Inc., 355 B.R. 225 (D.C. Haw. 2006).

260. *Id.; see also* Tomasello v. Rubin, 167 F.3d 612, 618 (D.C. Cir. 1999).

261. 18 U.S.C. § 2712(a).

262. 18 U.S.C. §§ 2712(b)(1)–(2).

263. 18 U.S.C. § 2712(b)(3).

264. 18 U.S.C. § 2712(c).

265. Walden v. City of Providence, 495 F. Supp. 2d 245 (D.R.I. 2007).

266. 18 U.S.C. § 2712(e)(1).

assistance in accordance with the terms of a court order, warrant, subpoena, statutory authorization, or certification under this law.[267]

6:84.   The Patriot Act

The Patriot Act expanded certain law enforcement powers, particularly as they relate to gaining foreign intelligence. The Patriot Act expanded the scope of the Foreign Intelligence Surveillance Act of 1978 (FISA). This relates to the foreign intelligence surveillance court that has jurisdiction to hear government applications to obtain foreign intelligence. The Patriot Act increased the government's ability to gain these orders by permitting roving wire taps and by authorizing warrantless wire taps in certain circumstances, as well as granting the government the ability to obtain "any tangible things" without proof of individual suspicion under other provisions of the Act.

The Patriot Act has impacted privacy laws and lessened the burdens upon law enforcement in obtaining electronic data.[268] If the Director of the Federal Bureau of Investigation requests subscriber and toll billing records related information or electronic communication transactional records, an ISP is required to produce these records.[269] As a precondition to the request, certain high-ranking FBI officials must certify in writing that the requested records are relevant to an authorized investigation to protect against international terrorism or clandestine intelligence activities. Such an investigation cannot be conducted solely on the basis of activities that are protected under a person's free speech rights under the First Amendment.[270] ISPs are prohibited from disclosing to anyone that the FBI has requested or obtained access to information under the Patriot Act.[271]

The Patriot Act also permits the execution of warrants on delayed notice, so that the target may not know of the search until after the search has occurred.[272]

V. Application of Monitoring Laws

6:85.   Viewing of computer screen or other devices as an interception

Mere viewing of a communication on a computer screen is insufficient to establish a violation of the ECPA. Indeed, one court has stated that "Congress had in mind more surreptitious threats to privacy than simply looking over one's shoulder at a computer

---

267. 18 U.S.C. § 2703(e).

268. 18 U.S.C. § 2709.

269. 18 U.S.C. § 2709(a).

270. 18 U.S.C. § 2709(b).

271. 18 U.S.C. § 2709(c).

272. 18 U.S.C. § 3103.

screen when it passed the ECPA."[273] Similarly, viewing a pager's memory by pressing a display button on the pager did not violate the ECPA.[274]

6:86.   Screenshots and the ECPA

The *Councilman* holding, discussed in this chapter, was recently adopted by the Southern District of Ohio when it found that the use of software that took screenshots of e-mails and other matters on a computer screen violated the ECPA.[275]

6:87.   Disclosure of information in excess of a privacy policy—No violation of the ECPA

In a case involving American Airlines, one district court held that the disclosure of information in violation of a privacy policy would not, by itself, give rise to a claim under the ECPA.[276] This holding is consistent with the holding in similar litigation against JetBlue.[277]

6:88.   Seizure of devices as an interception

In certain cases information, including stored communications, has been seized lawfully (in the case of government action) or stolen. While if otherwise illegal this may be a crime under other statutes, merely seizing a device that has stored electronic communications is not an interception of communications.[278]

6:89.   Unauthorized access to information constitutes a violation of the ECPA

In addition to the CFAA claims discussed elsewhere in this book, unauthorized access to confidential or protected material, if in electronic form, can serve as the basis of an ECPA claim, if the information is accessed via the Internet, or presumably other electronic means.[279]

---

273. Wesley College v. Pitts, 974 F. Supp. 375, 121 Ed. Law Rep. 136 (D. Del. 1997), aff'd, 172 F.3d 861 (3d Cir. 1998).

274. U.S. v. Meriwether, 917 F.2d 955, 960 (6th Cir. 1990).

275. Potter v. Havlicek, 2007 WL 539534, (S.D. Ohio 2007). The Court also relied upon the O'Brien v. O'Brien, 899 So.2d 1133 (Fla. Dist. Ct. App. 5th Dist. 2005) case, which is discussed in § 6:73.

276. In re American Airlines, Inc. Privacy Litigation, 370 F. Supp. 2d 552 (N.D. Tex. 2005); citing In re N.W. Airlines Privacy Litigation, 2004 WL 1278459, at *2 (D. Minn. 2004).

277. *In re* JetBlue Airways Corp. Privacy Litigation, 379 F. Supp. 2d 299, (E.D. N.Y. 2005).

278. Steve Jackson Games, Inc. v. U.S. Secret Service, 36 F.3d at 458 (holding that government seizure of computer with private e-mails on it was not an interception under Title I).

279. *See* Therapeutic Research Faculty v. NBTY, 488 F. Supp. 2d 991 (E.D. Cal. 2007) (holding that a claim could be stated under the ECPA against party that exceeded authorized use of password and thereby obtained additional access to licensed materials).

6:90. Disclosures of information to third parties

One case against Amazon.com sought to apply the ECPA in a novel way—the plaintiff argued that Amazon.com's disclosure of the plaintiff's information to a third party was an ECPA violation. The flaw in this argument was that the plaintiff had knowingly provided the information to Amazon.com. The court noted that because the plaintiff e-mailed his information directly to Amazon.com, there was no "interception," which is a predicate to liability under the Wiretap Act.[280] The plaintiff also argued that Amazon.com had violated the Stored Communication Act by disclosing this information to the third-party. The court noted the holding in *Andersen Consulting*,[281] and its requirement that the entity in question provides *to the public* remote computing or electronic communication service, and rejected this argument. While Amazon.com was indisputably an online retailer, it was not an entity that provided public remote computing or electronic communication service.[282]

6:91. ISP's liability for gathering a subscriber's e-mail

ISPs may have customers cancel accounts or switch e-mails names, and many ISPs may not immediately shut down these accounts. One user argued that this practice was a violation of the Wiretap Act because the ISP, Earthlink in this particular case, intercepted his e-mails within the meaning of the Wiretap Act.[283] The Second Circuit rejected this argument, finding that the gathering of the e-mails was part of the "ordinary course of business," and thus not an interception under the Wiretap Act.[284]

6:92. Use of illegally intercepted communications

One question that has created issues for courts is when it is proper for a person to use an illegally intercepted communication. Under Title I of the ECPA and most state laws, it is illegal for a person to knowingly disclose an illegally intercepted communication.[285] Thus, the knowledge of the defendant who discloses a communication that another has illegally obtained is often a critical issue.

This issue was examined in connection with an investigation of then-Speaker of the House Newt Gingrich.[286] In this case, two Florida residents used a police scanner to intercept a cellular phone call in which Speaker Gingrich was speaking to other House members regarding the ethics charges brought against Speaker Gingrich. A recording of this conversation was made and then given to a Democratic member of the House, who then disclosed it to the press.[287] The recording was in an envelope which had a letter attached to it when it was transmitted. The first issue that was presented, in a

---

280. Crowley v. CyberSource Corp., 166 F. Supp. 2d 1263, 1269 (N.D. Cal. 2001).

281. Andersen Consulting LLP v. UOP, 991 F. Supp. 1041 (N.D. Ill. 1998).

282. *Crowley*, 166 F. Supp. 2d at 1270.

283. Hall v. EarthLink Network, Inc., 396 F.3d 500 (2d Cir. 2005).

284. *Hall*, 396 F.3d at 508.

285. *See* 18 U.S.C. § 2511(1).

286. Boehner v. McDermott, 191 F.3d 463 (D.C. Cir. 1999), cert. granted, judgment vacated, 532 U.S. 1050, 121 S. Ct. 2190, 149 L. Ed. 2d 1022 (2001) ("Boehner I").

287. *Boehner*, 191 F.3d at 465.

series of cases, was whether the Wiretap Act's restriction on disclosure of wrongfully obtained communications was constitutional. The court applied a content-neutral test and concluded that this provision was constitutional, particularly where the defendant knew of the illegal nature of the interception and was the direct recipient of the communications from the individuals that violated the ECPA.[288]

After *Boehner I*, the Supreme Court decided *Bartnicki v. Vopper*.[289] This case addressed the same issues as *Boehner I*, and the Court held that the ECPA's restrictions on the disclosure of communications were unconstitutional, due to First Amendment concerns, in certain circumstances.[290] *Bartnicki* dealt with members of the press who had lawfully obtained recordings of communications, because they did not know the recordings had been illegally obtained by another.[291] Indeed, in this case, the defendants received the tapes anonymously and did not know who had recorded them, or if they were illegally obtained.[292] Though the ECPA is a content-neutral restriction, its application to defendants who did not know they had possession of illegally obtained communications was found to be unconstitutional by the Supreme Court. The Court, however, expressly stated that its decision did not apply to individuals who obtain information illegally.[293] It is important to note that this was an "as applied" challenge, and thus did not invalidate this portion of the ECPA, except to the extent that it was applied to individuals who did not know they had illegally obtained communications.[294]

After the *Bartnicki* case, the Eleventh Cirtcuit Court of Appeals was confronted with *Boehner II*, in which the trial court had granted summary judgment against the defendant, finding a violation of the ECPA.[295] In this case, the court of appeals noted the contents of the cover letter with the tapes, but also that the defendant had a communication with the interceptors of the communication in which they told him that they had used a scanner to intercept the call. The Eleventh Circuit concluded that this was direct evidence that the defendant knew the communication had been illegally obtained, and affirmed summary judgment against the defendant.

The First Circuit recently addressed similar issues when it ruled regarding the constitutionality of Massachusetts' wiretap law. In *Jean v. Massachusetts State Police*, 492 F.3d 24 (1st Cir. 2007), Ms. Jean received an video, which contained audio, of an allegedly illegal police search of a third-party's residence, that was captured by a "nanny cam."[296] Jean received the video and posted it on the Internet as part of a website that was critical of certain state officials.[297] It was assumed that, at the time she posted it, Jean was aware the video had been illegally obtained. Jean was threatened with criminal prosecution, and she brought a civil action to enjoin the state via a request for preliminary

---

288. *Boehner*, 191 F.3d, at 467-69.

289. Bartnicki v. Vopper, 532 U.S. 514, 121 S. Ct. 1753, 149 L. Ed. 2d 787 (2001).

290. *Id.*

291. *Id.* at 535.

292. *Id.* at 519, 525, 530-31(fn. 15), and 535.

293. *Id.* at 532, fn. 19.

294. *Id.* at 524-25.

295. Boehner v. McDermott, 332 F.3d 149 (D.C. Cir. 2006) ("Boehner II").

296. Jean v. Massachusetts State Police, 492 F.3d 24 (1st Cir. 2007).

297. *Id.*

injunction, arguing that the Massachusetts Wiretap Act violated her First Amendment rights if it was applied as the police were indicating.[298] The court of appeal, as did the district court, concluded that the case was controlled by the Supreme Court's ruling in *Bartnicki*. Among the main principles the *Jean* court identified were those discussed by *Bartnicki*, which included "removing an incentive for parties to intercept private conversations" and "minimizing the harm to persons whose conversations have been illegally intercepted."[299] The Court also noted *Bartnicki's* admonition that for truthful matters of public interest the state must have a need of the highest order if they seek to punish subsequent publications.[300]

Of particular import to the *Jean* court was that the conduct occurred in a private citizen's home and was not the interception of a private communication, like the cell phone call in *Bartnicki*. Ultimately, while the Court concluded that the Massachusetts statute criminalized Jean's conduct, the First Amendment precluded enforcement against Jean.[301]

In *United States v. Reed,* a case that presented somewhat unique circumstances, a party accused of wrongfully intercepting telephone calls by recording them attempted to bring an action against individuals who reviewed the tape without his consent, based upon § 2511(1)(c)–(d), which precludes intentionally disclosing or using the contents of a wire communication if the individual knows or has reason to know that the information was obtained through an improper interception.[302] The Ninth Circuit concluded that the party in this case, who allegedly illegally intercepted and recorded the calls, could not state a claim because it the interception was either legal and therefore no claim existed, or he would not have standing to assert claims derivative of his own illegal activity.[303]

6:93.   Review and recording of voicemail

The review and recording of voicemail by a third party is an "interception" under ECPA and therefore actionable.[304]

6:94.   Recording by spouses

As noted in the *O'Brien* case, neither state laws modeled after the ECPA, nor the ECPA itself, permit a spouse to monitor or intercept communications of another spouse.[305]

---

298. *Id.*, 492 F.3d 24.

299. *Id.*, 492 F.3d at 28.

300. *Id.*, 492 F.3d at 29.

301. *Id.*, 492 F.3d at 33.

302. United States v. Reed, 575 F.3d 900 (9th Cir. 2009).

303. *Id.*

304. United States v. Smith, 155 F.3d 1051 (9th Cir. 1998).

305. Pritchard v. Pritchard, 732 F.2d 372 (4th Cir. 1984). For a discussion of the O'Brien case, see § 6:73.

6:95.   Interspousal immunity

Another issue that is frequently litigated in ECPA cases is whether one spouse has the right to intercept the other spouse's communications. This originates from a Fifth Circuit case that many courts have followed.[306] Other courts have rejected this line of cases.[307]

6:96.   Stored Communication Act still applies to "post transmission" emails

In one case a defendant argued that the Stored Communications Act did not apply to emails that had already been read by the recipient. This argument was rejected.[308]

6:97.   Keystroke loggers and common law liability

One court addressed whether the use of a keystroke logger could give rise to common law invasion of privacy liability. The analysis is highly factually dependent, and certain of the common law claims were not found to give rise to liability.[309] In this case the purpose of the interception of communications via the passwords obtained by the keystroke logger (for use in litigation) was a factor that the court felt mitigated the allegations of improper activity.

---

306. *See* Simpson v. Simpson, 490 F.2d 803 (5th Cir. 1974) (rejected by, U. S. v. Jones, 542 F.2d 661 (6th Cir. 1976)) and (rejected by, Kratz v. Kratz, 477 F. Supp. 463 (E.D. Pa. 1979)) and (disapproved of by, State v. Shaw, 103 N.C. App. 268, 404 S.E.2d 887 (1991)) and (rejected by, People v. Otto, 2 Cal. 4th 1088, 9 Cal. Rptr. 2d 596, 831 P.2d 1178 (1992)) and (overruled by, Glazner v. Glazner, 347 F.3d 1212 (11th Cir. 2003)). Ohio state courts have also recognized this exception. *See* Beaber v. Beaber, 322 N.E.2d 910 (1974).

307. *See* United States v. Jones, 542 F.2d 661 (6th Cir. 1976); Fultz v. Gilliam, 942 F.2d 396, 404 (6th Cir. 1991); Potter v. Havlicek, 2007 WL 539534 (S.D. Ohio 2007).

308. Bailey v. Bailey, 2008 WL 324156 (E.D.Mich. February 6, 2008).

309. *Id.*

Chapter 7

Employee Privacy

I.   Overview

7:1.   Introduction

Employee privacy issues raise a number of concerns and are impacted by a number of laws. Employee monitoring raises privacy concerns related to wiretapping and the review of stored communications, as well as videotaping privacy issues. The laws related to these issues are covered primarily in other chapters, but decisions specific to employees are covered in this chapter. It should be noted that many employee privacy issues still devolve into an examination of whether the employee had a reasonable expectation of privacy, which is in essence an analysis that is very similar to that under the Fourth Amendment. Notably, for government employers, the analysis is based upon the Fourth Amendment.

The use of polygraphs on employees also raises privacy concerns, and the federal laws, as well as the implementing regulations, are covered in this chapter. Moreover, background checks also raise concerns when they are used in the employment context, and the Fair Credit Reporting Act (FCRA), as well as certain state analogues, impacts employers' use of these tools. Finally, certain questions regarding past minor drug convictions are barred in California, and these laws are also covered in this chapter.

7:2.   Employee privacy in the workplace

Employees can have expectations of privacy in the workplace. For example, if an employer provides the employee employer-owned equipment, such as a safe, file cabinet or other area, the purpose of which is to keep the employee's private papers, these areas can treated as private.[1] In certain cases, this has been extended to areas given over to an employee's exclusive use, even if the employee does not preclude entry into the space at all times.[2] However, access by other employees or the employer's policies can alter this result.[3]

In the case of public employees, the expectation of privacy is enforced under the Fourth Amendment.[4] While in certain cases this requires the public employer to obtain a warrant, in other cases it does not, as long as the search is for non-investigatory, work-related purposes, or the investigation is not a criminal investigation, but rather one for work-related misconduct.[5]

However, the expectation of privacy for both public and non-public employees can be defeated by a policy that announces that the employer can inspect the property, or disclose information, including sensitive forms of information, such as personnel files.[6] Indeed, some courts have held that the policies need not even be reasonable and that the lack of a policy could be considered to be "irresponsible."[7] This has been repeatedly

---

1.   O'Connor v. Ortega, 480 U.S. 709, 718-19, 107 S. Ct. 1492, 94 L. Ed. 2d 714 (1987); Muick v. Glenayre Electronics, 280 F.3d 741 (7th Cir. 2002), citing, Shields v. Burge, 874 F.2d 1201, 1203-04 (7th Cir. 1989); Leventhal v. Knapek, 266 F.3d 64, 73-74 (2d Cir. 2001); U.S. v. Taketa, 923 F.2d 665, 673 (9th Cir. 1991); Schowengerdt v. General Dynamics Corp., 823 F.2d 1328, 1335, 91 A.L.R. Fed. 201 (9th Cir. 1987); Gillard v. Schmidt, 579 F.2d 825, 828 (3d Cir. 1978) (search of employee's desk was unreasonable due to expectation of privacy).

2.   Schowengerdt v. General Dynamics Corp., 823 F.2d 1328, 1335, 91 A.L.R. Fed. 201 (9th Cir. 1987); U.S. v. Taketa, 923 F.2d 665, 673 (9th Cir. 1991) (failure of employee to lock office at all times did not defeat privacy claim for contents).

3.   U.S. v. Taketa, 923 F.2d at 673 (In the employment context "a valid regulation may defeat an otherwise reasonable expectation of workplace privacy.").

4.   Muick v. Glenayre Electronics, 280 F.3d at 743; *see also* O'Connor v. Ortega, 480 U.S. 709, 715, 107 S. Ct. 1492, 94 L. Ed. 2d 714 (1987); U.S. v. Simons, 206 F.3d 392, 398 (4th Cir. 2000) ("The Fourth Amendment prohibits 'unreasonable searches and seizures' by government agents, including government employers or supervisors.") In the case of government employees, a search can be permissible even without a warrant if it is reasonable, including as to its scope.

5.   O'Conner v. Ortega, 480 U.S at 725-26 ("[P]ublic employer intrusions on the constitutionally protected privacy interests of government employees for noninvestigatory, work-related purposes, as well as for investigations of work-related misconduct, should be judged by the standard of reasonableness under all the circumstances."); *see also* Wasson v. Sonoma County Jr. College Dist., 4 F. Supp. 2d 893, 127 Ed. Law Rep. 299 (N.D. Cal. 1997), aff'd on other grounds, 203 F.3d 659, 141 Ed. Law Rep. 995 (9th Cir. 2000).

6.   O'Connor v. Ortega, 480 U.S. 709, 107 S. Ct. 1492, 94 L. Ed. 2d 714 (1987) ("public employees' expectations of privacy ... may be reduced by virtue of actual office practices and procedures, or by legitimate regulation."); U.S. v. Simons, 206 F.3d 392, 398-99 (4th Cir. 2000); Schowengerdt v. U.S., 944 F.2d 483, 488-89 (9th Cir. 1991); American Postal Workers Union, Columbus Area Local AFL-CIO v. U.S. Postal Service, 871 F.2d 556, 560-61 (6th Cir. 1989); *see also* Gossmeyer v. McDonald, 128 F.3d 481, 490 (7th Cir. 1997); Sheppard v. Beerman, 18 F.3d 147, 152 (2d Cir. 1994); U.S. v. Bunkers, 521 F.2d 1217, 1220 (9th Cir. 1975); American Postal Workers Union, Columbus Area Local AFL-CIO v. U.S. Postal Service, 871 F.2d 556, 560 (6th Cir. 1989) (permitting search of employee lockers due to policy permitting inspection); Wasson, 4 F. Supp. 2d at 905-06 (existence of a monitoring and disclosure policy defeated claim of privacy in personnel file).

7.   Muick v. Glenayre Electronics, 280 F.3d at 743.

found to be the case in connection with employer-owned computers.[8] Some employees have argued that the existence of a password regime on a computer system supported a finding that there was a privacy right, but courts have typically rejected this argument.[9] However, certain courts, where policies only permit monitoring for limited purposes narrowly read these policies and do not permit monitoring for other purposes.[10]

Interestingly, the search of computer-related equipment has also been found to justify the intrusion into a locked office, desks, and cabinets, where they are employer-owned, particularly where other employees had keys to the area.[11]

However, some courts have held that the lack of a policy can create a reasonable expectation of privacy by the employee.[12] Other courts have gone to the other extreme and actually found that even when no policy exists, and the employee purchased the equipment, there was no reasonable expectation of privacy in an office.[13] In sum, courts do not look only to exclusive possession, but rather they consider whether there is a reasonable expectation of privacy given the totality of the circumstances.[14] A court in Florida recently analyzed workplace computer privacy issues and examined these types of factors. Particularly important to the court was that the employer had created an expectation of privacy: the computer user had a locked door and there were a limited number of keys; the employee was the only user of the computer; and the employee permitted limited use of his office, only with his consent. Also important to the court was the lack of a written computer policy that expressly disclaimed any privacy right,

---

8. *See, e.g.*, Muick v. Glenayre Electronics, 280 F.3d 741 (7th Cir. 2002); U.S. v. Angevine, 281 F.3d 1130, 1134-35 (10th Cir. 2002); U.S. v. Simons, 206 F.3d 392, 398 (4th Cir. 2000); U.S. v. Bailey, 272 F. Supp. 2d 822 (D. Neb. 2003) (Disclosure of monitoring and computer policy in employee handbook and on intranet defeated any claim of privacy regarding computer records by employee); Garrity v. John Hancock Mut. Life Ins. Co., 18 I.E.R. Cas. (BNA) 981, 146 Lab. Cas. (CCH) P 59541, 2002 WL 974676 (D. Mass. 2002) (Employee's knowledge that employer had technical ability to monitor e-mail defeated privacy claim). U.S. v. Angevine, 281 F.3d 1130 (10th Cir. 2002) (holding that computer ownership, splash screen and monitoring policy defeated employee privacy claim); Biby v. Board of Regents, of University of Nebraska at Lincoln, 419 F.3d 845, 201 Ed. Law Rep. 36 (8th Cir. 2005) (same); U.S. v. Thorn, 375 F.3d 679 (8th Cir. 2004), cert. granted, judgment vacated, 543 U.S. 1112, 125 S. Ct. 1065, 160 L. Ed. 2d 1050 (2005) and judgment reinstated, 413 F.3d 820 (8th Cir. 2005) (en banc) (warrantless search of computer upheld because of computer monitoring policy and search of office upheld because other employees had keys to access office) c.f. U.S. v. Blok, 188 F.2d 1019 (D.C. Cir. 1951) (warrantless search of employee's desk by government employer unreasonable).

9. U.S. v. Bailey, 272 F. Supp. 2d at 836.

10. *See, e.g.*, Briggs v. American Filter Co., 630 F.2d 414, 420 n. 8, (5th Cir. 1980).

11. U.S. v. Thorn, 375 F.3d 679, 683 (8th Cir. 2004), cert. granted, judgment vacated, 543 U.S. 1112, 125 S. Ct. 1065, 160 L. Ed. 2d 1050 (2005) and judgment reinstated, 413 F.3d 820 (8th Cir. 2005).

12. U.S. v. Slanina, 283 F.3d 670, 676-77 (5th Cir. 2002), cert. granted, judgment vacated, 537 U.S. 802, 123 S. Ct. 69, 154 L. Ed. 2d 3 (2002) (upholding search of government computer, but finding that the employee had a reasonable expectation of privacy due to the lack of a policy.); *Simons*, 206 F.3d at 399 (holding the lack of a policy created a legitimate expectation of privacy in an office).

13. Gossmeyer v. McDonald, 128 F.3d 481, 490 (7th Cir. 1997).

14. U.S. v. Taketa, 923 F.2d 665, 670-71 (9th Cir. 1991) (A valid fourth amendment claim requires a subjective expectation of privacy that is objectively reasonable. Even if we assume that Taketa had a subjective expectation of privacy in O'Brien's office, we cannot find such an expectation to be objectively reasonable. In the employment context, we have found a reasonable expectation of privacy to exist in an area "given over to [an employee's] exclusive use." O'Brien's office was given over to O'Brien's exclusive use and contained his personal desk and files; the fact that Taketa had access to it, and used it for his own illegal activities in conspiracy with O'Brien, does not lead us to find an objectively reasonable expectation of privacy.") (citations omitted).

as well as the fact that the computer was not accessible on a network, though it did have Internet access.[15] The court also rejected the employer's argument that merely because the employee had a supervisor, this necessarily meant that computer monitoring was permitted.[16]

It should be noted that searches have been upheld, even in cases where an employee is found to have a reasonable expectation of privacy, if the search is for an internal investigation and not, in the case of public employers, for law enforcement purposes.[17] In *Esser*, a postal employee argued that despite the prominent posting of a signed warning to postal employees that by entering the premises their purses, briefcases and other containers were subject to search, she did not waive her Fourth Amendment rights.[18] The Eleventh Circuit, in an unpublished decision, concluded that by entering the premises where there was a posted regulation informing individuals of the potential searches, Esser did not have a reasonable expectation of privacy in her purse. This was particularly true because the office rules required employees to read all posted regulations.

The Ninth Circuit addressed the issue of employee conduct on an employer owned network in *U.S. v. Ziegler*, and the court rejected an employee's argument to exclude evidence gathered off of the employer's network in the context of a criminal prosecution. Ziegler's employer had a policy of monitoring its employees' use of the Internet.[19] The employer also had dedicated employees in the IT department that routinely monitored employees' Internet use.[20] Ziegler was accused of accessing child pornography on the

---

15. State v. Young, 2007 WL 4480737 (Fla. App. 1 Dist.) ("The facts of the instant case indicate that the church had endowed Young with an expectation of privacy far beyond that which an average employee enjoys. Not only did the church install a special lock on the door, but it supplied only three keys to the door, two of which were in Young's sole possession. Additionally, Young had a recognized practice of allowing visitors into his office only with his permission or for limited purposes related to church business. Although Young's expectation of privacy would be more compelling if he had never allowed another person to use the office, such a condition would be unrealistic in any office setting. Young was required to have an objectively reasonable expectation of privacy, not a compelling expectation. It is difficult to imagine circumstances within a realistic business setting which would give rise to a more legitimate expectation of privacy. Young also had an objectively reasonable expectation of privacy in his office computer. Although the church owned the computer, Young was the sole regular user. Although the church administrator performed maintenance on the computer, there was no evidence that she or anyone other than Young stored personal files on the computer or used it for any purpose other than maintenance. Unlike in the federal cases finding no expectation of privacy in a workplace computer, the church in the instant case had no written policy or disclaimer regarding the use of the computer.").

16. State v. Young, 2007 WL 4480737 *7 (Fla. App. 1 Dist.) ("Thus, based on the other facts of this case, Young's expectation of privacy was legitimate, even in the face of a church policy allowing the district superintendent to supervise him. All employees have supervisors, but many employees may still have a legitimate expectation that others will not examine their personal files, even if these files are brought into the workplace.").

17. Taketa, 923 F.2d at 674 (general allegations, though not sufficient for probable cause, supported the initiation of an internal investigation and a warrantless search of an employee's work space because the search was reasonable.); accord, Zurcher v. Stanford Daily, 436 U.S. 547, 556, 98 S. Ct. 1970, 56 L. Ed. 2d 525 (1978) ("[t]he critical element in a reasonable search is not that the owner of the property is suspected of a crime but that there is reasonable cause to believe that the specific 'things' to be searched for and seized are located on the property to which entry is sought.").

18. United States v. Esser, 284 Fed. Appx. 757 (11th Cir. 2008) (unpublished).

19. U.S. v. Ziegler, 456 F.3d 1138, 1139-1140 (9th Cir. 2006), opinion withdrawn and superseded on reh'g, 474 F.3d 1184 (9th Cir. 2007), cert. denied, 128 S. Ct. 879, 169 L. Ed. 2d 738 (U.S. 2008).

20. U.S. v. Ziegler, 474 F.3d 1184 (9th Cir. 2007), cert. denied, 128 S. Ct. 879, 169 L. Ed. 2d 738 (U.S. 2008).

employer's network. The employer had "spot checked" Ziegler's system cache and found evidence that allegedly supported the allegations.[21] The employer had other employees enter Ziegler's locked office and copy his hard drive to gather additional evidence.[22]

Ziegler moved to exclude the evidence that was gathered from his hard drive, claiming that the search was done at the direction of the government and that since the search was conducted without a warrant, it violated his Fourth Amendment rights. The district court disagreed and held that Ziegler had no reasonable expectation of privacy in "the files he accessed on the Internet."[23] The appellate court acknowledged that the Fourth Amendment does protect people, not places, and that computers are in many cases their most private spaces.[24] However, it also noted that the ultimate analysis of privacy depends upon whether the expectation of privacy is reasonable in its context.[25]

Given the existence of a password on the computer, as well as the locked door to Ziegler's office, it was undisputed that he had a subjective expectation of privacy, so the ultimate issue the court considered was whether Ziegler had a reasonable expectation of privacy in his workplace computer, as well as the files that resided on it.[26] The court concluded that Ziegler did not have an expectation of privacy that was reasonable. Citing *Simons*, the court noted the Fourth Circuit's holding that an employer's Internet use policy that mandated that employees only use their workplace computer for business purposes, coupled with the reservation of audit rights to monitor compliance, including the implementation of a firewall, made any expectation of privacy by an employee unreasonable.[27]

This issue was addressed in *United States v. Maxwell*.[28] In this case, a service member allegedly used an AOL account to send sexually explicit e-mails to an Air Force officer and send child pornography.[29] The court determined that due to AOL's "contractual privacy protections," the government's search of the e-mails was improper.[30]

A similar conclusion was reached in *United States v. Monroe*.[31] In this case, the court rejected a service member's claim that he had a reasonable expectation of privacy in the government e-mail system.[32] However, this result can be altered by the conduct of the relevant government agency. In *United States v. Long*,[33] Long, a Marine Corps corporal,

---

21. U.S. v. Ziegler, 456 F.3d 1138 (9th Cir. 2006), opinion withdrawn and superseded on reh'g, 474 F.3d 1184 (9th Cir. 2007), cert. denied, 128 S. Ct. 879, 169 L. Ed. 2d 738 (U.S. 2008).

22. U.S. v. Zeigler, at 1141.

23. U.S. v. Zeigler, at 1142.

24. U.S. v. Zeigler, citing Katz v. U.S., 389 U.S. 347, 351, 88 S. Ct. 507, 19 L. Ed. 2d 576 (1967); U.S. v. Gourde, 440 F.3d 1065, 1077 (9th Cir. 2006), cert. denied, 127 S. Ct. 578, 166 L. Ed. 2d 432 (U.S. 2006) (en banc) (Kleinfeld, J., dissenting) c.f., U.S. v. Arnold, 523 F.3d 941 (9th Cir. 2008), as amended on denial of reh'g and reh'g en banc, 533 F.3d 1003 (9th Cir. 2008), cert. denied, 2009 WL 425169 (U.S. 2009).

25. U.S. v. Zeigler, 456 F. 3d at 1143.

26. U.S. v. Ziegler, 456 F.3d 1138 (9th Cir. 2006), opinion withdrawn and superseded on reh'g, 474 F.3d 1184 (9th Cir. 2007), cert. denied, 128 S. Ct. 879, 169 L. Ed. 2d 738 (U.S. 2008).

27. U.S. v. Zeigler, 456 F. 3d at 1143-44 citing U.S. v Simons, 206 F.3d 392, 398 (4th Cir. 2000).

28. U.S. v. Maxwell, 45 M.J. 406 (C.A.A.F. 1996).

29. *Maxwell*, 45 M.J. at 414.

30. *Id.*

31. U.S. v. Monroe, 52 M.J. 326, 330 (C.A.A.F. 2000).

32. Monroe, 52 M.J. at 330.

33. United States v. Long, 64 M.J. 57 (C.A.A.F. 2006).

argued that she had a reasonable expectation of privacy in her e-mail account, despite a banner that appeared each day informing her that monitoring was a possibility. The court examined the testimony of the network administrator, who testified that e-mails were not routinely monitored due to privacy concerns. Moreover, the court noted that the banner itself did not explicitly say that the Marines were going to monitor e-mails for law enforcement reasons.[34] This, coupled with the strict password policy, led the court to conclude that Long had a reasonable expectation of privacy in her e-mails, and therefore the search of her e-mails was improper.[35] As in *Ziegler*, the court in *Quon v. Arch Wireless Operating Co, Inc.* concerned itself not only with the monitoring policies established by an employer, but also focused upon how consistently that policy was actually implemented.[36]

The *Quon* case arose from the monitoring of employee communications on police department-provided pagers. Two of the four plaintiffs (Jeff Quon and Steve Trujillo) were both police officers. One of the other plaintiffs was a police dispatcher, and the fourth was Jeff Quon's wife. Jeff Quon and Steve Trujillo used department-provided pagers in the course and scope of their employment and also allegedly used them for personal use, including sending sexually-explicit messages. The department had a "general" policy of monitoring e-mail and other forms of communications and also banned personal use of systems, but the policies were not read to explicitly cover text messaging. Notably, Trujillo and Jeff Quon both signed the "general" policy, and both used the same form of technology—the department-provided pagers.

However, only Jeff Quon attended later meetings where the department allegedly stated that text messages were treated like e-mail and therefore covered by general policy. As in other cases noted above, there was also evidence of an informal policy to *not monitor* texting, which was evidenced by the fact that personal use was acknowledged and monitoring was not done unless the employee refused to pay for "excessive" personal use.

The provider in this case, Arch Wireless, kept a backup copy of the text messages. Since it paid for the devices, the department was identified as the "subscriber" under the Stored Communications Act. Based upon this conclusion, the department obtained copies of the content contained on the backup copy of the text messages from the service provider, without employee consent. The four plaintiffs sued, claiming that the disclosure of the content of communications violated the Stored Communications Act and their privacy rights, as well as other statutory protections. The court initially examined the scope of the Stored Communications Act and whether Arch Wireless was a "remote computing service" or an "electronic communication service," because the answer to that question would impact whether the content of the communications could be disclosed just to the recipients or also to the subscriber without consent. The court concluded that Arch Wireless was an electronic computing service and, as a result, it could not disclose the content of text messages to a subscriber without consent of a recipient. Thus, Arch Wireless's disclosure to the department, the subscriber, according

---

34. United States v. Long, 64 M.J. 57 (C.A.A.F. 2006).

35. *Id.*

36. Quon v. Arch Wireless Operating Co, Inc., 529 F.3d 892 (9th Cir.2008).

to the Ninth Circuit, violated the Stored Communications Act and the employees' privacy rights.

For three of the four plaintiffs, including Trujillo, the Ninth Circuit simply examined whether the users of text messaging have a reasonable expectation of privacy regarding text messages that are stored on the service provider's network, ultimately concluding that there was a reasonable expectation of privacy, at least as to the service provider. This expectation was not endless because the court noted that one of the recipients could have permitted the department to review the messages at issue. However, the court clearly stated that, as a matter of law, the plaintiffs had a reasonable expectation of privacy that the messages would not be reviewed absent the consent of a sender or recipient. Notably, even for Trujillo, who signed the same policy and used the same technology as Jeff Quon, the court did not apply the "general" policy.

In the case of Jeff Quon, the only plaintiff who attended the meeting at which it was announced that the "general" policy covered texting, the Ninth Circuit examined the general policy, noting "The Department's general 'Computer Usage, Internet and E-mail Policy' stated both that the use of computers 'for personal benefit is a significant violation of City of Ontario Policy' and that '[u]sers should have no expectation of privacy or confidentiality when using these resources.' Quon signed this Policy and attended a meeting in which it was made clear that the Policy also applied to use of the pagers. If that were all, this case would be analogous to the cases relied upon by the Appellees."[37] The cases cited by the appellees and referenced by the *Quon* court were all cases in which a policy defeated an employee's right of privacy, including the *Muick* case.[38] Thus, though both Trujillo and Jeff Quon signed the same policy, it was only applied to Jeff Quon because only he attended the meeting where the policy was applied to texting.

However, these were not the only facts considered in the *Quon* case. Despite the application of the "general" policy to texting, the release of the text messages was still held to be improper because of the "operational reality" regarding texting. The operational reality of the department was that text messages were not monitored in most cases, particularly if personal use was paid for, and that many of the employees were aware of this fact. Thus, despite having a policy, the employer's failure to consistently implement it proved fatal.

The defendants appealed to the Supreme Court, arguing that the search of the text messages was proper. Ultimately, the Supreme Court found that the search was proper, under a Fourth Amendment analysis, which is applicable to government employers.[39] In reaching this conclusion, the Supreme Court expressly limited the application of its ruling, and noted for purposes of this case it was assuming that a right of privacy existed. The Supreme Court found that under the Fourth Amendment the search was proper on two grounds: the department had reasonable grounds for suspecting that the search was necessary for a noninvestigatory work-related purpose; and that the search was not excessively intrusive. These findings supported a ruling that the search was proper.

---

37. *Id.* at 7022.
38. Muick v. Glenayre Electronics, 280 F.3d 741, 743 (7th Cir. 2002).
39. City of Ontario, California, et al v. Quon, et al, ___ S. Ct. ___ (slip op. June 17, 2010).

Since the Fourth Amendment does not apply to private employers, and the Supreme Court assumed, but did not decide, that there was a right of privacy in the text messages, the case does not have broad application, but two points are worth noting generally.

First, the reliance by the Supreme Court on an analysis that there was reasonable grounds for the search demonstrates that employers are in safer waters if they limit searches of employee communications to situations where they have grounds to suspect some form of misconduct.

Second, limiting the search in certain ways to the purpose of the investigation also seems to be a good practice based upon this decision.

It should be noted that merely inserting a computer into a network will not waive an otherwise reasonable expectation of privacy, particularly if there is no clear monitoring policy.[40] However, where there is a monitoring policy, a person's expectation of privacy can be diminished.[41] Moreover, at least one court has permitted law enforcement to use publicly available technology to identify an Internet user's IP address.[42]

In a case involving a person that used his personal computer on a military network, the Eleventh Circuit held that the individual did not have a reasonable expectation of privacy because his computer settings allowed anyone on the network to search his computer drive. Here, a civilian contractor working on a military base connected his personal laptop to the base network. He was aware that his activities on the base network were monitored. As part of a search of the network the military became aware of pornographic text and movies that were shared on the contractor's computer, and it should be noted that no special means of access of the computer were used. This finding led to the arrest of the contractor, as well as a further search of his apartment based upon a warrant. The contractor argued these actions violated his reasonable expectation of privacy. The court, comparing this situation to common areas in apartment complexes, held that the contractor did not have a reasonable expectation of privacy since the search in this case was really one of the network, not the computer *per se.* Thus, the court held that the search of the computer was proper.[43]

7:3.   Searches of government employees

In the government employer context, which requires a Fourth Amendment analysis, searches of computers have been found to be reasonable where a policy existed that disclosed the employer reserved the right to monitor communications, even where there were other statements indicating that files would be confidential.[44] In the government

---

40. U.S. v. Heckenkamp, 482 F.3d 1142 (9th Cir. 2007), cert. denied, 128 S. Ct. 635, 169 L. Ed. 2d 395 (U.S. 2007).

41. U.S. v. Angevine, 281 F.3d 1130 (10th Cir. 2002); U.S. v. Simons, 206 F.3d 392 (4th Cir. 2000).

42. State v. Jacobs, 2007 WL 1121289 (Minn. Ct. App. 2007), review denied, (June 27, 2007).

43. United States v. King, 509 F.3d 1138 (11th Cir. 2007).

44. Wasson v. Sonoma County Jr. College Dist., 4 F. Supp. 2d 893, 127 Ed. Law Rep. 299 (N.D. Cal. 1997), aff'd on other grounds, 203 F.3d 659, 141 Ed. Law Rep. 995 (9th Cir. 2000) (As for the Fourth Amendment claim, it has long been clearly established that searches and seizures of private property of employees by their government employers or supervisors are subject to the restraints of the Fourth Amendment. The Court noted, however, "[P]ublic employees' expectations of privacy in their offices, desks, and file cabinets, like similar expectations of employees in the private sector, may be reduced by virtue of actual office practices and procedures, or by legitimate regulation." Because of the variety of work environments in the public sector,

employer context, a warrant is not always required, even if the employee has a reasonable expectation of privacy. Indeed, reasonable suspicion can be sufficient if the government is attempting to investigate misconduct.[45]

7:4.   Internal investigations and invasion of privacy claims

As privacy becomes a more front-and-center issue, more and more plaintiffs raise privacy concerns in the context of investigations into employee misconduct. In *Warinner,* an employee was investigated as part of an undercover drug investigation at an automobile assembly plant.[46] As a result of the investigation, the plaintiff brought an invasion of privacy claim based upon an intrusion upon seclusion theory. The court first examined whether the plaintiff in the case had a reasonable expectation of privacy.[47] In this case, since the conduct at issue was a purported drug transaction with undercover investigators that did not occur at the plaintiffs' homes, the court concluded that there was no reasonable expectation of privacy.

The case also addressed whether the reports that were generated regarding the activity were "consumer" reports under the Fair Credit Reporting Act. The court noted that specifically excluded from the definition of a consumer report is any report containing information solely as to transactions or experiences between the consumer and the person making the report.[48] Reports regarding employees' drug use had been held not to be a consumer report based upon this exception.[49]

7:5.   Employee e-mails and the attorney-client privilege

In one of the first reported decisions on this issue, a bankruptcy court addressed the application of the attorney-client privilege to an employee who uses a corporate network to communicate with his personal attorney.[50] New York has specifically addressed the issue via statute that provides that any communication that is privileged under the attorney-client privilege does not lose its privileged nature simply because it is communicated

---

the question of whether an employee has a reasonable expectation of privacy must be addressed on a case-by-case basis. If the employee does have a reasonable expectation of privacy in the area that was searched, the Court must balance the invasion of those privacy interests against the government's need for supervision, control, and the efficient operation of the workplace ... Ordinarily, a search will be justified at its inception where there are reasonable grounds for suspecting that the search will turn up evidence that the employee is guilty of work-related misconduct.") (interal citiations omitted.); *see also* O'Connor v. Ortega, 480 U.S. 709, 725-26, 107 S. Ct. 1492, 94 L. Ed. 2d 714 (1987) ("[P]ublic employer intrusions on the constitutionally protected privacy interests of government employees for noninvestigatory, work-related purposes, as well as for investigations of work-related misconduct, should be judged by the standard of reasonableness under all the circumstances.").

45.   U.S. v. Taketa, 923 F.2d 665 (9th Cir. 1991).

46.   Warinner v. North American Securities Solutions Inc., 3:05-CV-00244-CRS-JDM (W.D. Ken. June 5, 2008).

47.   Webb v. Bob Smith Chevrolet Inc., 2005 WL 2065237, at * 6 (W.D. KY August 24, 2005) (McCall v. Courier-Journal and Louisville Times Co., 623 S.W.2d 882, 887 (1981); Price v. General Motors Corp., 1:99-CV-78-R, slip op. at 19 (W.D. KY 2001).

48.   15 U.S.C. § 1681(a)(d)(2)(A)(i).

49.   *See* Salazar v. Golden State Warriors, 124 F.Supp.2d 1155, 1158 (N.D. Cal. 2000).

50.   In re Asia Global Crossing, Ltd., 322 B.R. 247 (Bankr. S.D.N.Y. 2005).

by electronic means or because persons necessary for the delivery of the electronic communication may have access to the content of the communication.[51]

The court noted that it is generally accepted that attorneys can communicate, without fear of disclosure, with their clients via unencrypted e-mail.[52] This court examined the e-mail privacy cases as a starting point and noted that the application of the privilege must be consistent with objective and subjective components.[53] The court ultimately considered four factors when formulating its test to determine whether e-mails were privileged:

(1) Does the corporation maintain a policy banning personal or other objectionable use?

(2) Does the company monitor the use of the employee's computer or e-mail?

(3) Do third parties have a right of access to the computer or e-mails?

(4) Did the corporation notify the employee, or was the employee aware, of the use and monitoring policies?[54]

In this case, while the court found that third parties could review the e-mails because they were sent over the network and stored on the company's servers (a fact that is true in virtually all cases), the remaining factors were not met because the evidence was "equivocal" regarding the existence or notice of monitoring policies.[55] Thus, the court could not conclude that the privilege was inapplicable.[56]

Other courts have applied similar, but slightly different factors. In one case the court considered the non-enforcement of a computer monitoring policy, as well as traditional factors that included the reasonableness of the precautions taken by the producing party to prevent inadvertent disclosure; the delay, if any, in the party's actions in asserting an issue; and an examination of the issue of fairness.[57] Whether the computer was in a home office or an office that otherwise had restricted access has also been a consideration, though not a dispositive one.[58]

California courts have addressed the issue in a related context-protection of electronic files on a work computer.[59] In *Jiang*, the defendant used his work computer to create electronic files that were communications to his attorney. The employer had a computer use policy that stated there was no reasonable expectation of privacy, but it did not preclude personal use, in contrast to the policy in the *TBG* case.[60] Ultimately the court concluded that the defendant's communications were confidential under the attorney-client privilege and could not be used by the prosecution.[61]

---

51. N.Y.C.P.L.R. § 4548.

52. In re Asia Global Crossing, Ltd., 322 B.R. 247, 256 (Bankr. S.D. N.Y. 2005).

53. *Id.*, at 257.

54. In re Asia Global Crossing, Ltd., 322 B.R. 247 (Bankr. S.D. N.Y. 2005).

55. *Id.*

56. *Id.*, at 261.

57. Curto v. Medical World Communications, Inc., 2007 WL 1452106 (E.D. N.Y. 2007).

58. *Id.*

59. People v. Jiang, 131 Cal. App. 4th 1027 (2005).

60. *Id.*; cf TBG Ins. Services Corp. v. Superior Court of Los Angeles 117 Cal.Rptr.2d 155 (2002).

61. *Id.*

New York courts have reached different conclusions, at least where personal use is banned.[62] A court in New York recently addressed this issue, and applied *In re Asia Global Crossing*.[63] In *Scott*, a doctor used his employer's e-mail system to communicate with his personal lawyer in connection with an employment dispute. The employer, Beth Israel Hospital, was monitoring the doctor's e-mail and saw these communications.[64] The doctor brought a motion for protective order seeking the return of the e-mails.

Beth Israel had a computer use policy that disclosed their right to monitor and explicitly stated that the computer systems could not be used for personal use.[65] The court also noted that the attorney's e-mails contained a standard footer, which stated that the communications were privileged and confidential, and were for the intended recipient only.

The court applied *In re Asia Global Crossing*, and found that one of the key issues for its decision was the ban on personal use in the policy, particularly when the right to monitor was clearly disclosed. Other courts continue to find that attorney-client materials are privileged, even if sent on an employer's system.[66] In a webmail case, a court recently addressed these issues and came to a similar conclusion.[67] In this case, while the court noted that plaintiff Sims had no reasonable expectation of privacy in the contents of the laptop that was furnished by defendant Lakeside, including emails sent on his work account, web-based emails and any material he created to communicate with his attorney and his spouse were protected under the attorney client and marital privilege. This was true despite the fact that the employer had a policy that said computers were only for work use and that the employer reserved the right to inspect the laptop at any time.[68] Other recent decisions have more narrowly construed these privileges.[69]

While analysis of these cases reveal slightly inconsistent analysis, one key issue appears to be prohibiting personal use as part of the employer's computer use policy.

In a case that has gotten significant recent attention, *Stengart v. Loving Care Agency, Inc.*,[70] like *Mt. Olive*[71] before it, arose from the plaintiff's use of web-based email. In this case, the plaintiff used a company-issued computer to exchange e-mails with her lawyer through her personal, password-protected, web-based e-mail account. She utilized Yahoo's email service, which she used to communicate with her attorney. The appellate court noted that despite her use of the employer's computer system, she never saved her Yahoo ID or password on the company laptop. Moreover, the plaintiff's

---

62. Long v. Marubeni America Corp., 2006 WL 2998671 (S.D. N.Y. 2006).

63. Scott v. Beth Israel Medical Center Inc., 17 Misc. 3d 934, 847 N.Y.S.2d 436 (Sup 2007).

64. *Id.*

65. *Id.*

66. Sims v. Lakeside School, 2007 WL 2745367 (W.D. Wash. 2007) ("However, web-based e-mails generated by plaintiff Sims and any material he created to communicate with his attorney and his spouse are protected under the attorney-client privilege and the marital communications privilege.").

67. Sims v. Lasuch School, 2:06-CV-01412-RSM (W.D. Wash. September 20, 2007).

68. *Id.*, citing Muick v. Goenayre Electronics, 280 F.3d 741, 743 7th Cir. 2002.

69. United States v. General Maritime Management (Portugal) L.D.A., 2:08-CR-00393 (S.D. Tex. July 21, 2008).

70. Stengart v. Loving Care Agency, Inc., 201 N.J. 300, 990 A.2d 650 (N.J. Mar 30, 2010).

71. Fischer v. Mt. Olive Lutheran Church, 207 F. Supp. 2d 914, 925 (W.D. Wis. 2002).

lawyer's emails had a footer that disclosed that the emails were for the personal and confidential use of the intended recipient.

There was a dispute regarding whether there was an applicable employment policy, but the appellate court assumed that the policy applied, and it provided in relevant part:

> The company reserves and will exercise the right to review, audit, intercept, access, and disclose all matters on the company's media systems and services at any time, with or without notice....
>
> E-mail and voice mail messages, internet use and communication and computer files are considered part of the company's business and client records. Such communications are not to be considered private or personal to any individual employee.
>
> The principal purpose of electronic mail (*e-mail*) is for company business communications. Occasional personal use is permitted; however, the system should not be used to solicit for outside business ventures, charitable organizations, or for any political or religious purpose, unless authorized by the Director of Human Resources.

The policy also specifically prohibited "[c]ertain uses of the e-mail system" including sending inappropriate sexual, discriminatory, or harassing messages, chain letters, "[m]essages in violation of government laws," or messages relating to job searches, business activities unrelated to Loving Care, or political activities. The policy also warned employees that: "Abuse of the electronic communications system may result in disciplinary action up to and including separation of employment."

The defendant, Loving Care, after the plaintiff filed an employment lawsuit, hired a computer forensic expert to recover all files stored on the laptop including the e-mails, which had been automatically saved on the hard drive. Loving Care's attorneys reviewed the e-mails and used the information in the course of discovery.

The appellate court began its analysis by examining the policy itself:

> The Policy specifically reserves to Loving Care the right to review and access "all matters on the company's media systems and services at any time." In addition, e-mail messages are plainly "considered part of the company's business ... records."
>
> It is not clear from that language whether the use of personal, password-protected, web-based e-mail accounts via company equipment is covered. The Policy uses general language to refer to its "media systems and services" but does not define those terms. Elsewhere, the Policy prohibits certain uses of "the e-mail system," which appears to be a reference to company e-mail accounts. The Policy does not address personal accounts at all. In other words, employees do not have express notice that messages sent or received

on a personal, web-based e-mail account are subject to monitoring if company equipment is used to access the account.

The Policy also does not warn employees that the contents of such e-mails are stored on a hard drive and can be forensically retrieved and read by Loving Care.

The Policy goes on to declare that e-mails "are not to be considered private or personal to any individual employee." In the very next point, the Policy acknowledges that "[o]ccasional personal use [of e-mail] is permitted." As written, the Policy creates ambiguity about whether personal e-mail use is company or private property.

The scope of the written Policy, therefore, is not entirely clear.

The court then examined the scope of the attorney-client privilege, noting it applies to email,[72] and then examined the policy underlying the attorney-client privilege. Of note is that the court then examined many of the workplace privacy cases involving searches of computers in New Jersey, noting that these cases generally supported an employer's right to review information stored on its network, even if password protected.[73] The appellate court finally examined the other attorney-client email cases, drew a distinction between cases involving government action, and affirmed the trial court's decision, finding that Stengart could reasonably expect that e-mail communications with her lawyer through her personal account would remain private and that sending and receiving them via a company laptop did not eliminate the attorney-client privilege that protected them, particularly in light of the policy and the actions she took to protect her emails. This was particularly true because the emails in question did not create liability for the company or were not "illegal or inappropriate."

There are several key lessons in this case. First, a clear policy that disclosed that contents of electronic communications can be gathered even if not sent via the employer's email domain is something to be considered. Second, the appellate court clearly drew a distinction between a privacy right in non-privileged matters (particularly where illegal activity might occur), and privileged matters, so the application of this case beyond the attorney-client context may be limited. Third, an employer should think carefully before reviewing communications that are privileged, and not just private, and if it desires to try and review these types of communications, specific, clear disclosures should be made in the employment policies. Finally, given how these communications were captured, employers should consider what additional disclosures are needed for software solutions such as encryption and other scanning software that may review emails, particularly those not sent on the employer's email domain.

---

72. Seacoast Builders Corp. v. Rutgers, 358 N.J.Super. 524, 553, 818 A.2d 455 (App.Div.2003).
73. State v. M.A., 402 N.J.Super. 353, 954 A.2d 503 (App.Div.2008) (holding the defendant had no reasonable expectation of privacy in personal information he stored on a workplace computer under a separate password); *see also* Doe v. XYC Corp., 382 N.J.Super. 122, 887 A.2d 1156 (App.Div.2005).

National Economic Research Associates v. Evans,[74] is another case that precludes employers from looking at attorney-client emails. In this case, while there was a policy that discussed email monitoring, the policy did not clearly disclose that communications that were not part of the company's email system could be reviewed, and therefore the court found that review of attorney-client emails forensically pulled from a hard drive would be improper. Certain courts have even found an expectation of privacy in the use of an employer email system, rather than in webmail.[75]

7:6. Right to purchase creating an expectation of privacy

In a related area, a court in the Southern District of California recently held that a policy of permitting employees to purchase their work laptop upon departure could, at least potentially, create an expectation of privacy that could preclude a search of the computer.[76]

7:7. No general duty to monitor employee computer use

The Wisconsin Court of Appeals addressed whether, in general circumstances, an employer has a duty to monitor an employee's computer use.[77] In *Sigler*, the plaintiffs argued that the defendant corporation had a duty to prevent its employees from using company computers to harass others based upon the fact that it was foreseeable that the failure to properly train or supervise their employees could cause harm to another. The plaintiffs used the fact that the defendant employer had disciplined fourteen employees in 2003 for Internet technology-related offenses, it was foreseeable that harm could come to them due to a failure to train. It also argued that the individual defendant's low reviews should have been a clue of potential problems and that the defendant employer should have done regular monitoring. Ultimately, the court concluded that the plaintiffs had not demonstrated a duty of care, and therefore summary judgment was appropriate. This conclusion was based upon the fact that the only allegations against the defendant employer were that it provided the individual defendant with access to a computer and the Internet and that company policies prohibited personal use of computer resources. The court also concluded that a negligent supervision claim would also fail due to a variety of public policy factors.

7:8. Employee e-mails and the spousal privilege

One court recently held that e-mails sent to a person's spouse, even on an employer's system, are privileged.[78]

---

74. National Economic Research Associates v. Evans, 2006 WL 2440008 No. 15, at 337 (Mass.Super.Ct. Sept. 25, 2006),
75. Convertino v. U.S. Dep't of Justice, 674 F.Supp.2d 97 (D.D.C.2009) (finding reasonable expectation of privacy in attorney-client e-mails sent via employer's e-mail system).
76. Hilderman v. Enea TekSci, Inc., 551 F.Supp.2d 1183 (S.D.Cal. 2008).
77. Sigler vs. Kobinsky Appeal No. 2008 AP29 (2008).
78. Sims v. Lakeside School, 2007 WL 2745367 (W.D. Wash. 2007).

7:9.   NLRB's assessment of computer use policies

The NLRB has generally found certain limitations upon employees' use of communications systems to be valid.[79] However, where personal use is permitted, the NLRB has, at least in part, rejected employer's attempts to block union activity on e-mail.[80] However, where only charitable activity is permitted, union activity may be in certain cases blocked.[81]

7:10.   Other employee e-mail issues

One of the challenges frequently facing employers is when they can monitor employees e-mail communications. In most cases courts have found that this monitoring of employees is proper. First, there are a number of cases that hold that the review of stored communications is proper because employers do not offer service to the "public" and are therefore not subject to many of the restrictions.[82]

In *Andersen Consulting LLP v. UOP and Bickel & Brewer*,[83] the court addressed whether a company could review and disclose stored electronic communications—that is, e-mails—without violating the ECPA. Andersen was hired to perform consulting work for UOP and was eventually terminated.[84] UOP disclosed the contents of Andersen's e-mails on UOP's system. Andersen argued that this disclosure violated § 2702's restrictions. Andersen argued that § 2702 applied because UOP provided electronic communications service *to the public* when it gave Andersen e-mail service as part of the contract. Noting that the access granted Andersen was the same as granted to UOP's employees, the court rejected this argument, noting that § 2702 only applied to an entity that provided service to the public and that this service was not offered to the public at large.[85] The court also rejected Andersen's argument that the access was to the public because Andersen could communicate with third-parties. It also rejected Andersen's arguments because UOP did not independently provide Internet services because it purchased access from an Internet service provider.[86]

This result also seems correct for other reasons. In many cases, employers are reviewing stored communications in order to prevent or detect illegal acts, including violations of the CFAA or the theft of trade secrets. This also should permit the review of stored communications, particularly if there is a policy in place regarding these issues. Moreover, many cases have held that employees using their employer's e-mail system have no expectation of privacy and the review and monitoring of communications is therefore permitted.

---

79.   Mid Mountain Foods, Inc., 332 NLRB No. 19, slip op. at 2 (2000); The Guard Publishing Co., 351 NLRB No. 70 (December 16, 2007).

80.   The Guard Publishing Co., 351 NLRB No. 70 (December 16, 2007).

81.   *Id.*

82.   *See* Conner, 130 F. Supp. at 1377 (holding that the restrictions of 2702 limiting disclosure of stored communications are inapplicable to an employer who provides interoffice e-mail because it is not an electronic communication service to the "public").

83.   Andersen Consulting LLP v. UOP, 991 F. Supp. 1041 (N.D. Ill. 1998).

84.   *Id.,* at 1041.

85.   *Id.,* at 1042.

86.   *Id.,* at 1043.

This approach has been adopted by California courts. In one of the few published decisions in California regarding employee e-mail and privacy, a California court permitted e-mail monitoring of employees where the employee had acknowledged and agreed to a monitoring policy as part of an employee handbook.[87] Citing the California constitutional right to privacy, as well as California Supreme Court authorities, the court noted the strong privacy protections granted to California citizens, but ultimately concluded that the waiver of these protections via an employee handbook would be enforced.[88] Also, in an unpublished decision, the Second Appellate District of the California Court of Appeal addressed this issue in *Shoars v. Epson America, Inc.*,[89] when it interpreted California's then current version of the Wiretap Act. Ultimately, the court concluded that the monitoring system Epson had put in place, which included the monitoring and downloading of employee e-mail, did not violate California's wiretap law.

The Second Appellate District reached a similar conclusion in an unpublished 1993 case, also involving employee e-mails. The defendant had reviewed certain employee e-mails and determined that they were of a personal and non-business related nature and could be deemed offensive. The employees at issue had received unsatisfactory reviews and eventually filed a grievance based upon the fact that the defendant had invaded their privacy by reviewing and reading their e-mail messages. The court rejected the plaintiffs' claims, noting that they had signed a computer user registration form that informed users that computers were to be used only for business purposes. Moreover, one of the plaintiffs had learned from her coworkers that e-mail messages were monitored by the defendant, though this does not appear to have been in writing. The court rejected the plaintiffs' claims finding that based upon these facts there could be no reasonable expectation of privacy. It also rejected a claim under California Penal Code section 631 *et seq.*, since the monitoring was based upon the access that the defendant normally had to its systems, not a "cap." Moreover, the court also noted that the e-mail messages were retrieved from storage, not while they were on the wire, thereby dooming the 631 claim.

A similar issue was addressed by court in the Eastern District of Pennsylvania in *Smyth v. Pillsbury Co.*[90] In this case, the defendant allegedly informed all of its employees that all e-mail communications would remain "confidential and privileged." The defendant also stated that e-mail communications could not be intercepted and used against the defendants' employees as grounds for a termination or reprimand. The plaintiff sent e-mails to his supervisor, and the defendant at some point intercepted these e-mails, and then notified the plaintiff that his employment was being terminated for transmitting inappropriate and unprofessional comments over the e-mail system.

The court rejected any claim of privacy, finding that by transmitting the e-mails to a third party—his supervisor—the plaintiff lost any reasonable expectation of privacy, even considering the assurances made by the defendant regarding the privacy of the communications. The court also held that even if an employee could have a reasonable expectation of privacy in the contents of e-mail communications, the interception of

---

87.   TBG Ins. Services Corp. v. Superior Court, 96 Cal. App. 4th 443, 117 Cal. Rptr. 2d 155 (2d Dist. 2002).

88.   *Id.,* at 451-53.

89.   *Shoars v. Epson America, Inc.,* No. B 073234 (Cal. App. 2nd Dist. 1994) (unpublished opinion).

90.   Smyth v. Pillsbury Co., 914 F. Supp. 97 (E.D. Pa. 1996).

these e-mails would not be substantial and highly offensive. As such, the court dismissed the plaintiff's case.

There are two states that do restrict the monitoring of employee e-mails in ways that are somewhat unique. In Connecticut, any employer[91] who engages in any type of electronic monitoring[92] must give prior written notice to all employees[93] who may be affected, informing them of the types of monitoring that may occur. Employers must also post, in a conspicuous place that is readily available for viewing by its employees, a notice concerning the types of electronic monitoring that the employer may engage in. This posting satisfies the disclosure requirements.[94] However, these requirements do not apply if the employer has reasonable grounds to believe that employees are engaged in conduct that (i) violates the law, (ii) violates the legal rights of the employer or the employer's employees, or (iii) creates a hostile workplace environment; in such cases, the employer may monitor without prior written notice, if the electronic monitoring may produce evidence of this misconduct.[95] These requirements do not apply to a criminal investigation, and any information obtained in the course of a criminal investigation through the use of electronic monitoring may be used in a disciplinary proceeding against an employee.[96]

The Connecticut Labor Commissioner can request civil penalties for violation of this law in a maximum amount of $500 for the first violation, $1,000 for the second offense, and $3,000 for any subsequent offense.[97]

Delaware also has restricted the monitoring of employee e-mail. It is improper in Delaware for an employer,[98] or any agent or any representative of any employer, to monitor or otherwise intercept any telephone conversation or transmission, electronic mail or transmission, or Internet access or usage of or by a Delaware employee unless the employer either:

> (1) Provides an electronic notice of such monitoring or intercepting policies or activities to the employee at least once during each day the employee accesses the employer-provided e-mail or Internet access services; or

---

91. "Employer" means any person, firm or corporation, including the state and any political subdivision of the state which has employees. Conn. Gen. Stat. § 31-48d(a)(1).

92. "Electronic monitoring" means the collection of information on an employer's premises concerning employees' activities or communications by any means other than direct observation, including the use of a computer, telephone, wire, radio, camera, electromagnetic, photoelectronic or photo-optical systems, but not including the collection of information (A) for security purposes in common areas of the employer's premises which are held out for use by the public, or (B) which is prohibited under state or federal law. Conn. Gen. Stat. § 31-48d(a)(3).

93. "Employee" means any person who performs services for an employer in a business of the employer, if the employer has the right to control and direct the person as to (A) the result to be accomplished by the services, and (B) the details and means by which such result is accomplished. Conn. Gen. Stat. § 31-48d(a)(2).

94. Conn. Gen. Stat. § 31-48d(b)(1).

95. Conn. Gen. Stat. § 31-48d(b)(2).

96. Conn. Gen. Stat. § 31-48d(d).

97. Conn. Gen. Stat. § 31-48d(c).

98. As used in this section, "employer" includes any individual, corporation, partnership, firm or association with a place of business in Delaware and the State of Delaware or any agency or political subdivision thereof. Del. Code Ann. tit. 19 § 705(a).

(2) Has first given a 1-time notice to the employee of such monitoring or intercepting activity or policies. The notice required by this paragraph shall be in writing, in an electronic record, or in another electronic form and acknowledged by the employee either in writing or electronically.[99]

This law does not apply to processes that are designed to manage the type or volume of incoming or outgoing electronic mail or telephone voice mail or Internet usage, that are not targeted to monitor or intercept the electronic mail or telephone voice mail or Internet usage of a particular individual, and that are performed solely for the purpose of computer system maintenance or protection.[100]

Violation of this law gives rise to liability for a civil penalty of $100 per violation, and/or other permitted remedies.[101] However, violations of this law by an employer will not be admitted into evidence for the purpose of, or used as, a defense to criminal liability of any person.[102]

An issue that is becoming more commonly encountered in employee monitoring cases is whether monitoring of employee accessed e-mail accounts that are not based on the employer's server can be done without violating the ECPA. The courts that have considered this issue have questioned whether this violates the Stored Communications Act and have, at least in one case, let the matter proceed past summary judgment.[103] Other courts, even when they have affirmed the principle that employees do not have a reasonable expectation of privacy in shared or work computers, have held that employees do have a reasonable expectation of privacy in web-based e-mail programs that are not provided by their employer, apparently even if they are accessed on the employer's network.[104]

Finally, certain courts have drawn a distinction between privacy rights and attorney-client privilege and have held that review of privileged e-mails may not be proper in certain circumstances, particularly if a monitoring policy is not followed.

7:11.   Employee privacy

Indeed, employees have been held to have reasonable privacy expectations in company cell phones. This is particularly true where personal use is permitted and the employee therefore maintained a property interest in the phone, had a right to exclude others from using the phone, demonstrated a subjective expectation of privacy, and took normal precautions to maintain his privacy in the phone.[105]

---

99.   Del. Code Ann. tit. 19 § 705(b).

100. Del. Code Ann. tit. 19 § 705(e).

101. Del. Code Ann. tit. 19 § 705(c) to (d).

102. *Id.*

103. Fischer v. Mt. Olive Lutheran Church, 207 F. Supp. 2d 914, 925 (W.D. Wis. 2002). *See also* Sims v. Lakeside School, 2007 WL 2745367 (W.D. Wash. 2007).

104. Wilson v. Moreau, 440 F. Supp. 2d 81 (D.R.I. 2006), aff'd, 492 F.3d 50 (1st Cir. 2007).

105. U.S. v. Finley, 477 F.3d 250, 72 Fed. R. Evid. Serv. 377 (5th Cir. 2007), cert. denied, 127 S. Ct. 2065, 167 L. Ed. 2d 790 (U.S. 2007).

One other issue that courts have addressed in the employee context is whether an employee has a right of privacy in a computer that he brings to work and uses for work purposes.[106] In *Barrows*, the defendant brought his private computer to work, used file-sharing software, and frequently worked on that computer. He also put his personal computer on the employer's network. Most importantly, he did not have any password protection on his computer, and since his office was not private, anyone could have accessed his computer. Under these facts, the Tenth Circuit concluded that the defendant did not have a reasonable expectation of privacy.[107]

While it arises in the union context, which is subject to different scrutiny under the NLRA, other courts have held that the non-enforcement of a company's e-mail policy may impact its ability to preclude certain forms of communications.[108]

7:12.   Personal use of systems

One issue that seems to be an important factor in monitoring situations, particularly when the attorney-client privilege is implicated, is whether personal use of electronic systems is expressly prohibited. As discussed in this chapter, the analysis in certain cases hinges on whether employers have expressly stated that personal use is not permitted.

In certain cases in California, courts have found some expectation, even if not an absolute expectation, of privacy in a locked office, even where others had keys and there was an explicit policy stating that individuals could be monitored at the employer's facility.[109]

However, there are a number of cases that support a finding of no employee privacy.[110]

7:13.   Videotaping in workplace—Generally

In *Nelson v. Salem State College*, the Supreme Judicial Court of Massachusetts addressed whether an employee's right of privacy was violated due to videotaping in the work place. Video surveillance equipment was operated full-time and the plaintiff was unknowingly videotaped.[111] The court examined the plaintiff's expectation of privacy under the federal constitution and concluded that the plaintiff had an expectation of privacy that was expressed by her conduct, but that, given the general lack of privacy in the workplace, the expectation was not reasonable.[112] In light of this, the plaintiff had no expectation of privacy that could serve as a basis to object to the videotaping of the workplace.

---

106. U.S. v. Barrows, 481 F.3d 1246 (10th Cir. 2007).

107. Barrows, 481 F.3d 1246.

108. Media General Operations, Incorporated v. NLRB, 06-1023 (4th Cir. 2007) (unpublished).

109. Hernandez v. Hillsides, Inc., 48 Cal. Rptr. 3d 780 (Cal. App. 2d Dist. 2006), review granted and opinion superseded, 53 Cal. Rptr. 3d 801, 150 P.3d 692 (Cal. 2007); *see also* Sanders v. American Broadcasting Companies, Inc., 20 Cal. 4th 907, 85 Cal. Rptr. 2d 909, 978 P.2d 67 (1999).

110. Garrity v. John Hancock Mut. Life Ins. Co., 18 I.E.R. Cas. (BNA) 981, 146 Lab. Cas. (CCH) P 59541, 2002 WL 974676 (D. Mass. 2002); McLaren v. Microsoft Corp., 1999 WL 339015 (Tex. App. Dallas 1999).

111. Nelson v. Salem State College, 446 Mass. 525, 845 N.E.2d 338 (2006).

112. Nelson, 446 Mass. 533-534; *see also* Vega-Rodriguez v. Puerto Rico Telephone Co., 110 F.3d 174, 178 (1st Cir. 1997).

The court in *Hernandez v. Hillsides, Inc.*, considered whether a plaintiff had to prove that there was actual viewing of footage from a surveillance camera in order for a plaintiff to state a claim for invasion of privacy. This case involved two employees who occupied an office in which a camera had been installed. The evidence demonstrated that their employer had never viewed a videotape of them, because the camera, which had transmission capabilities, only transmitted after normal business hours, when the plaintiffs were not there. The court of appeal held that intrusion alone, even without actual viewing or recording, could serve as the basis of a claim and denied summary judgment for the defendant.[113]

While many cases have found videotaping to be problematic in certain circumstances, particularly if not disclosed, the NLRB found that union employees who were wrongfully videotaped had no remedy for the violation, even though some were fired based upon the misconduct that the videotaping demonstrated.[114]

In *Doe v. Dearborn Public Schools*, the district court addressed the appropriate scope of videotaping in a workplace.[115] In *Doe*, a school official placed a hidden video camera in a staff office that was located inside, but separated from, the male locker room at a high school. This was allegedly done to try to determine who had been committing theft in the locker room. The camera was ultimately discovered, and employees of the school complained regarding its presence. The plaintiffs in the case brought a number of claims including violation of their constitutional rights and common law claims, as well as others. In assessing whether the plaintiffs had a reasonable expectation of privacy, the court first examined the *Katz* matter[116] stating that a person had a reasonable expectation of privacy when the individual has manifested a subjective expectation of privacy in the object of the challenged search and society is willing to recognize that expectation as reasonable. In assessing the first prong of this test the court typically considers "what a person had an expectation of privacy in, for example, a home, office, phone booth or airplane."[117]

The court also noted that the Supreme Court has recognized that there are reasonable expectations of privacy even in a shared office.[118] In this case, though the plaintiffs did not engage in certain private activities in the locker room, including changing clothes (as other cases have focused on), the court still found that there was a reasonable expectation of privacy since the individuals were given exclusive use of the office. The court did note that certain use of video cameras might have been appropriate but indicated that the use in this case was overbroad.

---

113. Hernandez v. Hillsides, Inc., 48 Cal. Rptr. 3d 780 (Cal. App. 2d Dist. 2006), review granted and opinion superseded, 53 Cal. Rptr. 3d 801, 150 P.3d 692 (Cal. 2007); citing Harkey v. Abate, 131 Mich.App. 177 (1984); Carter v. Innisfree Hotel, Inc., 661 So. 2d 1174 (Ala. 1995); Hamberger v. Eastman, 106 N.H. 107, 206 A.2d 239, 11 A.L.R.3d 1288 (1964).

114. Anheuser-Busch, Inc. and Brewers and Maltsters, Local Union No. 6, affiliated with International Brotherhood of Teamsters, Case-14-CA-25299, September 29, 2007.

115. Doe v. Dearborn Public Schools, 2:06-CV-12369-DPH-RSW (E.D.Mich. March 31, 2008).

116. Katz v. U.S., 389 U.S. 347, 351, 88 S. Ct. 507 (1967).

117. Dow Chemical Co. v. United States, 749 F.2d 307, 312 (6th Cir. 1984); *see also* Oliver v. United States, 466 U.S. 170, 178 (1984).

118. O'Connor v. Ortega, 480 U.S. 709, 715-17 (1987).

CHAPTER 8

Controlling the Assault of Non-Solicited Pornography and Marketing Act (CAN-SPAM)

8:1. Overview

CAN-SPAM, or the Controlling the Assault of Non-Solicited Pornography and Marketing Act of 2003, was passed due to the legislative reaction to certain state e-mail laws, California's in particular. These state laws went far beyond what the federal government was willing to do, so CAN-SPAM was passed with the goal of preempting (in essence nullifying) the troublesome portions of state law. CAN-SPAM was not initially well received, though the criticism seems to have died down in recent times. The main criticism of CAN-SPAM is that it does not explicitly prohibit unsolicited e-mails. Despite this perceived shortcoming, CAN-SPAM has increased the FTC's ability to stop spam. States at this point seem to be taking a back seat to the FTC on these issues, though state-based e-mail actions still occur.

CAN-SPAM, like the Do-Not-Call and do-not-fax laws, has privacy implications, in addition to restricting marketing. CAN-SPAM almost exclusively regulates senders of e-mail that is "commercial" or is a "transactional or relationship message." Thus, one of the first issues in assessing the requirements of CAN-SPAM is to determine whether an e-mail is a "commercial" e-mail or it is a "transactional or relationship message."

A commercial e-mail is one that has as its primary purpose commercial advertisement and/or the promotion of a commercial product or service.[1]

A transactional or relationship message is one that

- facilitates, completes, or confirms a commercial transaction that the recipient has previously agreed to enter into with the sender;
- provides warranty information, product recall information, or safety or security information with respect to a commercial product or service used or purchased by the recipient;
- provides, for subscriptions, memberships, accounts, loans, or comparable ongoing commercial relationships involving the ongoing purchase or use by the recipient of products or services offered by the sender
    - o notification concerning a change in the terms or features,
    - o notification of a change in the recipient's standing or status, or
    - o at regular periodic intervals, account balance information or other type of account statement;
- provides information directly related to an employment relationship or related benefit plan in which the recipient is currently involved, participating, or enrolled; or
- delivers goods or services, including product updates or upgrades, that the recipient is entitled to receive under the terms of a transaction that the recipient has previously agreed to enter into with the sender.[2]

While there are limited categories to qualify as a transactional or relationship message, some portions of the law are read broadly. At least at the pleading stage, one court held that messages that fall within the "directly related to an employment relationship or related benefit plan..." exception do not have to be sent by the employer.[3]

8:2.   Defining an internet access service

Part of the definitional challenge of CAN-SPAM is finding out who an Internet Access Service is, because those entities have standing to bring a civil action for violation of CAN-SPAM. Generally speaking, an IAS is considered to be synonymous with an ISP though the definition refers to 47 U.S.C.A § 231(e)(4), which defines an IAS as "a service that enables users to access content, information, electronic mail, or other services offered over the internet and may also include access to proprietary content, information, and other services as part of a package of services offered to consumers. Such term does not include telecommunication services." When courts consider whether an entity is an IAS, the issue of whether internet access is provided is not a conclusive factor. If an entity provides "further" access, including entities such as Facebook,[4] the

---

1.   15 U.S.C. § 7702(2)(a).
2.   15 U.S.C. § 7702(17); 16 C.F.R. § 316.3(b).
3.   Aitken v. Communications Workers of America, 496 F. Supp. 2d 653, 666 (E.D. Va. 2007).
4.   Facebook, Inc. v. Connect U LLC, 489 F.Supp.2d 1087, 1094 (D. Cal. 2007).

entity will likely have standing to pursue a claim under CAN-SPAM.[5] This definition
was recently reaffirmed in *Haselton v. Quicken Loans, Inc.*[6]

8:3.   Primary purpose

The FTC has issued rules regarding the definition of "primary purpose," a phrase which
is key to determining whether an e-mail is a commercial e-mail and therefore subject
to many of the CAN-SPAM requirements. In determining whether an e-mail's "primary
purpose" is commercial or not, there are several different scenarios to consider. The
clearest scenario is where an e-mail consists exclusively of the commercial advertisement
or promotion of a commercial product or service. If this is the case, then the "primary
purpose" of the message is deemed to be commercial.[7]

If an electronic mail message contains both the commercial advertisement or
promotion of a commercial product or service and transactional or relationship content,
then the "primary purpose" of the message is considered commercial if (i) a recipient
reasonably interpreting the subject line of the e-mail message would likely conclude
that the e-mail contains the commercial advertisement or promotion of a commercial
product or service; or (ii) the e-mail's transactional or relationship content does not
appear, in whole or in substantial part, at the beginning of the body of the message.[8]

A third scenario is where an e-mail contains commercial content and content that
is neither commercial nor transactional or relationship oriented. Under this scenario,
the "primary purpose" of the e-mail will be deemed to be commercial if (i) A recipient
reasonably interpreting the subject line of the e-mail would likely conclude that the
message contains the commercial advertisement or promotion of a commercial product
or service; or (ii) a recipient reasonably interpreting the body of the e-mail would likely
conclude that the primary purpose of the e-mail is the commercial advertisement or
promotion of a commercial product or service.[9] Issues to be considered in assessing these
factors include the relative placement of the content that is the commercial advertisement
or promotion of a commercial product or service, (i.e., at the beginning of the body of
the message); the proportion of the message dedicated to commercial content; and how
color, graphics, type size, and style are used to highlight commercial content.[10]

Under the rules, it should be noted that in applying the term "commercial electronic
mail message,"[11] as defined in CAN-SPAM the "primary purpose" of an electronic
mail message will be deemed to be commercial based on the criteria in paragraphs (a)
(1) through (a)(3) and (b) of the rules, but these criteria do not include anything that

---

5.   *See also*, MySpace, Inc. v. The Globe.com, Inc., 2007 WL 1686966 (C.D. Cal. 2007) (broadly defining an
     IAS to include traditional ISPs, email providers and even most website owners).

6.   Haselton v. Quicken Loans, Inc., 2008 WL 4585314 (W.D. Wash. 2008).

7.   16 C.F.R. § 316.3(a)(1).

8.   16 C.F.R. § 316.3(a)(2).

9.   16 C.F.R. § 316.3(a)(3).

10. 16 C.F.R. § 316.3(a)(3)(ii).

11. The definition of the term "commercial electronic mail message" is the same as the definition of that term in
     the CAN-SPAM Act, 15 U.S.C. § 7702(2). 16 C.F.R. § 316.2(c). The definition of the term "electronic mail
     message" is the same as the definition of that term in the CAN-SPAM Act, 15 U.S.C. § 7702(6). 16 C.F.R.
     § 316.2(e).

is not commercial speech as commercial electronic mail messages.[12] If an electronic mail message consists exclusively of the commercial advertisement or promotion of a commercial product or service, then the "primary purpose" of the message is deemed to be commercial.[13] If an electronic mail message contains both the commercial advertisement or promotion of a commercial product or service as well as transactional or relationship content (as set forth below), then the "primary purpose" of the message is deemed to be commercial if (1) a recipient[14] reasonably interpreting the subject line of the electronic mail message would likely conclude that the message contains the commercial advertisement or promotion of a commercial product or service or (2) the electronic mail message's transactional or relationship content as set forth below does not appear, in whole or in substantial part, at the beginning of the body of the message.[15] If an electronic mail message contains both the commercial advertisement or promotion of a commercial product or service as well as other content that is not transactional or relationship content as set forth below, then the "primary purpose" of the message is deemed to be commercial if (1) a recipient reasonably interpreting the subject line of the electronic mail message would likely conclude that the message contains the commercial advertisement or promotion of a commercial product or service or (2) a recipient reasonably interpreting the body of the message would likely conclude that the primary purpose of the message is the commercial advertisement or promotion of a commercial product or service.[16] Relevant factors to this interpretation include the placement of content that is the commercial advertisement or promotion of a commercial product or service, in whole or in substantial part, at the beginning of the body of the message and the proportion of the message dedicated to such content, as well as how color, graphics, type size, and style are used to highlight commercial content.[17]

One of the issues that many companies face is whether an e-mail is "commercial." Courts, relying upon the regulations, have defined a commercial e-mail consistent with the meaning of "commercial" under the First Amendment.[18]

Certain other entities have argued that their not-for-profit status makes the e-mails they send inherently non-commercial. This argument has been rejected by courts.[19]

In applying the term "transactional or relationship message,"[20] the "primary purpose" of an electronic mail message is deemed to be transactional or relationship if the electronic mail message consists exclusively of transactional or relationship content, which is content to facilitate, complete, or confirm a commercial transaction

---

12. 16 C.F.R. § 316.3(a).

13. 16 C.F.R. § 316.3(a)(1).

14. The definition of the term "recipient" is the same as the definition of that term in the CAN-SPAM Act, 15 U.S.C. § 7702(14). 16 C.F.R. § 316.2(j).

15. 16 C.F.R. §§ 316.3(a)(2)(i)–(ii).

16. 16 C.F.R. §§ 316.3(a)(3)(i)–(ii).

17. 16 C.F.R. § 316.3(a)(3).

18. Aitken v. Communications Workers of America, 496 F. Supp. 2d 653, 662 (E.D. Va. 2007).

19. *Id.* at 663.

20. The definition of the term "transactional or relationship message" is the same as the definition of that term in the CAN-SPAM Act, 15 U.S.C. § 7702(17). 16 C.F.R. § 316.2(n).

that the recipient has previously agreed to enter into with the sender;[21] to provide warranty information, product recall information, or safety or security information with respect to a commercial product or service used or purchased by the recipient; to provide information directly related to an employment relationship or related benefit plan in which the recipient is currently involved, participating, or enrolled; to deliver goods or services, including product updates or upgrades, that the recipient is entitled to receive under the terms of a transaction that the recipient has previously agreed to enter into with the sender; or with respect to a subscription, membership, account, loan, or comparable ongoing commercial relationship involving the ongoing purchase or use by the recipient of products or services offered by the sender, to provide notification concerning a change in the terms or features, notification of a change in the recipient's standing or status, or at regular periodic intervals, account balance information or other type of account statement.[22]

8:4.   New CAN-SPAM rules

The FTC recently issued new rules regarding CAN-SPAM that address some of the open issues and also alter the primary purpose rules. The new rules attempt to clarify the definitions of "sender" and "person," verify that a post office box is permissible for the "valid physical postal address," and restrict conditions on opt-outs.

The new rules contain a definition of "primary purpose," a phase which is key to determining whether an e-mail is a commercial e-mail and therefore subject to many of the CAN-SPAM requirements. In applying the term "commercial electronic mail message"[23] defined in the CAN-SPAM Act, the "primary purpose" of an electronic mail message will be deemed to be commercial based on criteria set forth in the regulations.[24] If an electronic mail message consists exclusively of the commercial advertisement or promotion of a commercial product or service, then the "primary purpose" of the message will be deemed to be commercial.[25] If an electronic mail message contains both the commercial advertisement or promotion of a commercial product or service as well as transactional or relationship content, then the "primary purpose" of the message shall be deemed to be commercial if a recipient[26] reasonably interpreting the subject line of the electronic mail message would likely conclude that the message contains the commercial advertisement or promotion of a commercial product or service; or the electronic mail message's transactional or relationship content does not appear, in whole or in substantial part, at the beginning of the body of the message.[27]

---

21. The definition of the term "sender" is the same as the definition of that term in the CAN-SPAM Act, 15 U.S.C. 7702(16). 16 C.F.R. § 316.2(l).

22. 16 C.F.R. §§ 316.3(b)–(c)(5).

23. The definition of the term "commercial electronic mail message" is the same as the definition of that term in the CAN-SPAM Act, 15 U.S.C. § 7702(2). 16 C.F.R. § 316.2(c). The definition of the term "electronic mail message" is the same as the definition of that term in the CAN-SPAM Act, 15 U.S.C. § 7702(6). 16 C.F.R. § 316.2(e).

24. 16 C.F.R. § 316.3(a).

25. 16 C.F.R. § 316.3(a)(1).

26. The definition of the term "recipient" is the same as the definition of that term in the CAN-SPAM Act, 15 U.S.C. § 7702(14). 16 C.F.R. § 316.2(k).

27. 16 C.F.R. §§ 316.3(a)(2)(i)–(ii).

If an electronic mail message contains both the commercial advertisement or promotion of a commercial product or service as well as other content that is not transactional or relationship content, then the "primary purpose" of the message is deemed to be commercial if a recipient reasonably interpreting the subject line of the electronic mail message would likely conclude that the message contains the commercial advertisement or promotion of a commercial product or service; or a recipient reasonably interpreting the body of the message would likely conclude that the primary purpose of the message is the commercial advertisement or promotion of a commercial product or service. Factors illustrative of those relevant to this interpretation include the placement of content that is the commercial advertisement or promotion of a commercial product or service, in whole or in substantial part, at the beginning of the body of the message; the proportion of the message dedicated to such content; and how color, graphics, type size, and style are used to highlight commercial content.[28]

It should be noted that the FTC does not intend for these criteria to treat as a "commercial electronic mail message" anything that is not commercial speech.

In applying the term "transactional or relationship message"[29] defined in the CAN-SPAM Act, 15 U.S.C.A. § 7702(17), the "primary purpose" of an electronic mail message shall be deemed to be transactional or relationship if the electronic mail message consists exclusively of transactional or relationship content.[30] Transactional or relationship content of e-mail messages under the CAN-SPAM Act is content to facilitate, complete, or confirm a commercial transaction that the recipient has previously agreed to enter into with the sender;[31] to provide warranty information, product recall information, or safety or security information with respect to a commercial product or service used or purchased by the recipient; with respect to a subscription, membership, account, loan, or comparable ongoing commercial relationship involving the ongoing purchase or use by the recipient of products or services offered by the sender, to provide notification concerning a change in the terms or features; notification of a change in the recipient's standing or status; or at regular periodic intervals, account balance information or other type of account statement; to provide information directly related to an employment relationship or related benefit plan in which the recipient is currently involved, participating, or enrolled; or to deliver goods or services, including product updates or upgrades, that the recipient is entitled to receive under the terms of a transaction that the recipient has previously agreed to enter into with the sender.[32]

---

28. 16 C.F.R. §§ 316.3(a)(3)(i)–(ii).

29. The definition of the term "transactional or relationship messages" is the same as the definition of that term in the CAN-SPAM Act, 15 U.S.C. § 7702(17). 16 C.F.R. § 316.2(o).

30. 16 C.F.R. § 316.3(b).

31. The definition of the term "sender" is the same as the definition of that term in the CANSPAM Act, 15 U.S.C. § 7702(16), provided that, when more than one person's products, services, or Internet website are advertised or promoted in a single electronic mail message, each such person who is within the Act's definition will be deemed to be a "sender," except that, only one person will be deemed to be the "sender" of that message if such person: (A) is within the Act's definition of "sender"; (B) is identified in the "from" line as the sole sender of the message; and (C) is in compliance with 15 U.S.C. § 7704(a)(1), 15 U.S.C. § 7704(a)(2), 15 U.S.C. § 7704(a)(3)(A)(i), 15 U.S.C. § 7704(a)(5)(A), and 16 C.F.R. § 316.4. 16 C.F.R. § 316.2(m).

32. 16 C.F.R. §§ 316.3(c)(1)–(5).

8:5.   New CAN-SPAM rules—Prohibition on charging a fee or placing other requirements on recipients who wish to opt out

Neither a sender nor any person[33] acting on behalf of a sender may require that any recipient pay any fee, provide any information other than the recipient's electronic mail address[34] and opt-out preferences, or take any other steps except sending a reply electronic mail message or visiting a single Internet[35] Web page, in order to use a return electronic mail address or other Internet-based mechanism, required by 15 U.S.C.A. § 7704(a)(3), to submit a request not to receive future commercial electronic mail messages from a sender; or (b) have such a request honored as required by 15 U.S.C.A. § 7704(a)(3)(B) and (a)(4).[36]

8:6.   New CAN-SPAM rules—Sexually oriented e-mails and labeling

Any person who initiates,[37] to a protected computer,[38] the transmission of a commercial electronic mail message that includes sexually oriented material[39] must exclude sexually oriented materials from the subject heading for the electronic mail message and include in the subject heading the phrase "SEXUALLY-EXPLICIT:"[40] in capital letters as the first nineteen (19) characters at the beginning of the subject line and provide that the content of the message that is initially viewable by the recipient, when the message is opened by any recipient and absent any further actions by the recipient, include only the following information: the phrase "SEXUALLY-EXPLICIT:" in a clear and conspicuous manner; clear and conspicuous identification that the message is an advertisement or solicitation; clear and conspicuous notice of the opportunity of a recipient to decline to receive further commercial electronic mail messages from the sender; a functioning return electronic mail address or other Internet-based mechanism, clearly and conspicuously displayed, that a recipient may use to submit, in a manner specified in the message, a reply electronic mail message or other form of Internet-based communication requesting

---

33. "Person" means any individual, group, unincorporated association, limited or general partnership, corporation, or other business entity. 16 C.F.R. § 316.2(h).

34. The definition of the term "electronic mail address" is the same as the definition of that term in the CAN-SPAM Act, 15 U.S.C. § 7702(5). 16 C.F.R. § 316.2(d).

35. The definition of the term "Internet" is the same as the definition of that term in the CANSPAM Act, 15 U.S.C. § 7702(10). 16 C.F.R. § 316.2(g).

36. 16 C.F.R. §§ 316.4(a)–(b).

37. The definition of the term "initiate" is the same as the definition of that term in the CANSPAM Act, 15 U.S.C. § 7702(9). 16 C.F.R. § 316.2(f).

38. The definition of the term "protected computer" is the same as the definition of that term in the CAN-SPAM Act, 15 U.S.C. § 7702(13). 16 C.F.R. § 316.2(j).

39. The definition of the term "sexually oriented material" is the same as the definition of that term in the CAN-SPAM Act, 15 U.S.C. § 7704(d)(4). 16 C.F.R. § 316.2(n).

40. The phrase "SEXUALLY-EXPLICIT" comprises 17 characters, including the dash between the two words. The colon (:) and the space following the phrase are the 18 and 19th characters. This phrase consists of nineteen (19) characters and is identical to the phrase required in 316.5(a)(1) of this Rule. "Character" means an element of the American Standard Code for Information Interchange ("ASCII") character set. 16 C.F.R. § 316.2(b).

not to receive future commercial electronic mail messages from that sender at the electronic mail address where the message was received. The address or Internet-based mechanism must remain capable of receiving such messages or communications for no less than 30 days after the transmission of the original message.[41]

It must also contain a clear and conspicuous display of a valid physical postal address[42] of the sender; and any needed instructions on how to access, or activate a mechanism to access, the sexually oriented material, preceded by a clear and conspicuous statement that to avoid viewing the sexually oriented material, a recipient should delete the e-mail message without following such instructions.[43]

These requirements do not apply to the transmission of an electronic mail message if the recipient has given prior affirmative consent[44] to receipt of the message.[45]

8:7.   Defining senders of e-mail

Defining who is a "sender" of e-mail is important because CAN-SPAM almost exclusively regulates senders of e-mail. A sender of a commercial e-mail is one who initiates such a message and whose product, service, or Internet website is advertised or promoted by the message.[46] Moreover, if a company operates separate divisions or lines of business but holds itself out as, in essence, one business, the company itself will be treated as the sender of such message for purposes of CAN-SPAM.[47]

Initiating a message means to originate or transmit such message or to procure the origination or transmission of such message, but does not include actions that constitute routine conveyance of such message. It is worth noting that more than one person can be found to have initiated a message.[48] As noted above, the new CAN-SPAM rules contain a new definition of "sender" with attempts to address these perceived ambiguities.

8:8.   Affiliate issues and defining a "sender"

One of the issues that many companies have struggled with is who is a sender of e-mail. One of the first cases to address this issue in the context of the affiliate context was *U.S. v. Cyberheat, Inc.*[49] In this case, the FTC brought an enforcement action against a company that used an affiliate marketing program to promote its adult-oriented website. The FTC brought an enforcement action seeking injunctive relief against Cyberheat, claiming that it was vicariously liable for the violations of the adult-oriented labeling

---

41.   16 C.F.R. §§ 316.4(a)(1)–(2)(iv).

42.   "Valid physical postal address" means the sender's current street address, a post office box the sender has accurately registered with the United States Postal Service, or a private mailbox the sender has accurately registered with a commercial mail receiving agency that is established pursuant to United States Postal Service regulations. 16 C.F.R. § 316.2(p).

43.   16 C.F.R. § 316.4(a)(1)–(2)(vi).

44.   The definition of the term "affirmative consent" is the same as the definition of that term in the CAN-SPAM Act, 15 U.S.C. § 7702(1). 16 C.F.R. § 316.2(a).

45.   16 C.F.R. § 316.4(b).

46.   15 U.S.C. § 7702(16)(A).

47.   15 U.S.C. § 7702(16)(B).

48.   15 U.S.C. § 7702(9).

49.   U.S. v. Cyberheat, Inc., 2007-1 Trade Cas. (CCH) &p;75635, 2007 WL 686678 (D. Ariz. 2007).

requirement.[50] The court noted that given the content at issue, Cyberheat had a duty to ensure compliance with the requirements regarding sexually explicit material, a duty that it could only delegate "at its own peril."[51] That said, as the court examined the issues and the FTC's claim that there was in essence strict liability for violation of CAN-SPAM, it did not rule that Cyberheat was necessarily liable for the alleged violations. Ultimately the court concluded that the two main issues to determine whether Cyberheat would be liable for the violations of its affiliates were (1) did it exert control over the affiliates and (2) did it have knowledge of the violations.[52] In this case, the court concluded that these questions were ultimately questions for the jury because the evidence, at least at the summary judgment stage, was mixed.

8:9.   Affiliates and "intent" for "senders"

U.S. v. Impulse Media Group, Inc., provided further guidance regarding the nature of liability for other's conduct under CAN-SPAM, particularly in the affiliate context.[53] In this case the court addressed the meaning of the word "intentional" as it relates to who is a sender of e-mail. The defendant ran an affiliate program that did not specifically relate to commercial e-mails, but rather was an incentive-based system that seemed more geared to websites. One of the affiliates sent e-mails that did not comply with the adult labeling rule of CAN-SPAM and an enforcement action was brought against Impulse Media Group, the company that ran the affiliate program.[54] The court noted that Impulse Media itself did not send any e-mails, but rather was alleged to have "initiated" e-mails because it procured the transmission.[55] As noted above, a party procures an e-mail under CAN-SPAM when they intentionally "... pay or provide other consideration to, or induce, another person to initiate such a message on one's behalf."[56] Impulse Media was alleged to have procured e-mails due to the largely web-based affiliate program it was running that led to the commercial e-mails being sent by affiliates. The court rejected the plaintiff's argument that CAN-SPAM amounted to a strict liability statute, but it also did not accept Impulse Marketing's argument that both intent and knowledge of the violations were required in order to obtain injunctive relief.[57] The court ultimately concluded that the intent element required "a defendant actually intend to procure commercial e-mail when it solicits another party for services."[58] Thus, under this court's holding, a party could be liable for injunctive relief if it intentionally obtained commercial e-mails, whether it had knowledge or not of the violation, but could only be liable for a criminal violation if it also knew of the

---

50. *Cyberheat*, 2007 WL 686678, at *4.

51. *Cyberheat*, 2007 WL 686678, at *5.

52. *Cyberheat*, 2007 WL 686678, at *6.

53. U.S. v. Impulse Media Group, Inc., 2007 WL 1725560 (W.D. Wash. 2007).

54. *Impulse Media Group*, 2007 WL 1725560.

55. *Impulse Media Group*, 2007 WL 1725560, at *4.

56. *Id.*, 15 U.S.C. § 7702(12).

57. *Impulse Media Group*, 2007 WL 1725560, at *4.

58. *Impulse Media Group*, 2007 WL 1725560, at *5. The court drew a distinction between this element, and the knowledge element, which it stated required some knowledge of the violation of CAN-SPAM.

violations of CAN-SPAM.[59] In this case, the court concluded that the issue of intent was one for a jury because factors weighed in both directions.[60]

8:10.   Other vicarious liability holdings

Other courts have found that a principal has no liability for the alleged spam violations of its independent contractor, particularly if there are explicit directions on how to e-mail or instructions not to e-mail.[61]

8:11.   Purchase of leads and liability

Certain courts have indicated that the purchase of improper leads from affiliates, by itself, wasn't sufficient to create liability for spamming even if the addresses were obtained though improper means.[62]

8:12.   "Procuring" e-mails, conscious avoidance, and knowledge

The Northern District of California recently addressed what it means to procure an e-mail and whether the failure to investigate affiliates rendered a company liable for their alleged spam violations. In ASIS Internet Services v. Active Response Group, 2008 WL 2952809 (N.D. Cal. 2008), the defendant was alleged to have not done much of anything to investigate its affiliate marketers, though it did have a contract that contained provisions that mandated CAN-SPAM and legal compliance.[63] In this matter the plaintiff relied upon a portion of CAN-SPAM that required actual knowledge of violations, or conscious avoidance of knowledge, in order to show that an e-mail was "procured."[64]

The court noted that there were no cases defining what "conscious avoidance" of knowledge could mean under CAN-SPAM when a defendant's knowledge was considered, so it relied upon other cases from the criminal context, using the following definition: "[w]hen knowledge of the existence of a particular fact is an element of an offense, such knowledge is established if a person is aware of a high probability of its existence, unless he actually believes it does not exist."[65] This, however, requires more than mere negligence.

---

59.   *Impulse Media Group*, 2007 WL 1725560, at *5-6.

60.   The court considered the terms of the affiliate agreement, whether the defendant actually terminated anyone for violations of the spam restrictions, the type of technology and training the defendant gave its affiliates (including the fact that e-mail marketing did not appear to be part of it), as well as the fact that the defendant did not appear to have ever paid an affiliate for e-mail marketing. *Impulse Media Group*, 2007 WL 1725560, at *5-6.

61.   Fenn v. Redmond Ventures, Inc., 101 P.3d 387 (Utah 2004).

62.   AT&T Mobility LLC v. C&C Global Enterprises, LLC, 2007 WL 2001736 (N.D. Ga. 2007).

63.   ASIS Internet Services v. Optin Global, Inc., 2008 WL 1902217 (N.D. Cal. 2008).

64.   In any action based upon 15 U.S.C. § 7706(g)(1), the plaintiff must show knowledge in order to establish that an e-mail was procured. See 15 U.S.C. § 7706(g)(2).

65.   *ASIS*, 2008 WL 1902217 at *18, citing U.S. v. Nektalov, 461 F.3d 309, 314 (2d Cir. 2006) quoting Leary v. U.S., 395 U.S. 6, 89 S. Ct. 1532, 23 L. Ed. 2d 57 (1969).

When it considered the evidence, the court concluded that there was an insufficient showing of knowledge in this case:

> The Court nevertheless finds that Plaintiff has failed to point to evidence sufficient to establish a jury question as to whether Azoogle "procured" the Emails at issue in this case under the definition discussed above. Although ASIS has pointed to significant evidence that Azoogle, during the relevant time period, did little to investigate the third party vendors it engaged, there is no evidence in the record from which a jury could conclude that Azoogle, in contracting with Seamless Media, made a deliberate choice not to know that Seamless Media would engage third parties to send out spam on Azoogle's behalf. The evidence cited by ASIS to establish knowledge on Azoogle's part is entirely speculative. Even assuming it is true that the Emails were sent by a single individual and that the lead was typed into a web site that was copied from Azoogle's lowrateadvisors site, this is insufficient to show that Azoogle consciously avoided knowing that the Emails would be sent. Further, while ASIS relies primarily on the allegation that Azoogle failed to adequately investigate its third-party vendors, ASIS has pointed to no evidence that if Azoogle had investigated Seamless Media prior to entering into the Insertion Order, it would have learned facts sufficient to show that Seamless Media was likely to engage in CAN-SPAM violations. There is no evidence in the record that would put Azoogle on notice that Seamless Media, or Seamless Media's vendors, obtained leads from spammers. Indeed, the only evidence on this subject is that Seamless Media had a good reputation at the time, and was obliged by its contract with Azoogle to follow the law.[66]

8:13. Header and subject line information

CAN-SPAM regulates the content of header information, whether or not the e-mail is a commercial e-mail or a transactional or relationship e-mail. It is illegal to send an e-mail that contains header information that is materially false or materially misleading.[67] Examples of materially false or materially misleading header information include (i) header information that is technically accurate but includes an originating e-mail address, domain name, or Internet protocol address which was obtained by means of false or fraudulent pretenses or representations, or (ii) header information that fails to identify accurately a computer used to initiate the message because the person initiating the message knowingly uses another computer to relay or retransmit the message for purposes of disguising its origin.[68]

---

66. *ASIS*, 2008 WL 1902217 at *19.

67. 15 U.S.C. § 7704(a)(1).

68. 15 U.S.C. §§ 7704(a)(1)(a)–(c).

Materially false subject lines are also regulated, but only if they are contained in commercial e-mails.[69] It is unlawful to initiate the transmission of a commercial e-mail message with actual knowledge, or knowledge fairly implied on the basis of objective circumstances, that a subject heading of the message would be reasonably likely to mislead a recipient about a material fact regarding the contents or subject matter of the message.[70]

8:14.   Use of other names in the header of an e-mail

One device many companies use in e-mail marketing is using another name in the header of an e-mail. That may be done to make the commercial nature of the e-mail clearer, or it may occur if the website permits individuals to enter names of acquaintances who they think will want to receive commercial offers, and the company truly sending the e-mail wishes to personalize the recipient's experience. One court has held that this type of conduct does not violate CAN-SPAM, if there are other accurate identifiers of the company whose products or services are being promoted.[71] Since CAN-SPAM requires material misrepresentations in the headers, technically inaccurate statements, which are in essence corrected by other accurate disclosures in the e-mails, would not appear to be actionable under CAN-SPAM.[72] This holding has been applied by other courts as well, when they have found other state's e-mail laws to be preempted.[73] This issue was also addressed in the new CAN-SPAM rules discussed above.

8:15.   Requirements of commercial e-mails

Commercial e-mails must meet three requirements. First, they must have a clear and conspicuous identification that the message is an advertisement or solicitation. Second, there must be clear and conspicuous notice of the opportunity to opt-out of future commercial e-mails, as well as the inclusion of a return address or other mechanism that allows opt-out requests.[74] Third, each commercial e-mail must contain a valid physical postal address for the sender.[75]

One of the prior ambiguities in CAN-SPAM is what is meant by a "valid physical postal address." Many businesses use post office boxes to receive mail in the regular course of their business. It has been unclear, but is now acceptable, to use a post office box as the valid physical postal address, as set forth in the new rules. If a post office box is the normal address used then it should meet the requirements of CAN-SPAM. However, if a post office box is not generally used to collect mail then the use of a special "spam" post office box might not comply.

---

69.   15 U.S.C. § 7704(a)(2).

70.   *Id.*

71.   Omega World Travel, Inc. v. Mummagraphics, 469 F.2d 348, 358 (4th Cir. 2006).

72.   *Omega World Travel, Inc.*, 469 F.2d at 358.

73.   Gordon v. Virtumundo, Inc., 2007 WL 1459395 (W.D. Wash. 2007).

74.   15 U.S.C. §§ 7704(a)(3)(a)–(b), 7704(a)(5)(A)–(B).

75.   15 U.S.C. § 7704(a)(5)(a)(iii).

In *United States v. Cyberheat, Inc.*, the FTC finally provided some guidance about what a "valid physical postal address" is.[76] The FTC stated that a "valid physical postal address" is "a sender's current street address, a Post Office box a sender has registered with the United States Postal Service, or a private mailbox a sender has registered with a commercial mail receiving agency that is established pursuant to United States Postal Service regulations." This is consistent with the new rules.

Unlike many other statutory schemes, for purely commercial e-mails, CAN-SPAM did not mandate the use of any particular characters for the "advertisement" label. As such, there is no specific requirement that the characters "ADV:" appear. While CAN-SPAM is more flexible, there is an open question as to what "clear and conspicuous identification" is. It certainly could be met by a disclosure in the subject line, but that does not, on the face of the statute, appear to be required. Burying a disclosure in small text certainly would not be clear and conspicuous, but there is no real guidance about where the disclosure must be made and what language must be used. Using the word advertising or solicitation in the same font size as the remainder of the e-mail if the disclosure occurs in the beginning of the e-mail would appear to comply with CAN-SPAM. Other disclosure schemes might work as well, but until these issues are raised, or the FTC provides additional guidance, it is unclear what the outer boundaries are.

8:16.   What is "clear and conspicuous?"

While CAN-SPAM does not provide a definition of what "clear and conspicuous" means in the context of commercial e-mail labeling, federal courts have addressed the meaning of clear and conspicuous in other contexts.[77] In *Cole*, the Seventh Circuit addressed the meaning of clear and conspicuous under FCRA, a statutory scheme that also does not define the phrase. The court noted that in other contexts courts had relied upon the Uniform Commercial Code (U.C.C.) definition of conspicuous when interpreting this term.[78] Conspicuous is defined as "so written, displayed or presented that a reasonable person against which it is to operate ought to have noticed it."[79] Issues that the Seventh Circuit considered in the U.C.C. context were whether the notice appeared at the front or back of the document, whether the language was emphasized in some way, and whether the notice was set off from the rest of the document in order to draw attention to it.[80]

In *In re Bassett*, the Ninth Circuit reached a similar result when interpreting the meaning of "clear and conspicuous" in the bankruptcy context. The Ninth Circuit also relied upon cases interpreting the U.C.C. (using Nevada's definition), and stating that a term is conspicuous if "a reasonable person in the buyer's position would not have been surprised to find the [term] in the contract."[81] Judge Kozinski also noted that the

---

76.   United States v. Cyberheat, Inc., 2007 WL 686678 (D. Ariz. 2008).

77.   *See* Cole v. U.S. Capital, Inc., 389 F.3d 719 (7th Cir. 2004); In re Bassett, 285 F.3d 882 (9th Cir. 2002).

78.   Cole, 389 F.3d at 730.

79.   U.C.C. § 1-201(10).

80.   *Id.*

81.   *In re* Bassett, 285 F.3d 882, 885 (9th Cir. 2002).

mere use of capitalization does not make a term conspicuous.[82] The Ninth Circuit may also consider the placement of the disclosure, as well as the formatting of the type as well.[83]

8:17. Other labeling concerns

Labeling issues also raise concerns for industries in which advertising is heavily regulated because the definition of a commercial e-mail is likely inconsistent with the definition of advertising in other contexts. As such, other regulatory schemes may be triggered if an e-mail is labeled as an "advertisement."

8:18. Adult-oriented e-mails

Adult-oriented materials must include labeling in a slightly different form than identified above. The characters "SEXUALLY-EXPLICIT:"[84] must appear as the first nineteen characters of the subject line in capital letters.[85] This requirement exists so that individuals who view the subject line can determine whether they desire to open the e-mail without being required to view the text or any associated images.

The other distinction the FTC has drawn with adult-oriented e-mails versus standard commercial e-mails is that all of the required disclosures for commercial e-mails set forth below must appear in the first portion of the e-mail and above any adult content.[86] In the first viewable part of the e-mail there must also be clear and conspicuous identification that the message is an advertisement or solicitation, and there must also be the opportunity for a recipient to decline to receive further commercial electronic mail messages from the sender. There must also be a functioning return electronic mail address or other Internet-based mechanism that permits a recipient to submit a reply electronic mail message or other form of Internet-based communication that will stop future commercial e-mails from that sender. This e-mail address must remain capable of receiving such messages or communications for no less than 30 days after the transmission of the original message.[87]

Finally, there must also be a clear and conspicuous display of a valid physical postal address of the sender, as well as any needed instructions on how to access the sexually-oriented material. These instructions, however, must be preceded by a clear and conspicuous statement that to avoid viewing the sexually-oriented material, a recipient should delete the e-mail message without following the instructions.

---

82. *Id.* at 886 ("Lawyers who think that their caps lock keys are instant 'make conspicuous' buttons are deluded.").

83. *Id.*

84. The nineteen characters include the colon and the space after the colon.

85. 16 C.F.R. § 316.4(a)(1).

86. 16 C.F.R. § 316.4(a)(2).

87. *Id.*

8:19.   Liability for violation of adult labeling rule by affiliates

The FTC recently brought an action against Cyberheat for alleged violations of CAN-SPAM related to its affiliate program and other violations.[88] Specifically, Cyberheat was alleged to have violated the Adult Labeling Rule requirements, violated the requirement to provide a clear and conspicuous opt-out mechanism, and violated the requirement to provide a postal address. This conduct was allegedly engaged in via affiliates, and the ultimate resolution of the matter placed extensive program requirements on affiliate marketing, including that affiliates must provide certain personally identifiable information about their company to Cyberheat; that each affiliate be required via contract to provide identifying information to Cyberheat concerning any of that affiliate's sub-affiliates who initiate e-mails on Cyberheat's behalf; that affiliates be provided with a copy of the order and that they acknowledge the receipt of the order; that affiliates provide the e-mail addresses, the content, and the source of the e-mail addresses to Cyberheat at least seven days before e-mails are sent; and that Cyberheat affirmatively agree to the content and process used to generate the e-mails, the establishment and placement of a functioning opt-out mechanism, and numerous other requirements. A fine of $413,000 was also paid.

The case is important to note because it is one of the first cases regarding affiliate marketing, and it attempts to define the scope of affiliate marketing programs.

These placement requirements apply if an e-mail is sent without affirmative consent.[89] If the e-mail is sent with consent, presumably, the standard commercial e-mail rules would still apply, but the additional placement requirements would not be determined by the adult-oriented rules.

8:20.   Opt-out requests

The functional return e-mail address or other Internet-based mechanism that allows the recipient to opt-out of receiving future commercial e-mails is subject to specific form and timing requirements. If an Internet-based list or menu is used, then the recipient can be given the choice of selecting specific types of commercial e-mail the recipient wishes to receive as long as the recipient may choose not to receive any commercial e-mails.[90]

One court has indicated that merely having a valid reply to address in the header, without some indication that it is the appropriate way to opt out, may not comply with CAN-SPAM.[91]

Once an opt-out request is received, the sender must stop sending commercial e-mails to the recipient's e-mail address within 10 business days after receipt of an opt-out notice from the recipient.[92] Moreover, the sender cannot sell or otherwise transfer the recipient's e-mail address to another entity after receipt of the opt-out notice from the

---

88.   United States v. Cyberheat, Inc., 2007 WL 686678 (D. Ariz. 2008).

89.   16 C.F.R. § 316.4(b).

90.   15 U.S.C. § 7704(a)(3).

91.   Aitken v. Communications Workers of America, 496 F. Supp. 2d 653 (E.D. Va. 2007).

92.   15 U.S.C. §§ 7704(a)(4)(a)(i)–(iii).

recipient.[93] Finally, the sender must maintain a mechanism or e-mail address capable of receiving opt-out messages for a period not less than 30 days after transmission of the original commercial e-mail.[94]

8:21.   Role of affirmative consent

Affirmative consent under CAN-SPAM means the following:

> (1) The recipient expressly consented to receive the message, either in response to a clear and conspicuous request for such consent or at the recipient's own initiative; and

> (2) If the message is from a party other than the party to which the recipient communicated such consent, the recipient was given clear and conspicuous notice at the time the consent was communicated that the recipient's e-mail address could be transferred to such other party for the purpose of initiating commercial e-mail messages.[95]

Affirmative consent under CAN-SPAM does not dramatically reduce the requirements of CAN-SPAM. If consent is received to send commercial e-mails, the only alteration in a sender's obligation is that a commercial e-mail no longer needs to be labeled as an advertisement or solicitation.[96]

Affirmative consent in certain circumstances will permit multiple parties to send commercial e-mails. The affirmative consent to receive e-mails will include third parties if there is clear and conspicuous disclosure, at the time consent was obtained, that the recipient's e-mail address will be transferred to third parties.[97]

8:22.   Actual harm requirement

In order to state a claim under portions of CAN-SPAM, the electronic mail service provider must show that it was "adversely affected."[98] Prior cases, including *Hypertouch*, held that this requirement was met when it was shown that high spam traffic caused network disruption and increased costs.[99] This is in contrast to *Gordon v. Virtumundo, Inc.*[100]

One federal court recently addressed standing under CAN-SPAM and simultaneously made certain observations about the type of claims brought under spam laws by plaintiffs.[101] In *Gordon*, the plaintiff alleged he ran an IAS that had standing to bring

---

93.   15 U.S.C. § 7704(a)(4)(a)(iv).
94.   15 U.S.C. § 7704(a)(3)(A)(ii).
95.   15 U.S.C. § 7702(1).
96.   15 U.S.C. § 7704(a)(5)(B).
97.   15 U.S.C. § 7702(1)(B).
98.   *See* 15 U.S.C. § 7706(g)(1).
99.   *See* Hypertouch, Inc. v. Kennedy-Western University, 2006 WL 648688 (N.D. Cal. 2006).
100. Gordon v. Virtumundo, Inc., 2007 WL 1459395 (W.D. Wash. 2007).
101. *Id.*

a CAN-SPAM claim against the defendants as a "provider of Internet access service adversely affected by a violation."[102] The defendants moved for summary judgment, claiming that the plaintiff did not have standing to bring the claim because it did not qualify as an adversely affected Internet Access Service. As part of its analysis, the court noted the proliferation of these types of spam claims, that seek astronomical amounts of statutory damages, where little or no damage was suffered.[103] The court concluded that while in this case the plaintiffs might be able to show that they were an Internet Access Service, they could not show the necessary level of adverse effect.

> Specifically, Plaintiffs undisputedly have suffered no harm related to bandwidth, hardware, Internet connectivity, network integrity, overhead costs, fees, staffing, or equipment costs, and they have alleged absolutely no financial hardship or expense due to the e-mails they received from Defendants. Plaintiffs have spam filters available to them, and such filters continue to become more sophisticated. Nor do Plaintiffs allege they use "dial-up," the costs associated with which were specifically discussed by Congress (and likely are becoming an obsolete concern as high-speed broadband usage becomes the norm). Moreover, even if there is some negligible burden to be inferred from the mere fact that unwanted e-mails have come to Plaintiffs' domain, it is clear to the Court that whatever harm might exist due to that inconvenience, it is not enough to establish the "adverse effect" intended by Congress. Indeed, the only harm Plaintiffs have alleged is the type of harm typically experienced by most e-mail users.[104]

The court then noted that the type of harm necessary must be significant, particularly where only statutory damages were sought, and that in fact it appeared that plaintiffs had actually benefited, not suffered, from receiving spam due to their research endeavors and prolific litigation and settlements.[105]

One argument frequently made by defendants against IASs is that they must show a significant effect of a monetary or technical nature, directly caused by the e-mails at issue. This can be a difficult task depending upon the size of the IAS and the number of e-mails it receives. Some courts have accepted this argument. For example, in *Brosnan vs. Alik Mortgage LLC,* the court applied *Gordon* and *Hypertouch* and concluded that in order to meet this requirement, "The effects need to be more than the time and money spent dealing with spam. The effects must rise to a significant level of harm unique to an IAS. These harms include a substantial decreased bandwidth, expenditures of resources to manage the spam (hired staff, purchased equipment, increased server costs) and compromised network integrity."[106] In this case, as the plaintiff had not pled these facts, the court found he lacked standing under CAN-SPAM. However, this argument

---

102. *Id.* at *2.

103. *Id.* at *8.

104. *Id.* at *8.

105. *Id.* at *9.

106. Brosnan v. Alik Mortgage LLC, 2008 WL 413732 (N.D.Cal. 2008).

was soundly rejected by the district court in the Northern District of California in *ASIS Internet Services v. Active Response Group.*[107]

Courts have found that IASs, if they show harms that are unique to them, such as slowed networks and other similar harms, can state a claim under CAN-SPAM.[108] In *Ferguson*, the district court addressed whether an IAS had suffered sufficient harm to qualify under CAN-SPAM to state a civil cause of action.[109] The court noted that in order to be "adversely affected" an IAS had to show some costs or impact apart from what consumers suffer. In this unique case, which did not involve a large commercial ISP, the plaintiff was unable to show he suffered adverse effect. Indeed, in this case, he did not own a server, but "at best" rented service space. In fact the court noted that any network harm would likely be borne by his server company, Sonic.net. He also did not show he had to invest in new equipment or increase capacity or add new software due to the emails, nor did he show that he had to hire customer service personnel to deal with complaints. At best, he showed that he had to switch from a dial up connection to a broadband connection, and this impact was insufficient to meet the adverse effect standard.[110]

The Northern District of California recently addressed the actual harm and standing issue under CAN-SPAM.[111] In *Asis*, the plaintiff had allegedly had spam routed through its servers, but it had used a program called Postini to block the receipt of some of the e-mails. Moreover, there was not a significant amount of evidence showing actual harm. The defendant argued that therefore the plaintiff did not have standing to bring the claim because there was no actual harm.

Ultimately the court applied *Gordon*:

> This Court finds the reasoning of *Gordon* to be sound. Further, having carefully reviewed the evidence, the Court concludes that no reasonable jury could find, based on the undisputed evidence, that the Emails that are the subject of this action caused any significant adverse effect to ASIS. While there is some evidence that spam generally has imposed costs on ASIS over the years, there is no evidence that the Emails at issue in this action resulted in adverse effects to ASIS: there is *no* evidence in the record that any of the Emails either reached any active ASIS users (rather than being filtered by Postini) or were the subject of complaints to ASIS; there is *no* evidence in the record that ASIS had to increase its server capacity or experienced crashes as a result of the Emails; and there is *no* evidence in the record that ASIS experienced higher costs for filtering by Postini as a result of the Emails. Indeed, the monthly charge for filtering that Postini charged ASIS was somewhat lower in the second half of 2005 when the Emails were sent, than in the first half of 2005. In short, ASIS

---

107. ASIS Internet Services v. Active Response Group, 2008 WL 2952809 (N.D. Cal. 2008).

108. Haselton v. Quicken Loans, Inc., 2008 WL 4585314 (W.D. Wash. 2008).

109. Ferguson v. Quinstreet, Inc., 2008 WL 3166307 (W.D. Wash. 2008).

110. *Id.*

111. ASIS Internet Services v. Optin Global, Inc., 2008 WL 1902217 (N.D. Cal. 2008).

suffered no meaningful adverse effect as a result of the Emails of any kind. As a result, it does not have standing to assert its claims under the CAN-SPAM Act.[112]

8:23.　No misrepresentation in e-mails

In *Benson v. Oregon Processing Service, Inc.*, the court addressed a common situation in commercial e-mail cases—a plaintiff who does not follow the unsubscribe directions and instead collects the e-mails, presumably to increase his damage claim.[113] In this case, the plaintiff instead replied to the e-mail address that sent the e-mails, which was not a working e-mail address. Despite this, and because there was an opt-out mechanism (and the domain that was used in the e-mail was registered to the defendant) the court concluded the e-mails were not deceptive and were appropriate.[114]

8:24.　Spam as a defense to criminal charges

One of the issues that has been raised in criminal cases involving receipt of contraband via e-mail is that the recipient never sought the information out—in other words, the recipient was spammed.[115] In most cases these allegations related to the receipt of child pornography, which requires knowledge that the material is child pornography. In most cases, including in the *Kelley* case, this argument is rejected because there is other evidence showing intent. In certain cases, however, this argument might be appropriate.

8:25.　CAN-SPAM and mitigation defenses

One court in the Northern District of California has held that mitigation of damages is not a defense to an action under CAN-SPAM, and its civil penalties.[116] However, this court did not address whether other defenses that focus on the plaintiff's conduct, including unclean hands, laches, estoppels, and other similar defenses, are inappropriate. These defenses should be permitted in CAN-SPAM cases, particularly given the conduct of some plaintiffs.

8:26.　Standing to sue and enforcement

The FTC has jurisdiction to enforce most violations of CAN-SPAM as if they were unfair or deceptive acts or practices proscribed by the FTC Act.[117] While the FTC has few restrictions upon its jurisdiction, there are certain types of entities that the FTC cannot regulate. Entities that do not seek a profit are typically not within the jurisdiction

---

112. *ASIS*, 2008 WL 1902217 at *17.

113. Benson v. Oregon Processing Service, Inc., 136 Wash. App. 587 (Wash. App. 2007).

114. *Id.* at 592-593.

115. *See* United States v. Hay, 231 F.3d 630, 633-34 (9th Cir. 2000); United States v. Kelley, 482 F.3d 1047 (9th Cir. 2007).

116. Phillips v. Netblue, Inc., 2006 WL 3647116 (N.D. Cal. 2006).

117. 15 U.S.C. § 7706(a).

of the FTC. Moreover, certain industries are not within the jurisdiction of the FTC for CAN-SPAM issues, and other agencies have jurisdiction to enforce CAN-SPAM. The Office of the Comptroller of the Currency has jurisdiction to enforce CAN-SPAM against national banks and federal branches and federal agencies of foreign banks.[118]

The Federal Reserve Board has enforcement authority over member banks of the Federal Reserve System (other than national banks), branches and agencies of foreign banks (other than federal branches, federal agencies, and insured state branches of foreign banks), commercial lending companies owned or controlled by foreign banks, organizations operating under section 25 or 25A of the Federal Reserve Act,[119] and bank holding companies.[120]

The director of the Federal Deposit Insurance Corporation (FDIC) has authority to enforce CAN-SPAM against banks insured by the FDIC (other than members of the Federal Reserve System) and insured state branches of foreign banks.[121] The director of the Office of Thrift Supervision has jurisdiction over savings associations the deposits of which are insured by the FDIC.[122] Federally insured credit unions are subject to enforcement by the Board of the National Credit Union Administration.[123]

The Securities and Exchange Commission was not ignored by CAN-SPAM. The SEC has enforcement authority over any broker or dealer, investment companies or investment advisers. Enforcement against insurance companies was specifically reserved to the states where the state has a state insurance enforcement authority.[124] If none exists, CAN-SPAM places enforcement authority with the FTC.[125]

The Secretary of Transportation has the authority to enforce CAN-SPAM with respect to any air carrier or foreign air carrier, and the Secretary of Agriculture has the same authority regarding any entity subject to the Packers and Stockyards Act.[126] The Farm Credit Administration has enforcement rights with respect to any federal land bank, federal land bank association, federal intermediate credit bank, or production credit association.[127] Finally the Federal Communications Commission has authority to enforce compliance with CAN-SPAM against any person subject to the Communications Act of 1934.[128]

State governmental agencies are also permitted to enforce certain violations of CAN-SPAM. A state attorney general, official, or agency of the state may bring a civil action in a federal district court, on behalf of the residents of the state. A state attorney general can seek injunctive relief, damages, or statutory penalties arising out of allegations that a sender of e-mail used false or misleading transmission information,

---

118. 15 U.S.C. § 7706(b)(1)(a).

119. 12 U.S.C. §§ 601, 611.

120. 15 U.S.C. § 7706(b)(1)(B).

121. 15 U.S.C. § 7706(b)(1)(C).

122. 15 U.S.C. § 7706(b)(1)(d).

123. 15 U.S.C. § 7706(b)(3).

124. 15 U.S.C. § 7706(b)(6).

125. *Id.*

126. 15 U.S.C. §§ 7706(b)(7)–(8).

127. 15 U.S.C. § 7706(b)(9).

128. 15 U.S.C. § 7706(b)(10).

deceptive subject headings, or a pattern and practice of failing to provide opt-out mechanisms, honoring opt-outs, or failing to appropriately label e-mails.[129] While states can bring actions, they are somewhat restricted in their enforcement authority. Prior to filing an action the state must serve prior written notice of any action on the FTC or other appropriate federal agency and simultaneously provide that entity with a copy of its complaint, unless notice is not feasible.[130] At that point the FTC or other federal agency has the right to intervene in the action and, upon intervening, to be heard on all matters arising therein. The right to remove the action to the appropriate United States district court is also available, as is the right to file petitions for appeal.[131] States are also precluded from initiating actions if the FTC or other appropriate federal agency has initiated an action.[132]

Internet Access Services (IASs) are also permitted to bring a civil action seeking an injunction, actual damages, or statutory penalties.[133] An IAS is permitted to bring an action if it can demonstrate that a sender transmitted e-mails with false or misleading transmission information, engaged in address harvesting, dictionary attacks, automated creation of multiple e-mail accounts, or transmitted violative commercial e-mails through unauthorized access. IASs can also bring actions if a sender engaged in a pattern and practice of sending e-mails with deceptive subject headers, failing to provide opt-out mechanisms, failing to honor opt-outs, or failing to appropriately label e-mails.[134]

Notably, unlike many comparable state laws, CAN-SPAM does not provide a private right of action by effected recipients. In other words, people who receive improper e-mails cannot bring a claim against the sender of the e-mails.

8:27. Do-not-email list

Having seen the success of the Do-Not-Call laws, Congress, via a request for a report in CAN-SPAM, requested that the FTC examine and report to Congress regarding whether a Do-Not-Email registry was a viable option to regulate spam.[135] When proposed by Congress, acceptance of a Do-Not-Email registry faced two main hurdles: constitutional concerns that now have been largely addressed in the Do-Not-Call context, as well as practical concerns about the effectiveness of a Do-Not-Email registry. After examining the issue, and receiving public comments, the FTC recently rejected the concept of a Do-Not-Email registry.

The concept of a Do-Not-Email registry was predicated upon the creation of a centralized database of e-mail addresses. As with Do-Not-Call, it was anticipated that the FTC would create a list of consumer e-mails that would be off-limits to marketers that sent unsolicited e-mails. In the Do-Not-Call arena, consumers can call a telephone number or log onto a website and register their telephone number. Once a number is registered, it is placed in a database that all companies that do telephone solicitations

---

129. 15 U.S.C. §§ 7706(b)(1)–(3).
130. 15 U.S.C. § 7706(b)(5).
131. *Id.*
132. 15 U.S.C. § 7706(b)(8).
133. 15 U.S.C. § 7706(g)(3).
134. 15 U.S.C. § 7706(g)(1).
135. 15 U.S.C. § 7708.

must download and monitor. This database, which must be updated and maintained, provides guidance to marketers as to who they can and cannot call. If a number is on the list, it cannot be called for most forms of unsolicited marketing.

Obviously, for this type of model to work, the phone numbers must be disclosed to companies. This would also have been required of any Do-Not-Email list. While this system worked in the phone solicitation arena, it would likely have only increased the amount of spam e-mails.

If a Do-Not-Email database were created, it would have contained millions of e-mail addresses. While most U.S,-based companies would have downloaded this list and followed the restrictions of CAN-SPAM, companies not based in the United States could have used this list for more nefarious purposes.

In the hands of a company based in a country without any spam legislation, the list would be the Holy Grail of commercial e-mailers. It would contain a list of verified and confirmed e-mail addresses—indeed the very addresses that people are concerned enough about to protect via registration. If such a list were created, there would be no way for the FTC to enforce the violation of a Do-Not-Email list against a company that had no tie to a country with spam legislation. People would likely have seen an increase in the volume of e-mails that originate from countries that condone and permit these types of e-mails.

8:28. Inapplicability of header restrictions to statements in body of e-mail

CAN-SPAM expressly regulates false or misleading header information.[136] Courts have read this provision narrowly and have held that this does not restrict allegedly deceptive statements in the body of an e-mail.[137]

8:29. Other vicarious liability issues

As noted above, under most situations, only "senders" of e-mails have liability under CAN-SPAM. However, there are certain circumstances where third parties can have liability for the actions of others. It is illegal for a business to promote, or allow the promotion of its trade or business, or goods, products, property, or services in a commercial e-mail message that contains false or misleading headers or transmission information or deceptive subject lines under the following circumstances:

(1) the business knew, or should have known, in the ordinary course of trade or business, that the goods, products, property, or services sold, offered for sale, leased or offered for lease, or otherwise made available through that trade or business were being promoted in such a message;

(2) it received or expected to receive an economic benefit from such promotion; and

(3) it took no reasonable action:

(A) to prevent the transmission; or

---

136. 15 U.S.C. § 7704(a)(1).

137. Internet Access Service Providers LLC v. Real Networks, Inc., 2005 WL 1244961 (D. Idaho 2005).

(B) to detect the transmission and report it to the FTC.[138]

It should be noted that a person or company that only provides goods to a third party, but does not promote or allow the promotion of the goods, can still be liable in limited circumstances. This includes situations in which the person owns, or has a greater than 50-percent ownership or economic interest in, the trade or business of the person that committed the violation, or the person has actual knowledge that goods, products, property, or services are promoted in a violative e-mail and receives, or expects to receive, an economic benefit from such promotion.[139]

8:30.   Mere advertising insufficient to establish liability

Despite the vicarious liability provisions, courts have held that the mere existence of e-mail advertising regarding a party does not establish liability if the e-mail wasn't sent by the party and there is no evidence establishing knowledge or conscious avoidance of knowledge.[140] In *Hypertouch*, the plaintiff argued that the defendant was liable for CAN-SPAM violations resulting from e-mails that the defendant had not sent, but which advertised the defendant's services. The court noted that the mere existence of advertising was insufficient by itself to establish the knowledge required for CAN-SPAM liability under the vicarious liability provisions. The court also noted that the defendant had policies in place that required compliance with CAN-SPAM and used an outside expert to review its advertising.[141] These policies, coupled with the lack of evidence regarding knowledge, led the court to dismiss the claim.[142]

8:31.   Registration of e-mail accounts

Like many predecessor state laws, CAN-SPAM regulates who mechanically registers e-mail accounts, as well as how e-mails are sent in an attempt to control deceptive practices in relation to bulk commercial e-mailing. Therefore, knowingly taking any of the following acts is prohibited:

(1) accessing a computer without authorization and intentionally initiating the transmission of multiple commercial e-mail messages from or through such computer;

(2) using a computer to relay or retransmit multiple commercial e-mail messages, with the intent to deceive or mislead recipients, or any Internet access service, as to the origin of such messages;

(3) materially falsifying header information in multiple commercial e-mail messages and intentionally initiating the transmission of such messages;

(4) registering, using information that materially falsifies the identity of the actual registrant, for five or more e-mail accounts or online user accounts or two or more domain names, and intentionally initiating the transmission of multiple commercial e-mail messages from any combination of such accounts or domain names, or

---

138. 15 U.S.C. §§ 7705(a)(1)–(3).

139. 15 U.S.C. §§ 7705(b)(1)–(2).

140. Hypertouch, Inc. v. Kennedy-Western University, 2006 WL 648688 (N.D. Cal. 2006).

141. *Id.* at *5.

142. *Id.* at *6.

(5) falsely representing yourself to be the registrant or the legitimate successor in interest to the registrant of five or more Internet Protocol addresses, and intentionally initiating the transmission of multiple commercial e-mail messages from such addresses.[143]

8:32.   Automated scripts

The use of automated scripts to obtain e-mail addresses for mailing lists, sometimes called harvesting, is prohibited, as is the use of scripts to register multiple e-mail accounts. CAN-SPAM precludes anyone from transmitting or assisting in the origination of a commercial e-mail through the provision or selection of addresses to which the message will be transmitted, if the sender knows, or should have known the following:

(1) that the e-mail address of the recipient was obtained using an automated means from an Internet website or proprietary online service operated by another person, and such website or online service included, at the time the address was obtained, a notice stating that the operator of such website or online service will not give, sell, or otherwise transfer addresses maintained by such website or online service to any other party for the purposes of initiating, or enabling others to initiate, e-mail messages;

(2) that the e-mail address of the recipient was obtained using an automated means that generates possible e-mail addresses by combining names, letters, or numbers into numerous permutations;

(3) that scripts or other automated means were used to register for multiple e-mail accounts or online user accounts from which to transmit to a computer, or enabled another person to transmit to a computer, a commercial e-mail message that is unlawful as set forth above; or

(4) that an unlawful commercial e-mail message was knowingly sent via a computer or computer network that such person has accessed without authorization.[144]

8:33.   Restrictions upon wireless messaging[145]

No person or entity may initiate[146] any mobile service commercial message[147] unless that person or entity has the express prior authorization of the addressee; that person

---

143. 18 U.S.C. §§ 1037(a)(1)–(5).

144. 15 U.S.C. §§ 7704(b)(1)–(3).

145. It should be noted that, according to the FCC, these regulations apply to SMS messages even if the message is purely Internet-based. In the Matter of Rules and Regulations Implementing the Controlling the Assault of Non-Solicited Pornography and Marketing Act of 2003, CG Docket No. 04-53, published August 12, 2004, Section III A., 14 to 17.

146. "Initiate," with respect to a commercial electronic mail message, means to originate or transmit such messages or to procure the origination or transmission of such message, but shall not include actions that constitute routine conveyance of such message. For purposes of this paragraph, more than one person may be considered to have initiated a message. "Routine conveyance" means the transmission, routing, relaying, handling, or storing, through an automatic technical process, or an electronic mail message for which another person has identified the recipients or provided the recipient addresses. 47 C.F.R. § 64.3100(c)(6).

147. "Mobile Service Commercial Message" means a commercial electronic mail message that is transmitted directly to a wireless device that is utilized by a subscriber of a commercial mobile service (as such term is defined in section 332(d) of the Communications Act of 1934 (47 U.S.C. § 332(d)) in connection with such service. A commercial message is presumed to be a mobile service commercial message if it is sent or

or entity is forwarding that message to its own address; or that person or entity is forwarding to an address provided the following:

- The original sender has not provided any payment, consideration or other inducement to that person or entity and

- That message does not advertise or promote a product, service, or internet website of the person or entity forwarding the message; or

- The address to which that message is sent or directed does not include a reference to a domain name that has been posted on the FCC's wireless domain names list for a period of at least 30 days before that message was initiated, provided that the person or entity does not knowingly initiate a mobile service commercial message.[148]

Any person or entity initiating any mobile service commercial message must cease sending further messages within 10 days after receiving a request by a subscriber; include a functioning return electronic mail address or other Internet-based mechanism for the purpose of receiving requests to cease the initiating of mobile service commercial messages and/or commercial electronic mail messages[149] that is clearly and conspicuously displayed and that does not require the subscriber to view or hear further commercial content other than institutional identification; and, if consent was obtained electronically, provide to a recipient who electronically grants express prior authorization to send commercial electronic mail messages with a functioning option and clear and conspicuous instructions to reject further messages by the same electronic means that was used to obtain authorization.[150] A person initiating a mobile service commercial message is also required to ensure that the use of at least one option provided above for opt-outs does not result in additional charges to the subscriber; to identify themselves in the message in a form that will allow a subscriber to reasonably determine that the sender is the authorized entity; and for no less than 30 days after the transmission of any mobile service commercial message, to remain capable of receiving messages or communications made to the electronic mail address, other Internet-based mechanism, if applicable.[151]

---

directed to any address containing a reference, whether or not displayed, to an Internet domain listed on the FCC's wireless domain names list. 47 C.F.R. § 64.3100(7).

148. 47 C.F.R. § 64.3100(a).

149. "Commercial electronic mail message" means the term as defined in the CAN-SPAM Act, 15 U.S.C. § 7702. The term is defined as "an electronic message for which the primary purpose is commercial advertisement or promotion of a commercial product or service (including content on an Internet website operated for a commercial purpose)." The term "commercial electronic mail message" does not include a transactional or relationship message. 47 C.F.R. § 64.3100(c)(2). Electronic mail message means a message sent to a unique electronic mail address. 47 C.F.R. § 64.3100(c)(5). "Electronic mail address" means a destination, commonly expressed as a string of characters, consisting of a unique user name or mailbox and a reference to an Internet domain, whether or not displayed, to which an electronic mail message can be sent or delivered. 47 C.F.R. § 64.3100(c)(4).

150. 47 C.F.R. § 64.3100(b).

151. *Id.*

8:34.   Form of authorization

The express prior authorization contemplated by the rule may be obtained by oral or written means, including electronic methods.[152] If written authorization is obtained then it must contain the subscriber's signature, which can include an electronic signature as permitted by the E-Sign Act.[153] The authorization must include the electronic mail address to which the messages will be sent. If this is done via the Internet, then the website must allow the subscriber to input the specific electronic mail address to which the commercial messages may be sent.[154] This consent is typically only considered valid for the person seeking the authorization, and not for affiliated parties, unless the subscriber expressly agrees that affiliated parties may be included.[155]

Any request for express prior authorization must also include the following disclosures:

- that the subscriber is agreeing to receive mobile service commercial messages (mscms) sent to his/her wireless device from a particular sender, which includes clearly stating the identity of the business, individual, or other entity that will be sending the messages;
- that the subscriber may be charged by his/her wireless service provider in connection with receipt of such messages; and that the subscriber may revoke his/her authorization to receive mscms at any time.[156]

These notices must be clearly legible, use sufficiently large type, or, if audio, be of sufficiently loud volume, and be placed so as to be readily apparent to a wireless subscriber.[157] These disclosures must also be presented separately from any other authorizations in the document or oral presentation. If any portion of the notice is translated into another language, then all portions of the notice must be translated into the same language.[158]

8:35.   Additional restrictions upon CMRS providers

All Commercial Mobile Radio Service (CMRS)[159] providers must identify all electronic mail domain names[160] used to offer subscribers messaging specifically for wireless devices in connection with commercial mobile service in the manner and timeframe described in a public notice issued by the Consumer & Governmental Affairs Bureau

---

152. 47 C.F.R. § 64.3100(d).

153. 47 C.F.R. § 64.3100(d)(1).

154. 47 C.F.R. § 64.3100(d)(2).

155. 47 C.F.R. § 64.3100(d)(3).

156. 47 C.F.R. §§ 64.3100(d)(5)(A)–(B).

157. 47 C.F.R. § 64.3100(d)(6).

158. 47 C.F.R. § 64.3100(d)(6).

159. Commercial Mobile Radio Service provider means any provider that offers the services defined in 47 C.F.R. § 20.9. 47 C.F.R. § 64.3100(c)(1).

160. Domain name means any alphanumeric designation that is registered with or assigned by any domain name registrar, domain name registry, or other domain name registration authority as part of an electronic address on the Internet. 47 C.F.R. § 64.3100(c)(3).

in December 2004.[161] CMRS providers are also responsible for the continuing accuracy and completeness of the information provided to the FCC for its wireless domain name list.[162] This includes filing updates not less than 30 days before issuing subscribers a new or modified domain name, removing domain names that have not been issued or are no longer in use within six months of certain actions, and certifying that any domain name placed on the FCC's wireless domain names list is used for mobile service messaging.[163]

8:36. Penalties and damages

While Congress provided remedies for the states and IASs that bring actions to enforce CAN-SPAM, CAN-SPAM does not provide the FTC remedies that are specific to the statutory scheme. Instead, for purposes of FTC enforcement, violations of CAN-SPAM are considered violations of the FTC Act, and are therefore subject to the remedies that the FTC may obtain in FTC Act cases.[164] As such, the FTC can obtain the remedies available to it under 15 U.S.C.A. § 53(b), which include injunctive relief, disgorgement and restitution, as well as other "equitable" remedies the court is permitted to grant.[165]

States are permitted to seek actual damages or penalties of up to $250 per violation with a cap of $2 million.[166] The court can treble the award if it is shown that the defendant committed the violation willfully and knowingly or if the defendant's conduct included address harvesting, dictionary attacks, automated creation of multiple e-mail accounts via scripts, or relaying or transmitting violative commercial e-mails through unauthorized access.[167] Damages can be reduced if a defendant can demonstrate that it established and implemented, with due care, commercially reasonable practices and procedures designed to effectively prevent such violations, or that the violation occurred despite commercially reasonable efforts to maintain compliance with the above-referenced practices and procedures. Attorneys' fees are also recoverable.[168]

Moreover, criminal penalties are also available if a person intentionally sends multiple commercial e-mails in connection with (1) unauthorized access of a computer, (2) using relays or retransmitting with the intent to deceive, (3) materially false header information, (4) registering five or more e-mail accounts or two or more domain names with materially false information, or (5) falsely representing oneself to be the owner of five or more IP addresses,. A prison term of up to five years is available if these actions are undertaken in furtherance of a felony or if the defendant has previously

---

161. 47 C.F.R. § 64.3100(e). The FCC's online submission form is http://www.fcc.gov/cgb/policy/Domain-NameInput.html (last visited March 28, 2011). The FCC's original notice is http://hraunfoss.fcc.gov/edocs_public/attachmatch/DA-04-3944A1.pdf (last visited March 28, 2011).

162. 47 C.F.R. § 64.3100(f).

163. 47 C.F.R. §§ 64.3100(f)(1)–(3).

164. 15 U.S.C. § 7706(a).

165. 15 U.S.C. § 53(b). The relief available to the FTC is discussed more fully in chapter 15 of this book.

166. 15 U.S.C. § 7706(b)(3)(a)(B).

167. 15 U.S.C. § 7706(f)(3)(C).

168. 15 U.S.C. § 7706(b)(3)(D).

been convicted of conduct related to the improper distribution of multiple commercial e-mails.[169]

Fines and prison terms of up to three years are available for certain violations, depending upon the volume of e-mails, and the minimum penalty is a prison term of not more than one year.[170] Forfeiture of profits and equipment used in furtherance of any such crime is also required.[171]

Under the sentencing guidelines for CAN-SPAM, one factor a court is to consider is the amount of "loss" caused by the conduct.[172] In a recent decision a district court in Arizona noted that the defendant's gain cannot be used as an alternative measure of loss unless the true losses that resulted from the conduct cannot be easily calculated.[173] Thus, where the loss suffered as a result of the violations is low, though still ascertainable, the gain by the defendants cannot be used as an alternative measure.

In actions brought by IASs, an injunction or cease and desist order can be sought without a showing of intent to preclude commercial e-mails that contain false or misleading information, contain deceptive subject headings, are transmitted after objection, result from address harvesting or dictionary attacks, or were relayed or retransmitted through unauthorized access.[174]

IASs are also entitled to damages or statutory penalties. A $100 per e-mail statutory penalty is available for e-mails that have false or misleading transmission information and a $25 per e-mail statutory penalty is available for other violations.[175] For statutory violations excluding false or misleading transmission information, the statutory damages are capped at $1 million in actions by IASs.[176] Damages can be trebled based upon the same factors courts consider in actions brought by states.[177]

Similarly, damages can be reduced if a defendant can demonstrate that it established and implemented, with due care, commercially reasonable practices and procedures designed to effectively prevent such violations, or that the violation occurred despite commercially reasonable efforts to maintain compliance with the above-referenced practices and procedures.[178] Attorneys' fees are also recoverable.[179]

8:37. Pleading CAN-SPAM violations with particularity

One of the issues courts have had to address is whether allegations related to fraudulent or deceptive e-mails under CAN-SPAM or analogous state law must be plead with particularity. Many courts have concluded that these types of allegations must meet many

---

169. 18 U.S.C. § 1037(b)(1).
170. 18 U.S.C. § 1037(b)(2).
171. 18 U.S.C. § 1037(c).
172. United States v. Kilbride, 2007 WL 2774487 (D. Ariz. 2007).
173. *Id.*
174. 15 U.S.C. § 7706(b)(2).
175. 15 U.S.C. § 7706(8)(3).
176. 15 U.S.C. § 7706(8)(3)(B).
177. 15 U.S.C. § 7706(g)(3)(C).
178. 15 U.S.C. § 7706(8)(3)(D).
179. 15 U.S.C. § 7706(g)(4).

of the common law requirements of fraud, including being plead with particularity.[180] Indeed, certain plaintiffs will attempt to avoid identifying the e-mails that are at issue in a CAN-SPAM case, which in many cases hinders a defendant's defense to an action. A district court in Washington rejected a plaintiff's attempt to avoid giving notice of the nature of the action under CAN-SPAM and granted a motion for a more definite statement, requiring the plaintiff to identify the e-mails at issue in the case, including specifically, the e-mail address to which the e-mails were sent and the date on which they were sent.[181]

8:38.   Assignment of claims

A common practice in spam cases is for plaintiffs to try and assign claims or create some other convoluted argument to try and create standing for absent parties. Assignment of claims raises a number of issues, including the potential unauthorized practice of law. Moreover, courts in enforcing the TCPA have held that assignment of these types of personal injury claims is improper and void.[182] This is also true under state junk fax laws.[183]

8:39.   Preemption

CAN-SPAM specifically preempts any state laws or regulations that expressly regulate the use of e-mail to send commercial messages. However, state laws that regulate falsity or deception in e-mails are not preempted. CAN-SPAM does not explicitly effect any state laws that are not specific to e-mail, including state trespass, contract, or tort law. Finally, CAN-SPAM does not preempt laws that relate to acts of fraud or computer crime. However, this does not mean that CAN-SPAM does not impact these laws in certain ways.

Generally a court will begin any preemption analysis with two assumptions. First is the presumption that Congress did not intend to preempt the field of law.[184] Second, courts presume that the purpose of Congress is the "ultimate touchstone" in a case.[185] As such, preemption analysis does not seek to narrowly construe congressional intent, but rather seeks to fairly read the language, purpose, and structure of the statute at issue.[186]

One argument many plaintiffs have made is that an inaccuracy in an e-mail, however slight, renders the e-mail false or misleading, and therefore state law would not be preempted by CAN-SPAM in such a case. This argument has been directly rejected by federal courts, because they have interpreted the false or misleading exception to

---

180. *See* Gordon v. Virtumundo, Inc., 2007 WL 1459395 (W.D. Wash. 2007); *see also* ASIS Internet Services v. Optin Global, Inc., 65 Fed. R. Serv. 3d 404 (N.D. Cal. 2006).

181. Omni Innovations, LLC v. Impulse Marketing Group, Inc., 2007 WL 2110337 (W.D. Wash. 2007).

182. US Fax Law Center, Inc. v. iHire, Inc., 476 F.3d 1112 (10th Cir. 2007).

183. US Fax Law Center, Inc. v. Myron Corp., 159 P.3d 745 (Colo. Ct. App., 2006).

184. Omega World Travel, Inc. v. Mummagraphics, 469 F.3d 348, 353 (4th Cir. 2006); citing Maryland v. Louisiana, 451 U.S. 725, 746 (1981).

185. Omega World Travel, Inc. v. Mummagraphics, 469 F.3d 348, 352 (4th Cir. 2006); citing Medtronic, Inc. v. Lohr, 518 U.S. 470, 485 (1996).

186. *Id.*

preemption to require conduct equivalent to fraud.[187] The district court in the Central District of California addressed the level of fraud required to escape CAN-SPAM preemption, holding that common law fraud, including reliance, was required, and the mere failure to include a company name in an e-mail would not be considered a sufficient showing to defeat preemption by alleging fraud, citing the legislative history of CAN-SPAM and its direction that states not force e-mails to contain certain content.[188] The Northern District of California recently addressed the level of fraud needed in relation to CAN-SPAM's preemption clause.[189] In *Hoang*, the defendant was alleged to have falsely indicated that emails were coming from an email address on the Yahoo.com domain and the plaintiff brought an action for violation of California's commercial email law. The plaintiff alleged that the use of the Yahoo.com domain name in this way was a material misrepresentation, therefore supporting a finding that CAN-SPAM's preemption clause was not applicable to this case. The court found that this conduct was a material misrepresentation, sufficient to find that CAN-SPAM was preempted.[190] The court also held that the use of the same names in the header, as well as names in the subject line, were sufficiently false to support preemption. Ultimately, however, the court found that the plaintiffs had failed to prove damage as a result of their reliance upon a misrepresentation and therefore dismissed the claim.[191]

There are three types of preemption: express, field, and conflict preemption. "Express preemption occurs when Congress has considered the issue of preemption, has included in the legislation under consideration a provision expressly addressing that issue, and has explicitly provided therein that state law is preempted."[192] "When Congress has expressly defined the extent to which state law is preempted, a court will interpret the effect of the preemption language by focusing on the plain wording of the provision, but will narrowly construe the precise language of the preemption clause in light of the strong presumption against preemption."[193] Thus, where Congress expressly intended to preempt state law, the state law is of no effect.

---

187. Omega World Travel, Inc. v. Mummagraphics, 469 F.3d 348, 353-54 (4th Cir. 2006).

188. Kleffman v. Vonage Holdings Corp., 2007 WL 1518650 (C.D. Cal. 2007).

189. Hoang v. Reunion.com, Inc., 3:06-cv-03518-MMC (N.D. Cal. December 23, 2008).

190. *Id.* ("Contrary to defendant's argument, plaintiffs have sufficiently alleged, for purposes of § 7707(b)(1), that defendant's inclusion of a third-party's domain name in the subject emails was a false representation and that defendant knew such emails would convey a false representation, in that, according to plaintiffs, the emails were not sent by the yahoo.com addressees identified in the email or with their permission, but, rather, were sent by defendant, which authored the entirety of the language in the email. Further, plaintiffs, have sufficiently alleged the above-referenced representations were material and defendant intended the recipients to rely thereon, in that, according to plaintiffs, defendant intended the recipients to believe the emails had been authored and sent by the individuals whose yahoo.com email addresses were identified and to act on such belief by 'opening and reading' the emails, which in fact, contained a commercial advertisement for defendant's services.").

191. Hoang v. Reunion.com, Inc., 3:06-cv-03518-MMC (N.D. Cal. December 23, 2008); citing Omega World Travel, Inc. v. Mummagraphics, Inc., 469 F.3d 348, 354 (4th Cir. 2006); Ferron v. Echostar Satellite, LLC, 2008 WL 4377309, *6 (S.D. Ohio 2008); ASIS Internet Services v. Optin Global, Inc., 2008 WL 1902217, *19 (N.D. Cal. 2008); Kleffman v. Vonage Holdings Corp., 2007 WL 1518650, *3 (C.D. Cal. 2007).

192. Washington Mut. Bank v. Super. Ct., 75 Cal. App. 4th 773, 781 (1999) (citing Cipollone v. Liggett Group, Inc., 505 U.S. 504, 523 (1992)).

193. Washington Mutual Bank, 75 Cal. App. 4th at 782 (citing CSX Transp., Inc. v. Easterwood, 507 U.S. 658, 664 (1993) and Cipollone, 505 U.S. at 523).

However, there are other forms of preemption that are implicated by CAN-SPAM: conflict preemption and obstacle preemption. It is well settled that state law that conflicts with federal law is "without effect."[194] Conflict preemption occurs when it is impossible for a private party to comply with both federal and state law.[195] Obstacle preemption occurs when, under the circumstances of a particular case, the challenged state law stands as an obstacle to the accomplishment and execution of the full purposes and objectives of Congress.[196] As stated by the United States Supreme Court: "[w]hat is a sufficient obstacle is a matter of judgment, to be informed by examining the federal statute as a whole and identifying its purpose and intended effects ..."[197] Thus, in certain cases, conflicting state e-mail, or other laws, may be preempted by CAN-SPAM even though the law is not expressly preempted, particularly if the law in question would stand as an obstacle to the accomplishment and execution of the congressional objectives behind CAN-SPAM.

One area where this issue has been addressed is the preemptive effect of CAN-SPAM on state university e-mail policies.[198] In *White Buffalo Ventures, LLC v. University of Texas at Austin* the university had adopted certain regulations that precluded the plaintiff from sending certain e-mails through the university system. The issue ultimately involved a decision as to whether the university was acting as a state actor or as a service provider. Ultimately the court concluded that while there was preemption language that supported both sides, the university's restrictions as a service provider were valid under the Supremacy Clause.[199]

8:40.   Specificity requirements

The specificity in pleading requirement has also been applied to the damage allegations, and the failure to adequately plead damages may result in a court not having jurisdiction to hear the matter.[200]

---

194. Maryland v. Louisiana, 451 U.S. 725, 746 (1981).

195. Viva! Intern. Voice For Animals v. Adidas Promotional Retail Operations, Inc., 41 Cal. 4th 929, 63 Cal. Rptr. 3d 50, 162 P.3d 569 (2007).

196. Viva! Int'l Voice For Animals v. Adidas Promot'l Retail Operations, Inc., 134 Cal. App. 4th 133, (2005) (citing Crosby, 530 U.S. at 372-73); review granted and opinion superseded, 41 Cal. Rptr. 3d 69, 130 P.3d 930 (Cal. 2006) and judgment rev'd, 41 Cal. 4th 929, 63 Cal. Rptr. 3d 50, 162 P.3d 569 (2007).

197. Crosby v. National Foreign Trade Council, 530 U.S. 363, 373, 120 S. Ct. 2288, 2294 (2000).

198. White Buffalo Ventures, LLC v. University of Texas at Austin, 420 F.3d 366 (5th Cir. 2005).

199. *White Buffalo*, 420 F.3d at 373-74.

200. Brosnan v. Alki Mortg., LLC, 2008 WL 413732 (N.D.Cal. 2008).

CHAPTER 9

Restrictions on Telephones

9:1.   Telephone regulation introduction

Telephone companies are in one of the most regulated industries in connection with privacy and security issues. At the federal level, the Telecommunications Act restricts disclosure of certain private information regarding individuals. The Electronic Communications Privacy Act, discussed in chapter 6, also regulates the disclosure of records, as well as wiretapping.

Care should also be taken when subpoenas are issued for this type of records. Certain states, California among them, have restricted the ability of litigants to obtain telephone records via civil statutes, as well as via regulations placed upon the telephone companies. The pretexting debate also raises issues regarding telephone records, and many states have passed specific laws that address pretexting in the telephone record context.

9:2.   Telecommunications Act of 1996

The Telecommunications Act of 1996 places a general duty on telecommunications carriers to protect the privacy of several different types of entities and individuals. Telecommunications carriers have a duty to protect the confidentiality of proprietary information of, and relating to, other telecommunication carriers, equipment manufacturers, and customers, including telecommunication carriers reselling telecommunications services provided by a telecommunications carrier.[1]

9:3.   Confidentiality of carrier information

A telecommunications carrier that receives or obtains proprietary information from another carrier for purposes of providing a telecommunications service may use this information for this service, and cannot use the information for its own marketing efforts.[2]

9:4.   Customer proprietary network information

Unless otherwise permitted by law or the customer, any telecommunications carrier that receives or obtains customer proprietary network information[3] (CPNI) by virtue of providing a telecommunications service can only use, disclose, or permit access to individually identifiable customer proprietary network information when providing either the telecommunications service from which the information was derived, or services necessary to, or used in, the provision of telecommunications service, including the publishing of directories.[4] These restrictions do not prevent a telecommunications carrier from using, disclosing, or permitting access to aggregate customer information,[5] other than for certain purposes. Similarly, local exchange carriers may use, disclose, or permit access to aggregate customer information other than for certain purposes, but local exchange carriers can only do this if they provide the aggregate information to other carriers or persons on reasonable and nondiscriminatory terms and conditions and upon reasonable request.[6] However, telecommunications carriers must disclose customer proprietary network information, upon affirmative written request by the customer, to any person designated by the customer.[7]

9:5.   Exceptions to privacy restrictions

Telecommunications carriers can use, disclose, or permit access to customer proprietary network information obtained from its customers, either directly or indirectly through its agents, to initiate, render, bill, and collect for telecommunications services; to protect the rights or property of the carrier or to protect users of those services and other carriers from fraudulent, abusive, or unlawful use of, or subscription to, such services; or to

---

1.   47 U.S.C. § 222(a).

2.   47 U.S.C. § 222(b).

3.   The term "customer proprietary network information" means—(A) information that relates to the quantity, technical configuration, type, destination, location, and amount of use of a telecommunications service subscribed to by any customer of a telecommunications carrier, and that is made available to the carrier by the customer solely by virtue of the carrier-customer relationship; and (B) information contained in the bills pertaining to telephone exchange service or telephone toll service received by a customer of a carrier except that such term does not include subscriber list information. 47 U.S.C. § 222(h)(1).

4.   47 U.S.C. § 222(c)(1).

5.   The term "aggregate customer information" means collective data that relates to a group or category of services or customers, from which individual customer identities and characteristics have been removed. 47 U.S.C. § 222(h)(2).

6.   47 U.S.C. § 222(c)(3).

7.   47 U.S.C. § 222(c)(2).

provide any inbound telemarketing, referral, or administrative services to the customer for the duration of the call, if the call was initiated by the customer and the customer approves of the use of the information to provide the service.[8] Disclosure can also be made regarding call location information concerning the user of a commercial mobile service to a public safety answering point,[9] emergency medical service provider, or emergency dispatch provider, public safety, fire service, or law enforcement official, or hospital emergency or trauma care facility, in order to respond to the user's call for emergency services;[10] to the user's legal guardian or members of the user's immediate family of the user's location in an emergency situation that involves the risk of death or serious physical harm; or to providers of information or database management services solely for purposes of assisting in the delivery of emergency services in response to an emergency.[11]

9:6. Disclosure of subscriber list information

Any telecommunications carrier that provides telephone exchange services must provide subscriber list information[12] gathered in this capacity on a timely and unbundled basis, under nondiscriminatory and reasonable rates, terms, and conditions, to any person upon request if the purpose of the request is publishing directories in any format.[13]

9:7. Wireless location information

The restrictions placed upon the disclosure of wireless location information are higher, given the sensitivity of this information. Any disclosure of, or access to, call location information concerning the user of a commercial mobile service, other than permitted as referenced in § 9:5, or automatic crash notification information to any person other than for use in the operation of an automatic crash notification system, cannot be made without the prior authorization of the customer.[14]

9:8. Disclosure of information in connection with emergency services

Any telecommunications carrier that provides telephone exchange service must provide customer proprietary information (including information pertaining to subscribers whose

---

8. 47 U.S.C. §§ 222(d)(1)–(3).

9. The term "public safety answering point" means a facility that has been designated to receive emergency calls and route them to emergency service personnel. 47 U.S.C. § 222(h)(4).

10. The term "emergency services" means 9-1-1 emergency services and emergency notification services. 47 U.S.C. § 222(h)(5).

11. 47 U.S.C. § 222(d)(4)(A) to (C).

12. The term "subscriber list information" means any information (A) identifying the listed names of subscribers of a carrier and such subscribers' telephone numbers, addresses, or primary advertising classifications (as such classifications are assigned at the time of the establishment of such service), or any combination of such listed names, numbers, addresses, or classifications; and (B) that the carrier or an affiliate has published, caused to be published, or accepted for publication in any directory format. 47 U.S.C. § 222(h)(3).

13. 47 U.S.C. § 222(e).

14. 47 U.S.C. §§ 222(f)(1)–(2).

information is unlisted or unpublished) that is in its possession or control (including information pertaining to subscribers of other carriers) on a timely and unbundled basis, under nondiscriminatory and reasonable rates, terms, and conditions to providers of emergency services, and providers of emergency support services,[15] solely for purposes of delivering or assisting in the delivery of emergency services.[16]

9:9.   Private right of action under the Telecommunications Act of 1996

An issue presented to a federal court in Texas was whether there was an implied right of action against non-telecommunications companies under the Telecommunications Act of 1996, as well as whether the SCA covered records related to a list of numbers called by a person.[17] In *McEwen*, the defendants obtained information regarding telephone calls made by plaintiffs, allegedly in the context of an investigation related to the improper use of trade secrets.[18] The court concluded that there was no private right of action under the Telecommunications Act of 1996, except against "common carriers."[19]

9:10.   Telephone record regulations

In response to the prominence that pretexting has gained due to recent events, new federal regulations were enacted in 2007. The regulations created a number of new requirements (including carrier authentication requirements, notice to customers of account changes, notice of unauthorized disclosures, an annual CPNI certification, and additional requirements specific to providers of interconnected VoIP service) and they govern joint venture and independent contractor use of CPNI and include enforcement provisions.

9:11.   Use of customer proprietary network information without customer approval

Any telecommunications carrier[20] may use, disclose, or permit access to CPNI[21] for the purpose of providing or marketing service offerings among the categories of service (i.e., local, interexchange, and commercial mobile radio service) to which the

---

15.   The term "emergency support services" means information or data base management services used in support of emergency services. 47 U.S.C. § 222(h)(7).

16.   47 U.S.C. § 222(g).

17.   McEwen v. Sourceresources.com, 2007 WL 508874 (S.D. Tex. 2007).

18.   *Id.* at *2-3.

19.   *Id.* *6-7 (*citing* Conboy v. AT&T Corp., 241 F.3d 242 (2d Cir. 2001)).

20.   The terms "telecommunications carrier" or "carrier" shall have the same meaning as set forth in section 3(44) of the Communications Act of 1934, as amended, 47 U.S.C. § 153(44). For the purposes of this subpart, the term "telecommunications carrier" or "carrier" shall include an entity that provides interconnected VoIP service. 47 C.F.R. § 64.2003(o).

21.   Customer proprietary network information (CPNI). The term "customer proprietary network information (CPNI)" has the same meaning given to such term in section 222(h)(1) of the Communications Act of 1934, as amended, 47 U.S.C. 222(h)(1). 47 C.F.R. § 64.2003(g). Subscriber list information (SLI). The term "subscriber list information (SLI)" has the same meaning given to such term in § 222(h)(3) of the Communications Act of 1934, as amended, 47 U.S.C. § 222(h)(3). 47 C.F.R. § 64.2003(n).

customer[22] already subscribes from the same carrier, without customer approval.[23] If a telecommunications carrier provides different categories of service, and a customer subscribes to more than one category of service offered by the carrier, the carrier is permitted to share CPNI among the carrier's affiliated[24] entities that provide a service offering to the customer.[25] However, if a telecommunications carrier provides different categories of service, but a customer does not subscribe to more than one offering by the carrier, the carrier is not permitted to share CPNI with its affiliates, except as provided below.[26]

A telecommunications carrier may not use, disclose, or permit access to CPNI in order to market to a customer service offerings that are within a category of service to which the subscriber does not already subscribe from that carrier, unless that carrier has customer approval to do so, with certain limited exceptions.[27] A wireless provider may use, disclose, or permit access to CPNI derived from its providing commercial mobile radio service (CMRS), without customer approval, for the provision of customer premises equipment (CPE)[28] and information services.[29] A wireline carrier may use, disclose, or permit access to CPNI derived from its providing local exchange service or interexchange service, without customer approval, for the provision of CPE and call answering, voice mail or messaging, voice storage and retrieval services, fax store and forward, and protocol conversion.[30]

Despite this, a telecommunications carrier may not use, disclose, or permit access to CPNI to identify or track customers that call competing service providers. For example, a local exchange carrier may not use local service CPNI to track all customers that call local service competitors.[31]

A telecommunications carrier is permitted to use, disclose, or permit access to CPNI, without customer approval, if it is providing inside wiring installation, maintenance, and repair services, as well as for the purpose of conducting research on the health effects of CMRS.[32]

Additionally, local exchange carriers (LECs),[33] CMRS providers, and entities that provide interconnected VoIP service as that term is defined in § 9:3 of this chapter may use CPNI, without customer approval, to market services formerly known as adjunct-to-

---

22. Customer. A customer of a telecommunications carrier is a person or entity to which the telecommunications carrier is currently providing service. 47 C.F.R. § 64.2003(f).

23. 47 C.F.R. § 64.2005(a).

24. Affiliate. The term "affiliate" has the same meaning given such term in section 3(1) of the Communications Act of 1934, as amended, 47 U.S.C. § 153(1). 47 C.F.R. § 64.2003(c).

25. 47 C.F.R. § 64.2005(a)(1).

26. 47 C.F.R. § 64.2005(a)(2).

27. 47 C.F.R. § 64.2005(b).

28. The term "customer premises equipment (CPE)" has the same meaning given to such term in section 3(14) of the Communications Act of 1934, as amended, 47 U.S.C. § 153(14). 47 C.F.R. § 64.2003(h).

29. 47 C.F.R. § 64.2005(b)(1).

30. *Id.*

31. 47 C.F.R. § 64.2005(b)(2).

32. 47 C.F.R. §§ 64.2005(c)(1)–(2).

33. The term "local exchange carrier" has the same meaning given to such term in section 3(26) of the Communications Act of 1934, as amended, 47 U.S.C. § 153(26). 47 C.F.R. § 64.2003(j).

basic services, such as, but not limited to, speed dialing, computer-provided directory assistance, call monitoring, call tracing, call blocking, call return, repeat dialing, call tracking, call waiting, caller I.D., call forwarding, and other features.[34]

Telecommunications carriers may also use, disclose, or permit access to CPNI to protect the rights or property of the carrier, or to protect users of those services and other carriers from fraudulent, abusive, or unlawful use of, or subscription to, such services.[35]

9:12.   Approval required for use of customer proprietary network information

Customer approval can be obtained through written, oral, or electronic methods.[36] However, a telecommunications carrier relying on oral methods bears the burden of proof to show that the approval was given in compliance with these rules.[37] An approval or disapproval to use, disclose, or permit access to a customer's CPNI must remain in effect until the customer revokes or limits the approval or disapproval.[38] Telecommunications carriers must also maintain records of approvals in any form for at least one year.[39]

9:13.   Use of opt-out and opt-in approval process

Telecommunications carriers may, subject to opt-out approval[40] or opt-in approval,[41] use its customers' individually identifiable CPNI for the purpose of marketing communications-related services[42] to that customer.[43] A telecommunications carrier may, subject to opt-out

---

34. This section is subject to OMB approval. 47 C.F.R. § 64.2005(c)(3).

35. 47 C.F.R. § 64.2005(d).

36. 47 C.F.R. § 64.2007(a).

37. 47 C.F.R. § 64.2007(a)(1).

38. 47 C.F.R. § 64.2007(a)(2).

39. 47 C.F.R. § 64.2005(a)(3).

40. The term "opt-out approval" refers to a method for obtaining customer consent to use, disclose, or permit access to the customer's CPNI. Under this approval method, a customer is deemed to have consented to the use, disclosure, or access to the customer's CPNI if the customer has failed to object thereto within the waiting period described in § 64.2008(d)(1) after the customer is provided appropriate notification of the carrier's request for consent consistent with the rules in this subpart. 47 C.F.R. § 64.2003(l).

41. The term "opt-in approval" refers to a method for obtaining customer consent to use, disclose, or permit access to the customer's CPNI. This approval method requires that the carrier obtain from the customer affirmative, express consent allowing the requested CPNI usage, disclosure, or access after the customer is provided appropriate notification of the carrier's request consistent with the requirements set forth in this subpart. 47 C.F.R. § 64.2003(k).

42. The term "communications-related services" means telecommunications services, information services typically provided by telecommunications carriers, and services related to the provision or maintenance of customer premises equipment. 47 C.F.R. § 64.2003(e). Information services typically provided by telecommunications carriers. The phrase "information services typically provided by telecommunications carriers" means only those information services (as defined in section 3(20) of the Communication Act of 1934, as amended, 47 U.S.C. § 153(20)) that are typically provided by telecommunications carriers, such as Internet access or voice mail services. Such phrase "information services typically provided by telecommunications carriers," as used in this subpart, shall not include retail consumer services provided using Internet Web sites (such as travel reservation services or mortgage lending services), whether or not such services may otherwise be considered to be information services. 47 C.F.R. § 64.2003(i).

43. 47 C.F.R. § 64.2007(b).

approval or opt-in approval, disclose its customer's individually identifiable CPNI, for the purpose of marketing communications-related services to that customer, to its agents and its affiliates that provide communications-related services.[44] A telecommunications carrier may also permit these persons or entities to obtain access to CPNI for these purposes.[45] Except for use and disclosure of CPNI that is permitted without customer approval under § 64.2005, or that is described in this paragraph, or as otherwise provided in § 222 of the Communications Act of 1934, a telecommunications carrier may only use, disclose, or permit access to its customer's individually identifiable CPNI subject to opt-in approval.[46]

9:14.   Notice for use of customer proprietary network information

Prior to any solicitation for customer approval, a telecommunications carrier must provide notification to the customer of the customer's right to restrict use of, disclosure of, and access to that customer's CPNI.[47] Telecommunications carriers must also maintain, for at least one year, records of notification in any form.[48]

Telecommunication carriers must also provide individual notice to customers when they solicit approval to use, disclose, or permit access to customers' CPNI.[49] The notice must provide sufficient information to enable the customer to make an informed decision as to whether to permit a carrier to use, disclose, or permit access to, the customer's CPNI.[50] There are a number of form and content requirements, including that

- the notification must state that the customer has a right, and the carrier has a duty, under federal law, to protect the confidentiality of CPNI;
- the notification must specify the types of information that constitute CPNI and the specific entities that will receive the CPNI, describe the purposes for which CPNI will be used, and inform the customer of his or her right to disapprove those uses, and deny or withdraw access to CPNI at any time;
- the notification must advise the customer of the precise steps the customer must take in order to grant or deny access to CPNI, and must clearly state that a denial of approval will not affect the provision of any services to which the customer subscribes, though carriers may provide a brief statement, in clear and neutral language, describing consequences directly resulting from the lack of access to CPNI;
- the notification must be comprehensible and must not be misleading;
- if written notification is provided, the notice must be clearly legible, use sufficiently large type, and be placed in an area so as to be readily apparent to a customer;

---

44.   *Id.*
45.   *Id.*
46.   *Id.*
47.   47 C.F.R. § 64.2008(a)(1).
48.   47 C.F.R. § 64.2008(a)(2).
49.   47 C.F.R. § 64.2008(b).
50.   47 C.F.R. § 64.2008(c).

- if any portion of a notification is translated into another language, then all portions of the notification must be translated into that language;
- a carrier may not include in the notification any statement attempting to encourage a customer to freeze third-party access to CPNI; and
- the notification must state that any approval or denial of approval for the use of CPNI outside of the service to which the customer already subscribes from that carrier is valid until the customer affirmatively revokes or limits such approval or denial.[51]

There is also a mandatory requirement that a telecommunications carrier's solicitation for approval be proximate to the notification of a customer's CPNI rights.[52] While not mandatory, there may be a statement in the notification that the customer's approval to use CPNI may enhance the carrier's ability to offer products and services tailored to the customer's needs, as well as that the carrier may be compelled to disclose CPNI to any person upon affirmative written request by the customer.[53]

9:15. Notice requirements for opt-outs

A telecommunications carrier must provide notification to obtain opt-out approval through electronic or written methods, but not by oral communication, except as provided below.[54] These notices must comply with the above.[55] Additionally, carriers must wait a 30-day minimum period of time after giving customers notice and an opportunity to opt out before assuming customer approval to use, disclose, or permit access to CPNI.[56] A carrier may, in its discretion, provide for a longer period.[57] Carriers have an affirmative duty to notify customers as to the applicable waiting period for a response before approval is assumed.[58]

The timing of when the notice begins to run is dependent on the form of notice. With electronic notice, the waiting period begins to run from the date when the notification was sent.[59] If the notice is by mail, the waiting period begins to run on the date following the mailing date.[60]

Carriers who use the opt-out mechanism must provide notice to their customers every two years.[61]

---

51.   47 C.F.R. §§ 64.2008(c)(1)–(6), 64.2008(c)(8)–(9).

52.   47 C.F.R. § 64.2008(c)(10).

53.   47 C.F.R. § 64.2008(c)(7).

54.   47 C.F.R. § 64.2008(d).

55.   *Id.*

56.   47 C.F.R. § 64.2008(d)(1).

57.   *Id.*

58.   *Id.*

59.   47 C.F.R. § 64.2008(d)(1)(i).

60.   47 C.F.R. § 64.2008(d)(1)(ii).

61.   47 C.F.R. § 64.2008(d)(2).

9:16.   Additional burdens on e-mail notice

Telecommunications carriers that use e-mail to provide opt-out notices must comply with additional requirements: carriers must obtain express, verifiable, prior approval from consumers to send notices via e-mail regarding their service in general, or CPNI in particular; carriers must allow customers to reply directly to e-mails containing CPNI notices in order to opt out; opt-out e-mail notices that are returned to the carrier as undeliverable must be sent to the customer in another form before carriers may consider the customer to have received notice; carriers that use e-mail to send CPNI notices must ensure that the subject line of the message clearly and accurately identifies the subject matter of the e-mail; and telecommunications carriers must make available to every customer a method to opt out that is of no additional cost to the customer and that is available 24 hours a day, 7 days a week.[62] Carriers may satisfy this requirement through a combination of methods, so long as all customers have the ability to opt out at no cost and are able to effectuate that choice whenever they choose.[63]

9:17.   Notice requirements for opt-in requests

A telecommunications carrier may provide notification to obtain opt-in approval through oral, written, or electronic methods.[64] The contents of any such notification must comply with the requirements stated in 47 C.F.R. § 64.2008(c).[65]

9:18.   Notice requirements for one-time use of CPNI

Carriers may use oral notice to obtain limited, one-time use of CPNI for inbound and outbound customer telephone contacts for the duration of the call, regardless of whether carriers use opt-out or opt-in approval based on the nature of the contact.[66] The contents of any such notification must comply with the requirements of 47 C.F.R. § 64.2008(c), except that telecommunications carriers may omit certain notices if they are not relevant to why the carrier seeks CPNI,[67] Such exceptions include that carriers need not advise customers that if they have opted-out previously, no action is needed to maintain the opt-out election; carriers need not advise customers that they may share CPNI with their affiliates or third parties and need not name those entities, if the limited CPNI usage will not result in use by, or disclosure to, an affiliate or third party; carriers need not disclose the means by which a customer can deny or withdraw future access to CPNI, so long as carriers explain to customers that the scope of the approval the carrier seeks is limited to one-time use; and carriers may omit disclosure of the precise steps a customer must take in order to grant or deny access to CPNI,

---

62.   47 C.F.R. §§ 64.2008(d)(3)(i)–(v).

63.   47 C.F.R. § 64.2008(d)(3)(v).

64.   47 C.F.R. § 64.2008(e).

65.   *Id.*

66.   47 C.F.R. § 64.2008(f)(1).

67.   47 C.F.R. § 64.2008(f)(2).

as long as the carrier clearly communicates that the customer can deny access to his CPNI for the call.[68]

9:19.   Safeguards on use of CPNI

Telecommunications carriers must implement a system by which the status of a customer's CPNI approval can be clearly established prior to the use of CPNI.[69] Telecommunications carriers must also train their personnel as to when they are and are not authorized to use CPNI, and carriers must have an explicit disciplinary process in place.[70] Carriers are also required to maintain a record, electronically or in some other manner, of their own and their affiliates' sales and marketing campaigns that use their customers' CPNI.[71] All carriers must maintain a record of all instances where CPNI was disclosed or provided to third parties, or where third parties were allowed access to CPNI.[72] The record must include a description of each campaign, the specific CPNI that was used in the campaign, and what products and services were offered as a part of the campaign, and this must be retained for at least one year.[73]

Telecommunications carriers must also establish a supervisory review process regarding carrier compliance with the rules in this portion of the regulations for outbound marketing situations and maintain records of carrier compliance for a minimum period of one year.[74] This includes the specific requirement that sales personnel must obtain supervisory approval of any proposed outbound marketing request for customer approval.[75]

9:20.   Compliance statements

A telecommunications carrier is required to have an officer, as an agent of the carrier, sign and file with the FCC a compliance certificate on an annual basis.[76] The officer must state in the certification that he has personal knowledge that the company has established operating procedures that are adequate to ensure compliance with the rules in this portion of the regulations.[77] The carrier must provide a statement accompanying the certificate explaining how its operating procedures ensure that it is or is not in compliance with the rules in this subpart.[78] In addition, the carrier must include an explanation of any actions taken against data brokers and a summary of all customer complaints received in the past year concerning the unauthorized release of CPNI.[79]

---

68.   47 C.F.R. §§ 64.2008(f)(2)(i)–(iv).

69.   47 C.F.R. § 64.2009(a).

70.   47 C.F.R. § 64.2009(b).

71.   47 C.F.R. § 64.2009(c).

72.   *Id.*

73.   *Id.*

74.   47 C.F.R. § 64.2009(d).

75.   *Id.*

76.   47 C.F.R. § 64.2009(e). This portion of the regulations are pending OMB approval.

77.   47 C.F.R. § 64.2009(e).

78.   *Id.*

79.   *Id.*

This filing must be made annually with the Enforcement Bureau on or before March 1 in EB Docket No. 06-36, for data pertaining to the previous calendar year.[80]

9:21.   Notices to the Commission regarding opt-outs

Carriers must provide written notice within five business days to the Commission of any instance where the opt-out mechanisms do not work properly to such a degree that a consumer's inability to opt out is more than an anomaly.[81] The notice must be in the form of a letter and must include the carrier's name, a description of the opt-out mechanisms used, the problems experienced, the remedy proposed and when it was or will be implemented, whether the relevant state commissions has been notified (including whether it has taken any action), a copy of the notice provided to customers, and contact information.[82] The notice must be submitted even if the carrier offers other methods by which consumers may opt out.[83]

9:22.   Safeguards on the disclosure of CPNI— Password requirements

In order to establish a password, a telecommunications carrier must authenticate the customer without the use of readily available biographical information[84] or account information.[85] [86] Telecommunications carriers may create a back-up customer authentication method in the event of a lost or forgotten password, but the back-up customer authentication method may not prompt the customer for readily available biographical information, or account information.[87] If a customer cannot provide the correct password or the correct response for the back-up customer authentication method, the customer must establish a new password under a procedure that complies with this paragraph.[88]

9:23.   Safeguards on the disclosure of CPNI— General requirements

Telecommunications carriers must take reasonable measures to discover and protect against attempts to gain unauthorized access to CPNI.[89] Telecommunications carriers

---

80.   47 C.F.R. § 64.2009(e).

81.   47 C.F.R. § 64.2009(f).

82.   47 C.F.R. § 64.2009(f)(1).

83.   47 C.F.R. § 64.2009(f)(2).

84.   "Readily available biographical information" is information drawn from the customer's life history and includes such things as the customer's social security number, or the last four digits of that number; mother's maiden name; home address; or date of birth. 47 C.F.R. § 64.2003(m).

85.   "Account information" is information that is specifically connected to the customer's service relationship with the carrier, including such things as an account number or any component thereof, the telephone number associated with the account, or the bill's amount. 47 C.F.R. § 64.2003(a).

86   47 C.F.R. § 64.2010(e).

87.   *Id.*

88.   *Id.*

89.   47 C.F.R. § 64.2010(a).

must properly authenticate a customer prior to disclosing CPNI based on customer-initiated telephone contact, online account access, or an in-store visit.[90]

9:24. Safeguards on the disclosure of CPNI— Telephone access

Telecommunications carriers may only disclose call detail information[91] over the telephone, based on customer-initiated telephone contact, if the customer first provides the carrier with a password, as described below, that is not prompted by the carrier asking for readily available biographical information or account information.[92] If the customer does not provide a password, the telecommunications carrier may only disclose call detail information by sending it to the customer's address of record[93] or by calling the customer at the telephone number of record.[94] If the customer is able to provide call detail information to the telecommunications carrier during a customer-initiated call without the telecommunications carrier's assistance, then the telecommunications carrier is permitted to discuss the call detail information provided by the customer.[95]

9:25. Safeguards on the disclosure of CPNI—Online access

A telecommunications carrier must authenticate a customer without the use of readily available biographical information or account information, prior to allowing the customer online access to CPNI related to a telecommunications service[96] account.[97] Once the customer is authenticated, the customer may only obtain online access to CPNI related to a telecommunications service account through a password that is not prompted by the carrier asking for readily available biographical information or account information.[98]

---

90. *Id.*

91. "Call detail information" is any information that pertains to the transmission of specific telephone calls, including, for outbound calls, the number called, and the time, location, or duration of any call and, for inbound calls, the number from which the call was placed, and the time, location, or duration of any call. 47 C.F.R. § 64.2003(d).

92. 47 C.F.R. § 64.2010(b).

93. An "address of record," whether postal or electronic, is an address that the carrier has associated with the customer's account for at least 30 days. 47 C.F.R. § 64.2003(b).

94. "Telephone number of record" is the telephone number associated with the underlying service, not the telephone number supplied as a customer's "contact information." 47 C.F.R. § 64.2003(q). 47 C.F.R. § 64.2010(b).

95. 47 C.F.R. § 64.2010(b).

96. The term "telecommunications service" has the same meaning given to such term in section 3(46) of the Communications Act of 1934, as amended, 47 U.S.C. § 153(46). 47 C.F.R. § 64.2003(p).

97. 47 C.F.R. § 64.2010(c).

98. *Id.*

9:26.   Safeguards on the disclosure of CPNI—In-store access

A telecommunications carrier may disclose CPNI to a customer who, at a carrier's retail location, presents to the telecommunications carrier or its agent a valid photo ID[99] matching the customer's account information.[100]

9:27.   Safeguards on the disclosure of CPNI—Notification of account changes

Telecommunications carriers must notify customers immediately whenever a password, customer response to a back-up means of authentication for lost or forgotten passwords, online account, or address of record is created or changed.[101] This notification is not required when the customer initiates service, including the selection of a password at service initiation.[102] Notification may be made through a carrier-originated voicemail or text message to the telephone number of record, or by mail to the address of record, but it must not reveal the changed information or be sent to the new account information.[103]

9:28.   Safeguards on the disclosure of CPNI—Business customer exception

Telecommunications carriers may vary the authentication regimes via contract for services that are provided to business customers that have both a dedicated account representative and a contract that specifically addresses the carriers' protection of CPNI.[104]

9:29.   Notification of CPNI security breaches

The regulations also impose notice obligations on carriers, which include notice to the government and notice to consumers. Unlike most other security breach laws, this law creates an explicit requirement to go to law enforcement first and gives law enforcement the ability to delay notice, which is a common element in security breach laws.

9:30.   Notification of CPNI security breaches— What is a breach?

A breach under these regulations has a different definition than under most security breach laws. Under these regulations, a "breach" has occurred when a person, without authorization or exceeding authorization, has intentionally gained access to, used, or disclosed CPNI.[105] The definition does not hinge on acquisition, and at some level

---

99. A "valid photo ID" is a government-issued means of personal identification with a photograph such as a driver's license, passport, or comparable ID that is not expired. 47 C.F.R. § 64.2003(r).

100. 47 C.F.R. § 64.2010(d).

101. 47 C.F.R. § 64.2010(f).

102. *Id.*

103. *Id.*

104. 47 C.F.R. § 64.2010(g).

105. 47 C.F.R. § 64.2011(e).

incorporates the standards from the CFAA regarding authority. Given that access is required, but not acquisition, this law will have broad application to carriers.

9:31. Notification of CPNI security breaches— Notice requirements

There are two disclosure requirements under this law. The first requires electronic notice to the United States Secret Service (USSS) and the FBI as soon as practicable and in no event later than seven business days after reasonable determination of the breach.[106] The Commission is required to maintain a link to the reporting facility at http://www.fcc.gov/eb/cpni.[107] The carrier shall not notify its customers or disclose the breach publicly, whether voluntarily or under state or local law or these rules, until it has completed the process of notifying law enforcement.[108] It should be noted that notwithstanding any state law to the contrary, the carrier is generally precluded from notifying customers or disclosing the breach to the public until seven full business days have passed after notification to the USSS and the FBI except as provided in 47 C.F.R. § 64.2011(b)(2) and (b)(3).[109]

However, if the carrier believes that there is an extraordinarily urgent need to notify any class of affected customers sooner than otherwise permitted, in order to avoid immediate and irreparable harm, it must indicate in its notification to the government and may proceed to immediately notify its affected customers only after consultation with the relevant investigating agency.[110] The carrier must cooperate with the relevant investigating agency's request to minimize any adverse effects of customer notification.[111] If the relevant investigating agency determines that public disclosure or notice to customers would impede or compromise an ongoing or potential criminal investigation or national security, the agency may direct the carrier not to so disclose or notify for an initial period of up to 30 days.[112] The period may be extended by the agency as reasonably necessary in the judgment of the agency.[113] If such a direction is given, the agency must notify the carrier when it appears that public disclosure or notice to affected customers will no longer impede or compromise a criminal investigation or national security.[114] The agency must also provide in writing its initial direction to the carrier, any subsequent extension, and any notification that notice will no longer impede or compromise a criminal investigation or national security.[115] These writings must be contemporaneously logged on the same reporting facility that contains records of notifications filed by carriers.[116]

---

106. 47 C.F.R. §§ 64.2011(a)–(b).
107. 47 C.F.R. § 64.2011(b).
108. 47 C.F.R. § 64.2011(a).
109. 47 C.F.R. § 64.2011(b)(1).
110. 47 C.F.R. § 64.2011(2).
111. 47 C.F.R. § 64.2011(b)(2).
112. 47 C.F.R. § 64.2011(b)(3).
113. *Id.*
114. *Id.*
115. *Id.*
116. *Id.*

The second notification requires notice to customers only after it has completed the process outlined above.[117]

There are also recordkeeping requirements, which require a carrier to maintain a record, electronically or in some other manner, of any breaches discovered, notifications made to the USSS and the FBI, and notifications made to customers.[118] The record must include, if available, dates of discovery and notification, a detailed description of the CPNI that was the subject of the breach, and the circumstances of the breach.[119] These records must be maintained by the carriers for a minimum of two years.[120]

9:32.   Notification of CPNI security breaches—Preemption

These regulations do not supersede any statute, regulation, order, or interpretation in any state, except to the extent that such statute, regulation, order, or interpretation is inconsistent with the provisions of this regulation, and then only to the extent of the inconsistency.[121]

9:33.   Federal Do-Not-Call law

The federal Do-Not-Call law is generally viewed as one of the more successful attempts to protect consumer privacy. Though it is framed in the terms of restrictions on marketing activity, it is truly a privacy statute that is simply specific to a method of communicating certain messages. The hallmark of the law is the Do-Not-Call list, an opt-in list that consumers can place themselves on. This act by a consumer precludes many forms of telephone communications, particularly those that promote commercial services, unless there is a pre-existing relationship between the business and the consumer. The Do-Not-Call law also has record retention requirements, as well as disclosure requirements in many cases.

Many states have followed the federal government's lead and enacted their own laws, which are in large part driven by the existence of the Do-Not-Call registry. These laws also can contain restrictions on the use of prerecorded messages, and these restrictions may not be contained in the same section of the code in which the Do-Not-Call law was placed. Indeed, some states have placed restrictions on recorded messages and auto-dialers in the public utilities code. It should be noted that certain state laws actually regulate direct mail and other written solicitations under their Do-Not-Call laws if the writing attempts to solicit a call. In order to ensure compliance, a review of applicable state laws is frequently required.

---

117. 47 C.F.R. § 64.2011(c).

118. 47 C.F.R. § 64.2011(d).

119. *Id.*

120. *Id.*

121. 47 C.F.R. § 64.2011(f).

It is a violation of the Do-Not-Call law[122] if a telemarketer[123] or a seller[124] causes a telemarketer to cause any telephone to ring, or to engage any person[125] in telephone conversation, repeatedly or continuously with intent to annoy, abuse, or harass any person at the called number, or deny or interfere in any way, directly or indirectly, with a person's right to be placed on any registry of names and/or telephone numbers of persons who do not wish to receive outbound telephone calls.[126] It is also improper to initiate an outbound call when that person previously has stated that he or she does not wish to receive an outbound telephone call made by or on behalf of the seller whose goods or services are being offered or made on behalf of the charitable organization for which a charitable contribution[127] is being solicited, or that person's telephone number is on the "Do-Not-Call" registry, maintained by the Commission, of persons who do not wish to receive outbound telephone calls to induce the purchase of goods or services unless the seller

- has obtained the express agreement, in writing, of such person to place calls to that person. Such written agreement shall clearly evidence such person's authorization that calls made by or on behalf of a specific party may be placed to that person, and shall include the telephone number to which the calls may be placed and the signature, including a valid electronic signature, of that person; or
- has an established business relationship[128] with such person, and that person has not stated that he or she does not wish to receive outbound telephone calls under the above-referenced portions of this rule.[129]

It is also an illegal act to abandon[130] an outbound call.[131] It also an illegal act to sell, rent, lease, purchase, or use any list established to comply with the Do-Not-Call list for any purpose except compliance with the provisions of the rule or otherwise to prevent telephone calls to telephone numbers on such lists.[132]

---

122. This law is also known as the Telephone Consumer Protection Act, or TCPA.
123. "Telemarketer" means any person who, in connection with telemarketing, initiates or receives telephone calls to or from a customer or donor. 16 C.F.R. § 310.2(bb).
124. "Seller" means any person who, in connection with a telemarketing transaction, provides, offers to provide, or arranges for others to provide goods or services to the customer in exchange for consideration. 16 C.F.R. § 310.2(z).
125. "Person" means any individual, group, unincorporated association, limited or general partnership, corporation, or other business entity. 16 C.F.R. § 310.2(v).
126. Outbound telephone call means a telephone call initiated by a telemarketer to induce the purchase of goods or services or to solicit a charitable contribution. 16 C.F.R. § 310.2(u). 16 C.F.R. §§ 310.4(b)(1)(i)–(ii).
127. Charitable contribution means any donation or gift of money or any other thing of value. 16 C.F.R. § 310.2(f).
128. Established business relationship means a relationship between a seller and a consumer based on: (1) the consumer's purchase, rental, or lease of the seller's goods or services or a financial transaction between the consumer and seller, within the eighteen (18) months immediately preceding the date of a telemarketing call; or (2) the consumer's inquiry or application regarding a product or service offered by the seller, within the three (3) months immediately preceding the date of a telemarketing call. 16 C.F.R. § 310.2(n).
129. 16 C.F.R. §§ 310.4(b)(1)(iii)(A)–(B).
130. An outbound telephone call is "abandoned" under this section if a person answers it and the telemarketer does not connect the call to a sales representative within 2 seconds of the person's completed greeting.
131. 16 C.F.R. § 310.4(b)(1)(iv).
132. 16 C.F.R. § 310.4(b)(2).

It is also improper if the seller and telemarketer is initiating any outbound telephone call that delivers a prerecorded message, other than a prerecorded message permitted for compliance with the call abandonment safe harbor in § 310.4(b)(4)(iii), unless in any such call to induce the purchase of any good or service, the seller has obtained from the recipient of the call an express agreement, in writing, that evidences the willingness of the recipient of the call to receive calls that deliver prerecorded messages by or on behalf of a specific seller and that includes such person's telephone number and signature.[133] The seller must obtain the agreement only after a clear and conspicuous disclosure that the purpose of the agreement is to authorize the seller to place prerecorded calls to such person, and the seller must not require, directly or indirectly, that the agreement be executed as a condition of purchasing any good or service.[134]

Additionally, in any such call to induce the purchase of any good or service, or to induce a charitable contribution from a member of, or previous donor to, a non-profit charitable organization on whose behalf the call is made, the seller or telemarketer also must allow the telephone to ring for at least 15 seconds or 4 rings before disconnecting an unanswered call; and within 2 seconds after the completed greeting of the person called, plays a prerecorded message that promptly provides the disclosures required by § 310.4(d) or (e), followed immediately by a disclosure of one or both of the following:

- in the case of a call that could be answered in person by a consumer, that the person called can use an automated interactive voice and/or keypress-activated opt-out mechanism to assert a Do-Not-Call request pursuant to § 310.4(b)(1)(iii)(A) at any time during the message.[135] The mechanism must automatically add the number called to the seller's entity-specific Do-Not-Call list; once invoked, immediately disconnect the call; and be available for use at any time during the message.

- in the case of a call that could be answered by an answering machine or voicemail service, that the person called can use a toll-free telephone number to assert a Do-Not-Call request pursuant to § 310.4(b)(1)(iii)(A).[136] The number provided must connect directly to an automated interactive voice or keypress-activated opt-out mechanism that automatically adds the number called to the seller's entity-specific Do-Not-Call list; immediately thereafter disconnects the call; and is accessible at any time throughout the duration of the telemarketing campaign.[137]

The call must also comply with all other requirements of these regulations and other applicable federal and state laws.[138] Any call that complies with all applicable

---

133. For purposes of this Rule, the term "signature" shall include an electronic or digital form of signature, to the extent that such form of signature is recognized as a valid signature under applicable federal law or state contract law.

134. 16 C.F.R. §§ 310.4(b)(v)(A)(i)–(iv).

135. 16 C.F.R. §§ 310.4(b)(v)(B)(i)–(ii)(A)(1).

136. 16 C.F.R. §§ 310.4(b)(v)(B)(i)–(ii)(A)(2)–(3).

137. 16 C.F.R. §§ 310.4(b)(v)(B)(i)–(ii)(B)(1)–(3).

138. 16 C.F.R. § 310.4(b)(v)(B)(iii).

requirements of 16 C.F.R. § 310.4(b)(v) shall not be deemed to violate § 310.4(b)(1)(iv).[139]

9:34.   Exception for HIPAA

The above restrictions do not apply to any outbound telephone call that delivers a prerecorded healthcare message made by, or on behalf of, a covered entity or its business associate, as those terms are defined in the HIPAA Privacy Rule.[140]

9:35.   Federal Do-Not-Call law—Defenses

It is a defense to any action for a violation of these provisions if the seller or telemarketer can demonstrate that, as part of its routine business practice

(1) it has established and implemented written procedures to comply with 16 C.F.R. §§ 310.4(b)(1)(ii) and (iii);

(2) it has trained its personnel, and any entity assisting in its compliance, in the procedures established pursuant to 16 C.F.R. § 310.4(b)(3)(i);

(3) it or another person acting on its behalf has maintained and recorded a list of telephone numbers it may not contact, in compliance with 16 C.F.R. § 310.4(b)(1)(iii)(A);

(4) it uses a process to prevent telemarketing[141] to any telephone number on any list established pursuant to 16 C.F.R. § 310.4(b)(3)(iii) or 16 C.F.R. § 310.4(b)(1)(iii)(B), employing a version of the "Do-Not-Call" registry obtained from the Commission no more than 31 days prior to the date any call is made, and maintains records documenting this process;

(5) it or another person acting on its behalf monitors and enforces compliance with the procedures established pursuant to § 310.4(b)(3)(i); and

(6) any subsequent call otherwise violating § 310.4(b)(1)(ii) or (iii) is the result of error.[142]

There is similarly no liability for abandoning calls when the following measures are in use:

- The seller or telemarketer employs technology that ensures abandonment of no more than 3 percent of all calls answered by a person, measured per day per calling

---

139. 16 C.F.R. § 310.4(b)(v)(C).

140. 16 C.F.R. § 310.4(b)(v)(D).

141. Telemarketing means a plan, program, or campaign which is conducted to induce the purchase of goods or services or a charitable contribution, by use of one or more telephones and which involves more than one interstate telephone call. The term does not include the solicitation of sales through the mailing of a catalog which contains a written description or illustration of the goods or services offered for sale; includes the business address of the seller; includes multiple pages of written material or illustrations; and has been issued not less frequently than once a year, when the person making the solicitation does not solicit customers by telephone but only receives calls initiated by customers in response to the catalog and during those calls takes orders only without further solicitation. For purposes of the previous sentence, the term "further solicitation" does not include providing the customer with information about, or attempting to sell, any other item included in the same catalog which prompted the customer's call or in a substantially similar catalog. 16 C.F.R. § 310.2(cc).

142. 16 C.F.R. §§ 310.4(b)(3)(i)–(vi).

campaign, if less than 30 days, or separately over each successive 30-day period or portion thereof that the campaign continues.

- The seller or telemarketer, for each telemarketing call placed, allows the telephone to ring for at least 15 seconds or 4 rings before disconnecting an unanswered call.

- Whenever a sales representative is not available to speak with the person answering the call within 2 seconds after the person's completed greeting, the seller or telemarketer promptly plays a recorded message that states the name and telephone number of the seller on whose behalf the call was placed.

- The seller or telemarketer complies with the record retention requirements.[143]

9:36.   Federal Do-Not-Call law—Calling times

It is a violation of the Do-Not-Call regulations for a telemarketer, without prior consent, to engage in outbound telephone calls to a person's residence at any time other than between 8:00 a.m. and 9:00 p.m. local time at the called person's location.[144]

9:37.   Federal Do-Not-Call law—Required disclosures

Generally, it is a violation of the Do-Not-Call regulations for a telemarketer to induce the purchase of goods or services or to fail to disclose truthfully, promptly, and in a clear and conspicuous manner to the person receiving the call, the following information:

(1) the identity of the seller;

(2) that the purpose of the call is to sell goods or services;

(3) the nature of the goods or services; and

(4) that no purchase or payment is necessary to be able to win a prize[145] or participate in a prize promotion[146] if a prize promotion is offered and that any purchase or payment will not increase the person's chances of winning.[147]

---

143. 16 C.F.R. § 310.4(b)(4).

144. 16 C.F.R. § 310.4(c).

145. Prize means anything offered, or purportedly offered, and given, or purportedly given, to a person by chance. For purposes of this definition, chance exists if a person is guaranteed to receive an item and, at the time of the offer or purported offer, the telemarketer does not identify the specific item that the person will receive. 16 C.F.R. § 310.2(x).

146. Prize promotion means: (1) A sweepstakes or other game of chance; or (2) An oral or written express or implied representation that a person has won, has been selected to receive, or may be eligible to receive a prize or purported prize. 16 C.F.R. § 310.2(y).

147. 16 C.F.R. § 310.4(d). This disclosure must be made before or in conjunction with the description of the prize to the person called. If requested by that person, the telemarketer must disclose the no-purchase/no-payment entry method for the prize promotion. However, in any internal upsell for the sale of goods or services, the seller or telemarketer must provide the disclosures listed in this portion of the law only to the extent that the information in the upsell differs from the disclosures provided in the initial telemarketing transaction.

9:38.　Federal Do-Not-Call law—Required disclosures— Charitable solicitations

It is also illegal for a telemarketer in an outbound telephone call to induce a charitable contribution, to fail to disclose truthfully, promptly, and in a clear and conspicuous manner to the person receiving the call, the following information:

(1) the identity of the charitable organization on behalf of which the request is being made; and

(2) that the purpose of the call is to solicit a charitable contribution.[148]

The TCPA's application to charitable fundraising was initially challenged. While the law is inapplicable to in-house charity fundraising because the FTC typically does not have jurisdiction over not-for-profit businesses, it was thought to apply to for profit entities that did fundraising for charitable entities. This viewpoint was affirmed by the Fourth Circuit when it rejected a constitutional challenge to the TCPA.[149]

9:39.　Federal Do-Not-Call law—Required disclosures— Recordkeeping requirements

A seller or telemarketer must keep, for a period of 24 months from the date the record is produced, the following information regarding its telemarketing activities:

(1) all substantially different advertising, brochures, telemarketing scripts, and promotional materials;

(2) the name and last known address of each prize recipient and the prize awarded for prizes that are represented, directly or by implication, to have a value of $25.00 or more;

(3) the name and last known address of each customer,[150] the goods or services purchased, the date such goods or services were shipped or provided, and the amount paid by the customer for the goods or services;

(4) the name, any fictitious name used, the last known home address and telephone number, and the job title(s) for all current and former employees directly involved in telephone sales or solicitations; provided, however, that if the seller or telemarketer permits fictitious names to be used by employees, each fictitious name must be traceable to only one specific employee; and

(5) all verifiable authorizations or records of express informed consent or express agreement required to be provided or received under this rule.[151]

These records can be kept in any form and in the same manner, format, or place as they keep such records in the ordinary course of business.[152] The seller and a telemarketer calling on behalf of the seller may, by written agreement, allocate responsibility between themselves for the recordkeeping required by the regulations.[153]

---

148. 16 C.F.R. § 310.4(e).

149. National Federation of the Blind v. FTC, 420 F.3d 331 (4th Cir. 2005).

150. Customer means any person who is or may be required to pay for goods or services offered through telemar-keting. 16 C.F.R. § 310.2(l).

151. 16 C.F.R. §§ 310.5(a)(1)–(5).

152. 16 C.F.R. § 310.5(b).

153. 16 C.F.R. § 310.5(c).

The solicitation of charitable contributions is not subject to the provisions of the Do-Not-Call list. Certain other pay-per-call services, franchising, and other acts are exempted as well.[154]

9:40. TCPA's application to SMS

In certain circumstances, including if auto-dialers are used and messages are sent to cell phones, the TCPA has been held to apply to e-mail or other electronic messaging.[155]

9:41. Autodialer and facsimile restrictions

No person or entity may initiate any telephone call (other than a call made for emergency purposes[156] or made with the prior express consent of the called party) using an automatic telephone dialing system[157] or an artificial or prerecorded voice to any emergency telephone line, including any 911 line and any emergency line of a hospital, medical physician or service office, health care facility, poison control center, or fire protection or law enforcement agency; to the telephone line of any guest room or patient room of a hospital, health care facility, elderly home, or similar establishment; or to any telephone number assigned to a paging service, cellular telephone service, specialized mobile radio service, or other radio common carrier service, or any service for which the called party is charged for the call.[158] However, a person will not be liable for violating the last portion of this provision when the call is placed to a wireless number that has been ported from wireline service and such call is a voice call; not knowingly made to a wireless number; and made within 15 days of the porting of the number from wireline to wireless service, provided the number is not already on the national Do-Not-Call registry or caller's company-specific Do-Not-Call list.[159]

It is also illegal for a person to initiate any telephone call to any residential line using an artificial or prerecorded voice to deliver a message without the prior express consent of the called party, unless the call is made for emergency purposes; is not made for a commercial purpose; is made for a commercial purpose but does not include or introduce an unsolicited advertisement[160] or constitute a telephone solicitation;[161] is

---

154. 16 C.F.R. § 310.6(b).

155. Joffe v. Acacia Mortg. Corp., 211 Ariz. 325, 121 P.3d 831 (Ct. App. Div. 1, 2005).

156. The term emergency purposes means calls made necessary in any situation affecting the health and safety of consumers. 47 C.F.R. § 64.1200(f)(3).

157. The terms automatic telephone dialing system and autodialer mean equipment which has the capacity to store or produce telephone numbers to be called using a random or sequential number generator and to dial such numbers. 47 C.F.R. § 64.1200(f)(1).

158. 47 C.F.R. §§ 64.1200(a)(1)(i)–(iii).

159. 47 C.F.R. § 64.1200(a)(1)(iv).

160. The term unsolicited advertisement means any material advertising the commercial availability or quality of any property, goods, or services which is transmitted to any person without that person's prior express invitation or permission, in writing or otherwise. 47 C.F.R. § 64.1200(f)(13).

161. The term telephone solicitation means the initiation of a telephone call or message for the purpose of encouraging the purchase or rental of, or investment in, property, goods, or services, which is transmitted to any person, but such term does not include a call or message (i) To any person with that person's prior express invitation or permission; (ii) To any person with whom the caller has an established business relationship; or (iii) By or on behalf of a tax-exempt nonprofit organization. 47 C.F.R. § 64.1200(f)(12).

made to any person with whom the caller has an established business relationship[162] at the time the call is made; or is made by or on behalf of a tax-exempt nonprofit organization.[163] It is also illegal to use a telephone facsimile machine,[164] computer, or other device to send an unsolicited advertisement to a telephone facsimile machine, unless the unsolicited advertisement is from a sender[165] with an established business relationship with the recipient and the sender obtained the number of the telephone facsimile machine through the voluntary communication of such number by the recipient directly to the sender, within the context of such established business relationship; or a directory, advertisement, or site on the Internet to which the recipient voluntarily agreed to make available its facsimile number for public distribution.[166] If a sender obtains the facsimile number from the recipient's own directory, advertisement, or Internet site, it will be presumed that the number was voluntarily made available for public distribution, unless the materials explicitly note that unsolicited advertisements are not accepted at the specified facsimile number. If a sender obtains the facsimile number from other sources, the sender must take reasonable steps to verify that the recipient agreed to make the number available for public distribution.[167]

This does not apply in the case of an unsolicited advertisement that is sent based on an established business relationship with the recipient that was in existence before July 9, 2005 if the sender also possessed the facsimile machine number of the recipient before July 9, 2005.[168] There is a rebuttable presumption that if a valid established business relationship was formed prior to July 9, 2005, the sender possessed the facsimile number prior to such date as well.The advertisement must also contain a notice that informs the recipient of the ability and means to avoid future unsolicited advertisements.[169]

---

162. The term established business relationship for purposes of telephone solicitations means a prior or existing relationship formed by a voluntary two-way communication between a person or entity and a residential subscriber with or without an exchange of consideration, on the basis of the subscriber's purchase or transaction with the entity within the eighteen (18) months immediately preceding the date of the telephone call or on the basis of the subscriber's inquiry or application regarding products or services offered by the entity within the three months immediately preceding the date of the call, which relationship has not been previously terminated by either party. The subscriber's seller-specific Do-Not-Call request, as set forth in paragraph (d)(3) of this section, terminates an established business relationship for purposes of telemarketing and telephone solicitation even if the subscriber continues to do business with the seller. The subscriber's established business relationship with a particular business entity does not extend to affiliated entities unless the subscriber would reasonably expect them to be included given the nature and type of goods or services offered by the affiliate and the identity of the affiliate. 47 C.F.R. § 64.1200(f)(4).

163. 47 C.F.R. §§ 64.1200(a)(2)(i)–(v).

164. The term telephone facsimile machine means equipment that has the capacity to transcribe text or images, or both, from paper into an electronic signal and to transmit that signal over a regular telephone line, or to transcribe text or images (or both) from an electronic signal received over a regular telephone line onto paper. 47 C.F.R. § 64.1200(f)(11).

165. The term sender means the person or entity on whose behalf a facsimile unsolicited advertisement is sent or whose goods or services are advertised or promoted in the unsolicited advertisement. 47 C.F.R. § 64.1200(f)(8).

166. 47 C.F.R. §§ 64.1200(a)(3)(i)–(ii)(B).

167. 47 C.F.R. § 64.1200(a)(3)(ii).

168. 47 C.F.R. § 64.1200(a)(3)(ii)(C).

169. 47 C.F.R. § 64.1200(a)(3)(iii).

A notice contained in an advertisement complies with the requirements under this paragraph only if the notice is clear and conspicuous[170] and on the first page of the advertisement; the notice states that the recipient may make a request to the sender of the advertisement not to send any future advertisements to a telephone facsimile machine or machines and that failure to comply within 30 days with such a request meeting the requirements is unlawful; the notice sets forth the requirements for an opt-out request; the telephone and facsimile numbers and cost-free mechanism identified in the notice must permit an individual or business to make an opt-out request 24 hours a day, 7 days a week; the notice includes a domestic contact telephone number and facsimile machine number for the recipient to transmit such a request to the sender; and if neither the required telephone number nor facsimile machine number is a toll-free number, a separate cost-free mechanism including a website address or e-mail address, for a recipient to transmit a request pursuant to such notice to the sender of the advertisement.[171] A local telephone number also shall constitute a cost-free mechanism so long as recipients are local and will not incur any long distance or other separate charges for calls made to such number.

A facsimile advertisement that is sent to a recipient that has provided prior express invitation or permission to the sender must include an opt-out notice that complies with specific requirements.[172] A request not to send future unsolicited advertisements to a telephone facsimile machine complies with the requirements under this subparagraph only if the request identifies the telephone number or numbers of the telephone facsimile machine or machines to which the request relates; the request is made to the telephone number, facsimile number, website address or e-mail address identified in the sender's facsimile advertisement; and the person making the request has not, subsequent to such request, provided express invitation or permission to the sender, in writing or otherwise, to send such advertisements to such person at such telephone facsimile machine.[173]

A sender that receives a proper request not to send future unsolicited advertisements must honor that request within the shortest reasonable time from the date of such request, not to exceed 30 days, and is prohibited from sending unsolicited advertisements to the recipient unless the recipient subsequently provides prior express invitation or permission to the sender. The recipient's opt-out request terminates the established business relationship exemption for purposes of sending future unsolicited advertisements. If such requests are recorded or maintained by a party other than the sender on whose behalf the unsolicited advertisement is sent, the sender will be liable for any failures to honor the opt-out request.[174] A facsimile broadcaster[175] will be liable for violations, including the inclusion of opt-out notices on unsolicited advertisements, if it demonstrates

---

170. The term clear and conspicuous for purposes of paragraph (a)(3)(iii)(A) of this section means a notice that would be apparent to the reasonable consumer, separate and distinguishable from the advertising copy or other disclosures, and placed at either the top or bottom of the facsimile. 47 C.F.R. § 64.1200(f)(2).

171. 47 C.F.R. §§ 64.1200(a)(3)(iii)(A)–(E).

172. 47 C.F.R. § 64.1200(a)(3)(iv).

173. 47 C.F.R. §§ 64.1200(a)(3)(v)(A)–(C).

174. 47 C.F.R. § 64.1200(a)(vi).

175. The term facsimile broadcaster means a person or entity that transmits messages to telephone facsimile machines on behalf of another person or entity for a fee. 47 C.F.R. § 64.1200(f)(6).

a high degree of involvement in, or actual notice of, the unlawful activity and fails to take steps to prevent such facsimile transmissions.[176]

It is also illegal for a person or entity to use an automatic telephone dialing system in such a way that two or more telephone lines of a multi-line business are engaged simultaneously; disconnect an unanswered telemarketing[177] call prior to at least 15 seconds or 4 rings; or abandon[178] more than 3 percent of all telemarketing calls that are answered live by a person, or measured over a 30-day period.[179] Whenever a sales representative is not available to speak with the person answering the call, that person must receive, within two seconds after the called person's completed greeting, a prerecorded identification message that states only the name and telephone number of the business, entity, or individual on whose behalf the call was placed, and that the call was for "telemarketing purposes." The person must provide a telephone number to permit any individual to make a Do-Not-Call request during regular business hours for the duration of the telemarketing campaign. The telephone number may not be a 900 number or any other number for which charges exceed local or long distance transmission charges. The seller[180] or telemarketer[181] must maintain records establishing compliance with this paragraph.[182]

A call for telemarketing purposes that delivers an artificial or prerecorded voice message to a residential telephone line that is assigned to a person who either has granted prior express consent for the call to be made or has an established business relationship with the caller shall not be considered an abandoned call if the message begins within two seconds of the called person's completed greeting.[183]

It should also be noted that calls made by or on behalf of tax-exempt nonprofit organizations are not covered.[184]

Finally, it is also illegal to use any technology to dial any telephone number for the purpose of determining whether the line is a facsimile or voice line.[185]

---

176. 47 C.F.R. § 64.1200(a)(3)(vii).

177. The term telemarketing means the initiation of a telephone call or message for the purpose of encouraging the purchase or rental of, or investment in, property, goods, or services, which is transmitted to any person. 47 C.F.R. § 64.1200(f)(10).

178. A call is "abandoned" if it is not connected to a live sales representative within two (2) seconds of the called person's completed greeting.

179. 47 C.F.R. §§ 64.1200(a)(4)–(6).

180. The term seller means the person or entity on whose behalf a telephone call or message is initiated for the purpose of encouraging the purchase or rental of, or investment in, property, goods, or services, which is transmitted to any person. 47 C.F.R. § 64.1200(f)(7).

181. The term telemarketer means the person or entity that initiates a telephone call or message for the purpose of encouraging the purchase or rental of, or investment in, property, goods, or services, which is transmitted to any person. 47 C.F.R. § 64.1200(f)(9).

182. 47 C.F.R. § 64.1200(a)(6).

183. 47 C.F.R. § 64.1200(a)(6)(i).

184. 47 C.F.R. § 64.1200(a)(6)(ii).

185. 47 C.F.R. § 64.1200(a)(7).

9:42.   Artificial or prerecorded messages

All artificial or prerecorded telephone messages must at the beginning of the message, state clearly the identity of the business, individual, or other entity that is responsible for initiating the call. If a business is responsible for initiating the call, the name under which the entity is registered to conduct business with the state corporation commission (or comparable regulatory authority) must be stated, and during or after the message, the telephone number (other than that of the autodialer or prerecorded message player that placed the call) of such business, other entity, or individual must also be clearly stated.[186] The telephone number provided may not be a 900 number or any other number for which charges exceed local or long distance transmission charges. For telemarketing messages to residential telephone subscribers, such telephone number must permit any individual to make a Do-Not-Call request during regular business hours for the duration of the telemarketing campaign.

9:43.   Improper initiation of telephone solicitations

No person or entity can initiate any telephone solicitation to any residential telephone subscriber before the hour of 8 a.m. or after 9 p.m. (local time at the called party's location), or to a residential telephone subscriber who has registered his or her telephone number on the national Do-Not-Call registry maintained by the federal government.[187] Do-not-call registrations must be honored indefinitely, or until the registration is cancelled by the consumer or the telephone number is removed by the database administrator.

Any person or entity making telephone solicitations (or on whose behalf telephone solicitations are made) will not be liable for violating this requirement if it can demonstrate that the violation is the result of error and that as part of its routine business practice, it meets the following standards: it has established and implemented written procedures to comply with the national Do-Not-Call rules; it has trained its personnel, and any entity assisting in its compliance, in procedures established pursuant to the national Do-Not-Call rules; it has maintained and recorded a list of telephone numbers that the seller may not contact; it uses a process to prevent telephone solicitations to any telephone number on any list established pursuant to the Do-Not-Call rules, employing a version of the national Do-Not-Call registry obtained from the administrator of the registry no more than 31 days prior to the date any call is made, and maintains records documenting this process; and it uses a process to ensure that it does not sell, rent, lease, purchase, or use the national Do-Not-Call database, or any part thereof, for any purpose except compliance with this section and any such state or federal law to prevent telephone solicitations to telephone numbers registered on the national database.[188] The person or entity must purchase access to the relevant Do-Not-Call data from the administrator of the national database and does not participate in any arrangement to share the cost of accessing the national database, including any arrangement with telemarketers who may not divide the costs to access the national database among various client sellers.[189]

---

186. 47 C.F.R. §§ 64.1200(b)(1)–(2).

187. 47 C.F.R. §§ 64.1200(c)(1)–(2).

188. 47 C.F.R. §§ 64.1200(c)(2)(i)(A)–(E).

189. 47 C.F.R. § 64.1200(c)(2)(i)(E).

Any person or entity making telephone solicitations (or on whose behalf telephone solicitations are made) will also not be liable for violating this requirement if it can demonstrate that it has obtained the subscriber's prior express invitation or permission. Such permission must be evidenced by a signed, written agreement between the consumer and seller that states that the consumer agrees to be contacted by this seller and includes the telephone number to which the calls may be placed unless the telemarketer making the call has a personal relationship[190] with the recipient of the call.[191]

It is also illegal for any person to initiate any call for telemarketing purposes to a residential telephone subscriber unless such person or entity has instituted procedures for maintaining a list of persons who request not to receive telemarketing calls made by or on behalf of that person or entity.[192] The procedures instituted must meet the following minimum standards:

- persons or entities making calls for telemarketing purposes must have a written policy, available upon demand, for maintaining a Do-Not-Call list;
- personnel engaged in any aspect of telemarketing must be informed and trained in the existence and use of the Do-Not-Call list; and
- if a person or entity making a call for telemarketing purposes (or on whose behalf such a call is made) receives a request from a residential telephone subscriber not to receive calls from that person or entity, the person or entity must record the request and place the subscriber's name, if provided, and telephone number on the Do-Not-Call list at the time the request is made.[193]

As part of the procedures, persons or entities making calls for telemarketing purposes (or on whose behalf such calls are made) must honor a residential subscriber's Do-Not-Call request within a reasonable time, not to exceed 30 days, from the date such request is made.[194] If these requests are recorded or maintained by a party other than the person or entity on whose behalf the telemarketing call is made, the person or entity on whose behalf the telemarketing call is made will be liable for any failures to honor the Do-Not-Call request.[195] A person or entity making a call for telemarketing purposes must obtain a consumer's prior express permission to share or forward the consumer's request not to be called to a party other than the person or entity on whose behalf a telemarketing call is made or an affiliated entity.[196]

The procedures must also include other requirements, including the following:

- a person or entity making a call for telemarketing purposes must provide the called party with the name of the individual caller, the name of the person or entity on whose behalf the call is being made, and a telephone number or address at which the person or entity may be contacted, but it should be noted that the telephone

---

190. The term personal relationship means any family member, friend, or acquaintance of the telemarketer making the call. 47 C.F.R. § 64.1200(f)(14).
191. 47 C.F.R. §§ 64.1200(c)(2)(ii)–(iii).
192. 47 C.F.R. § 64.1200(d).
193. 47 C.F.R. §§ 64.1200(d)(1)–(3).
194. 47 C.F.R. § 64.1200(d)(3).
195. *Id.*
196. *Id.*

number provided may not be a 900 number or any other number for which charges exceed local or long distance transmission charges;

- in the absence of a specific request by the subscriber to the contrary, a residential subscriber's Do-Not-Call request shall apply to the particular business entity making the call (or on whose behalf a call is made), and will not apply to affiliated entities unless the consumer reasonably would expect them to be included given the identification of the caller and the product being advertised; and

- a person or entity making calls for telemarketing purposes must maintain a record of a consumer's request not to receive further telemarketing calls.[197]

A Do-Not-Call request must be honored for five years from the time the request is made.[198]

It should be noted that tax-exempt nonprofit organizations are not required to comply with § 64.1200(d).[199]

9:44. Exemptions

The requirements of § 64.1200(c) to (d) are applicable to any person or entity making telephone solicitations or telemarketing calls to wireless telephone numbers to the extent described in the Commission's Report and Order, CG Docket No. 02-278, FCC-03-153, "Rules and Regulations Implementing the Telephone Consumer Protection Act of 1991."[200]

9:45. Additional requirements

When providing local exchange service, persons or entities must provide an annual notice, via an insert in the subscriber's bill, of the right to give or revoke a notification of an objection to receiving telephone solicitations pursuant to the national Do-Not-Call database maintained by the federal government and the methods by which such rights may be exercised by the subscriber.[201] The notice must be clear and conspicuous and include, at a minimum, the Internet address and toll-free number that residential telephone subscribers may use to register on the national database.[202] When providing service to any person or entity for the purpose of making telephone solicitations, a one-time notification to such person or entity of the national Do-Not-Call requirements, including, at a minimum, citation to § 64.1200 and 16 C.F.R. 310 must be given.[203] Failure to receive this notification will not serve as a defense to any person or entity making telephone solicitations from violations of this section.[204]

---

197. 47 C.F.R. §§ 64.1200(d)(4)–(6).
198. 47 C.F.R. § 64.1200(d)(6).
199. 47 C.F.R. § 64.1200(d)(7).
200. 47 C.F.R. § 64.1200(e).
201. 47 C.F.R. § 64.1200(g)(1).
202. *Id.*
203. 47 C.F.R. § 64.1200(g)(2).
204. *Id.*

9:46.   Additional autodialer issues

Some have attempted to interpret state autodialer laws as being only applicable to calls with a commercial purpose. Certain state courts, including the Indiana Supreme Court have recently interpreted their restrictions on autodialers as applying to all calls, and not just calls with a commercial purpose.[205]

9:47.   Federal Do-Not-Fax law

Do-not-fax laws also exist, and follow a similar model to the Do-Not-Call laws.

Under the federal statute, it is improper to use any telephone facsimile machine,[206] computer, or other device to send to a telephone facsimile machine an unsolicited advertisement,[207] unless (1) the unsolicited advertisement is from a sender with an established business relationship with the recipient[208]and (2) the sender obtained the number of the telephone facsimile machine through the voluntary communication of such number, within the context of such established business relationship, from the recipient of the unsolicited advertisement, or a directory, advertisement, or site on the Internet to which the recipient voluntarily agreed to make available its facsimile number for public distribution.

This restriction does not apply if such a fax is sent based upon an established business relationship with the recipient that was in existence before July 9, 2005, if the sender possessed the facsimile machine number of the recipient before such date of enactment, and the unsolicited advertisement meets the notice requirements identified below.

It should be noted that this exception does not apply when the consumer has expressly opted-out of receiving such communications.[209]

California has passed its own version of Do-Not-Fax, which is much broader than the federal law. However, there is pending litigation regarding whether California's law is preempted by the federal law and the trial court has already found that the California statute is preempted.

---

205. State of Indiana v. American Family Voices, Inc., No. 31S00-0803-CV-139 (December 23, 2008).

206. The term "telephone facsimile machine" means equipment which has the capacity (A) to transcribe text or images, or both, from paper into an electronic signal and to transmit that signal over a regular telephone line, or (B) to transcribe text or images (or both) from an electronic signal received over a regular telephone line onto paper. 47 U.S.C. § 227(a)(3).

207. The term "unsolicited advertisement" means any material advertising the commercial availability or quality of any property, goods, or services which is transmitted to any person without that person's prior express invitation or permission, in writing or otherwise. 47 U.S.C. § 227(a)(5).

208. The term "established business relationship," for purposes only of section 1:16 of this chapter, shall have the meaning given the term in section 64.1200 of title 47, Code of Federal Regulations, as in effect on January 1, 2003, except that—(A) such term shall include a relationship between a person or entity and a business subscriber subject to the same terms applicable under such section to a relationship between a person or entity and a residential subscriber; and (B) an established business relationship shall be subject to any time limitation established pursuant to paragraph (2)(G). 47 U.S.C. § 227(a)(2).

209. 47 U.S.C. § 227(c).

9:48. Do-Not-Fax—the established business relationship in the business context

One argument that has been made by plaintiffs in the Do-Not-Fax context is that the established business relationship exception to the Do-Not-Fax law does not include businesses. This argument has been rejected, though review of the decision has been granted by the California Supreme Court.[210]

9:49. Federal Do-Not-Fax law—Opt-outs

Any unsolicited advertisement that is sent via fax must contain a clear and conspicuous disclosure on the first page of the advertisement that states that the recipient may request that the sender of the unsolicited advertisement not send any future unsolicited advertisements to a telephone facsimile machine or machines. It must also disclose that the failure to comply within the shortest reasonable time as determined by the FCC is unlawful.[211] The notice must also contain a domestic contact telephone and facsimile machine number for the recipient to transmit such a request to the sender and a cost-free mechanism for a recipient to transmit an opt-out request.[212] The telephone and facsimile machine numbers and the cost-free mechanism must permit an individual or business to make such a request at any time on any day of the week.

In order to be effective, the opt-out must identify the telephone number or numbers of the telephone facsimile machine or machines to which the request relates; the request must be made to the telephone or facsimile number of the sender of such an unsolicited advertisement provided above, or by any other method of communication as determined by the FCC and the person making the request has not, subsequent to such request, provided express invitation or permission to the sender, in writing or otherwise, to send advertisements to the person at the telephone facsimile machine.[213]

A private right of action, including statutory penalties, is permitted by the law.

9:50. CALEA and broadband access and VoIP

One of the issues that has captured significant attention recently regarding telecommunications regulation is the applicability of FCC regulation to VoIP. While the Supreme Court answered that question in the *Brand X* case and rejected the application of the Telecommunications Act to VoIP, the merging of traditional telecommunications products and broadband and VoIP products has created other issues. One issue is the application of the Communications Assistance for Law Enforcement Act (CALEA) to broadband and VoIP.[214] In *American Council*, the D.C. Court of Appeals addressed whether CALEA applied to broadband and VoIP providers. Ultimately, the court examined

---

210. Catalyst Strategic Design, Inc. v. Kaiser Foundation Health Plan, Inc., 153 Cal. App. 4th 1328 (2007), rehearing granted.

211. 47 U.S.C. §§ 227(b)(2)(D)(i)–(iii).

212. 47 U.S.C. § 227(b)(2)(D)(iv).

213. 47 U.S.C. § 227(b)(2)(E).

214. American Council on Educ. v. FCC, 451 F.3d 226 (D.C. Cir. 2006).

the differing (and broader) structure of CALEA in relation to the Telecommunications Act of 1996.

Despite the inapplicability of the Telecommunications Act, CALEA was found to apply to broadband and VoIP and thus required these providers to permit law enforcement access.[215]

One court recently addressed whether CALEA applied to VoIP carriers, as well as broadband ISPs.[216] The FCC concluded, via regulations it promulgated, that both VoIP and broadband ISPs were subject to CALEA, to the extent that they qualified as "telecommunications carriers."[217] The FCC determined that VoIP replaced traditional telephone service and broadband service replaced traditional dial-up access.[218] After extensive analysis of CALEA, as well as the Telecommunications Act of 1996, the Court of Appeal upheld the FCC determination that these entities had to comply with CALEA.[219]

9:51. Slamming

"Slamming" occurs when a telephone company improperly changes a consumer's telecommunications carrier by not following the FCC regulations.[220] Most violations relate to a change that is made without the consent of the consumer. Fines of up to 150 percent of the charges to the subscriber, payable to the proper carrier, are available, as are other remedies.[221] Consumers have the right under this law to freeze their telephone number to prevent a change.[222]

9:52. Instant messaging and SMS technology

Instant messaging presents many similar issues to e-mail, including privacy concerns. While there are few legal regulations specific to instant messaging, it raises compliance issues under the CFAA and the ECPA, among other statutes. Certain industries are required to retain instant messages and potentially monitor the communications. The FCC wireless rules can apply to certain forms of SMS, as can the Do-Not-Call restrictions. In other cases, employers may want to proactively monitor these communications in order to obtain evidence of employee misconduct or for other reasons.

---

215. *Id.* at 230-31.
216. American Council on Educ. v. FCC, 451 F.3d 226 (D.C. Cir. 2006).
217. *Id.*
218. *Id.* at 229.
219. *Id.* at 236.
220. 47 C.F.R. § 64.1120.
221. 47 C.F.R. § 64.1140.
222. 47 C.F.R. § 64.1190.

CHAPTER 10

Financial Privacy

I.   Introduction

10:1.   Financial privacy and security in general

This chapter presents an overview of the financial privacy and security laws at the federal level including, Gramm-Leach-Bliley,[1] the Right to Financial Privacy Act,[2] the Fair Credit Reporting Act,[3] and its well publicized amendment, the Fair and Accurate Credit Transactions Act of 2003 (FACT Act), as well as the relevant regulations interpreting these laws.

As a general principle, financial data is one of the most heavily regulated types of data. The importance of the data, coupled with the likelihood of identity theft if there is an improper acquisition, has lead to extensive regulations. Generally, these laws restrict the disclosure of information (including to "affiliates"), require data security, require the implementation of response plans to address the unauthorized access of consumer information, require the destruction of data when it is no longer needed, regulate the

---

1.   15 U.S.C. §§ 6801 *et seq.*
2.   12 U.S.C. §§ 3401 *et seq.*
3.   15 U.S.C. §§ 1681a *et seq.*

notices that must be given to consumers, and provide for procedures to ensure the accuracy of information that is maintained.

One issue regarding the FACT Act should be noted. While the Act has received extensive attention, it was an amendment to an existing law—the Fair Credit Reporting Act, also known as FCRA. The FACT Act did not create a new or separate statutory scheme, but instead added or amended numerous parts of FCRA, including those parts regarding identity theft reporting and fraud alerts. There are also specific regulations that have been promulgated under the FACT Act. As discussed below, this rule, unlike FCRA, Gramm-Leach-Bliley, or other similar laws, applies to all businesses subject to the FTC's jurisdiction, and does not just apply to financial institutions or consumer reporting agencies.

II. Gramm-Leach-Bliley Act

10:2.   Application in general

Given the sensitive nature of financial information, Congress determined that financial institutions should be required to protect the privacy of their customers. Gramm-Leach-Bliley (GLB) accomplishes this goal through the imposition of privacy and security regulations on certain financial institutions, if they collect "non-public personal information."

The first question to consider in assessing whether GLB applies is whether the business in question is a "financial institution," because GLB only applies to financial institutions. A financial institutions is, with certain exceptions, any institution that engages in "financial activities," including but not limited to the following:

- lending, exchanging, transferring, investing for others, or safeguarding money or securities;
- insuring, guaranteeing, or indemnifying against loss, harm, damage, illness, disability, or death, or providing and issuing annuities, and acting as principal, agent, or broker for purposes of the foregoing, in any state;
- providing financial, investment, or economic advisory services, including advising an investment company;
- issuing or selling instruments representing interests in pools of assets permissible for a bank to hold directly; or
- underwriting, dealing in, or making a market in securities.[4]

The second issue to be considered in determining if GLB applies is whether non-public personal information is involved. "Non-public personal information" means personally identifiable financial information that

- is provided by a consumer to a financial institution;

---

4.   12 U.S.C. § 1843(k).

- results from any transaction with the consumer or any service performed for the consumer; or is otherwise obtained by a financial institution.[5]

10:3. Statutory requirements of Gramm-Leach-Bliley

Gramm-Leach-Bliley was enacted to ensure that financial institutions met their obligations to customers to protect customer privacy and to implement safeguards to protect customers' information. As such, financial institutions[6] are required to protect customer privacy and to implement administrative, technical, and physical safeguards

- to ensure the security and confidentiality of customer records and information;
- to protect against any anticipated threats or hazards to the security or integrity of such records; and
- to protect against unauthorized access to or use of such records or information which could result in substantial harm or inconvenience to any customer.[7]

While the statute sets broad goals, the implementation of these standards was left to the FTC and other agencies as part of the rulemaking process.[8] Thus, while understanding the GLB statutes is important, many requirements are contained in the rules discussed below, as well as the Safeguards Rule, which relates to information security. Thus, a general discussion of the statutory requirements is included, but particular attention should be paid to the implementing rules.

One of the main requirements of GLB is that notice must be given to consumers[9] regarding a variety of issues. At the time a customer relationship[10] is established with a consumer, and not less than annually thereafter during the relationship, a financial institution must provide clear and conspicuous disclosure to the consumer, in writing, electronic, or other form permitted by the regulations of the financial institution's policies and practices with respect to the following:

---

5. 16 C.F.R. §§ 313.3(n)(1)–(o)(1).

6. "Financial institution" means any institution the business of which is engaging in financial activities as described in 12 U.S.C. § 1843(k), or persons subject to CFTC regulation. However, the term "financial institution" does not include any person or entity with respect to any financial activity that is subject to the jurisdiction of the Commodity Futures Trading Commission under the Commodity Exchange Act. 15 U.S.C. § 6809(3). It also does not include Federal Agricultural Mortgage Corporation or any entity chartered and operating under the Farm Credit Act of 1971 or other secondary market institutions. 15 U.S.C. §§ 6809(3) (B)–(D).

7. 15 U.S.C. §§ 6801(b)(1)–(3).

8. 15 U.S.C. § 6801(b).

9. "Consumer" means an individual who obtains, from a financial institution, financial products or services which are to be used primarily for personal, family, or household purposes, and also means the legal representative of such an individual. 15 U.S.C. § 6809(9).

10. "Time of establishing a customer relationship" is to be defined by the regulations prescribed under this law, and shall, in the case of a financial institution engaged in extending credit directly to consumers to finance purchases of goods or services, mean the time of establishing the credit relationship with the consumer. 15 U.S.C. § 6809(11).

- disclosing non-public personal information[11] to affiliates[12] and non-affiliated third parties,[13] including the categories of information that may be disclosed;
- disclosing non-public personal information of persons who have ceased to be customers of the financial institution; and
- protecting the non-public personal information of consumers.[14]

These disclosures should include the policies and practices of the institution regarding the disclosure of non-public personal information to nonaffiliated third-parties, (excluding agents of the institution), the categories of persons to whom the information may be disclosed, and the policies and practices of the institution with respect to disclosing of non-public personal information of persons who have ceased to be customers of the financial institution.[15] Additionally, required statements mandated by FCRA, the categories of non-public personal information that are collected by the financial institution, and the policies that the institution maintains to protect the confidentiality and security of non-public personal information in accordance must also be disclosed.[16]

Financial institutions are precluded from directly, or indirectly through an affiliate, disclosing non-public personal information to a third party, unless the financial institution meets several requirements. The financial institution must provide the consumer a notice that complies with the requirements discussed above.[17] It must also provide to the consumer the following:

- clear and conspicuous disclosure that such information may be disclosed to such third party;
- an opportunity, before the disclosure of the information, to opt out of any disclosure to a third-party; and
- an explanation of how the consumer can exercise that non-disclosure option.[18]

This requirement does not prevent a financial institution from providing non-public personal information to a non-affiliated third party to perform services for or functions on behalf of the financial institution, including marketing of the financial institution's

---

11. "Non-public personal information" means personally identifiable financial information: (i) provided by a consumer to a financial institution; (ii) resulting from any transaction with the consumer or any service performed for the consumer; or (iii) otherwise obtained by the financial institution. 15 U.S.C. § 6809(4)(A). It also includes any list, description, or other grouping of consumers (and publicly available information pertaining to them) that is derived using any nonpublic personal information other than publicly available information; but does not include any list, description, or other grouping of consumers (and publicly available information pertaining to them) that is derived without using any non-public personal information. 15 U.S.C. § 6809(4)(C). It also does not include information that is defined as public information under the regulations. 15 U.S.C. § 6809(4)(B).

12. "Affiliate" means any company that controls, is controlled by, or is under common control with another company. 15 U.S.C. § 6809(6).

13. "Non-affiliated third party" means any entity that is not an affiliate of, or related by common ownership or affiliated by corporate control with, the financial institution, but does not include a joint employee of such institution. 15 U.S.C. § 6809(5).

14. 15 U.S.C. § 6803(a).

15. 15 U.S.C. §§ 6803(b)(1)(A)–(B).

16. 15 U.S.C. §§ 6803(b)(2)–(4).

17. 15 U.S.C. § 6802(a).

18. 15 U.S.C. §§ 6802(b)(1)(A)–(C).

own products or services. Disclosures related to financial products or services offered pursuant to joint agreements[19] between two or more financial institutions that comply with the requirements of GLB are permitted, if the financial institution fully discloses the information sharing and enters into a contractual agreement with the third party that requires the third party to maintain the confidentiality of the information.[20]

Non-affiliated third parties that receive non-public personal information from a financial institution may not, directly or through an affiliate, disclose the information to any other person that is a non-affiliated third party of both the financial institution and the receiving party, unless the disclosure would be proper if made directly to the other party by the financial institution.[21]

A financial institution may not disclose to any non-affiliated third party, other than to a consumer reporting agency, a consumer's account number or other form of access number or access code for a credit card account, deposit account, or transaction account for use in telemarketing, direct mail marketing, or other marketing through electronic mail to the consumer.[22]

GLB does not prohibit the disclosure of non-public personal information if the disclosure is necessary to effect, administer, or enforce a transaction[23] requested or authorized by the consumer, in connection with servicing or processing a financial product or service requested or authorized by the consumer, or to maintain or service the consumer's account with the financial institution, or with another entity as part of a private label credit card program or other extension of credit on behalf of such entity. It also does not prohibit disclosures related to a proposed or actual securitization,

---

19. "Joint agreement" means a formal written contract pursuant to which two or more financial institutions jointly offer, endorse, or sponsor a financial product or service, and as may be further defined in the regulations prescribed this law. 15 U.S.C. § 6809(10).

20. 15 U.S.C. § 6802(b)(2).

21. 15 U.S.C. § 6802(c).

22. 15 U.S.C. § 6802(d).

23. "As necessary to effect, administer, or enforce the transaction" means: (A) the disclosure is required, or is a usual, appropriate, or acceptable method, to carry out the transaction or the product or service business of which the transaction is a part, and record or service or maintain the consumer's account in the ordinary course of providing the financial service or financial product, or to administer or service benefits or claims relating to the transaction or the product or service business of which it is a part, and includes (i) providing the consumer or the consumer's agent or broker with a confirmation, statement, or other record of the transaction, or information on the status or value of the financial service or financial product; and (ii) the accrual or recognition of incentives or bonuses associated with the transaction that are provided by the financial institution or any other party; (B) the disclosure is required, or is one of the lawful or appropriate methods, to enforce the rights of the financial institution or of other persons engaged in carrying out the financial transaction, or providing the product or service; (C) the disclosure is required, or is a usual, appropriate, or acceptable method, for insurance underwriting at the consumer's request or for reinsurance purposes, or for any of the following purposes as they relate to a consumer's insurance: Account administration, reporting, investigating, or preventing fraud or material misrepresentation, processing premium payments, processing insurance claims, administering insurance benefits (including utilization review activities), participating in research projects, or as otherwise required or specifically permitted by Federal or State law; or (D) the disclosure is required, or is a usual, appropriate or acceptable method, in connection with—(i) the authorization, settlement, billing, processing, clearing, transferring, reconciling, or collection of amounts charged, debited, or otherwise paid using a debit, credit or other payment card, check, or account number, or by other payment means; (ii) the transfer of receivables, accounts or interests therein; or (iii) the audit of debit, credit or other payment information. 15 U.S.C. § 6809(7).

secondary market sale (including sales of servicing rights), or similar transaction related to a transaction of the consumer.[24]

GLB does not preclude the disclosure of non-public personal information to the extent specifically permitted or required under other provisions of law and, in accordance with the Right to Financial Privacy Act of 1978,[25] to law enforcement agencies (including certain regulators, a state insurance authority,[26] or the FTC), self-regulatory organizations, or for an investigation on a matter related to public safety. It also does not prohibit disclosure to a consumer reporting agency in accordance with FCRA, or if required to comply with federal, state, or local laws, rules, and other applicable legal requirements. It permits disclosures made to comply with a properly authorized investigation, subpoena, or summons or to respond to judicial process or government regulatory authorities having jurisdiction over the financial institution for examination, compliance, or other purposes as authorized by law.[27]

Disclosure can be made to protect the confidentiality or security of the financial institution's records pertaining to the consumer, the service, product, or the transaction, to protect against or prevent actual or potential fraud, unauthorized transactions, claims, or other liability, for required institutional risk control, or for resolving customer disputes or inquiries. Disclosure can also be made to persons holding a legal or beneficial interest relating to the consumer or to persons acting in a fiduciary or representative capacity on behalf of the consumer.[28]

Finally, disclosure can be made with the consent, or at the direction, of the consumer, to provide information to insurance rate advisory organizations; guaranty funds or agencies of the financial institution; persons assessing the institution's compliance with industry standards; and the institution's attorneys, accountants, and auditors, or in connection with a proposed or actual sale, merger, transfer, or exchange of all or a portion of a business or operating unit if the disclosure of non-public personal information concerns solely consumers of such business or unit.[29]

There are a number of agencies that have enforcement authority, depending upon the type of financial institution.[30] The FTC and state insurance authorities, as well as the federal functional regulators[31] all have enforcement power.[32]

GLB preempts any state law that provides lesser protection, but does not preempt any state law that provides customers greater protections.[33]

---

24. 15 U.S.C. §§ 6802(e)(1)–(3).

25. 12 U.S.C. §§ 3401 *et seq.*

26. "State insurance authority" means, in the case of any person engaged in providing insurance, the state insurance authority of the state in which the person is domiciled. 15 U.S.C. § 6809(8).

27. 15 U.S.C. §§ 6802(e)(5)(6), (8).

28. 15 U.S.C. §§ 6802(e)(3)(A)–(E).

29. 15 U.S.C. §§ 6802(e)(2), (4), (7).

30. 15 U.S.C. § 6805(a).

31. "Federal functional regulator" means—(A) the Board of Governors of the Federal Reserve System; (B) the Office of the Comptroller of the Currency; (C) the Board of Directors of the Federal Deposit Insurance Corporation; (D) the Director of the Office of Thrift Supervision; (E) the National Credit Union Administration Board; and (F) the Securities and Exchange Commission. 15 U.S.C. § 6809(2).

32. 15 U.S.C. § 6805.

33. 15 U.S.C. §§ 6807(a)–(b).

10:4. Financial Privacy Rule

If GLB applies, the Financial Privacy Rule is also applicable to GLB-covered entities.

The Office of Comptroller of the Currency, the Federal Reserve System, the Federal Deposit Insurance Corporation, the Office of Thrift Supervision, the National Credit Union Administration, the Federal Trade Commission, the Commodity Futures Trading Commission and the Security and Exchange Commission have all issued rules on the privacy of financial information, which now include the often discussed model privacy notice. At this time many financial institutions are taking a wait and see approach to the model notice, as it is suggested and provides a safe harbor, but it is not mandated at this time. The Office of Comptroller of the Currency's version of the rule is available at 12 C.F.R. §§ 40 *et seq.*

10:5. Federal Financial Institutions Examinations Council requirements

In July 2006, the Federal Financial Institutions Examinations Council issued a booklet providing extensive requirements that supplement the requirements of GLB for entities that are regulated by the FFIEC.[34]

10:6. Security provisions

The security provisions of GLB are discussed in chapter 11.

10:7. The interplay of GLB and FCRA

While GLB and FCRA apply to many of the same entities, it is important to note that GLB will not be construed as modifying FCRA.[35]

III. Fair Credit Reporting Act

10:8. Overview of FCRA

The Fair Credit Reporting Act (FCRA) regulates consumer credit reporting agencies'[36] use of consumer reports.[37] As such, it is an act that must be considered because it, like

---

34. This provides extensive requirements that can be found at http://ithandbook.ffiec.gov/.

35. American Bankers Ass'n. v. Gould, 412 F.3d 1081, 1088 (9th Cir. 2005).

36. A "consumer reporting agency" means any person which, for monetary fees, dues, or on a cooperative nonprofit basis, regularly engages in whole or in part in the practice of assembling or evaluating consumer credit information or other information on consumers for the purpose of furnishing consumer reports to third parties, and which uses any means or facility of interstate commerce for the purpose of preparing or furnishing consumer reports. 15 U.S.C. § 1681(a)(f).

37. A "consumer report" means any written, oral, or other communication of any information by a consumer

GLB, impacts certain aspects of financial privacy.[38] FCRA restricts consumer reporting agencies from placing certain information in consumer credit reports, including the following:

- bankruptcy cases that are older than ten years;
- civil suits that are more than seven years old, or the statute of limitations has expired, whichever is longer;
- paid tax liens that, from date of payment, are older than seven years;
- accounts placed for collection or charged to profit and loss that are older than seven years; and
- any other adverse item of information that is older than seven years.[39]

FCRA also contains a number of other restrictions, including restrictions on the disclosure of medical information.[40] FCRA also addresses issues of identity theft. If a consumer gives notice that there is a suspicion that identity theft has occurred, the credit reporting agency has certain obligations, including duties to include a fraud alert in the file of the consumer and to provide that alert along with any credit score generated for a period of not less than 90 days.[41] A consumer reporting agency must also refer the information regarding the fraud alert under this paragraph to certain other consumer reporting agencies.

10:9.   Misuse of credit reports and jurisdiction

One issue that has arisen in the FCRA context is whether viewing the credit report of a consumer gives rise to jurisdiction in the consumer's home state for a FCRA violation. Generally, most courts will find that the improper viewing of a consumer report under FCRA will give rise to jurisdiction in the consumer's home state, because the conduct is purposefully directed at the resident of the forum state.[42]

---

reporting agency bearing on a consumer's credit worthiness, credit standing, credit capacity, character, general reputation, personal characteristics, or mode of living which is used or expected to be used or collected in whole or in part for the purpose of serving as a factor in establishing the consumer's eligibility for— (A) credit or insurance to be used primarily for personal, family, or household purposes; (B) employment purposes; or (C) any other purpose authorized under section 1681b. 15 U.S.C. § 1681(a)(d)(1). There are certain exclusions from the definition of a "consumer report" contained in other subsections.

38.   15 U.S.C. § 1681.

39.   15 U.S.C. § 1681(c)(a). These periods can run from a variety of different points, which are discussed in the text of (a).

40.   15 U.S.C. § 1681b(g)(3).

41.   15 U.S.C. § 1681c-1(a)(1).

42.   Myers v. Bennett Law Offices, 238 F.3d 1068 (9th Cir. 2001); Cole v. American Family Mutual Ins. Co., 333 F. Supp. 2d 1038 (D. Kan. 2004); Andrews v. Prestige Ford Garland Ltd. Partnership, 2005 WL 3297339 (W.D. Ok. 2005); Bils v. Nixon Hargrave, Devans & Doyle, 880 P.2d 743 (1994); Smith v. Cutler, 504 F. Supp. 2d 1162 (D. N.M. 2007).

10:10. What do credit reporting agencies do?

It is helpful to understand what credit reporting agencies do as a general background to FCRA. One court summarized it as collecting information about consumers' credit experience and reselling the information for various purposes.[43]

10:11. Furnishing of consumer reports

Subject to the other requirements of FCRA, a consumer reporting agency may only disclose a consumer report[44] in certain circumstances. Disclosure can be made in response to a court order or a subpoena issued in connection with proceedings before a federal grand jury or in accordance with the written instructions of the consumer. Disclosure can also be made to a person that the consumer reporting agency has reason to believe intends to use the information in connection with a credit transaction involving the consumer, if it involves the extension of credit to or review or collection of an account of the consumer, if the information is used for employment purposes,[45] in connection with the underwriting of insurance involving the consumer.[46]

Disclosure can also be made to a person that the consumer reporting agency has reason to believe intends to use the information in connection with a determination of the consumer's eligibility for a license or other benefit granted by a governmental instrumentality required by law to consider an applicant's financial responsibility or status. This also extends to uses as a potential investor or servicer, or current insurer, in connection with a valuation of, or an assessment of the credit or prepayment risks associated with, an existing credit obligation, or based upon a legitimate business need for the information in connection with a business transaction that is initiated by the

---

43. Consumer Data Industry Ass'n v. Swanson, 2007 WL 2219389 (D.Minn. 2007).

44. "Consumer report" means any written, oral, or other communication of any information by a consumer reporting agency bearing on a consumer's credit worthiness, credit standing, credit capacity, character, general reputation, personal characteristics, or mode of living which is used or expected to be used or collected in whole or in part for the purpose of serving as a factor in establishing the consumer's eligibility for—(A) credit or insurance to be used primarily for personal, family, or household purposes; (B) employment purposes; or (C) any other purpose authorized under FCRA. 15 U.S.C. § 1681a(d)(1). "Consumer report" does not include—(A) subject to section 1681s-3 of this title, any—(i) report containing information solely as to transactions or experiences between the consumer and the person making the report; (ii) communication of that information among persons related by common ownership or affiliated by corporate control; or (iii) communication of other information among persons related by common ownership or affiliated by corporate control, if it is clearly and conspicuously disclosed to the consumer that the information may be communicated among such persons and the consumer is given the opportunity, before the time that the information is initially communicated, to direct that such information not be communicated among such persons; (B) any authorization or approval of a specific extension of credit directly or indirectly by the issuer of a credit card or similar device; (C) any report in which a person who has been requested by a third party to make a specific extension of credit directly or indirectly to a consumer conveys his or her decision with respect to such request, if the third party advises the consumer of the name and address of the person to whom the request was made, and such person makes the disclosures to the consumer required under section 1681m of this title; or (D) a communication described in subsection (o) or (x) of this section. 15 U.S.C. § 1681a(d)(2).

45. "Employment purposes" when used in connection with a consumer report means a report used for the purpose of evaluating a consumer for employment, promotion, reassignment or retention as an employee. § 1681a(h).

46. 15 U.S.C. §§ 1681b(a)(1)–(3)(c).

consumer. Disclosure related to review an account to determine whether the consumer continues to meet the terms of the account is legitimate under the rules.[47]

Disclosure can also be made in response to a request by the head of a state or local child support enforcement agency[48] (or a state or local government official authorized by the head of such an agency), if the person making the request certifies to the consumer reporting agency that the disclosure is needed for the purpose of establishing an individual's capacity to make child support payments and determining the appropriate level of such payments, if the paternity of the consumer for the child to which the obligation relates has been established or acknowledged by the consumer in accordance with the laws under which the obligation arises and the person has provided at least 10 days' prior notice[49] to the consumer whose report is requested, that the report will be requested, that the report will be kept confidential, and that it will be used solely for these purposes and not for any other purpose.[50] Finally, disclosure can be made to an agency administering a state plan under 42 U.S.C. § 654 related to a child support award.[51]

10:12. Protection of medical information

Consumer reporting agencies may not disclose medical information[52] for employment purposes, or in connection with a credit or insurance transaction, or disclose a consumer report that contains medical information (other than medical contact information treated in the manner required under 15 U.S.C. § 605(a)(6)) about a consumer, unless certain criteria are met.[53] These criteria include if the information is furnished in connection with an insurance transaction and if the consumer affirmatively consents to the furnishing of the report.[54] Disclosure is also permitted if the information is furnished for employment purposes or in connection with a credit transaction, the information is relevant to process or effects the employment or credit transaction, and the consumer provides specific written consent for the furnishing of the report that describes in clear and conspicuous language the use for which the information will be furnished.[55]

---

47. 15 U.S.C. §§ 1681b(a)(3)(d)–(f).

48. "State or local child support enforcement agency" means a state or local agency that administers a state or local program for establishing and enforcing child support obligations. 15 U.S.C. § 1681a(j)(2).

49. Notice must be by certified or registered mail to the last known address of the consumer. 15 U.S.C. § 1681b(a)(4)(c).

50. 15 U.S.C. § 1681b(a)(4).

51. 15 U.S.C. § 1681b(a)(5).

52. "Medical information"—(1) means information or data, whether oral or recorded, in any form or medium, created by or derived from a health care provider or the consumer, that relates to—(A) the past, present, or future physical, mental, or behavioral health or condition of an individual; (B) the provision of health care to an individual; or (C) the payment for the provision of health care to an individual. (2) does not include the age or gender of a consumer, demographic information about the consumer, including a consumer's residence address or e-mail address, or any other information about a consumer that does not relate to the physical, mental, or behavioral health or condition of a consumer, including the existence or value of any insurance policy. 15 U.S.C. § 1681a(i). "Overdue support" has the meaning given to such term in 42 U.S.C. § 666(e). 15 U.S.C. § 1681a(j)(1).

53. 15 U.S.C. § 1681b(g)(1).

54. 15 U.S.C. § 1681b(g)(1)(A).

55. 15 U.S.C. § 1681b(g)(1)(B).

Finally, disclosure is permitted if the information to be furnished pertains solely to transactions, accounts, or balances relating to debts arising from the receipt of medical services, products, or devices, where the information, other than account status or amounts, is restricted or reported using codes that do not identify, or do not provide information sufficient to infer, the specific provider or the nature of such services, products, or devices.[56] Redisclosure of this information by the recipient is also precluded, except to the extent that disclosure is necessary to fulfill the purpose of the original disclosure.[57]

Creditors are also prohibited from obtaining or using medical information of a consumer if it is related to any determination of the consumer's eligibility or continued eligibility for credit.[58] There are certain exceptions to this restriction, including certain activities related to insurance, purposes authorized by HIPAA, or other federal agencies or certain state agencies.[59] There are additional restrictions upon the use and disclosure of medical information under the FACT Act.

10:13. Disclosures to governmental entities

Disclosure of a consumer's name, address, former addresses, places of employment, or former places of employment to a governmental agency is permitted, notwithstanding the other restrictions of FCRA.[60]

10:14. Disclosures to consumers

Consumer reporting agencies must, upon the request of the consumer, clearly and accurately disclose all information in the consumer's file at the time of a request. This requirement does not require a consumer reporting agency to disclose any information concerning credit scores, other risk scores, or predictors related to the consumer.[61] It should be noted that disclosure of the first five digits of the consumer's social security number, or other similar identification number, should not be made if the consumer has previously requested that the social security number not be disclosed and the credit reporting agency has been provided with adequate proof of identity.[62]

Consumer reporting agencies must also disclose of the sources of information for most reports; the identification of each person who has procured a report during certain time periods (depending upon the purpose of the request); the dates, original payees, and amounts of any checks upon which any adverse characterization of the consumer is based; and a record of all inquiries received by the agency during the one year period preceding the request that identify the consumer in connection with a credit or insurance transaction that was not initiated by the consumer. A statement that the consumer may request and obtain a credit score must also be made if the consumer

---

56. 15 U.S.C. § 1681b(g)(1)(C).
57. 15 U.S.C. § 1681b(g)(4).
58. 15 U.S.C. § 1681b(g)(2).
59. 15 U.S.C. § 1681b(g)(3).
60. 15 U.S.C. § 1681(f).
61. 15 U.S.C. § 1681g(a)(1)(B).
62. 15 U.S.C. § 1681g(a)(1)(A).

only requests the credit file and not the credit score.[63] A summary of the consumer's rights to obtain and dispute information, as well as a summary of identity theft rights, must also be included.[64]

A victim[65] of identity theft also has the right to receive certain information from the entity that provided credit or consideration related to the transaction that resulted from identity theft. The consumer can receive information regarding the transaction if the consumer makes a written request that is mailed to a business entity at an address specified by that entity and, if asked for by the business, the consumer provides information regarding the transaction at issue, including the date and any other identifying information if known to the consumer.[66] These disclosures must be made without charge.[67]

Before this information can be provided the victim must verify his identity and the fact of an identity theft occurrence. A person can verify his identity by presenting a government issued identification card, personally identifying information of the same type that was provided by the unauthorized person, or personally identifying information that the business entity typically requests from new applicants or for new transactions, including any documentation described in the first two options, unless the business, in its discretion otherwise has a high degree of confidence that it knows the identity of the person making the request.[68]

Proof of the identity theft assertion can be given by a copy of the police report evidencing the claim of identity theft and, at the business's election, either a properly completed copy of a standardized affidavit prepared by the FTC, if available, or an affidavit of fact that is acceptable to the business.[69]

A business entity may decline to provide information in response to a request if it, in the exercise of good faith, determines the following:

- that FCRA does not require disclosure;
- that the business entity, after reviewing the information provided, does not have a high degree of confidence in knowing the true identity of the individual requesting the information;
- that the request for the information is based on a misrepresentation of fact by the individual requesting the information relevant to the request for information; or
- that the information requested is internet navigational data or similar information about a person's visit to a website or online service.[70]

It is a defense to an enforcement action for disclosure of information if the business made the disclosure in good faith pursuant to the disclosure requirements.[71] Moreover,

---

63.　15 U.S.C. §§ 1681(a)(2)–(6).

64.　15 U.S.C. §§ 1681(c)–(d).

65.　"Victim" means a consumer whose means of identification or financial information has been used or transferred (or has been alleged to have been used or transferred) without the authority of that consumer, with the intent to commit, or to aid or abet, an identity theft or a similar crime. 15 U.S.C. § 1681g(e)(11).

66.　15 U.S.C. § 1681g(e)(3).

67.　15 U.S.C. § 1681g(e)(4).

68.　15 U.S.C. §§ 1681g(e)(2)(A)(i)–(iii).

69.　15 U.S.C. §§ 1681g(e)(2)(B)(i)–(ii).

70.　15 U.S.C. § 1681g(e)(5).

71.　15 U.S.C. § 1681g(e)(6).

many of the enforcement and remedial statutes are not applicable to disclosures by businesses under these requirements.[72] It is also a defense for a business to establish that it has made a reasonable search of its records and the requested records are not available.[73]

10:15. Affiliate sharing

Affiliate sharing has presented one of the more difficult issues, given California's foray into financial privacy via S.B. 1. As discussed below, the affiliate sharing provisions of FCRA doomed California's law because FCRA was held to preempt California's inconsistent requirements.

A person that is affiliated by corporate control or under common ownership cannot use information that would be considered a consumer report but for the exclusion of 15 U.S.C. § 1681a(d)(2)(A),[74] to make a solicitation[75] for marketing purposes to a consumer regarding its products or services unless there has been clear and conspicuous disclosure to the consumer that the information may be communicated among affiliates for marketing purposes and the consumer is given the opportunity to opt-out of the sharing of information and marketing in a simple way.[76]

The notice must be clear, conspicuous and concise, and it must allow the consumer the opportunity to prohibit all solicitations. The opt-out may allow the consumer to choose from different options when electing not to receive solicitations, including the types of entities and information covered by the opt-out and which methods of delivering solicitations the consumer wants to prohibit.[77] The opt-out must be effective for at least five years, unless revoked earlier by the consumer.[78] However, the information may not be used even at the end of the opt-out period unless the consumer receives a notice and an opportunity, using a simple method, to extend the opt-out for another period of at least five years.[79]

Despite the clear and conspicuous requirement, the required notice to consumer can be combined with other notices required by FCRA.[80]

The restrictions upon affiliate sharing do not apply to the following:

- using information to make a solicitation for marketing purposes to a consumer with whom the person has a pre-existing business relationship;[81]

---

72. *Id.*

73. 15 U.S.C. § 1681g(e)(10).

74. This section excludes from the definition of a consumer report any information that is provided by an affiliate.

75. "Solicitation" means the marketing of a product or service initiated by a person to a particular consumer that is based on an exchange of information described in subsection (a) of this section, and is intended to encourage the consumer to purchase such product or service, but does not include communications that are directed at the general public or determined not to be a solicitation by the regulations prescribed under this section. 15 U.S.C. § 1681s-3(d)(2).

76. 15 U.S.C. §§ 1681s-3(a)(1)(A)–(B).

77. 15 U.S.C. §§ 1681s-3(a)(2)(A)–(B).

78. 15 U.S.C. § 1681s-3(a)(2)(A).

79. 15 U.S.C. § 1681s-3(a)(2)(B).

80. 15 U.S.C. § 1681s-3(b).

81. "Pre-existing business relationship" means a relationship between a person, or a person's licensed agent,

- using information to facilitate communications to an individual for whose benefit the person provides employee benefit or other services pursuant to a contract with an employer related to and arising out of the current employment relationship or status of the individual as a participant or beneficiary of an employee benefit plan;
- using information to perform services on behalf of another person related by common ownership or affiliated by corporate control, except that this exemption does not permit a person to send solicitations on behalf of another person, if such other person would not be permitted to send the solicitation on its own behalf as a result of the election of the consumer;
- using information in response to a communication initiated by the consumer;
- using information in response to solicitations authorized or requested by the consumer; or
- if compliance with this section would prevent compliance by that person with any provision of state insurance laws pertaining to unfair discrimination in any state in which the person is lawfully doing business.[82]

Many of the restrictions of FCRA are triggered by information consisting of a "consumer report." One issue regarding the definition of "consumer report" under FCRA is important to note. A consumer report does not include any communications between persons related by common ownership or control if the information relates solely to transactions or experiences between the consumer and the person making the report.[83] Thus, sharing between affiliates typically does not trigger the portions of FCRA that restrict disclosure of consumer reports.

There is also a second exemption to FCRA that relates to affiliate sharing. A consumer report does not include communications of other information among persons that are under common ownership or affiliated by corporate control if there is a clear and conspicuous disclosure to the consumer that the information may be shared and is also given the opportunity to opt-out.[84]

This provision was found to broadly preempt California's Financial Information Privacy Act. In *American Bankers Ass'n. v. Gould*,[85] the Ninth Circuit addressed the preemptive effect of FCRA on S.B. 1 in a case brought by the financial services industry. FCRA has a specific preemption clause that preempts all state laws regarding affiliate sharing, with the exception of a Vermont statute.[86] The court examined the language of FCRA, including recent amendments regarding the sharing of information between

---

and a consumer, based on—(A) a financial contract between a person and a consumer which is in force; (B) the purchase, rental, or lease by the consumer of that person's goods or services, or a financial transaction (including holding an active account or a policy in force or having another continuing relationship) between the consumer and that person during the 18-month period immediately preceding the date on which the consumer is sent a solicitation covered by this section; (C) an inquiry or application by the consumer regarding a product or service offered by that person, during the 3-month period immediately preceding the date on which the consumer is sent a solicitation covered by this section; or (D) any other pre-existing customer relationship defined in the regulations implementing this section. 15 U.S.C. § 1681s-3(d)(1).

82. 15 U.S.C. § 1681s-3(a)(4).
83. 15 U.S.C. §§ 1681a(d)(2)(A)(i)–(iii); American Bankers Ass'n. v. Gould, 412 F.3d 1081 (9th Cir. 2005).
84. 15 U.S.C. § 1681a(d)(2)(A)(iii); American Bankers Ass'n. v. Gould, 412 F.3d 1081 (9th Cir. 2005).
85. American Bankers Ass'n. v. Gould, 412 F.3d 1081 (9th Cir. 2005).
86. *American Bankers Ass'n*, 412 F.3d at 1087.

affiliates and ultimately concluded that the provisions of S.B. 1 that attempted to regulate the sharing of information were preempted by FCRA.[87] The preemption issue was finally settled, at least by the trial court, when the case was remanded.[88] On remand, the trial court held that, in light of the Ninth Circuit's first holding, the affiliate sharing portion of S.B. 1, was preempted and could not be severed.[89] The Ninth Circuit ultimately rejected the district court's finding that no part of S.B. 1 survived and held that non-preempted portions should be severed, finding that the regulation of consumer report information that is otherwise covered by FCRA was preempted, but that the affiliate sharing provision otherwise survived.[90]

10:16. Exclusions for individuals reporting "first hand" experience

As noted above, while FCRA generally governs the use of consumer reports for employment purposes, there are certain exceptions to this rule. Section 1681a(d)(2)(A)(I) excludes from the definition of a "consumer report" "any ... report containing information solely as to transactions or experiences between the consumer and the person making the report." This has been interpreted as permitting employers to report certain information regarding employees, including information provided by third parties, without creating a consumer report.[91] This includes reports regarding employees' drug use, because these have been held not to be a consumer report based upon this exception.[92]

10:17. Defining an "offer of credit" under FCRA

One of the issues frequently raised under FCRA is what a "firm offer of credit or insurance" is, because the acquisition and use of certain information under FCRA is only permitted if it is in relation to such a firm offer of credit or insurance.[93] Courts, including the Seventh Circuit, have held that it is improper to bundle an offer of credit with a product, so as to promote the product, if the offer of credit does not have value if viewed alone.[94] This holding led plaintiffs to conclude that courts must analyze this issue not in just situations of offers of merchandise and credit, but also to decide whether an offer of credit alone is valuable enough to permit the use of consumers' credit files. This has been presented in scenarios where the plaintiffs

---

87. *Id.*

88. *See* American Bankers Ass'n v. Lockyer, 2005 WL 2452798 (E.D. Cal. 2005); rev'd and remanded, 541 F.3d 1214 (9th Cir. 2008).

89. American Bankers Ass'n v. Lockyer, 2005 WL 2452798 (E.D. Cal. 2005); rev'd and remanded, 541 F.3d 1214 (9th Cir. 2008).

90. American Bankers Ass'n v. Lockyer, 541 F.3d 1214 (9th Cir. 2008).

91. Owner-Operator Independent Drivers Ass'n, Inc. v. USIS Commercial, 537 F.3d 1184 (10th Cir. 2008) (holding that report regarding truck drivers in computerized system was not a consumer report because it was generated based upon information that employers provided, including information that could be characterized as being in letters of recommendation.); *see also* Hodge v. Texaco, Inc., 975 F.2d 1093, 1096 (5th Cir. 1992).

92. *See* Salazar v. Golden State Warriors, 124 F.Supp.2d 1155, 1158 (N.D. Cal. 2000).

93. 15 U.S.C. § 1681b(c)(1)(B)(i).

94. *See* Cole v. U.S. Capital, Inc., 389 F.3d 709 (7th Cir. 2004).

argue that a firm offer of credit was not made because not all of the material terms of the offer of credit were disclosed at the time of the solicitation.[95] The Seventh Circuit rejected any valuation other than an offer of credit if it was not bundled with merchandise, finding that the offer merely needed to be "firm," not valuable. The distinction the court drew was that the *Cole* test was used to determine whether the offer was one for merchandise, an impermissible offer, versus one of credit.[96] Thus, the court in this case concluded, "When credit histories are used to offer credit, or insurance, and nothing else but, the right question is whether the offer is "firm" rather than whether it is "valuable."

The court also examined whether the promise of "free merchandise" means that the offer is not one of credit. This was done in the context of Murray v New Cingular Wireless Services and the court concluded that phone service itself was not credit, but that the offer of phone service was on credit because the services were provided before payment was due, and that deferred payment is "credit" under FCRA,[97] which incorporates a broad definition of "credit" from the Equal Credit Opportunity Act.[98] Indeed, the court noted, "A "free phone" is anything but free as it cannot be had apart from the service plan; payments for service include the cost of the phone, which is amoritzed over the length of the contract."[99] The court then examined whether the offer had to contain all material terms to be a firm offer of credit. The court rejected this as well, because a "firm offer" is defined by statute in 15 U.S.C. § 1681A. The sole inquiry into this definition is whether the offer will be honored if the verification checks out, not whether the terms appear in an initial mailing as in this case.

The Seventh Circuit devised a test that a statement that is "much smaller" than the principal type on the page cannot be conspicuous.[100]

10:18. Restrictions upon credit card receipts

The FACT Act restrictions upon printing credit card and debit card numbers on receipts became operative three years after the enactment of the FACT Act.[101] Unless otherwise permitted, a person that accepts credit cards or debit cards for the transaction of business is not permitted to print more than the last five digits of the card number or print the expiration date on any receipt provided to the cardholder at the point of the sale or transaction.[102] This requirement only applies to receipts that are electronically printed, and does not apply to transactions in which the sole means of recording a credit card or debit card account number is by handwriting or by an imprint or copy of the card.[103]

This provision of the law had a phased-in effective date. For machines that were in use before January 1, 2005, the law did not become effective until three years after

95. Murray v. New Cingular Wireless Services, Inc., 523 F.3d 719 (7th Cir. 2008).

96. *See* Murray v. GMAC Mortgage Corp., 434 F.3d 948 (7th Cir. 2006).

97. 15 U.S.C. § 1681A(r)(5) incorporating by reference the definition of "credit" at 15 U.S.C. § 1691A(d).

98. Murray v. New Cingular Wireless Services, Inc., 523 F.3d 719 (7th Cir. 2008).

99. *Id.*

100. Cole v. U.S. Capital, Inc., 389 F.3d 709, 731 (7th Cir. 2004).

101. 15 U.S.C. § 1681c(g)(3).

102. 15 U.S.C. § 1681c(g)(1).

103. 15 U.S.C. § 1681c(g)(2).

the date the FACT Act was passed, which was December 4, 2003.[104] The law became effective within one year for machines that were in use after January 1, 2005, and is now fully effective.[105]

There has been litigation under this provision, and one of the issues that has been raised is whether Internet receipts are covered. Cases have decided this issue both ways; some have found that the Internet is not covered,[106] and others support a finding that the Internet is covered.[107]

10:19. Electronic receipt and truncation of credit card numbers

A lawsuit against 1-800-FLOWERS.com was one of a multitude of consumer class actions arising from the FACT Act's requirement that credit card numbers be truncated. In this case, the court concluded that a receipt transmitted electronically to the consumer, even where the business does not actually print the receipt, falls within the FACT Act restriction.[108] The court relied upon the *Vasquez-Torres vs. Stub Hub, Inc.* decision.[109]

The court also rejected the defendant's argument that the receipt was not completed at the "point of sale." The point of sale concept is important under the FACT Act, as well as under certain state laws that restrict the collection of information at the "point of sale." In *Ehrheart vs. Bose Corp.*,[110] the district court concluded that point of sale was not necessarily limited to the concept of a "precise location within a store." The *Bose* court rejected such a narrow, technical reading of the statute.

10:20. Civil liability

Any person that negligently fails to comply with the requirements of FCRA is liable for actual damages, as well as attorneys' fees.[111] Additionally, a court can award attorneys' fees if it finds that a party made an unsuccessful pleading or motion in bad faith.[112]

In the case of willful non-compliance, the court can award actual damages or statutory damages of not less than $100 or not more than $1,000, or in the case of an individual that obtains a consumer report under false pretenses, actual damages or a civil penalty of $1,000, whichever is greater.[113] Punitive damages, as well as attorneys' fees are also recoverable.[114]

---

104. 15 U.S.C. § 1681c(g)(3)(A).

105. 15 U.S.C. § 1681c(g)(3)(B).

106. Grabein v. Jupiterimages Corp., 2008 WL 2704451 (S.D. Fla. 2008); Haslam v. Federated Dep't Stores, Inc., 2008 WL 5574762 (S.D. Fla. 2008); Edwin King v. Movietickets.com, 555 F. Supp. 2d 1339 (S.D.Fla. 2008); Smith v. Zazzle.com, Inc., 589 F. Supp. 2d 1345 (S.D. Fla. 2008).

107. Grabein v. 1-800-Flowers.com, Inc., 2008 WL 343179 (S.D. Fla. 2008).

108. Cradein vs. 1-800-FLOWERS.COM, Inc., 07-22235-CIV-HUCK (S.D. Sl. 2008).

109. Vasquez-Torres vs. Stub Hub, Inc., 2007 U.S. Dist. LEXIS 63719, *7 (C.D. Cal. July 2, 2007).

110. Ehrheart vs. Bose Corp., 2008 WL 64491 (W.D. Pa. 2008).

111. 15 U.S.C. §§ 1681o(a)(1)–(2).

112. 15 U.S.C. § 1681o(b).

113. 15 U.S.C. §§ 1681n(a)(1)(a)–(b).

114. 15 U.S.C. §§ 1681n(a)(2)–(3).

The Supreme Court has now addressed what the word "willfully" means in the context of FCRA's remedial provisions. "Willfully" has been construed to include both knowing and reckless violations of FCRA, as it does in other civil contexts.[115] Even prior to the Supreme Court's decision, it had been held that to establish willfulness it must be shown that a defendant knowingly and intentionally acted with conscious disregard, though a plaintiff need not show malice or evil motive.[116]

If a person obtains a consumer report from a consumer reporting agency under false pretenses or knowingly without a permissible purpose, the plaintiff can recover actual damages or $1,000, whichever is greater, and attorneys' fees.[117]

Knowingly and willfully obtaining information regarding a consumer from a consumer reporting agency under false pretenses is also a crime that is punishable by a fine, a prison term of not more than two years, or both.[118] Moreover, it is also a crime for any officer or employee of a consumer reporting agency to knowingly and willfully provide information from a consumer's file to an unauthorized person. This crime is also punishable by a fine, a prison term of not more than two years, or both.[119]

10:21. FCRA and litigation

While FCRA has proved to be a fertile ground for plaintiffs' claims, not all violations give rise to a private right of action. For example, violation of 15 U.S.C. § 1681s-2(a), by itself does not give rise to a private right of action.[120]

Similarly under FCRA, merely being deterred from applying for credit is insufficient to establish damage for a civil cause of action.[121] However, a plaintiff can succeed if the plaintiff shows conduct was a causal factor in the denial of credit.[122]

---

115. Safeco Ins. Co. of America v. Burr, 127 S. Ct. 2201, 167 L. Ed. 2d 1045 (2007).

116. Bakker vs. McKinnon, 152 F.3d 1007, 1013 (8th Cir. 1998); Cushman vs. Transunion Corp, 115 F.3d 220, 226 (3rd Cir. 1997); Pinner vs. Schmidt, 805 F.2d 1258, 1263 (5th Cir. 1986).

117. 15 U.S.C. § 1681n(b).

118. 15 U.S.C. § 1681q.

119. 15 U.S.C. § 1681r.

120. Brewer v. Transunion, L.L.C., 453 F. Supp. 2d 1346, (S.D. Ala. 2006).

121. Tinsley vs. TRW Inc., 879 F.Supp. 550, 552 (D. Md. 1995); Renniger vs. Chex Systems, No. 98C669, 1998 U.S. Dist. LEXIS 8528 (N.D. Ill. May 22, 1998).

122. Craybill vs. Transunion LLC, 259 F.3d 662, 664 7th Cir. 2001 (actual damages require some causal relationship between the violation of the statute and loss of credit or some other harm); Philbin vs. Transunion Corp., 101 F.3d 957, 963 (3rd Cir. 1996); Casella vs. Equifax Credit Information Services, 56 F.3d 469, 473 (2nd Cir. 1995).

10:22. Liability for dissemination of truthful information

In an unpublished decision, the Eleventh Circuit addressed whether a consumer reporting agency could be sued for sending a return check that contained a notation of "NSF/Non-Redepositable." In this case the consumer had stopped payment on a check. The court held that there was no evidence showing that the information was untrue or that it was done with malice or willful intent.[123]

10:23. Recovery of emotional distress under FCRA

Emotional distress is recoverable under FCRA. In certain cases, it requires a showing that the consumer reporting agency disseminated inaccurate information and someone viewed it.[124]

10:24. FCRA and accurate reporting defenses under § 1681i(1)(a)

Accurate reporting is a defense to claims under FCRA for claims under §§ 1681e(b) and 1681i.[125] However a declaration from a plaintiff has been held to be sufficient to create a material issue of fact on summary judgment.

10:25. Expert testimony regarding violations of FCRA

The District of Columbia Court of Appeal recently addressed whether the Fair Credit Reporting Act requires a plaintiff to produce expert testimony regarding violations of § 1681e(b) regarding whether the defense procedures were reasonable. In this case, the court concluded that FCRA did not require such a showing.[126] The court noted that the touchstone of judging the reasonableness of procedures is "what a reasonably prudent person would do under the circumstances."[127] The standard involves weighing the potential harm from any inaccuracies against the burdens associated with safeguarding accuracy.[128] Thus, where the potential harm that can result is great and the burden of safeguards is small, the consumer reporting agency has, in all likelihood, a duty to clarify inaccurate or incomplete information.[129]

10:26. FACT Act rules on affiliate marketing

New rules regarding affiliate marketing, an issue that has presented difficult issues for financial institutions, present new compliance issues. In addressing affiliate marketing,

---

123. Lofton-Taylor vs. Verizon Wireless, 262 Fed. Appx. 999, 2008 WL 189853 (11th Cir. 2008).

124. Millstone vs. O'Hanlon Reports, Inc., 528 F.2d 829, 834-835 (8th Cir. 1976); Casella vs. Equifax Credit Information Services, 56 F.3d 469, 475 (2nd Cir. 1995).

125. Fahey vs. Experian Information Solutions, Inc., 571 F. Supp. 2d 1082 (E.D. Miss. 2008) (citing Cahlin vs. General Motors Acceptance Corp., 936 F.2d 1151, 1156, 1160 (11th Cir. 1991)).

126. Wilson vs. CARCO, Inc., 518 F.3d 40 (D.C. Cir. 2008).

127. *Wilson*, 518 F.3d at 42 (citing Stewart v. Credit Bureau, Inc., 734 F.2d 47, 51 (D.C. Cir. 1984). (Per curiam)).

128. Stewart v. Credit Bureau, Inc., 734 F.2d 47, 51 (D.C. Cir. 1984).

129. Coropoulus vs. Credit Bureau, Inc., 734 F.2d 37, 42 (D.C. Cir. 1984).

one must first understand what an "affiliate" is. Under the regulations, an "affiliate" is any company[130] that is related by common ownership or common corporate control with another company.[131] This definition is key to understanding the scope of the regulations.

The affiliate marketing regulations are intended to apply to insured state non-member banks, insured state licensed branches of foreign banks, and subsidiaries of these entities (except for brokers, dealers, persons[132] providing insurance, investment companies, and investment advisers).[133]

10:27. FACT Act rules on affiliate marketing—Defining a "pre-existing" relationship

One of the key issues with affiliate marketing is defining what a "pre-existing business relationship" is. The regulations define it thus:

> The term "pre-existing business relationship" means a relationship between a person, or a person's licensed agent, and a consumer[134] based on—(A) A financial contract between the person and the consumer which is in force on the date on which the consumer is sent a solicitation[135] covered by this subpart; (B) The purchase, rental, or lease by the consumer of the person's goods or services, or a financial transaction (including holding an active account or a policy in force or having another continuing relationship) between the consumer and the person, during the 18-month period immediately preceding the date on which the consumer is sent a solicitation covered by this subpart; or (C) An inquiry or application by the consumer regarding a product or service offered by that person during the three-month period immediately preceding the date on which the consumer is sent a solicitation covered by this subpart.[136]

The regulations also offer a number of examples related to the definition of a "pre-existing relationship," including the following:

- If a consumer has a time deposit account, such as a certificate of deposit, at a depository institution that is currently in force, the depository institution has a pre-existing business relationship with the consumer and can use eligibility information it

---

130. Company means any corporation, limited liability company, business trust, general or limited partnership, association, or similar organization. 12 C.F.R. § 334.3(d).

131. 12 C.F.R. § 334.3(b).

132. "Person" means any individual, partnership, corporation, trust, estate cooperative, association, government or governmental subdivision or agency, or other entity. 12 C.F.R. § 334.3(l).

133. 12 C.F.R. § 334.20(a).

134. "Consumer" means an individual. 12 C.F.R. § 334.3(e).

135. The term "eligibility information" means any information the communication of which would be a consumer report if the exclusions from the definition of "consumer report" in section 603(d)(2)(A) of the Act did not apply. Eligibility information does not include aggregate or blind data that does not contain personal identifiers such as account numbers, names, or addresses. 12 C.F.R. § 334.20(b)(3).

136. 12 C.F.R. § 334.20(b)(4)(i).

receives from its affiliates to make solicitations to the consumer about its products or services.

- If a consumer obtained a certificate of deposit from a depository institution, but did not renew the certificate at maturity, the depository institution has a pre-existing business relationship with the consumer and can use eligibility information it receives from its affiliates to make solicitations to the consumer about its products or services for 18 months after the date of maturity of the certificate of deposit.

- If a consumer obtains a mortgage, the mortgage lender has a pre-existing business relationship with the consumer. If the mortgage lender sells the consumer's entire loan to an investor, the mortgage lender has a pre-existing business relationship with the consumer and can use eligibility information it receives from its affiliates to make solicitations to the consumer about its products or services for 18 months after the date it sells the loan, and the investor has a pre-existing business relationship with the consumer upon purchasing the loan. If, however, the mortgage lender sells a fractional interest in the consumer's loan to an investor but also retains an ownership interest in the loan, the mortgage lender continues to have a pre-existing business relationship with the consumer, but the investor does not have a pre-existing business relationship with the consumer. If the mortgage lender retains ownership of the loan, but sells ownership of the servicing rights to the consumer's loan, the mortgage lender continues to have a pre-existing business relationship with the consumer. The purchaser of the servicing rights also has a pre-existing business relationship with the consumer as of the date it purchases ownership of the servicing rights, but only if it collects payments from or otherwise deals directly with the consumer on a continuing basis.

- If a consumer applies to a depository institution for a product or service that it offers, but does not obtain a product or service from or enter into a financial contract or transaction with the institution, the depository institution has a pre-existing business relationship with the consumer and can therefore use eligibility information it receives from an affiliate to make solicitations to the consumer about its products or services for three months after the date of the application.

- If a consumer makes a telephone inquiry to a depository institution about its products or services and provides contact information to the institution, but does not obtain a product or service from or enter into a financial contract or transaction with the institution, the depository institution has a pre-existing business relationship with the consumer and can therefore use eligibility information it receives from an affiliate to make solicitations to the consumer about its products or services for three months after the date of the inquiry.

- If a consumer makes an inquiry to a depository institution by e-mail about its products or services, but does not obtain a product or service from or enter into a financial contract or transaction with the institution, the depository institution has a pre-existing business relationship with the consumer and can therefore use eligibility information it receives from an affiliate to make solicitations to the consumer about its services for three months after the date of the inquiry.

- If a consumer has an existing relationship with a depository institution that is part of a group of affiliated companies, makes a telephone call to the centralized call center for the group of affiliated companies to inquire about products or services offered by the insurance affiliate, and provides contact information to the call center, the call constitutes an inquiry to the insurance affiliate that offers those products or services. The insurance affiliate has a pre-existing business relationship with the consumer and can therefore use eligibility information it receives from its affiliated depository institution to make solicitations to the consumer about its products or services for three months after the date of the inquiry.[137]

The regulations also offer examples of what situations do not give rise to a pre-existing business relationship:

- If a consumer makes a telephone call to a centralized call center for a group of affiliated companies to inquire about the consumer's existing account at a depository institution, the call does not constitute an inquiry to any affiliate other than the depository institution that holds the consumer's account and does not establish a pre-existing business relationship between the consumer and any affiliate of the account-holding depository institution.

- If a consumer who has a deposit account with a depository institution makes a telephone call to an affiliate of the institution to ask about the affiliate's retail locations and hours, but does not make an inquiry about the affiliate's products or services, the call does not constitute an inquiry and does not establish a pre-existing business relationship between the consumer and the affiliate. Also, the affiliate's capture of the consumer's telephone number does not constitute an inquiry and does not establish a pre-existing business relationship between the consumer and the affiliate.

- If a consumer makes a telephone call to a depository institution in response to an advertisement that offers a free promotional item to consumers who call a toll-free number, but the advertisement does not indicate that the depository institution's products or services will be marketed to consumers who call in response, the call does not create a pre-existing business relationship between the consumer and the depository institution because the consumer has not made an inquiry about a product or service offered by the institution, but has merely responded to an offer for a free promotional item.[138]

---

137. 12 C.F.R. §§ 334.20(b)(4)(ii)(A)–(G).
138. 12 C.F.R. §§ 334.20(b)(4)(iii)(A)–(C).

10:28. FACT Act rules on affiliate marketing—Initial notice and opt-out requirements

Covered entities generally cannot use eligibility information[139] about a consumer that they receive from an affiliate[140] to make a solicitation for marketing purposes[141] to the consumer, unless

- it is clearly and conspicuously disclosed to the consumer in writing or, if the consumer agrees, electronically, in a concise[142] notice that the entity may use eligibility information about that consumer received from an affiliate to make solicitations for marketing purposes to the consumer;
- the consumer is provided a reasonable opportunity and a reasonable and simple method to opt out, or prohibit the entity from using eligibility information to make solicitations for marketing purposes to the consumer; and
- the consumer has not opted out.[143]

The regulations provide the following example:

> A consumer has a homeowner's insurance policy with an insurance company. The insurance company furnishes eligibility information about the consumer to its affiliated depository institution. Based on that eligibility information, the depository institution wants to make a solicitation to the consumer about its home equity loan products. The depository institution does not have a pre-existing business relationship with the consumer and none of the other exceptions apply. The depository institution is prohibited from using eligibility information received from its insurance affiliate to make

---

139. The term "eligibility information" means any information the communication of which would be a consumer report if the exclusions from the definition of "consumer report" in section 603(d)(2)(A) of the Act did not apply. Eligibility information does not include aggregate or blind data that does not contain personal identifiers such as account numbers, names, or addresses. 12 C.F.R. § 334.20(b)(3).

140. "Affiliate" means any company that is related by common ownership or common corporate control with another company. 12 C.F.R. § 334.3(b). "Common ownership or common corporate control" means a relationship between two companies under which: (1) One company has, with respect to the other company: (i) Ownership, control, or power to vote 25 percent or more of the outstanding shares of any class of voting security of a company, directly or indirectly, or acting through one or more other persons; (ii) Control in any manner over the election of a majority of the directors, trustees, or general partners (or individuals exercising similar functions) of a company; or (iii) The power to exercise, directly or indirectly, a controlling influence over the management or policies of a company, as the FDIC determines; or (2) Any other person has, with respect to both companies, a relationship described in paragraphs (i)(1)(i) through (i)(1)(iii) of this section. 12 C.F.R. § 334.3(i).

141. For purposes of this subpart, the entity makes a solicitation for marketing purposes if—(i) the entity receives eligibility information from an affiliate; (ii) the entity uses that eligibility information to do one or more of the following: (A) Identify the consumer or type of consumer to receive a solicitation; (B) Establish criteria used to select the consumer to receive a solicitation; or (C) Decide which of the entity's products or services to market to the consumer or tailor a solicitation to that consumer; and (iii) As a result of the use of the eligibility information, the consumer is provided a solicitation. 12 C.F.R. § 334.21(b)(1).

142. The term "concise" means a reasonably brief expression or statement. Combination with other required disclosures. A notice required by this subpart may be concise even if it is combined with other disclosures required or authorized by federal or state law. 12 C.F.R. §§ 334.20(b)(2)(i)–(ii).

143. 12 C.F.R. §§ 334.21(a)(1)(i)–(iii).

solicitations to the consumer about its home equity loan products unless the consumer is given a notice and opportunity to opt out and the consumer does not opt out.[144]

10:29. FACT Act rules on affiliate marketing—Who can provide notice

In certain cases the notice required by these regulations can be provide by an affiliate that has or has previously had a pre-existing business relationship with the consumer, or as part of a joint notice from two or more members of an affiliated group of companies, provided that at least one of the affiliates on the joint notice has or has previously had a pre-existing business relationship with the consumer.[145]

10:30. FACT Act rules on affiliate marketing—Use of eligibility information from an affiliate

It is permitted for entities to receive[146] eligibility information from an affiliate in various ways, including when the affiliate places that information into a common database that the entity may access.[147] Unless an entity[148] has used eligibility information that it received from an affiliate in a compliant manner, it is not considered to be a solicitation subject to these regulations if the affiliate: uses its own eligibility information that it obtained in connection with a pre-existing business relationship it has or had with the consumer to market the entity's products or services to the consumer; or directs its service provider to use the affiliate's own eligibility information that it obtained in connection with a pre-existing business relationship it has or had with the consumer to market the entity's products or services to the consumer, and the entity does not communicate directly with the service provider regarding that use.[149]

10:31. FACT Act Rules on affiliate marketing—Use of eligibility information by a service provider

An entity does not make a solicitation subject to these regulations if a service provider receives eligibility information from an affiliate that the affiliate obtained in connection with a pre-existing business relationship it has or had with the consumer and uses that

---

144. 12 C.F.R. § 334.21(a)(2).

145. 12 C.F.R. §§ 334.21(a)(3)(i)–(ii).

146. "Except as provided in paragraph (b)(5) of this section, you receive or use an affiliate's eligibility information if a service provider acting on your behalf (whether an affiliate or a nonaffiliated third party) receives or uses that information in the manner described in paragraphs (b)(1)(i) or (b)(1)(ii) of this section. All relevant facts and circumstances will determine whether a person is acting as your service provider when it receives or uses an affiliate's eligibility information in connection with marketing your products and services." 12 C.F.R. § 334.21(b)(3).

147. 12 C.F.R. § 334.21(b)(2).

148. The regulations use the term "You," which means a person described in paragraph (a) of 12 C.F.R. § 334.20(b)(6).

149. 12 C.F.R. § 334.21(b)(4).

eligibility information to market products or services to the consumer, so long as the following conditions are met:

- The affiliate controls access to and use of its eligibility information by the service provider (including the right to establish the specific terms and conditions under which the service provider may use such information to market the entity's products or services);
- The affiliate establishes specific terms and conditions under which the service provider may access and use the affiliate's eligibility information to market the entity's products and services (or those of affiliates generally) to the consumer, such as the identity of the affiliated companies whose products or services may be marketed to the consumer by the service provider, the types of products or services of affiliated companies that may be marketed, and the number of times the consumer may receive marketing materials, and periodically evaluates the service provider's compliance with those terms and conditions;
- The affiliate requires the service provider to implement reasonable policies and procedures designed to ensure that the service provider uses the affiliate's eligibility information in accordance with the terms and conditions established by the affiliate relating to the marketing of the entity's products or services;
- The affiliate is identified on or with the marketing materials provided to the consumer; and
- The entity does not improperly use the affiliate's eligibility information.[150]

The regulations provide a number of examples of these situations.[151]

10:32. FACT Act Rules on affiliate marketing—Writing requirements

Certain requirements must be set forth in a writing between the affiliate and the service provider, including the specific terms and conditions established by the affiliate.[152]

10:33. FACT Act Rules on affiliate marketing—Exceptions to eligibility information regulations

These regulations do not apply to entities that use eligibility information that they receive from an affiliate to make a solicitation for marketing purposes to a consumer with whom the entity has a pre-existing business relationship; to facilitate communications to an individual for whose benefit the entity provides employee benefit or other services pursuant to a contract with an employer related to and arising out of the current employment relationship or status of the individual as a participant or beneficiary of an employee benefit plan; to perform services on behalf of an affiliate, except that this subparagraph shall not be construed as permitting the entity to send solicitations on behalf of an affiliate if the affiliate would not be permitted to send the solicitation as

---

150. 12 C.F.R. §§ 334.21(b)(5)(i)(A)–(E).
151. 12 C.F.R. §§ 334.21(b)(6)(i)–(vi).
152. 12 C.F.R. § 334.21(b)(5)(ii).

a result of the election of the consumer to opt out under this subpart; in response to a communication about the entity's products or services initiated by the consumer; in response to an authorization or request by the consumer to receive solicitations; or if the entity's compliance with this subpart would prevent the entity from complying with any provision of state insurance laws pertaining to unfair discrimination in any state in which the entity is lawfully doing business.[153] The regulations provide a number of examples of the exceptions.[154]

10:34. FACT Act Rules on affiliate marketing—Scope and duration of opt-out

Except as otherwise provided, the consumer's election to opt out prohibits any affiliate covered by the opt-out notice from using eligibility information received from another affiliate as described in the notice to make solicitations to the consumer.[155] If the consumer establishes a continuing relationship with the entity or its affiliate, an opt-out notice may apply to eligibility information obtained in connection with a single continuing relationship or multiple continuing relationships that the consumer establishes with the entity or its affiliates, including continuing relationships established subsequent to delivery of the opt-out notice, so long as the notice adequately describes the continuing relationships covered by the opt-out; or any other transaction between the consumer and the entity or its affiliates as described in the notice.[156] If there is no continuing relationship between a consumer and the entity or its affiliate, and the entity or its affiliate obtains eligibility information about a consumer in connection with a transaction with the consumer, such as an isolated transaction or a credit application that is denied, an opt-out notice provided to the consumer only applies to eligibility information obtained in connection with that transaction.[157] A consumer may be given the opportunity to choose from a menu of alternatives when electing to prohibit solicitations, such as by electing to prohibit solicitations from certain types of affiliates covered by the opt-out notice but not other types of affiliates covered by the notice, electing to prohibit solicitations based on certain types of eligibility information but not other types of eligibility information, or electing to prohibit solicitations by certain methods of delivery but not other methods of delivery. However, one of the alternatives must allow the consumer to prohibit all solicitations from all of the affiliates that are covered by the notice.[158]

The regulations offer a number of examples of continuing and non-continuing relationships.[159]

---

153. 12 C.F.R. §§ 334.21(c)(1)–(6).

154. 12 C.F.R. § 334.21(d).

155. 12 C.F.R. § 334.22(1).

156. 12 C.F.R. §§ 334.22(2)(A)–(B).

157. 12 C.F.R. § 334.22(3).

158. 12 C.F.R. § 334.22(4).

159. 12 C.F.R. § 334.22.

10:35. FACT Act Rules on affiliate marketing—Notice following termination of all continuing relationships

A consumer must be given a new opt-out notice if, after all continuing relationships with the entity or its affiliates are terminated, the consumer subsequently establishes another continuing relationship with the entity or its affiliates and the consumer's eligibility information is to be used to make a solicitation.[160] The new opt-out notice must apply, at a minimum, to eligibility information obtained in connection with the new continuing relationship.[161] Consistent with paragraph (b) of this portion of the regulations, the consumer's decision not to opt out after receiving the new opt-out notice would not override a prior opt-out election by the consumer that applies to eligibility information obtained in connection with a terminated relationship, regardless of whether the new opt-out notice applies to eligibility information obtained in connection with the terminated relationship.[162] The regulations provide examples of these scenarios.[163]

A consumer's choice to opt-out must be effective for at least five years beginning when the consumer's opt-out election is received and implemented, unless the consumer subsequently revokes the opt-out in writing or, if the consumer agrees, electronically.[164] An opt-out period of more than five years may be established, including an opt-out period that does not expire unless revoked by the consumer.[165] The consumer has the right to opt out at any time.[166]

10:36. FACT Act Rules on affiliate marketing—Contents of an opt-out notice

The notice must be clear, conspicuous, and concise, and must accurately disclose the name of the affiliate(s) providing the notice;[167] a list of the affiliates or types of affiliates whose use of eligibility information is covered by the notice, which may include companies that become affiliates after the notice is provided to the consumer;[168] a general

---

160. 12 C.F.R. § 334.22(5).

161. *Id.*

162. *Id.*

163. *Id.*

164. 12 C.F.R. § 334.22(5)(b).

165. *Id.*

166. 12 C.F.R. § 334.22(5)(c).

167. If the notice is provided jointly by multiple affiliates and each affiliate shares a common name, such as "ABC," then the notice may indicate that it is being provided by multiple companies with the ABC name or multiple companies in the ABC group or family of companies, for example, by stating that the notice is provided by "all of the ABC companies," "the ABC banking, credit card, insurance, and securities companies," or by listing the name of each affiliate providing the notice. But if the affiliates providing the joint notice do not all share a common name, then the notice must either separately identify each affiliate by name or identify each of the common names used by those affiliates, for example, by stating that the notice is provided by "all of the ABC and XYZ companies" or by "the ABC banking and credit card companies and the XYZ insurance companies." 12 C.F.R. § 334.23(a)(1)(i).

168. If each affiliate covered by the notice shares a common name, such as "ABC," then the notice may indicate that it applies to multiple companies with the ABC name or multiple companies in the ABC group or family of companies, for example, by stating that the notice is provided by "all of the ABC companies," "the ABC banking, credit card, insurance, and securities companies," or by listing the name of each affiliate providing the notice. But if the affiliates covered by the notice do not all share a common name, then the notice must

description of the types of eligibility information that may be used to make solicitations to the consumer; that the consumer may elect to limit the use of eligibility information to make solicitations to the consumer; that the consumer's election will apply for the specified period of time stated in the notice and, if applicable, that the consumer will be allowed to renew the election once that period expires; if the notice is provided to consumers who may have previously opted out, such as if a notice is provided to consumers annually, that the consumer who has chosen to limit solicitations does not need to act again until the consumer receives a renewal notice; and a reasonable and simple method for the consumer to opt out.[169]

If the consumer is afforded a broader right to opt out of receiving marketing than is required by this subpart, the requirements of this section may be satisfied by providing the consumer with a clear, conspicuous, and concise notice that accurately discloses the consumer's opt-out rights.[170] A notice required by this subpart may be coordinated and consolidated with any other notice or disclosure required to be issued under any other provision of law by the entity providing the notice, including but not limited to the notice described in § 603(d)(2)(A)(iii) of the Act and the Gramm-Leach-Bliley Act privacy notice.[171]

A notice or other disclosure that is equivalent to the notice required by this subpart, and that is provided to a consumer together with disclosures required by any other provision of law, satisfies the requirements of this section.[172]

If two or more consumers jointly obtain a product or service, a single opt-out notice may be provided to the joint consumers. Any of the joint consumers may exercise the right to opt out.[173] The opt-out notice must explain how an opt-out direction by a joint consumer will be treated.[174] An opt-out direction by a joint consumer may be treated as applying to all of the associated joint consumers, or each joint consumer may be permitted to opt out separately.[175] If each joint consumer is permitted to opt out separately, one of the joint consumers must be permitted to opt out on behalf of all of the joint consumers and the joint consumers must be permitted to exercise their separate rights to opt out in a single response.[176] It should be noted that it is impermissible to require all joint consumers to opt out before implementing any opt-out direction.[177]

---

either separately identify each covered affiliate by name or identify each of the common names used by those affiliates, for example, by stating that the notice applies to "all of the ABC and XYZ companies" or to "the ABC banking and credit card companies and the XYZ insurance companies." 12 C.F.R. § 334.23(a)(1)(i).

169. 12 C.F.R. §§ 334.23(a)(1)(i)–(vii).

170. 12 C.F.R. § 334.23(a)(3).

171. 12 C.F.R. § 334.23(b).

172. 12 C.F.R. § 334.23(c).

173. 12 C.F.R. § 334.23(a)(2)(i).

174. 12 C.F.R. § 334.23(a)(2)(ii).

175. *Id.*

176. *Id.*

177. 12 C.F.R. § 334.23(a)(2)(iii).

10:37. FACT Act rules on affiliate marketing—Reasonable opportunity to opt out

An entity cannot use eligibility information about a consumer that it receives from an affiliate to make a solicitation to the consumer about the entity's products or services, unless the consumer is provided a reasonable opportunity to opt out, as required by § 334.21(a)(1)(ii).[178] The regulations provide a number of examples of a reasonable opportunity to opt out.[179]

10:38. FACT Act rules on affiliate marketing—Reasonable and simple methods of opting out

In addition, the regulations also require that an entity not use eligibility information about a consumer that it receives from an affiliate to make a solicitation to the consumer about the entity's products or services, unless the consumer is provided a reasonable and simple method to opt out, as required by 12 C.F.R. § 334.21(a)(1)(ii).[180] The regulations also provide examples of reasonable and simple methods of opting out.[181] A consumer

---

178. 12 C.F.R. § 334.24(a).

179. The consumer is given a reasonable opportunity to opt out if: (1) By mail. The opt-out notice is mailed to the consumer. The consumer is given 30 days from the date the notice is mailed to elect to opt out by any reasonable means. (2) By electronic means. (i) The opt-out notice is provided electronically to the consumer, such as by posting the notice at an Internet Web site at which the consumer has obtained a product or service. The consumer acknowledges receipt of the electronic notice. The consumer is given 30 days after the date the consumer acknowledges receipt to elect to opt out by any reasonable means. (ii) The opt-out notice is provided to the consumer by e-mail where the consumer has agreed to receive disclosures by e-mail from the person sending the notice. The consumer is given 30 days after the e-mail is sent to elect to opt out by any reasonable means. (3) At the time of an electronic transaction. The opt-out notice is provided to the consumer at the time of an electronic transaction, such as a transaction conducted on an Internet Web site. The consumer is required to decide, as a necessary part of proceeding with the transaction, whether to opt out before completing the transaction. There is a simple process that the consumer may use to opt out at that time using the same mechanism through which the transaction is conducted. (4) At the time of an in-person transaction. The opt-out notice is provided to the consumer in writing at the time of an in-person transaction. The consumer is required to decide, as a necessary part of proceeding with the transaction, whether to opt out before completing the transaction, and is not permitted to complete the transaction without making a choice. There is a simple process that the consumer may use during the course of the in-person transaction to opt out, such as completing a form that requires consumers to write a "yes" or "no" to indicate their opt-out preference or that requires the consumer to check one of two blank check boxes—one that allows consumers to indicate that they want to opt out and one that allows consumers to indicate that they do not want to opt out. (5) By including in a privacy notice. The opt-out notice is included in a Gramm-Leach-Bliley Act privacy notice. The consumer is allowed to exercise the opt-out within a reasonable period of time and in the same manner as the opt-out under that privacy notice. 12 C.F.R. § 334.24(b).

180. 12 C.F.R. § 334.25(a).

181. Reasonable and simple opt-out methods. Reasonable and simple methods for exercising the opt-out right include—(i) Designating a check-off box in a prominent position on the opt-out form; (ii) Including a reply form and a self-addressed envelope together with the opt-out notice; (iii) Providing an electronic means to opt out, such as a form that can be electronically mailed or processed at an Internet Web site, if the consumer agrees to the electronic delivery of information; (iv) Providing a toll-free telephone number that consumers may call to opt out; or (v) Allowing consumers to exercise all of their opt-out rights described in a consolidated opt-out notice that includes the privacy opt-out under the Gramm-Leach-Bliley Act, 15 U.S.C. 6801 *et seq.*, the affiliate sharing opt-out under the Act, and the affiliate marketing opt-out under the Act, by a single method, such as by calling a single toll-free telephone number. 12 C.F.R. § 334.25(b)(1). Opt-out methods that are not reasonable and simple. Reasonable and simple methods for exercising an opt-out right do not include—(i) Requiring the consumer to write his or her own letter; (ii) Requiring the consumer to call or

can be required to opt out through a specific means, as long as that means is reasonable and simple for that consumer.[182]

10:39. FACT Act rules on affiliate marketing—Delivery of opt-out notices

An opt-out notice must be provided so that each consumer can reasonably be expected to receive actual notice.[183] For opt-out notices provided electronically, the notice may be provided in compliance with either the electronic disclosure provisions in this subpart or federal law regarding e-signatures.[184] The regulations provide examples of reasonable expectations of actual notice, as well as examples of situations that will not provide reasonable expectations of actual notice.[185]

10:40. FACT Act rules on affiliate marketing—Renewal of opt-out

After the opt-out period expires an entity may not make solicitations based upon eligibility information received from an affiliate to a consumer who previously opted out, unless the consumer has been given an appropriate renewal notice and a reasonable opportunity and a reasonable and simple method to renew the opt-out, and the consumer does not renew the opt-out; or an exception in § 334.21(c) applies.[186] As noted above, each opt-out renewal must be effective for five years.[187]

The notice referenced above must be provided by the affiliate that provided the previous opt-out notice, or its successor; or as part of a joint renewal notice from two or more members of an affiliated group of companies, or their successors, that jointly provided the previous opt-out notice.[188] There are certain specific requirements

---

write to obtain a form for opting out, rather than including the form with the opt-out notice; (iii) Requiring the consumer who receives the opt-out notice in electronic form only, such as through posting at an Internet Web site, to opt out solely by paper mail or by visiting a different Web site without providing a link to that site. 12 C.F.R. § 334.25(b)(2).

182. 12 C.F.R. § 334.25(c).

183. 12 C.F.R. § 334.26(a).

184. *Id.*

185. A consumer may reasonably be expected to receive actual notice if the affiliate providing the notice: (1) Hand-delivers a printed copy of the notice to the consumer; (2) Mails a printed copy of the notice to the last known mailing address of the consumer; (3) Provides a notice by e-mail to a consumer who has agreed to receive electronic disclosures by e-mail from the affiliate providing the notice; or (4) Posts the notice on the Internet Web site at which the consumer obtained a product or service electronically and requires the consumer to acknowledge receipt of the notice. 12 C.F.R. § 334.26(b). A consumer may not reasonably be expected to receive actual notice if the affiliate providing the notice: (1) Only posts the notice on a sign in a branch or office or generally publishes the notice in a newspaper; (2) Sends the notice via e-mail to a consumer who has not agreed to receive electronic disclosures by e-mail from the affiliate providing the notice; or (3) Posts the notice on an Internet Web site without requiring the consumer to acknowledge receipt of the notice. 12 C.F.R. § 334.26(c).

186. 12 C.F.R. §§ 334.27(a)(1)(i)(1)–(2).

187. 12 C.F.R. § 334.27(a)(2).

188. 12 C.F.R. §§ 334.27(a)(3)(i)–(ii).

regarding the content of the renewal notice, including that it is clear, conspicuous, and concise.[189]

10:41. FACT Act rules on affiliate marketing—Timing of renewal notice

A renewal notice may be provided to the consumer either within a reasonable period of time before the expiration of the opt-out period, or any time after the expiration of the opt-out period but before solicitations that would have been prohibited by the expired opt-out are made to the consumer.[190] It can be provided in combination with the requisite GLB notice, if required, if certain timing issues are met.[191]

10:42. FACT Act rules on affiliate marketing—Effective date

While the regulations became effective on January 1, 2008, compliance was not mandatory until October 1, 2008.

10:43. FACT Act regulations regarding address discrepancies

These regulations apply to a user of consumer reports that receives a notice of address discrepancy[192] from a consumer reporting agency and that is an insured state non-

---

189. The renewal notice must be clear, conspicuous, and concise, and must accurately disclose: (1) The name of the affiliate(s) providing the notice. If the notice is provided jointly by multiple affiliates and each affiliate shares a common name, such as "ABC," then the notice may indicate that it is being provided by multiple companies with the ABC name or multiple companies in the ABC group or family of companies, for example, by stating that the notice is provided by "all of the ABC companies," "the ABC banking, credit card, insurance, and securities companies," or by listing the name of each affiliate providing the notice. But if the affiliates providing the joint notice do not all share a common name, then the notice must either separately identify each affiliate by name or identify each of the common names used by those affiliates, for example, by stating that the notice is provided by "all of the ABC and XYZ companies" or by "the ABC banking and credit card companies and the XYZ insurance companies;" (2) A list of the affiliates or types of affiliates whose use of eligibility information is covered by the notice, which may include companies that become affiliates after the notice is provided to the consumer. If each affiliate covered by the notice shares a common name, such as "ABC," then the notice may indicate that it applies to multiple companies with the ABC name or multiple companies in the ABC group or family of companies, for example, by stating that the notice is provided by "all of the ABC companies," "the ABC banking, credit card, insurance, and securities companies," or by listing the name of each affiliate providing the notice. But if the affiliates covered by the notice do not all share a common name, then the notice must either separately identify each covered affiliate by name or identify each of the common names used by those affiliates, for example, by stating that the notice applies to "all of the ABC and XYZ companies" or to "the ABC banking and credit card companies and the XYZ insurance companies;" (3) A general description of the types of eligibility information that may be used to make solicitations to the consumer; (4) That the consumer previously elected to limit the use of certain information to make solicitations to the consumer; (5) That the consumer's election has expired or is about to expire; (6) That the consumer may elect to renew the consumer's previous election; (7) If applicable, that the consumer's election to renew will apply for the specified period of time stated in the notice and that the consumer will be allowed to renew the election once that period expires; and (8) A reasonable and simple method for the consumer to opt out. 12 C.F.R. § 334.27(b).

190. 12 C.F.R. §§ 334.27(c)(1)(i)–(ii).

191. 12 C.F.R. § 334.27(c)(2).

192. For purposes of this section, a notice of address discrepancy means a notice sent to a user by a consumer reporting agency pursuant to 15 U.S.C. § 1681c(h)(1), that informs the user of a substantial difference between the address for the consumer that the user provided to request the consumer report and the address(es) in the agency's file for the consumer. 12 C.F.R. § 334.82(b).

member bank, insured state licensed branch of a foreign bank, or a subsidiary of such entities (except brokers, dealers, persons providing insurance, investment companies, and investment advisers).[193]

A user must develop and implement reasonable policies and procedures designed to enable the user to form a reasonable belief that a consumer report relates to the consumer about whom it has requested the report, when the user receives a notice of address discrepancy.[194] The regulations contain examples of reasonable policies and procedures.[195]

A user must develop and implement reasonable policies and procedures for furnishing an address for the consumer that the user has reasonably confirmed is accurate to the consumer reporting agency from whom it received the notice of address discrepancy when the user can form a reasonable belief that the consumer report relates to the consumer about whom the user requested the report; establishes a continuing relationship with the consumer; and regularly and in the ordinary course of business, furnishes information to the consumer reporting agency from which the notice of address discrepancy relating to the consumer was obtained.[196] There are a number of examples of how a user can reasonably confirm an address is accurate.[197]

These policies and procedures must provide that the user will furnish the consumer's address that the user has reasonably confirmed is accurate to the consumer reporting agency as part of the information it regularly furnishes for the reporting period in which it establishes a relationship with the consumer.[198]

10:44. FACT Act and Red Flag regulations

These regulations generally apply to financial institutions or creditors. There are a number of different regulations that are all nearly identical, that differ solely regarding what the basis of jurisdiction is, typically based on the type of entity involved. In its broadest form, the regulations cover any creditor that is subject to the FTC Act. For ease of reference, only the regulations found at 12 C.F.R. § 334.90 are covered.[199]

---

193. 12 C.F.R. § 334.82(a).

194. 12 C.F.R. § 334.82(c).

195. Examples of reasonable policies and procedures. (i) Comparing the information in the consumer report provided by the consumer reporting agency with information the user: (A) Obtains and uses to verify the consumer's identity in accordance with the requirements of the Customer Information Program (CIP) rules implementing 31 U.S.C. § 5318(l) (31 C.F.R. § 103.121); (B) Maintains in its own records, such as applications, change of address notifications, other customer account records, or retained CIP documentation; or (C) Obtains from third-party sources; or (ii) Verifying the information in the consumer report provided by the consumer reporting agency with the consumer. 12 C.F.R. § 334.28(c)(2).

196. 12 C.F.R. §§ 334.82(d)(1)(i)–(iii).

197. The user may reasonably confirm an address is accurate by: (i) Verifying the address with the consumer about whom it has requested the report; (ii) Reviewing its own records to verify the address of the consumer; (iii) Verifying the address through third-party sources; or (iv) Using other reasonable means.

198. 12 C.F.R. § 334.82(d)(3).

199. 12 C.F.R. § 334.90(a).

10:45. Periodic identification of covered accounts

Each financial institution[200] or creditor[201] must periodically determine whether it offers or maintains covered accounts.[202] As a part of this determination, a financial institution or creditor must conduct a risk assessment to determine whether it offers or maintains covered accounts described in paragraph (b)(3)(ii) of this section, taking into consideration the following:

- the methods it provides to open its accounts;
- the methods it provides to access its accounts; and
- its previous experiences with identity theft.[203]

10:46. Establishment an identity theft prevention program

Financial institutions and creditors that offer or maintain one or more covered accounts must develop and implement a written identity theft prevention program (program) that is designed to detect, prevent, and mitigate identity theft[204] in connection with the opening of a covered account or any existing covered account. The program must be

---

200. Financial institution has the same meaning as in 15 U.S.C. 1681a(t). 12 C.F.R. § 334.90(b)(7).

201. Initially, the FTC stated that because the term creditor has the same meaning as in 15 U.S.C. 1681a(r)(5), the definition would then apply to lenders such as banks, finance companies, automobile dealers, mortgage brokers, utility companies, and telecommunications companies as well as any situation in which delivery of goods or services preceded payment. 12 C.F.R. § 334.90(b)(5). Controversy over the broad interpretation of the term creditor and the potential that deferral of payment would apply to almost everyone caused the FTC to delay enforcement several times and caused Congress to amend the statute. The Red Flag Program Clarification Act of 2010 (Pub. Law 111-319) limits the definition of "creditor" under the FCRA to entities that:

    1. obtain or use consumer reports, directly or indirectly, in connection with a credit transaction;

    2. furnish information to consumer reporting agencies (*see* 15 U.S.C. 1681s-2) in connection with a credit transaction; or

    3. advance funds to or on behalf of a person (based on the person's obligation to repay the funds or repayable from property pledged by or on behalf of the person).

    Importantly, the amendment specifically excludes from the definition of "creditor" entities that advance funds "to or on behalf of a person for expenses incidental to a service provided by the creditor to that person." This exclusion means that entities that both provide a product or service and allow customers to pay for the product or service at a later time would not be subject to the Red Flags Rule, provided such entities do not engage in the activities enumerated in bullets (1) or (2) above.

202. Covered account means: (i) An account that a financial institution or creditor offers or maintains, primarily for personal, family, or household purposes, that involves or is designed to permit multiple payments or transactions, such as a credit card account, mortgage loan, automobile loan, margin account, cell phone account, utility account, checking account, or savings account; and (ii) Any other account that the financial institution or creditor offers or maintains for which there is a reasonably foreseeable risk to customers or to the safety and soundness of the financial institution or creditor from identity theft, including financial, operational, compliance, reputation, or litigation risks. 12 C.F.R. § 334.90(b)(3). Account means a continuing relationship established by a person with a financial institution or creditor to obtain a product or service for personal, family, household or business purposes. Account includes: (i) An extension of credit, such as the purchase of property or services involving a deferred payment; and (ii) A deposit account. 12 C.F.R. § 334.90(b)(1).

203. 12 C.F.R. §§ 334.90(c)(1)–(3).

204. Identity theft has the same meaning as in 16 C.F.R. 603.2(a). 12 C.F.R. § 334.90(b)(8).

appropriate to the size and complexity of the financial institution or creditor and the nature and scope of its activities.[205]

The program must include reasonable policies and procedures to

- identify relevant "red flags"[206] for the covered accounts that the financial institution or creditor offers or maintains, and incorporate those red flags into its Program;
- detect red flags that have been incorporated into the program of the financial institution or creditor;
- respond appropriately to any red flags that are detected to prevent and mitigate identity theft; and
- ensure the program (including the red flags determined to be relevant) is updated periodically, to reflect changes in risks to customers[207] and to the safety and soundness of the financial institution or creditor from identity theft.[208]

10:47. Administration of the program

Financial institutions and creditors, if required to implement a program, must also provide for the continued administration of the program and must

- obtain approval of the initial written program from either its board of directors[209] or an appropriate committee of the board of directors;
- involve the board of directors, an appropriate committee thereof, or a designated employee at the level of senior management in the oversight, development, implementation and administration of the program;
- train staff, as necessary, to effectively implement the program; and
- exercise appropriate and effective oversight of service provider[210] arrangements.[211]

10:48. Effective date

While the regulations became effective on January 1, 2008, compliance only became mandatory on December 31, 2010.

---

205. 12 C.F.R. § 334.90(d)(1).
206. "Red flag" means a pattern, practice, or specific activity that indicates the possible existence of identity theft. 12 C.F.R. § 334.90(b)(9).
207. Customer means a person that has a covered account with a financial institution or creditor. 12 C.F.R. § 334.90(b)(6).
208. 12 C.F.R. §§ 334.90(d)(2)(i)–(iv).
209. The term board of directors includes: (i) In the case of a branch or agency of a foreign bank, the managing official in charge of the branch or agency; and (ii) In the case of any other creditor that does not have a board of directors, a designated employee at the level of senior management. 12 C.F.R. § 334.90(b)(2).
210. Service provider means a person that provides a service directly to the financial institution or creditor. 12 C.F.R. § 334.90(b)(10).
211. 12 C.F.R. §§ 334.90(e)(1)–(4).

10:49. Administrative enforcement

The FTC generally has enforcement authority for violations of FCRA, and the violation of FCRA is considered to be an unfair or deceptive act or practice in violation of Section 5(a) of the FTC Act, and therefore subject to enforcement under Section 5(b).[212] In addition to those penalties, the FTC is also authorized to seek a civil penalty of up to $2,500 per violation if there is a showing that there was a knowing violation that was part of a pattern and practice of violations.[213] The civil penalty cannot be imposed unless the person has previously been enjoined from or ordered not to commit the violation and the person violates the injunction.[214]

The FTC does not have jurisdiction over certain types of entities and other administrative agencies are granted administrative enforcement authority.[215] For certain violations, the chief law enforcement officer of a state is also permitted to bring an action seeking an injunction and, on behalf of the residents of the state, to seek to recover damages, civil penalties in the case of negligent or willful violations, and attorneys' fees.[216]

If an action is filed by a state, the state must serve prior written notice upon the FTC or appropriate federal agency, as well as a copy of the complaint.[217] The FTC or other federal agency has the ability to intervene in the action, to remove the action, and to file petitions for appeal.[218]

10:50. FCRA and preemption of state law claims

There are in essence three different views of the preemptive effect of FCRA on state law claims for damages. One view is that FCRA completely preempts state law claims.[219] Other courts have held that FCRA only preempts state law claims after notice of a dispute.[220] A third series of courts have adopted what is known as the statutory approach, which finds that FCRA preempts state law claims based upon state statutes.[221]

In *Beyer v. Firstar Bank N.A.*,[222] the plaintiff had a dispute with a bank and a collection agency regarding a balance on his credit card. The collection agency and the plaintiff entered a settlement agreement that the bank never entered or agreed to. The plaintiff later determined that a negative entry was entered in his credit report, and he sued originally under Iowa law and then under FCRA. The district court entered judgment against the plaintiff, who then appealed the decision. The Eighth Circuit affirmed the judgment, finding that the plaintiff could not prove the malice or willful

212. 15 U.S.C. § 1681s(a)(1).

213. 15 U.S.C. § 1681s(a)(2)(A).

214. 15 U.S.C. § 1681s(a)(3).

215. 15 U.S.C. § 1681s(b).

216. 15 U.S.C. §§ 1681s(c)(1), (4)–(5).

217. 15 U.S.C. § 1681s(c)(2).

218. *Id.*

219. *See, e.g.*, Riley v. GMAC, 226 F. Supp. 2d 1316 (S.D. Ala. 2002).

220. Woltersdorf v. Pentagon Federal Credit Union, 320 F. Supp. 2d 1222 (N.D. Ala. 2004).

221. *See* Johnson v. Citimortgage, Inc., 351 F. Supp. 2d 1368 (N.D. Ga. 2004); Brewer v. Transunion, L.L.C., 453 F. Supp. 2d 1346 (S.D. Ala. 2006).

222. Beyer v. Firstar Bank N.A., 447 F.3d 1106 (8th Cir. 2006).

intent required for his claims to avoid preemption by FCRA. The appellate court also held that even if the claims were not preempted, the failure of the plaintiff to produce evidence that he had satisfied the debt in question required that judgment be entered in the bank's favor.

10:51. Regulation S-P

Regulation S-P is a regulation implemented by the SEC that applies to brokers, dealers, and investment companies, as well as to investment advisers that are registered with the Commission. It also applies to foreign (non-resident) brokers, dealers, investment companies and investment advisers that are registered with the Commission if they have non-public personal information about individuals who obtain financial products or services primarily for personal, family, or household purposes.[223] This does not apply to information about companies or about individuals who obtain financial products or services primarily for business, commercial, or agricultural purposes and in any case does not apply to foreign (non-resident) brokers, dealers, investment companies, and investment advisers that are not registered with the Commission.[224]

Much of Regulation S-P tracks the Financial Privacy Rule implemented under GLB. The portions of Regulation S-P that generally track the Financial Privacy Rule are not discussed here because of the similarities. However, Regulation S-P contains one section that is not contained in the Financial Privacy Rule which implements certain other requirements under GLB and FCRA, and this section is discussed below.

Every broker, dealer, and investment company, and every investment adviser registered with the Commission must adopt written policies and procedures that address administrative, technical, and physical safeguards for the protection of customer records and information.[225] These written policies and procedures must be reasonably designed to ensure the security and confidentiality of customer records and information; protect against any anticipated threats or hazards to the security or integrity of customer records and information; and protect against unauthorized access to or use of customer records or information that could result in substantial harm or inconvenience to any customer.[226]

There is also a data destruction requirement that generally tracks the FACT Act requirements. Every broker and dealer other than notice-registered broker-dealers,[227] every investment company, and every investment adviser and transfer agent[228] registered with the Commission, that maintains or otherwise possesses consumer report information[229]

---

223. 17 C.F.R. § 248.1(b).

224. *Id.*

225. 17 C.F.R. § 248.30(a).

226. 17 C.F.R. §§ 248.30(a)(1)–(3).

227. "Notice-registered broker-dealers" means a broker or dealer registered by notice with the Commission under section 15(b)(11) of the Securities Exchange Act of 1934 (15 U.S.C. 78o(b)(11)). 17 C.F.R. § 248.1(b)(1)(iv).

228. "Transfer agent" has the same meaning as in section 3(a)(25) of the Securities Exchange Act of 1934 (15 U.S.C. 78c(a)(25)). 17 C.F.R. § 248.1(b)(1)(v).

229. "Consumer report information" means any record about an individual, whether in paper, electronic or other form, that is a consumer report or is derived from a consumer report. Consumer report information also means a compilation of such records. Consumer report information does not include information that does not identify individuals, such as aggregate information or blind data. 17 C.F.R. § 248.1(b)(1)(ii). Consumer

for a business purpose must properly dispose of the information by taking reasonable measures to protect against unauthorized access to or use of the information in connection with its disposal.[230] Given the data retention requirements on certain entities, the SEC clearly stated that this regulation in no way can be construed to require any broker, dealer, or investment company, or any investment adviser or transfer agent registered with the Commission to maintain or destroy any record pertaining to an individual that is not imposed under other law or to alter or affect any requirement imposed under any other provision of law to maintain or destroy any of those records.[231]

The SEC has recently issued proposed revisions to Regulation S-P that would cause covered entities to implement new information security policies, as well as provide notice of security breaches. The information security policies would in all likelihood track what has been done under GLB, and the relevant factors for development of a comprehensive information security policy would include involving the board of directors, assessing risk, managing and controlling risk, overseeing service provider arrangements, adjusting the program, and reporting to the board.

Notice to customers, as well as to the relevant regulator, of breaches of information security are also likely to be requirements of a revised Regulation S-P. Other proposed changes include increased recordkeeping of privacy and safeguarding policies, as well as limited exceptions to the disclosure requirements when an employee departs if the disclosure is limited to customer names; a description of the types of accounts and products held by the customers; and customer contact information. This exception would apply if notice is given to the entity on or before the separation date.[232]

10:52. FCRA preemption and mortgage-trigger lists

One practice that has drawn recent legislative attention is the sale of mortgage-trigger lists—lists of people who have had a particular lender request information about them.[233] Minnesota recently passed a law that prohibits the sale of these lists, but the law was held to be preempted by FCRA because this practice is regulated by 15 U.S.C. § 1681b(c).[234]

---

report has the same meaning as in section 603(d) of the Fair Credit Reporting Act (15 U.S.C. 1681a(d)). 17 C.F.R. § 248.1(b)(1)(i).

230. "Disposal" means: (A) The discarding or abandonment of consumer report information; or (B) The sale, donation, or transfer of any medium, including computer equipment, on which consumer report information is stored. 17 C.F.R. § 248.1(b)(1)(iiii). 17 C.F.R. § 248.30(2)(i).

231. 17 C.F.R. §§ 248.30(2)(ii)(A)–(B).

232. *See* www.sec.gov/rules/proposed/2008/34-57427.pdf, last visited March 1, 2011.

233. Consumer Data Industry Ass'n v. Swanson, 2007 WL 2219389 (D. Minn. 2007).

234. *Id.*

CHAPTER 11

Data Security and Destruction

I. Introduction

11:1. In general

Data security and destruction present legal issues, as well as, in certain cases, complicated technical issues. This chapter examines the federal and state laws that require businesses to maintain adequate security and to destroy data. Compliance with other standards, including those imposed by credit card companies, is also discussed. Finally, common issues with security incidents and investigations are also discussed.

Though federal and state statutes have been the norm, states are beginning to adopt detailed regulations regarding data security. Massachusetts is the first, and other states are likely to follow this path.

II. Federal Law

11:2. Impact of Sarbanes-Oxley and federal obstruction laws on data destruction

The Sarbanes-Oxley Act (SOX) and other federal laws can impact data destruction in several ways. Destruction of data in certain cases can be a felony. If someone corruptly alters, destroys, mutilates, or conceals a record, document, or other object, or attempts to do so, with the intent to impair the object's integrity or availability for use in an official proceeding, it is a crime punishable by a fine, a prison term not to exceed 20 years, or both.[1] It should be noted that there does not need to be a pending action or investigation for a violation to be found.[2] Similarly, it is not a defense to a charge that the record or document is inadmissible or privileged.[3]

It is also a crime if a person knowingly alters, destroys, mutilates, conceals, covers up, falsifies, or makes a false entry in any record, document, or tangible object with the intent to impede, obstruct, or influence the investigation or proper administration of any matter within the jurisdiction of any department or agency of the United States or any case filed under Title 11 (bankruptcy cases), or in relation to or contemplation of either of the above.[4] The crime is punishable by a fine, a prison term not to exceed 20 years, or both.[5]

Auditors are also precluded from destroying certain records. Any accountant who conducts an audit of an issuer of securities to which section 10A(a) of the Securities Exchange Act of 1934 applies must maintain all audit or review workpapers for a period of five years from the end of the fiscal period in which the audit or review was concluded.[6]

Public companies are now required to adopt certain policies for their audit committees. This can impact privacy, particularly that of employees in certain ways. Specifically, the audit committee must establish procedures for the following:

- the receipt, retention, and treatment of complaints received by the issuer regarding accounting, internal accounting controls, or auditing matters; and
- the confidential, anonymous submission by employees of the issuer of concerns regarding questionable accounting or auditing matters.[7]

SOX also impacts data destruction and retention in other ways that may apply in conjunction with a number of other statutes that restrict data destruction and require retention.[8] SOX 404 is one issue that occupies a significant amount of resources at

---

1. 18 U.S.C. § 1512(c)(1).
2. 18 U.S.C. § 1512(f)(1).
3. 18 U.S.C. § 1512(f)(2).
4. 18 U.S.C. § 1519.
5. *Id.*
6. 18 U.S.C. § 1520(a)(1).
7. 15 U.S.C. § 78f.
8. *See, e.g.*, 15 U.S.C. §§ 7211, 7213, 7262; 18 U.S.C. §§ 1503, 1505, 1520.

public companies covered by the rule.[9] SOX 404 requires company management to assess the internal controls of the company, including IT and data security in a number of ways, particularly they affect a company's financial condition.

To the extent that an individual discloses weaknesses in a company's IT controls, companies are precluded from discriminating or retaliating against whistleblowers.[10]

Finally, the SOX 404 certification requirements concern, among other things, the integrity of the company's financial systems and internal controls. While there is no specific mention of data security either within the statute or associated regulations. Meanwhile, the integrity of data is a core component of information security. Therefore, any information system controls of companies subject to Sarbanes Oxley would need to address information security as part of their SOX preparations and audits.

11:3.   Document retention issues for broker-dealers

Any broker-dealer that is subject to Rule 17a-3 of the Securities and Exchange Act of 1934 must, in essence, retain all communications regarding its business, including internal communications such as e-mails.[11] Typically the broker-dealers must retain these records for a period of not less than three years, with the first two years' retention being in an accessible place. In addition, NASD rules imposed stricter burdens on broker-dealers.[12] The stock exchanges, including the NYSE, have their own rules relating to these issues as well, and the failure to meet these standards, particularly the NASD rule, has led to significant fines.

11:4.   Gramm-Leach-Bliley Act—Safeguards Rule

The Safeguards Rule implements certain provisions of GLB and identifies the standards for developing, implementing, and maintaining reasonable administrative, technical, and physical safeguards to protect the security, confidentiality, and integrity of customer information.[13] The Safeguards Rule applies to the handling of customer information by financial institutions that are subject to the FTC's jurisdiction.[14]

Financial institutions are required to develop, implement, and maintain a comprehensive information security program[15] that is written in one or more readily

---

9.   On September 15, 2010, the SEC issued final rule 33-9142 that permanently exempts registrations that are with accelerated or large accelerated filer under Rule 12b-2 of the Securities Exchange Act of 1934 from 404(b) internal control requirements. See www.sec.gov/rules/final/2010/33-9142.pdf (last visited March 25, 2011).

10. 18 U.S.C. § 1514A.

11. Rule 17a-4(b).

12. *See* NASD Rule 3110. The NASD has now been replaced by Financial Industry Regulatory Authority (FINRA) as the relevant regulatory body, but the rules remain the same.

13. "Customer information" means any record containing nonpublic personal information as defined in 16 C.F.R. § 313.3(n), about a customer of a financial institution, whether in paper, electronic, or other form, that is handled or maintained by or on behalf of the financial institution or its affiliates 16 C.F.R. § 314.2(b); 16 C.F.R. § 314.1(a).

14. Except as modified by this part or unless the context otherwise requires, the terms used in this part have the same meaning as set forth in the Commission's rule governing the Privacy of Consumer Financial Information, 16 C.F.R. § 313; 16 C.F.R. § 314.2(a); 16 C.F.R. § 314.1(b).

15. "Information security program" means the administrative, technical, or physical safeguards you use to

accessible parts and contains administrative, technical, and physical safeguards that are appropriate to the entity's size and complexity, the nature and scope of its activities, and the sensitivity of any customer information at issue.[16] The information security program must meet certain objectives:

- to ensure the security and confidentiality of customer information;
- to protect against any anticipated threats or hazards to the security or integrity of such information; and
- to protect against unauthorized access to or use of such information that could result in substantial harm or inconvenience to any customer.[17]

There are certain required elements that the information security program must contain. First, the financial institution must designate an employee or employees to coordinate the information security program.[18] Second, the financial institution must identify reasonably foreseeable internal and external risks to the security, confidentiality, and integrity of customer information that could result in the unauthorized disclosure, misuse, alteration, destruction, or other compromise of such information, and assess the sufficiency of any safeguards in place to control these risks.[19] At a minimum, the risk assessment should include consideration of risks in each relevant area of operations, including the following:

- employee training[20] and management;
- information systems, including network and software design, as well as information processing, storage, transmission, and disposal; and
- detecting, preventing and responding to attacks, intrusions, or other systems' failures.[21]

Third, the financial institution must design and implement information safeguards to control the risks identified through the risk assessment, and regularly test or otherwise monitor the effectiveness of the safeguards' key controls, systems, and procedures.[22] Fourth, the financial institution must oversee its service providers,[23] by taking reasonable steps to select and retain service providers that are capable of maintaining appropriate safeguards for the customer information at issue, and requiring the service providers by contract to implement and maintain such safeguards.[24] Fifth, the financial institution

---

access, collect, distribute, process, protect, store, use, transmit, dispose of, or otherwise handle customer information. 16 C.F.R. § 314.2(c).

16.   16 C.F.R. § 314.3(a).

17.   16 C.F.R. § 314.3(b).

18.   16 C.F.R. § 314.4(a).

19.   16 C.F.R. § 314.4(b).

20.   Training should include common risks, IT issues, training for IT staff on the difference between service packs if necessary, and other relevant issues.

21.   16 C.F.R. § 314.4(b).

22.   16 C.F.R. § 314.4(c).

23.   "Service provider" means any person or entity that receives, maintains, processes, or otherwise is permitted access to customer information through its provision of services directly to a financial institution that is subject to this part. 16 C.F.R. § 314.2(d).

24.   16 C.F.R. § 314.4(d).

must evaluate and adjust its information security program in light of the results of the testing and monitoring required by the third requirement, any material changes to operations or business arrangements, or any other circumstances that the financial institution knows or has reason to know may have a material impact on the information security program.[25]

11:5. Security and incident response guidelines

The federal agencies that regulate banks have issued joint guidance regarding security and incident response guidelines, as authorized by GLB. For ease of reference, the regulations from the Office of the Comptroller of the Currency are discussed below, but the regulations from all of the agencies are identical.

Each bank is required to implement a comprehensive written information security program that includes administrative, technical, and physical safeguards appropriate to the size and complexity of the bank and the nature and scope of its activities. This does not require the implementation of a uniform set of policies, but all elements of the information security program must be coordinated.[26] The information security program must be designed to ensure the security and confidentiality of customer[27] information,[28] protect against any anticipated threats or hazards to the security or integrity of such information, and protect against unauthorized access to or use of such information that could result in substantial harm or inconvenience to any customer.[29]

11:6. Development and implementation of information security program

There are a number of required elements for the implementation of an information security plan. They include: Involve the Board of Directors, Assess Risk, Manage and Control Risk, Oversee Service Provider Arrangements, Adjust the Program, and Report to the Board.

11:7. Development and implementation of information security program—Involve the board of directors

There must be adequate oversight of the development and implementation of the information security plan. As such, the board of directors[30] or an appropriate committee of the board of each bank must approve the written information security program, oversee the development, implementation, and maintenance of the bank's information

---

25. 16 C.F.R. § 314.4(e).

26. 12 C.F.R. Pt. 30, App. B, II(A).

27. Customer means any customer of the bank as defined in § 40.3(h) of this chapter. 12 C.F.R. Pt. 30, App. B, I(C)(2)(b).

28. Customer information means any record containing nonpublic personal information, as defined in § 40.3(n) of this chapter, about a customer, whether in paper, electronic, or other form, that is maintained by or on behalf of the bank. 12 C.F.R. Pt. 30, App. B, I(C)(2)(c).

29. 12 C.F.R. Pt. 30, App. B, II(B).

30. Board of directors, in the case of a branch or agency of a foreign bank, means the managing official in charge of the branch or agency. 12 C.F.R. Pt. 30, App. B, I(C)(2)(a).

security program, including assigning specific responsibility for its implementation and reviewing reports from management.[31]

11:8. Development and implementation of information security program—Assess risk

Banks are required to identify reasonably foreseeable internal and external threats that could result in unauthorized disclosure, misuse, alteration, or destruction of customer information or customer information systems,[32] assess the likelihood and potential damage of these threats, factoring in the sensitivity of customer information, and assess the sufficiency of policies, procedures, customer information systems, and other arrangements in place to control risks.[33]

11:9. Development and implementation of information security program—Manage and control risk

The regulations also require banks to design the information security program to control the identified risks, commensurate with the sensitivity of the information, as well as the complexity and scope of the bank's activities.[34] Consideration must also be given as to whether the following security measures are appropriate for the bank, and if so, those measures must be adopted:[35]

- access controls on customer information systems, including controls to authenticate and permit access only to authorized individuals and controls to prevent employees from providing customer information to unauthorized individuals who may seek to obtain this information through fraudulent means;
- access restrictions at physical locations containing customer information, such as buildings, computer facilities, and records storage facilities to permit access only to authorized individuals;
- encryption of electronic customer information, including while in transit or in storage on networks or systems to which unauthorized individuals may have access;
- procedures designed to ensure that customer information system modifications are consistent with the bank's information security program;
- dual control procedures, segregation of duties, and employee background checks for employees with responsibilities for or access to customer information;
- monitoring systems and procedures to detect actual and attempted attacks on or intrusions into customer information systems;

---

31. 12 C.F.R. Pt. 30, App. B, III(A).
32. Customer information systems means any methods used to access, collect, store, use, transmit, protect, or dispose of customer information. 12 C.F.R. Pt. 30, App. B, I(C)(2)(d).
33. 12 C.F.R. Pt. 30, App. B, III(B).
34. 12 C.F.R. Pt. 30, App. B, III(C)(1).
35. 12 C.F.R. Pt. 30, App. B, III(C)(1).

- response programs that specify actions to be taken when the bank suspects or detects that unauthorized individuals have gained access to customer information systems, including appropriate reports to regulatory and law enforcement agencies; and

- measures to protect against destruction, loss, or damage of customer information due to potential environmental hazards, such as fire and water damage or techno-logical failures.[36]

Training must also be given to the bank's staff to implement the bank's information security program.[37] Regular testing of the key controls, systems and procedures of the information security program is also required. The frequency and nature of such tests are determined by the bank's risk assessment and tests should be conducted or reviewed by independent third parties or staff independent of those that develop or maintain the security programs.[38]

11:10. Development and implementation of information security program—Oversee service provider arrangements

The OCC has also placed restrictions on banks relative to their service provider[39] arrangements.[40] Banks are required to exercise appropriate due diligence in selecting their service providers; to require, by contract, the service providers to implement appropriate measures designed to meet the objectives of these guidelines; and where indicated by the bank's risk assessment, to monitor their service providers to confirm that they satisfy their obligations.[41] The monitoring must include the review of audits, summaries of test results, or other equivalent evaluations of the service providers.[42]

11:11. Development and implementation of information security program—Adjust the program

Banks are also required to monitor, evaluate, and adjust, as appropriate, the information security program in light of any relevant changes in technology, the sensitivity of customer information, internal or external threats to information, and the banks' own changing business arrangements, including mergers and acquisitions, alliances and joint ventures, outsourcing arrangements, and changes to customer information systems.[43]

---

36. 12 C.F.R. Pt. 30, App. B, III(C)(1)(a)–(h).

37. 12 C.F.R. Pt. 30, App. B, III(C)(2).

38. 12 C.F.R. Pt. 30, App. B, III(C)(3).

39. "Service provider" means any person or entity that maintains, processes, or otherwise is permitted access to customer information through its provision of services directly to the bank. 12 C.F.R. Pt. 30, App. B, I(C) (2)(e).

40. 12 C.F.R. Pt. 30, App. B, III(D).

41. 12 C.F.R. Pt. 30, App. B, III(D)(1)–(3).

42. 12 C.F.R. Pt. 30, App. B, III(D)(3).

43. 12 C.F.R. Pt. 30, App. B, III(E).

11:12. Development and implementation of information security program—Report to the board

Reporting to the board or an appropriate committee of the board at least annually is also required by the guidelines.[44] The report should describe the overall status of the information security program and the bank's compliance with the guidelines. The reports should also discuss material matters related to its program, addressing issues such as risk assessment; risk management and control decisions; service provider arrangements; results of testing; security breaches or violations and management's responses; and recommendations for changes in the information security program.[45]

11:13. FTC security suggestions

The FTC has made several suggestions regarding compliance with security requirements. One suggestion is that employee references should be checked prior to hiring employees who will have access to customer information. Moreover, the FTC has suggested that all new employees sign an agreement to follow the confidentiality and security standards for handling customer information. Training of employees regarding the maintenance of security, confidentiality, and integrity of customer information is also suggested, as is regular instruction of employees on the institution's policy, and the legal requirements, to keep customer information secure and confidential.

Limiting access to customer information to employees who have a business reason for seeing such information is also an FTC recommendation. If the policy is not followed then the FTC suggests that disciplinary measures be imposed. Security of information systems is also a regulated area. Information systems include network and software design, and information processing, storage, transmission, retrieval, and disposal.

FTC suggestions regarding information security also include storing records in a secure area, providing for secure data transmission (with clear instructions and simple security tools) when customer information is transmitted, and ensuring that if sensitive information is sent via e-mail it is password protected so that only authorized employees have access to the information.

Customer information should also be disposed of in a secure manner. This can include hiring or designating a records retention manager to supervise the disposal of records containing nonpublic personal information, shredding or recycling customer information recorded on paper, and storing it in a secure area until a recycling service picks it up. Disposal of outdated customer information and the permanent deletion of all information on computers, diskettes, magnetic tapes, hard drives, or any other electronic media that contain customer information are also suggested. The implementation of appropriate oversight or audit procedures to detect the improper disclosure or theft of customer information is also a FTC recommendation.

Effective security management can also include the prevention, detection, and response to attacks, intrusions, or other system failures. The following practices have also been suggested by the FTC:

---

44.   12 C.F.R. Pt. 30, App. B, III(F).

45.   *Id.*

- following a written contingency plan to address any breaches of physical, administrative or technical safeguards;
- checking with software vendors regularly to obtain and install patches that resolve software vulnerabilities;
- using anti-virus software that updates automatically;
- maintaining up-to-date firewalls, particularly if broadband Internet access is used; and
- providing central management of security tools for employees and passing along updates about any security risks or breaches.

Taking steps to preserve the security, confidentiality, and integrity of customer information in the event of a computer or other technological failure, including frequent backup is also recommended. Finally, notifying customers promptly if their non-public personal information is subject to loss, damage, or unauthorized access is also something suggested by the FTC.

11:14. FACT Act document destruction rule

The Fair and Accurate Credit Transactions Act of 2003 (FACT Act) amended provisions of the Fair Credit Reporting Act (FCRA) and also called for the FTC to implement certain rules. Included among these rules was the Document Destruction Rule. The rule is designed to reduce the risk of consumer fraud and related harms, including identity theft, created by improper disposal of consumer information.[46] This rule became effective on June 1, 2005.[47]

Unlike FCRA, Gramm-Leach-Bliley (GLB), and other federal financial privacy and security statutes, this rule applies to any person over whom the FTC has jurisdiction, who, for a business purpose, maintains or otherwise possesses consumer information.[48]

Any person who maintains or otherwise possesses consumer information for a business purpose must properly dispose of such information by taking "reasonable measures to protect against unauthorized access to or use of the information in connection with its disposal."[49] The rule does not directly delineate every act that must be taken to comply with this rule, but the FTC has given examples of what it considers to be reasonable measures, including the following:

- implementing and monitoring compliance with policies and procedures that require the burning, pulverizing, or shredding of papers containing consumer information so that the information cannot practicably be read or reconstructed;

---

46. 16 C.F.R. § 682.2(a).

47. 16 C.F.R. § 682.5.

48. "Consumer information" means any record about an individual, whether in paper, electronic, or other form, that is a consumer report or is derived from a consumer report. Consumer information also means a compilation of such records. Consumer information does not include information that does not identify individuals, such as aggregate information or blind data. 16 C.F.R. § 682.1(b). It should be noted that the definitions from FCRA apply unless otherwise modified. 16 C.F.R. § 682.1(a). 16 C.F.R. § 682.2(b).

49. "Dispose," "disposing," or "disposal" means: (1) The discarding or abandonment of consumer information, or (2) The sale, donation, or transfer of any medium, including computer equipment, upon which consumer information is stored. 16 C.F.R. § 682.1(c).16 C.F.R. § 682.3(a).

- implementing and monitoring compliance with policies and procedures that require the destruction or erasure of electronic media containing consumer information so that the information cannot practicably be read or reconstructed;

- after due diligence,[50] entering into and monitoring compliance with a contract with another party engaged in the business of record destruction to dispose of material, specifically identified as consumer information, in a manner consistent with this rule;

- for persons or entities who maintain or otherwise possess consumer information through their provision of services directly to a person subject to this rule, implementing and monitoring compliance with policies and procedures that protect against unauthorized or unintentional disposal of consumer information, and disposing of such information as required by this rule;

- for persons subject to GLB and the Safeguards Rule, incorporating the proper disposal of consumer information as required by this rule into the information security program required by the Safeguards Rule.[51]

- It should be noted that these examples are illustrative only and are not exclusive or exhaustive methods for complying with the rule.[52]

One federal court in California has held that the allegation that a defendant placed more than five digits of a credit card on a computer screen was sufficient to allege, at least at the motion to dismiss stage, that the defendant had violated the FACT Act.[53]

III. Selected State Provisions

A. *California*

11:15. Data security law

California's data security law is applicable if a business licenses or owns unredacted or unencrypted "personal information"[54] regarding a California resident. If a business

---

50. Due diligence can include reviewing an independent audit of the disposal company's operations and/or its compliance with this rule, obtaining information about the disposal company from several references or other reliable sources, requiring that the disposal company be certified by a recognized trade association or similar third party, reviewing and evaluating the disposal company's information security policies or procedures, or taking other appropriate measures to determine the competency and integrity of the potential disposal company.

51. 16 C.F.R. § 682.3(b).

52. *Id.*

53. Vasquez-Torres v. Stubhub, Inc., CV 07-1328-PSG(SSx) (C.D. Cal. July 2, 2007).

54. "Personal information" means an individual's first name or first initial and his or her last name in combination with any one or more of the following data elements, when either the name or the date elements are not encrypted or redacted: (A) Social security number; (B) Driver's license number or California identification card number; (C) Account number, credit or debit card number, in combination with any required security

licenses or owns such information, then it must implement and maintain reasonable security practices and procedures that are appropriate to the nature of the information. This seems to place a sliding scale on businesses depending upon the nature of the information collected. Social security and account numbers, as well as medical information,[55] typically are considered to be more sensitive types of information and thus might be subject to higher security requirements.

There are also additional restrictions upon businesses that disclose personal information to non-affiliated third parities. If a business discloses information to a third party pursuant to an agreement, then that agreement must require the third party to meet the data security standards noted above.[56]

California recognized that there were other federal and state laws that impacted security of information. Compliance with any of the other laws, if it provides greater protection, constitutes compliance with the California law.[57]

California also places an affirmative obligation on businesses to destroy consumer's records, if they contain personal information, when the records are no longer needed. This obligation applies whether the record is in electronic form or not.[58] Businesses are required to (1) shred, (2) erase, or (3) otherwise modify the personal information in those records to make it unreadable or undecipherable through any means.[59]

11:16. Auto dealers and data security

It is illegal for any manufacturer, manufacturer branch, distributor, or distributor branch licensed under the California Vehicle Code to access, modify, or extract information from a confidential dealer computer record[60] without obtaining the prior written consent of the dealer and without maintaining administrative, technical, and physical safeguards to protect the security, confidentiality, and integrity of the information.[61] This requirement in no way limits duty that a dealer may have to safeguard the security and privacy of records maintained by the dealer.[62]

It is also improper for any manufacturer, manufacturer branch, distributor, or distributor branch licensed under the California Vehicle Code to use electronic, contractual, or other means to prevent or interfere with the lawful efforts of a dealer to comply with federal and state data security and privacy laws.[63] It is also a prohibited act for any dealer

---

code, access code, or password that would permit access to an individual's financial account; or (D) Medical information. Cal. Civ. Code §§ 1798.81.5(d)(1)(a) to (d).

55. "Medical information" means any individually identifiable information, in electronic or physical form, regarding the individual's medical history or medical treatment or diagnosis by a health care professional. Cal. Civ. Code § 1798.81.5(d)(1)(D)(2).

56. Cal. Civ. Code § 1798.81.5(c).

57. Cal. Civ. Code § 1798.81.5(e)(5).

58. Cal. Civ. Code § 1798.81.

59. Id.

60. "Confidential dealer computer record" means a computer record residing on the dealer's computer system that contains, in whole or in part, any personally identifiable consumer data, or the dealer's financial or other proprietary data. Cal. Vehicle Code § 11713.25(c)(1).

61. Cal. Vehicle Code § 11713.3(v)(1).

62. Cal. Vehicle Code § 11713.3(v)(2).

63. Cal. Vehicle Code § 11713.3(w)(1)(A).

to prevent or interfere with the ability of a dealer to ensure that specific data accessed from the dealer's computer system is within the scope of consent specified above, or to monitor specific data accessed from or written to the dealer's computer system.[64] This requirement also in no way limits duty that a dealer may have to safeguard the security and privacy of records maintained by the dealer.[65]

11:17. Restrictions on computer vendors

It is illegal for any computer vendor[66] to access, modify, or extract information from a confidential dealer computer record or personally identifiable consumer data[67] from a dealer without first obtaining express written consent from the dealer and without maintaining administrative, technical, and physical safeguards to protect the security, confidentiality, and integrity of the information.[68] Express consent[69] granted by a dealer can be revoked upon 10-day written notice to the vendor, or a shorter period agreed to by the vendor and the dealer.[70] It is also illegal to require a dealer as a condition of doing or continuing to do business, to give express consent to perform the activities specified above, unless consent is limited to permitting access to personally identifiable consumer data to the extent necessary to protect against or prevent actual or potential fraud, unauthorized transactions, claims, or other liability, or to protect against breaches of confidentiality or security of consumer records; to comply with institutional risk control or to resolve consumer disputes or inquiries; to comply with federal, state, or local laws, rules, and other applicable legal requirements, including lawful requirements of a law enforcement or governmental agency; to comply with lawful requirements of a self-regulatory organization or as necessary to perform an investigation on a matter related to public safety; to comply with a properly authorized civil, criminal, or regulatory investigation, or subpoena or summons by federal, state, or local authorities; or to make other use of personally identifiable consumer data with the express written consent of the consumer that has not been revoked by the consumer.[71]

It is also illegal to use electronic, contractual, or other means to prevent or interfere with the lawful efforts of a dealer to comply with federal and state data security and privacy laws and to maintain the security, integrity, and confidentiality of confidential

---

64. Cal. Vehicle Code § 11713.3(w)(1)(B).

65. Cal. Vehicle Code § 11713.3(w)(2).

66. "Computer vendor" means a person, other than a manufacturer, manufacturer branch, distributor, or distributor branch, who in the ordinary course of that person's business configured, sold, leased, licensed, maintained, or otherwise made available to a dealer, a dealer computer system. Cal. Vehicle Code § 11713.25(c)(2).

67. "Personally identifiable consumer data" means information that is any of the following: (A) Information of the type specified in subparagraph (A) of paragraph (6) of subdivision (e) of Section 1798.83 of the Civil Code. (B) Information that is nonpublic personal information as defined in Section 313.3(n)(1) of Title 16 of the Code of Federal Regulations. (C) Information that is nonpublic personal information as defined in subdivision (a) of Section 4052 of the Financial Code. Cal. Vehicle Code § 11713.25(c)(5).

68. Cal. Vehicle Code § 11713.25(a)(1).

69. "Express consent" means the unrevoked written consent signed by a dealer that specifically describes the data that may be accessed, the means by which it may be accessed, the purpose for which it may be used, and the person or class of persons to whom it may be disclosed. Cal. Vehicle Code § 11713.25(c)(4).

70. Cal. Vehicle Code § 11713.25(b).

71. Cal. Vehicle Code § 11713.25(a)(2)(A) to (B)(vi).

dealer computer records, including, but not limited to, the ability of a dealer to monitor specific data accessed from or written to the dealer computer system,[72] and any attempted waiver of this protection is void.[73]

11:18. Restrictions on network security

Any device that includes an integrated and enabled wireless access point,[74] such as a premises-based wireless network router or wireless access bridge, that is for use in a small office,[75] home office, or residential setting and that is sold as new in California for use in a small office, home office, or residential setting must be manufactured to comply with one of the following requirements.[76] The first option is to include in its software a security warning that comes up as part of the configuration process of the device.[77] The warning must advise the consumer how to protect his or her wireless network connection from unauthorized access. This requirement can be met by providing the consumer with instructions to protect his or her wireless network connection from unauthorized access, which may refer to a product manual, the manufacturer's Internet website, or a consumer protection Internet website that contains accurate information advising the consumer on how to protect his or her wireless network connection from unauthorized access.[78]

The second option is to have attached to the device a temporary warning sticker that must be removed by the consumer in order to allow its use.[79] The warning must advise the consumer how to protect his or her wireless network connection from unauthorized access.[80] This requirement may be met by advising the consumer that his or her wireless network connection may be accessible by an unauthorized user and referring the consumer to a product manual, the manufacturer's Internet website, or a consumer protection Internet website that contains accurate information advising the consumer on how to protect his or her wireless network connection from unauthorized access.[81]

The third option is to provide other protection on the device that does all of the following: advises the consumer that his or her wireless network connection may be

---

72. "Dealer computer system" means a computer system or computerized application primarily designed for use by and sold to a motor vehicle dealer that, by ownership, lease, license, or otherwise, is used by and in the ordinary course of business of a dealer. Cal. Vehicle Code § 11713.25(c)(3).

73. Cal. Vehicle Code § 11713.25(a)(3).

74. "Wireless access point" means a device, such as a premises-based wireless network router or a wireless network bridge, that allows wireless clients to connect to it in order to create a wireless network for the purpose of connecting to an Internet service provider. Cal. Bus. & Prof. Code § 22948.5(d). "Wireless client" means a wireless device that connects to a wireless network for the purpose of connecting to an Internet service provider. Cal. Bus. & Prof. Code § 22948.5(e).

75. "Small office" means a business with 50 or fewer employees within the company. Cal. Bus. & Prof. Code § 22948.5(b).

76. Cal. Bus. & Prof. Code § 22948.6(a).

77. Cal. Bus. & Prof. Code § 22948.6(a)(1).

78. Id.

79. Cal. Bus. & Prof. Code § 22948.6(a)(2).

80. Id.

81. Id.

accessible by an unauthorized user; advises the consumer how to protect his or her wireless network connection from unauthorized access; and requires an affirmative action by the consumer prior to allowing use of the product.[82] It should be noted that additional information may also be available in the product manual or on the manufacturer's Internet website.[83]

The fourth, and final, option is to provide, prior to allowing use of the device, other protection that is enabled without an affirmative act by the consumer, to protect the consumer's wireless network connection from unauthorized access.[84]

This law only applies to devices that include an integrated and enabled wireless access point, that are used in a federally unlicensed[85] spectrum,[86] and that are manufactured on or after October 1, 2007.[87]

B.   Massachusetts

11:19. Data destruction

When an agency[88] or person[89] disposes of paper documents containing personal information[90] the documents must be redacted, burned, pulverized, or shredded so that personal data cannot practically be read or reconstructed.[91] For electronic media and other non-paper media containing personal information the media must be destroyed or erased so that personal information cannot practically be read or reconstructed.[92] Any agency or person disposing of personal information may contract with a third party to dispose of personal information in accordance with this law.[93] Any third party hired to dispose of material containing personal information must implement and

---

82. Cal. Bus. & Prof. Code §§ 22948.6(a)(3)(A)–(C).

83. Cal. Bus. & Prof. Code § 22948.6(a)(3).

84. Cal. Bus. & Prof. Code § 22948.6(a)(4).

85. "Federally unlicensed spectrum" means a spectrum for which the Federal Communications Commission does not issue a specific license to a user, but instead certifies equipment that may be used in a segment of spectrum designated for shared use. Cal. Bus. & Prof. Code § 22948.5(a).

86. "Spectrum" means the range of frequencies over which electromagnetic signals can be sent, including radio, television, wireless Internet connectivity, and every other communication enabled by radio waves. Cal. Bus. & Prof. Code § 22948.5(c).

87. Cal. Bus. & Prof. Code § 22948.6(b) to (c).

88. "Agency," any county, city, town, or constitutional office or any agency thereof, including but not limited to, any department, division, bureau, board, commission or committee thereof, or any authority created by the general court to serve a public purpose, having either statewide or local jurisdiction. M.G.L. c 93I Section 1.

89. "Person," a natural person, corporation, association, partnership or other legal entity. *Id.*

90. "Personal information," a resident's first name and last name or first initial and last name in combination with any one or more of the following data elements that relate to the resident: a. Social Security number; b. driver's license number or Massachusetts identification card number; c. financial account number, or credit or debit card number, with or without any required security code, access code, personal identification number or password that would permit access to a resident's financial account; or d. a biometric indicator. *Id.*

91. *Id.* Section 2(a).

92. *Id.* Section 2(b).

93. *Id.* Section 2.

monitor compliance with policies and procedures that prohibit unauthorized access to or acquisition of or use of personal information during the collection, transportation, and disposal of personal information.[94]

11:20. Enforcement

Any agency or person who violates the provisions of this law is subject to a civil fine of not more than $100 per data subject[95] affected.[96] The fine cannot exceed $50,000 for each instance of improper disposal.[97] The attorney general may file a civil action in the superior or district court to recover the penalties.[98] Additionally, the attorney general may bring an action pursuant to section 4 of chapter 93A against a person or otherwise to remedy violations of this law and for other relief that may be appropriate.[99]

11:21. Data security regulations

Massachusetts enacted regulations via an order that went into effect September 19, 2008. The order establishes rules and regulations for safeguarding personal information owned or licensed by state agencies[100] in the executive department. State agencies must develop, implement, and maintain written information security programs governing their collection, use, dissemination, storage, retention, and destruction of personal information.[101]

The programs must include provisions that relate to the protection of information stored or maintained in electronic form; must address, without limitation, administrative, technical, and physical safeguards; and must comply with all federal and state privacy and information security laws and regulations.

Further, these programs must ensure that agencies collect the minimum quantity of personal information reasonably needed to accomplish the legitimate purpose for which the information is collected; securely store and protect the information against unauthorized access, destruction, use, modification, disclosure, or loss; provide access to and destroy the information as soon as it is no longer needed or required to be maintained by state or federal record retention requirements.

---

94. *Id.*

95. "Data subject," an individual to whom personal information refers. *Id.* Section 1.

96. *Id.* Section 2.

97. *Id.*

98. *Id.*

99. *Id.* Section 3.

100. "State agencies" (or "agencies") shall include all executive offices, boards, commissions, agencies, departments, divisions, councils, bureaus, and offices, now existing and hereafter established. Mass. Exec. Order No. 504.

101. "Personal information" a resident's first name and last name or first initial and last name in combination with any 1 or more of the following data elements that relate to such resident: (a) Social Security number; (b) driver's license number or state-issued identification card number; or (c) financial account number, or credit or debit card number, with or without any required security code, access code, personal identification number or password, that would permit access to a resident's financial account; provided, however, that "Personal information" shall not include information that is lawfully obtained from publicly available information, or from federal, state or local government records lawfully made available to the general public. Mass. Gen. Laws ch. 93H, § 1; Mass. Exec. Order No. 504.

This order also requires that all contracts entered into by a state agency after January 1, 2009 contain provisions requiring the agency's contractors to certify that they have read Executive Order 504; that they have reviewed and will comply with all information security programs, plans, guidelines, standards, and policies that apply to the work performed for the contracting agency; that they will communicate these provisions to and enforce these provisions against their subcontractors; and that they will implement and maintain any other reasonable and appropriate security procedures and practices necessary to protect the personal information to which they are given access under the contract from unauthorized access, destruction, use, modification, disclosure, or loss.

11:22. Standards for the protection of personal information of residents of the commonwealth

This regulation implements the provisions of M.G.L. c. 93H relative to the standards to be met by persons who own or license personal information about a resident of the Commonwealth of Massachusetts. This regulation establishes minimum standards to be met in connection with the safeguarding of personal information contained in both paper and electronic records.[102] The objectives of this regulation are to ensure the security and confidentiality of customer information in a manner fully consistent with industry standards; protect against anticipated threats or hazards to the security or integrity of such information; and protect against unauthorized access to or use of such information that may result in substantial harm or inconvenience to any consumer.[103] The provisions of this regulation apply to all persons that own or license personal information about a resident of the Commonwealth of Massachusetts.[104]

11:23. Duty to protect and standards for protecting personal information

Every person[105] that owns or licenses[106] personal information[107] about a resident of the commonwealth shall develop, implement, and maintain a comprehensive information

---

102. 201 Mass. Code Regs. 17.01(1).

103. *Id.*

104. 201 Mass. Code Regs. 17.01(2).

105. "Person" means a natural person, corporation, association, partnership or other legal entity, other than an agency, executive office, department, board, commission, bureau, division or authority of the Commonwealth, or any of its branches, or any political subdivision thereof. 201 Mass. Code Regs. 17.02.

106. "Owns or licenses" means the person receives, stores, maintains, processes, or otherwise has access to personal information in connection with the provision of goods or services or in connection with employment. 201 Mass. Code Regs. 17.02.

107. "Personal information" means a Massachusetts resident's first name and last name or first initial and last name in combination with any one or more of the following data elements that relate to such resident: (a) social security number; (b) driver's license number or state-issued identification card number; or (c) financial account number, or credit or debit card number, with or without any required security code, access code, personal identification number or password, that would permit access to a resident's financial account; provided, however, that "Personal information" shall not include information that is lawfully obtained from publicly available information, or from federal, state or local government records lawfully made available to the general public. 201 Mass. Code Regs. 17.02.

security program that is written in one or more readily accessible parts and contains administrative, technical, and physical safeguards that are appropriate to the size, scope and type of business of the person obligated to safeguard the personal information under such comprehensive information security program; the amount of resources available to such person; the amount of stored data; and the need for security and confidentiality of both consumer and employee information. The safeguards contained in such program must be consistent with the safeguards for protection of personal information and information of a similar character set forth in any state or federal regulations by which the person who owns or licenses such information may be regulated.[108]

Every comprehensive information security program must include, but shall not be limited to the following:

- designating one or more employees to maintain the comprehensive information security program;
- identifying and assessing reasonably foreseeable internal and external risks to the security, confidentiality, and/or integrity of any electronic,[109] paper, or other records[110] containing personal information, and evaluating and improving, where necessary, the effectiveness of the current safeguards for limiting such risks, including but not limited to
   o ongoing employee (including temporary and contract employee) training,
   o employee compliance with policies and procedures, and
   o means for detecting and preventing security system failures;
- developing security policies for employees relating to the storage, access and transportation of records containing personal information outside of business premises;
- imposing disciplinary measures for violations of the comprehensive information security program rules;
- preventing terminated employees from accessing records containing personal information;
- overseeing service providers,[111] by
   o taking reasonable steps to select and retain third-party service providers that are capable of maintaining appropriate security measures to protect such personal information consistent with these regulations and any applicable federal regulations, and
   o requiring such third-party service providers by contract to implement and maintain such appropriate security measures for personal information, provided, however, that until March 1, 2012, a contract a person has entered into with a third party service provider to perform services for said person or functions on

---

108. 201 Mass. Code Regs. 17.03(1)(a)–(d).

109. "Electronic" means relating to technology having electrical, digital, magnetic, wireless, optical, electromagnetic or similar capabilities. 201 Mass. Code Regs. 17.02.

110. "Record or Records" means any material upon which written, drawn, spoken, visual, or electromagnetic information or images are recorded or preserved, regardless of physical form or characteristics. 201 Mass. Code Regs. 17.02.

111. "Service provider" means any person that receives, stores, maintains, processes, or otherwise is permitted access to personal information through its provision of services directly to a person that is subject to this regulation. 201 Code Mass. Regs. 17.02.

said person's behalf satisfies the provisions of 17.03(2)(f)(2) even if the contract does not include a requirement that the third party service provider maintain such appropriate safeguards, as long as said person entered into the contract no later than March 1, 2010.

- reasonably restricting physical access to records containing personal information and storing such records and data in locked facilities, storage areas or containers;

- Regular monitoring to ensure that the comprehensive information security program is operating in a manner reasonably calculated to prevent unauthorized access to or unauthorized use of personal information; and upgrading information safeguards as necessary to limit risks;

- reviewing the scope of the security measures at least annually or whenever there is a material change in business practices that may reasonably implicate the security or integrity of records containing personal information; and

- documenting responsive actions taken in connection with any incident involving a breach of security[112] and performing mandatory post-incident reviews of events and actions taken, if any, to make changes in business practices relating to protection of personal information.[113]

11:24. Computer system security requirements

Every person that owns or licenses personal information about a resident of the commonwealth and electronically stores or transmits such information shall include in its written, comprehensive information security program the establishment and maintenance of a security system covering its computers, including any wireless system, that, at a minimum, and to the extent technically feasible, shall have the following elements:

- Secure user authentication protocols including the following:
  o control of user IDs and other identifiers,
  o a reasonably secure method of assigning and selecting passwords, or use of unique identifier technologies, such as biometrics or token devices,
  o control of data security passwords to ensure that such passwords are kept in a location and/or format that does not compromise the security of the data they protect,
  o restricting access to active users and active user accounts only, and
  o blocking access to user identification after multiple unsuccessful attempts to gain access or the limitation placed on access for the particular system;
- Secure access control measures that

---

112. "Breach of security" means the unauthorized acquisition or unauthorized use of unencrypted data or, encrypted electronic data and the confidential process or key that is capable of compromising the security, confidentiality, or integrity of personal information, maintained by a person or agency that creates a substantial risk of identity theft or fraud against a resident of the commonwealth. A good faith but unauthorized acquisition of personal information by a person or agency, or employee or agent thereof, for the lawful purposes of such person or agency, is not a breach of security unless the personal information is used in an unauthorized manner or subject to further unauthorized disclosure. 201 Mass. Code Regs. 17.02.

113. 201 Mass. Code Regs. 17.03(2)(a)–(j).

- o restrict access to records and files containing personal information to those who need such information to perform their job duties; and

- o assign unique identifications plus passwords, which are not vendor supplied default passwords, to each person with computer access, that are reasonably designed to maintain the integrity of the security of the access controls;

- encryption of all transmitted records and files containing personal information that will travel across public networks, and encryption of all data containing personal information to be transmitted wirelessly;

- reasonable monitoring of systems, for unauthorized use of or access to personal information;

- encryption of all personal information stored on laptops or other portable devices;

- for files containing personal information on a system that is connected to the Internet, reasonably up-to-date firewall protection and operating system security patches, reasonably designed to maintain the integrity of the personal information;

- reasonably up-to-date versions of system security agent software, which must include malware protection, and reasonably up-to-date patches and virus definitions, or a version of such software that can still be supported with up-to-date patches and virus definitions, and is set to receive the most current security updates on a regular basis; and

- education and training of employees on the proper use of the computer security system and the importance of personal information security.[114]

11.25. Effective date

Every person who owns or licenses personal information about a resident of the Commonwealth Massachusetts must have been in full compliance with the regulations on or before March 1, 2010.[115]

Enforcement of data security regulations has already begun as the Massachusetts Attorney General released a Final Judgment By Consent against the Briar Group restaurant chain for failing to take measures to protect consumer data.[116]

C. Nevada

11:26. Overview

A business[117] that maintains records that contain personal information[118] concerning customers must take reasonable steps to ensure the destruction of those records when

---

114. 201 Mass. Code Regs. 17.04(1)–(8).

115. 201 Mass. Code Regs. 17.05.

116 Commonwealth of Massachusetts v. Briar Group LLC, Sup. Ct. no. 11-185 (filed March 28, 2011).

117. "Business" means a proprietorship, corporation, partnership, association, trust, unincorporated organization or other enterprise doing business in Nevada. Nev. Rev. Stat. § 603A.200(2)(a).

118. "Personal information" means a natural person's first name or first initial and last name in combination with any one or more of the following data elements, when the name and data elements are not encrypted: 1.

the business decides that it will no longer maintain the records.[119] "Reasonable measures to ensure the destruction" as used in the statute means any method that modifies the records containing the personal information in such a way as to render the personal information contained in the records unreadable or undecipherable. This includes the following:

(1) shredding of the record containing the personal information; or

(2) erasing of the personal information from the records.[120]

Nevada also requires a data collector[121] that maintains records which contain personal information to implement and maintain reasonable security measures to protect those records from unauthorized access, acquisition, destruction, use, modification, or disclosure. Any contract for the disclosure of the personal information of a resident of Nevada that is maintained by a data collector must include a provision requiring the person to whom the information is disclosed to implement and maintain reasonable security measures to protect those records from unauthorized access, acquisition, destruction, use, modification or disclosure.[122]

If an entity is regulated by state or federal law that requires a data collector to provide greater protection to records that contain personal information and the entity is in compliance with the provisions of that law, the data collector is deemed to be in compliance with the provisions of Nevada law.[123]

11:27. Data security

If a data collector doing business in Nevada accepts a payment card[124] in connection with a sale of goods or services, the data collector shall comply with the current version of the Payment Card Industry (PCI) Data Security Standard, as adopted by the PCI Security Standards Council or its successor organization, with respect to those transactions, not later than the date for compliance set forth in the Payment Card Industry (PCI) Data Security Standard or by the PCI Security Standards Council or its successor organization.[125] A data collector doing business in Nevada to whom this first requirement does not apply shall not transfer any personal information through an electronic, non-voice transmission other than a facsimile[126] to a person outside of the

---

Social security number or employer identification number. 2. Driver's license number or identification card number. 3. Account number, credit card number or debit card number, in combination with any required security code, access code or password that would permit access to the person's financial account. The term does not include publicly available information that is lawfully made available to the general public. Nev. Rev. Stat. § 603A.040.

119. Nev. Rev. Stat. § 603A.200.

120. Nev. Rev. Stat. § 603A.200(2)(b).

121. "Data collector" means any governmental agency, institution of higher education, corporation, financial institution or retail operator or any other type of business entity or association that, for any purpose, whether by automated collection or otherwise, handles, collects, disseminates or otherwise deals with nonpublic personal information. Nev. Rev. Stat. § 603A.030.

122. Nev. Rev. Stat. § 603A.210.

123. Nev. Rev. Stat. § 603A.210(3).

124. "Payment card" has the meaning ascribed to it in Nev. Rev. Stat. § 205.602. Nev. Rev. Stat. § 603A(5)(d).

125. Nev. Rev. Stat. § 603A(1).

126. "Facsimile" means an electronic transmission between two dedicated fax machines using Group 3 or Group 4 digital formats that conform to the International Telecommunications Union T.4 or T.38 standards or

secure system of the data collector unless the data collector uses encryption[127] to ensure the security of electronic transmission; nor move any data storage device[128] containing personal information beyond the logical or physical controls of the data collector or its data storage contractor unless the data collector uses encryption to ensure the security of the information.[129]

11:28. Safe harbor

Compliance with these requirements offers a data collector a limited safe harbor in the event of a breach. A data collector shall not be liable for damages for a breach of the security of the system data if the data collector is in compliance with this section and the breach is not caused by the gross negligence or intentional misconduct of the data collector, its officers, employees, or agents.[130]

11:29. Exceptions

The requirements of this section do not apply to a telecommunication provider[131] acting solely in the role of conveying the communications of other persons, regardless of the mode of conveyance used, including, without limitation optical, wire line and wireless facilities, nor do they apply to analog transmission and digital subscriber line transmission, voice over Internet protocol, and other digital transmission technology.[132] It also does not apply to data transmission over a secure, private communication channel for approval or processing of negotiable instruments, electronic fund transfers, or similar payment methods; or issuance of reports regarding account closures due to fraud, substantial overdrafts, abuse of automatic teller machines or related information regarding a customer.[133]

---

computer modems that conform to the International Telecommunications Union T.31 or T.32 standards. The term does not include onward transmission to a third device after protocol conversion, including, but not limited to, any data storage device. Nev. Rev. Stat. § 603A(5)(c).

127. "Encryption" means the protection of data in electronic or optical form, in storage or in transit, using: (1) An encryption technology that has been adopted by an established standards setting body, including, but not limited to, the Federal Information Processing Standards issued by the National Institute of Standards and Technology, which renders such data indecipherable in the absence of associated cryptographic keys necessary to enable decryption of such data; and (2) Appropriate management and safeguards of cryptographic keys to protect the integrity of the encryption using guidelines promulgated by an established standards setting body, including, but not limited to, the National Institute of Standards and Technology. Nev. Rev. Stat. §§ 603A(5)(b)(1)–(2).

128. "Data storage device" means any device that stores information or data from any electronic or optical medium, including, but not limited to, computers, cellular telephones, magnetic tape, electronic computer drives and optical computer drives, and the medium itself. Nev. Rev. Stat. § 603A(5)(a).

129. Nev. Rev. Stat. §§ 603A(2)(a)–(b).

130. Nev. Rev. Stat. §§ 603A(3)(a)–(b).

131. "Telecommunication provider" has the meaning ascribed to it in Nev. Rev. Stat. § 704.027. Nev. Rev. Stat. § 603A(5)(e).

132. Nev. Rev. Stat. §§ 603A(4)(a)(1)–(3).

133. Nev. Rev. Stat. §§ 603A(b)(1)–(2).

11:30. Effective date

This law became effective on January 1, 2010.

11:31. Injunctive relief

While this law does not directly state that it has remedies, it has been placed in chapter 603A of the Nevada code, and § 603A.920 provides that if the Attorney General or a district attorney of any county has reason to believe that any person is violating, proposes to violate, or has violated the provisions of this chapter, he or she may bring an action against that person to obtain a temporary or permanent injunction against the violation.[134]

D. New York

11:32. Data destruction

The state of New York has enacted a statute requiring the destruction of records that contain personally identifiable information. The law precludes any business from disposing of a record containing personal identifying information unless one of the following is done:

- shredding before disposal;
- destruction of the personal identifying information in the record;
- modification of the record to make the personal information unreadable; or
- taking action that is consistent with industry standards that the business reasonably believes will ensure that unauthorized individuals cannot access the data.[135]

11:33. Data destruction—New York City

Any person licensed under Chapter 2 of the Administrative Code, or under state laws enforced by the department,[136] must discard of an individual's personal identifying information[137] in a manner that is intended to prevent retrieval of the information.[138]

As with the security breach law passed by New York City, questions could be raised about preemption in many cases by other laws. However, given the number of

---

134. Nev. Rev. Stat. § 603A.920.

135. N.Y. Gen. Bus. Law § 399-h(2).

136. The term "department" refers to the Department of Consumer Affairs.

137. The term "personal identifying information" shall mean any person's date of birth, social security number, driver's license number, non-driver photo identification card number, financial services account number or code, savings account number or code, checking account number or code, brokerage account number or code, credit card account number or code, debit card number or code, automated teller machine number or code, personal identification number, mother's maiden name, computer system password, electronic signature or unique biometric data that is a fingerprint, voice print, retinal image or iris image of another person. This term shall apply to all such data, notwithstanding the method by which such information is maintained. NY City Administrative Code § 20-117(a)(1).

138. NY City Administrative Code § 20-117(g).

companies that have a presence in New York City, this law must be considered when information is being disposed of.

E. Oregon

11:34. Data security

Any person[139] that owns, maintains or otherwise possesses data that includes a consumer's[140] personal information[141] that is used in the course of the person's business, vocation, occupation, or volunteer activities must develop, implement, and maintain reasonable safeguards to protect the security, confidentiality, and integrity of the personal information, including disposal of the data.[142] The following is deemed to be compliance with the requirement: a person that complies with a state or federal law providing greater protection to personal information than that provided by this law; a person that is subject to and complies with regulations promulgated pursuant to GLB; or a person that is subject to and complies with regulations implementing HIPAA.[143] Additionally a person can comply by implementing an information security program that includes the following:

- administrative safeguards such as the following, in which the person
    - designates one or more employees to coordinate the security program,
    - identifies reasonably foreseeable internal and external risk,
    - assesses the sufficiency of safeguards in place to control the identified risks,
    - trains and manages employees in the security program practices and procedures,

---

139. "Person" means any individual, private or public corporation, partnership, cooperative, association, estate, limited liability company, organization or other entity, whether or not organized to operate at a profit, or a public body as defined in ORS 174.109. Or. Rev. Stat § 646A.602(10).

140. "Consumer" means an individual who is also a resident of this state. Or. Rev. Stat. § 646A.602(2).

141. "Personal information" means a consumer's first name or first initial and last name in combination with any one or more of the following data elements, when the data elements are not rendered unusable through encryption, redaction or other methods, or when the data elements are encrypted and the encryption key has also been acquired: (A) Social Security number; (B) Driver license number or state identification card number issued by the Department of Transportation; (C) Passport number or other United States issued identification number; or (D) Financial account number, credit or debit card number, in combination with any required security code, access code or password that would permit access to a consumer's financial account. Means any of the data elements or any combination of the data elements described in paragraph (a) of this subsection when not combined with the consumer's first name or first initial and last name and when the data elements are not rendered unusable through encryption, redaction or other methods, if the information obtained would be sufficient to permit a person to commit identity theft against the consumer whose information was compromised. Does not include information, other than a Social Security number, in a federal, state or local government record that is lawfully made available to the public. Or. Rev. Stat. §§ 646A.602(11)(a)–(c). "Redacted" means altered or truncated so that no more than the last four digits of a Social Security number, driver license number, state identification card number, account number or credit or debit card number is accessible as part of the data. Or. Rev. Stat. § 646A.602(12). "Encryption" means the use of an algorithmic process to transform data into a form in which the data is rendered unreadable or unusable without the use of a confidential process or key. Or. Rev. Stat. § 646A.602(6).

142. Or. Rev. Stat. § 646A.622.

143. Or. Rev. Stat. § 646A.622(2)(a) to (c).

- o selects service providers capable of maintaining appropriate safeguards, and requires those safeguards by contract, and
  - o adjusts the security program in light of business changes or new circumstances;
- technical safeguards, such as the following, in which the person
  - o assesses risks in network and software design,
  - o assesses risks in information processing, transmission and storage,
  - o detects, prevents and responds to attacks or system failures, and
  - o regularly tests and monitors the effectiveness of key controls, systems and procedures, and
- physical safeguards, such as the following, in which the person
  - o assesses risks of information storage and disposal,
  - o detects, prevents and responds to intrusions,
  - o protects against unauthorized access to or use of personal information during or after the collection, transportation, and destruction or disposal of the information, and
  - o disposes of personal information after it is no longer needed for business purposes or as required by local, state, or federal law by burning, pulverizing, shredding, or modifying a physical record and by destroying or erasing electronic media so that the information cannot be read or reconstructed.[144]

A person is deemed to comply with the requirements of Or. Rev. Stat. § 646A.602(d)(C)(iv) if he contracts with another person engaged in the business of record destruction to dispose of personal information in a manner consistent with Or. Rev. Stat. § 646A.602(d)(C)(iv).[145]

Notwithstanding these requirements, a person that is an owner of a small business as defined in § 285B.123(3) complies with subsection (1) of this law if the person's information security and disposal program contains administrative, technical and physical safeguards and disposal measures appropriate to the size and complexity of the small business, the nature and scope of its activities, and the sensitivity of the personal information collected from or about consumers.[146]

11:35. Enforcement

The director of the Department of Consumer and Business Services may make any public or private investigations within or outside this state as the director deems necessary to determine whether a person has violated any provision of this law; may require or permit a person to file a statement in writing, under oath or otherwise as the director determines, as to all the facts and circumstances concerning the matter to be investigated; and may administer oaths and affirmations, subpoena witnesses, compel attendance, take evidence and require the production of books, papers, correspondence, memoranda, agreements or other documents or records that the director deems relevant

---

144. Or. Rev. Stat. § 646A.622(2)(d)(A)–(C).
145. Or. Rev. Stat. § 646A.622(3).
146. Or. Rev. Stat. § 646A.622(4).

or material to the inquiry.[147] If a person fails to comply with a subpoena so issued or a party or witness refuses to testify on any matters, the judge of the circuit court or of any county, on the application of the director, shall compel obedience by proceedings for contempt as in the case of disobedience of the requirements of a subpoena issued from such court or a refusal to testify therein.[148] If the director has reason to believe that any person has engaged or is engaging in any violation of this Act, the director may issue an order, subject to Chapter 183, directed to the person to cease and desist from the violation, or require the person to pay compensation to consumers injured by the violation.[149] The director may order compensation to consumers only upon a finding that enforcement of the rights of the consumers by private civil action would be so burdensome or expensive as to be impractical.[150]

In addition to any other penalties and enforcement provisions provided by law, any person who violates or who procures, aids, or abets in the violation of this law subject to a penalty of not more than $1,000 for every violation.[151] Each violation is a separate offense and, in the case of a continuing violation, each day's continuance is a separate violation, but the maximum penalty for any occurrence cannot exceed $500,000.[152] Civil penalties under this law can be imposed as provided in § 183.745.[153]

IV. Common Security-Related Issues

11:36. Loss of laptop computers

One data security issue that has received a significant amount of attention is the frequent loss of laptop computers containing personally identifiable information. Typically, the loss of a laptop containing personally identifiable information will trigger an inquiry under the Notice of Security Breach Statutes as to whether there is an event that gives rise to notice to consumers. However, courts have also had to address the issues of data security and data loss in cases involving the loss of a laptop computer.[154] In *Guin*, the defendant Brazos permitted an employee to keep unencrypted nonpublic customer data on a laptop computer that was ultimately stolen from the employee's house. Brazos was a nonprofit corporation that originated and serviced student loans. Brazos ultimately was unable to determine which of its customers' information was contained on the laptop, and it became aware that it was required at that point by California law to give notice

---

147. Or. Rev. Stat. §§ 646A.624(1)(a)–(c).
148. Or. Rev. Stat. § 646A.624(2).
149. Or. Rev. Stat. § 646A.624(3).
150. *Id.*
151. Or. Rev. Stat. § 646A.624(4)(a).
152. Or. Rev. Stat. § 646A.624(4)(b).
153. Or. Rev. Stat. § 646A.624(4)(c).
154. *See* Guin v. Brazos Higher Educ. Service Corp., Inc., 2006 WL 288483 (D. Minn. 2006).

to its customers.[155] Brazos ultimately decided to send a notification letter to all of its customers. The plaintiff sought additional information, including from the consumer reporting agencies, and neither he nor any other customer to Brazos's knowledge had experienced any type of fraud as a result of the loss of the laptop. Guin argued that Brazos had breached its security obligations under GLB. The court rejected this, and dismissed Guin's case finding that at the time of the burglary Brazos had written security policies, current risk assessment reports, and proper safeguards for customers' personal information as required by GLB. The court also affirmatively stated that GLB did not prohibit someone from working with sensitive data on a laptop and rejected Guin's argument that any information contained on the laptop should be encrypted. The court also rejected Guin's argument that Brazos had failed to act reasonably, noting the policies that it had in place and the training that it gave its employees.

The court also rejected Guin's claim, noting that he could not show actual loss or damage.[156]

Interestingly, the *Guin* court added another hurdle to privacy claims by plaintiffs—that of causation. The general rule is that an intervening criminal act of a third party will break the chain of causation, even if damages exist, thereby creating a defense for the other parties who did not engage in criminal conduct. The *Guin* court also stated that even if damage had existed, it would be due to the intervening criminal act of a third party, and therefore, any damages that resulted would not be foreseeable to Brazos.[157]

11:37. What are "reasonable" technological safeguards

In an action under the Fair Debt Collection Act, the Seventh Circuit had the opportunity to discuss what constitutes reasonable technological safeguards in the context of a defense to a civil action under the Fair Debt Collection Act. While the particular factual scenario is not critical, the Court's formulation of what is "reasonable" is noteworthy.

> The word "reasonable" in the Fair Debt Collection Practices Act defense cannot be equated to "state of the art," which is to say, at the technological frontier. For then whenever a new, more powerful search program came on the market, debt collectors who failed to purchase it post haste would find themselves sued by clients of Mr. Philipps seeking statutory damages on top of any actual damages they might have suffered. The investment would be disproportionate to the slight aggregate harms resulting from the handful of dunning letters that modest procedures occasionally let through the sieve.[158]

---

155. *Guin*, 2006 WL 288483 (D.C. Minn. 2006).

156. *Guin*, 2006 WL 288483 (D.C. Minn. 2006). *See also* Reliance Ins. Co. v. Arneson, 322 N.W.2d 604, 607 (Minn. 1982).

157. *Guin*, 2006 WL 288483 (D.C. Minn. 2006); Hilligoss v. Cross Companies, 304 Minn. 546, 228 N.W.2d 585, 586 (1975); Funchess v. Cecil Newman Corp., 632 N.W.2d 666, 674 (Minn. 2001); *see also* Bigbee v. Pacific Tel. & Tel. Co., 34 Cal. 3d 49, 192 Cal. Rptr. 857, 665 P.2d 947 (1983); Rosh v. Cave Imaging Systems, Inc., 26 Cal. App. 4th 1225, 32 Cal. Rptr. 2d 136 (6th Dist. 1994).

158. Ross v. RJM Acquisitions Funding LLC, 480 F.3d 493 (7th Cir. 2007).

The import of this case is that it may provide companies some guidance when statutes impose requirements for "reasonable" safeguards or security. While it is not a security case per se, the Fair Debt Collections Act is, at its core, a privacy statute, so this may be persuasive authority when the word reasonable is defined in the context of technological safeguards.

11:38. Payment card industry compliance

The credit card industry has implemented security standards in order to try and prevent fraudulent or improper changes. There are 12 requirements, which are organized by five principles, under the Payment Card Industry (PCI) Data Security Standards. The failure to comply with these standards can have a number of consequences, including fines and restrictions on the entity that violates the requirements. It should be noted that these requirements apply to both electronic and traditional brick and mortar businesses.

The first principle is to build and maintain a secure network. Under this principle, there are two requirements—to install and maintain a firewall configuration to protect data and not to use vendor supplied defaults for passwords or other security parameters. The second principle is to protect cardholder data. This requires protecting stored data and to encrypt the transmission of data and sensitive information across public networks.

The third principle is to maintain a vulnerability management program. This requires that entities use and regularly update anti-virus software and develop and maintain secure systems and applications. The fourth principle is to implement and maintain strong access control measures. This principle has three requirements: restricting access to data to a "need-to-know" basis, assigning a unique ID to each person with computer access, and restricting physical access to cardholder data.

The fourth identified principle is regularly monitoring and testing networks, which requires tracking and monitoring all access to network resources and cardholder data and regular testing of security systems and processes. The final principle is to maintain an information security policy, which requires that a policy be in place to address information security.

There are a number of quite detailed sub-points to each requirement, the discussion of which is beyond the scope of this book, that should be reviewed as part of a compliance program.

11:39. Putting it together

The differing legal and technical standards make determining whether adequate security is in place a difficult and fact-specific task. However, certain steps are universal, and this section attempts to lay out general compliance strategies, as well as issues to consider in assessing security.

The first step in determining security requirements is to determine what legal or other requirements are placed upon a business. This can include an assessment of the business line of the company (for example, a "covered entity" under HIPAA) as well as the type of data that is collected. As more fully discussed in other chapters, whether data is collected from non-U.S. residents should also be considered.

These determinations will give you a good start in determining the scope of the requirements you are dealing with. The next step is to determine what internal processes, if any, are in place to verify compliance with these requirements. This will permit you to determine whether the security measures in place meet the burdens of the law and other requirements.

Controlling access to data is an important issue to assess and consider. This should include assessing what restrictions are placed upon individuals who access data, what qualifications are required for these people, as well as what consequences exist for the failure to follow appropriate restrictions. Appropriate password policies should also be in place. An assessment of whether there are any risk factors or especially sensitive data that might require additional access control is also a good step. This should include ensuring that there is adequate security for the data, where it resides, and for any backups.

Also important is ensuring that there is appropriate security contained in the software or other applications that are utilized, including a determination that the software has been tested sufficiently to avoid failures that could cause data compromises. This can include testing for vulnerabilities to common attacks or to more sophisticated attacks for high value data.

Monitoring network security is also an important point. This includes examining the network architecture, the monitoring process for intrusions and inappropriate use, assessing firewalls, and assessing remote access policies. Determining the extent of Internet and e-mail security is also important when assessing security issues. This includes examining what e-mail security controls to implement, what policies are in place to restrict Internet or e-mail use for non-business purposes, whether a virus scan is done on information received via the Internet or e-mail, and whether there is content filtering in place to ensure that inappropriate sites are not accessed.

Screening of personnel is also an important issue to consider because many incidents result from either employees, or former employees, taking inappropriate actions. Appropriate background checks on employees, particularly those who have access to sensitive data, should be performed. Assessing the confidentiality or non-disclosure agreements that are in place, the training regarding privacy and security that is provided to employees, and the management steps in place to retrieve confidential information from terminated employees are also important. Also, whether data is processed or stored outside the United States, particularly in countries with lower data privacy and security requirements, should be assessed.

Physical security must also be considered. The use of badges or other identification documents for employees and visitors is often a key first step. Having passive forms of monitoring, guards in key locations, and electronic measures to control data access are often key to information security. As many of the data incidents show, policies should be in place that govern the removal of sensitive data on removable media, whether on CD-ROM, back-up tape, a laptop, or other form of removable media.

Incident management is another issue that must be addressed when determining whether appropriate security controls are in place. This includes having an existing process to monitor whether an incident has taken place. Internal reporting processes should also be included so that any delays in reporting to appropriate managers are minimized.

Having up-to-date and appropriate virus detection and internal controls and notification should also be considered as part of the plan. Monitoring of statistical data regarding virus or other similar incidents should also be done. In the event an incident does happen, a disaster recovery plan, including policies and procedures regarding data backup and recovery, should be in place so that it can be quickly implemented.

Given the growing concern of electronic records management, including in the litigation context, thought should be given to records management issues, including how a "litigation hold," or records freeze, would be implemented. Finally, an assessment of what auditing procedures are in place to test compliance with the security plan is an important capstone to ensuring data security.

11:40. Incident response

Many companies do not have an incident response plan in place, even though they process or handle personally identifiable information. While not legally required, having a plan in place will simplify the critical first steps of incident response.

When responding to an incident, one should be aware that there are four somewhat-competing goals that are in play. Companies need to "plug the leak" and take steps to make changes to prevent further exploitation of the risk factor that led to the incident; preserve all relevant evidence for potential criminal and civil claims against the perpetrator; get the system up again, if it was taken down, so that business interruption can be minimized; and assess what, if any, personally identifying information was accessed so that any required notices can be given.

Thought should be given to quickly identifying and retaining outside technical consultants to handle many of these issues because there are specific steps required in certain instances to preserve evidence. Many companies will retain these consultants through a lawyer or law firm so that their reports and communications are privileged under the attorney work-product doctrine. The investigative steps taken vary on the type of incident (e.g., theft of physical property that contains data versus a hacking incident) so a detailed analysis of all of the steps is beyond the scope of this book.

Once an investigation into an incident has begun, clear chains of information flow must be in place so that the individuals responding to the incident are not unknowingly working at cross-purposes, and information can be shared so that the investigation can proceed more efficiently. If sufficient evidence is gathered to support a prosecution, law enforcement should be contacted, and a packet of information should be gathered and presented to the appropriate individuals.

11:41. Addressing the data destruction/retention conundrum

There are no easy answers when balancing a company's data destruction and retention requirements. There are a number of data retention requirements, including the now infamous "litigation hold." However, as identity theft becomes more of an issue, more states, as well as the federal government, are requiring companies to destroy sensitive data after it is no longer needed. At this time there is no clear guidance on how to chart a course through, for example, the destruction requirements of the FACT Act and a company's other obligations, particularly if there is no pending claim but there is arguably a potential claim that the data relates to. In these cases given the significant liability that can result from the destruction of data, it may be the best course to retain the data and rely upon the retention requirements to claim that there was still a legitimate need to retain the data.

CHAPTER 12

Notice of Security Breaches

I. Introduction

12:1. Overview of notice of security breach laws

Just a few short years ago, California was the only state that had enacted a law that required notice to consumers if there was a security breach involving personally identifiable information. Now 46 states, the District of Columbia, Puerto Rico, and New York City have enacted laws that require notice, and the Office of the Comptroller of the Currency has issued notice of security breach recommendations for banks as well. HIPAA has also recently been amended to provide for notice of security breaches as well, and those rules are discussed below.

There are a number of issues that companies must face in order to understand their obligations under these laws. One of the first issues that must be considered is under what circumstances notice must be given. In most cases, notice must be given when a company has a reasonable belief that there has been an unauthorized acquisition of unencrypted data. Certain laws expressly state that they only apply to unencrypted data, and others define personally identifiable data as identifying data that is unencrypted, so it is important to closely review the definitions of these laws, which are included in the footnotes contained in this chapter. States also vary on what information is covered by these statutes. For example, Arkansas, California, Delaware, and others include medical information in their definitions of personal information. In Georgia a password is sufficient personal information to trigger notice if it would allow access to identifying information. Montana, Nevada, North Dakota and Rhode Island also have broad definitions of personal information.

The form of notice is an issue that varies from state to state as well. As more states adopt these laws, there is more of recognition that notice via telephone or state-wide media is acceptable. This is true even where the criteria for substitute notice are not met.

Also, certain states have placed a requirement in their laws that notice be sent to the consumer reporting agencies if more than 1,000 consumers are affected. Generally speaking this letter should simply set forth basic facts regarding the incident, but should not include the names of effected consumers.

Another issue that states approach differently is whether a company can decline to provide notice if it, or law enforcement, makes a determination that there is not a great likelihood of harm. While certain states have followed this path, the vast majority of states do not permit companies to exercise this level of discretion. Some states also differ slightly on the form of notice that can be used for direct or substitute notice.

These differences aside, there are many common elements in these laws. Almost all require some form of direct notice unless giving notice would compromise a law enforcement investigation or the security of the system. The exception is Illinois, which appears to require notice independent of law enforcement concerns. Substitute notice is also permitted under all of these laws based upon the cost and number of consumers that should receive notice. Most also recognize that federal law may preempt these laws in certain industries, particularly the financial industry, and compliance with federal law in many circumstances will be deemed to be compliance with the state laws.

12:2. Data security legislation

There has been a significant amount of speculation over whether comprehensive data security legislation, including security breach requirements at the federal level, will pass. The federal government has not yet acted, and the reason for legislative inaction seems to be a debate over whether notice is required in all circumstances, as California law requires, or if notice will only be required if there is a reasonable likelihood of harm, as states like Florida have legislated.

While at first blush California's approach seems to protect consumers more, it is not at all clear that more frequent notice makes sense from a policy perspective. Many consumers, after receiving a number of notices, may not pay as much attention to them as they would if they received fewer of them and received them only when there was a significant risk of harm. Notices, however, also raise another issue—phishing and pharming attacks.

After significant breaches, identity thieves will often circulate e-mails claiming to be companies that will assist with the security breach if recipient/consumer will only give them your personally identifiable information. While there are legitimate monitoring companies out there, there are also many who try to exploit those whom they perceive as being vulnerable to attack.

Overall, imposing some level of rational thought and consideration of the risk of harm seems to be the legislative approach that makes the most sense.

On the data security front, one of the more interesting debates about federal legislation is whether a general data security duty will be folded into GLB and enforced by the Federal Trade Commission in the same way. While this has the advantage of drawing on an existing infrastructure, it is a path that no other country has taken. If anything, it seems to make more sense to have a dedicated privacy and security enforcement agency, whether part of the FTC or not, that would include GLB within its scope, recognizing that there are other federal agencies with jurisdiction over financial institutions.

12:3.   Theft of laptop computers

Loss of laptop computers continues to be one of the more common occurrences giving rise to a security breach. One of the factors that many practitioners examine when assessing whether there is a likelihood of harm to consumers, which is a factor under many security breach statutes, is whether the theft appeared directed to obtaining information or whether it was a theft that was directed to obtaining the hardware only. One court has adopted this type of analysis when it rejected a plaintiff's claim, finding that any damages that could result from the theft of a laptop were not conjectural and hypothetical, including because the plaintiffs had not alleged that the thief had taken the laptop in order to obtain their information or that the information had actually been used.[1]

12:4.   Steps to comply with notice of security breach laws

The first step companies should take in most cases is consulting their existing security or incident response plan, if one exists. The plan should identify employees and their responsibilities in case of an incident. This should include a forensic component if possible so that the company can quickly address and assess the scope and cause of the security breach. The plan should also provide for a quick determination and repair of any security vulnerability. Addressing the circumstances under which the company will contact law enforcement should also be included. Steps should be taken to assess the type of information that has been potentially compromised.

Given the number of laws now in place, there should be a person designated to determine, if possible, the residence and number of consumers whose information has been compromised and then determine the scope of the disclosure obligation, which should include whether there is just a disclosure obligation to the consumers or whether other entities should be contacted. If the notice statute permits the company to decline to provide notice, the company should take all appropriate steps to assess and document the circumstances that support its decision to decline to provide notice. All of this must be done quite quickly as the vast majority of these statutes require notice to be given soon after the incident.

One other concern regarding pre-incident compliance should be noted. Companies that have a security plan in place that is consistent with the notice requirements of

---

1.   Randolph v. ING Life Ins. & Annuity Co., 486 F. Supp. 2d 1 (D.D.C. 2007); Ruiz v. Gap, Inc., 2009 WL 941162 (N.D.Cal. 2009) (offer of credit insurance cuts off potential damages in security breach case).

these statutes are generally permitted to follow their own procedures in case of a data security incident. Having a security plan that is compliant in place before an incident gives the company the advantage of having time to think and work through issues before an incident occurs, though this is not directly required by any of the statutes.

As a final note, companies should also assess whether there is an independent obligation to provide notice in the case of a data security incident even if there is no statute requiring notice. For example, the Ohio attorney general had filed litigation claiming that the failure to give notice to Ohio consumers after a data security incident was an unlawful business practice, even though at that time there was no statute directly requiring it.

12:5. Access

One of the key issues in a security breach is whether access equals acquisition. There have not been any cases that have decided whether mere access equates to a reasonable belief that an acquisition occurred, but one case decided by the Third Circuit provides some guidance.[2] In this case, former employees repeatedly accessed the plaintiffs' servers, allegedly in order to obtain confidential information. Indeed, there were allegedly over 125 accesses by one defendant over a 7-day period.[3] In rejecting the Computer Fraud and Abuse Act (CFAA) claim, the court noted that the plaintiffs had not established a CFAA claim because mere access did not establish a taking or use of information.

> The PC plaintiffs urge that we draw inferences of intent and the obtaining of valuable information from the mere fact that unauthorized access has been shown, and ask defendants to rebut these inferences by demonstrating the innocence of their actions. However, the elements of the claims asserted are part of a *plaintiff's* burden. That information was taken does not follow mere access. Access could be accidental, and, even if access were purposeful and unauthorized, information could be viewed but not used or taken. Furthermore, without a showing of some taking, or use, of information, it is difficult to prove intent to defraud, and indeed, the PC plaintiffs have not shown that they can do so.[4]

This issue was also addressed in a case involving ChoicePoint in relation to an alleged violation of FCRA. In that case, the plaintiffs' alleged that ChoicePoint had violated FCRA because there was an improper "communication" of the plaintiffs' consumer report.[5] The case arose from the allegation that improper individuals had accessed certain computerized data possessed by ChoicePoint. In this case the plaintiffs could not demonstrate that any information had actually been transmitted to the improper individuals and instead argued that in order to prove a communication, they need not demonstrate that any information was sent or received. The court rejected this argument,

---

2.   P.C. Yonkers, Inc. v. Celebrations The Party and Seasonal Superstore, LLC, 428 F.3d. 504 (3rd Cir. 2006).

3.   *Id.*

4.   *Id.*

5.   Harrington v. ChoicePoint Inc., 2:05-cv-01294-MRP-JWJ (C.D.Cal. October 11, 2006).

finding that no "communication" had occurred and noting that the plaintiffs' definition of a communication was "... at odds with the plain meaning of that word, which at minimum requires some act of transmission from one source or another."[6]

Additionally in this case, the court also rejected a claim of communication where the server logs maintained by ChoicePoint demonstrated that all of the plaintiffs' information was accessed, because the "fraudsters" only accessed the first page of certain reports and did not request additional information. This case also would seem to support the view that merely viewing information is insufficient to establish an acquisition of data under the security breach statutes, and to provide companies the ability to defeat claims of access where server logs, or presumably review of bandwidth logs, support the conclusion that information was not acquired.

12:6.   Form of notice

Compliance issues with the notice of security breach laws are now just beginning to be litigated. One of the open issues with these statutes was what exact disclosures were required. One court, while not directly holding what was required, did offer some insights that are helpful. In *Kahle v. Litton Loan Servicing LP*, there was a theft of hard drives that resulted in the defendant having to give notice to a number of individuals, including the plaintiff. In this case, the defendant's disclosure informed the effected individuals of (i) the type of information at issue, (ii) the location of the Federal Trade Commission Website that could provide them assistance, (iii) a toll-free number to answer questions regarding the breach, and (iv) a recommendation that the consumers place a fraud alert on their consumer report.[7] This case, at least implicitly, indicated that this statement was helpful, particularly if the recommendation was not taken by the plaintiff, in establishing that the defendant did not cause any injury due to the breach, if any existed.[8]

II.   Gramm-Leach-Bliley Act Requirements

12:7.   Response programs for unauthorized access to customer information and customer notice

A bank is required to develop a response program related to unauthorized access of customer information that, at minimum, contains procedures related to the following:

- assessing the nature and scope of an incident and identifying what customer information systems and types of customer information have been accessed or misused;

---

6.   Harrington, 2:05-cv-01294-MRP-JWJ.

7.   Kahle v. Litton Loan Servicing, LP, 486 F. Supp. 2d 705 (S.D. Ohio 2007).

8.   *Id.*

- notifying its primary federal regulator as soon as possible when the institution becomes aware of an incident involving unauthorized access to or use of sensitive customer information;

- consistent with the Agencies' Suspicious Activity Report ("SAR") regulations, notifying appropriate law enforcement authorities, in addition to filing a timely SAR in situations involving federal criminal violations requiring immediate attention, such as when a reportable violation is ongoing;

- taking appropriate steps to contain and control the incident to prevent further unauthorized access to or use of customer information, for example, by monitoring, freezing, or closing affected accounts, while preserving records and other evidence; and

- notifying customers when warranted.[9]

While it is ultimately the financial institution's burden to notify its customers and its regulators of an incident involving the unauthorized access to customer information systems if maintained by an independent service provider, the financial institution may authorize or contract with its service provider to notify the institution's customers or regulator on its behalf.[10]

12:8.   Notice to customers of unauthorized access, content and delivery

The importance of customer notice is considered a "key" part of a financial institution's duty to protect customers' information against unauthorized access or use.[11] When a financial institution becomes aware of an incident of unauthorized access to sensitive customer information,[12] the institution should conduct a reasonable investigation to promptly determine the likelihood that the information has been or will be misused.[13] If it is determined that misuse of customer information has occurred or is reasonably possible, the financial institution should notify the affected customers as soon as possible.[14] Customer notice may be delayed if an appropriate law enforcement agency determines that notification will interfere with a criminal investigation and provides the institution with a written request for delaying the notice.[15] However, the institution

---

9.   Interagency Guidance on Response Programs for Unauthorized Access to Customer Information and Customer Notice, (II)(A)(1)(a)–(e), 70 Fed. Reg. 15736 (March 29, 2005).

10.   *Id.* at (II)(A)(2).

11.   *Id.* at (III).

12.   Sensitive customer information means a customer's name, address, or telephone number, in conjunction with the customer's social security number, driver's license number, account number, credit or debit card number, or a personal identification number or password that would permit access to the customer's account. Sensitive customer information also includes any combination of components of customer information that would allow someone to log onto or access the customer's account, such as user name and password or password and account number. *Id.* at (III)(A)(1).

13.   *Id.* at (III)(A).

14.   *Id.*

15.   *Id.*

should notify its customers as soon as notification will no longer interfere with the investigation.[16]

If a financial institution, based upon its investigation, can determine from its logs or other data precisely which customers' information has been improperly accessed, it can limit notification to only those customers with regard to whom the institution determines that misuse of their information has occurred or is reasonably possible. If the financial institution determines that there has been access and it is reasonable to believe that misuse will occur, but the institution is unable to identify which specific customers' information has been accessed, it should notify all customers in the group.[17]

Notice to customers should be given in a clear and conspicuous manner.[18] The notice should describe the incident in general terms and describe the type of customer information that was the subject of unauthorized access or use. It also should generally describe what the institution has done to protect the customers' information from further unauthorized access.[19] In addition, the notice should include a telephone number that customers can call for further information and assistance, should remind customers of the need to remain vigilant over the next 12 to 24 months, and inform them to promptly report incidents of suspected identity theft to the institution.[20] It is suggested that the notice include the following additional items, if appropriate:

- a recommendation that the customer review account statements and immediately report any suspicious activity to the institution;
- a description of fraud alerts and an explanation of how the customer may place a fraud alert in the customer's consumer reports to put the customer's creditors on notice that the customer may be a victim of fraud;
- a recommendation that the customer periodically obtain credit reports from each nationwide credit reporting agency and have information relating to fraudulent transactions deleted;
- an explanation of how the customer may obtain a credit report free of charge; and
- information about the availability of the FTC's online guidance regarding steps a consumer can take to protect against identity theft. The notice should encourage the customer to report any incidents of identity theft to the FTC, and should provide the FTC's website address and toll-free telephone number that customers may use to obtain the identity theft guidance and report suspected incidents of identity theft.[21]

Financial institutions are also encouraged, but not required, to notify the nationwide consumer reporting agencies prior to sending notices to a large number of customers that include contact information for the reporting agencies.[22]

Customer notice should be delivered in any manner designed to ensure that a customer can reasonably be expected to receive it. This can include contacting

---

16. *Id.*
17. *Id.* at (III)(A)(2).
18. *Id.* at (III)(B)(1).
19. *Id.*
20. *Id.*
21. *Id.*
22. *Id.* at (III)(B)(2).

customers by telephone or by mail, or by e-mail for those customers for whom the institution has a valid e-mail address and who have agreed to receive communications electronically.[23]

III. HIPAA and PHR Breaches

12:9.   HIPAA and Personal Health Records Breaches

There are a number of statutes and regulations that impact the unauthorized access or acquisition of HIPAA regulated data and information that is in personal health records (PHRs). Because PHRs fall outside the scope of HIPAA, the FTC has issued PHR breach rules and HHS has issued HIPAA breach rules. The statutes, including the temporary regulations, as well as the final regulations, follow.

One of the key issues under HIPAA is defining "unsecured protected health information"—that is, the information that triggers a breach. Under the statute, the term "unsecured protected health information" means protected health information that is not secured through the use of a technology or methodology specified by the secretary in guidance.[24] There was a back-up definition[25] in case the secretary did not issue a definition, but the secretary issued the requisite regulations and therefore it did not come into effect.

12:10. Defining a "breach"

One of the first key changes to HIPAA was the incorporation of the rules regarding unauthorized access to protected health information (PHI). The term "breach" is defined as "the unauthorized acquisition, access, use, or disclosure of protected health information which compromises the security or privacy of such information, except where an unauthorized person to whom such information is disclosed would not reasonably have been able to retain such information."[26] It does not include any unintentional acquisition, access, or use of protected health information by an employee or individual acting under the authority of a covered entity or business associate if such acquisition, access, or use was made in good faith and within the course and scope of the employment or other professional relationship of such employee or individual, respectively, with the covered entity or business associate; and the information is not further acquired,

---

23.   *Id.* at (III)(C).

24.   42 U.S.C. § 17932(h)(1)(A). The term "protected health information" has the meaning given such term in section 160.103 of title 45, Code of Federal Regulations. 42 U.S.C. § 17921(12).

25.   In the case that the secretary does not issue guidance under paragraph (2) by the date specified in such paragraph, for purposes of this section, the term "unsecured protected health information" shall mean protected health information that is not secured by a technology standard that renders protected health information unusable, unreadable, or indecipherable to unauthorized individuals and is developed or endorsed by a standards developing organization that is accredited by the American National Standards Institute.

26.   42 U.S.C. § 17921(1)(A).

accessed, used, or disclosed by any person.[27] It also does not include any inadvertent disclosure from an individual who is otherwise authorized to access protected health information at a facility operated by a covered entity or business associate to another similarly situated individual at same facility, and any such information received as a result of such disclosure is not further acquired, accessed, used, or disclosed without authorization by any person.[28]

The regulations changed the definition originally provided in the HITECH Act,[29] and now a breach is defined as the acquisition, access, use, or disclosure of protected health information in a manner not permitted under subpart E (Privacy Rule)[30] of this part which compromises the security or privacy of the protected health information.[31] For purposes of this definition, "compromises the security or privacy of the protected health information" means the unauthorized use or disclosure poses a significant risk of financial, reputational, or other harm to the individual. A use or disclosure of protected health information that does not include the identifiers listed at § 164.514(e)(2), date of birth, and zip code does not compromise the security or privacy of the protected health information.[32]

The definition of breach excludes (i) any unintentional acquisition, access, or use of protected health information by a workforce member or person acting under the authority of a covered entity or a business associate, if such acquisition, access, or use was made in good faith and within the scope of authority and does not result in further use or disclosure in a manner not permitted under the Privacy Rule; (ii) any inadvertent disclosure by a person who is authorized to access protected health information at a covered entity or business associate to another person authorized to access protected health information at the same covered entity or business associate, or organized health care arrangement in which the covered entity participates, and the information received as a result of such disclosure is not further used or disclosed in a manner not permitted under the Privacy Rule; or a disclosure of protected health information where a covered entity or business associate has a good faith belief that an unauthorized person to whom the disclosure was made would not reasonably have been able to retain such information.[33]

---

27. 42 U.S.C. § 17921(1)(B)(i).

28. 42 U.S.C. §§ 17921(1)(B)(ii)–(iii).

29. American Recovery and Reinvestment Act of 2009, Pub. L. 111–5, Title XIII, Subtitle D of the Health Information Technology for Economic and Clinical Health Act (HITECH Act), addresses the privacy and security concerns associated with the electronic transmission of health information. HITECH Act § 13402(a) providing a notice obligation without regard to the qualification of whether such an event compromises the security or privacy of the health information.

30. 45 C.F.R. Part 164 addresses the security and privacy of protected health information. Subpart A are general provisions, while subpart C constitutes the Security Rule, subpart D constitutes the Breach Notification Rule, and subpart E constitutes the Privacy Rule.

31. 45 C.F.R. 164.402. It is important to note that the source of subpart D (Breach Notification Rule) is an interim final rule with request for comments that, at time of publication, is undergoing review and potential revision in an eventual final rule. 74 Fed. Reg. 42740 (August 24, 2009).

32. *Id.*

33. 45 C.F.R. § 164.400.

12:11. Statutory requirements

A covered entity that accesses, maintains, retains, modifies, records, stores, destroys, or otherwise holds, uses, or discloses[34] unsecured protected health information (as defined in subsection (h)(1)) shall, in the case of a breach of such information that is discovered by the covered entity, notify each individual whose unsecured protected health information has been, or is reasonably believed by the covered entity to have been, accessed, acquired, or disclosed as a result of such breach.[35] A business associate of a covered entity that accesses, maintains, retains, modifies, records, stores, destroys, or otherwise holds, uses, or discloses unsecured protected health information shall, following the discovery of a breach of such information, notify the covered entity of such breach. The notice must include the identification of each individual whose unsecured protected health information has been, or is reasonably believed by the business associate to have been, accessed, acquired, or disclosed during such breach.[36]

The statute directly addresses when a breach is treated as discovered. A breach shall be treated as discovered by a covered entity or by a business associate as of the first day on which such breach is known to such entity or associate, respectively, (including any person, other than the individual committing the breach, that is an employee, officer, or other agent of such entity or associate, respectively) or should reasonably have been known to such entity or associate (or person) to have occurred.[37]

The covered entity involved (or business associate involved in the case of a notification required under subsection § 17932(b)), shall have the burden of demonstrating that all notifications were made as required under this part, including evidence demonstrating the necessity of any delay.[38]

12:12. Timing of notice

Subject to the requirements of § 17932(g), all notifications required under this section shall be made without unreasonable delay and in no case later than 60 calendar days after the discovery of a breach by the covered entity involved (or business associate involved in the case of a notification required under § 17932(b)).[39] If a law enforcement official determines that a notification, notice, or posting required under this section would impede a criminal investigation or cause damage to national security, such notification, notice, or posting shall be delayed in the same manner as provided under section 164.528(a)(2) of title 45, Code of Federal Regulations, in the case of a disclosure covered under such section.[40]

---

34. The terms "disclose" and "disclosure" have the meaning given the term "disclosure" in section 160.103 of title 45, Code of Federal Regulations. 42 U.S.C. § 17921(4).
35. 42 U.S.C. § 17932(a).
36. 42 U.S.C. § 17932(b).
37. 42 U.S.C. § 17932(c).
38. 42 U.S.C. § 17932(d)(2).
39. 42 U.S.C. § 17932(d)(1).
40. 42 U.S.C. § 17932(g).

12:13. Form of notice

Notice required under this section to be provided to an individual, with respect to a breach, typically must be provided promptly and via written notification by first-class mail to the individual (or the next of kin of the individual if the individual is deceased) at the last known address of the individual or the next of kin, respectively, or, if specified as a preference by the individual, by electronic mail. The notification may be provided in one or more mailings as information is available.[41] In the case in which there is insufficient, or out-of-date contact information (including a phone number, e-mail address, or any other form of appropriate communication) that precludes direct written or, if specified by the individual, electronic notification to the individual, a substitute form of notice must be provided, including, in the case that there are 10 or more individuals for which there is insufficient or out-of-date contact information, a conspicuous posting for a period determined by the secretary on the home page of the website of the covered entity involved or notice in major print or broadcast media, including major media in geographic areas where the individuals affected by the breach likely reside. Such a notice in media or web posting will include a toll-free phone number where an individual can learn whether or not the individual's unsecured protected health information is possibly included in the breach.[42]

In any case deemed by the covered entity involved to require urgency because of possible imminent misuse of unsecured protected health information, the covered entity, in addition to direct notice provided, may provide information to individuals by telephone or other means, as appropriate.[43]

Regardless of the method by which notice is provided to individuals, notice of a breach shall include, to the extent possible, the following: a brief description of what happened, including the date of the breach and the date of the discovery of the breach, if known; a description of the types of unsecured protected health information that were involved in the breach (such as full name, social security number, date of birth, home address, account number, or disability code); the steps individuals should take to protect themselves from potential harm resulting from the breach; a brief description of what the covered entity involved is doing to investigate the breach, to mitigate losses, and to protect against any further breaches; and contact procedures for individuals to ask questions or learn additional information, which shall include a toll-free telephone number, an e-mail address, website, or postal address.[44]

12:14. Notice to other entities

Notice must be provided to prominent media outlets serving a state[45] or jurisdiction, following the discovery of a breach, if the unsecured protected health information of more than 500 residents of such state or jurisdiction is, or is reasonably believed to

---

41.   42 U.S.C. § 17932(e)(1)(A).

42.   42 U.S.C. § 17932(e)(1)(B).

43.   42 U.S.C. § 17932(e)(1)(C).

44.   42 U.S.C. § 17932(f)(1)–(5).

45.   The term "State" means each of the several States, the District of Columbia, Puerto Rico, the Virgin Islands, Guam, American Samoa, and the Northern Mariana Islands. 42 U.S.C. § 17921(15).

have been, accessed, acquired, or disclosed during the breach.[46] Notice must also be provided to the secretary by covered entities of unsecured protected health information that has been acquired or disclosed in a breach. If the breach was with respect to 500 or more individuals, then such notice must be provided immediately.[47] If the breach was with respect to fewer than 500 individuals, the covered entity may maintain a log of any such breach occurring and annually submit such a log to the secretary documenting such breaches occurring during the year involved.[48] The secretary shall make available to the public on the Internet website of the Department of Health and Human Services a list that identifies each covered entity involved in a breach in which the unsecured protected health information of more than 500 individuals is acquired or disclosed.[49]

12:15. Report to Congress on breaches

The secretary is required to give to the Committee on Finance and the Committee on Health, Education, Labor, and Pensions of the Senate and the Committee on Ways and Means and the Committee on Energy and Commerce of the House of Representatives annual reports regarding breaches for which notice was provided to the secretary under subsection § 17932(e)(3).[50] The report must include the number and nature of breaches and actions taken in response to breaches.[51]

12:16. Requirement to issue regulations

As discussed below, the secretary issued interim final regulations that applied to breaches that were discovered on or after the date that was 30 days after the publication of the regulations.[52]

12:17. Breach notification requirement for vendors of personal health records and other non-HIPAA covered entities

In contrast with the interim final rule that HHS issued, the FTC issued a final rule to address notifications for health breaches within its scope.[53] Because the data within personal health records or PHRs is sensitive but outside the scope of HIPAA, the FTC has jurisdiction over those organizations that provide PHRs to consumers.

---

46.   42 U.S.C. § 17932(e)(2).

47.   42 U.S.C. § 17932(e)(3).

48.   42 U.S.C. § 17932(e)(3).

49.   42 U.S.C. § 17932(e)(4).

50.   42 U.S.C. § 17932(i)(1).

51.   42 U.S.C. §§ 17932(i)(2)(A)–(B).

52.   42 U.S.C. § 17932(j). See 74 Fed. Reg. 42740 (August 24, 2009). See also section 12:23 *et seq* below for a detailed review of the HHS requirements.

53.   Health Breach Notification Rule: Final Rule, 16 C.F.R. Part 318, published in 74 Fed. Reg. 42962 (August 25, 2009).

In accordance with § 17937(c), each vendor of personal health records,[54] following the discovery of a breach of security[55] of unsecured PHR identifiable health information[56] that is in a personal health record maintained or offered by such vendor, and each entity described in clause (ii), (iii), or (iv) of section 17953(b)(1)(A) of this title, following the discovery of a breach of security of such information that is obtained through a product or service provided by such entity, shall notify each individual who is a citizen or resident of the United States whose unsecured PHR identifiable health information was acquired by an unauthorized person as a result of such a breach of security and notify the Federal Trade Commission.[57]

12:18. Notification by third party service providers

A third party service provider that provides services to a vendor of personal health records or to an entity described in clause (ii), (iii). or (iv) of section 17953(b)(1)(A) of this title in connection with the offering or maintenance of a personal health record or a related product or service and that accesses, maintains, retains, modifies, records, stores, destroys, or otherwise holds, uses, or discloses unsecured PHR identifiable health information in such a record as a result of such services shall, following the discovery of a breach of security of such information, notify the vendor or entity, respectively, of such breach. The notice shall include the identification of each individual whose unsecured PHR identifiable health information has been, or is reasonably believed to have been, accessed, acquired, or disclosed during such breach.[58]

---

54. The term "vendor of personal health records" means an entity, other than a covered entity (as defined in paragraph (3)), that offers or maintains a personal health record. 42 U.S.C. § 17921(18). The term "personal health record" means an electronic record of PHR identifiable health information (as defined in section 17937(f)(2) of this title) on an individual that can be drawn from multiple sources and that is managed, shared, and controlled by or primarily for the individual. 42 U.S.C. § 17921(11).

55. Breach of security The term "breach of security" means, with respect to unsecured PHR identifiable health information of an individual in a personal health record, acquisition of such information without the authorization of the individual. 42 U.S.C. § 17937(f)(1).

56. Unsecured PHR identifiable health information **(A)** Subject to subparagraph **(B)**, the term "unsecured PHR identifiable health information" means PHR identifiable health information that is not protected through the use of a technology or methodology specified by the Secretary in the guidance issued under section 17932(h)(2) of this title. (B) Exception in case timely guidance not issued In the case that the Secretary does not issue guidance under section 17932(h)(2) of this title by the date specified in such section, for purposes of this section, the term "unsecured PHR identifiable health information" shall mean PHR identifiable health information that is not secured by a technology standard that renders protected health information unusable, unreadable, or indecipherable to unauthorized individuals and that is developed or endorsed by a standards developing organization that is accredited by the American National Standards Institute. 42 U.S.C. § 17937(f)(3). PHR identifiable health information. The term "PHR identifiable health information" means individually identifiable health information, as defined in section 1320d(6) of this title, and includes, with respect to an individual, information—**(A)** that is provided by or on behalf of the individual; and **(B)** that identifies the individual or with respect to which there is a reasonable basis to believe that the information can be used to identify the individual. 42 U.S.C. § 17937(f)(2).

57. 42 U.S.C. § 17937(a)(1)–(2).

58. 42 U.S.C. § 17937(b).

12:19. Application of requirements for timeliness, method, and content of notifications

Section 17932(c)–(f) applies to a notification required under subsection (a) and a vendor of personal health records, an entity described in subsection (a) and a third party service provider described in subsection (b), with respect to a breach of security under subsection (a) of unsecured PHR identifiable health information in such records maintained or offered by such vendor, in a manner specified by the Federal Trade Commission.[59]

12:20. Notification of the Secretary

Upon receipt of a notification of a breach of security under this law, the Federal Trade Commission must notify the secretary of the breach.[60]

12:21. Enforcement

A violation of § 17937(a) or (b) will be treated as an unfair and deceptive act or practice in violation of a regulation under § 57a(a)(1)(B) of Title 15 regarding unfair or deceptive acts or practices.[61]

12:22. Regulations and effective date

To carry out this portion of the law, the Federal Trade Commission was required to, and did, promulgate interim final regulations. The provisions of this section only apply to breaches of security that are discovered on or after the date that is 30 days after the date of publication of such interim final regulations.[62] If Congress enacts new legislation establishing requirements for notification in the case of a breach of security, requirements that apply to entities that are not covered entities or business associates, the provisions of this section shall not apply to breaches of security discovered on or after the effective date of regulations implementing such legislation.[63]

---

59. 42 U.S.C. § 17937(c).
60. 42 U.S.C. § 17937(d).
61. 42 U.S.C. § 17937(e). For further discussion of FTC enforcement authority and history, please see chapter 15.
62. 42 U.S.C. § 17937(g)(1).
63. 42 U.S.C. § 17937(g)(2).

IV. HIPAA Breach Regulations

12:23. Applicability

The interim final breach regulations issued by HHS apply to breaches of protected health information occurring on or after September 23, 2009.[64] As noted elsewhere, these interim final rules are expected to be finalized the latter half of 2011.

12:24. Notification to individuals

A covered entity shall, following the discovery of a breach[65] of unsecured protected health information,[66] notify each individual whose unsecured protected health information has been, or is reasonably believed by the covered entity to have been, accessed, acquired, used, or disclosed as a result of such breach.[67]

12:25. Discovery of breaches

For purposes of notification, as well as under §§ 164.406(a) and 164.408(a), a breach is treated as discovered by a covered entity as of the first day on which such breach is known to the covered entity or, by exercising reasonable diligence, would have been known to the covered entity. A covered entity is deemed to have knowledge of a breach if such breach is known or, by exercising reasonable diligence, would have been known to any person, other than the person committing the breach, who is a workforce member or agent of the covered entity (determined in accordance with the federal common law of agency).[68]

---

64. 45 C.F.R. § 164.400.

65. Breach means the acquisition, access, use, or disclosure of protected health information in a manner not permitted under subpart E of this part which compromises the security or privacy of the protected health information. (1)(i) For purposes of this definition, compromises the security or privacy of the protected health information means poses a significant risk of financial, reputational, or other harm to the individual. (ii) A use or disclosure of protected health information that does not include the identifiers listed at § 164.514(e)(2), date of birth, and zip code does not compromise the security or privacy of the protected health information. (2) Breach excludes: (i) Any unintentional acquisition, access, or use of protected health information by a workforce member or person acting under the authority of a covered entity or a business associate, if such acquisition, access, or use was made in good faith and within the scope of authority and does not result in further use or disclosure in a manner not permitted under subpart E of this part. (ii) Any inadvertent disclosure by a person who is authorized to access protected health information at a covered entity or business associate to another person authorized to access protected health information at the same covered entity or business associate, or organized health care arrangement in which the covered entity participates, and the information received as a result of such disclosure is not further used or disclosed in a manner not permitted under subpart E of this part. (iii) A disclosure of protected health information where a covered entity or business associate has a good faith belief that an unauthorized person to whom the disclosure was made would not reasonably have been able to retain such information. 45 C.F.R. § 164.400.

66. Unsecured protected health information means protected health information that is not rendered unusable, unreadable, or indecipherable to unauthorized individuals through the use of a technology or methodology specified by the Secretary in the guidance issued under section 13402(h)(2) of Public Law 111-5 on the HHS website. 45 C.F.R. § 164.400.

67. 45 C.F.R. § 164.404(a)(1).

68. 45 C.F.R. § 164.404(a)(2).

12:26. Timing of notice

Except as provided below, a covered entity must provide notification without unreasonable delay and in no case later than 60 calendar days after discovery of a breach.[69] If a law enforcement official[70] states to a covered entity or business associate that a notification, notice, or posting required under this subpart would impede a criminal investigation or cause damage to national security, a covered entity or business associate must, if the statement is in writing and specifies the time for which a delay is required, delay such notification, notice, or posting for the time period specified by the official; or if the statement is made orally, document the statement, including the identity of the official making the statement, and delay the notification, notice, or posting temporarily and no longer than 30 days from the date of the oral statement, unless an appropriate written statement is submitted during that time.[71]

12:27. Form of notice

Notice must include, to the extent possible, a brief description of what happened, including the date of the breach and the date of the discovery of the breach, if known; a description of the types of unsecured protected health information that were involved in the breach (such as whether full name, social security number, date of birth, home address, account number, diagnosis, disability code, or other types of information were involved); any steps individuals should take to protect themselves from potential harm resulting from the breach; a brief description of what the covered entity involved is doing to investigate the breach, to mitigate harm to individuals, and to protect against any further breaches; and contact procedures for individuals to ask questions or learn additional information, which shall include a toll-free telephone number, an e-mail address, website, or postal address.[72] The notice must be written in plain language.[73]

Written notice by first-class mail to the individual at the last known address of the individual or, if the individual agrees to electronic notice and such agreement has not been withdrawn, by electronic mail. The notification may be provided in one or more mailings as information is available.[74] If the covered entity knows the individual is deceased and has the address of the next of kin or personal representative of the individual (as specified under § 164.502(g)(4) of subpart E), written notification by first-class mail to either the next of kin or personal representative of the deceased individual is acceptable. In the case in which there is insufficient or out-of-date contact information that precludes written notification to the individual a substitute form of notice reasonably calculated to reach the individual shall be provided. Substitute notice need not be provided in

---

69. 45 C.F.R. § 164.404(b).

70. Law enforcement official means an officer or employee of any agency or authority of the United States, a State, a territory, a political subdivision of a State or territory, or an Indian tribe, who is empowered by law to: (1) Investigate or conduct an official inquiry into a potential violation of law; or (2) Prosecute or otherwise conduct a criminal, civil, or administrative proceeding arising from an alleged violation of law. 45 C.F.R. § 164.103.

71. 45 C.F.R. §§ 164.412(a)–(b).

72. 45 C.F.R. §§ 164.412(c)(1)(A)–(E).

73. 45 C.F.R. § 164.412(c)(2).

74. 45 C.F.R. § 164.412(d)(1)(i).

the case in which there is insufficient or out-of-date contact information that precludes written notification to the next of kin or personal representative of the individual.[75] In the case in which there is insufficient or out-of-date contact information for fewer than 10 individuals, then such substitute notice may be provided by an alternative form of written notice, telephone, or other means.[76] If there is insufficient or out-of-date contact information for 10 or more individuals, then such substitute notice must be in the form of either a conspicuous posting for a period of 90 days on the home page of the website of the covered entity involved or conspicuous notice in major print or broadcast media in geographic areas where the individuals affected by the breach likely reside; with additional notice in urgent situations. In any case deemed by the covered entity to require urgency because of possible imminent misuse of unsecured protected health information, the covered entity may provide information to individuals by telephone or other means, as appropriate, in addition to written or substitute notice.[77] It must also include a toll-free phone number that remains active for at least 90 days where an individual can learn whether the individual's unsecured protected health information may be included in the breach.[78]

12:28. Notification to the media

For a breach of unsecured protected health information involving more than 500 residents of a state[79] or jurisdiction, a covered entity shall, following the discovery of the breach as provided in § 164.404(a)(2), notify prominent media outlets serving the state or jurisdiction.[80] A covered entity must provide this notification without unreasonable delay and in no case later than 60 calendar days after discovery of a breach.[81] This notification must meet the requirements of § 164.404(c).[82]

12:29. Notification to the secretary

A covered entity must, following the discovery of a breach of unsecured protected health information as provided in § 164.404(a)(2), notify the secretary.[83] For breaches of unsecured protected health information involving 500 or more individuals, a covered entity must, except as provided in § 164.412, provide the notification contemporaneously with the notice required by § 164.404(a) and in the manner specified on the Department of Health and Human Services (HHS) website.[84] For breaches of unsecured protected health information involving less than 500 individuals, a covered entity must maintain a log or other documentation of such breaches and, not later than 60 days after the

---

75. 45 C.F.R. § 164.412(d)(2).
76. 45 C.F.R. § 164.412(d)(2)(i).
77. 45 C.F.R. § 164.412(d)(2)(ii)(A).
78. 45 C.F.R. § 164.412(d)(2)(ii)(B).
79. For purposes of this section, State includes American Samoa and the Northern Mariana Islands.
80. 45 C.F.R. § 164.406(a).
81. 45 C.F.R. § 164.406(b).
82. 45 C.F.R. § 164.406(c).
83. 45 C.F.R. § 164.408(a).
84. 45 C.F.R. § 164.408(b).

end of each calendar year, provide the notification for breaches occurring during the preceding calendar year, in the manner specified on the HHS website.[85]

12:30. Notification by a business associate

A business associate must, following the discovery of a breach of unsecured protected health information, notify the covered entity of such breach.[86] A breach is treated as discovered by a business associate as of the first day on which such breach is known to the business associate or, by exercising reasonable diligence, would have been known to the business associate. A business associate shall be deemed to have knowledge of a breach if the breach is known, or by exercising reasonable diligence would have been known, to any person, other than the person committing the breach, who is an employee, officer, or other agent of the business associate (determined in accordance with the federal common law of agency).[87]

12:31. Timing of notice—business associate

Except as provided in § 164.412, a business associate shall provide notice without unreasonable delay and in no case later than 60 calendar days after discovery of a breach.[88]

12:32. Form of notice

The notice must include, to the extent possible, the identification of each individual whose unsecured protected health information has been, or is reasonably believed by the business associate to have been, accessed, acquired, used, or disclosed during the breach.[89] A business associate must provide the covered entity with any other available information that the covered entity is required to include in notification to the individual under § 164.404(c) at the time of the notification or promptly thereafter as information becomes available.[90]

12:33. Administrative requirements and burdens of proof

A covered entity is required to comply with the administrative requirements of §§ 164.530(b), (d), (e), (g), (h), (i), and (j) with respect to the requirements of this subpart.[91] In the event of a use or disclosure in violation of the Privacy Rule, the covered entity or business associate, as applicable, must have the burden of demonstrating that all notifications were made as required by this subpart or that the use or disclosure did not constitute a breach, as defined at § 164.402.[92]

---

85. 45 C.F.R. § 164.408(c).
86. 45 C.F.R. § 164.410(a)(1).
87. 45 C.F.R. § 164.410(a)(2).
88. 45 C.F.R. § 164.410(b).
89. 45 C.F.R. § 164.410(c)(1).
90. 45 C.F.R. § 164.410(c)(2).
91. 45 C.F.R. § 164.414(a).
92. 45 C.F.R. § 164.414(b).

12:34. FTC PHR breach rule

The "Health Breach Notification Rule," implements section 13407 of the American Recovery and Reinvestment Act of 2009. It applies to foreign and domestic vendors[93] of personal health records,[94] PHR related entities,[95] and third-party service providers,[96] irrespective of any jurisdictional tests in the Federal Trade Commission (FTC) Act, that maintain information of U.S. citizens or residents.[97] It does not apply to HIPAA–covered entities,[98] or to any other entity to the extent that it engages in activities as a business associate[99] of a HIPAA–covered entity.[100] This part preempts state[101] law as set forth in section 13421 of the American Recovery and Reinvestment Act of 2009.[102]

12:35. Breach notification requirements

In accordance with §§ 318.4, 318.5, and 318.6, each vendor of personal health records,[103] following the discovery of a breach of security[104] of unsecured[105] PHR identifiable health

93. "Vendor of personal health records" means an entity, other than a HIPAA–covered entity or an entity to the extent that it engages in activities as a business associate of a HIPAA–covered entity, that offers or maintains a personal health record. 16 C.F.R. § 318.2(j).

94. "Personal health record" means an electronic record of PHR identifiable health information on an individual that can be drawn from multiple sources and that is managed, shared, and controlled by or primarily for the individual. 16 C.F.R. § 318.2(d).

95. "PHR related entity" means an entity, other than a HIPAA–covered entity or an entity to the extent that it engages in activities as a business associate of a HIPAA–covered entity, that: (1) Offers products or services through the website of a vendor of personal health records; (2) Offers products or services through the websites of HIPAA–covered entities that offer individuals personal health records; or (3) Accesses information in a personal health record or sends information to a personal health record. 16 C.F.R. § 318.2(f).

96. "Third-party service provider" means an entity that: (1) Provides services to a vendor of personal health records in connection with the offering or maintenance of a personal health record or to a PHR related entity in connection with a product or service offered by that entity; and (2) Accesses, maintains, retains, modifies, records, stores, destroys, or otherwise holds, uses, or discloses unsecured PHR identifiable health information as a result of such services. 16 C.F.R. § 318.2(h).

97. 16 C.F.R. § 318.1(a).

98. "HIPAA–covered entity" means a covered entity under the Health Insurance Portability and Accountability Act, Public Law 104–191, 110 Stat. 1936, as defined in 45 CFR 160.103. 16 C.F.R. § 318.2(c).

99. "Business associate" means a business associate under the Health Insurance Portability and Accountability Act, Public Law 104–191, 110 Stat. 1936, as defined in 45 CFR 160.103. 16 C.F.R. § 318.2(b).

100. 16 C.F.R. § 318.1(a).

101. State means any of the several states, the District of Columbia, Puerto Rico, the Virgin Islands, Guam, American Samoa and the Northern Mariana Islands. 16 C.F.R. § 318.2(g).

102. 16 C.F.R. § 318.1(b).

103. "Vendor of personal health records" means an entity, other than a HIPAA–covered entity or an entity to the extent that it engages in activities as a business associate of a HIPAA–covered entity, that offers or maintains a personal health record. 16 C.F.R. § 318.2(j).

104. "Breach of security" means, with respect to unsecured PHR identifiable health information of an individual in a personal health record, acquisition of such information without the authorization of the individual. Unauthorized acquisition will be presumed to include unauthorized access to unsecured PHR identifiable health information unless the vendor of personal health records, PHR related entity, or third party service provider that experienced the breach has reliable evidence showing that there has not been, or could not reasonably have been, unauthorized acquisition of such information. 16 C.F.R. § 318.2(a).

105. "Unsecured" means PHR identifiable information that is not protected through the use of a technology or methodology specified by the Secretary of Health and Human Services in the guidance issued under section 13402(h)(2) of the American Reinvestment and Recovery Act of 2009. 16 C.F.R. § 318.2(i).

information[106] that is in a personal health record maintained or offered by such vendor, and each PHR related entity, following the discovery of a breach of security of such information that is obtained through a product or service provided by such entity, shall notify each individual who is a citizen or resident of the United States whose unsecured PHR identifiable health information was acquired by an unauthorized person as a result of such breach of security and notify the Federal Trade Commission.[107] A third party service provider shall, following the discovery of a breach of security, provide notice of the breach to an official designated in a written contract by the vendor of personal health records or the PHR related entity to receive such notices or, if such a designation is not made, to a senior official at the vendor of personal health records or PHR related entity to which it provides services, and obtain acknowledgment from such official that such notice was received. The notification must include the identification of each customer of the vendor of personal health records or PHR related entity whose unsecured PHR identifiable health information has been, or is reasonably believed to have been, acquired during such breach. For purposes of ensuring implementation of this requirement, vendors of personal health records and PHR related entities shall notify third-party service providers of their status as vendors of personal health records or PHR related entities subject to this part.[108] A breach of security shall be treated as discovered as of the first day on which such breach is known or reasonably should have been known to the vendor of personal health records, PHR related entity, or third-party service provider, respectively. Such vendor, entity, or third-party service provider shall be deemed to have knowledge of a breach if such breach is known, or reasonably should have been known, to any person, other than the person committing the breach, who is an employee, officer, or other agent of such vendor of personal health records, PHR related entity, or third party service provider.[109]

12:36. Timing of notice

Except as provided in § 318.4(c) of this section and § 318.5(c), all notifications required under §§ 318.3(a)(1), 318.3(b), and 318.5(b) shall be sent without unreasonable delay and in no case later than 60 calendar days after the discovery of a breach of security.[110] The vendor of personal health records, PHR related entity, and third-party service provider involved shall have the burden of demonstrating that all notifications were made as required under this part, including evidence demonstrating the necessity of any delay.[111] If a law enforcement official determines that a notification, notice, or posting required under this part would impede a criminal investigation or cause damage to

---

106. "PHR identifiable health information" means "individually identifiable health information," as defined in section 1171(6) of the Social Security Act (42 U.S.C. 1320d(6)), and, with respect to an individual, information: (1) That is provided by or on behalf of the individual; and (2) That identifies the individual or with respect to which there is a reasonable basis to believe that the information can be used to identify the individual. 16 C.F.R. § 318.2(e).

107. 16 C.F.R. § 318.3(a)(1)–(2).

108. 16 C.F.R. § 318.3(b).

109. 16 C.F.R. § 318.3(b).

110. 16 C.F.R. § 318.4(a).

111. 16 C.F.R. § 318.4(b).

national security, such notification, notice, or posting shall be delayed. This paragraph shall be implemented in the same manner as provided under 45 C.F.R. § 164.528(a)(2), in the case of a disclosure covered under such section.[112]

12:37. Form of notice

A vendor of personal health records or PHR related entity that discovers a breach of security shall provide notice of such breach to an individual promptly, as described in § 318.4, in the form of written notice, by first-class mail to the individual at the last known address of the individual, or by e-mail, if the individual is given a clear, conspicuous, and reasonable opportunity to receive notification by first-class mail, and the individual does not exercise that choice. If the individual is deceased, the vendor of personal health records or PHR related entity that discovered the breach must provide such notice to the next of kin of the individual if the individual had provided contact information for his or her next of kin, along with authorization to contact them. The notice may be provided in one or more mailings as information is available.[113] If, after making reasonable efforts to contact all individuals to whom notice is required under § 318.3(a), through the means provided in paragraph (a)(1) of this section, the vendor of personal health records or PHR related entity finds that contact information for ten or more individuals is insufficient or out-of-date, the vendor of personal health records or PHR related entity shall provide substitute notice, which shall be reasonably calculated to reach the individuals affected by the breach, in the following form: through a conspicuous posting for a period of 90 days on the home page of its website; or in major print or broadcast media, including major media in geographic areas where the individuals affected by the breach likely reside. Such a notice in media or web posting shall include a toll-free phone number, which shall remain active for at least 90 days, where an individual can learn whether or not the individual's unsecured PHR identifiable health information may be included in the breach.[114]

In any case deemed by the vendor of personal health records or PHR related entity to require urgency because of possible imminent misuse of unsecured PHR identifiable health information, that entity may provide information to individuals by telephone or other means, as appropriate, in addition to written or substitute notice.[115]

Regardless of the method by which notice is provided to individuals under § 318.5, notice of a breach of security must be in plain language and include, to the extent possible, the following: a brief description of what happened, including the date of the breach and the date of the discovery of the breach, if known; a description of the types of unsecured PHR identifiable health information that were involved in the breach (such as full name, social security number, date of birth, home address, account number, or disability code); steps individuals should take to protect themselves from potential harm resulting from the breach; a brief description of what the entity that suffered the breach is doing to investigate the breach, to mitigate harm, and to protect

---

112. 16 C.F.R. § 318.4(c).
113. 16 C.F.R. § 318.5(a)(1).
114. 16 C.F.R. §§ 318.5(a)(2)(i)–(ii).
115. 16 C.F.R. § 318.5(a)(3).

against any further breaches; and contact procedures for individuals to ask questions or learn additional information, which shall include a toll-free telephone number, an e-mail address, website, or postal address.[116]

12:38. Notice to other entities

A vendor of personal health records or PHR related entity shall provide notice to prominent media outlets serving a state[117] or jurisdiction, following the discovery of a breach of security, if the unsecured PHR identifiable health information of 500 or more residents of such state or jurisdiction is, or is reasonably believed to have been, acquired during such breach.[118] Vendors of personal health records and PHR related entities shall provide notice to the Federal Trade Commission following the discovery of a breach of security. If the breach involves the unsecured PHR identifiable health information of 500 or more individuals, then such notice shall be provided as soon as possible and in no case later than ten business days following the date of discovery of the breach. If the breach involves the unsecured PHR identifiable health information of fewer than 500 individuals, the vendor of personal health records or PHR related entity may maintain a log of any such breach, and submit such a log annually to the Federal Trade Commission no later than 60 calendar days following the end of the calendar year, documenting breaches from the preceding calendar year. All notices pursuant to this paragraph shall be provided according to instructions at the Federal Trade Commission's website.[119]

12:39. Enforcement

A violation of this part shall be treated as an unfair or deceptive act or practice in violation of a regulation under § 18(a)(1)(B) of the Federal Trade Commission Act (15 U.S.C. 57a(a)(1)(B)) regarding unfair or deceptive acts or practices.[120]

12:40. Effective date

These regulations apply to breaches of security that are discovered on or after September 24, 2009.[121]

12:41. Centers for Medicare & Medicaid Services requirements

The Centers for Medicare & Medicaid Services (CMS) has issued requirements for incidents entitled the "CMS Information Security Incident Handling and Breach Analysis/ Notification Procedure," and version 2.3 of this document was issued on December 3,

---

116. 16 C.F.R. § 318.6(a)–(e).
117. State means any of the several States, the District of Columbia, Puerto Rico, the Virgin Islands, Guam, American Samoa and the Northern Mariana Islands. 16 C.F.R. § 318.2(g).
118. 16 C.F.R. § 318.5(b).
119. 16 C.F.R. § 318.5(c).
120. 16 C.F.R. § 318.7(c).
121. 16 C.F.R. § 318.8.

2010.[122] It is applicable to CMS employees, contractors, and other business partners and sets the timing of disclosure to CMS of an incident, depending on the category of the incident. Reporting can be required as quickly as 1 hour. This means that PHI lost relating to a Medicare/Medicaid patient is subject to strict notice obligations.

V.   General

12:42. Veterans administration security breach and data security regulations

In light of a well publicized security breach involving the Department of Veterans Affairs, the federal government had little choice but to act to place new security requirements on the department. The Department of Veterans Affairs Information Security Act, which was was signed by President Bush in 2006, places additional security training requirements, information security requirements, as well as notice of certain forms of security breaches to Congress.[123] The law also places certain requirements on the Secretary of Veterans Affairs to ensure that these requirements are met.[124]

In the event of a security breach involving "sensitive personal information," there must be an independent risk analysis of the data breach to assess the potential for misuse and, if there is a reasonable risk, the department must offer credit protection services, as provided by regulations that are to be adopted by the secretary.[125] Additionally, there are additional security requirements that must be placed in contracts that involve sensitive personal information.[126]

---

122. Full details regarding the requirements can be found at https://www.cms.gov/informationsecurity/down-loads/incident_handling_procedure.pdf (last visited May 12, 2011).

123. 38 U.S.C. §§ 5721 *et seq.*

124. *Id.*

125. 38 U.S.C. § 5724.

126. 38 U.S.C. § 5725.

Chapter 13

Constitutional and Statutory Issues— Privacy Rights and Restrictions

13:1.   Introduction

Privacy statutes are not a new phenomenon, although the specificity and number of new statutes is a creature of recent times. However, many states have already placed broad privacy protections in statutes and, in some cases, the state constitutions. A selection of these state laws and constitutional rights are covered in this chapter, as is the federal Video Voyeur Act. Also, certain restrictions upon privacy are also covered. As is obvious from the divergent interpretations and statutory burdens and rights, privacy in many cases is still a state-by-state analysis, and certain states, in addition to those identified below, have found implicit privacy rights in their constitutions.

I. Federal Provisions

13:2. Fourth Amendment and privacy

The Fourth Amendment to the Constitution has received interesting treatment from the courts in connection with privacy issues. It states:

> The right of the people to be secure in their persons, houses, papers, and effects, against unreasonable searches and seizures, shall not be violated, and no warrants shall issue, but upon probable cause, supported by oath or affirmation, and particularly describing the place to be searched, and the persons or things to be seized.[1]

The Fourth Amendment has typically been viewed as limited privacy protection, tied to more general protections against improper gathering of specific, tangible items, though courts recently seem to be framing Fourth Amendment issues in the context of broader privacy concerns.[2] While the existence of constitutional of privacy is not questioned by courts, it is also clear that government interference with privacy rights is proper if permitted by the Constitution.[3]

> The ultimate question, therefore, is whether one's claim to privacy from government intrusion is reasonable in light of all the surrounding circumstances ... In considering the reasonableness of asserted privacy expectations, the Court has recognized that no single factor invariably will be determinative. Thus, the Court has examined whether a person invoking the protection of the Fourth Amendment took normal precautions to maintain his privacy—that is, precautions customarily taken by those seeking privacy. Similarly, the Court has looked to the way a person has used a location, to determine whether the Fourth Amendment should protect his expectations of privacy ... The Court on occasion also has looked to history to discern whether certain types of government intrusion were perceived to be objectionable by the Framers of the Fourth Amendment. And, as the Court states today, property rights reflect society's explicit recognition of a person's authority to act as he wishes in certain areas, and therefore should be considered in determining whether an individual's expectations of privacy are reasonable.[4]

---

1. U.S. Const. amend. IV.
2. Katz v. U.S., 389 U.S. 347, 350, 88 S. Ct. 507, 19 L. Ed. 2d 576 (1967) ("Secondly, the Fourth Amendment cannot be translated into a general constitutional 'right to privacy.' That Amendment protects individual privacy against certain kinds of governmental intrusion, but its protections go further and often have nothing to do with privacy at all. Other provisions of the Constitution protect personal privacy from other forms of governmental invasion.").
3. Katz v. U.S., 389 U.S. at 351, fn. 5 ("Virtually every governmental action interferes with personal privacy to some degree. The question in each case is whether that interference violates a command of the United States Constitution.").
4. Raskas v. Illinois, 439 U.S. 128, 152-153 (1978) (citations omitted).

In applying this standard, courts have found certain disclosures to be inconsistent with a reasonable expectation of privacy, including with bank and other records.[5] This is also true in connection with records related to Internet subscription information,[6] as well as information that is displayed on the Internet.[7]

One issue that has surfaced in the privacy realm related to searches is a doctrine that permits government to search areas that were already searched by private citizens.[8] In the Internet context, this doctrine has been used to justify searches of otherwise protected areas on the Internet. This can result from a person's giving a password to a third party, thus defeating a claim of a reasonable expectation of privacy, or because the expectation of privacy can effectively be destroyed by a private search.[9]

13:3.   The *Leon* warrant exception and wiretap warrants

There is a good faith exception to the general warrant requirement, which resulted from the Supreme Court's holding in *United States v. Leon*.[10] While this exception was created by the Courts to address issues under the Fourth Amendment, it is not explicitly referenced in the ECPA, which has its own warrant requirements, which set exclusion from evidence as the consequence of the violation of the ECPA's warrant requirement.[11] The Seventh, Eighth and Eleventh Circuits have previously held that the *Leon* good faith exception applies to warrants under the ECPA.[12] However, the Sixth Circuit recently reached a different conclusion, relying upon the express text of § 2515, finding there is no good faith exception to the warrant requirement in the ECPA and therefore excluding the evidence at issue in that case.[13]

13:4.   Cell phone privacy and third parties

Absent some unique facts under the Fourth Amendment, someone who is not a subscriber may not have standing to challenge a government search on privacy grounds.[14]

---

5.   Smith v. Maryland, 442 U.S. 735 (1979) (no reasonable expectation of privacy in the telephone numbers dialed by a telephone subscriber); United States v. Payner, 447 U.S. 727, 731-32 (1980) (same for records given to a bank officer); United States v. Miller, 425 U.S. 435 (1976); *see also* United States v. White, 401 U.S. 745 (1971) (no expectation of privacy in confidences exchanged in a private conversation).

6.   United States v. Cox, 190 F. Supp. 2d 330, 332 (N.D.N.Y. 2002).

7.   United States v. Gines-Perez, 214 F. Supp. 2d 205, 225 (D.P.R. 2002) ("[I]t strikes the Court as obvious that a claim to privacy is unavailable to someone who places information on an indisputably, public medium, such as the Internet, without taking any measures to protect the information.").

8.   United States v. D'Andrea, 497 F. Supp. 2d 117 (D. Mass. 2007), *citing,* United States v. Jacobsen, 446 U.S. 109, 115 (1984) ("The additional invasions of [a defendant's] privacy by the Government agent must be tested by the degree to which they exceeded the scope of the private search.").

9.   U.S. v. D'Andrea, 497 F. Supp. 2d 117 (D. Mass. 2007); *see also,* United States v. Runyan, 275 F.3d 449, 464-465 (5th Cir. 2001); Paul v. State, 57 P.3d 702-03 (2002).

10.   United States v. Leon, 468 U.S. 897 (1984).

11.   18 U.S.C. § 2515, discussed in Section 5:31.

12.   *See* United States v. Wen, 477 F.3d 896 (7th Cir. 2006); United States v. Moore, 41 F.3d 370, 376 (8th Cir. 1994), *cert. denied,* 514 U.S. 1121 (1995); United States v. Malekzadeh, 855 F.2d 1492, 1497 (11th Cir. 1988), *cert. denied,* 489 U.S. 1024 (1989), 489 U.S. 1029 (1989).

13.   United States v. Rice, 478 F.3d 704 (6th Cir. 2007).

14.   Washington v. Clay, 145 Wash. App. 1040, 2008 WL 2721282 (Wash. App. Div. 1 2008).

13:5. Fourteenth Amendment and privacy

In addition to the Fourth Amendment, the Fourteenth Amendment also provides some privacy protection to individuals.[15] This protection includes a parent's right to try to limit, in certain circumstances, the disclosure of a child's name on the Internet.[16] The Fourteenth Amendment's privacy protection has also extended to certain financial information, as well as serving as the basis for other "fundamental" rights under the federal constitution.

An Ohio federal court assessed whether economic damage, particularly identity theft, was sufficient to support a constitutional claim for violation of an individual's privacy rights.[17] In *Lambert*, the plaintiff had her name and social security number posted on a state run Internet site after she received a speeding ticket. She was later the victim of identity theft, allegedly as a result of the posting, and sued alleging violations of her federal and state constitutional rights, as well as Ohio common law.[18] The court first analyzed the parameters of the existence of a constitutional right to privacy in the Sixth Circuit, noting that one will only be found when the interest at stake concerns "those personal rights that can be deemed 'fundamental' or 'implicit' in the concept of ordered liberty."[19] In sum, the court expressed the Sixth Circuit test as a two-step process for analyzing informational right-to-privacy claims: (1) the interest at stake must implicate either a fundamental right or one implicit in the concept of ordered liberty; and (2) the government's interest in disseminating the information must be balanced against the individual's interest in keeping the information private.[20]

Here the court concluded that because the only risk identified was that of financial harm, it did not meet the first test and therefore, the court rejected the plaintiff's argument that she had a constitutional right of privacy in her social security number.[21]

13:6. The Fifth Amendment and compelling disclosure of passwords

One issue that the district court in Vermont addressed was whether a criminal defendant could be compelled to provide the police a password that was necessary to access certain encrypted files on a laptop. The court concluded that compelling the defendant in this case to provide the password was akin to compelling him to produce a key to a locked container, which would admit the container was his and he had control over it, and the disclosure would therefore violate his right against self-incrimination.

---

15. *See* Whalen v. Roe, 429 U.S. 600 (1977); Barry v. New York, 712 F.2d 1554 (2nd Cir. 1983); Doe v. City of New York, 15 F.3d 264 (2nd Cir. 1994); Securities Industry and Financial Markets Ass'n v. Garfield, 469 F. Supp. 2d 25 (D. Conn. 2007).

16. Securities Industry and Financial Markets Ass'n v. Garfield, 469 F. Supp. 2d 25 (D. Conn. 2007).

17. Lambert v. Hartmann, 2006 WL 3833529 (S.D. Ohio 2006).

18. *Lambert*, 2006 WL 3833529 at *1.

19. Lambert v. Hartmann, 2006 WL 3833529 at *4 (S.D. Ohio 2006) (citing J.P. v. DeSanti, 653 F.2d 1080, 1090 (6th Cir. 1981)); Kallstrom v. City of Columbus, 136 F.3d 1055, 1061 (6th Cir. 1998).

20. *Lambert*, 2006 WL 3833529 at *4 (citing Bloch v. Ribar, 156 F.3d 673, 684 (6th Cir. 1998)); DeSanti, 653 F.2d at 1090-91.

21. *Lambert*, 2006 WL 3833529 at *2 (citing Lawson v. Baxter, 2006 WL 3004069, *2, n. 1 (W.D. Mich. October 20, 2006)); Pitts v. Perkins Local School Board, 2006 WL 1050675, *2 (N.D. Ohio 2006).

> Compelling Boucher to enter the password forces him to produce evidence that could be used to incriminate him. Producing the password, as if it were a key to a locked container, forces Boucher to produce the contents of his laptop ... Entering a password into the computer implicitly communicates facts. By entering the password Boucher would be disclosing the fact that he knows the password and has control over the files on drive Z. The procedure is equivalent to asking Boucher, 'Do you know the password to the laptop?' If Boucher does know the password, he would be faced with the forbidden trilemma; incriminate himself, lie under oath, or find himself in contempt of court.[22]

13:7.   Computer searches of home computers

Individuals generally have a reasonable expectation of privacy in their home computers.[23] However, this can be diminished by certain acts, particularly sending information to a third party, obviously limited to the information that was conveyed.[24] At the point of conveyance, typically upon receipt, the sender's privacy expectation is reduced in the information that was sent.[25]

These cases indicate the difficulty some courts have had with the permissible scope of computer searches. This is particularly true when the computers are not in the office setting, but rather in the home setting. Typically searches of a home can be accomplished without a warrant if consent is given by a person with actual, or apparent, authority to consent to the search.[26] A person has actual authority to consent to a search "if that third party has either (1) mutual use of the property by virtue of joint access, or (2) control for most purposes."[27] Apparent authority is a test that relies upon the totality-of-the circumstances that looks at whether the facts available to the officers would lead a reasonable officer to conclude that the third party had authority to consent to the search.[28] Other courts have held that easy physical access to a premises containing a computer can support a finding of apparent authority, even where actual authority does not exist.[29]

---

22. In re Boucher, 2007 WL 4246473 at *2 (D. Vt. 2007).

23. United States v. Lifshitz, 369 F.3d 173 (2nd Cir. 2004).

24. *See* Smith v. Maryland, 442 U.S. 735, 743-44 (1979); United States v. Miller, 425 U.S. 435 (1976); *see also* Guest v. Leis, 255 F.3d 325, 333 (6th Cir. 2001); *Lifshitz*, 369 F.3d at 190; United States v. Maxwell, 45 M.J. 406, 418 (C.A.A.F. 1996); United States v. King, 55 F.3d 1193, 1195-96 (privacy interest in letter terminates upon delivery); Minnesota v. Jacobs, 2007 WL 1121289 (Minn. Ct. App. April 17, 2007).

25. *Lifshitz*, 369 F.3d at 190.

26. *See, e.g.*, Illinois v. Rodriguez, 497 U.S. 177, 181 (1990); United States v. Rith, 164 F.3d 1323, 1328 (10th Cir. 1999); United States v. Matlock, 415 U.S. 164, 171 (1974).

27. *Rith*, 164 F.3d at 1329.

28. Rodriguez, 497 U.S. at 188; Georgia v. Randolph, 126 S. Ct. 1515, 1520 (2006); United States v. Andrus, 483 F.3d 711 (10th Cir. 2007), decision clarified on denial of reh'g, 499 F.3d 1162 (10th Cir. 2007) and cert. denied, 128 S. Ct. 1738, 170 L. Ed. 2d 542 (2008).

29. U.S. v. Sager, 2008 WL 45358 (N.D. Ind. 2008).

This test also, according to recent Supreme Court guidance, requires an inquiry into societal expectations.[30] Thus, searches of certain areas, despite a stated consent by a third-party, may be unreasonable as a matter of law, given their private nature.

Examples of such areas can include suitcases, footlockers, strongboxes, and other locked areas.[31] Home computers present a difficult scenario for some courts as they have struggled with whether they are more like the traditionally private areas that cannot be searched with apparent authority, analogizing them, particularly where password protection is present, to locked storage.[32] In one of the more colorful discussions of the issue, one Ninth Circuit justice offered the following:

> [F]or most people, their computers are their most private spaces. People commonly talk about the bedroom as a very private space, yet when they have parties, all the guests—including perfect strangers—are invited to toss their coats on the bed. But if one of those guests is caught exploring the host's computer, that will be his last invitation.[33]

Recently, the Tenth Circuit addressed this issue in a slightly unusual context. While upholding a search of a computer based upon apparent authority, the majority seemed to indicate issues that could exist in future cases. In *Andrus*, the police searched an individual's computer based upon the consent of the suspect's father, who owned the house in which the suspect lived. While the father indisputably did not have actual authority to authorize the search, the court of appeal held that he had apparent authority to authorize the search, including because he paid the Internet access bill, among other factors.[34] However, the issue that the court seemed to want to address, but felt it could not, was the role of password protection. The defendant offered no evidence regarding the prevalence of password protection, and so the majority felt that it could not address the password issue, though it clearly felt that it could be a determinative issue.[35] It was particularly troubled because the forensic examiners employed by law enforcement typically use a program, EnCase, which bypasses password protection, to gather evidence.

Given that the court could not address the password issue, it focused instead on other cases that examined the location of the computer in the house, whether multiple parties had access to the computer, or if the person who is asked to consent to the search has disclaimed control or ownership of the computer.[36] This case ultimately upheld the

---

30. Randolph, 126 S. Ct. at 1522 ("The constant element in assessing Fourth Amendment reasonableness in consent cases ... is the great significance given to widely shared societal expectations.").

31. United States v. Block, 590 F.2d 535, 541 (4th Cir. 1978); United States v. Salinas-Cano, 959 F.2d 861, 865 (10th Cir. 1992).

32. *Andrus*, 483 F.3d 711 (citing Trulock v. Freeh, 275 F.3d 391, 403 (4th Cir. 2001)); U.S. v. Aaron, 33 Fed. Appx. 180, 184 (6th Cir. 2002).

33. United States v. Gourde, 40 F.3d 1065, 1077 (9th Cir. 2006) (*en banc*) (Kleinfeld, J. dissenting).

34. U.S. v. Andrus, 483 F.3d 711 (10th Cir. 2007).

35. *Andrus*, 483 F.3d 711.

36. *Andrus*, 483 F.3d 711 (citing United States v. Buckner, 472 F.3d 551, 555-56 (4th Cir. 2007); United States v. Morgan, 435 F.3d 660, 663 (6th Cir. 2006); United States v. Smith, 27 F. Supp. 2d 1111, 1116 (C.D. Ill. 1998)).

search in this case, apparently in part because the defendant had waived the password protection argument, but it may signal issues for law enforcement, especially where EnCase is used, if the files are password protected.[37]

13:8.   Fourth Amendment and an "untimely" search of a computer

In an issue of first impression, a court in Washington did not suppress evidence found on a computer seized within the timeframe of the warrant, though the evidence was gathered after the return date on the warrant through a continuing forensic examination. The court found that there was no prejudice to the defendant and the time was not unreasonable.[38]

13:9.   Providing a computer to a third-party for repairs as a waiver of privacy

In an issue that appears to be one of first impression—though it will likely recur—a court in Texas held that a person waives any privacy rights under the Fourth Amendment in a computer if he leaves private information on a computer that is submitted for repairs.[39]

13:10. Peer-to-peer and privacy

At least one court in the Central District of California has noted that the opening of a computer to a peer-to-peer network may have implications for privacy on the computer, including what may appear to be a waiver of privacy rights.[40] In particular, courts have held that utilizing file sharing in a way that opens up a computer to the Internet can defeat a reasonable expectation of privacy in the computer's contents, as well as subscriber information.[41] Another court addressed the impact on a defendant's expectation of privacy when peer-to-peer software is used on a computer.[42] Like other courts, the court in *Borowy*, concluded that the use of peer-to-peer software defeated an expectation of privacy in the files that are exposed on the Internet.[43]

---

37.   *Andrus*, 483 F.3d 711., fns. 6, 8.

38.   State v. Grenning, 142 Wash. App. 518, 174 P.3d 706 (2008).

39.   Signorelli v. State, 2007 WL 4723210 (Tex. App.-Beaumont 2008).

40.   Columbia Pictures, Inc. v. Bunnell, 245 F.R.D. 443, 69 Fed. R. Serv. 3d 173 (C.D. Cal. 2007) (citing In re Verizon Internet Servs., 257 F. Supp. 2d 244, 267 (D. D.C. 2003) (stating "if an individual subscriber opens his computer to permit others, through peer-to-peer file-sharing, to download materials from that computer, it is hard to understand just what privacy expectation he or she has after essentially opening the computer to the world."), rev'd, 351 F.3d 1229 (D.C. Cir. 2003).

41.   U.S. v. Kennedy, 81 F. Supp. 2d 1103 (D. Kan. 2000).

42.   United States v. Borowy, 577 F. Supp. 2d 1133 (D. Nev. 2008).

43.   *Id.* ("In this case, Borowy did not have a legitimate expectation of privacy in files he made available to others using P2P software. First, it is not apparent that Borowy had a subjective expectation of privacy in these files ... Second, even assuming Borowy had a subjective expectation of privacy, his expectation was objectively unreasonable.") (citing United States v. Perrine, 518 F.3d 1196, 1205 (10th Cir. 2008)).

13:11. Computer searches and special needs exceptions to the warrant requirement

Even where no warrant is obtained, and a party has a reasonable expectation of privacy, searches of computers can still occur. One such scenario is under the "special needs" exception, which permits warrantless searches where "... 'special needs', beyond the normal need for law enforcement, make the warrant and probable-cause requirement impracticable.'"[44] In computer cases, where the integrity of a network or e-mail system are implicated, special needs have been found to exist, thus obviating the need for a warrant in certain circumstances, particularly if the target has a history of network intrusions.[45]

13:12. Warrantless search of computers of probationers

One court recently addressed the propriety of the warrantless search of a probationer's computer. The Sixth Circuit rejected the application of the *Griffin* special needs test in the case, because it concluded there was no basis to find the government implemented a procedure that required reasonable suspicion, an element of the *Griffin* test.[46] However, the Sixth Circuit did not invalidate the search and instead found it proper under the totality of the circumstances test expressed in *United States v. Knights*[47] if the search was reasonable.[48] In this case, the court concluded the search was reasonable because the probationer's terms of release included the right of the government to check his computer for Internet connectivity.

13:13. Seizure of information beyond a warrant

In *United States v. Comprehensive Drug Testing, Inc.*, the government issued both subpoenas and search warrants for the test results of a small subset of players that were allegedly implicated in steroid use.[49] The warrants were served and the government received, as part of that response, information regarding testing results of a number of other players. One of the objections raised by the players' association was that the large-scale removal of information, including other test results, was improper. Applying *Tamura*, the Ninth Circuit in its initial opinion concluded the gathering of information that included other non-responsive information was not improper.[50]

However, this decision was heard *en banc* and the Ninth Circuit reversed the ruling, in part. Of particular concern was the government's use of the plain view doctrine, or

---

44. United States v. Heckenkamp, 482 F.3d 1142 (9th Cir. 2007) (citing New Jersey v. T.L.O., 469 U.S. 325, 351 (1985); Griffin v. Wisconsin, 483 U.S. 868, 873 (1987)).

45. Heckenkamp, 482 F.3d 1142.

46. The "special needs" exception permitting search of a probationer's home is set forth in Griffin v. Wisconsin, 483 U.S. 868, 873 (1987).

47. United States v. Knights, 534 U.S. 112 (2001).

48. United States v. Herndon, 501 F.3d 683 (6th Cir. 2007).

49. United States v. Comprehensive Drug Testing, 473 F.3d 915 (9th Cir. 2006), opinion withdrawn and super-seded on reh'g, 513 F.3d 1085, 69 Fed. R. Serv. 3d 1365 (9th Cir. 2008), reh'g en banc granted, 545 F.3d 1106 (9th Cir. 2008).

50. *Comprehensive Drug Testing*, 473 F.3d 915 (citing United States v. Tamura, 694 F.2d 591 (9th Cir. 1982)).

other similar doctrines, to justify the seizure of computerized information beyond the seizable information the government was entitled to obtain. If the government did not agree to this then the Ninth Circuit stated that the court should require a third-party to segregate the seizable and non-seizable information, or deny the warrant. The Ninth Circuit also laid out a framework, and made other statements regarding the necessary disclosures regarding the risks of concealment and destruction of evidence.

13:14. Reasonable expectation of privacy and false identities

One issue courts have addressed is whether a person can have a reasonable expectation of privacy when a person uses a pseudonym. While generally a person can have a reasonable expectation of privacy using a pseudonym, a person that fraudulently uses someone else's identity does not have a reasonable expectation of privacy.[51]

13:15. Requests for identification of online book purchasers

In a recent case involving Amazon.com, a federal grand jury sought information regarding a bookseller related to an investigation for tax evasion and wire fraud by the seller.[52] While the customers were not the target of the investigation, the government sought information related to purchases of books by the seller's clients.[53] Amazon provided certain information to the government, but citing First Amendment concerns, refused to identify the customers.[54] The government and Amazon.com sought to resolve the dispute via an agreed-upon mechanism which would have disclosed certain information, but were unable to do so. The court rejected the proposed methodology and did not compel disclosure of the information, but rather it put in place a system that permitted individual customers to volunteer to come forward.[55]

13:16. Discovery of e-mail addresses

The Ninth Circuit recently addressed an issue of first impression regarding e-mail addresses—whether a warrant was required before the government could discover a list of e-mail addresses mailed by a defendant, as well as the volume of bytes mailed. The Ninth Circuit concluded that a list of e-mail addresses was comparable to discovery of phone numbers called and gathered via a pen register, and therefore the government

---

51. United States v. Villarreal, 963 F.2d 770, 774 (5th Cir. 1992); United States v. Johnson, Slip Op. 08-4031 (10th Cir. 2009).

52. In re Grand Jury Subpoena to Amazon.com Dated August 7, 2006, 246 F.R.D. 570, 2007 WL 4197490 (W.D. Wis. 2007).

53. Id.

54. Id.

55. In re Grand Jury Subpoena to Amazon.com Dated August 7, 2006, 246 F.R.D. 570, 574 (W.D. Wis. 2007) ("Nonetheless, I have concluded that at this juncture (and perhaps at every juncture), the government is not entitled to unfettered access to the identities of even a small sample of this group of book buyers without each book buyer's permission. Everyone involved in this dispute agrees that the book buyers have done nothing wrong and face no direct scrutiny; accordingly, they should not be put unnecessarily to the embarrassment of an unsolicited FBI interview that might specifically deter them from future recorded book purchases or generally deter others who learn of this investigation.").

could obtain the list of e-mail addresses without a warrant.[56] The court analogized this situation also to cases that permitted the government to review the addresses of letters that were sent via U.S. Mail, though the contents of the sealed letters or e-mails could not be reviewed as part of this discovery.[57]

13:17. IP addresses and expectations of privacy

The court in the Southern District of California recently found that subscribers do not have a reasonable expectation of privacy in IP login histories and IP addressing information.[58]

13:18. Warrants and videotaping

Many courts have held that warrants to conduct video surveillance must meet the higher standards of Title I of the ECPA, though ultimately this is a constitutional question because the ECPA does not expressly cover videotaping.[59] The standards imposed by certain courts, including by the *Cuevas-Sanchez* court were as follows:

- the judge issuing the warrant must find that normal investigative procedures have been tried and have failed or reasonably appear to be unlikely to succeed if tried or to be too dangerous;

- the warrant must contain a particular description of the type of communication sought to be intercepted, and a statement of the particular offense to which it relates;

- the warrant must not allow the period of interception to be longer than is necessary to achieve the objective of the authorization, or in any event longer than thirty days (though extensions are possible); and

- the warrant must require that the interception "be conducted in such a way as to minimize the interception of communications not otherwise subject to interception under [Title III].[60]

---

56. United States v. Forrester, 495 F.3d 1041 (9th Cir. 2007), opinion amended and superseded on denial of reh'g, 512 F.3d 500 (9th Cir. 2008), cert. denied, 129 S. Ct. 249, 172 L. Ed. 2d 188 (2008).

57. *See* United States v. Jacobsen, 466 U.S. 109 (1984); United States v. Van Leeuwen, 397 U.S. 249 (1970); Ex parte Jackson, 96 U.S. 727 (1877); United States v. Hernandez, 313 F.3d 1206 (9th Cir. 2002).

58. United States v. Li, 2008 WL 789899 (S.D. Cal. 2008). It should be noted that this decision relied upon the prior version of *Forrester*.

59. *See, e.g.,* United States v. Cuevas-Sanchez, 821 F.2d 248, 251-52 (5th Cir. 1987) ("Because Title III does not include video surveillance techniques, we must decide what standards should guide a court in issuing these orders; whether to adopt its technical requirements verbatim or to use Title III as a guide for the constitutional standard. The Second and Seventh Circuits have chosen the latter path. These two Courts considered a court's power to issue warrants and the constitutional standards governing valid warrants in all cases. They then borrowed the provisions in Title III that implement those constitutional standards for application in the context of video surveillance.") (citations omitted); citing United States v. Biasucci, 786 F.2d 504, 510 (2nd Cir.), *cert. denied,* 479 U.S. 827, 107 S. Ct. 104, 93 L. Ed. 2d 54 (1986).

60. Cuevas-Sanchez, 821 F.2d at 252. (Internal citations and punctuation omitted).

13:19. Federal regulations of personnel records

The federal government has specific regulations regarding the use, maintenance and security of personnel records[61] it maintains. This includes regulations regarding the collection and use of information, safeguarding information, including additional restrictions on automated records; disposition of records; and retention and disclosure of records.[62]

13:20. Federal Video Voyeur Act

It is illegal for a person to knowingly and with intent capture[63] an image of a private area of an individual[64] without their consent, under circumstances in which the individual has a reasonable expectation of privacy.[65] This crime is punishable by a fine, a prison term of not more than 1 year, or both.[66]

13:21. Videotaping

Other courts have examined the issue of spouses secretly videotaping each other.[67] Most cases, not surprisingly, hold that this type of activity violates privacy rights, though courts do recognize that there are some diminished expectations of privacy in shared spaces.

13:22. Searches due to terrorist concerns on public transportation

Concerns over national security and terrorist incidents in the United States have led to a number of more structured search regimes being used on public transportation. While courts have recognized that passengers may have a legitimate expectation of

---

61. "Personnel record" means any record concerning an individual that is maintained and used in the personnel management or personnel policy setting process. (For purposes of this part, this term is not limited just to those personnel records in a system of records and subject to the Privacy Act). 5 C.F.R. § 293.102.

62. 5 C.F.R. §§ 293.101 to 293.509.

63. The term "capture," with respect to an image, means to videotape, photograph, film, record by any means, or broadcast. 18 U.S.C. § 1801(b)(1). The term "broadcast" means to electronically transmit a visual image with the intent that it be viewed by a person or persons. 18 U.S.C. § 1801(b)(2).

64. The term "a private area of the individual" means the naked or undergarment clad genitals, pubic area, buttocks, or female breast of that individual. 18 U.S.C. § 1801(b)(3). The term "female breast" means any portion of the female breast below the top of the areola. 18 U.S.C. § 1801(b)(4).

65. The term "under circumstances in which that individual has a reasonable expectation of privacy" means: (A) circumstances in which a reasonable person would believe that he or she could disrobe in privacy, without being concerned that an image of a private area of the individual was being captured; or (B) circumstances in which a reasonable person would believe that a private area of the individual would not be visible to the public, regardless of whether that person is in a public or private place. 18 U.S.C. § 1801(b)(5); 18 U.S.C. § 1801(a).

66. 18 U.S.C. § 1801(a).

67. Miller v. Brooks, 472 S.E.2d 350 (N.C. Ct. App. 1996); In re Marriage of Tigges, 758 N.W.2d 824 (Iowa 2008); Clayton v. Richards, 47 S.W.3d 149 (Tex. App. 2001).

privacy in their bags or persons, these searches have generally been upheld, typically under the "special needs" doctrine.[68]

13:23. Border searches generally

Searches at the borders are typically considered to raise lesser constitutional issues than normal searches—indeed these searches do not require probable cause or a warrant, or even a reasonable suspicion.[69] However, there are also extended border searches that can also occur without a warrant, but these require a slightly higher showing. These cases typically require a showing that an individual crossed a border; law enforcement seized the person sufficiently soon after the crossing to be reasonably confident that the condition of the person did not change; and there was a reasonable suspicion that the individual violated a criminal law.[70]

A very good summary of the law of border searches was recently provided by the Sixth Circuit in an unpublished decision:

> Two accepted applications of the guarantee frame today's dispute. At one extreme: police officers may not seize individuals minding their own business on a public street and search their belongings without probable cause and a warrant—or at least reasonable suspicion under some circumstances. At the other extreme: customs officials may stop and search individuals and their luggage before they board any airplane or when they enter the country by air without a warrant and without reasonable suspicion or probable cause. Border searches "are reasonable simply by virtue of the fact that they occur at the border," where the sovereign has a right to "regulate the collection of duties and to prevent the introduction of contraband into this country[.]" Between the extremes: while the ban on "unreasonable searches and seizures" gives law enforcement more latitude to search and seize travelers (and their luggage) as they board airplanes and as they enter the country by air, it still has force within an airport. Law enforcement may not search people and their luggage simply because they happen to be in an airport. And even when law enforcement has a legitimate ground for searching an individual or her suitcase, the length and manner of the detention still may violate the Fourth Amendment.[71]

---

68.   Cassidy v. Chertoff, 471 F.3d 67 (2nd Cir. 2006); MacWade v. Kelly, 460 F.3d 260 (2nd Cir. 2006).

69.   United States v. Montoya de Hernandez, 473 U.S. 531, 538 (1985); United States v. Ramsey, 431 U.S. 606, 616 (1977); United States v. Flores-Montano, 541 U.S. 149, 152-53 (2004).

70.   United States v. Yang, 286 F.3d 940, 949 (7th Cir. 2002); United States v. Cardenas, 9 F.3d 1139, 1153 (5th Cir. 1993); United States v. McGinnis, 2007 WL 2617171 (6th Cir. 2007).

71.   United States v. McGinnis, 2007 WL 2617171, at *4 (6th Cir. 2007).

13:24. Searches of computers at borders

Generally the government is permitted to conduct routine searches of people that are entering the United States without probable cause, reasonable suspicion, or a warrant.[72] This has been held to include review of a laptop computer.[73] However, other courts have found searches of this scope to be improper.[74]

In *U.S. v. Arnold*, the court examined the appropriate scope of a search of a computer when the government had no reasonable suspicion to support the search.[75] The defendant in this case argued that laptop computers were unlike other "closed containers" and more akin to homes or a person's mind.[76] The Ninth Circuit revised the district court's ruling that reasonable suspicion was required to search a laptop or other personal electronic storage devices at the border.[77] An important factor in this decision appeared to be the portability of the device, as opposed to home computers, which are not portable. The Ninth Circuit recently reheard this case *en banc* and permitted a border search of a computer without requiring particularized suspicion.[78] The court relied, in part, on cases that permit searches of briefcases, luggage, "purse, wallet, or pockets" and papers found in containers.[79]

The U.S. Immigration and Customs Enforcement issued directive 7-6.0 on Border Searches of Documents and Electronic Media, effective July 16, 2008, which sets forth additional information regarding the policies and procedures regarding border searches.

---

72. *See* United States v. Romm, 455 F.3d 990, 996 (9th Cir. 2006); *citing* United States v. Montoya de Hernandez, 473 U.S. 531, 538 (1985).

73. United States v. Romm, 455 F.3d 990, 996 (9th Cir. 2006).

74. United States v. Arnold, 454 F. Supp. 2d 999 (C.D. Cal. 2006), as amended on denial of reh'g and reh'g en banc, 533 F.3d 1003 (9th Cir. 2008), cert. denied, 2009 WL 425169 (U.S. 2009).

75. United States v. Arnold, 523 F.3d 941 (9th Cir. 2008).

76. U.S. v. Arnold, 523 F.3d 941 (9th Cir. 2008), as amended on denial of reh'g and reh'g en banc, 533 F.3d 1003 (9th Cir. 2008), cert. denied, 2009 WL 425169 (U.S. 2009).

77. U.S. v. Arnold, 523 F.3d 941 (9th Cir. 2008).

78. U.S. v. Arnold, 533 F.3d 1003 (9th Cir. 2008).

79. United States v. Tsai, 282 F.3d 690, 696 (9th Cir. 2002); Henderson v. United States, 390 F.2d 805, 808 (9th Cir. 1967); United States v. Grayson, 597 F.2d 1225, 1228-29 (9th Cir. 1979).

CHAPTER 14

Health Information and Privacy and Security

I. Introduction

14:1.   Importance of health privacy

Health information is among the most sensitive and private information available regarding a person. As such, there are a number of laws at both the state and federal level, which protect health information. The protections that are available can vary significantly. Most obviously, while many states recognize the doctor-patient privilege, this does not exist under federal law.[1] Many states have in fact regulated health privacy in a much more restrictive way than HIPAA. State law is also important to consider. Many states have gone beyond the restrictions of HIPAA and have passed legislation regarding HIV status, medical marketing, and even data security. A selection of the

---

1.   Taylor v. Dean, 2006 WL 4756452 (M.D. Fla. 2006).

more burdensome laws is discussed in this chapter. Not surprisingly, California does lead the way in this area, having passed a number of laws, though recent amendments have expanded healthcare providers' ability to disclose certain information. Other states have regulated pharmacy disclosures in unique ways, and some of those laws are also discussed below. In the wrongful disclosure of medical records context, certain state courts have also held that certain forms of negligence can support a finding of punitive damages.[2]

14:2.   Restrictions on disclosure—prescription drug information

Certain states have enacted restrictions on the disclosure of physicians' prescribing habits in a stated attempt to control prescription drug costs. Initially, these laws faced serious, successful legal challenges. Recently, the First Circuit Court of Appeals addressed these issues in *IMS Health, Inc. v. Ayotte*.[3] In this case, certain organizations challenged the New Hampshire law that restricted the disclosure of physicians prescribing histories for use in detailing. While the laws face challenges based upon the fact they reportedly restricted speech, the First Circuit did not accept this at face value and, in fact, concluded that the challenged portions of the law regulate conduct not speech. The court also concluded that even assuming speech was regulated and therefore First Amendment issues were present, the law passed constitutional scrutiny and therefore did not violate the First Amendment. This was true, though the court noted that even informational data could be considered speech.[4]

The court concluded that the law regulated conduct, not speech, because what the law truly restricted, in view of the First Circuit, was the data miners' ability to aggregate, compile, and transfer information for narrowly defined commercial ends. The court rejected this argument.

In assessing the First Amendment issues, the court noted that the plaintiffs in the case, the data miners, lack standing to assert the rights of the pharmaceutical companies, the detailers, or the physicians themselves based upon the law. Thus, it is possible that the court could reach a different conclusion depending upon the plaintiff at issue.

---

2.   Randi A.J. v. Long Island Surgi-Center, 842 N.Y.S. 2d 558 (N.Y. A.D. 2 Dept., 2007) ("In other contexts, however, it is well-settled that conduct warranting an award of punitive damages 'need not be intentionally harmful but may consist of actions which constitute willful or wanton negligence or recklessness.' ... We decline to hold, as our dissenting colleagues apparently would, that only conduct done with evil motive or in bad faith warrants deterrence through punitive damages. Courts in this state have long recognized that those who, without specifically intending to cause harm, nevertheless engage in grossly negligent or reckless conduct showing an utter disregard for the safety or rights of others, may also be deserving of the imposition of punitive damages.") (citations omitted).

3.   IMS Health, Inc. v. Ayotte, 550 F.3d 42 (1st Cir. 2008).

4.   *Id.* (citing Universal City Studios, Inc. v. Corley, 273 F.3d 429, 446-47 (2d Cir. 2001) ("Even dry information, devoid of advocacy, political relevance or artistic expression, has been accorded First Amendment protection.")); *see also* Va. Vd. of Pharm. v. Va. Citizen's Consumer Council, Inc., 425 U.S. 748, 770 (1976).

II. Health Insurance Portability and Accountability Act

A. *In general*

14:3. Background

The Health Insurance Portability and Accountability Act (HIPAA) arose ironically not from concerns over privacy, but as part of the national debate over national health care. There was a need to increase the efficiency of information sharing if healthcare reform was going to be a possibility. While the law has significant privacy implications, it was not a law directed exclusively at privacy. Indeed, many inexperienced practitioners refer to this law as "HIPPA," thinking privacy somehow made its way into the title of the law.

HIPAA was, for several years, the focus of extensive compliance programs, particularly in the healthcare field. While HIPAA still remains an issue, and compliance must be monitored, the mystery surrounding HIPAA seems to be dissipating.

Litigation under HIPAA has been scarce. While certain individuals have tried to bring private claims for violations of HIPAA, courts have consistently held that no private right of action exists under this law. Thus, enforcement is largely left to the government agencies that have jurisdiction under HIPAA.

14:4. Overview of Act

The Health Insurance Portability and Accountability Act (HIPAA) governs the use and disclosure of protected health information through the imposition of privacy, security, and reporting requirements, as well as marketing restrictions.

Protected health information is "individually identifiable health information" that is not contained in education or employment records[5] and includes any information that is written, oral, or transmitted by or stored in electronic media.[6] Individually identifiable information is defined as information that is a subset of health information, including demographic information collected from an individual that

---

5.   45 C.F.R. § 160.103.

6.   *Id.*

(1) is created or received by a health care provider,[7] health plan,[8] employer, or health care clearinghouse;[9] and

(2) relates to the past, present, or future mental health or condition of an individual; the provision of health care to an individual; or the past, present, or future payment for the provision of the health care to an individual; and

(3) identifies the individual or with respect to which there is a reasonable basis to believe the information can be used to identify the individual.[10]

14:5. Inapplicability to employers

The definition of PHI specifically excludes information stored in employment records, so HIPAA is generally inapplicable to employers.

---

7.   The term "health care provider" includes a provider of services (as defined in section 1861(u) [42 U.S.C. § 1395x(u)]), a provider of medical or other health services (as defined in section 1861(s) [42 U.S.C. § 1395x(s)]), and any other person furnishing health care services or supplies. 45 C.F.R. § 160.013.

8.   The term "health plan" means an individual or group plan that provides, or pays the cost of, medical care (as such term is defined in section 2791 of the Public Health Service Act [42 U.S.C. § 300gg-91]). Such term includes the following, and any combination thereof:

    (A) A group health plan (as defined in section 3(1) of ERISA, 29 U.S.C. § 1002(l)), but only if the plan—(i) has 50 or more participants (as defined in section 3(7) of the Employee Retirement Income Security Act of 1974 [29 U.S.C. § 1002(7)]); or (ii) is administered by an entity other than the employer who established and maintains the plan.

    (B) A health insurance issuer (as defined in section 2791(b) of the Public Health Service Act [42 U.S.C. § 300gg-91(b)]).

    (C) A health maintenance organization (as defined in section 2791(b) of the Public Health Service Act [42 U.S.C. § 300gg-91(b)]).

    (D) Parts A, B, or C of the Medicare program under title XVIII [42 U.S.C. §§ 1395c *et seq.*, 1395j *et seq.* or 1395w-21 *et seq.*].

    (E) The Medicaid program under title XIX [42 U.S.C. §§ 1396 *et seq.*].

    (F) A Medicare supplemental policy (as defined in section 1882(g)(1) [42 U.S.C. § 1395ss(g)(1)]).

    (G) A long-term care policy, including a nursing home fixed indemnity policy (unless the secretary determines that such a policy does not provide sufficiently comprehensive coverage of a benefit so that the policy should be treated as a health plan).

    (H) An employee welfare benefit plan or any other arrangement which is established or maintained for the purpose of offering or providing health benefits to the employees of 2 or more employers.

    (I) The health care program for active military personnel under title 10, United States Code.

    (J) The veterans health care program under chapter 17 of title 38, United States Code [38 U.S.C. §§ 1701 *et seq.*].

    (K) The Civilian Health and Medical Program of the Uniformed Services (CHAMPUS), as defined in section 1072(4) of title 10, United States Code.

    (L) The Indian health service program under the Indian Health Care Improvement Act (25 U.S.C. §§ 1601 *et seq.*).

    (M) The Federal Employees Health Benefit Plan under chapter 89 of title 5, United States Code [5 U.S.C. §§ 8901 *et seq.*]. 42 U.S.C. § 1320(d)(5).

9.   The term "health care clearinghouse" means a public or private entity that processes or facilitates the processing of nonstandard data elements of health information into standard data elements. 45 C.F.R. § 160.103.

10.   45 C.F.R. § 160.103.

14:6.   Privacy and security requirements

There are a number of privacy and security[11] requirements in HIPAA. These rules are discussed in full below. It should be noted that the rules regarding privacy and security under HIPAA apply to health plans and health care clearinghouses (including as a business associate), as well as to health care providers who transmit health information in electronic form in connection with a covered transaction[12].[13] It should also be noted that certain entities can be hybrids or may be components of a covered entity. There are specific guidelines regarding the application of the security and privacy rules to these entities.[14]

14:7.   New statutory requirements under ARRA

There were a number of new statutory requirements, as well as new regulations created under new rulemaking authority, as a result of the ARRA. The new statutory requirements are discussed first, with the new regulations discussed later in the chapter.

On February 17, 2009, President Barack Obama signed into law the American Recovery and Reinvestment Act of 2009 (ARRA) (commonly referred to as the Federal Stimulus Package), which contained the provisions of the Health Information Technology for Economic and Clinical Health Act (HITECH Act).

The HITECH Act affects covered entities and business associates[15] alike, as well as vendors of personal health records and health information exchange organizations.

---

11.   "Security" or "Security measures" encompass all of the administrative, physical, and technical safeguards in an information system. 45 C.F.R. 164.304.

12.   "Transaction" means the transmission of information between two parties to carry out financial or administrative activities related to health care. It includes the following types of information transmissions: (1) Health care claims or equivalent encounter information. (2) Health care payment and remittance advice. (3) Coordination of benefits. (4) Health care claim status. (5) Enrollment and disenrollment in a health plan. (6) Eligibility for a health plan. (7) Health plan premium payments. (8) Referral certification and authorization. (9) First report of injury. (10) Health claims attachments. (11) Other transactions that the secretary may prescribe by regulation. 45 C.F.R. § 160.103.

13.   45 C.F.R. § 164.101.

14.   45 C.F.R. § 164.105.

15.   Business associate: (1) Except as provided in paragraph (2) of this definition, business associate means, with respect to a covered entity, a person who: (i) On behalf of such covered entity or of an organized health care arrangement (as defined in § 164.501 of this subchapter) in which the covered entity participates, but other than in the capacity of a member of the workforce of such covered entity or arrangement, performs, or assists in the performance of: (A) A function or activity involving the use or disclosure of individually identifiable health information, including claims processing or administration, data analysis, processing or administration, utilization review, quality assurance, billing, benefit management, practice management, and repricing; or (B) Any other function or activity regulated by this subchapter; or (ii) Provides, other than in the capacity of a member of the workforce of such covered entity, legal, actuarial, accounting, consulting, data aggregation (as defined in § 164.501 of this subchapter), management, administrative, accreditation, or financial services to or for such covered entity, or to or for an organized health care arrangement in which the covered entity participates, where the provision of the service involves the disclosure of individually identifiable health information from such covered entity or arrangement, or from another business associate of such covered entity or arrangement, to the person. (2) A covered entity participating in an organized health care arrangement that performs a function or activity as described by paragraph (1)(i) of this definition for or on behalf of such organized health care arrangement, or that provides a service as described in paragraph (1)(ii) of this definition to or for such organized health care arrangement, does not, simply through the performance of such function or activity or the provision of such service, become a business associate of

The HITECH Act also resolved an unanswered question regarding security breaches—whether notice was required under HIPAA. The HITECH Act requires that patients be notified of any unauthorized acquisition, access, use[16] or disclosure of their unsecured protected health information[17] (Unsecured PHI)[18] that compromises the privacy or security of such information, though there are some exceptions related to unintentional or inadvertent use or disclosure by employees or authorized individuals within the "same facility."

14:8. Application of knowledge elements associated with contracts

Section 164.504(e)(1)(ii) of title 45, Code of Federal Regulations, applies to a business associate described in subsection (a), with respect to compliance with such subsection, in the same manner that such section applies to a covered entity, with respect to compliance with the standards in sections 164.502(e) and 164.504(e) of such title, except that in applying such section 164.504(e)(1)(ii) each reference to the business associate, with respect to a contract, shall be treated as a reference to the covered entity involved in such contract.[19]

14:9. Application of civil and criminal penalties

In the case of a business associate that violates any provision of § 17934(a) or (b), the provisions of sections 1176 and 1177 of the Social Security Act (42 U.S.C. §§ 1320d-5, 1320d-6) shall apply to the business associate with respect to such violation in the same manner as such provisions apply to a person who violates a provision of part C of title XI of such Act.[20]

---

other covered entities participating in such organized health care arrangement. (3) A covered entity may be a business associate of another covered entity. 45 C.F.R. § 160.103.

16. "Use" means, with respect to individually identifiable health information, the sharing, employment, application, utilization, examination, or analysis of such information within an entity that maintains such information. 45 C.F.R. § 160.103.

17. "Protected health information" means individually identifiable health information: (1) Except as provided in paragraph (2) of this definition, that is: (i) Transmitted by electronic media; (ii) Maintained in electronic media; or (iii) Transmitted or maintained in any other form or medium. (2) Protected health information excludes individually identifiable health information in: (i) Education records covered by the Family Educational Rights and Privacy Act, as amended, 20 U.S.C. § 1232g; (ii) Records described at 20 U.S.C. § 1232g(a)(4)(B)(iv); and (iii) Employment records held by a covered entity in its role as employer. 45 C.F.R. § 160.103. Electronic media means: (1) Electronic storage media including memory devices in computers (hard drives) and any removable/transportable digital memory medium, such as magnetic tape or disk, optical disk, or digital memory card; or (2) Transmission media used to exchange information already in electronic storage media. Transmission media include, for example, the internet (wide-open), extranet (using internet technology to link a business with information accessible only to collaborating parties), leased lines, dial-up lines, private networks, and the physical movement of removable/transportable electronic storage media. Certain transmissions, including of paper, via facsimile, and of voice, via telephone, are not considered to be transmissions via electronic media, because the information being exchanged did not exist in electronic form before the transmission. 45 C.F.R. § 160.103.

18. The Department of Health and Human Services (HHS) is required to define the term "Unsecured PHI" within 60 days. If such guidance is not issued, the HITECH Act defines "Unsecured PHI" as any PHI that is not secured by a technology standard that renders it unusable, unreadable, or indecipherable to unauthorized individuals, and is developed or endorsed by a standards developing organization that is accredited by the American National Standards Institute.

19. 42 U.S.C. § 17934(b).

20. 42 U.S.C. § 17934(c).

As more fully discussed below, the HITECH Act increases civil penalty amounts based upon the level of intent and neglect (i.e., whether the violation was made without knowledge, due to reasonable cause, or due to willful neglect). For violations determined to have been made without knowledge, penalties start at $100 per violation, not to exceed $25,000. For violations based on reasonable cause, penalties start at $1,000 per violation, not to exceed $100,000. For violations due to willful neglect, penalties start at $10,000, not to exceed $250,000. For violations due to willful neglect that are not corrected, penalties start at $50,000, not to exceed $1.5 million.

While as noted in this chapter, HIPAA does not currently provide for a private right of action, the HITECH Act heightens HIPAA enforcement by authorizing state attorneys general to file suit on behalf of their residents. Courts will be able to award damages, costs, and attorneys' fees related to violations of HIPAA.

14:10. Business associate contracts required for certain entities

Each organization, with respect to a covered entity, that provides data transmission of protected health information to such entity (or its business associate) and that requires access on a routine basis to such protected health information, such as a health information exchange organization, regional health information organization, e-prescribing gateway, or each vendor that contracts with a covered entity to allow that covered entity to offer a personal health record to patients as part of its electronic health record, is required to enter into a written contract (or other written arrangement) described in section 164.502(e)(2) of title 45, Code of Federal Regulations and a written contract (or other arrangement) described in section 164.308(b) of such title, with such entity and shall be treated as a business associate of the covered entity for purposes of the provisions of this subchapter and subparts C and E of part 164 of title 45, Code of Federal Regulations, as such provisions are in effect as of February 17, 2009.[21]

14:11. Improved enforcement under the Social Security Act

Any violation by a covered entity under this subchapter is subject to enforcement and penalties under section 1320d-5 and 1320d-6 of this title.[22]

14:12. Effective date and regulations

The amendments made above shall apply to penalties imposed on or after the date that is 24 months after February 17, 2009.[23] Not later than 18 months after February 17, 2009, the Secretary of Health and Human Services shall promulgate regulations to implement these amendments.[24]

---

21.   42 U.S.C. § 17938.
22.   42 U.S.C. § 17939(a).
23.   42 U.S.C. § 17939(b)(1).
24.   42 U.S.C. § 17939(b)(2).

14:13. Distribution of certain civil monetary penalties collected

Subject to the regulation promulgated pursuant to paragraph (c)(3), any civil monetary penalty or monetary settlement collected with respect to an offense punishable under this subchapter or section 1320d-5 of this title insofar as such section relates to privacy or security must be transferred to the Office for Civil Rights of the Department of Health and Human Services to be used for purposes of enforcing the provisions of this subchapter and subparts C and E of part 164 of title 45, Code of Federal Regulations, as such provisions are in effect as of February 17, 2009.[25] Not later than 18 months after February 17, 2009, the Comptroller General shall submit to the secretary a report including recommendations for a methodology under which an individual who is harmed by an act that constitutes an offense referred to in paragraph (1) may receive a percentage of any civil monetary penalty or monetary settlement collected with respect to such offense.[26]

14:14. Establishment of methodology to distribute percentage of CMPS collected to harmed individuals

Not later than 3 years after February 17, 2009, the secretary must establish by regulation and based on the recommendations submitted under paragraph (2), a methodology under which an individual who is harmed by an act that constitutes an offense referred to in paragraph (1) may receive a percentage of any civil monetary penalty or monetary settlement collected with respect to such offense.[27] The methodology under paragraph (3) shall be applied with respect to civil monetary penalties or monetary settlements imposed on or after the effective date of the regulation.[28]

14:15. Effective date

The amendments made by this subsection shall apply to violations occurring after February 17, 2009.[29]

14:16. Audits

The secretary shall provide for periodic audits to ensure that covered entities and business associates that are subject to the requirements of this subchapter and subparts C and E of part 164 of title 45, Code of Federal Regulations, as such provisions are in effect as of February 17, 2009, comply with such requirements.[30]

---

25. 42 U.S.C. § 17939(c)(1).
26. 42 U.S.C. § 17939(c)(2).
27. 42 U.S.C. § 17939(c)(3).
28. 42 U.S.C. § 17939(c)(4).
29. 42 U.S.C. § 17939(c)(4).
30. 42 U.S.C. § 17940.

14:17. Relationship to other laws—HIPAA state preemption

Section 1178 of the Social Security Act (42 U.S.C. § 1320d-7) shall apply to a provision or requirement under this subchapter in the same manner that such section applies to a provision or requirement under part C of title XI of such Act or a standard or implementation specification adopted or established under sections 1172 through 1174 of such Act.[31]

14:18. Relationship to other laws—HIPAA

The standards governing the privacy and security of individually identifiable health information promulgated by the secretary under sections 262(a) and 264 of the Health Insurance Portability and Accountability Act of 1996 shall remain in effect to the extent that they are consistent with this subchapter. The secretary shall by rule amend such federal regulations as required to make such regulations consistent with this subchapter.[32]

14:19. Construction of law

Nothing in this subchapter shall constitute a waiver of any privilege otherwise applicable to an individual with respect to the protected health information of such individual.[33]

14:20. Reports on compliance

For the first year beginning after February 17, 2009 and annually thereafter, the Secretary shall prepare and submit to the Committee on Health, Education, Labor, and Pensions of the Senate and the Committee on Ways and Means and the Committee on Energy and Commerce of the House of Representatives a report concerning complaints of alleged violations of law, including the provisions of this subchapter as well as the provisions of subparts C and E of part 164 of title 45, Code of Federal Regulations, (as such provisions are in effect as of February 17, 2009) relating to privacy and security of health information that are received by the secretary during the year for which the report is being prepared. Each such report shall include, with respect to such complaints received during the year, the number of such complaints; the number of such complaints resolved informally, a summary of the types of such complaints so resolved, and the number of covered entities that received technical assistance from the secretary during such year in order to achieve compliance with such provisions and the types of such technical assistance provided; the number of such complaints that have resulted in the imposition of civil monetary penalties or have been resolved through monetary settlements, including the nature of the complaints involved and the amount paid in each penalty or settlement; the number of compliance reviews conducted and the outcome of each such review; the number of subpoenas or inquiries issued; the secretary's plan for improving compliance with and enforcement of such provisions

---

31. 42 U.S.C. § 17951(a).

32. 42 U.S.C. § 17951(b).

33. 42 U.S.C. § 17951(c).

for the following year; and the number of audits performed and a summary of audit findings pursuant to section 17940 of this title.[34]

Each report must be made available to the public on the Internet website of the Department of Health and Human Services.[35]

14:21. Study and report on application of privacy and security requirements to non-HIPAA covered entities

The Secretary of HHS, in consultation with the Federal Trade Commission, was directed to conduct a study and submit a report on privacy and security requirements for entities that are not covered entities or business associates by February 17, 2010, the anniversary of the law. Several months overdue as of March 2011, the study and report should include the following:

- requirements relating to security, privacy, and notification in the case of a breach of security or privacy (including the applicability of an exemption to notification in the case of individually identifiable health information that has been rendered unusable, unreadable, or indecipherable through technologies or methodologies recognized by appropriate professional organization or standard setting[36] bodies to provide effective security for the information) that should be applied to the following:
  - o vendors of personal health records,
  - o entities that offer products or services through the website of a vendor of personal health records,
  - o entities that are not covered entities and that offer products or services through the websites of covered entities that offer individuals personal health records,
  - o entities that are not covered entities and that access information in a personal health record or send information to a personal health record, and
  - o third party service providers used by a vendor or entity described in clause (i), (ii), (iii), or (iv) to assist in providing personal health record products or services;
- a determination of which federal government agency is best equipped to enforce such requirements recommended to be applied to such vendors, entities, and service providers under subparagraph (A); and
- a timeframe for implementing regulations based on such findings.[37]

The Secretary shall submit to the Committee on Finance, the Committee on Health, Education, Labor, and Pensions, and the Committee on Commerce of the Senate and the Committee on Ways and Means and the Committee on Energy and Commerce of the House of Representatives a report on the findings of the study under paragraph (1) and

---

34.　42 U.S.C. § 17953(a)(1)(A)–(G).

35.　42 U.S.C. § 17953(a)(2).

36.　Standard setting organization (SSO) means an organization accredited by the American National Standards Institute that develops and maintains standards for information transactions or data elements, or any other standard that is necessary for, or will facilitate the implementation of, this part. 45 C.F.R. § 160.103.

37.　42 U.S.C. §§ 17953(b)(1)(A)–(C).

shall include in such report recommendations on the privacy and security requirements described in such paragraph.[38]

14:22. Guidance on implementation specification to de-identify protected health information

The Secretary shall, in consultation with stakeholders, issue guidance on how best to implement the requirements for the de-identification of protected health information under section 164.514(b) of title 45, Code of Federal Regulations.[39]

14:23. GAO report on treatment disclosures

The Comptroller General of the United States shall submit to the Committee on Health, Education, Labor, and Pensions of the Senate and the Committee on Ways and Means and the Committee on Energy and Commerce of the House of Representatives a report on the best practices related to the disclosure among health care providers of protected health information of an individual for purposes of treatment of such individual. The report must include an examination of the best practices implemented by states[40] and by other entities, such as health information exchanges and regional health information organizations, an examination of the extent to which such best practices are successful with respect to the quality of the resulting health care provided to the individual and with respect to the ability of the health care provider to manage such best practices, and an examination of the use of electronic informed consent for disclosing protected health information for treatment, payment, and health care operations.[41]

14:24. Report required

Not later than five years after February 17, 2009, the Government Accountability Office shall submit to Congress and the Secretary of Health and Human Services a report on the impact of any of the provisions of this Act on health insurance premiums, overall health care costs, adoption of electronic health records by providers, and reduction in medical errors and other quality improvements.[42]

14:25. Study

The secretary shall study the definition of "psychotherapy notes" in section 164.501 of title 45, Code of Federal Regulations, with regard to including test data that is related to direct responses, scores, items, forms, protocols, manuals, or other materials that are part of a mental health evaluation, as determined by the mental health professional

---

38. 42 U.S.C. § 17953(b)(2).

39. 42 U.S.C. § 17953(c).

40. State refers to one of the following: (1) For a health plan established or regulated by Federal law, State has the meaning set forth in the applicable section of the United States Code for such health plan. (2) For all other purposes, State means any of the several States, the District of Columbia, the Commonwealth of Puerto Rico, the Virgin Islands, and Guam. 45 C.F.R. § 160.103.

41. 42 U.S.C. § 17953(d).

42. 42 U.S.C. § 17953(e).

providing treatment or evaluation in such definitions and may, based on such study, issue regulations to revise such definition.[43]

14:26. Restrictions on certain disclosures and sales of health information; accounting of certain protected health information disclosures; access to certain information in electronic format

In the case that an individual requests under paragraph (a)(1)(i)(A) of section 164.522 of title 45, Code of Federal Regulations, that a covered entity restrict the disclosure of the protected health information of the individual, notwithstanding paragraph (a)(1) (ii) of such section, the covered entity must comply with the requested restriction if except as otherwise required by law, the disclosure is to a health plan[44] for purposes of carrying out payment[45] or health care operations[46] (and is not for purposes of carrying out treatment[47]); and the protected health information pertains solely to a health care item or service for which the health care provider[48] involved has been paid out of pocket in full.[49]

14:27. Disclosures required to be limited to the limited data set or the minimum necessary

Subject to subparagraph § 17935(b)(1)(B), a covered entity shall be treated as being in compliance with 45 C.F.R. 164.502(b)(1) with respect to the use, disclosure, or request of protected health information described in such section, only if the covered entity limits such protected health information, to the extent practicable, to the limited data set (as defined in section 164.514(e)(2)) or, if needed by such entity, to the minimum necessary to accomplish the intended purpose of such use, disclosure, or request, respectively.[50] Moreover, the secretary was required to issue guidance on what is the "minimum necessary" for purposes of subpart E of part 164 of title 45, Code of Federal Regulation. In issuing such guidance the secretary shall take into consideration the guidance under section 17953(c) of this title and the information necessary to improve

---

43. 42 U.S.C. § 17953(f).

44. The term "health plan" has the meaning given such term in section 160.103 of title 45, Code of Federal Regulations. 42 U.S.C. § 17921(8).

45. The term "payment" has the meaning given such term in section 164.501 of title 45, Code of Federal Regulations. 42 U.S.C. § 17921(10).

46. The term "health care operation" has the meaning given such term in section 164.501 of title 45, Code of Federal Regulations. 42 U.S.C. § 17921(6).

47. The term "treatment" has the meaning given such term in section 164.501 of title 45, Code of Federal Regulations. 42 U.S.C. § 17921(16).

48. The term "health care provider" has the meaning given such term in section 160.103 of title 45, Code of Federal Regulations. 42 U.S.C. § 17921(7).

49. 42 U.S.C. §§ 17935(a)(1)–(2).

50. 42 U.S.C. § 17935(b)(1)(A).

patient outcomes and to detect, prevent, and manage chronic disease.[51] The requirements of 42 U.S.C. § 17935(b)(1)(A) do not apply now that guidance has been issued.[52]

14:28. Determination of minimum necessary

For the requirements of § 17935(b)(1), in the case of the disclosure of protected health information, the covered entity or business associate disclosing such information shall determine what constitutes the minimum necessary to accomplish the intended purpose of such disclosure.[53]

14:29. Application of exceptions

The exceptions described in section 164.502(b)(2) of title 45, Code of Federal Regulations, shall apply to the requirement under paragraph (1) as of the effective date described in section 13423 in the same manner that such exceptions apply to section 164.502(b)(1) of such title before the date.[54]

14:30. Exception

Nothing in this subsection shall be construed as affecting the use, disclosure, or request of protected health information that has been de-identified.[55]

14:31. Accounting of certain protected health information disclosures required if covered entity uses electronic health record

In applying section 164.528 of title 45, Code of Federal Regulations, in the case that a covered entity uses or maintains an electronic health record[56] with respect to protected health information, the exception under paragraph (a)(1)(i) of such section does not apply to disclosures through an electronic health record made by such entity of such information, and an individual shall have a right to receive an accounting of disclosures described in such paragraph of such information made by such covered entity during only the three years prior to the date on which the accounting is requested.[57]

14:32. Regulations

The secretary was required to promulgate regulations on what information shall be collected about each disclosure referred to in paragraph (1), not later than six months

---

51. 42 U.S.C. § 17935(b)(1)(B).
52. 42 U.S.C. § 17935(b)(1)(C).
53. 42 U.S.C. § 17935(b)(2).
54. 42 U.S.C. § 17935(b)(3).
55. 42 U.S.C. § 17935(b)(4).
56. The term "electronic health record" means an electronic record of health-related information on an individual that is created, gathered, managed, and consulted by authorized health care clinicians and staff. 42 U.S.C. § 17921(5).
57. 42 U.S.C. § 17935(c)(1)(A)–(B).

after the date on which the secretary adopts standards on accounting for disclosure described in the section 300jj-12(b)(2)(B)(iv) of this title. The regulations shall only require such information to be collected through an electronic health record in a manner that takes into account the interests of the individuals in learning the circumstances under which their protected health information is being disclosed and takes into account the administrative burden of accounting for such disclosures.[58]

14:33. Response to requests for accounting

In response to a request from an individual for an accounting, a covered entity shall elect to provide either an accounting, as specified under paragraph (1), for disclosures of protected health information that are made by such covered entity and by a business associate acting on behalf of the covered entity, or an accounting, as specified under paragraph (1), for disclosures that are made by such covered entity and provide a list of all business associates acting on behalf of the covered entity, including contact information for such associates (such as mailing address, phone, and e-mail address).[59] A business associate included on the second list identified above must provide an accounting of disclosures (as required under paragraph (1) for a covered entity) made by the business associate upon a request made by an individual directly to the business associate for such an accounting.[60]

14:34. Effective date

In the case of a covered entity insofar as it acquired an electronic health record as of January 1, 2009, paragraph (1) shall apply to disclosures, with respect to protected health information, made by the covered entity from such a record on and after January 1, 2014.[61] In the case of a covered entity insofar as it acquires an electronic health record after January 1, 2009, paragraph (1) shall apply to disclosures, with respect to protected health information, made by the covered entity from such record on and after the later of the following: January 1, 2011 or the date that it acquires an electronic health record.[62] The secretary may set an effective date that is later that the date specified under subparagraph (A) or (B) if the secretary determines that such later date is necessary, but in no case may the date specified under subparagraph (A) be later than 2016, or subparagraph (B) be later than 2013.[63]

14:35. Prohibition on sale of electronic health records or protected health information

Except as provided in paragraph (2), a covered entity or business associate shall not directly or indirectly receive remuneration in exchange for any protected health

---

58.   42 U.S.C. § 17935(c)(2).
59.   42 U.S.C. §§ 17935(c)(3)(A)–(B).
60.   42 U.S.C. § 17935(c)(3)(B).
61.   42 U.S.C. § 17935(c)(4)(A).
62.   42 U.S.C. §§ 17935(c)(4)(B)(i)–(ii).
63.   42 U.S.C. §§ 17935(c)(4)(C)(i)–(ii).

information of an individual unless the covered entity obtained from the individual, in accordance with section 164.508 of title 45, Code of Federal Regulations, a valid authorization that includes, in accordance with such section, a specification of whether the protected health information can be further exchanged for remuneration by the entity receiving protected health information of that individual.[64] This restriction does not apply if

- the purpose of the exchange is for public health activities (as described in section 164.512(b) of title 45, Code of Federal Regulations);
- the purpose of the exchange is for research (as described in sections 164.501 and 164.512(i) of title 45, Code of Federal Regulations) and the price charged reflects the costs of preparation and transmittal of the data for such purpose;
- the purpose of the exchange is for the treatment of the individual, subject to any regulation that the secretary may promulgate to prevent protected health information from inappropriate access, use, or disclosure;
- the purpose of the exchange is the health care operation specifically described in subparagraph (iv) of paragraph (6) of the definition of healthcare operations in section 164.501 of title 45, Code of Federal Regulations;
- the purpose of the exchange is for remuneration that is provided by a covered entity to a business associate for activities involving the exchange of protected health information that the business associate undertakes on behalf of and at the specific request of the covered entity pursuant to a business associate agreement;
- the purpose of the exchange is to provide an individual with a copy of the individual's protected health information pursuant to section 164.524 of title 45, Code of Federal Regulations; or
- the purpose of the exchange is otherwise determined by the secretary in regulations to be similarly necessary and appropriate as the exceptions provided in subparagraphs (A) through (F).[65]

14:36. Regulations regarding the prohibition of sale

Not later than 18 months after February 17, 2009, the secretary shall promulgate regulations to carry out this subsection. In promulgating such regulations, the secretary must evaluate the impact of restricting the exception described in paragraph (2)(A) to require that the price charged for the purposes described in such paragraph reflects the costs of the preparation and transmittal of the data for such purpose, on research or public health activities, including those conducted by or for the use of the Food and Drug Administration, and the secretary may further restrict the exception described in paragraph (2)(A) to require that the price charged for the purposes described in such paragraph reflects the costs of the preparation and transmittal of the data for such

---

64.   42 U.S.C. § 17935(d)(1).

65.   42 U.S.C. §§ 17935(d)(2)(A)–(G).

purpose, if the secretary finds that such further restriction will not impede such research or public health activities.[66]

14:37. Effective date

The restrictions of § 17935(d)(1) shall apply to exchanges occurring on or after the date that is six months after the date of the promulgation of final regulations implementing this subsection.[67]

14:38. Access to certain information in electronic format

In applying section 164.524 of title 45, Code of Federal Regulations, in the case that a covered entity uses or maintains an electronic health record with respect to protected health information of an individual, the individual shall have a right to obtain from such covered entity a copy of such information in an electronic format and, if the individual chooses, to direct the covered entity to transmit such copy directly to an entity or person designated by the individual, provided that any such choice is clear, conspicuous, and specific.[68] Notwithstanding paragraph (c)(4) of this section, any fee that the covered entity may impose for providing such individual with a copy of such information (or a summary or explanation of such information) if such copy (or summary or explanation) is in an electronic form shall not be greater than the entity's labor costs in responding to the request for the copy (or summary or explanation).[69]

14:39. Conditions on certain contacts as part of health care operations—marketing

A communication by a covered entity or business associate that is about a product or service and that encourages recipients of the communication to purchase or use the product or service shall not be considered a health care operation for purposes of subpart E of part 164 of title 45, Code of Federal Regulations, unless the communication is made as described in subparagraph (i), (ii), or (iii) of paragraph (1) of the definition of marketing in section 164.501 of such title.[70]

A communication by a covered entity or business associate that is described in subparagraph (i), (ii), or (iii) of paragraph (1) of the definition of marketing in section 164.501 of title 45, Code of Federal Regulations, shall not be considered a health care operation for purposes of subpart E of part 164 of title 45, Code of Federal Regulations if the covered entity receives or has received direct or indirect payment[71] in exchange for making such communication, except where

---

66. 42 U.S.C. §§ 17935(d)(3)(A)–(B).

67. 42 U.S.C. § 17935(d)(4).

68. 42 U.S.C. § 17935(e)(1).

69. 42 U.S.C. § 17935(e)(2).

70. 42 U.S.C. § 17936(a)(1).

71. For purposes of paragraph (2), the term "direct or indirect payment" shall not include any payment for treatment (as defined in section 164.501 of title 45, Code of Federal Regulations) of an individual. 42 U.S.C. § 17936(a)(4).

- such communication describes only a drug or biologic that is currently being prescribed for the recipient of the communication; and
- any payment received by such covered entity in exchange for making a communication described in clause (i) is reasonable in amount[72];
- each of the following conditions apply:
  - o the communication is made by the covered entity, and
  - o the covered entity making such communication obtains from the recipient of the communication, in accordance with section 164.508 of title 45, Code of Federal Regulations, a valid authorization (as described in paragraph (b) of such section) with respect to such communication; or
- each of the following conditions apply:
  - o the communication is made by a business associate on behalf of the covered entity, and
  - o the communication is consistent with the written contract (or other written arrangement described in section 164.502(e)(2) of such title) between such business associate and covered entity.[73]

14:40. Opportunity to opt out of fundraising

The secretary shall by rule provide that any written fundraising communication that is a healthcare operation as defined under section 164.501 of title 45, Code of Federal Regulations, shall, in a clear and conspicuous manner, provide an opportunity for the recipient of the communications to elect not to receive any further such communication. When an individual elects not to receive any further such communication, such election shall be treated as a revocation of authorization under section 164.508 of title 45, Code of Federal Regulations.[74]

14:41. Effective date

This section shall apply to written communications occurring on or after the effective date specified under section 13423.[75]

B. Scope of HIPAA Regulations and Enforcement

14:42. Statutory basis and purpose

The requirements of this subchapter implement sections 1171 through 1179 of the Social Security Act[76] (the Act), as added by section 262 of Public Law 104-191, section 264

---

72. For purposes of paragraph (2), the term "reasonable in amount" shall have the meaning given such term by the secretary by regulation. 42 U.S.C. § 17936(a)(3).

73. 42 U.S.C. §§ 17936(a)(2)(A)–(C).

74. 42 U.S.C. § 17936(b).

75. 42 U.S.C. § 17936(c).

76. "Act" means the Social Security Act. 45 C.F.R. § 160.103.

of Public Law 104-191, section 13402 of Public Law 111-5, and section 13410(d) of Public Law 111-5.[77]

14:43. Applicability

Except as otherwise provided, the standards, requirements, and implementation[78] specifications adopted under this subchapter apply to the following entities: a health plan[79]; a health care clearinghouse[80]; a health care[81] provider[82] who transmits any

---

77. 45 C.F.R. § 160.101.

78. "Implementation specification" means specific requirements or instructions for implementing a standard. 45 C.F.R. § 160.103.

79. "Health plan" means an individual or group plan that provides, or pays the cost of, medical care (as defined in section 2791(a)(2) of the PHS Act, 42 U.S.C. § 300gg-91(a)(2)). (1) Health plan includes the following, singly or in combination: (i) A group health plan, as defined in this section. (ii) A health insurance issuer, as defined in this section. (iii) An HMO, as defined in this section. (iv) Part A or Part B of the Medicare program under title XVIII of the Act. (v) The Medicaid program under title XIX of the Act, 42 U.S.C. § 1396, *et seq.* (vi) An issuer of a Medicare supplemental policy (as defined in section 1882(g)(1) of the Act, 42 U.S.C. § 1395ss(g)(1)). (vii) An issuer of a long-term care policy, excluding a nursing home fixed-indemnity policy. (viii) An employee welfare benefit plan or any other arrangement that is established or maintained for the purpose of offering or providing health benefits to the employees of two or more employers. (ix) The health care program for active military personnel under title 10 of the United States Code. (x) The veterans health care program under 38 U.S.C. chapter 17. (xi) The Civilian Health and Medical Program of the Uniformed Services (CHAMPUS) (as defined in 10 U.S.C. § 1072(4)). (xii) The Indian Health Service program under the Indian Health Care Improvement Act, 25 U.S.C. § 1601, *et seq.* (xiii) The Federal Employees Health Benefits Program under 5 U.S.C. § 8902, *et seq.* (xiv) An approved State child health plan under title XXI of the Act, providing benefits for child health assistance that meet the requirements of section 2103 of the Act, 42 U.S.C. § 1397, *et seq.* (xv) The Medicare+Choice program under Part C of title XVIII of the Act, 42 U.S.C. § 1395w-21 through 1395w-28. (xvi) A high risk pool that is a mechanism established under State law to provide health insurance coverage or comparable coverage to eligible individuals. (xvii) Any other individual or group plan, or combination of individual or group plans, that provides or pays for the cost of medical care (as defined in section 2791(a)(2) of the PHS Act, 42 U.S.C. § 300gg-91(a)(2)). (2) Health plan excludes: (i) Any policy, plan, or program to the extent that it provides, or pays for the cost of, excepted benefits that are listed in section 2791(c)(1) of the PHS Act, 42 U.S.C. § 300gg-91(c)(1); and (ii) A government-funded program (other than one listed in paragraph (1)(i)–(xvi) of this definition): (A) Whose principal purpose is other than providing, or paying the cost of, health care; or (B) Whose principal activity is: (1) The direct provision of health care to persons; or (2) The making of grants to fund the direct provision of health care to persons. 45 C.F.R. § 160.103.

80. "Health care clearinghouse" means a public or private entity, including a billing service, repricing company, community health management information system or community health information system, and "value-added" networks and switches, that does either of the following functions: (1) Processes or facilitates the processing of health information received from another entity in a nonstandard format or containing nonstandard data content into standard data elements or a standard transaction. (2) Receives a standard transaction from another entity and processes or facilitates the processing of health information into nonstandard format or nonstandard data content for the receiving entity. 45 C.F.R. § 160.103.

81. "Health care" means care, services, or supplies related to the health of an individual. Health care includes, but is not limited to, the following: (1) Preventive, diagnostic, therapeutic, rehabilitative, maintenance, or palliative care, and counseling, service, assessment, or procedure with respect to the physical or mental condition, or functional status, of an individual or that affects the structure or function of the body; and (2) Sale or dispensing of a drug, device, equipment, or other item in accordance with a prescription. 45 C.F.R. § 160.103.

82. "Health care provider" means a provider of services (as defined in section 1861(u) of the Act, 42 U.S.C. § 1395x(u)), a provider of medical or health services (as defined in section 1861(s) of the Act, 42 U.S.C. § 1395x(s)), and any other person or organization who furnishes, bills, or is paid for health care in the normal course of business. 45 C.F.R. § 160.103.

health information[83] in electronic form in connection with a transaction covered by this subchapter.[84] To the extent required under the Social Security Act, 42 U.S.C. § 1320a-7c(a)(5), nothing in this subchapter shall be construed to diminish the authority of any Inspector General, including such authority as provided in the Inspector General Act of 1978, as amended (5 U.S.C. App.).[85]

14:44. Modifications

Except as provided in paragraph (b) of this section, the secretary[86] may adopt a modification to a standard or implementation specification adopted under this subchapter no more frequently than once every 12 months.[87] The secretary may adopt a modification at any time during the first year after the standard or implementation specification is initially adopted, if the secretary determines that the modification is necessary to permit compliance with the standard or implementation specification.[88] The secretary was required to establish the compliance date[89] for any standard or implementation specification modified under this section. The compliance date for a modification was to be no earlier than 180 days after the effective date of the final rule in which the secretary adopts the modification. The secretary could consider the extent of the modification and the time needed to comply with the modification in determining the compliance date for the modification. The secretary was permitted to extend the compliance date for small health plans,[90] as the secretary determines is appropriate.[91]

14:45. General rule and exceptions—Preemption

A standard, requirement, or implementation specification adopted under this subchapter that is contrary[92] to a provision of state law[93] preempts the provision of state law. This

---

83. "Health information" means any information, whether oral or recorded in any form or medium, that: (1) Is created or received by a health care provider, health plan, public health authority, employer, life insurer, school or university, or health care clearinghouse; and (2) Relates to the past, present, or future physical or mental health or condition of an individual; the provision of health care to an individual; or the past, present, or future payment for the provision of health care to an individual. 45 C.F.R. § 160.103.

84. 45 C.F.R. §§ 160.102(a)(1)–(3).

85. 45 C.F.R. § 160.102(b).

86. "Secretary" means the Secretary of Health and Human Services or any other officer or employee of HHS to whom the authority involved has been delegated. 45 C.F.R. § 160.103.

87. 45 C.F.R. § 160.104(a).

88. 45 C.F.R. § 160.104(b).

89. Compliance date means the date by which a covered entity must comply with a standard, implementation specification, requirement, or modification adopted under this subchapter. 45 C.F.R. § 160.103.

90. "Small health plan" means a health plan with annual receipts of $5 million or less. 45 C.F.R. § 160.103.

91. 45 C.F.R. §§ 160.104(c)(1)–(3).

92. "Contrary," when used to compare a provision of State law to a standard, requirement, or implementation specification adopted under this subchapter, means: (1) A covered entity would find it impossible to comply with both the State and federal requirements; or (2) The provision of state law stands as an obstacle to the accomplishment and execution of the full purposes and objectives of part C of title XI of the Act, section 264 of Public Law 104-191, or section 13402 of Public Law 111-5, as applicable. 45 C.F.R. § 160.202.

93. "State law" means a constitution, statute, regulation, rule, common law, or other state action having the force and effect of law. 45 C.F.R. § 160.202.

general rule applies, except if one or more of the following exceptions exists.[94] The first is a determination is made by the secretary under § 160.204 that the provision of state law is necessary: to prevent fraud and abuse related to the provision of or payment for health care; to ensure appropriate state regulation of insurance and health plans to the extent expressly authorized by statute or regulation; for state reporting on health care delivery or costs; or for purposes of serving a compelling need related to public health, safety, or welfare, and, if a standard, requirement, or implementation specification under 45 C.F.R. Part 164 is at issue, if the secretary determines that the intrusion into privacy is warranted when balanced against the need to be served.[95]

The second exception is if it has as its principal purpose the regulation of the manufacture, registration, distribution, dispensing, or other control of any controlled substances (as defined in 21 U.S.C. § 802), or that is deemed a controlled substance by state law.[96]

Moreover, a third exception is if the provision of state law relates to the privacy of individually identifiable health information[97] and is more stringent[98] than a standard, requirement, or implementation specification adopted under the Privacy Rule.[99] A fourth is if the provision of state law, including state procedures established under such law, as applicable, provides for the reporting of disease or injury, child abuse, birth, or

---

94.   45 C.F.R. § 160.203.

95.   45 C.F.R. §§ 160.203(a)(1)(i)–(iv).

96.   45 C.F.R. § 160.203(a)(2).

97.   "Relates to the privacy of individually identifiable health information" means, with respect to a state law, that the state law has the specific purpose of protecting the privacy of health information or affects the privacy of health information in a direct, clear, and substantial way. 45 C.F.R. § 160.202. Individually identifiable health information is information that is a subset of health information, including demographic information collected from an individual, and: (1) Is created or received by a health care provider, health plan, employer, or health care clearinghouse; and (2) Relates to the past, present, or future physical or mental health or condition of an individual; the provision of health care to an individual; or the past, present, or future payment for the provision of health care to an individual; and (i) That identifies the individual; or (ii) With respect to which there is a reasonable basis to believe the information can be used to identify the individual. 45 C.F.R. § 160.103.

98.   "More stringent" means, in the context of a comparison of a provision of state law and a standard, requirement, or implementation specification adopted under subpart E of part 164 of this subchapter, a state law that meets one or more of the following criteria: (1) With respect to a use or disclosure, the law prohibits or restricts a use or disclosure in circumstances under which such use or disclosure otherwise would be permitted under this subchapter, except if the disclosure is: (i) Required by the secretary in connection with determining whether a covered entity is in compliance with this subchapter; or (ii) To the individual who is the subject of the individually identifiable health information. (2) With respect to the rights of an individual, who is the subject of the individually identifiable health information, regarding access to or amendment of individually identifiable health information, permits greater rights of access or amendment, as applicable. (3) With respect to information to be provided to an individual who is the subject of the individually identifiable health information about a use, a disclosure, rights, and remedies, provides the greater amount of information. (4) With respect to the form, substance, or the need for express legal permission from an individual, who is the subject of the individually identifiable health information, for use or disclosure of individually identifiable health information, provides requirements that narrow the scope or duration, increase the privacy protections afforded (such as by expanding the criteria for), or reduce the coercive effect of the circumstances surrounding the express legal permission, as applicable. (5) With respect to recordkeeping or requirements relating to accounting of disclosures, provides for the retention or reporting of more detailed information or for a longer duration. (6) With respect to any other matter, provides greater privacy protection for the individual who is the subject of the individually identifiable health information. 45 C.F.R. § 160.202.

99.   45 C.F.R. § 160.203(b).

death, or for the conduct of public health surveillance, investigation, or intervention.[100] Finally, the fifth is if the provision of state law requires a health plan to report, or to provide access to, information for the purpose of management audits, financial audits, program monitoring and evaluation, or the licensure or certification of facilities or individuals.[101] [102]

14:46. Process for requesting exception determinations

A request to except a provision of state law from preemption under § 160.203(a) may be submitted to the secretary. A request by a state must be submitted through its chief elected official, or his or her designee. The request must be in writing and include the following information: the state law for which the exception is requested; the particular standard, requirement, or implementation specification for which the exception is requested; the part of the standard or other provision that will not be implemented based on the exception or the additional data to be collected based on the exception, as appropriate; how health care providers, health plans, and other entities would be affected by the exception; the reasons why the state law should not be preempted by the federal standard, requirement, or implementation specification, including how the state law meets one or more of the criteria at § 160.203(a); and any other information the secretary may request in order to make the determination.[103] Requests for exception under this section must be submitted to the secretary at an address that will be published in the Federal Register. Until the secretary's determination is made, the standard, requirement, or implementation specification under this subchapter remains in effect.[104] The secretary's determination under this section will be made on the basis of the extent to which the information provided and other factors demonstrate that one or more of the criteria at § 160.203(a) has been met.[105]

14:47. Duration of effectiveness of exception determinations

An exception granted under this subpart remains in effect until either the state law or the federal standard, requirement, or implementation specification that provided the basis for the exception is materially changed such that the ground for the exception no longer exists; or the secretary revokes the exception, based on a determination that the ground supporting the need for the exception no longer exists.[106]

---

100. 45 C.F.R. § 160.203(c).

101. Individual means the person who is the subject of protected health information. 45 C.F.R. § 160.103.

102. 45 C.F.R. § 160.203(d).

103. 45 C.F.R. §§ 160.204(a)(1)–(5).

104. 45 C.F.R. § 160.204(b).

105. 45 C.F.R. § 160.204(c).

106. 45 C.F.R. § 160.205(a)–(b).

14:48. Applicability

This subpart applies to actions by the secretary, covered entities, and others with respect to ascertaining the compliance by covered entities with, and the enforcement of, the applicable provisions of this part 160 and parts 162 and 164 of this subchapter.[107]

14:49. Principles for achieving compliance

The secretary will, to the extent practicable, seek the cooperation of covered entities in obtaining compliance with the applicable administrative simplification provisions.[108] The Secretary may provide technical assistance to covered entities to help them comply voluntarily with the applicable administrative simplification provisions.[109]

14:50. Complaints to the secretary

A person[110] who believes a covered entity[111] is not complying with the administrative simplification provisions may file a complaint with the secretary.[112] Complaints under this section must meet the following requirements: a complaint must be filed in writing, either on paper or electronically; a complaint must name the person that is the subject of the complaint and describe the acts or omissions believed to be in violation of the applicable administrative simplification provisions; a complaint must be filed within 180 days of when the complainant knew or should have known that the act or omission complained of occurred, unless this time limit is waived by the secretary for good cause shown; the secretary may prescribe additional procedures for the filing of complaints, as well as the place and manner of filing, by notice in the Federal Register.[113]

The secretary may investigate complaints filed under this section. Such investigation may include a review of the pertinent policies, procedures, or practices of the covered entity and of the circumstances regarding any alleged violation. At the time of initial written communication with the covered entity about the complaint, the secretary will describe the acts and/or omissions that are the basis of the complaint.[114]

---

107. 45 C.F.R. § 160.300.

108. 45 C.F.R. § 160.304(a); Administrative simplification provision means any requirement or prohibition established by: (1) 42 U.S.C. §§ 1320d–1320d-4, 1320d-7, and 1320d-8; (2) Section 264 of Pub.L. 104-191; or (3) This subchapter. 45 C.F.R. § 160.302.

109. 45 C.F.R. § 160.304(b).

110. "Person" means a natural person, trust or estate, partnership, corporation, professional association or corporation, or other entity, public or private. 45 C.F.R. § 160.103.

111. "Covered entity" means: (1) A health plan. (2) A health care clearinghouse. (3) A health care provider who transmits any health information in electronic form in connection with a transaction covered by this subchapter. 45 C.F.R. § 160.103.

112. 45 C.F.R. § 160.306(a).

113. 45 C.F.R. § 160.306(b)(1)–(4).

114. 45 C.F.R. § 160.306(c).

14:51. Compliance reviews

The secretary may conduct compliance reviews to determine whether covered entities are complying with the applicable administrative simplification provisions.[115]

14:52. Responsibilities of covered entities

A covered entity must keep such records and submit such compliance reports, in such time and manner and containing such information, as the secretary may determine to be necessary to enable the secretary to ascertain whether the covered entity has complied or is complying with the applicable administrative simplification provisions.[116] A covered entity must also cooperate with the secretary, if the secretary undertakes an investigation or compliance review of the policies, procedures, or practices of the covered entity to determine whether it is complying with the applicable administrative simplification provisions.[117]

There are also mandates regarding access to information. A covered entity must permit access by the secretary during normal business hours to its facilities, books, records, accounts, and other sources of information, including protected health information, that are pertinent to ascertaining compliance with the applicable administrative simplification provisions. If the secretary determines that exigent circumstances exist, such as when documents may be hidden or destroyed, a covered entity must permit access by the secretary at any time and without notice.[118] If any information required of a covered entity under this section is in the exclusive possession of any other agency, institution, or person and the other agency, institution, or person fails or refuses to furnish the information, the covered entity must so certify and set forth what efforts it has made to obtain the information.[119] Protected health information obtained by the secretary in connection with an investigation or compliance review under this subpart will not be disclosed by the secretary, except if necessary for ascertaining or enforcing compliance with the applicable administrative simplification provisions, or if otherwise required by law.[120]

14:53. Secretarial action regarding complaints and compliance reviews

If an investigation of a complaint pursuant to § 160.306 or a compliance review pursuant to § 160.308 indicates noncompliance, the secretary will attempt to reach a resolution of the matter satisfactory to the secretary by informal means. Informal means may include demonstrated compliance or a completed corrective action plan or other agreement.[121] If the matter is resolved by informal means, the secretary will so

---

115. 45 C.F.R. § 160.308.
116. 45 C.F.R. § 160.310(a).
117. 45 C.F.R. § 160.310(b).
118. 45 C.F.R. § 160.310(c)(1).
119. 45 C.F.R. § 160.310(c)(2).
120. 45 C.F.R. § 160.310(c)(3).
121. 45 C.F.R. § 160.312(a)(1).

inform the covered entity and, if the matter arose from a complaint, the complainant, in writing.[122] If the matter is not resolved by informal means, the secretary will so inform the covered entity and provide the covered entity an opportunity to submit written evidence of any mitigating factors or affirmative defenses for consideration under §§ 160.408 and 160.410 of this part. The covered entity must submit any such evidence to the secretary within 30 days (computed in the same manner as prescribed under § 160.526 of this part) of receipt of such notification; and if, following action pursuant to paragraph (a)(3)(i) of this section, the secretary finds that a civil money penalty[123] should be imposed, inform the covered entity of such finding in a notice of proposed determination in accordance with § 160.420 of this part.[124]

If, after an investigation pursuant to § 160.306 or a compliance review pursuant to § 160.308, the secretary determines that further action is not warranted, the secretary will so inform the covered entity and, if the matter arose from a complaint, the complainant, in writing.[125]

14:54. Investigational subpoenas and inquiries

The secretary may issue subpoenas in accordance with 42 U.S.C. §§ 405(d) and (e), 1320a-7a(j), and 1320d-5 to require the attendance and testimony of witnesses and the production of any other evidence during an investigation or compliance review pursuant to this part.[126] A subpoena issued under this paragraph must state the name of the person[127] (including the entity, if applicable) to whom the subpoena is addressed; state the statutory authority for the subpoena; indicate the date, time, and place that the testimony will take place; include a reasonably specific description of any documents or items required to be produced; and if the subpoena is addressed to an entity, describe with reasonable particularity the subject matter on which testimony is required. In that event, the entity must designate one or more natural persons who will testify on its behalf, and must state as to each such person that person's name and address and the matters on which he or she will testify. The designated person must testify as to matters known or reasonably available to the entity.[128] A subpoena under this section must be served by delivering a copy to the natural person named in the subpoena or to the entity named in the subpoena at its last principal place of business; or registered or certified mail addressed to the natural person at his or her last known dwelling place or to the entity at its last known principal place of business.[129] A verified return by the natural person serving the subpoena setting forth the manner of service or, in the

---

122. 45 C.F.R. § 160.312(a)(2).

123. "Civil money penalty" or "penalty" means the amount determined under § 160.404 of this part and includes the plural of these terms. 45 C.F.R. § 160.302.

124. 45 C.F.R. §§ 160.312(a)(3)(i)–(iii).

125. 45 C.F.R. § 160.312(b).

126. 45 C.F.R. § 160.314(a).

127. For purposes of this paragraph, a person other than a natural person is termed an "entity."

128. 45 C.F.R. §§ 160.314(a)(1)(i)–(v).

129. 45 C.F.R. §§ 160.314(a)(2)(i)–(ii).

case of service by registered or certified mail, the signed return post office receipt, constitutes proof of service.[130]

Witnesses are entitled to the same fees and mileage as witnesses in the district courts of the United States (28 U.S.C. §§ 1821 and 1825). Fees need not be paid at the time the subpoena is served. A subpoena under this section is enforceable through the district court of the United States for the district where the subpoenaed natural person resides or is found or where the entity transacts business.[131]

14:55. Investigational inquiries are non-public investigational proceedings conducted by the secretary

Testimony at investigational inquiries will be taken under oath or affirmation.[132] Attendance of non-witnesses is discretionary with the secretary, except that a witness is entitled to be accompanied, represented, and advised by an attorney.[133] Representatives of the secretary are entitled to attend and ask questions.[134] A witness has the opportunity to clarify his or her answers on the record following questioning by the secretary.[135] Any claim of privilege must be asserted by the witness on the record and objections must be asserted on the record. Errors of any kind that might be corrected if promptly presented will be deemed to be waived unless reasonable objection is made at the investigational inquiry. Except where the objection is on the grounds of privilege, the question will be answered on the record, subject to objection.[136] If a witness refuses to answer any question not privileged or to produce requested documents or items, or engages in conduct likely to delay or obstruct the investigational inquiry, the secretary may seek enforcement of the subpoena under paragraph (a)(5) of this section.[137] The proceedings will be recorded and transcribed. The witness is entitled to a copy of the transcript, upon payment of prescribed costs, except that, for good cause, the witness may be limited to inspection of the official transcript of his or her testimony.[138]

Where the witness will be provided a copy of the transcript, the transcript will be submitted to the witness for signature. The witness may submit to the secretary written proposed corrections to the transcript, with such corrections attached to the transcript. If the witness does not return a signed copy of the transcript or proposed corrections within 30 days (computed in the same manner as prescribed under § 160.526 of this part) of its being submitted to him or her for signature, the witness will be deemed to have agreed that the transcript is true and accurate.[139] Where, as provided in paragraph (b)(8) of this section, the witness is limited to inspecting the transcript, the witness will have the opportunity at the time of inspection to propose corrections to the transcript,

---

130. 45 C.F.R. § 160.314(a)(3).
131. 45 C.F.R. §§ 160.314(a)(4)–(5).
132. 45 C.F.R. § 160.314(b)(1).
133. 45 C.F.R. § 160.314(b)(2).
134. 45 C.F.R. § 160.314(b)(3).
135. 45 C.F.R. § 160.314(b)(4).
136. 45 C.F.R. §§ 160.314(b)(5)–(6).
137. 45 C.F.R. § 160.314(b)(7).
138. 45 C.F.R. § 160.314(b)(8).
139. 45 C.F.R. § 160.314(b)(9)(i)(A).

with corrections attached to the transcript. The witness will also have the opportunity to sign the transcript. If the witness does not sign the transcript or offer corrections within 30 days (computed in the same manner as prescribed under § 160.526 of this part) of receipt of notice of the opportunity to inspect the transcript, the witness will be deemed to have agreed that the transcript is true and accurate.[140] The secretary's proposed corrections to the record of transcript will be attached to the transcript.[141]

Consistent with § 160.310(c)(3), testimony and other evidence obtained in an investigational inquiry may be used by HHS[142] in any of its activities and may be used or offered into evidence in any administrative or judicial proceeding.[143]

14:56. Refraining from intimidation or retaliation

A covered entity may not threaten, intimidate, coerce, harass, discriminate against, or take any other retaliatory action against any individual or other person for filing of a complaint under § 160.306; testifying, assisting, or participating in an investigation, compliance review, proceeding, or hearing under this part; or opposing any act or practice made unlawful by this subchapter, provided the individual or person has a good faith belief that the practice opposed is unlawful, and the manner of opposition is reasonable and does not involve a disclosure[144] of protected health information in violation of subpart E of part 164 of this subchapter.[145]

14:57. Basis for a civil money penalty

Subject to § 160.410, the secretary will impose a civil money penalty upon a covered entity if the secretary determines that the covered entity has violated[146] an administrative simplification provision.[147] Except as provided in paragraph (b)(2) of this section, if the secretary determines that more than one covered entity was responsible for a violation, the secretary will impose a civil money penalty against each such covered entity.[148] A covered entity that is a member of an affiliated covered entity, in accordance with § 164.105(b) of this subchapter, is jointly and severally liable for a civil money penalty for a violation of part 164 of this subchapter based on an act or omission of the affiliated covered entity, unless it is established that another member of the affiliated covered entity was responsible for the violation.[149] A covered entity is liable, in accordance with the federal common law of agency, for a civil money penalty for a violation based on the

---

140. 45 C.F.R. § 160.314(b)(9)(i)(B).

141. 45 C.F.R. § 160.314(b)(9)(ii).

142. "HHS" stands for the Department of Health and Human Services. 45 C.F.R. § 160.103.

143. 45 C.F.R. § 160.314(c).

144. "Disclosure" means the release, transfer, provision of, access to, or divulging in any other manner of information outside the entity holding the information. 45 C.F.R. § 160.103.

145. 45 C.F.R. § 160.316(a)–(c).

146. "Violation" or "violate" means, as the context may require, failure to comply with an administrative simplification provision. 45 C.F.R. § 160.302.

147. 45 C.F.R. § 160.402(a).

148. 45 C.F.R. § 160.402(b)(1).

149. 45 C.F.R. § 160.402(b)(2).

act or omission of any agent of the covered entity, including a workforce[150] member, acting within the scope of the agency, unless the agent is a business associate of the covered entity; the covered entity has complied, with respect to such business associate, with the applicable requirements of §§ 164.308(b) and 164.502(e) of this subchapter; and the covered entity did not know of a pattern of activity or practice of the business associate, and fail to act as required by §§ 164.314(a)(1)(ii) and 164.504(e)(1)(ii) of this subchapter, as applicable.[151]

14:58. Amount of a civil money penalty

The amount of a civil money penalty will be determined in accordance within certain limitations, and §§ 160.406, 160.408, and 160.412.[152] The amount of a civil money penalty that may be imposed is subject to the following limitations:

- For violations that occurred prior to February 18, 2009, the secretary may not impose a civil money penalty in the amount of more than $100 for each violation, or in excess of $25,000 for identical violations during a calendar year (January 1 through the following December 31).

- For violations occurring on or after February 18, 2009, the secretary may not impose a civil money penalty for a violation in which it is established that the covered entity did not know and, by exercising reasonable diligence,[153] would not have known that the covered entity violated such provision, in the amount of less than $100 or more than $50,000 for each violation, or in excess of $1,500,000 for identical violations during a calendar year (January 1 through the following December 31).[154]

- For a violation in which it is established that the violation was due to reasonable cause[155] and not to willful neglect,[156] the secretary may not impose a civil money penalty in the amount of less than $1,000 or more than $50,000 for each violation, or in excess of $1,500,000 for identical violations during a calendar year (January 1 through the following December 31).[157]

- For a violation in which it is established that the violation was due to willful neglect and was corrected during the 30-day period beginning on the first date the covered entity liable for the penalty knew, or, by exercising reasonable diligence, would have known that the violation occurred, the secretary may not impose a civil money

---

150. "Workforce" means employees, volunteers, trainees, and other persons whose conduct, in the performance of work for a covered entity, is under the direct control of such entity, whether or not they are paid by the covered entity. 45 C.F.R. § 160.103.

151. 45 C.F.R. § 160.402(c)(1)–(3).

152. 45 C.F.R. § 160.404(a).

153. Reasonable diligence means the business care and prudence expected from a person seeking to satisfy a legal requirement under similar circumstances. 45 C.F.R. § 160.401.

154. 45 C.F.R. § 160.404(b)(1)(i)–(ii).

155. Reasonable cause means circumstances that would make it unreasonable for the covered entity, despite the exercise of ordinary business care and prudence, to comply with the administrative simplification provision violated. 45 C.F.R. § 160.401.

156. Willful neglect means conscious, intentional failure or reckless indifference to the obligation to comply with the administrative simplification provision violated. 45 C.F.R. § 160.401.

157. 45 C.F.R. § 160.404(b)(2)(i)–(ii).

penalty in the amount of less than $10,000 or more than $50,000 for each violation, or in excess of $1,500,000 for identical violations during a calendar year (January 1 through the following December 31).[158]

- For a violation in which it is established that the violation was due to willful neglect and was not corrected during the 30-day period beginning on the first date the covered entity liable for the penalty knew, or, by exercising reasonable diligence, would have known that the violation occurred, the secretary may not impose a civil money penalty in the amount of less than $50,000 for each violation, or in excess of $1,500,000 for identical violations during a calendar year (January 1 through the following December 31).[159]

If a requirement or prohibition in one administrative simplification provision is repeated in a more general form in another administrative simplification provision in the same subpart, a civil money penalty may be imposed for a violation of only one of these administrative simplification provisions.[160]

14:59. Violations of an identical requirement or prohibition

The secretary will determine the number of violations of an administrative simplification provision based on the nature of the covered entity's obligation to act or not act under the provision that is violated, such as its obligation to act in a certain manner, or within a certain time, or to act or not act with respect to certain persons. In the case of continuing violation of a provision, a separate violation occurs each day the covered entity is in violation of the provision.[161]

14:60. Factors considered in determining the amount of a civil money penalty

In determining the amount of any civil money penalty, the secretary may consider as aggravating or mitigating factors, as appropriate, any of the following:

- the nature of the violation, in light of the purpose of the rule violated;
- the circumstances, including the consequences, of the violation, including but not limited to the time period during which the violation(s) occurred, whether the violation caused physical harm, whether the violation hindered or facilitated an individual's ability to obtain health care, and whether the violation resulted in financial harm;
- the degree of culpability of the covered entity, including but not limited to whether the violation was intentional, and whether the violation was beyond the direct control of the covered entity;
- any history of prior compliance with the administrative simplification provisions, including violations, by the covered entity, including but not limited to whether

---

158. 45 C.F.R. § 160.404(b)(2)(iii).
159. 45 C.F.R. § 160.404(b)(2)(iv).
160. 45 C.F.R. § 160.404(b)(3).
161. 45 C.F.R. § 160.406.

the current violation is the same or similar to prior violations, whether and to what extent the covered entity has attempted to correct previous violations, how the covered entity has responded to technical assistance from the secretary provided in the context of a compliance effort, and how the covered entity has responded to prior complaints;

- the financial condition of the covered entity, including but not limited to whether the covered entity had financial difficulties that affected its ability to comply, whether the imposition of a civil money penalty would jeopardize the ability of the covered entity to continue to provide, or to pay for, health care, and the size of the covered entity; and

- such other matters as justice may require.[162]

14:61. Affirmative defenses

For violations occurring prior to February 18, 2009, the secretary may not impose a civil money penalty on a covered entity for a violation if the covered entity establishes that an affirmative defense exists with respect to the violations, including the following: the violation is an act punishable under 42 U.S.C. § 1320d-6; the covered entity establishes, to the satisfaction of the secretary, that it did not have knowledge of the violation, determined in accordance with the federal common law of agency, and, by exercising reasonable diligence, would not have known that the violation occurred; or the violation is due to reasonable cause and not willful neglect, and corrected during either the 30-day period beginning on the first date the covered entity liable for the penalty knew, or by exercising reasonable diligence would have known, that the violation occurred, or such additional period as the secretary determines to be appropriate based on the nature and extent of the failure to comply.[163]

For violations occurring on or after February 18, 2009, the secretary may not impose a civil money penalty on a covered entity for a violation if the covered entity establishes that an affirmative defense exists with respect to the violations, including the following: the violation is an act punishable under 42 U.S.C. § 1320d-6; or the covered entity establishes to the satisfaction of the secretary that the violation is not due to willful neglect, and corrected during either the 30-day period beginning on the first date the covered entity liable for the penalty knew, or, by exercising reasonable diligence, would have known that the violation occurred, or such additional period as the secretary determines to be appropriate based on the nature and extent of the failure to comply.[164]

14:62. Waiver

For violations due to reasonable cause and not willful neglect that are not corrected within the period described in § 160.410(a)(3)(ii) or (b)(2)(ii), as applicable, the secretary

---

162. 45 C.F.R. §§ 160.408(a)–(f).

163. 45 C.F.R. §§ 160.410(a)(1)–(3).

164. 45 C.F.R. §§ 160.410(b)(1)–(2).

may waive the civil money penalty, in whole or in part, to the extent that the payment of the penalty would be excessive relative to the violation.[165]

14:63. Limitations

No action under this subpart may be entertained unless commenced by the secretary, in accordance with § 160.420, within six years from the date of the occurrence of the violation.[166]

14:64. Authority to settle

Nothing in this subpart limits the authority of the secretary to settle any issue or case or to compromise any penalty.[167]

14:65. Penalty not exclusive

Except as otherwise provided by 42 U.S.C. § 1320d-5(b)(1), a penalty imposed under this part is in addition to any other penalty prescribed by law.[168]

14:66. Notice of proposed determination

If a penalty is proposed in accordance with this part, the secretary must deliver or send by certified mail with return receipt requested, to the respondent,[169] written notice of the secretary's intent to impose a penalty. This notice of proposed determination must include reference to the statutory basis for the penalty; a description of the findings of fact regarding the violations with respect to which the penalty is proposed (except that, in any case where the secretary is relying upon a statistical sampling study in accordance with § 160.536 of this part, the notice must provide a copy of the study relied upon by the secretary); the reasons why the violations subject the respondent to a penalty; the amount of the proposed penalty and a reference to the subparagraph of § 160.404 upon which it is based; any circumstances described in § 160.408 that were considered in determining the amount of the proposed penalty; and instructions for responding to the notice, including a statement of the respondent's right to a hearing, a statement that failure to request a hearing within 90 days permits the imposition of the proposed penalty without the right to a hearing under § 160.504 or a right of appeal under § 160.548 of this part, and the address to which the hearing request must be sent.[170]

The respondent may request a hearing before an ALJ[171] on the proposed penalty by filing a request in accordance with § 160.504 of this part.[172]

---

165. 45 C.F.R. § 160.412.

166. 45 C.F.R. § 160.414.

167. 45 C.F.R. § 160.416.

168. 45 C.F.R. § 160.418.

169. "Respondent" means a covered entity upon which the secretary has imposed, or proposes to impose, a civil money penalty. 45 C.F.R. § 160.302.

170. 45 C.F.R. §§ 160.420(a)(1)–(6).

171. "ALJ" means Administrative Law Judge. 45 C.F.R. § 160.302.

172. 45 C.F.R. § 160.420(b).

14:67. Failure to request a hearing

If the respondent does not request a hearing within the time prescribed by § 160.504 of this part and the matter is not settled pursuant to § 160.416, the secretary will impose the proposed penalty or any lesser penalty permitted by 42 U.S.C. § 1320d-5. The Secretary will notify the respondent by certified mail, return receipt requested, of any penalty that has been imposed and of the means by which the respondent may satisfy the penalty, and the penalty is final on receipt of the notice. The respondent has no right to appeal a penalty under § 160.548 of this part with respect to which the respondent has not timely requested a hearing.[173]

14:68. Collection of penalty

Once a determination of the secretary to impose a penalty has become final, the penalty will be collected by the secretary, subject to the first sentence of 42 U.S.C. § 1320a-7a(f).[174] The penalty may be recovered in a civil action brought in the United States district court for the district where the respondent resides, is found, or is located.[175] The amount of a penalty, when finally determined, or the amount agreed upon in compromise, may be deducted from any sum then or later owing by the United States, or by a state agency, to the respondent.[176] Matters that were raised or that could have been raised in a hearing before an ALJ, or in an appeal under 42 U.S.C. § 1320a-7a(e), may not be raised as a defense in a civil action by the United States to collect a penalty under this part.[177]

14:69. Notification of the public and other agencies

Whenever a proposed penalty becomes final, the secretary will notify, in such manner as the secretary deems appropriate, the public and the following organizations and entities thereof and the reason it was imposed: the appropriate state or local medical or professional organization, the appropriate state agency or agencies administering or supervising the administration of state health care programs (as defined in 42 U.S.C. § 1320a-7(h)), the appropriate utilization and quality control peer review organization, and the appropriate state or local licensing agency or organization (including the agency specified in 42 U.S.C. §§ 1395aa(a), 1396a(a)(33)).[178]

---

173. 45 C.F.R. § 160.422.
174. 45 C.F.R. § 160.424(a).
175. 45 C.F.R. § 160.424(b).
176. 45 C.F.R. § 160.424(c).
177. 45 C.F.R. § 160.424(d).
178. 45 C.F.R. § 160.426.

C.   Security

14:70.   Statutory basis for security and privacy regulations

The provisions of this part are adopted pursuant to the secretary's authority to prescribe standards, requirements, and implementation specifications under part C of title XI of the Act, section 264 of Public Law 104-191, and section 13402 of Public Law 111-5.[179]

14:71.   Applicability of regulations

Except as otherwise provided, the standards, requirements, and implementation specifications adopted under this part apply to the following entities: a health plan; a health care clearinghouse; a health care provider who transmits any health information in electronic form in connection with a transaction covered by this subchapter.[180]

When a health care clearinghouse creates or receives protected health information as a business associate[181] of another covered entity, or other than as a business associate of a covered entity, the clearinghouse must comply with § 164.105 relating to organizational requirements for covered entities, including the designation of health care components[182] of a covered entity.[183]

14:72.   Organizational requirements—hybrid entities

If a covered entity is a hybrid entity,[184] the requirements of subparts C and E of this part, other than the requirements of this section, § 164.314, and § 164.504, apply only to the health care component(s) of the entity, as specified in this section.[185]   It should be noted that in applying a provision of subparts C and E of this part, other than the requirements of this section, § 164.314, and § 164.504, to a hybrid entity

- a reference in such provision to a "covered entity" refers to a health care component of the covered entity;
- a reference in such provision to a "health plan," "covered health care provider," or "health care clearinghouse," refers to a health care component of the covered entity if such health care component performs the functions of a health plan, health care provider, or health care clearinghouse, as applicable;

---

179. 45 C.F.R. § 164.102.

180. 45 C.F.R. §§ 164.104(a)(1)–(3).

181. "Business associate" means a business associate under the Health Insurance Portability and Accountability Act, Public Law 104–191, 110 Stat. 1936, as defined in 45 CFR 160.103. 16 C.F.R. § 318.2(b).

182. Health care component means a component or combination of components of a hybrid entity designated by the hybrid entity in accordance with § 164.105(a)(2)(iii)(C). 45 C.F.R. § 164.103.

183. 45 C.F.R. § 164.104(b).

184. Hybrid entity means a single legal entity: (1) That is a covered entity; (2) Whose business activities include both covered and non-covered functions; and (3) That designates health care components in accordance with paragraph § 164.105(a)(2)(iii)(C). 45 C.F.R. § 164.103.

185. 45 C.F.R. § 164.105(a)(1).

- a reference in such provision to "protected health information" refers to protected health information that is created or received by or on behalf of the health care component of the covered entity; and

- a reference in such provision to "electronic protected health information"[186] refers to electronic protected health information that is created, received, maintained, or transmitted by or on behalf of the health care component of the covered entity.[187]

The covered entity that is a hybrid entity must ensure that a health care component of the entity complies with the applicable requirements of this section and subparts C and E of this part. In particular, and without limiting this requirement, such covered entity must ensure that

- its health care component does not disclose protected health information to another component of the covered entity in circumstances in which subpart E of this part would prohibit such disclosure if the health care component and the other component were separate and distinct legal entities;

- its health care component protects electronic protected health information with respect to another component of the covered entity to the same extent that it would be required under subpart C of this part to protect such information if the health care component and the other component were separate and distinct legal entities;

- a component that is described by paragraph (a)(2)(iii)(C)(2) of this section does not use or disclose protected health information that it creates or receives from or on behalf of the health care component in a way prohibited by subpart E of this part;

- a component that is described by paragraph (a)(2)(iii)(C)(2) of this section that creates, receives, maintains, or transmits electronic protected health information on behalf of the health care component is in compliance with subpart C of this part; and

- if a person performs duties for both the health care component in the capacity of a member of the workforce of such component and for another component of the entity in the same capacity with respect to that component, such workforce member must not use or disclose protected health information created or received in the course of or incident to the member's work for the health care component in a way prohibited by subpart E of this part.[188]

A covered entity that is a hybrid entity has the following responsibilities:

- For purposes of subpart C of part 160 of this subchapter, pertaining to compliance and enforcement, the covered entity has the responsibility of complying with subpart E of this part.

- The covered entity is responsible for complying with § 164.316(a) and § 164.530(i), pertaining to the implementation of policies and procedures to ensure compliance with applicable requirements of this section and subparts C and E of this part, including the safeguard requirements in paragraph (a)(2)(ii) of this section.

---

186. Electronic protected health information means information that comes within paragraphs (1)(i) or (1)(ii) of the definition of protected health information as specified in this section. 45 C.F.R. § 160.103.

187. 45 C.F.R. §§ 164.105(a)(2)(i)(A)–(D).

188. 45 C.F.R. §§ 164.105(a)(2)(ii)(A)–(E).

- The covered entity is responsible for designating the components that are part of one or more health care components of the covered entity and documenting the designation in accordance with paragraph (c) of this section, provided that, if the covered entity designates a health care component or components, it must include any component that would meet the definition of covered entity if it were a separate legal entity. Health care component(s) also may include a component only to the extent that it performs covered functions[189] or activities that would make such component a business associate of a component that performs covered functions if the two components were separate legal entities.[190]

Legally separate covered entities that are affiliated may designate themselves as a single covered entity for purposes of subparts C and E of this part.[191] Legally separate covered entities may designate themselves (including any health care component of such covered entity) as a single affiliated covered entity, for purposes of subparts C and E of this part, if all of the covered entities designated are under common ownership[192] or control.[193] The designation of an affiliated covered entity must be documented and the documentation maintained as required by paragraph (c) of this section.[194]

14:73. Safeguard requirements for affiliated covered entities

An affiliated covered entity must ensure that the affiliated covered entity's creation, receipt, maintenance, or transmission of electronic protected health information complies with the applicable requirements of subpart C of this part; the affiliated covered entity's use and disclosure of protected health information comply with the applicable requirements of subpart E of this part; and if the affiliated covered entity combines the functions of a health plan, health care provider, or health care clearinghouse, the affiliated covered entity complies with § 164.308(a)(4)(ii)(A) and § 164.504(g), as applicable.[195]

14:74. Documentation

A covered entity must maintain a written or electronic record of a designation as required by paragraphs (a) or (b) of this section.[196] A covered entity must retain the documentation as required by paragraph (c)(1) of this section for six years from the date of its creation or the date when it last was in effect, whichever is later.[197]

---

189. Covered functions means those functions of a covered entity the performance of which makes the entity a health plan, health care provider, or health care clearinghouse. 45 C.F.R. § 164.103.
190. 45 C.F.R. §§ 164.105(a)(2)(iii)(A)–(C).
191. 45 C.F.R. § 164.105(b)(1).
192. Common ownership exists if an entity or entities possess an ownership or equity interest of 5 percent or more in another entity. 45 C.F.R. § 164.103.
193. 45 C.F.R. § 164.105(b)(2)(i)(A); Common control exists if an entity has the power, directly or indirectly, significantly to influence or direct the actions or policies of another entity. 45 C.F.R. § 164.103.
194. 45 C.F.R. § 164.105(b)(2)(i)(B).
195. 45 C.F.R. §§ 164.105(b)(2)(ii)(A)–(C).
196. 45 C.F.R. § 164.105(c)(1).
197. 45 C.F.R. § 164.105(c)(2).

14:75. Relationship to other portions of the regulations

In complying with the requirements of this part, covered entities are required to comply with the applicable provisions of parts 160 and 162 of this subchapter.[198]

14:76. Applicability

A covered entity must comply with the applicable standards, implementation specifications, and requirements of this subpart with respect to electronic protected health information.[199]

14:77. In general

Covered entities must ensure the confidentiality,[200] integrity,[201] and availability[202] of all electronic protected health information the covered entity creates, receives, maintains, or transmits; protect against any reasonably anticipated threats or hazards to the security[203] or integrity of such information; protect against any reasonably anticipated uses or disclosures of such information that are not permitted or required under subpart E of this part; and ensure compliance with this subpart by its workforce.[204]   Covered entities may use any security measures that allow the covered entity to reasonably and appropriately implement the standards and implementation specifications as specified in this subpart.[205]   In deciding which security measures to use, a covered entity must take into account the following factors: the size, complexity, and capabilities of the covered entity; the covered entity's technical infrastructure, hardware, and software security capabilities; the costs of security measures; and the probability and criticality of potential risks to electronic protected health information.[206]   A covered entity must comply with the standards as provided in this section and in § 164.308, § 164.310, § 164.312, § 164.314, and § 164.316 with respect to all electronic protected health information.[207]

When a standard adopted in § 164.308, § 164.310, § 164.312, § 164.314, or § 164.316 includes required implementation specifications, a covered entity must implement the implementation specifications.[208]   When a standard adopted in § 164.308, § 164.310,

---

198. 45 C.F.R. § 164.106.

199. 45 C.F.R. § 164.302.

200. "Confidentiality" means the property that data or information is not made available or disclosed to unauthorized persons or processes. 45 C.F.R. § 164.304.

201. "Integrity" means the property that data or information have not been altered or destroyed in an unauthorized manner. 45 C.F.R. § 164.304.

202. "Availability" means the property that data or information is accessible and useable upon demand by an authorized person. 45 C.F.R. § 164.304.

203. "Security" or "Security measures" encompass all of the administrative, physical, and technical safeguards in an information system. 45 C.F.R. § 164.304.

204. 45 C.F.R. §§ 164.306(a)(1)–(4).

205. 45 C.F.R. § 164.306(b)(1).

206. 45 C.F.R. §§ 164.306(b)(2)(i)–(iv).

207. 45 C.F.R. § 164.306(c).

208. 45 C.F.R. § 164.306(d)(2).

§ 164.312, § 164.314, or § 164.316 includes addressable implementation specifications, a covered entity must

- assess whether each implementation specification is a reasonable and appropriate safeguard in its environment, when analyzed with reference to the likely contribution to protecting the entity's electronic protected health information; and
- as applicable to the entity
  o implement the implementation specification if reasonable and appropriate, or

if implementing the implementation specification is not reasonable and appropriate, document why it would not be reasonable and appropriate to implement the implementation specification and implement an equivalent alternative measure if reasonable and appropriate.[209]

Security measures implemented to comply with standards and implementation specifications adopted under § 164.105 and this subpart must be reviewed and modified as needed to continue provision of reasonable and appropriate protection of electronic protected health information as described at § 164.316.[210]

14:78. Application of security provisions and penalties to business associates of covered entities

In what is one of the major changes to HIPAA, business associates are now directly covered by the security requirements and certain privacy requirements of HIPAA, which has required modification to many existing business associate agreements. Now, §§ 164.308, 164.310, 164.312, and 164.316 of title 45, Code of Federal Regulations, apply to a business associate[211] of a covered entity[212] in the same manner that such sections apply to the covered entity.[213] The additional requirements of this title that relate to security and that are made applicable with respect to covered entities shall also be applicable to such a business associate and must be incorporated into the business associate agreement between the business associate and the covered entity.[214] In the case of a business associate that violates any security provision specified in subsection (a), sections 1320d-5 and 1320d-6 of this title shall apply to the business associate with respect to such violation in the same manner such sections apply to a covered entity that violates such security provision.[215]

---

209. 45 C.F.R. §§ 164.306(d)(3)(A)–(B).

210. 45 C.F.R. § 164.306(e).

211. The term "business associate" has the meaning given such term in section 160.103 of title 45, Code of Federal Regulations. 42 U.S.C. § 17921(2).

212. The term "covered entity" has the meaning given such term in section 160.103 of title 45, Code of Federal Regulations. 42 U.S.C. § 17921(3).

213. 42 U.S.C. § 17931(a).

214. *Id.*

215. 42 U.S.C. § 17931(b).

14:79. Security management process

A covered entity and business associate must implement policies and procedures to prevent, detect, contain and correct security violations.[216]

14:80. Security management process—Risk analysis

Covered entities and business associates are required to conduct an accurate and thorough assessment of the potential risks and vulnerabilities to the confidentiality, integrity, and availability of electronic protected health information held by the covered entity.[217]

14:81. Security management process—Risk management

It is also required that covered entities and business associates implement security measures sufficient to reduce risks and vulnerabilities to a reasonable and appropriate level to comply with the general security requirements.[218]

14:82. Security management process—Sanction policy

Entities subject to HIPAA are also required to sanction employees who fail to comply with the security policies and procedures of the covered entity or business associate, as appropriate.[219]

14:83. Security management process—Information system activity review

Implementation of procedures to regularly review records of information system[220] activity, such as audit logs, access[221] reports, and security incident[222] tracking reports is also required.[223]

---

216. 45 C.F.R. § 164.308(a)(1)(i).

217. 45 C.F.R. § 164.308(a)(1)(ii)(A).

218. 45 C.F.R. § 164.308(a)(1)(ii)(A).

219. 45 C.F.R. § 164.308(a)(1)(ii)(C).

220. "Information system" means an interconnected set of information resources under the same direct management control that shares common functionality. A system normally includes hardware, software, information, data, applications, communications, and people. 45 C.F.R. § 164.304.

221. "Access" means the ability or the means necessary to read, write, modify, or communicate data/information or otherwise use any system resource. (This definition applies to "access" as used in this subpart, not as used in subpart E of this part.) 45 C.F.R. § 164.304.

222. "Security incident" means the attempted or successful unauthorized access, use, disclosure, modification, or destruction of information or interference with system operations in an information system. 45 C.F.R. § 164.304.

223. 45 C.F.R. § 164.308(a)(1)(ii)(D).

14:84. Assigned security responsibility

Covered entities and business associates must identify a security official who is responsible for the development and implementation of the policies and procedures required by HIPAA.[224]

14:85. Workforce security

HIPAA also requires that covered entities and business associates implement policies and procedures to ensure that all members of their workforces have appropriate access to electronic protected health information and to prevent the workers who do not have access from obtaining access to electronic protected health information.[225]

    HIPAA also provides some implementation suggestions, but these are "addressable" and not necessarily required, as discussed above.

14:86. Workforce security—Authorization and/or supervision

Covered entities and business associates must consider implementing procedures for the authorization and/or supervision of workforce members who work with electronic protected health information or in locations where it might be accessed.[226]

14:87. Workforce security—Workforce clearance procedure

Procedures should be implemented to determine that the access of a workforce member to electronic protected health information is appropriate.[227]

14:88. Workforce security—Termination procedures

Procedures for terminating access to electronic protected health information when the employment of a workforce member ends or as required by determinations made as specified in the workforce clearance procedure should be considered.[228]

14:89. Information access management

Covered entities and business associates must implement policies and procedures for authorizing access to electronic protected health information that are consistent with the applicable requirements.[229]

---

224. 45 C.F.R. § 164.308(a)(2).
225. 45 C.F.R. § 164.308(a)(3)(i).
226. 45 C.F.R. § 164.308(3)(ii)(A).
227. 45 C.F.R. § 164.308(3)(ii)(B).
228. 45 C.F.R. § 164.308(a)(3)(ii)(C).
229. 45 C.F.R. § 164.308(a)(4)(i).

14:90. Information access management—Isolating health care clearinghouse functions

This regulation requires a health care clearinghouse that is part of a larger organization to implement policies and procedures that protect the electronic protected health information of the clearinghouse from unauthorized access by the larger organization.[230]

14:91. Information access management—Access authorization

This implementation is "addressable," so not necessarily required. Thus, covered entities and business associates should consider implementing policies and procedures for granting access to electronic protected health information, for example, through access to a workstation,[231] transaction, program, process, or other mechanism.[232]

14:92. Information access management—Access establishment and modification

This implementation is also addressable. Covered entities and business associates should consider implementing policies and procedures that, based upon the entity's access authorization policies, establish, document, review, and modify a user's[233] right of access to a workstation, transaction, program, or process.[234]

14:93. Security awareness and training

Covered entities and business associates must implement a security awareness and training program for all managers and members of their workforces.[235] All of these implementation points are addressable.

14:94. Security awareness and training-Security reminders

This relates to periodic security updates.[236]

---

230. 45 C.F.R. § 164.308(a)(4)(ii)(A).

231. "Workstation" means an electronic computing device, for example, a laptop or desktop computer, or any other device that performs similar functions, and electronic media stored in its immediate environment. 45 C.F.R. § 164.304.

232. 45 C.F.R. § 164.308(a)(4)(ii)(B).

233. "User" means a person or entity with authorized access. 45 C.F.R. § 164.304.

234. 45 C.F.R. § 164.308(a)(4)(ii)(C).

235. 45 C.F.R. § 164.308(a)(5)(i).

236. 45 C.F.R. § 164.308(a)(5)(ii)(A).

14:95. Security awareness and training—Protection from malicious software

This implementation relates to procedures for guarding against, detecting, and reporting malicious software.[237]

14:96. Security awareness and training—Log-in monitoring

Covered entities and business associates must consider procedures for monitoring log-in attempts and reporting discrepancies.[238]

14:97. Security awareness and training— Password management

This relates to procedures for creating, changing, and safeguarding passwords.[239]

14:98. Security incident procedures

Covered entities and business associates must implement policies and procedures to address security incidents.[240]

14:99. Security incident procedures—Response and Reporting

HIPAA requires that covered entities identify and respond to suspected or known security incidents; mitigate, to the extent practicable, the harmful effects of known security incidents; and document security incidents and their outcomes.[241]

14:100. Contingency plan

Covered entities and business associates must establish and implement, as needed, policies and procedures for responding to emergent situations or other occurrences that damage the systems that contain electronic health information.[242]

14:101. Contingency plan—Data backup plan

HIPAA requires the establishment and implementation of procedures to create and maintain retrievable exact copies of electronic protected health information.[243]

---

237. Malicious software means software, for example, a virus, designed to damage or disrupt a system. 45 C.F.R. § 164.304.
238. 45 C.F.R. § 164.308(a)(5)(ii)(C).
239. 45 C.F.R. § 164.308(a)(5)(ii)(D). "Password" means confidential authentication information composed of a string of characters. 45 C.F.R. § 164.304.
240. 45 C.F.R. § 164.308(a)(6)(i).
241. 45 C.F.R. § 164.308(a)(6)(ii).
242. 45 C.F.R. § 164.308(a)(7)(i).
243. 45 C.F.R. § 164.308(a)(7)(ii)(A).

14:102. Contingency plan—Disaster recovery plan

A disaster discovery plan must be established and implemented as needed and must provide procedures to restore any loss of data.[244]

14:103. Contingency plan—Emergency mode operation plan

Covered entities and business associates must establish, and implement as needed, procedures to enable continuation of critical business processes for protection of the security of electronic protected health information while operating in emergency mode.[245]

14:104. Contingency plan—Testing and revision procedures

This implementation is addressable. It suggests implementing procedures for periodic testing and revision of contingency plans.[246]

14:105. Contingency plan—Applications and data criticality analysis

This implementation is also addressable. It contemplates assessment of the relative criticality of specific applications and data in support of other contingency plan components.[247]

14:106. Evaluation

Covered entities and business associates must perform periodic technical and non-technical evaluations, based at least initially upon the standards implemented under HIPAA, and thereafter in response to environmental or operational changes affecting the security of electronic protected health information. These evaluations must establish the extent to which an entity's security policies and procedures meet the requirements of HIPAA.[248]

14:107. Business associate contracts and other agreements

A covered entity, in accordance with § 164.306, may permit a business associate to create, receive, maintain, or transmit electronic protected health information on the covered entity's behalf only if the covered entity obtains satisfactory assurances, in accordance with § 164.314(a) that the business associate will appropriately safeguard the information.[249] A covered entity must document the satisfactory assurances required

---

244. 45 C.F.R. § 164.308(a)(7)(ii)(B).
245. 45 C.F.R. § 164.308(a)(7)(ii)(C).
246. 45 C.F.R. § 164.308(a)(7)(ii)(D).
247. 45 C.F.R. § 164.308(a)(7)(ii)(E).
248. 45 C.F.R. § 164.308(a)(8).
249. 45 C.F.R. § 164.308(b)(1).

by paragraph (b)(1) of this section through a written contract or other arrangement with the business associate that meets the applicable requirements of § 164.314(a).[250]

This standard does not apply with respect to the transmission by a covered entity of electronic protected health information to a health care provider concerning the treatment of an individual; the transmission of electronic protected health information by a group health plan or an HMO[251] or health insurance issuer[252] on behalf of a group health plan to a plan sponsor,[253] to the extent that the requirements of § 164.314(b) and § 164.504(f) apply and are met; or the transmission of electronic protected health information from or to other agencies providing the services at § 164.502(e)(1)(ii)(C), when the covered entity is a health plan that is a government program providing public benefits, if the requirements of § 164.502(e)(1)(ii)(C) are met.[254]

A covered entity that violates the satisfactory assurances it provided as a business associate of another covered entity will be in noncompliance with the standards, implementation specifications, and requirements of this paragraph and § 164.314(a).[255]

14:108. Physical safeguards

A covered entity and business associate must implement policies and procedures to limit physical access[256] to its electronic information systems[257] and the facility or facilities[258] in which they are housed, while ensuring that properly authorized access is allowed.[259] This includes contingency operations, which is an addressable portion of the regulations, which includes establishing and implementing as needed procedures that allow facility access in support of restoration of lost data under the disaster recovery plan and emergency mode operations plan in the event of an emergency.[260] Other addressable portions of the regulations include facility security plans, access control and validation

---

250. 45 C.F.R. § 164.308(b)(4).

251. "Health maintenance organization" (HMO) (as defined in section 2791(b)(3) of the PHS Act, 42 U.S.C. § 300gg-91(b)(3) and used in the definition of health plan in this section) means a federally qualified HMO, an organization recognized as an HMO under state law, or a similar organization regulated for solvency under state law in the same manner and to the same extent as such an HMO. 45 C.F.R. § 160.103.

252. "Health insurance issuer" (as defined in section 2791(b)(2) of the PHS Act, 42 U.S.C. § 300gg-91(b)(2) and used in the definition of health plan in this section) means an insurance company, insurance service, or insurance organization (including an HMO) that is licensed to engage in the business of insurance in a state and is subject to state law that regulates insurance. Such term does not include a group health plan. 45 C.F.R. § 160.103.

253. Plan sponsor is defined as defined at section 3(16)(B) of ERISA, 29 U.S.C. § 1002(16)(B). 45 C.F.R. § 164.103.

254. 45 C.F.R. §§ 164.308(b)(2)(i)–(iii).

255. 45 C.F.R. § 164.308(b)(3).

256. "Access" means the ability or the means necessary to read, write, modify, or communicate data/information or otherwise use any system resource. (This definition applies to "access" as used in this subpart, not as used in subparts D or E of this part.) 45 C.F.R. § 164.304.

257. "Information system" means an interconnected set of information resources under the same direct management control that shares common functionality. A system normally includes hardware, software, information, data, applications, communications, and people. 45 C.F.R. § 164.304.

258. Facility means the physical premises and the interior and exterior of a building(s). 45 C.F.R. § 164.304.

259. 45 C.F.R. § 164.310(a)(1).

260. 45 C.F.R. § 164.310(a)(2)(i).

procedures and maintenance records. These require, if applicable, implementing policies and procedures to safeguard the facility and the equipment therein from unauthorized physical access, tampering, and theft, implementing procedures to control and validate a person's access to facilities based on their role or function, including visitor control, and control of access to software programs for testing and revision, and implementing policies and procedures to document repairs and modifications to the physical components of a facility which are related to security (for example, hardware, walls, doors, and locks).[261] Workstation use and security are also issues that must be dealt with.[262] Standards regarding device and media controls, including the required implementations of disposal and media reuse, as well as the addressable implementations of accountability and data backup and storage is also a HIPAA standard.[263]

14:109. Device and media controls

A covered entity as well as business associate must implement policies and procedures that govern the receipt and removal of hardware and electronic media that contain electronic protected health information into and out of a facility,[264] and the movement of these items within the facility.[265] The implementation specifications include disposal, media reuse, as well as addressable requirements of accountability and data backup and storage. Disposal requires implementing policies and procedures to address the final disposition of electronic protected health information, and/or the hardware or electronic media on which it is stored.[266] Media reuse requires procedures for removal of electronic protected health information from electronic media before the media are made available for reuse.[267] Accountability requires maintaining a record of the movements of hardware and electronic media and any person responsible for these.[268] Data backup and storage requires creating a retrievable, exact copy of electronic protected health information, when needed, before movement of equipment.[269]

14:110. Technical safeguards

HIPAA also sets standards and implementations for technical safeguards[270] which require the implementation of technical policies and procedures for electronic information

---

261. 45 C.F.R. §§ 164.310(a)(2)(i)–(iv).

262. 45 C.F.R. §§ 164.310(b) to (c).

263. 45 C.F.R. § 164.310(d).

264. Facility means the physical premises and the interior and exterior of a building(s). 45 C.F.R. § 164.304.

265. 45 C.F.R. § 164.310(d)(1).

266. 45 C.F.R. § 164.310(d)(2)(i).

267. 45 C.F.R. § 164.310(d)(2)(ii).

268. 45 C.F.R. § 164.310(d)(2)(iii).

269. 45 C.F.R. § 164.310(d)(2)(iv).

270. "Technical safeguards" means the technology and the policy and procedures for its use that protect electronic protected health information and control access to it. 45 C.F.R. § 164.304.

systems[271] that maintain electronic protected health information to allow access[272] only to those persons or software programs that have been granted access rights as specified in § 164.308(a)(4).[273] Access control, which is implemented through the requirements of unique user identification and emergency access procedures, as well as the addressable implementations of automatic logoff and encryption[274] and decryption are also contemplated.[275] Audit controls, as well as integrity, which is implemented through the addressable requirement that there be a mechanism to authenticate electronic protected health information, are also HIPAA standards.[276] Person or entity authentication and transmission security, which is implemented by the addressable requirements of integrity controls and encryption, are also required.[277]

Unique user[278] identification, which is implemented though the assignment of a unique name and/or number for identifying and tracking user identity, is required, as is emergency access procedure, which requires covered entities to establish and implement as needed procedures for obtaining necessary electronic protected health information during an emergency.[279]

Automatic logoff can be implemented through electronic procedures that terminate an electronic session after a predetermined time of inactivity, and encryption[280] and decryption is implemented though a mechanism to encrypt and decrypt electronic protected health information.[281]

Audit controls require the implementation of hardware, software, and/or procedural mechanisms that record and examine activity in information systems that contain or use electronic protected health information.[282] Integrity requires the implementation of policies and procedures to protect electronic protected health information from improper alteration or destruction, including through the addressable specification of creating a mechanism to authenticate electronic protected health information and implementing electronic mechanisms to corroborate that electronic protected health information has not been altered or destroyed in an unauthorized manner.[283]

---

271. "Information system" means an interconnected set of information resources under the same direct management control that shares common functionality. A system normally includes hardware, software, information, data, applications, communications, and people. 45 C.F.R. § 164.304.

272. "Access" means the ability or the means necessary to read, write, modify, or communicate data/information or otherwise use any system resource. (This definition applies to "access" as used in this subpart, not as used in subparts D or E of this part.) 45 C.F.R. § 164.304.

273. 45 C.F.R. § 164.312(a)(1).

274. "Encryption" means the use of an algorithmic process to transform data into a form in which there is a low probability of assigning meaning without use of a confidential process or key. 45 C.F.R. § 164.304.

275. 45 C.F.R. §§ 164.312(a)(1) to (2).

276. 45 C.F.R. §§ 164.312(b) to (c)(2).

277. 45 C.F.R. §§ 164.312(d) to (e)(2).

278. "User" means a person or entity with authorized access. 45 C.F.R. § 164.304.

279. 45 C.F.R. §§ 164.312(a)(2)(i)–(ii).

280. "Encryption" means the use of an algorithmic process to transform data into a form in which there is a low probability of assigning meaning without use of a confidential process or key. 45 C.F.R. § 164.304.

281. 45 C.F.R. §§ 164.312(a)(2)(iii)–(iv).

282. 45 C.F.R. § 164.312(b).

283. 45 C.F.R. §§ 164.312(c)(1)–(2).

Person or entity authentication[284] requires the implementation of procedures to verify that a person or entity seeking access to electronic protected health information is the one claimed, and transmission security[285] requires the implementation of technical security measures to guard against unauthorized access to electronic protected health information that is being transmitted over an electronic communications network.[286] The addressable integrity controls specification suggests the implementation of security measures to ensure that electronically transmitted electronic protected health information is not improperly modified without detection until disposed of, and encryption is implemented via a mechanism to encrypt electronic protected health information whenever deemed appropriate.[287]

14:111. Organizational requirements

Covered entities and business associates are also required to meet certain organizational requirements, which include the entry of business associate agreements or other arrangements. (If a business associate entered into a subcontract, then that subcontractor would also become a business associate.) This includes requirements that the business associate meet technical and security requirements, as well as many other requirements.[288] The contract must provide that the business associate will implement administrative,[289] physical,[290] and technical safeguards[291] that reasonably and appropriately protect the confidentiality,[292] integrity,[293] and availability[294] of the electronic protected health information that it creates, receives, maintains, or transmits on behalf of the covered entity as required by this subpart; it must ensure that any agent, including a subcontractor, to whom it provides such information, agrees to implement reasonable and appropriate safeguards to protect it; it must report to the covered entity any security incident[295]

---

284. Authentication means the corroboration that a person is the one claimed. 45 C.F.R. § 164.304.

285. Security or Security measures encompass all of the administrative, physical, and technical safeguards in an information system. 45 C.F.R. § 164.304.

286. 45 C.F.R. § 164.312(d)–(e)(1).

287. 45 C.F.R. § 164.312(e)(2)(i)–(ii).

288. 45 C.F.R. § 164.314.

289. Administrative safeguards are administrative actions, and policies and procedures, to manage the selection, development, implementation, and maintenance of security measures to protect electronic protected health information and to manage the conduct of the covered entity's workforce in relation to the protection of that information. 45 C.F.R. § 164.304.

290. Physical safeguards are physical measures, policies, and procedures to protect a covered entity's electronic information systems and related buildings and equipment, from natural and environmental hazards, and unauthorized intrusion. 45 C.F.R. § 164.304.

291. Technical safeguards means the technology and the policy and procedures for its use that protect electronic protected health information and control access to it. 45 C.F.R. § 164.304.

292. Confidentiality means the property that data or information is not made available or disclosed to unauthorized persons or processes. 45 C.F.R. § 164.304.

293. Integrity means the property that data or information have not been altered or destroyed in an unauthorized manner. 45 C.F.R. § 164.304.

294. Availability means the property that data or information is accessible and useable upon demand by an authorized person. 45 C.F.R. § 164.304.

295. Security incident means the attempted or successful unauthorized access, use, disclosure, modification, or destruction of information or interference with system operations in an information system. 45 C.F.R. § 164.304.

of which it becomes aware; and it must authorize termination of the contract by the covered entity, if the covered entity determines that the business associate has violated a material term of the contract.[296] When a covered entity and its business associate are both governmental entities, the covered entity is in compliance with § 164.314(a)(1) if it enters into a memorandum of understanding with the business associate that contains terms that accomplish the objectives of § 164.314(a)(2)(i), or if other law (including regulations adopted by the covered entity or its business associate) contains requirements applicable to the business associate that accomplish the objectives of § 164.314(a)(2)(i).[297]

If a business associate is required by law[298] to perform a function or activity on behalf of a covered entity or to provide a service described in the definition of business associate as specified in § 160.103 of this subchapter to a covered entity, the covered entity may permit the business associate to create, receive, maintain, or transmit electronic protected health information on its behalf to the extent necessary to comply with the legal mandate without meeting the requirements of paragraph (a)(2)(i) of this section, provided that the covered entity attempts in good faith to obtain satisfactory assurances as required by paragraph (a)(2)(ii)(A) of this section, and documents the attempt and the reasons that these assurances cannot be obtained.[299] The covered entity may omit from its other arrangements authorization of the termination of the contract by the covered entity, as required by § 164.314(a)(2)(i)(D) of this section, if such authorization is inconsistent with the statutory obligations of the covered entity or its business associate.[300]

A covered entity is not in compliance with the standards in § 164.502(e) and § 164.314(a) if the covered entity knew of a pattern of an activity or practice of the business associate that constituted a material breach or violation of the business associate's obligation under the contract or other arrangement, unless the covered entity took reasonable steps to cure the breach or end the violation, as applicable, and, if such steps were unsuccessful, terminated the contract or arrangement, if feasible, or if termination is not feasible, reported the problem to the secretary.[301] Group plans must also take steps to ensure that the plan documents reasonably and appropriately safeguard electronic protected health information.[302]

---

296. 45 C.F.R. §§ 164.314(a)(2)(i)(A)–(D).

297. 45 C.F.R. §§ 164.314(a)(2)(ii)(A)(1)–(2).

298. Required by law means a mandate contained in law that compels an entity to make a use or disclosure of protected health information and that is enforceable in a court of law. Required by law includes, but is not limited to, court orders and court-ordered warrants; subpoenas or summons issued by a court, grand jury, a governmental or tribal inspector general, or an administrative body authorized to require the production of information; a civil or an authorized investigative demand; Medicare conditions of participation with respect to health care providers participating in the program; and statutes or regulations that require the production of information, including statutes or regulations that require such information if payment is sought under a government program providing public benefits. 45 C.F.R. § 164.103.

299. 45 C.F.R. § 164.314(a)(2)(ii)(B).

300. 45 C.F.R. § 164.314(a)(2)(ii)(C).

301. 45 C.F.R. § 164.314(a)(1)(ii)(A)–(B).

302. 45 C.F.R. § 164.314(b)(1).

14:112. Organizational requirements—Requirements for group health plans

Except when the only electronic protected health information disclosed to a plan sponsor[303] is disclosed pursuant to § 164.504(f)(1)(ii) or (iii), or as authorized under § 164.508, a group health plan[304] must ensure that its plan documents provide that the plan sponsor will reasonably and appropriately safeguard electronic protected health information created, received, maintained, or transmitted to or by the plan sponsor on behalf of the group health plan.[305] This must be implemented by amending the plan documents of the group health plan to incorporate provisions to require the plan sponsor to implement administrative, physical, and technical safeguards that reasonably and appropriately protect the confidentiality, integrity, and availability of the electronic protected health information that it creates, receives, maintains, or transmits on behalf of the group health plan; to ensure that the adequate separation required by § 164.504(f)(2)(iii) is supported by reasonable and appropriate security measures; ensure that any agent, including a subcontractor, to whom it provides this information agrees to implement reasonable and appropriate security measures to protect the information; and report to the group health plan any security incident of which it becomes aware.[306]

14:113. Policies and procedures

Covered entities and business associates must adopt reasonable and appropriate policies and procedures to comply with these standards, implementation specifications and other requirements of HIPAA, taking into account the factors identified by HIPAA, including under § 164.302(b).[307] These policies and procedures must be in written (including electronic) form for certain specified periods of time.[308] Moreover, if an action, activity, or assessment is required to be documented, it must be maintained in written format. Documentation required by this section must be retained for six years from the date of its creation or the date when it was last in effect, whichever is greater.[309] The documentation must be made available to the people responsible for implementing procedures to which the documentation pertains, and the documentation must be reviewed periodically and

---

303. Plan sponsor is defined as defined at section 3(16)(B) of ERISA, 29 U.S.C. § 1002(16)(B). 45 C.F.R. § 164.103.

304. "Group health plan" (also see definition of health plan in this section) means an employee welfare benefit plan (as defined in section 3(1) of the Employee Retirement Income and Security Act of 1974 (ERISA), 29 U.S.C. § 1002(1)), including insured and self-insured plans, to the extent that the plan provides medical care (as defined in section 2791(a)(2) of the Public Health Service Act (PHS Act), 42 U.S.C. § 300gg-91(a)(2)), including items and services paid for as medical care, to employees or their dependents directly or through insurance, reimbursement, or otherwise, that: (1) Has 50 or more participants (as defined in section 3(7) of ERISA, 29 U.S.C. § 1002(7)); or (2) Is administered by an entity other than the employer that established and maintains the plan. 45 C.F.R. § 160.103.

305. 45 C.F.R. § 164.314(b)(1).

306. 45 C.F.R. §§ 164.314(b)(2)(i)–(iv).

307. 45 C.F.R. § 164.316(a).

308. 45 C.F.R. § 164.316(b)(2).

309. 45 C.F.R. § 164.316(b)(2)(i).

updated as needed, in response to environmental or operational changes affecting the security of the electronic protected health information.[310]

D. Privacy

14:114. Application of privacy provisions and penalties to business associates

If a business associate of a covered entity obtains or creates protected health information pursuant to a written contract (or other written arrangement) described in 45 C.F.R. § 164.502(e)(2), with a covered entity, the business associate may use and disclose such protected health information only if such use or disclosure, respectively, is in compliance with each applicable requirement of section § 164.504(e).[311] The additional requirements of this subchapter that relate to privacy and that are made applicable with respect to covered entities are also applicable to such a business associate and must be incorporated into the business associate agreement between the business associate and the covered entity.[312]

14:115. Applicability

Except as otherwise provided, the standards, requirements, and implementation specifications of this subpart apply to covered entities with respect to protected health information.[313] While the HITECH Act largely focused on the application of the Security Role to Business Associates, the HITECH Act and subsequent regulations also apply limited aspects of the privacy Role directing to Business Associates.

14:116. Application to Health care clearinghouses

Health care clearinghouses must comply with the standards, requirements, and implementation specifications as set forth below. When a health care clearinghouse creates or receives protected health information as a business associate of another covered entity, the clearinghouse must comply with the following:

- Section 164.500 relating to applicability;
- Section 164.501 relating to definitions;
- Section 164.502 relating to uses and disclosures of protected health information, except that a clearinghouse is prohibited from using or disclosing protected health information other than as permitted in the business associate contract under which it created or received the protected health information;
- Section 164.504 relating to the organizational requirements for covered entities;

---

310. 45 C.F.R. §§ 164.316(b)(2)(ii)–(iii).

311. 42 U.S.C. § 17934(a).

312. 42 U.S.C. § 17934(a).

313. 45 C.F.R. § 164.500(a).

- Section 164.512 relating to uses and disclosures for which individual authorization or an opportunity to agree or object is not required, except that a clearinghouse is prohibited from using or disclosing protected health information other than as permitted in the business associate contract under which it created or received the protected health information;

- Section 164.532 relating to transition requirements; and

- Section 164.534 relating to compliance dates for initial implementation of the privacy standards.[314]

When a health care clearinghouse creates or receives protected health information other than as a business associate of a covered entity, the clearinghouse must comply with all of the standards, requirements, and implementation specifications of this subpart.[315]

14:117. Exceptions

The standards, requirements, and implementation specifications of this subpart do not apply to the Department of Defense or to any other federal agency, or non-governmental organization acting on its behalf, when providing health care to overseas foreign national beneficiaries.[316]

14:118. Uses and disclosures of de-identified protected health information

A covered entity may not use or disclose protected health information, except as permitted or required by the Privacy Rule or by 45 C.F.R. Part 160 subpart C.[317] A covered entity is permitted to use or disclose protected health information as follows: to the individual; for treatment, payment, or health care operations, as permitted by and in compliance with § 164.506; incident to a use or disclosure otherwise permitted or required by this subpart, provided that the covered entity has complied with the applicable requirements of § 164.502(b), § 164.514(d), and § 164.530(c) with respect to such otherwise permitted or required use or disclosure; pursuant to and in compliance with a valid authorization under § 164.508; pursuant to an agreement under, or as otherwise permitted by, § 164.510; and as permitted by and in compliance with this section, § 164.512, or § 164.514(e), (f), or (g).[318]

A covered entity is required to disclose protected health information to an individual, when requested under, and required by § 164.524 or § 164.528, and when required by HHS to investigate or determine the covered entity's compliance.[319]

---

314. 45 C.F.R. §§ 164.500(b)(1)(i)–(vii).

315. 45 C.F.R. § 164.500(b)(2).

316. 45 C.F.R. § 164.500(c).

317. 45 C.F.R. § 164.502(a).

318. 45 C.F.R. §§ 164.502(a)(1)(i)–(vi)

319. 45 C.F.R. §§ 164.502(a)(2)(i)–(ii).

14:119. Minimum necessary

When using or disclosing protected health information or when requesting protected health information from another covered entity, a covered entity must make reasonable efforts to limit protected health information to the minimum necessary to accomplish the intended purpose of the use, disclosure, or request.[320]

This requirement does not apply to disclosures to or requests by a health care provider for treatment; uses or disclosures made to the individual, as permitted under paragraph (a)(1)(i) of this section or as required by paragraph (a)(2)(i) of this section; uses or disclosures made pursuant to an authorization under § 164.508; certain disclosures made to HHS; uses or disclosures that are required by law, as described by § 164.512(a); and uses or disclosures that are required for compliance with applicable requirements of this subchapter.[321]

14:120. Uses and disclosures of protected health information subject to an agreed upon restriction

A covered entity that has agreed to a restriction pursuant to § 164.522(a)(1) may not use or disclose the protected health information covered by the restriction in violation of such restriction, except as otherwise provided in § 164.522(a).[322]

14:121. Creation of not individually identifiable information

A covered entity may use protected health information to create information that is not individually identifiable health information or may disclose protected health information only to a business associate for such purpose, whether or not the de-identified information is to be used by the covered entity.[323] Health information that meets the standard and implementation specifications for de-identification under § 164.514(a) and (b) is considered not to be individually identifiable health information (i.e., de-identified).[324] The requirements of this subpart do not apply to information that has been de-identified in accordance with the applicable requirements of § 164.514, provided that disclosure of a code or other means of record identification designed to enable coded or otherwise de-identified information to be re-identified constitutes disclosure of protected health information, and if de-identified information is re-identified, a covered entity may use or disclose such re-identified information only as permitted or required by this subpart.[325]

---

320. 45 C.F.R. § 164.502(b)(1).
321. 45 C.F.R. §§ 164.502(b)(2)(i)–(vi).
322. 45 C.F.R. § 164.502(c).
323. 45 C.F.R. § 164.502(d)(1).
324. 45 C.F.R. § 164.502(d)(2).
325. 45 C.F.R. § 164.502(d)(2).

14:122. Disclosures to business associates

A covered entity may disclose protected health information to a business associate and may allow a business associate to create or receive protected health information on its behalf, if the covered entity obtains satisfactory assurance that the business associate will appropriately safeguard the information.[326] This standard does not apply with respect to disclosures by a covered entity to a health care provider concerning the treatment[327] of the individual; with respect to disclosures by a group health plan or a health insurance issuer or HMO with respect to a group health plan to the plan sponsor, to the extent that the requirements of § 164.504(f) apply and are met; or with respect to uses or disclosures by a health plan that is a government program providing public benefits, if eligibility for or enrollment in the health plan is determined by an agency other than the agency administering the health plan, or if the protected health information used to determine enrollment or eligibility in the health plan is collected by an agency other than the agency administering the health plan, and such activity is authorized by law, with respect to the collection and sharing of individually identifiable health information for the performance of such functions by the health plan and the agency other than the agency administering the health plan.[328]

A covered entity that violates the satisfactory assurances it provided as a business associate of another covered entity will be in noncompliance with the standards, implementation specifications, and requirements of this paragraph and § 164.504(e).[329] A covered entity must implement this requirement by documenting the satisfactory assurances required by paragraph (e)(1) of this section through a written contract or other written agreement or arrangement with the business associate that meets the applicable requirements of § 164.504(e).[330]

14:123. Deceased individuals

A covered entity must comply with the requirements of this subpart with respect to the protected health information of a deceased individual.[331]

14:124. Personal representatives

A covered entity must, except as provided in § 164.502(g)(3) and (g)(5), treat a personal representative as the individual .[332] With respect to adults and emancipated minors if under applicable law a person has authority to act on behalf of an individual who is an adult or an emancipated minor in making decisions related to health care, a covered

---

326. 45 C.F.R. § 164.502(e)(1)(i).

327. "Treatment" means the provision, coordination, or management of health care and related services by one or more health care providers, including the coordination or management of health care by a health care provider with a third party; consultation between health care providers relating to a patient; or the referral of a patient for health care from one health care provider to another. 45 C.F.R. § 164.501.

328. 45 C.F.R. §§ 164.502(e)(1)(ii)(A)–(C).

329. 45 C.F.R. § 164.502(e)(1)(iii).

330. 45 C.F.R. § 164.502(e)(2).

331. 45 C.F.R. § 164.502(f).

332. 45 C.F.R. § 164.502(g)(1).

entity must treat such person as a personal representative, with respect to protected health information relevant to such personal representation.[333]

14:125. Adults and emancipated minors

If under applicable law a parent, guardian, or other person acting *in loco parentis* has authority to act on behalf of an individual who is an unemancipated minor in making decisions related to health care, a covered entity must treat such person as a personal representative, with respect to protected health information relevant to the personal representation, except that such person may not be a personal representative of an unemancipated minor, and the minor has the authority to act as an individual, with respect to protected health information pertaining to a health care service, if the minor consents to such health care service; no other consent to such health care service is required by law, regardless of whether the consent of another person has also been obtained; and the minor has not requested that such person be treated as the personal representative; the minor may lawfully obtain such health care service without the consent of a parent, guardian, or other person acting in loco parentis, and the minor, a court, or another person authorized by law consents to such health care service; or a parent, guardian, or other person acting in loco parentis assents to an agreement of confidentiality between a covered health care provider and the minor with respect to such health care service.[334]

However, if and to the extent, permitted or required by an applicable provision of state or other law, including applicable case law, a covered entity may disclose, or provide access in accordance with § 164.524 to, protected health information about an unemancipated minor to a parent, guardian, or other person acting in loco parentis.[335] If, and to the extent, prohibited by an applicable provision of state or other law, including applicable case law, a covered entity may not disclose, or provide access in accordance with § 164.524 to, protected health information about an unemancipated minor to a parent, guardian, or other person acting in loco parentis.[336] Finally, where the parent, guardian, or other person acting in loco parentis, is not the personal representative under paragraphs (g)(3)(i)(A), (B), or (C) of this section and where there is no applicable access provision under state or other law, including case law, a covered entity may provide or deny access under § 164.524 to a parent, guardian, or other person acting in loco parentis, if such action is consistent with state or other applicable law, provided that such decision must be made by a licensed health care professional, in the exercise of professional judgment.[337]

14:126. Deceased individuals

For deceased individuals, if under applicable law an executor, administrator, or other person has authority to act on behalf of a deceased individual or of the individual's

---

333. 45 C.F.R. § 164.502(g)(2).

334. 45 C.F.R. §§ 164.502(g)(3)(i)(A)–(C).

335. 45 C.F.R. § 164.502(g)(3)(ii)(A).

336. 45 C.F.R. § 164.502(g)(3)(ii)(B).

337. 45 C.F.R. § 164.502(g)(3)(ii)(C).

estate, a covered entity must treat such person as a personal representative under this subchapter, with respect to protected health information relevant to the personal representation.[338]

14:127. Confidential communications

A covered health care provider or health plan must comply with the applicable requirements of § 164.522(b) in communicating protected health information.[339]

14:128. Abuse, neglect, endangerment situations

Notwithstanding a state law or any requirement of this paragraph to the contrary, a covered entity may elect not to treat a person as the personal representative of an individual if the covered entity has a reasonable belief that the individual has been or may be subjected to domestic violence, abuse, or neglect by such person; or treating such person as the personal representative could endanger the individual, and the covered entity, in the exercise of professional judgment, decides that it is not in the best interest of the individual to treat the person as the individual's personal representative.[340]

14:129. Processing and disclosures with notice

A covered entity that is required by § 164.520 to have a notice may not use or disclose protected health information in a manner inconsistent with such notice. A covered entity that is required by § 164.520(b)(1)(iii) to include a specific statement in its notice if it intends to engage in an activity listed in §§ 164.520(b)(1)(iii)(A)–(C), may not use or disclose protected health information for such activities, unless the required statement is included in the notice.[341]

E.   Uses and disclosures

14:130. Business associate contracts

The contract or other arrangement between the covered entity and the business associate required by § 164.502(e)(2) must meet the requirements of paragraph (e)(2) or (e)(3), as applicable.[342] A covered entity is not in compliance with the standards in § 164.502(e) and paragraph (e) of this section, if the covered entity knew of a pattern of activity or practice of the business associate that constituted a material breach or violation of the business associate's obligation under the contract or other arrangement, unless the covered entity took reasonable steps to cure the breach or end the violation, as applicable, and,

---

338. 45 C.F.R. § 164.502(g)(4).
339. 45 C.F.R. § 164.502(h).
340. 45 C.F.R. §§ 164.502(g)(5)(i)–(ii).
341. 45 C.F.R. § 164.502(i).
342. 45 C.F.R. § 164.504(e)(1)(i).

if such steps were unsuccessful terminated the contract or arrangement, if feasible, or if termination is not feasible, reported the problem to the secretary.[343]

A contract between the covered entity and a business associate must establish the permitted and required uses and disclosures of such information by the business associate. The contract may not authorize the business associate to use or further disclose the information in a manner that would violate the requirements of this subpart, if done by the covered entity, except that the contract may permit the business associate to use and disclose protected health information for the proper management and administration of the business associate, as provided in paragraph (e)(4) of this section, and the contract may permit the business associate to provide data aggregation[344] services relating to the health care operations[345] of the covered entity.[346]

The agreement must also provide that the business associate will not use or further disclose the information other than as permitted or required by the contract or as required by law; will use appropriate safeguards to prevent use or disclosure of the information other than as provided for by its contract; will report to the covered entity any use or disclosure of the information not provided for by its contract of which it becomes aware; will ensure that any agents, including a subcontractor, to whom it provides protected

---

343. 45 C.F.R. § 164.504(e)(1)(ii)(A)–(B).

344. "Data aggregation" means, with respect to protected health information created or received by a business associate in its capacity as the business associate of a covered entity, the combining of such protected health information by the business associate with the protected health information received by the business associate in its capacity as a business associate of another covered entity, to permit data analyses that relate to the health care operations of the respective covered entities. 45 C.F.R. § 164.501.

345. "Health care operations" means any of the following activities of the covered entity to the extent that the activities are related to covered functions: (1) Conducting quality assessment and improvement activities, including outcomes evaluation and development of clinical guidelines, provided that the obtaining of generalizable knowledge is not the primary purpose of any studies resulting from such activities; population-based activities relating to improving health or reducing health care costs, protocol development, case management and care coordination, contacting of health care providers and patients with information about treatment alternatives; and related functions that do not include treatment; (2) Reviewing the competence or qualifications of health care professionals, evaluating practitioner and provider performance, health plan performance, conducting training programs in which students, trainees, or practitioners in areas of health care learn under supervision to practice or improve their skills as health care providers, training of non-health care professionals, accreditation, certification, licensing, or credentialing activities; (3) Underwriting, premium rating, and other activities relating to the creation, renewal or replacement of a contract of health insurance or health benefits, and ceding, securing, or placing a contract for reinsurance of risk relating to claims for health care (including stop-loss insurance and excess of loss insurance), provided that the requirements of § 164.514(g) are met, if applicable; (4) Conducting or arranging for medical review, legal services, and auditing functions, including fraud and abuse detection and compliance programs; (5) Business planning and development, such as conducting cost-management and planning-related analyses related to managing and operating the entity, including formulary development and administration, development or improvement of methods of payment or coverage policies; and (6) Business management and general administrative activities of the entity, including, but not limited to: (i) Management activities relating to implementation of and compliance with the requirements of this subchapter; (ii) Customer service, including the provision of data analyses for policy holders, plan sponsors, or other customers, provided that protected health information is not disclosed to such policy holder, plan sponsor, or customer. (iii) Resolution of internal grievances; (iv) The sale, transfer, merger, or consolidation of all or part of the covered entity with another covered entity, or an entity that following such activity will become a covered entity and due diligence related to such activity; and (v) Consistent with the applicable requirements of § 164.514, creating de-identified health information or a limited data set, and fundraising for the benefit of the covered entity. 45 C.F.R. § 164.501.

346. 45 C.F.R. §§ 164.504(e)(2)(i)(A)–(B).

health information received from, or created or received by the business associate on behalf of, the covered entity agrees to the same restrictions and conditions that apply to the business associate with respect to such information; will make available protected health information in accordance with § 164.524; will make available protected health information for amendment and incorporate any amendments to protected health information in accordance with § 164.526; will make available the information required to provide an accounting of disclosures in accordance with § 164.528; will make its internal practices, books, and records relating to the use and disclosure of protected health information received from, or created or received by the business associate on behalf of, the covered entity available to the secretary for purposes of determining the covered entity's compliance with this subpart; and at termination of the contract, if feasible, will return or destroy all protected health information received from, or created or received by the business associate on behalf of, the covered entity that the business associate still maintains in any form and retain no copies of such information or, if such return or destruction is not feasible, the business associate will extend the protections of the contract to the information and limit further uses and disclosures to those purposes that make the return or destruction of the information infeasible.[347]

The agreement must also allow termination of the contract by the covered entity, if the covered entity determines that the business associate has violated a material term of the contract.[348]

14:131. Other arrangements for business associate agreements

If a covered entity and its business associate are both governmental entities the covered entity may comply with paragraph (e) of this section by entering into a memorandum of understanding with the business associate that contains terms that accomplish the objectives of paragraph (e)(2).[349] The covered entity may comply with paragraph (e), if other law (including regulations adopted by the covered entity or its business associate) contains requirements applicable to the business associate that accomplish the objectives of paragraph (e)(2).[350]

Moreover, if a business associate is required by law to perform a function or activity on behalf of a covered entity or to provide a service described in the definition of business associate in § 160.103 to a covered entity, such covered entity may disclose protected health information to the business associate to the extent necessary to comply with the legal mandate without meeting the requirements of this paragraph (e), provided that the covered entity attempts in good faith to obtain satisfactory assurances as required by paragraph (e)(3)(i), and, if such attempt fails, documents the attempt and the reasons that such assurances cannot be obtained.[351] The covered entity may omit from its other arrangements the termination authorization required by paragraph (e)(2)

---

347. 45 C.F.R. §§ 164.504(e)(2)(ii)(A)–(I).
348. 45 C.F.R. § 164.504(e)(2)(iii).
349. 45 C.F.R. § 164.504(e)(3)(i)(A).
350. 45 C.F.R. § 164.504(e)(3)(i)(B).
351. 45 C.F.R. § 164.504(e)(3)(ii).

(iii), if such authorization is inconsistent with the statutory obligations of the covered entity or its business associate.[352]

The contract or other arrangement between the covered entity and the business associate may permit the business associate to use the information received by the business associate in its capacity as a business associate to the covered entity, if necessary for the proper management and administration of the business associate or to carry out the legal responsibilities of the business associate.[353] The contract or other arrangement between the covered entity and the business associate may permit the business associate to disclose the information received by the business associate in its capacity as a business associate for the purposes described in paragraph (e)(4)(i), if the disclosure is required by law or the business associate obtains reasonable assurances from the person to whom the information is disclosed that it will be held confidentially and used or further disclosed only as required by law or for the purpose for which it was disclosed to the person, and the person notifies the business associate of any instances of which it is aware in which the confidentiality of the information has been breached.[354]

14:132 Requirements for group health plans

Except as provided under paragraph (f)(1)(ii) or (iii) or as otherwise authorized under § 164.508, a group health plan, in order to disclose protected health information to the plan sponsor or to provide for or permit the disclosure of protected health information to the plan sponsor by a health insurance issuer or HMO with respect to the group health plan, must ensure that the plan documents restrict uses and disclosures of such information by the plan sponsor consistent with the requirements of this subpart.[355] The group health plan, or a health insurance issuer or HMO with respect to the group health plan, may disclose summary health information[356] to the plan sponsor, if the plan sponsor requests the summary health information for the purpose of obtaining premium bids from health plans for providing health insurance coverage under the group health plan, or modifying, amending, or terminating the group health plan.[357] The group health plan, or a health insurance issuer or HMO with respect to the group health plan, may disclose to the plan sponsor information on whether the individual is participating in the group health plan or is enrolled in or has disenrolled from a health insurance issuer or HMO offered by the plan.[358]

---

352. 45 C.F.R. § 164.504(e)(3)(iii).

353. 45 C.F.R. §§ 164.504(e)(4)(i)(A)–(B).

354. 45 C.F.R. §§ 164.504(e)(4)(ii)(A)–(B).

355. 45 C.F.R. § 164.504(f)(1)(i).

356. Summary health information means information, that may be individually identifiable health information, and: (1) That summarizes the claims history, claims expenses, or type of claims experienced by individuals for whom a plan sponsor has provided health benefits under a group health plan; and (2) From which the information described at § 164.514(b)(2)(i) has been deleted, except that the geographic information described in § 164.514(b)(2)(i)(B) need only be aggregated to the level of a five digit zip code. 45 C.F.R. § 164.504(a).

357. 45 C.F.R. § 164.504(f)(1)(ii)(A)–(B).

358. 45 C.F.R. § 164.504(f)(1)(iii).

The plan documents of the group health plan must be amended to incorporate provisions to establish the permitted and required uses and disclosures of such information by the plan sponsor, provided that such permitted and required uses and disclosures may not be inconsistent with this subpart, and to provide that the group health plan will disclose protected health information to the plan sponsor only upon receipt of a certification by the plan sponsor that the plan documents have been amended to incorporate the following provisions and that the plan sponsor agrees to not use or further disclose the information other than as permitted or required by the plan documents or as required by law; to ensure that any agents, including a subcontractor, to whom it provides protected health information received from the group health plan agree to the same restrictions and conditions that apply to the plan sponsor with respect to such information; to not use or disclose the information for employment-related actions and decisions or in connection with any other benefit or employee benefit plan of the plan sponsor; to report to the group health plan any use or disclosure of the information that is inconsistent with the uses or disclosures provided for of which it becomes aware; to make available protected health information in accordance with § 164.524; to make available protected health information for amendment and incorporate any amendments to protected health information in accordance with § 164.526; to make available the information required to provide an accounting of disclosures in accordance with § 164.528; to make its internal practices, books, and records relating to the use and disclosure of protected health information received from the group health plan available to the secretary for purposes of determining compliance by the group health plan with this subpart; if feasible, to return or destroy all protected health information received from the group health plan that the sponsor still maintains in any form and to retain no copies of such information when no longer needed for the purpose for which disclosure was made, except that, if such return or destruction is not feasible, to limit further uses and disclosures to those purposes that make the return or destruction of the information infeasible; and to ensure that the adequate separation required in paragraph (f)(2)(iii) is established.[359]

Plan documents also must describe those employees or classes of employees or other persons under the control of the plan sponsor to be given access to the protected health information to be disclosed, provided that any employee or person who receives protected health information relating to payment[360] under, health care operations of, or other matters pertaining to the group health plan in the ordinary course of business must

---

359. 45 C.F.R. § 164.504(f)(2)(i)–(ii).

360. Payment means: (1) The activities undertaken by: (i) A health plan to obtain premiums or to determine or fulfill its responsibility for coverage and provision of benefits under the health plan; or (ii) A health care provider or health plan to obtain or provide reimbursement for the provision of health care; and (2) The activities in paragraph (1) of this definition relate to the individual to whom health care is provided and include, but are not limited to: (i) Determinations of eligibility or coverage (including coordination of benefits or the determination of cost sharing amounts), and adjudication or subrogation of health benefit claims; (ii) Risk adjusting amounts due based on enrollee health status and demographic characteristics; (iii) Billing, claims management, collection activities, obtaining payment under a contract for reinsurance (including stop-loss insurance and excess of loss insurance), and related health care data processing; (iv) Review of health care services with respect to medical necessity, coverage under a health plan, appropriateness of care, or justification of charges; (v) Utilization review activities, including precertification and preauthorization of services, concurrent and retrospective review of services; and (vi) Disclosure to consumer reporting agencies of any of the following protected health information relating to collection of premiums or reimbursement: (A)

be included in such description; restrict the access to and use by such employees and other persons described in paragraph (f)(2)(iii)(A) to the plan administration functions[361] that the plan sponsor performs for the group health plan; and provide an effective mechanism for resolving any issues of noncompliance by persons described in paragraph (f)(2)(iii)(A) with the plan document provisions required by this paragraph.[362]

14:133. Uses and disclosures by group health plans

A group health plan may disclose protected health information to a plan sponsor to carry out plan administration functions that the plan sponsor performs only consistent with the provisions of paragraph (f)(2); it may not permit a health insurance issuer or HMO with respect to the group health plan to disclose protected health information to the plan sponsor except as permitted by this paragraph; it may not disclose and may not permit a health insurance issuer or HMO to disclose protected health information to a plan sponsor as otherwise permitted by this paragraph unless a statement required by § 164.520(b)(1)(iii)(C) is included in the appropriate notice; and it may not disclose protected health information to the plan sponsor for the purpose of employment-related actions or decisions or in connection with any other benefit or employee benefit plan of the plan sponsor.[363]

14:134. Requirements for a covered entity with multiple covered functions

A covered entity that performs multiple covered functions that would make the entity any combination of a health plan, a covered health care provider, and a health care clearinghouse, must comply with the standards, requirements, and implementation specifications of this subpart, as applicable to the health plan, health care provider, or health care clearinghouse covered functions performed.[364] A covered entity that performs multiple covered functions may use or disclose the protected health information of individuals who receive the covered entity's health plan or health care provider services, but not both, only for purposes related to the appropriate function being performed.[365]

Name and address; (B) Date of birth; (C) Social security number; (D) Payment history; (E) Account number; and (F) Name and address of the health care provider and/or health plan. 45 C.F.R. § 164.501.

361. Plan administration functions means administration functions performed by the plan sponsor of a group health plan on behalf of the group health plan and excludes functions performed by the plan sponsor in connection with any other benefit or benefit plan of the plan sponsor. 45 C.F.R. § 164.504(a).

362. 45 C.F.R. § 164.504(f)(2)(iii)(A)–(C).

363. 45 C.F.R. §§ 164.504(f)(3)(i)–(iv).

364. 45 C.F.R. § 164.504(g)(1).

365. 45 C.F.R. § 164.504(g)(2).

14:135. Uses and disclosures to carry out treatment, payment, or health care operations

Consent and authorization under HIPAA are different concepts. Consent permits a covered entity to use the information to carry out treatment, payment, or health care operations.[366] Consent, however, does not permit the use of information for which authorization is needed.[367]

Except with respect to uses or disclosures that require an authorization under §§ 164.508(a)(2) and (3), a covered entity may use or disclose protected health information for treatment, payment, or health care operations as set forth in § 164.506(c), provided that such use or disclosure is consistent with other applicable requirements of this subpart.[368] A covered entity may obtain consent of the individual to use or disclose protected health information to carry out treatment, payment, or health care operations.[369] Consent shall not be effective to permit a use or disclosure of protected health information when an authorization, under § 164.508, is required or when another condition must be met for such use or disclosure to be permissible under this subpart.[370]

14:136. Treatment, payment, or health care operations

A covered entity may use or disclose protected health information for its own treatment, payment, or health care operations.[371] A covered entity may disclose protected health information for treatment activities of a health care provider.[372] A covered entity may disclose protected health information to another covered entity or a health care provider for the payment activities of the entity that receives the information.[373] A covered entity may disclose protected health information to another covered entity for health care operations activities of the entity that receives the information, if each entity either has or had a relationship with the individual who is the subject of the protected health information being requested, the protected health information pertains to such relationship, and the disclosure is for a purpose listed in paragraph (1) or (2) of the definition of health care operations or for the purpose of health care fraud and abuse detection or compliance.[374] A covered entity that participates in an organized health care arrangement[375] may disclose protected health information about an individual to

---

366. 45 C.F.R. § 164.506(b).

367. 45 C.F.R. § 164.506(b)(2).

368. 45 C.F.R. § 164.506(a).

369. 45 C.F.R. § 164.506(b)(1).

370. 45 C.F.R. § 164.506(b)(2).

371. 45 C.F.R. § 164.506(c)(1).

372. 45 C.F.R. § 164.506(c)(2).

373. 45 C.F.R. § 164.506(c)(3).

374. 45 C.F.R. §§ 164.506(c)(4)(i)–(ii).

375. "Organized health care arrangement" means: (1) A clinically integrated care setting in which individuals typically receive health care from more than one health care provider; (2) An organized system of health care in which more than one covered entity participates and in which the participating covered entities: (i) Hold themselves out to the public as participating in a joint arrangement; and (ii) Participate in joint activities that include at least one of the following: (A) Utilization review, in which health care decisions by participating covered entities are reviewed by other participating covered entities or by a third party on their

another covered entity that participates in the organized health care arrangement for any health care operations activities of the organized health care arrangement.[376]

14:137. Uses and disclosures for which an authorization is required

Except as otherwise permitted or required by this subchapter, a covered entity may not use or disclose protected health information without an authorization that is valid under this section. When a covered entity obtains or receives a valid authorization for its use or disclosure of protected health information, such use or disclosure must be consistent with such authorization.[377] Notwithstanding any provision of this subpart, other than the transition provisions in § 164.532, a covered entity must obtain an authorization for any use or disclosure of psychotherapy notes,[378] except

- to carry out the following treatment, payment, or health care operations: use by the originator of the psychotherapy notes for treatment; use or disclosure by the covered entity for its own training programs in which students, trainees, or practitioners in mental health learn under supervision to practice or improve their skills in group, joint, family, or individual counseling; or use or disclosure by the covered entity to defend itself in a legal action or other proceeding brought by the individual; and
- if the use or disclosure is required by § 164.502(a)(2)(ii) or permitted by § 164.512(a), § 164.512(d) with respect to the oversight of the originator of the psychotherapy notes, § 164.512(g)(1), or § 164.512(j)(1)(i).[379]

Notwithstanding any provision of this subpart, other than the transition provisions in § 164.532, a covered entity must obtain an authorization for any use or disclosure

---

behalf; (B) Quality assessment and improvement activities, in which treatment provided by participating entities is assessed by other participating covered entities or by a third party on their behalf; or (C) Payment activities, if the financial risk for delivering health care is shared, in part or in whole, by participating covered entities through the joint arrangement and if protected health information created or received by a covered entity is reviewed by other participating covered entities or by a third party on their behalf for the purpose of administering the sharing of financial risk. (3) A group health plan and a health insurance issuer or HMO with respect to such group health plan, but only with respect to protected health information created or received by such health insurance issuer or HMO that relates to individuals who are or who have been participants or beneficiaries in such group health plan; (4) A group health plan and one or more other group health plans each of which are maintained by the same plan sponsor; or (5) The group health plans described in paragraph (4) of this definition and health insurance issuers or HMOs with respect to such group health plans, but only with respect to protected health information created or received by such health insurance issuers or HMOs that relates to individuals who are or have been participants or beneficiaries in any of such group health plans. 45 C.F.R. § 160.103.

376. 45 C.F.R. § 164.506(c)(5).

377. 45 C.F.R. § 164.508(a)(1).

378. "Psychotherapy notes" means notes recorded (in any medium) by a health care provider who is a mental health professional documenting or analyzing the contents of conversation during a private counseling session or a group, joint, or family counseling session and that are separated from the rest of the individual's medical record. Psychotherapy notes excludes medication prescription and monitoring, counseling session start and stop times, the modalities and frequencies of treatment furnished, results of clinical tests, and any summary of the following items: Diagnosis, functional status, the treatment plan, symptoms, prognosis, and progress to date. 45 C.F.R. § 164.501.

379. 45 C.F.R. § 164.508(a)(2).

of protected health information for marketing,[380] except if the communication is in the form of a face-to-face communication made by a covered entity to an individual or a promotional gift of nominal value provided by the covered entity.[381] If the marketing involves direct or indirect remuneration to the covered entity from a third party, the authorization must state that such remuneration is involved.[382]

14:138. Valid authorization

A valid authorization is a document that meets the requirements in paragraphs § 164.508(a) (3)(ii), (c)(1), and (c)(2) of this section, as applicable.[383] A valid authorization may contain elements or information in addition to the elements required by this section, provided that such additional elements or information are not inconsistent with the elements required by this section.[384] An authorization is not valid, if the document submitted has any of the following defects: the expiration date has passed or the expiration event is known by the covered entity to have occurred; the authorization has not been filled out completely, with respect to an element described by paragraph § 164.508(c), if applicable; the authorization is known by the covered entity to have been revoked; the authorization violates paragraph § 164.508(b)(3) or (4), if applicable; or any material information in the authorization is known by the covered entity to be false.[385]

An authorization for use or disclosure of protected health information may not be combined with any other document to create a compound authorization, except as follows: an authorization for the use or disclosure of protected health information for a research[386] study may be combined with any other type of written permission for the same research study, including another authorization for the use or disclosure of protected health information for such research or a consent to participate in such research; an authorization for a use or disclosure of psychotherapy notes may only be combined with another authorization for a use or disclosure of psychotherapy notes; an authorization under this section, other than an authorization for a use or disclosure of psychotherapy notes, may be combined with any other such authorization under

---

380. "Marketing" means: (1) To make a communication about a product or service that encourages recipients of the communication to purchase or use the product or service, unless the communication is made: (i) To describe a health-related product or service (or payment for such product or service) that is provided by, or included in a plan of benefits of, the covered entity making the communication, including communications about: the entities participating in a health care provider network or health plan network; replacement of, or enhancements to, a health plan; and health-related products or services available only to a health plan enrollee that add value to, but are not part of, a plan of benefits. (ii) For treatment of the individual; or (iii) For case management or care coordination for the individual, or to direct or recommend alternative treatments, therapies, health care providers, or settings of care to the individual. (2) An arrangement between a covered entity and any other entity whereby the covered entity discloses protected health information to the other entity, in exchange for direct or indirect remuneration, for the other entity or its affiliate to make a communication about its own product or service that encourages recipients of the communication to purchase or use that product or service. 45 C.F.R. § 164.501.

381. 45 C.F.R. § 164.508(a)(3)(i).

382. 45 C.F.R. § 164.508(a)(3)(ii).

383. 45 C.F.R. § 164.508(b)(1)(i).

384. 45 C.F.R. § 164.508(b)(1)(ii).

385. 45 C.F.R. §§ 164.508(b)(2)(A)–(E).

386. "Research" means a systematic investigation, including research development, testing, and evaluation, designed to develop or contribute to generalizable knowledge. 45 C.F.R. § 164.501.

this section, except when a covered entity has conditioned the provision of treatment, payment, enrollment in the health plan, or eligibility for benefits under paragraph (b) (4) on the provision of one of the authorizations.[387]

A covered entity may not condition the provision to an individual of treatment, payment, enrollment in the health plan, or eligibility for benefits on the provision of an authorization, except a covered health care provider may condition the provision of research-related treatment on provision of an authorization for the use or disclosure of protected health information for such research.[388] A health plan may condition enrollment in the health plan or eligibility for benefits on provision of an authorization requested by the health plan prior to an individual's enrollment in the health plan, if the authorization sought is for the health plan's eligibility or enrollment determinations relating to the individual or for its underwriting or risk rating determinations and the authorization is not for a use or disclosure of psychotherapy notes under paragraph (a) (2).[389] A covered entity may condition the provision of health care that is solely for the purpose of creating protected health information for disclosure to a third party on provision of an authorization for the disclosure of the protected health information to such third party.[390]

An individual may revoke an authorization provided under this section at any time, provided that the revocation is in writing, except to the extent that the covered entity has taken action in reliance thereon; or if the authorization was obtained as a condition of obtaining insurance coverage, other law provides the insurer with the right to contest a claim under the policy or the policy itself.[391]

A covered entity must document and retain any signed authorization as required by § 164.530(j).[392]

14:139. Other requirements of authorizations

A valid authorization under this section must contain at least the following elements: a description of the information to be used or disclosed that identifies the information in a specific and meaningful fashion; the name or other specific identification of the person(s), or class of persons, authorized to make the requested use or disclosure; the name or other specific identification of the person(s), or class of persons, to whom the covered entity may make the requested use or disclosure; a description of each purpose of the requested use or disclosure. The statement "at the request of the individual" is a sufficient description of the purpose when an individual initiates the authorization and does not, or elects not to, provide a statement of the purpose; an expiration date or an expiration event that relates to the individual or the purpose of the use or disclosure;[393]

---

387. 45 C.F.R. §§ 164.508(b)(3)(i)–(iii).

388. 45 C.F.R. § 164.508(b)(4)(i).

389. 45 C.F.R. § 164.508(b)(4)(ii).

390. 45 C.F.R. § 164.508(b)(4)(iii).

391. 45 C.F.R. §§ 164.508(b)(5)(i)–(ii).

392. 45 C.F.R. § 164.508(b)(6).

393. The statement "end of the research study," "none," or similar language is sufficient if the authorization is for a use or disclosure of protected health information for research, including for the creation and maintenance of a research database or research repository.

and signature of the individual and date. If the authorization is signed by a personal representative of the individual, a description of such representative's authority to act for the individual must also be provided.[394]

In addition, the authorization must contain statements adequate to place the individual on notice of the individual's right to revoke the authorization in writing, and must also contain either the exceptions to the right to revoke and a description of how the individual may revoke the authorization, or to the extent that the information in § 164.508(c)(2)(i)(A) is included in the notice required by § 164.520, a reference to the covered entity's notice.[395] It must also place the individual on notice of the ability or inability to condition treatment, payment, enrollment, or eligibility for benefits on the authorization, by stating either the covered entity may not condition treatment, payment, enrollment, or eligibility for benefits on whether the individual signs the authorization when the prohibition on conditioning of authorizations in paragraph (b)(4) of this section applies; or the consequences to the individual of a refusal to sign the authorization when, in accordance with paragraph (b)(4), the covered entity can condition treatment, enrollment in the health plan, or eligibility for benefits on failure to obtain such authorization.[396] It must also disclose the potential for information disclosed pursuant to the authorization to be subject to redisclosure by the recipient and no longer be protected by this subpart.[397]

Additionally, the authorization must be written in plain language and if a covered entity seeks an authorization from an individual for a use or disclosure of protected health information, the covered entity must provide the individual with a copy of the signed authorization.[398]

14:140. Uses and disclosures requiring an opportunity for the individual to agree or to object

A covered entity may use or disclose protected health information, provided that the individual is informed in advance of the use or disclosure and has the opportunity to agree to or prohibit or restrict the use or disclosure, in accordance with the applicable requirements of this section. The covered entity may orally inform the individual of, and obtain the individual's oral agreement or objection to, a permitted use or disclosure.[399]

Except when an objection is expressed in accordance with paragraphs (a)(2) or (3), a covered health care provider may use the following protected health information to maintain a directory of individuals in its facility: the individual's name; the individual's location in the covered health care provider's facility; the individual's condition described in general terms that does not communicate specific medical information about the

---

394. 45 C.F.R. §§ 164.508(c)(i)–(vi).

395. 45 C.F.R. §§ 164.508(c)(2)(i)(1)–(2).

396. 45 C.F.R. §§ 164.508(c)(2)(ii)(A)–(B).

397. 45 C.F.R. § 164.508(c)(2)(iii).

398. 45 C.F.R. §§ 164.508(c)(3)–(4).

399. 45 C.F.R. § 164.510.

individual; and the individual's religious affiliation.[400] Moreover, except when an objection is expressed in accordance with paragraphs (a)(2) or (3), a covered health care provider may disclose for directory purposes such information to members of the clergy, or, except for religious affiliation, to other persons who ask for the individual by name.[401]

A covered health care provider must inform an individual of the protected health information that it may include in a directory and the persons to whom it may disclose such information (including disclosures to clergy of information regarding religious affiliation) and provide the individual with the opportunity to restrict or prohibit some or all of the uses or disclosures permitted by § 164.510(a)(1).[402] If the opportunity to object to uses or disclosures required by paragraph (a)(2) cannot practicably be provided because of the individual's incapacity or an emergency treatment circumstance, a covered health care provider may use or disclose some or all of the protected health information permitted by paragraph (a)(1) for the facility's directory, if such disclosure is consistent with a prior expressed preference of the individual, if any, that is known to the covered health care provider; and in the individual's best interest as determined by the covered health care provider, in the exercise of professional judgment.[403] The covered health care provider must inform the individual and provide an opportunity to object to uses or disclosures for directory purposes as required by paragraph (a)(2) when it becomes practicable to do so.

14:141. Uses and disclosures for involvement in the individual's care and notification purposes

A covered entity may, in accordance with paragraphs (b)(2) or (3), disclose to a family member, other relative, or a close personal friend of the individual, or any other person identified by the individual, the protected health information directly relevant to such person's involvement with the individual's care or payment related to the individual's health care.[404] A covered entity may use or disclose protected health information to notify, or assist in the notification of (including identifying or locating), a family member, a personal representative of the individual, or another person responsible for the care of the individual of the individual's location, general condition, or death. Any such use or disclosure of protected health information for such notification purposes must be in accordance with § 164.510(b)(2), (3), or (4), as applicable.[405]

If the individual is present for, or otherwise available prior to, a use or disclosure permitted by § 164.510(b)(1) and has the capacity to make health care decisions, the covered entity may use or disclose the protected health information if it obtains the individual's agreement; provides the individual with the opportunity to object to the disclosure, and the individual does not express an objection; or reasonably infers from

---

400. 45 C.F.R. §§ 164.510(a)(1)(i)(A)–(D).

401. 45 C.F.R. §§ 164.510(a)(1)(ii)(A)–(B).

402. 45 C.F.R. § 164.510(a)(2).

403. 45 C.F.R. §§ 164.510(a)(3)(i)–(ii).

404. 45 C.F.R. § 164.510(b)(1)(i).

405. 45 C.F.R. § 164.510(b)(1)(ii).

the circumstances, based the exercise of professional judgment, that the individual does not object to the disclosure.[406]

If the individual is not present, or the opportunity to agree or object to the use or disclosure cannot practicably be provided because of the individual's incapacity or an emergency circumstance, the covered entity may, in the exercise of professional judgment, determine whether the disclosure is in the best interests of the individual and, if so, disclose only the protected health information that is directly relevant to the person's involvement with the individual's health care. A covered entity may use professional judgment and its experience with common practice to make reasonable inferences of the individual's best interest in allowing a person to act on behalf of the individual to pick up filled prescriptions, medical supplies, X-rays, or other similar forms of protected health information.[407] A covered entity may use or disclose protected health information to a public or private entity authorized by law or by its charter to assist in disaster relief efforts, for the purpose of coordinating with such entities the uses or disclosures permitted by paragraph (b)(1)(ii). The requirements in paragraphs (b)(2) and (3) apply to such uses and disclosure to the extent that the covered entity, in the exercise of professional judgment, determines that the requirements do not interfere with the ability to respond to the emergency circumstances.[408]

14:142. Uses without consent

A covered entity may use or disclose protected health information without the written authorization of the individual, as described in § 164.508, or the opportunity for the individual to agree or object as described in § 164.510, in the situations covered by this section, subject to applicable requirements. When the covered entity is required to inform the individual of, or when the individual may agree to, a use or disclosure permitted by this section, the covered entity's information and the individual's agreement may be given orally.[409] A covered entity may use or disclose protected health information to the extent that such use or disclosure is required by law and the use or disclosure complies with and is limited to the relevant requirements of such law.[410] A covered entity must meet the requirements described in paragraph (c), (e), or (f) for uses or disclosures required by law.[411]

14:143. Uses and disclosures for public health activities

A covered entity may disclose protected health information for the public health activities and purposes described in this paragraph to the following:

- a public health authority that is authorized by law to collect or receive such information for the purpose of preventing or controlling disease, injury, or disability,

---

406. 45 C.F.R. § 164.510(b)(2)(i)–(iii).
407. 45 C.F.R. § 164.510(b)(3).
408. 45 C.F.R. § 164.510(b)(4).
409. 45 C.F.R. § 164.512(a).
410. 45 C.F.R. § 164.512(a)(1).
411. 45 C.F.R. § 164.512(a)(2).

including, but not limited to, the reporting of disease, injury, vital events such as birth or death, and the conduct of public health surveillance, public health investigations, and public health interventions; or, at the direction of a public health authority, to an official of a foreign government agency that is acting in collaboration with a public health authority;

- a public health authority or other appropriate government authority authorized by law to receive reports of child abuse or neglect;

- a person subject to the jurisdiction of the Food and Drug Administration (FDA) with respect to an FDA-regulated product or activity for which that person has responsibility, for the purpose of activities related to the quality, safety or effectiveness of such FDA-regulated product or activity, including the following:

  o to collect or report adverse events (or similar activities with respect to food or dietary supplements), product defects or problems (including problems with the use or labeling of a product), or biological product deviations,

  o to track FDA-regulated products,

  o to enable product recalls, repairs, or replacement, or lookback (including locating and notifying individuals who have received products that have been recalled, withdrawn, or are the subject of lookback), or

  o to conduct post marketing surveillance;

- a person who may have been exposed to a communicable disease or may otherwise be at risk of contracting or spreading a disease or condition, if the covered entity or public health authority is authorized by law to notify such person as necessary in the conduct of a public health intervention or investigation; or

- an employer, about an individual who is a member of the workforce of the employer, if

  o the covered entity is a covered health care provider who is a member of the workforce of such employer or who provides health care to the individual at the request of the employer

    ▶ to conduct an evaluation relating to medical surveillance of the workplace, or

    ▶ to evaluate whether the individual has a work-related illness or injury,

  o the protected health information that is disclosed consists of findings concerning a work-related illness or injury or a workplace-related medical surveillance;

  o the employer needs such findings in order to comply with its obligations, under 29 C.F.R. parts 1904 through 1928, 30 C.F.R. parts 50 through 90, or under state law having a similar purpose, to record such illness or injury or to carry out responsibilities for workplace medical surveillance; and

  o the covered health care provider provides written notice to the individual that protected health information relating to the medical surveillance of the workplace and work-related illnesses and injuries is disclosed to the employer

    ▶ by giving a copy of the notice to the individual at the time the health care is provided, or

> ▶ if the health care is provided on the work site of the employer, by posting the notice in a prominent place at the location where the health care is provided.[412]

If the covered entity also is a public health authority, the covered entity is permitted to use protected health information in all cases in which it is permitted to disclose such information for public health activities under § 164.512(b)(1).[413]

14:144. Disclosures about victims of abuse, neglect or domestic violence

Except for reports of child abuse or neglect permitted by paragraph § 164.512(b)(1)(ii), a covered entity may disclose protected health information about an individual whom the covered entity reasonably believes to be a victim of abuse, neglect, or domestic violence to a government authority, including a social service or protective services agency, authorized by law to receive reports of such abuse, neglect, or domestic violence to the extent the disclosure is required by law and the disclosure complies with and is limited to the relevant requirements of such law; if the individual agrees to the disclosure; or to the extent the disclosure is expressly authorized by statute or regulation and, the covered entity, in the exercise of professional judgment, believes the disclosure is necessary to prevent serious harm to the individual or other potential victims, or if the individual is unable to agree because of incapacity, a law enforcement or other public official authorized to receive the report represents that the protected health information for which disclosure is sought is not intended to be used against the individual and that an immediate enforcement activity that depends upon the disclosure would be materially and adversely affected by waiting until the individual is able to agree to the disclosure.[414]

A covered entity that makes a disclosure permitted by paragraph § 164.512(c)(1) must promptly inform the individual that such a report has been or will be made, except if the covered entity, in the exercise of professional judgment, believes informing the individual would place the individual at risk of serious harm, or the covered entity would be informing a personal representative, and the covered entity reasonably believes the personal representative is responsible for the abuse, neglect, or other injury, and that informing such person would not be in the best interests of the individual as determined by the covered entity, in the exercise of professional judgment.[415]

14:145. Uses and disclosures for health oversight activities

A covered entity may disclose protected health information to a health oversight agency for oversight activities authorized by law, including audits; civil, administrative, or criminal investigations; inspections; licensure or disciplinary actions; civil, administrative, or criminal proceedings or actions; or other activities necessary for appropriate oversight

---

412. 45 C.F.R. §§ 164.512(b)(1)(i)–(v).

413. 45 C.F.R. § 164.512(b)(2).

414. 45 C.F.R. § 164.512(c)(1)(i)–(iii).

415. 45 C.F.R. § 164.512(c)(2)(i)–(ii).

of the health care system, government benefit programs for which health information is relevant to beneficiary eligibility, entities subject to government regulatory programs for which health information is necessary for determining compliance with program standards, or entities subject to civil rights laws for which health information is necessary for determining compliance.[416] For the purpose of the disclosures permitted by paragraph (d)(1), a health oversight activity does not include an investigation or other activity in which the individual is the subject of the investigation or activity and such investigation or other activity does not arise out of and is not directly related to the receipt of health care; a claim for public benefits related to health; or qualification for, or receipt of, public benefits or services when a patient's health is integral to the claim for public benefits or services.[417]

Notwithstanding paragraph (d)(2), if a health oversight activity or investigation is conducted in conjunction with an oversight activity or investigation relating to a claim for public benefits not related to health, the joint activity or investigation is considered a health oversight activity for purposes of paragraph (d).[418] If a covered entity also is a health oversight agency, the covered entity may use protected health information for health oversight activities as permitted by paragraph (d) of this section.[419]

14:146. Disclosures for judicial and administrative proceedings

A covered entity may disclose protected health information in the course of any judicial or administrative proceeding in response to an order of a court or administrative tribunal, provided that the covered entity discloses only the protected health information expressly authorized by such order, or in response to a subpoena, discovery request, or other lawful process, that is not accompanied by an order of a court or administrative tribunal, if the covered entity receives satisfactory assurance, as described in paragraph (e)(1)(iii), from the party seeking the information that reasonable efforts have been made by such party to ensure that the individual who is the subject of the protected health information that has been requested has been given notice of the request, or the covered entity receives satisfactory assurance, as described in paragraph (e)(1)(iv), from the party seeking the information that reasonable efforts have been made by such party to secure a qualified protective order[420] that meets the requirements of paragraph (e)(1)(v).[421]

Notwithstanding paragraph (e)(1)(ii), a covered entity may disclose protected health information in response to lawful process described in paragraph (e)(1)(ii) without receiving satisfactory assurance under paragraph (e)(1)(ii)(A) or (B) if the covered

---

416. 45 C.F.R. §§ 164.512(d)(1)(i)–(iv).

417. 45 C.F.R. §§ 164.512(d)(2)(i)–(iii).

418. 45 C.F.R. § 164.512(d)(3).

419. 45 C.F.R. § 164.512(d)(4).

420. For purposes of paragraph (e)(1) of this section, a "qualified protective order" means, with respect to protected health information requested under paragraph (e)(1)(ii) of this section, an order of a court or of an administrative tribunal or a stipulation by the parties to the litigation or administrative proceeding that: (A) Prohibits the parties from using or disclosing the protected health information for any purpose other than the litigation or proceeding for which such information was requested; and (B) Requires the return to the covered entity or destruction of the protected health information (including all copies made) at the end of the litigation or proceeding. 45 C.F.R. § 164.512(e)(1)(v).

421. 45 C.F.R. §§ 164.512(e)(1)(i)–(ii).

entity makes reasonable efforts to provide notice to the individual sufficient to meet the requirements of paragraph (e)(1)(iii)or to seek a qualified protective order sufficient to meet the requirements of paragraph (e)(1)(iv).[422]

These provisions do not supersede other provisions of this section that otherwise permit or restrict uses or disclosures of protected health information.[423]

14:147. Defining satisfactory assurances

For the purposes of § 164.512(e)(1)(ii)(A), a covered entity receives satisfactory assurances from a party seeking protecting health information if the covered entity receives from such party a written statement and accompanying documentation demonstrating that the party requesting such information has made a good faith attempt to provide written notice to the individual (or, if the individual's location is unknown, to mail a notice to the individual's last known address); that the notice included sufficient information about the litigation or proceeding in which the protected health information is requested to permit the individual to raise an objection to the court or administrative tribunal; and that the time for the individual to raise objections to the court or administrative tribunal has elapsed, and no objections were filed, or all objections filed by the individual have been resolved by the court or the administrative tribunal and the disclosures being sought are consistent with such resolution.[424]

Moreover, for the purposes of paragraph (e)(1)(ii)(B), a covered entity receives satisfactory assurances from a party seeking protected health information, if the covered entity receives from such party a written statement and accompanying documentation demonstrating that the parties to the dispute giving rise to the request for information have agreed to a qualified protective order and have presented it to the court or administrative tribunal with jurisdiction over the dispute, or that the party seeking the protected health information has requested a qualified protective order from such court or administrative tribunal.[425]

14:148. Disclosures for law enforcement purposes

A covered entity may disclose protected health information for a law enforcement purpose to a law enforcement official if the conditions in paragraphs (f)(1) through (f)(6) are met, as applicable.[426] Pursuant to process and as otherwise required by law. A covered entity may disclose protected health information as required by law, including laws that require the reporting of certain types of wounds or other physical injuries, except for laws subject to paragraph (b)(1)(ii) or (c)(1)(i), or in compliance with and as limited by the relevant requirements of a court order or court-ordered warrant, or a subpoena or summons issued by a judicial officer, a grand jury subpoena, an administrative request, including an administrative subpoena or summons, a civil or an authorized investigative demand, or similar process authorized under law, provided

---

422. 45 C.F.R. § 164.512(e)(1)(vi).
423. 45 C.F.R. § 164.512(e)(2).
424. 45 C.F.R. § 164.512(e)(1)(iii).
425. 45 C.F.R. §§ 164.512(e)(1)(iv)(A)–(B).
426. 45 C.F.R. § 164.512(f).

that the information sought is relevant and material to a legitimate law enforcement inquiry, the request is specific and limited in scope to the extent reasonably practicable in light of the purpose for which the information is sought. The previous conditions apply if de-identified information could not reasonably be used.[427]

14:149. Limited information for identification and location purposes

Except for disclosures required by law as permitted by paragraph (f)(1), a covered entity may disclose protected health information in response to a law enforcement official's request for such information for the purpose of identifying or locating a suspect, fugitive, material witness, or missing person, provided that the covered entity may disclose only the following information: name and address; date and place of birth; Social Security number; ABO blood type and Rh factor; type of injury; date and time of treatment; date and time of death, if applicable; and a description of distinguishing physical characteristics, including height, weight, gender, race, hair and eye color, presence or absence of facial hair (beard or moustache), scars, and tattoos; and except as permitted by paragraph (f)(2)(i), the covered entity may not disclose for the purposes of identification or location under paragraph (f)(2) any protected health information related to the individual's DNA or DNA analysis, dental records, or typing, samples, or analysis of body fluids or tissue.[428]

14:150. Victims of a crime

Except for disclosures required by law as permitted by § 164.512(f)(1), a covered entity may disclose protected health information in response to a law enforcement official's request for such information about an individual who is or is suspected to be a victim of a crime, other than disclosures that are subject to paragraph (b) or (c), if the individual agrees to the disclosure, or the covered entity is unable to obtain the individual's agreement because of incapacity or other emergency circumstance, provided that the law enforcement official represents that such information is needed to determine whether a violation of law by a person other than the victim has occurred, and such information is not intended to be used against the victim; the law enforcement official represents that immediate law enforcement activity that depends upon the disclosure would be materially and adversely affected by waiting until the individual is able to agree to the disclosure; and the disclosure is in the best interests of the individual as determined by the covered entity, in the exercise of professional judgment.[429]

14:151. Decedents

A covered entity may disclose protected health information about an individual who has died to a law enforcement official for the purpose of alerting law enforcement of

---

427. 45 C.F.R. §§ 164.512(f)(1)(i)–(ii).
428. 45 C.F.R. §§ 164.512(f)(2)(i)–(ii).
429. 45 C.F.R. § 164.512(f)(3)(i)–(ii).

the death of the individual if the covered entity has a suspicion that such death may have resulted from criminal conduct.[430]

14:152. Crime on premises

A covered entity may disclose to a law enforcement official protected health information that the covered entity believes in good faith constitutes evidence of criminal conduct that occurred on the premises of the covered entity.[431]

14:153. Reporting crime in emergencies

A covered health care provider providing emergency health care in response to a medical emergency, other than such emergency on the premises of the covered health care provider, may disclose protected health information to a law enforcement official if such disclosure appears necessary to alert law enforcement to the commission and nature of a crime, the location of such crime or of the victim(s) of such crime, and the identity, description, and location of the perpetrator of such crime.[432] If a covered health care provider believes that the medical emergency described in paragraph (f) (6)(i) is the result of abuse, neglect, or domestic violence of the individual in need of emergency health care, paragraph (f)(6)(i)does not apply and any disclosure to a law enforcement official for law enforcement purposes is subject to paragraph (c).[433]

14:154. Disclosures for workers' compensation

A covered entity may disclose protected health information as authorized by and to the extent necessary to comply with laws relating to workers' compensation or other similar programs, established by law, that provide benefits for work-related injuries or illness without regard to fault.[434]

14:155. Other requirements relating to uses and disclosures of protected health information—de-identified data

Health information that does not identify an individual and with respect to which there is no reasonable basis to believe that the information can be used to identify an individual is not individually identifiable health information.[435] A covered entity may determine that health information is not individually identifiable health information only if a person with appropriate knowledge of and experience with generally accepted statistical and scientific principles and methods for rendering information not individually identifiable applying such principles and methods, determines that the risk is very small that the information could be used, alone or in combination with other reasonably available

---

430. 45 C.F.R. § 164.512(f)(4).
431. 45 C.F.R. § 164.512(f)(5).
432. 45 C.F.R. § 164.512(f)(6)(i)(A)–(C).
433. 45 C.F.R. § 164.512(f)(6)(ii).
434. 45 C.F.R. § 164.512(l).
435. 45 C.F.R. § 164.514(a).

information, by an anticipated recipient to identify an individual who is a subject of the information, and documents the methods and results of the analysis that justify such determination; or if the following identifiers of the individual or of relatives, employers,[436] or household members of the individual, are removed:

- names;
- all geographic subdivisions smaller than a state, including street address, city, county, precinct, zip code, and their equivalent geocodes, except for the initial three digits of a zip code if, according to the current publicly available data from the Bureau of the Census,
  - ○ the geographic unit formed by combining all zip codes with the same three initial digits contains more than 20,000 people, and
  - ○ the initial three digits of a zip code for all such geographic units containing 20,000 or fewer people is changed to 000;
- all elements of dates (except year) for dates directly related to an individual, including birth date, admission date, discharge date, date of death; and all ages over 89 and all elements of dates (including year) indicative of such age, except that such ages and elements may be aggregated into a single category of age 90 or older;
- telephone numbers;
- fax numbers;
- electronic mail addresses;
- social security numbers;
- medical record numbers;
- health plan beneficiary numbers;
- account numbers;
- certificate/license numbers;
- vehicle identifiers and serial numbers, including license plate numbers;
- device identifiers and serial numbers;
- web uniform resource locators (URLs);
- Internet protocol (IP) address numbers;
- biometric identifiers, including finger and voice prints;
- full face photographic images and any comparable images; and
- any other unique identifying number, characteristic, or code, except as permitted by paragraph (c) of this section; and
- the covered entity does not have actual knowledge that the information could be used alone or in combination with other information to identify an individual who is a subject of the information.[437]

---

436. "Employer" is defined as it is in 26 U.S.C. 3401(d). 45 C.F.R. § 160.103.
437. 45 C.F.R. § 164.514(b)(1)–(2).

14:156. Re-identification

A covered entity may assign a code or other means of record identification to allow information de-identified under this section to be re-identified by the covered entity, provided that the code or other means of record identification is not derived from or related to information about the individual and is not otherwise capable of being translated so as to identify the individual, and the covered entity does not use or disclose the code or other means of record identification for any other purpose, and does not disclose the mechanism for re-identification.[438]

14:157. Minimum necessary uses of PHI

In order to comply with § 164.502(b) and this section, a covered entity must meet the requirements of § 164.514(d)(2) through (d)(5) with respect to a request for, or the use and disclosure of, protected health information.[439] A covered entity must identify those persons or classes of persons, as appropriate, in its workforce who need access to protected health information to carry out their duties, and for each such person or class of persons, the category or categories of protected health information to which access is needed and any conditions appropriate to such access.[440] A covered entity must make reasonable efforts to limit the access of such persons or classes identified in paragraph (d)(2)(i)(A) to protected health information consistent with paragraph (d)(2)(i)(B).[441]

14:158. Minimum necessary disclosures of PHI

For any type of disclosure that it makes on a routine and recurring basis, a covered entity must implement policies and procedures (which may be standard protocols) that limit the protected health information disclosed to the amount reasonably necessary to achieve the purpose of the disclosure.[442] For all other disclosures, a covered entity must develop criteria designed to limit the protected health information disclosed to the information reasonably necessary to accomplish the purpose for which disclosure is sought and review requests for disclosure on an individual basis in accordance with such criteria.[443]

A covered entity may rely, if such reliance is reasonable under the circumstances, on a requested disclosure as the minimum necessary for the stated purpose when making disclosures to public officials that are permitted under § 164.512, if the public official represents that the information requested is the minimum necessary for the stated purpose(s); when the information is requested by another covered entity; when the information is requested by a professional who is a member of its workforce or is a business associate of the covered entity for the purpose of providing professional services

---

438. 45 C.F.R. § 164.514(c)(1)–(2).
439. 45 C.F.R. § 164.514(d)(1).
440. 45 C.F.R. § 164.514(d)(2)(i)(A)–(B).
441. 45 C.F.R. § 164.514(d)(2)(ii).
442. 45 C.F.R. § 164.514(d)(3)(i).
443. 45 C.F.R. § 164.514(d)(3)(ii).

to the covered entity, if the professional represents that the information requested is the minimum necessary for the stated purpose(s); or when documentation or representations that comply with the applicable requirements of § 164.512(i) have been provided by a person requesting the information for research purposes.[444]

14:159. Minimum necessary requests for PHI

A covered entity must limit any request for protected health information to that which is reasonably necessary to accomplish the purpose for which the request is made, when requesting such information from other covered entities.[445] For a request that is made on a routine and recurring basis, a covered entity must implement policies and procedures (which may be standard protocols) that limit the protected health information requested to the amount reasonably necessary to accomplish the purpose for which the request is made.[446] For all other requests, a covered entity must develop criteria designed to limit the request for protected health information to the information reasonably necessary to accomplish the purpose for which the request is made and review requests for disclosure on an individual basis in accordance with such criteria.[447] For all uses, disclosures, or requests to which the requirements in paragraph (d) apply, a covered entity may not use, disclose or request an entire medical record, except when the entire medical record is specifically justified as the amount that is reasonably necessary to accomplish the purpose of the use, disclosure, or request.[448]

14:160. Limited data set

A covered entity may use or disclose a limited data set that meets the requirements of paragraphs § 164.514(e)(2) and (e)(3) if the covered entity enters into a data use agreement with the limited data set recipient, in accordance with paragraph (e)(4).[449] A limited data set is protected health information that excludes the following direct identifiers of the individual or of relatives, employers, or household members of the individual: names; postal address information, other than town or city, state, and zip code; telephone numbers; fax numbers; electronic mail addresses; social security numbers; medical record numbers; health plan beneficiary numbers; account numbers; certificate/license numbers; vehicle identifiers and serial numbers, including license plate numbers; device identifiers and serial numbers; Web uniform resource locators (URLs); Internet protocol (IP) address numbers; biometric identifiers, including finger and voice prints; and full face photographic images and any comparable images.[450]

A covered entity may use or disclose a limited data set under paragraph (e)(1) only for the purposes of research, public health, or health care operations.[451] A covered

---

444. 45 C.F.R. § 164.514(d)(3)(iii)(A)–(D).
445. 45 C.F.R. § 164.514(d)(4)(i).
446. 45 C.F.R. § 164.514(d)(4)(ii).
447. 45 C.F.R. §§ 164.514(d)(4)(iii)(A)–(B).
448. 45 C.F.R. § 164.514(d)(5).
449. 45 C.F.R. § 164.514(e)(1).
450. 45 C.F.R. §§ 164.514(e)(2)(i)–(xvi).
451. 45 C.F.R. § 164.514(e)(3)(i).

entity may use protected health information to create a limited data set that meets the requirements of paragraph (e)(2), or disclose protected health information only to a business associate for such purpose, whether or not the limited data set is to be used by the covered entity.[452]

A covered entity may use or disclose a limited data set under paragraph (e)(1) only if the covered entity obtains satisfactory assurance, in the form of a data use agreement that meets the requirements of this section, that the limited data set recipient will only use or disclose the protected health information for limited purposes.[453] A data use agreement between the covered entity and the limited data set recipient must

- establish the permitted uses and disclosures of such information by the limited data set recipient, consistent with paragraph (e)(3). The data use agreement may not authorize the limited data set recipient to use or further disclose the information in a manner that would violate the requirements of this subpart, if done by the covered entity;
- establish who is permitted to use or receive the limited data set; and
- provide that the limited data set recipient will
  - o not use or further disclose the information other than as permitted by the data use agreement or as otherwise required by law;
  - o use appropriate safeguards to prevent use or disclosure of the information other than as provided for by the data use agreement;
  - o report to the covered entity any use or disclosure of the information not provided for by its data use agreement of which it becomes aware;
  - o ensure that any agents, including a subcontractor, to whom it provides the limited data set agrees to the same restrictions and conditions that apply to the limited data set recipient with respect to such information; and
  - o not identify the information nor contact the individuals.[454]

A covered entity is not in compliance with the standards in paragraph § 164.514(e) if the covered entity knew of a pattern of activity or practice of the limited data set recipient that constituted a material breach or violation of the data use agreement, unless the covered entity took reasonable steps to cure the breach or end the violation, as applicable, and, if such steps were unsuccessful, discontinued disclosure of protected health information to the recipient and reported the problem to the secretary.[455]

A covered entity that is a limited data set recipient and violates a data use agreement will be in noncompliance with the standards, implementation specifications, and requirements of paragraph (e).

14:161. Uses for fundraising

A covered entity may use, or disclose to a business associate or to an institutionally related foundation, the following protected health information for the purpose of

---

452. 45 C.F.R. § 164.514(e)(3)(ii).
453. 45 C.F.R. § 164.514(e)(4)(i).
454. 45 C.F.R. §§ 164.514(e)(4)(ii)(A)–(C).
455. 45 C.F.R. §§ 164.514(e)(4)(iii)(A)–(B).

raising funds for its own benefit, without an authorization meeting the requirements of § 164.508: demographic information relating to an individual and dates of health care provided to an individual.[456] Moreover, the covered entity may not use or disclose protected health information for fundraising purposes as otherwise permitted by paragraph (f)(1) unless a statement required by § 164.520(b)(1)(iii)(B) is included in the covered entity's notice; the covered entity must include in any fundraising materials it sends to an individual under this paragraph a description of how the individual may opt out of receiving any further fundraising communications; and the covered entity must make reasonable efforts to ensure that individuals who decide to opt out of receiving future fundraising communications are not sent such communications.[457]

14:162. Uses and disclosures for underwriting and related purposes

If a health plan receives protected health information for the purpose of underwriting, premium rating, or other activities relating to the creation, renewal, or replacement of a contract of health insurance or health benefits, and if such health insurance or health benefits are not placed with the health plan, such health plan may not use or disclose such protected health information for any other purpose, except as may be required by law.[458]

14:163. Verification requirements

Prior to any disclosure permitted by this subpart, a covered entity must, except with respect to disclosures under § 164.510, verify the identity of a person requesting protected health information and the authority of any such person to have access to protected health information under this subpart, if the identity or any such authority of such person is not known to the covered entity, and must obtain any documentation, statements, or representations, whether oral or written, from the person requesting the protected health information when such documentation, statement, or representation is a condition of the disclosure.[459]

14:164. Right to notice of privacy practices for PHI

Except as provided by paragraph § 164.520(a)(2) or (3), an individual has a right to adequate notice of the uses and disclosures of protected health information that may be made by the covered entity, and of the individual's rights and the covered entity's legal duties with respect to protected health information.[460] An individual enrolled in a group health plan has a right to notice from the group health plan, if, and to the extent that, such an individual does not receive health benefits under the group health plan through an insurance contract with a health insurance issuer or HMO; or from the

---

456. 45 C.F.R. §§ 164.514(f)(1)(A)–(B).

457. 45 C.F.R. §§ 164.514(f)(2)(i)–(iii).

458. 45 C.F.R. § 164.514(g).

459. 45 C.F.R. §§ 164.514(h)(1)(i)–(ii).

460. 45 C.F.R. § 164.520(a)(1).

health insurance issuer or HMO with respect to the group health plan through which such individuals receive their health benefits under the group health plan.[461] A group health plan that provides health benefits solely through an insurance contract with a health insurance issuer or HMO, and that creates or receives protected health information in addition to summary health information as defined in § 164.504(a) or information on whether the individual is participating in the group health plan, or is enrolled in or has disenrolled from a health insurance issuer or HMO offered by the plan, must (A) maintain a notice under this section; and (B) provide such notice upon request to any person. The provisions of paragraph (c)(1) do not apply to such group health plan.[462] A group health plan that provides health benefits solely through an insurance contract with a health insurance issuer or HMO, and does not create or receive protected health information other than summary health information as defined in § 164.504(a) or information on whether an individual is participating in the group health plan, or is enrolled in or has disenrolled from a health insurance issuer or HMO offered by the plan, is not required to maintain or provide a notice under this section.[463] However, an inmate[464] does not have a right to notice under this section, and the requirements of this section do not apply to a correctional institution[465] that is a covered entity.[466]

There are regulations regarding the content of the notice. The covered entity must provide a notice that is written in plain language and that contains the elements required by § 164.520(b)(1).[467] The notice must contain the following statement as a header or otherwise prominently displayed: "THIS NOTICE DESCRIBES HOW MEDICAL INFORMATION ABOUT YOU MAY BE USED AND DISCLOSED AND HOW YOU CAN GET ACCESS TO THIS INFORMATION. PLEASE REVIEW IT CAREFULLY."[468] The notice must also contain the following:

- a description, including at least one example, of the types of uses and disclosures that the covered entity is permitted by this subpart to make for each of the following purposes: treatment, payment, and health care operations;
- a description of each of the other purposes for which the covered entity is permitted or required by this subpart to use or disclose protected health information without the individual's written authorization;

---

461. 45 C.F.R. § 164.520(a)(2)(i)(A)–(B).

462. 45 C.F.R. § 164.520(a)(2)(ii)(A)–(B).

463. 45 C.F.R. § 164.520(a)(2)(iii).

464. Inmate means a person incarcerated in or otherwise confined to a correctional institution. 45 C.F.R. § 164.501.

465. Correctional institution means any penal or correctional facility, jail, reformatory, detention center, work farm, halfway house, or residential community program center operated by, or under contract to, the United States, a state, a territory, a political subdivision of a state or territory, or an Indian tribe, for the confinement or rehabilitation of persons charged with or convicted of a criminal offense or other persons held in lawful custody. Other persons held in lawful custody includes juvenile offenders adjudicated delinquent, aliens detained awaiting deportation, persons committed to mental institutions through the criminal justice system, witnesses, or others awaiting charges or trial. 45 C.F.R. § 164.501.

466. 45 C.F.R. § 164.520(a)(3).

467. 45 C.F.R. § 164.520(b)(1).

468. 45 C.F.R. § 164.520(b)(1)(i).

- if a use or disclosure for any purpose described in paragraphs (b)(1)(ii)(A) or (B) is prohibited or materially limited by other applicable law, the description of such use or disclosure must reflect the more stringent law as defined in § 160.202;
- for each purpose described in paragraph (b)(1)(ii)(A) or (B), the description must include sufficient detail to place the individual on notice of the uses and disclosures that are permitted or required by this subpart and other applicable law;
- a statement that other uses and disclosures will be made only with the individual's written authorization and that the individual may revoke such authorization as provided by § 164.508(b)(5).[469]

If the covered entity intends to engage in any of the following activities, the description required by paragraph (b)(1)(ii)(A) must include a separate statement, as applicable, that the covered entity may contact the individual to provide appointment reminders or information about treatment alternatives or other health-related benefits and services that may be of interest to the individual; that the covered entity may contact the individual to raise funds for the covered entity; or that a group health plan, or a health insurance issuer or HMO with respect to a group health plan, may disclose protected health information to the sponsor of the plan.[470]

The notice must contain a statement of the individual's rights with respect to protected health information and a brief description of how the individual may exercise these rights, as follows: the right to request restrictions on certain uses and disclosures of protected health information as provided by § 164.522(a), including a statement that the covered entity is not required to agree to a requested restriction; the right to receive confidential communications of protected health information as provided by § 164.522(b), as applicable; the right to inspect and copy protected health information as provided by § 164.524; the right to amend protected health information as provided by § 164.526; the right to receive an accounting of disclosures of protected health information as provided by § 164.528; and the right of an individual, including an individual who has agreed to receive the notice electronically in accordance with paragraph (c)(3), to obtain a paper copy of the notice from the covered entity upon request.[471]

The notice must contain the following: a statement that the covered entity is required by law to maintain the privacy of protected health information and to provide individuals with notice of its legal duties and privacy practices with respect to protected health information; a statement that the covered entity is required to abide by the terms of the notice currently in effect; and for the covered entity to apply a change in a privacy practice that is described in the notice to protected health information that the covered entity created or received prior to issuing a revised notice, in accordance with § 164.530(i)(2)(ii), a statement that it reserves the right to change the terms of its notice and to make the new notice provisions effective for all protected health information that it maintains. The statement must also describe how it will provide individuals with a revised notice.[472]

---

469. 45 C.F.R. § 164.520(b)(1)(ii)(A)–(E).
470. 45 C.F.R. § 164.520(b)(1)(iii)(A)–(C).
471. 45 C.F.R. §§ 164.520(b)(1)(iv)(A)–(F).
472. 45 C.F.R. §§ 164.520(b)(1)(v)(A)–(C).

The notice must contain a statement that individuals may complain to the covered entity and to the secretary if they believe their privacy rights have been violated, a brief description of how the individual may file a complaint with the covered entity, and a statement that the individual will not be retaliated against for filing a complaint.[473] The notice must contain the name, or title, and telephone number of a person or office to contact for further information as required by § 164.530(a)(1)(ii).[474] The notice must also contain the date on which the notice is first in effect, which may not be earlier than the date on which the notice is printed or otherwise published.[475]

There are also optional elements for the notice. In addition to the information required by paragraph (b)(1), if a covered entity elects to limit the uses or disclosures that it is permitted to make, the covered entity may describe its more limited uses or disclosures in its notice, provided that the covered entity may not include in its notice a limitation affecting its right to make a use or disclosure that is required by law or permitted by § 164.512(j)(1)(i).[476] For the covered entity to apply a change in its more limited uses and disclosures to protected health information created or received prior to issuing a revised notice, in accordance with § 164.530(i)(2)(ii), the notice must include the statements required by paragraph (b)(1)(v)(C).[477]

The covered entity must promptly revise and distribute its notice whenever there is a material change to the uses or disclosures, the individual's rights, the covered entity's legal duties, or other privacy practices stated in the notice. Except when required by law, a material change to any term of the notice may not be implemented prior to the effective date of the notice in which such material change is reflected.[478]

A covered entity must make the required notice available on request to any person and to individuals as specified in § 164.520(c)(1) through (c)(3), as applicable.[479] There are also specific requirements for health plans. A health plan must provide notice no later than the compliance date for the health plan, to individuals then covered by the plan; thereafter, at the time of enrollment, to individuals who are new enrollees; and within 60 days of a material revision to the notice, to individuals then covered by the plan.[480] No less frequently than once every three years, the health plan must notify individuals then covered by the plan of the availability of the notice and how to obtain the notice.[481]

A health plan meets these requirements if notice is provided to the named insured of a policy under which coverage is provided to the named insured and one or more dependents.[482] If a health plan has more than one notice, it satisfies the requirements

---

473. 45 C.F.R. § 164.520(b)(1)(vi).
474. 45 C.F.R. § 164.520(b)(1)(vii).
475. 45 C.F.R. § 164.520(b)(1)(viii).
476. 45 C.F.R. § 164.520(b)(2)(i).
477. 45 C.F.R. § 164.520(b)(2)(ii).
478. 45 C.F.R. § 164.520(b)(3).
479. 45 C.F.R. § 164.520(c).
480. 45 C.F.R. §§ 164.520(c)(1)(i)(A)–(C).
481. 45 C.F.R. § 164.520(c)(1)(ii).
482. 45 C.F.R. § 164.520(c)(1)(iii).

by providing the notice that is relevant to the individual or other person requesting the notice.[483]

There are also specific requirements for certain covered health care providers. A covered health care provider that has a direct treatment relationship[484] with an individual must

- provide the notice no later than the date of the first service delivery, including service delivered electronically, to such individual after the compliance date for the covered health care provider, or in an emergency treatment situation, as soon as reasonably practicable after the emergency treatment situation;

- except in an emergency treatment situation, make a good faith effort to obtain a written acknowledgment of receipt of the notice provided in accordance with paragraph (c)(2)(i), and if not obtained, document its good faith efforts to obtain such acknowledgment and the reason why the acknowledgment was not obtained;

- if the covered health care provider maintains a physical service delivery site have the notice available at the service delivery site for individuals to request to take with them, and post the notice in a clear and prominent location where it is reasonable to expect individuals seeking service from the covered health care provider to be able to read the notice; and

- whenever the notice is revised, make the notice available upon request on or after the effective date of the revision and promptly comply with the requirements of paragraph (c)(2)(iii), if applicable.[485]

14:165. Requirements for electronic notice

A covered entity that maintains a web site that provides information about the covered entity's customer services or benefits must prominently post its notice on the web site and make the notice available electronically through the web site.[486] A covered entity may provide the notice required by this section to an individual by e-mail, if the individual agrees to electronic notice and such agreement has not been withdrawn. If the covered entity knows that the e-mail transmission has failed, a paper copy of the notice must be provided to the individual. Provision of electronic notice by the covered entity will satisfy the provision requirements of paragraph (c) when timely made in accordance with paragraph (c)(1) or (2).[487] For purposes of paragraph (c)(2)(i), if the first service delivery to an individual is delivered electronically, the covered health care provider must provide electronic notice automatically and contemporaneously in response to the individual's first request for service. The requirements in paragraph (c)(2)(ii) apply to

---

483. 45 C.F.R. § 164.520(c)(1)(iv).

484. "Direct treatment relationship" means a treatment relationship between an individual and a health care provider that is not an indirect treatment relationship. 45 C.F.R. § 164.501.

485. 45 C.F.R.§ 164.520(c)(2)(i)–(iv).

486. 45 C.F.R.§ 164.520(c)(3)(i).

487. 45 C.F.R.§ 164.520(c)(3)(ii).

electronic notice.[488] The individual who is the recipient of electronic notice retains the right to obtain a paper copy of the notice from a covered entity upon request.[489]

14:166 Joint notice by separate covered entities

Covered entities that participate in organized health care arrangements may comply by a joint notice, provided that

- the covered entities participating in the organized health care arrangement agree to abide by the terms of the notice with respect to protected health information created or received by the covered entity as part of its participation in the organized health care arrangement;
- the joint notice meets the implementation specifications in paragraph (b) of this section, except that the statements required by this section may be altered to reflect the fact that the notice covers more than one covered entity, and
  o describes with reasonable specificity the covered entities, or class of entities, to which the joint notice applies,
  o describes with reasonable specificity the service delivery sites, or classes of service delivery sites, to which the joint notice applies, and
  o if applicable, states that the covered entities participating in the organized health care arrangement will share protected health information with each other, as necessary to carry out treatment, payment, or health care operations relating to the organized health care arrangement;
- the covered entities included in the joint notice must provide the notice to individuals in accordance with the applicable implementation specifications of paragraph (c). Provision of the joint notice to an individual by any one of the covered entities included in the joint notice will satisfy the provision requirement of paragraph (c) with respect to all others covered by the joint notice.[490]

A covered entity must document compliance with the notice requirements, as required by § 164.530(j), by retaining copies of the notices issued by the covered entity and, if applicable, any written acknowledgments of receipt of the notice or documentation of good faith efforts to obtain such written acknowledgment, in accordance with paragraph (c)(2)(ii).[491]

14:167. Rights to request privacy protection for PHI

A covered entity must permit an individual to request that the covered entity restrict uses or disclosures of protected health information about the individual to carry out treatment, payment, or health care operations; and disclosures permitted under § 164.510(b).[492] A

---

488. 45 C.F.R. § 164.520(c)(3)(iii).
489. 45 C.F.R. § 164.520(c)(3)(iv).
490. 45 C.F.R. § 164.520(d)(1)–(3).
491. 45 C.F.R. § 164.520(e).
492. 45 C.F.R. §§ 164.522(a)(1)(i)(A)–(B).

covered entity is not required to agree to a restriction.[493] A covered entity that agrees to a restriction under paragraph (a)(1)(i) may not use or disclose protected health information in violation of such restriction, except that, if the individual who requested the restriction is in need of emergency treatment and the restricted protected health information is needed to provide the emergency treatment, the covered entity may use the restricted protected health information, or may disclose such information to a health care provider, to provide such treatment to the individual.[494] If restricted protected health information is disclosed to a health care provider for emergency treatment under paragraph (a)(1)(iii), the covered entity must request that such health care provider not further use or disclose the information.[495] A restriction agreed to by a covered entity under paragraph (a), is not effective under this subpart to prevent uses or disclosures permitted or required under §§ 164.502(a)(2)(ii), 164.510(a) or 164.512.[496]

A covered entity may terminate its agreement to a restriction, if the individual agrees to or requests the termination in writing; the individual orally agrees to the termination and the oral agreement is documented; or the covered entity informs the individual that it is terminating its agreement to a restriction, except that such termination is only effective with respect to protected health information created or received after it has so informed the individual.[497]

A covered entity that agrees to a restriction must document the restriction in accordance with § 164.530(j).[498]

14:168. Confidential communications requirements

A covered health care provider must permit individuals to request and must accommodate reasonable requests by individuals to receive communications of protected health information from the covered health care provider by alternative means or at alternative locations.[499] A health plan must permit individuals to request and must accommodate reasonable requests by individuals to receive communications of protected health information from the health plan by alternative means or at alternative locations, if the individual clearly states that the disclosure of all or part of that information could endanger the individual.[500]

A covered entity may require the individual to make a request for a confidential communication described in § 164.522(b)(1) in writing.[501] A covered entity may condition the provision of a reasonable accommodation on, when appropriate, information as to how payment, if any, will be handled, and specification of an alternative address or other method of contact.[502] A covered health care provider may not require an

---

493. 45 C.F.R. § 164.522(a)(1)(ii).
494. 45 C.F.R. § 164.522(a)(1)(iii).
495. 45 C.F.R. § 164.522(a)(1)(iv).
496. 45 C.F.R. § 164.522(a)(1)(v).
497. 45 C.F.R. §§ 164.522(a)(2)(i)–(iii).
498. 45 C.F.R. § 164.522(a)(3).
499. 45 C.F.R. § 164.522(b)(1)(i).
500. 45 C.F.R. § 164.522(b)(1)(ii).
501. 45 C.F.R. § 164.522(b)(2)(i).
502. 45 C.F.R. §§ 164.522(b)(2)(ii)(A)–(B).

explanation from the individual as to the basis for the request as a condition of providing communications on a confidential basis.[503] A health plan may require that a request contain a statement that disclosure of all or part of the information to which the request pertains could endanger the individual.[504]

14:169. Access of individuals to protected health information

Except as otherwise provided in § 164.524(a)(2) or (a)(3), an individual has a right of access to inspect and obtain a copy of protected health information about the individual in a designated record set,[505] for as long as the protected health information is maintained in the designated record set, except for psychotherapy notes; information compiled in reasonable anticipation of, or for use in, a civil, criminal, or administrative action or proceeding; and protected health information maintained by a covered entity that is subject to the Clinical Laboratory Improvements Amendments of 1988, 42 U.S.C. § 263a, to the extent the provision of access to the individual would be prohibited by law, or exempt from the Clinical Laboratory Improvements Amendments of 1988, pursuant to 42 C.F.R. § 493.3(a)(2).[506]

A covered entity may deny an individual access without providing the individual an opportunity for review in a number of circumstances. First, a covered entity may deny an individual access if the protected health information is excepted from the right of access by paragraph (a)(1).[507] Second, a covered entity that is a correctional institution or a covered health care provider acting under the direction of the correctional institution may deny, in whole or in part, an inmate's request to obtain a copy of protected health information, if obtaining such copy would jeopardize the health, safety, security, custody, or rehabilitation of the individual or of other inmates, or the safety of any officer, employee, or other person at the correctional institution or responsible for the transporting of the inmate.[508] Third, an individual's access to protected health information created or obtained by a covered health care provider in the course of research that includes treatment may be temporarily suspended for as long as the research is in progress, provided that the individual has agreed to the denial of access when consenting to participate in the research that includes treatment, and the covered health care provider has informed the individual that the right of access will be reinstated upon completion of the research.[509] Fourth, an individual's access to protected health information that is contained in records that are subject to the Privacy Act, 5 U.S.C.

---

503. 45 C.F.R. § 164.522(b)(2)(iii).

504. 45 C.F.R. § 164.522(b)(2)(iv).

505. "Designated record set" means: (1) A group of records maintained by or for a covered entity that is: (i) The medical records and billing records about individuals maintained by or for a covered health care provider; (ii) The enrollment, payment, claims adjudication, and case or medical management record systems maintained by or for a health plan; or (iii) Used, in whole or in part, by or for the covered entity to make decisions about individuals. (2) For purposes of this paragraph, the term record means any item, collection, or grouping of information that includes protected health information and is maintained, collected, used, or disseminated by or for a covered entity. 45 C.F.R. § 164.501.

506. 45 C.F.R. § 164.524(a)(1)(i)–(iii).

507. 45 C.F.R. § 164.524(a)(2)(i).

508. 45 C.F.R. § 164.524(a)(2)(ii).

509. 45 C.F.R. § 164.524(a)(2)(iii).

§ 552a, may be denied, if the denial of access under the Privacy Act would meet the requirements of that law.[510]

Finally, an individual's access may be denied if the protected health information was obtained from someone other than a health care provider under a promise of confidentiality and the access requested would be reasonably likely to reveal the source of the information.[511]

A covered entity may deny an individual access, provided that the individual is given a right to have such denials reviewed, as required by paragraph (a)(4), in certain circumstances,[512] including the following: a licensed health care professional has determined, in the exercise of professional judgment, that the access requested is reasonably likely to endanger the life or physical safety of the individual or another person; the protected health information makes reference to another person (unless such other person is a health care provider) and a licensed health care professional has determined, in the exercise of professional judgment, that the access requested is reasonably likely to cause substantial harm to such other person; or the request for access is made by the individual's personal representative and a licensed health care professional has determined, in the exercise of professional judgment, that the provision of access to such personal representative is reasonably likely to cause substantial harm to the individual or another person.[513]

14:170. Review of denial of access

If access is denied on a ground permitted under paragraph (a)(3), the individual has the right to have the denial reviewed by a licensed health care professional who is designated by the covered entity to act as a reviewing official and who did not participate in the original decision to deny. The covered entity must provide or deny access in accordance with the determination of the reviewing official under § 164.524(d)(4).[514]

14:171. Requests for access and timely action

The covered entity must permit an individual to request access to inspect or to obtain a copy of the protected health information about the individual that is maintained in a designated record set. The covered entity may require individuals to make requests for access in writing, provided that it informs individuals of such a requirement.[515] Except as provided in paragraph (b)(2)(ii), the covered entity must act on a request for access no later than 30 days after receipt of the request as follows: if the covered entity grants the request, in whole or in part, it must inform the individual of the acceptance of the request and provide the access requested, in accordance with paragraph (c).[516] If the covered entity denies the request, in whole or in part, it must provide the individual

---

510. 45 C.F.R. § 164.524(a)(2)(iv).
511. 45 C.F.R. § 164.524(a)(2)(v).
512. 45 C.F.R. § 164.524(a)(3).
513. 45 C.F.R. §§ 164.524(a)(3)(i)–(iii).
514. 45 C.F.R. § 164.524(a)(4).
515. 45 C.F.R. § 164.524(b)(1).
516. 45 C.F.R. § 164.524(b)(2)(i)(A).

with a written denial, in accordance with paragraph (d).[517] If the request for access is for protected health information that is not maintained or accessible to the covered entity on-site, the covered entity must take an action required by paragraph (b)(2)(i) by no later than 60 days from the receipt of such a request.[518] If the covered entity is unable to take an action required by paragraph (b)(2)(i)(A) or (B) within the time required by paragraph (b)(2)(i) or (ii), as applicable, the covered entity may extend the time for such actions by no more than 30 days, provided that the covered entity, within the time limit set by paragraph (b)(2)(i) or (ii), as applicable, provides the individual with a written statement of the reasons for the delay and the date by which the covered entity will complete its action on the request, and the covered entity may have only one such extension of time for action on a request for access.[519]

14:172. Providing access

If the covered entity provides an individual with access, in whole or in part, to protected health information, the covered entity must meet certain requirements.[520] The covered entity must provide the access requested by individuals, including inspection or obtaining a copy, or both, of the protected health information about them in designated record sets. If the same protected health information that is the subject of a request for access is maintained in more than one designated record set or at more than one location, the covered entity need only produce the protected health information once in response to a request for access.[521] The covered entity must provide the individual with access to the protected health information in the form or format requested by the individual, if it is readily producible in such form or format; or, if not, in a readable hard copy form or such other form or format as agreed to by the covered entity and the individual.[522] The covered entity may provide the individual with a summary of the protected health information requested, in lieu of providing access to the protected health information or may provide an explanation of the protected health information to which access has been provided, if the individual agrees in advance to such a summary or explanation and the individual agrees in advance to the fees imposed, if any, by the covered entity for such summary or explanation.[523]

The covered entity must provide the access as requested by the individual in a timely manner as required by paragraph (b)(2), including arranging with the individual for a convenient time and place to inspect or obtain a copy of the protected health information, or mailing the copy of the protected health information at the individual's request. The covered entity may discuss the scope, format, and other aspects of the request for access with the individual as necessary to facilitate the timely provision of access.[524] If the individual requests a copy of the protected health information

---

517. 45 C.F.R. § 164.524(b)(2)(i)(B).
518. 45 C.F.R. § 164.524(b)(2)(ii).
519. 45 C.F.R. §§ 164.524(b)(2)(iii)(A)–(B).
520. 45 C.F.R. § 164.524(c).
521. 45 C.F.R. § 164.524(c)(1).
522. 45 C.F.R. § 164.524(c)(2)(i).
523. 45 C.F.R. §§ 164.524(c)(2)(ii)(A)–(B).
524. 45 C.F.R. § 164.524(c)(3).

or agrees to a summary or explanation of such information, the covered entity may impose a reasonable, cost-based fee, provided that the fee includes only the cost of copying, including the cost of supplies for and labor of copying, the protected health information requested by the individual; postage, when the individual has requested the copy, or the summary or explanation, be mailed; and preparing an explanation or summary of the protected health information, if agreed to by the individual as required by paragraph (c)(2)(ii).[525]

14:173. Denial of access

If the covered entity denies access, in whole or in part, to protected health information, the covered entity must meet certain requirements.[526] The covered entity must, to the extent possible, give the individual access to any other protected health information requested, after excluding the protected health information as to which the covered entity has a ground to deny access.[527] The covered entity must provide a timely, written denial to the individual, in accordance with paragraph (b)(2). The denial must be in plain language and contain the following: the basis for the denial; if applicable, a statement of the individual's review rights under § 164.524(a)(4), including a description of how the individual may exercise such review rights; and a description of how the individual may complain to the covered entity pursuant to the complaint procedures in § 164.530(d) or to the secretary pursuant to the procedures in § 160.306. The description must include the name, or title, and telephone number of the contact person or office designated in § 164.530(a)(1)(ii).[528] If the covered entity does not maintain the protected health information that is the subject of the individual's request for access, and the covered entity knows where the requested information is maintained, the covered entity must inform the individual where to direct the request for access.[529] If the individual has requested a review of a denial under paragraph (a)(4), the covered entity must designate a licensed health care professional, who was not directly involved in the denial to review the decision to deny access. The covered entity must promptly refer a request for review to such designated reviewing official. The designated reviewing official must determine, within a reasonable period of time, whether or not to deny the access requested based on the standards in paragraph (a)(3). The covered entity must promptly provide written notice to the individual of the determination of the designated reviewing official and take other action as required by this section to carry out the designated reviewing official's determination.[530]

A covered entity must document the following and retain the documentation as required by § 164.530(j): the designated record sets that are subject to access by individuals, and the titles of the persons or offices responsible for receiving and processing requests for access by individuals.[531]

---

525. 45 C.F.R. §§ 164.524(c)(4)(i)–(iii).

526. 45 C.F.R. § 164.524(d).

527. 45 C.F.R. § 164.524(d)(1).

528. 45 C.F.R. § 164.524(d)(2)(i)–(iii).

529. 45 C.F.R. § 164.524(d)(3).

530. 45 C.F.R. § 164.524(d)(4).

531. 45 C.F.R. § 164.524(e)(1)–(2).

14:174. Amendment of Protected Health Information

An individual has the right to have a covered entity amend protected health information or a record about the individual in a designated record set for as long as the protected health information is maintained in the designated record set.[532] A covered entity may deny an individual's request for amendment, if it determines that the protected health information or record that is the subject of the request was not created by the covered entity, unless the individual provides a reasonable basis to believe that the originator of protected health information is no longer available to act on the requested amendment; is not part of the designated record set; would not be available for inspection under § 164.524; or is accurate and complete.[533]

The covered entity must permit an individual to request that the covered entity amend the protected health information maintained in the designated record set. The covered entity may require individuals to make requests for amendment in writing and to provide a reason to support a requested amendment, provided that it informs individuals in advance of such requirements.[534] The covered entity must act on the individual's request for an amendment no later than 60 days after receipt of such a request, if the covered entity grants the requested amendment, in whole or in part, it must take the actions required by § 164.526(c)(1) and (2), or if the covered entity denies the requested amendment, in whole or in part, it must provide the individual with a written denial, in accordance with paragraph (d)(1).[535] If the covered entity is unable to act on the amendment within the time required by § 164.526(b)(2)(i), the covered entity may extend the time for such action by no more than 30 days, provided that the covered entity, within the time limit set by paragraph (b)(2)(i), provides the individual with a written statement of the reasons for the delay and the date by which the covered entity will complete its action on the request, and the covered entity may have only one such extension of time for action on a request for an amendment.[536]

14:175. Actions on notices of amendment

A covered entity that is informed by another covered entity of an amendment to an individual's protected health information, in accordance with § 164.526(c)(3) of this section, must amend the protected health information in designated record sets as provided by paragraph (c)(1).[537]

---

532. 45 C.F.R. § 164.526(a)(1).
533. 45 C.F.R. §§ 164.526(a)(2)(i)–(iv).
534. 45 C.F.R. § 164.526(b)(1).
535. 45 C.F.R. §§ 164.526(b)(2)(i)(A)–(B).
536. 45 C.F.R. §§ 164.526(b)(2)(ii)(A)–(B).
537. 45 C.F.R. § 164.526(e).

14:176. Documentation

A covered entity must document the titles of the persons or offices responsible for receiving and processing requests for amendments by individuals and retain the documentation as required by § 164.530(j).[538]

14:177. Accounting of disclosures of protected health information

An individual has a right to receive an accounting of disclosures of protected health information made by a covered entity in the six years prior to the date on which the accounting is requested, except for the following disclosures: to carry out treatment, payment and health care operations as provided in § 164.506; to individuals of protected health information about them as provided in § 164.502; incident to a use or disclosure otherwise permitted or required by this subpart, as provided in § 164.502; pursuant to an authorization as provided in § 164.508; for the facility's directory or to persons involved in the individual's care or other notification purposes as provided in § 164.510; for national security or intelligence purposes as provided in § 164.512(k)(2); to correctional institutions or law enforcement officials as provided in § 164.512(k)(5); as part of a limited data set in accordance with § 164.514(e); or that occurred prior to the compliance date for the covered entity.[539]

14:178. Content of the accounting

The covered entity must provide the individual with a written accounting that meets certain requirements.[540] Except as otherwise provided by § 164.528(a), the accounting must include disclosures of protected health information that occurred during the six years (or such shorter time period at the request of the individual as provided in paragraph (a)(3)) prior to the date of the request for an accounting, including disclosures to or by business associates of the covered entity.[541] Except as otherwise provided by § 164.528(b)(3) or (b)(4), the accounting must include for each disclosure: the date of the disclosure; the name of the entity or person who received the protected health information and, if known, the address of such entity or person; a brief description of the protected health information disclosed; and a brief statement of the purpose of the disclosure that reasonably informs the individual of the basis for the disclosure or, in lieu of such statement, a copy of a written request for a disclosure under §§ 164.502(a)(2)(ii) or 164.512, if any.[542] If, during the period covered by the accounting, the covered entity has made multiple disclosures of protected health information to the same person or entity for a single purpose under §§ 164.502(a)(2)(ii) or 164.512, the accounting may, with respect to such multiple disclosures, provide: the information required by paragraph (b)(2) for the first disclosure during the accounting period; the frequency,

---

538. 45 C.F.R. § 164.526(f).

539. 45 C.F.R. §§ 164.528(a)(1)(i)–(ix).

540. 45 C.F.R. § 164.528(b).

541. 45 C.F.R. § 164.528(b)(1).

542. 45 C.F.R. §§ 164.528(b)(2)(i)–(iv).

periodicity, or number of the disclosures made during the accounting period; and the date of the last such disclosure during the accounting period.[543]

14:179. Providing the accounting

The covered entity must act on the individual's request for an accounting, no later than 60 days after receipt of such a request, and either provide the individual with the accounting, or if the covered entity is unable to provide the accounting within the time required by § 164.528(c)(1), the covered entity may extend the time to provide the accounting by no more than 30 days, provided that the covered entity, within the time limit set by paragraph (c)(1), provides the individual with a written statement of the reasons for the delay and the date by which the covered entity will provide the accounting, and the covered entity may have only one such extension of time for action on a request for an accounting.[544] The covered entity must provide the first accounting to an individual in any 12-month period without charge. The covered entity may impose a reasonable, cost-based fee for each subsequent request for an accounting by the same individual within the 12-month period, provided that the covered entity informs the individual in advance of the fee and provides the individual with an opportunity to withdraw or modify the request for a subsequent accounting in order to avoid or reduce the fee.[545]

14:180. Documentation

A covered entity must document the following and retain the documentation as required by § 164.530(j): the information required to be included in an accounting under paragraph (b) of this section for disclosures of protected health information that are subject to an accounting under paragraph (a); the written accounting that is provided to the individual under this section; and the titles of the persons or offices responsible for receiving and processing requests for an accounting by individuals.[546]

14:181. Personal designation

A covered entity must designate a privacy official who is responsible for the development and implementation of the policies and procedures of the entity.[547] A covered entity must designate a contact person or office who is responsible for receiving complaints under this section and who is able to provide further information about matters covered by the notice required by § 164.520.[548]

A covered entity must document the personnel designations in paragraph (a)(1) of this section as required by § 164.530(j).[549] A covered entity must train all members of

---

543. 45 C.F.R. §§ 164.528(b)(3)(i)–(iii).
544. 45 C.F.R. §§ 164.528(c)(1)(i)–(ii).
545. 45 C.F.R. § 164.528(c)(2).
546. 45 C.F.R. §§ 164.528(d)(1)–(3).
547. 45 C.F.R. § 164.530(a)(1)(i).
548. 45 C.F.R. § 164.530(a)(1)(ii).
549. 45 C.F.R. § 164.530(a)(2).

its workforce on the policies and procedures with respect to protected health information required by the Privacy Rule and the Breach Notification Rule, as necessary and appropriate for the members of the workforce to carry out their functions within the covered entity.[550]

A covered entity must provide training that meets the requirements of paragraph (b)(1), as follows: to each member of the covered entity's workforce by no later than the compliance date for the covered entity; thereafter, to each new member of the workforce within a reasonable period of time after the person joins the covered entity's workforce; and to each member of the covered entity's workforce whose functions are affected by a material change in the policies or procedures required by this subpart or subpart D of this part, within a reasonable period of time after the material change becomes effective in accordance with paragraph (i).[551]

A covered entity must document that the training as described in paragraph (b)(2) (i) has been provided, as required by paragraph (j).[552]

14:182. Safeguards

A covered entity must have in place appropriate administrative, technical, and physical safeguards to protect the privacy of protected health information.[553] A covered entity must reasonably safeguard protected health information from any intentional or unintentional use or disclosure that is in violation of the standards, implementation specifications or other requirements of the Privacy Rule.[554] A covered entity must reasonably safeguard protected health information to limit incidental uses or disclosures made pursuant to an otherwise permitted or required use or disclosure.[555]

14:183. Complaints to the covered entity

A covered entity must provide a process for individuals to make complaints concerning the covered entity's policies and procedures required by the Privacy Rule and the Breach Notification Rule or the covered entity's compliance with such policies and procedures.[556] As required by paragraph (j), a covered entity must document all complaints received, and their disposition, if any.[557]

---

550. 45 C.F.R. § 164.530(b)(1).
551. 45 C.F.R. §§ 164.530(b)(2)(i)(A)–(C).
552. 45 C.F.R. § 164.530(b)(2)(ii).
553. 45 C.F.R. § 164.530(c)(1).
554. 45 C.F.R. § 164.530(c)(2)(i).
555. 45 C.F.R. § 164.530(c)(2)(ii).
556. 45 C.F.R. § 164.530(d)(1).
557. 45 C.F.R. § 164.530(d)(2).

14:184. Documentation of complaints

A covered entity must have and apply appropriate sanctions against members of its workforce who fail to comply with the privacy policies and procedures of the covered entity or the requirements of the Privacy and Breach Notification Rules. This standard does not apply to a member of the covered entity's workforce with respect to actions that are covered by and that meet the conditions of § 164.502(j) or paragraph (g) (2).[558] As required by paragraph (j) of this section, a covered entity must document the sanctions that are applied, if any.[559]

14:185. Mitigation

A covered entity must mitigate, to the extent practicable, any harmful effect that is known to the covered entity of a use or disclosure of protected health information in violation of its policies and procedures or the requirements of this subpart by the covered entity or its business associate.[560]

14:186. Refraining from intimidating or retaliatory acts

A covered entity may not intimidate, threaten, coerce, discriminate against, or take other retaliatory action against any individual for the exercise by the individual of any right established, or for participation in any process provided for, by the Privacy or Breach Notification Rules, including the filing of a complaint under this section, and must refrain from intimidation and retaliation as provided in § 160.316.[561]

14:187. No waiver of rights

A covered entity may not require individuals to waive their rights under § 160.306, as a condition of the provision of treatment, payment, enrollment in a health plan, or eligibility for benefits.[562]

14:188. Policies and procedures

A covered entity must implement policies and procedures with respect to protected health information that are designed to comply with the standards, implementation specifications, or other requirements. The policies and procedures must be reasonably designed, taking into account the size of and the type of activities that relate to protected health information undertaken by the covered entity, to ensure such compliance. This standard is not to be construed to permit or excuse an action that violates any other standard, implementation specification, or other requirement of the Privacy Rule.[563]

---

558. 45 C.F.R. § 164.530(e)(1).

559. 45 C.F.R. § 164.530(e)(2).

560. 45 C.F.R. § 164.530(f).

561. 45 C.F.R. §§ 164.530(g)(1)–(2).

562. 45 C.F.R. § 164.530(h).

563. 45 C.F.R. § 164.530(i)(1).

A covered entity must change its policies and procedures as necessary and appropriate to comply with changes in the law, including the standards, requirements, and implementation specifications of the Privacy and Breach Notification Rules.[564] When a covered entity changes a privacy practice that is stated in the notice described in § 164.520, and makes corresponding changes to its policies and procedures, it may make the changes effective for protected health information that it created or received prior to the effective date of the notice revision, if the covered entity has, in accordance with § 164.520(b)(1)(v)(C), included in the notice a statement reserving its right to make such a change in its privacy practices.[565] A covered entity may make any other changes to policies and procedures at any time, provided that the changes are documented and implemented in accordance with § 164.530(i)(5).[566]

Whenever there is a change in law that necessitates a change to the covered entity's policies or procedures, the covered entity must promptly document and implement the revised policy or procedure. If the change in law materially affects the content of the notice required by § 164.520, the covered entity must promptly make the appropriate revisions to the notice in accordance with § 164.520(b)(3). Nothing in this paragraph may be used by a covered entity to excuse a failure to comply with the law.[567]

14:189. Changes to privacy practices stated in the notice

To implement a change as provided by paragraph (i)(2)(ii), a covered entity must do the following: ensure that the policy or procedure, as revised to reflect a change in the covered entity's privacy practice as stated in its notice, complies with the standards, requirements, and implementation specifications of the Privacy Rule; document the policy or procedure, as revised, as required by § 164.530(j); and revise the notice as required by § 164.520(b)(3) to state the changed practice and make the revised notice available as required by § 164.520(c). The covered entity may not implement a change to a policy or procedure prior to the effective date of the revised notice.[568]

If a covered entity has not reserved its right under § 164.520(b)(1)(v)(C) to change a privacy practice that is stated in the notice, the covered entity is bound by the privacy practices as stated in the notice with respect to protected health information created or received while such notice is in effect. A covered entity may change a privacy practice that is stated in the notice, and the related policies and procedures, without having reserved the right to do so, provided that such change meets the implementation specifications in paragraphs (i)(4)(i)(A)–(C) of this section and the change is effective only with respect to protected health information created or received after the effective date of the notice.[569]

This language supports retroactive changes to an entity's privacy practices, if it has reserved the right to modify these practices in the privacy notices.

---

564. 45 C.F.R. § 164.530(i)(2)(i).
565. 45 C.F.R. § 164.530(i)(2)(ii).
566. 45 C.F.R. § 164.530(i)(2)(iii).
567. 45 C.F.R. § 164.530(i)(3).
568. 45 C.F.R. § 164.530(i)(4)(i)(A)–(C).
569. 45 C.F.R. §§ 164.530(i)(4)(ii)(A)–(B).

14:190. Changes to other policies or procedures

A covered entity may change, at any time, a policy or procedure that does not materially affect the content of the notice required by § 164.520, provided that the policy or procedure, as revised, complies with the standards, requirements, and implementation specifications of this subpart, and that, prior to the effective date of the change, the policy or procedure, as revised, is documented as required by paragraph (j).[570]

14:191. Documentation

A covered entity must maintain the following: the policies and procedures provided for in paragraph (i) of this section in written or electronic form; if a communication is required by this subpart to be in writing, such writing, or an electronic copy, as documentation; if an action, activity, or designation is required by this subpart to be documented, a written or electronic record of such action, activity, or designation; and documentation sufficient to meet its burden of proof under § 164.414(b).[571]

14:192. Retention period

A covered entity must retain the documentation discussed above for six years from the date of its creation or the date when it last was in effect, whichever is later.[572]

14:193. Group health plans

A group health plan is not subject to the standards or implementation specifications in paragraphs (a) through (f) and (i) of this section, to the extent that the group health plan provides health benefits solely through an insurance contract with a health insurance issuer or an HMO and the group health plan does not create or receive protected health information, except for summary health information as defined in § 164.504(a), or information on whether the individual is participating in the group health plan, or is enrolled in or has disenrolled from a health insurance issuer or HMO offered by the plan.[573] A group health plan described in paragraph (k)(1) is subject to the standard and implementation specification in paragraph (j) only with respect to plan documents amended in accordance with § 164.504(f).[574]

---

570. 45 C.F.R. §§ 164.530(i)(5)(i)–(ii).

571. 45 C.F.R. §§ 164.530(j)(1)(i)–(iv).

572. 45 C.F.R. § 164.530(j)(2).

573. 45 C.F.R. §§ 164.530(k)(1)(i)–(ii).

574. 45 C.F.R. § 164.530(k)(2).

14:194. Use and disclosure of information

Notwithstanding §§ 164.508 and 164.512(i), a covered entity may use or disclose protected health information, consistent with § 164.532(b) and (c), pursuant to an authorization or other express legal permission obtained from an individual permitting the use or disclosure of protected health information, informed consent of the individual to participate in research, or a waiver of informed consent by an IRB.[575] Notwithstanding any provisions in § 164.508, a covered entity may use or disclose protected health information that it created or received prior to the applicable compliance date of this subpart pursuant to an authorization or other express legal permission obtained from an individual prior to the applicable compliance date of this subpart, provided that the authorization or other express legal permission specifically permits such use or disclosure and there is no agreed-to restriction in accordance with § 164.522(a).[576]

Notwithstanding any provisions in §§ 164.508 and 164.512(i), a covered entity may, to the extent allowed by one of the following permissions, use or disclose, for research, protected health information that it created or received either before or after the applicable compliance date of the Privacy Rule, provided that there is no agreed-to restriction in accordance with § 164.522(a), and the covered entity has obtained, prior to the applicable compliance date, an authorization or other express legal permission from an individual to use or disclose protected health information for the research; the informed consent of the individual to participate in the research; or a waiver, by an IRB, of informed consent for the research, in accordance with 7 C.F.R. § 1c.116(d), 10 C.F.R. § 745.116(d), 14 C.F.R. § 1230.116(d), 15 C.F.R. § 27.116(d), 16 C.F.R. § 1028.116(d), 21 C.F.R. § 50.24, 22 C.F.R. § 225.116(d), 24 C.F.R. § 60.116(d), 28 C.F.R. § 46.116(d), 32 C.F.R. § 219.116(d), 34 C.F.R. § 97.116(d), 38 C.F.R. § 16.116(d), 40 C.F.R. § 26.116(d), 45 C.F.R. § 46.116(d), 45 C.F.R. § 690.116(d), or 49 C.F.R. § 11.116(d), provided that a covered entity must obtain authorization in accordance with § 164.508 if, after the compliance date, informed consent is sought from an individual participating in the research.[577]

14:195. Effect of prior contracts or other arrangements with business associates

Notwithstanding any other provisions of the Privacy Rule, a covered entity, other than a small health plan, may disclose protected health information to a business associate and may allow a business associate to create, receive, or use protected health information on its behalf pursuant to a written contract or other written arrangement with such business associate that does not comply with §§ 164.502(e) and 164.504(e) consistent with the requirements, and only for such time, set forth in paragraph (e).[578]

Notwithstanding other sections of the Privacy Rule, a covered entity, other than a small health plan, is deemed to be in compliance with the documentation and contract

---

575. 45 C.F.R. § 164.532(a).
576. 45 C.F.R. § 164.532(b).
577. 45 C.F.R. §§ 164.532(c)(1)–(3).
578. 45 C.F.R. § 164.532(d).

requirements of §§ 164.502(e) and 164.504(e), with respect to a particular business associate relationship, for the time period set forth in § 164.532(e)(2), if prior to October 15, 2002, such covered entity has entered into and is operating pursuant to a written contract or other written arrangement with a business associate for such business associate to perform functions or activities or provide services that make the entity a business associate, and the contract or other arrangement was not renewed or modified from October 15, 2002, until the compliance date set forth in § 164.534.[579] A prior contract or other arrangement that meets the qualification requirements in paragraph (e), was deemed compliant until the earlier of the date such contract or other arrangement is renewed or modified on or after the compliance date set forth in § 164.534; or April 14, 2004.[580]

Nothing in this section shall alter the requirements of a covered entity to comply with 45 C.F.R part 160, subpart C (Compliance and Investigations) and §§ 164.524, 164.526, 164.528, and 164.530(f) with respect to protected health information held by a business associate.[581]

14:196. Compliance dates for initial implementation of the privacy standards

Covered health care providers had to comply with the applicable requirements of the Privacy Rule no later than April 14, 2003.[582] Health plans other than small health plans had to comply with the applicable requirements no later than April 14, 2003; small health plans, by April 14, 2004.[583] Health care clearinghouses had to comply with the applicable requirements of this subpart no later than April 14, 2003.[584]

14:197. Public records laws and HIPAA protections

Under certain state laws, ambulance companies, as well as other entities are covered by public records laws that mandate disclosures of certain limited forms of information.[585] In a recent Attorney General opinion, the Wisconsin Attorney General offered guidance on the interaction of HIPAA and public records laws, as well as the ambulance disclosure laws. Relying upon a number of decisions, the Attorney General concluded that HIPAA would not preclude disclosure of information under state public records laws, because HIPAA does not preclude disclosures that are "required by law."[586]

While the contents of 911 tapes are frequently treated as public records, a court in Louisiana has held that 911 tapes generated by a medical emergency are confidential

---

579. 45 C.F.R. §§ 164.532(e)(1)(i)–(ii).

580. 45 C.F.R. § 164.532(e)(2)(i)–(ii).

581. 45 C.F.R. § 164.532(e)(3).

582. 45 C.F.R. § 164.534(a).

583. 45 C.F.R. § 164.534(b).

584. 45 C.F.R. § 164.534(c).

585. See, e.g., Wis. Stat. Ann. § 146.50(12)(b).

586. State of Wisconsin Department of Justice, I-03-07, September 27, 2007; citing, State ex rel. Enquirer v. Daniels, 844 N.E.2d 1181 (2006); Abbott v. Texas Dept. of Mental Health, 212 S.W.3d 648 (2006); Protection & Advocacy System, Inc. v. Freudenthal, 412 F. Supp. 2d 1211, 1216-17 (D. Wyo. 2006).

under HIPAA and therefore cannot be disclosed under the Louisiana public records law.[587]

14:198. State Medicaid restrictions and HIPAA

While certain state laws can expand disclosures of HIPAA covered information, more restrictive state laws, including those that preclude the disclosure of certain information that would be permitted by HIPAA, will govern what information is disclosed by state agencies, at least in the opinion of the Attorney General of Tennessee.[588]

14:199. De-identified information

A covered entity can make protected health information anonymous and thereby create non-identifiable health information, which would not be subject to the HIPAA restrictions.[589] If the ability to re-identify the information exists, then the information is considered to be identifiable information.[590]

14:200. Disclosures to business associates

There are a number of requirements related to disclosures to business associates. A covered entity can disclose protected health information to a business associate and permit that business associate to create or receive protected health information on its behalf if the covered entity obtains satisfactory assurances from the business associate that it will appropriately safeguard the information.[591] There are a number of exceptions to this general requirement, as well as implementation standards that require the assurances to be in writing.[592]

14:201. Restrictions and exceptions

Any covered entity that is required to provide notice of its privacy practices under HIPAA is precluded from using or disclosing information in a way inconsistent with that notice.[593]

There are a number of exceptions available to covered entities, including relating to abuse of elders or dependent individuals, whistle-blowers or victims of crimes.[594] Disclosure to certain governmental entities is also permitted.[595]

Business associate agreements must have a number of requirements, including the establishment of permitted uses of the information, identify appropriate safeguards,

---

587. Hill v. East Baton Rouge Parrish Department of Emergency Medical Services, 925 So. 2d 17, 34 Media L. Rep. 1154 (2005).

588. State of Tennessee, Office of the Attorney General, Opinion No. 07-165, December 14, 2007.

589. 45 C.F.R. § 164.502(d).

590. 45 C.F.R. § 164.502(d).

591. 45 C.F.R. § 164.502(e)(1).

592. 45 C.F.R. § 164.502(e)(2).

593. 45 C.F.R. § 164.502(i).

594. 45 C.F.R. § 164.502(j).

595. 45 C.F.R. § 164.502(j).

reporting requirements, procedures for the amendment or correction of health information, and, if feasible, provide for destruction of the information upon termination of the agreement.[596]

---

596. 45 C.F.R. § 164.504(e)(1).

Chapter 15

Federal Trade Commission Act and Enforcement Under the FTC Act

15:1. Generally

The Federal Trade Commission Act (FTC Act) originally began as a statutory scheme that protected competing businesses, not consumers, from unfair methods of competition. In 1938, Section 5 of the Act was amended, and the FTC Act was extended to cover consumers as well.[1] The 1938 amendments also granted the FTC more flexibility in addressing practices before they have reached a conclusion and had a significant and long term effect.[2]

---

1. F.T.C. v. Colgate-Palmolive Co., 380 U.S. 374, 85 S. Ct. 1035, 1042 (1965); Guziak v. F. T. C., 361 F.2d 700, 703 (8th Cir. 1966).

2. Fashion Originators' Guild of America v. Federal Trade Commission, 312 U.S. 457, 312 U.S. 668, 61 S. Ct. 703, 707, 48 U.S.P.Q. 483 (1941) ("And as previously pointed out, it was the object of the Federal Trade Commission Act to reach not merely in their fruition but also in their incipiency combinations which could lead to these and other trade restraints and practices deemed undesirable."); Keasbey & Mattison Co. v. Federal Trade Commission, 159 F.2d 940, 73 U.S.P.Q. 203 (C.C.A. 6th Cir. 1947); Ford Motor Co. v. Federal Trade Commission, 120 F.2d 175 (C.C.A. 6th Cir. 1941).

There are two main sections that identify the deceptive conduct that is actionable under the FTC Act—15 U.S.C. §§ 45 and 52.[3] The interaction and structure of these portions of the FTC Act are important because other states, including California, have adopted this structure in their "Little FTC Act" statutes.

Section 45 regulates unfair and deceptive trade practices generally. Section 52 makes false advertising illegal independently of Section 45, but it should be noted that a violation of Section 52 is also a violation of Section 45.

15:2. Prohibited conduct

Section 45 of the Federal Trade Commission Act makes "unfair methods of competition in or affecting commerce, and unfair or deceptive acts or practices in or affecting commerce" unlawful.[4] The FTC also has jurisdiction to address deceptive trade practices.

The FTC has summarized the laws in this area in the following way: the FTC has determined that a representation, omission or practice is *deceptive* if it is likely to

- mislead consumers acting reasonably, and
- affect consumers' behavior or decisions about the product or service.

In addition, an act or practice is unfair if the injury it causes, or is likely to cause, is substantial, not outweighed by other benefits to consumers or competition, and not reasonably avoidable to consumers.[5]

15:3. Additional guidance regarding unfairness

Defining "unfair conduct" is of critical importance in the privacy and security arena because, as discussed below, unfairness has become an independent basis for FTC enforcement action, even where there is no misrepresentation or deceptive conduct. While the unfairness doctrine is an evolving one, the FTC did provide some guidance regarding what constitutes an unfair practice in a statement in 1980. The Commission stated that "[u]njustified consumer injury is the primary focus of the FTC Act"[6] and also noted "that to justify a finding of unfairness, any consumer injury must satisfy three tests: (1) the injury must be substantial; (2) it must be not outweighed by any offsetting benefits to consumers or competition; and (3) the injury must be one that consumers could not reasonably have avoided."[7] The FTC also stated that, "[a]lthough public policy" has been listed "as a separate consideration, it is used most frequently by the Commission as a means of providing additional evidence on the degree of consumer injury caused by specific practices."[8] Section 45(m) was later amended to include this expressly.

---

3. These sections are also referred to as Sections 5 and 12 of the FTC Act. All citations and references in this discussion use the section numbers from Title 15.

4. 15 U.S.C. § 45(a)(1).

5. See http://www.ftc.gov/ogc/brfovrvw.shtm (last visited March 29, 2011).

6. *See* http://www.ftc.gov/os/2003/06/dotcomment.htm (citing Unfairness Statement at 2, 104 F.T.C. at 1073).

7. *See* http://www.ftc.gov/os/2003/06/dotcomment.htm; Unfairness Statement at 2, 104 F.T.C. at 1073-74.

8. *See* http://www.ftc.gov/os/2003/06/dotcomment.htm; Unfairness Statement at 2, 104 F.T.C. at 1075.

The *Accusearch* case is one of the few recent litigated cases that provides guidance on the scope of unfair practices under the FTC Act. Abika.com is a website that has sold various personal data, including telephone records. The FTC brought suit against the operator of the website.[9] The FTC alleged that Accusearch's trade in telephone records violated the Telecommunications Act and also constituted an unfair practice in violation of § 5(a) of the FTC Act. Accusearch argued that it had not violated § 5 of the FTC Act because the Telecommunications Act did not apply to its activities and therefore its actions were not unfair under the FTC Act. The court of appeals rejected this argument, finding that the FTC need not prove independent illegality to establish that a practice is unfair.[10] The court of appeals also rejected Accusearch's argument that the FTC could not bring the action because it lacked power to enforce the Telecommunications Act.[11]

15:4.   Overview of relief

The FTC has several choices regarding how to proceed when it has determined that a deceptive trade practice is occurring. The FTC may bring suit in federal court to obtain a temporary restraining order (TRO) or preliminary injunction pending the initiation of administrative action.[12] Alternatively, the FTC may proceed exclusively in federal court by filing a complaint. Permanent injunctions and ancillary relief, including temporary or preliminary injunctive relief, are available to the FTC.[13]

In essence, the FTC has two methods of getting relief—administrative action, and filing in district court. Retrospective relief is only available if a district court action is filed, though in certain cases the FTC can proceed under § 57(B), though this also requires a later filing in district court.

15:5.   Relief available under Section 53(b)

Section 53(b) permits the FTC to bring an action in federal district court and secure appropriate equitable relief, including restitution and disgorgement.[14] The FTC is also authorized to prevent persons subject to its jurisdiction from engaging in unfair and deceptive acts or practices.[15] If the FTC chooses it can bring an administrative action against a defendant and simultaneously seek a TRO or preliminary injunction pending the initiation of administrative action.[16] Alternatively, the FTC may proceed entirely in

---

9.   FTC v. Accusearch, 570 F.3d 1187 (10th Cir. 2009).

10.   *Id.* (citing Spiegel, Inc. v. FTC, 540 F.2d 287, 291-94 (7th Cir. 1976)).

11.   *Id.* (citing Am. Fin. Servs. Ass'n v. FTC, 767 F.2d 957, 983 (D.C.Cir. 1985)).

12.   15 U.S.C. § 53(b).

13.   15 U.S.C. § 53(b); F.T.C. v. Gem Merchandising Corp., 87 F.3d 466, 468-69, 1996-2 Trade Cas. (CCH) P 71467 (11th Cir. 1996); F.T.C. v. World Travel Vacation Brokers, Inc., 861 F.2d 1020, 1026, 1988-2 Trade Cas. (CCH) P 68333, 12 Fed. R. Serv. 3d 1034 (7th Cir. 1988); F.T.C. v. Gill, 71 F. Supp. 2d 1030, 1047 (C.D. Cal. 1999), aff'd, 265 F.3d 944, 2001-2 Trade Cas. (CCH) P 73412 (9th Cir. 2001).

14.   F.T.C. v. AmeriDebt, Inc., 343 F. Supp. 2d 451, 455-56, 2004-2 Trade Cas. (CCH) P 74624 (D. Md. 2004).

15.   15 U.S.C. § 45(a) (2).

16.   15 U.S.C. § 53(b).

federal court, seeking a permanent injunction and ancillary relief, including temporary or preliminary injunctive relief.[17]

15:6. Remedies

In addition to injunctive relief under Section 53(b), the FTC can seek asset freezes,[18] the appointment of a receiver,[19] disgorgement, as well as restitution of ill-gotten gains.[20]

15:7. FTC's Privacy agenda

Despite the lack of comprehensive federal privacy statutes, companies can face enforcement actions if the FTC believes that a company's conduct constitutes a deceptive trade practice or the conduct violates one of the many statutes that the FTC enforces, including the Children's Online Privacy Protection Act (COPPA), Gramm-Leach-Bliley (GLB), and many others. The FTC has announced a privacy agenda that provides some insight into what the FTC considers to be improper practices. Moreover, additional guidance is available via examination of the enforcement actions brought by the FTC regarding privacy practices.

The FTC's privacy agenda includes stepping up enforcement of spam laws, including limiting chain letters and pyramid schemes. The FTC also has committed to increasing assistance to victims of identity theft, including identifying patterns in conduct reported by consumers and creating a unified fraud affidavit for victims of identity theft.

Enforcing companies' privacy promises is also a focal point of the FTC's agenda. Of particular import are cases involving sensitive information, transfers of information as part of bankruptcies, as well as practices that violate the European Union Safe Harbor program. Increasing enforcement of GLB, as well as the COPPA are also top FTC goals.

---

17.   F.T.C. v. Gem Merchandising Corp., 87 F.3d 466, 468-69, 1996-2 Trade Cas. (CCH) P 71467 (11th Cir. 1996); F.T.C. v. World Travel Vacation Brokers, Inc., 861 F.2d 1020, 1026, 1988-2 Trade Cas. (CCH) P 68333, 12 Fed. R. Serv. 3d 1034 (7th Cir. 1988); F.T.C. v. Gill, 71 F. Supp. 2d 1030, 1047 (C.D. Cal. 1999), aff'd, 265 F.3d 944, 2001-2 Trade Cas. (CCH) P 73412 (9th Cir. 2001); Federal Trade Com'n v. Productive Marketing, Inc., 136 F. Supp. 2d 1096, 1100-1102, 2001-1 Trade Cas. (CCH) P 73305 (C.D. Cal. 2001); F.T.C. v. Commonwealth Marketing Group, Inc., 72 F. Supp. 2d 530, 535, 1999-2 Trade Cas. (CCH) P 72610 (W.D. Pa. 1999); F.T.C. v. Crescent Pub. Group, Inc., 129 F. Supp. 2d 311, 332-33, 2001-1 Trade Cas. (CCH) P 73165 (S.D. N.Y. 2001); F.T.C. v. Verity Intern., Ltd., 124 F. Supp. 2d 193, 2001-1 Trade Cas. (CCH) P 73129 (S.D. N.Y. 2000); F.T.C. v. Think Achievement Corp., 144 F. Supp. 2d 1013, 1015, 2000-2 Trade Cas. (CCH) P 73089 (N.D. Ind. 2000), aff'd, 312 F.3d 259, 2002-2 Trade Cas. (CCH) P 73880 (7th Cir. 2002).

18.   F.T.C. v. H. N. Singer, Inc., 668 F.2d 1107, 1982-1 Trade Cas. (CCH) P 64569 (9th Cir. 1982); F.T.C. v. World Wide Factors, Ltd., 882 F.2d 344 (9th Cir. 1989).

19.   F.T.C. v. U.S. Oil & Gas Corp., 748 F.2d 1431, 1984-2 Trade Cas. (CCH) P 66332 (11th Cir. 1984).

20.   F.T.C. v. Febre, 128 F.3d 530, 1997-2 Trade Cas. (CCH) P 71950 (7th Cir. 1997); F.T.C. v. Mylan Laboratories, Inc., 62 F. Supp. 2d 25, 1999-2 Trade Cas. (CCH) P 72573 (D.D.C. 1999), on reconsideration in part, 99 F. Supp. 2d 1, 2000-1 Trade Cas. (CCH) P 72778 (D.D.C. 1999).

15:8.   Section 5 cases—In the Matter of Geocities

Geocities[21] was the first privacy enforcement action brought by the FTC. It was based upon the classic FTC theory—false or misleading statements. In this matter, the FTC alleged that Geocities had made misrepresentations in its privacy policy, including that it would only use the certain personally identifiable information that it collected from its customers, including children, to send specific e-mail advertising offers. The FTC asserted that in fact Geocities sold and rented the list and otherwise disclosed the information of its customers in ways that were not disclosed in the privacy policy. As with most FTC privacy matters, the case resolved via a consent decree that placed heightened burdens on Geocities, including specific disclosure requirements for its online privacy policy.

15:9.   Section 5 cases—In the Matter of Liberty Financial Companies, Inc.

The *Liberty Financial*[22] enforcement matter also presents a then-typical fact pattern for FTC enforcement. In this case, Liberty Financial allegedly made misrepresentations in its privacy policy regarding the fact that responses to online surveys would be anonymous, when in fact they were not. The FTC believed this representation, coupled with Liberty Financial's actual practices, was false and misleading. The matter resolved via consent decree and, like Geocities, Liberty Financial was required to place a privacy policy with specific format requirements on its website, make certain reports to the FTC, and not make certain misrepresentations regarding its privacy practices. Though this case represented a traditional enforcement pattern, the next case offered an insight into where the FTC would be heading several years later.

15:10. Section 5 cases—In the Matter of ReverseAuction.com, Inc.

The FTC filed a complaint against ReverseAuction.com[23] based upon the allegation that the company had wrongfully signed into eBay's website and obtained personally identifiable information about users, including e-mail addresses and eBay ratings. Reverseauction.com then allegedly took this information and spammed the eBay users, falsely representing that the users' eBay accounts were going to expire. ReverseAuction.com was a competitor of eBay, and it was alleged to have done this to promote its own website.

This matter resolved via a stipulated consent agreement, which specifically made no admission of the facts or of wrongdoing by ReverseAuction.com. However, the company did agree to not make certain representations regarding competitors, to give certain notices, and to keep certain records that could be disclosed to the FTC.

While neither the consent decree nor the alleged conduct that led to it were notable, the statement of then Commissioner Mozelle Thompson in connection with

---

21.   http://www.ftc.gov/os/caselist/c3850.shtm (last visited March 29, 2011).

22.   http://www.ftc.gov/os/caselist/9823522.shtm (last visited March 29, 2011).

23.   http://www.ftc.gov/os/caselist/reverseauction/index.shtm (last visited March 29, 2011).

the resolution of this matter, provides some insight into the FTC's current enforcement theories. Commissioner Thompson wrote a statement regarding the theories pursued against ReverseAuction.com in which he asserted that not only was the company's conduct deceptive, the standard FTC theory in privacy enforcement matters, but the alleged acts, even if not deceptive, were also unfair and therefore also violated Section 5 of the Act, and Commissioner Thompson proceeded to analyze the conduct under the "unfairness" framework noted above.

Although this case was a business-to-business case resolved in 2000, the theory stated by Commissioner Thompson—that privacy or security violations could be unfair practices apart from whether deception was involved—has now served as the basis for several enforcement actions. This statement certainly is relevant to the *CartManager*[24] enforcement action (at least in part), as well as *DSW*[25] and those cases that followed where the FTC explicitly pursued the theory that the lack of data security was itself an unfair practice.

15:11. Section 5 cases—FTC v. Toysmart.com

In this case the FTC alleged that Toysmart.com[26], because it attempted to sell customer information in violation of its privacy policy, misrepresented the fact that customer information would never be shared with third parties. The settlement with the FTC required the then-bankrupt Toysmart.com to obtain opt-in consent from its customers before information could be transferred to a bankruptcy purchaser. This case is in large part what led to the changes to the bankruptcy code referenced in chapter 2.

15:12. Section 5 cases—FTC v. Rennert

In this case[27] the FTC alleged that an online pharmacy made misrepresentations regarding medical and pharmaceutical facilities, as well as the level of privacy and security afforded to customers' information. The FTC also alleged that the defendants used the customer information to generate spam and also improperly debited customers' credit cards.

The matter resolved with a variety of requirements being placed upon the defendants, including restrictions from selling, renting, leasing transferring or otherwise disclosing customer information without express authorization from the customer. There were also disclosure requirements regarding the defendants' privacy policies, as well as increased information security requirements.

15:13. Section 5 cases—In the Matter of Eli Lilly and Company

Eli Lilly[28] was one of the first FTC actions that addressed, at least implicitly, a company's voluntary assumption of heightened privacy burdens to representations made to consumers. This matter arose from an e-mail that Eli Lilly sent to customers taking Prozac. Instead

---

24.   http://www.ftc.gov/os/caselist/0423068/0423068.shtm (last visited March 29, 2011).
25.   http://www.ftc.gov/os/caselist/0523096/0523096.shtm (last visited March 29, 2011).
26.   http://www.ftc.gov/os/caselist/x000075.shtm (last visited March 29, 2011).
27.   http://www.ftc.gov/os/caselist/9923245/9923245.shtm (last visited March 29, 2011).
28.   http://www.ftc.gov/os/caselist/0123214/0123214.shtm (last visited March 29, 2011).

of masking the names in the e-mail, Eli Lilly included all of the customers' names in the e-mail. The company had made specific representations on its website regarding its concern for customer privacy on its website, and these representations were relied upon by the FTC in its assertion that Eli Lilly had violated the FTC Act. The case is generally perceived as supporting the view that the FTC will read statements regarding concern for customer privacy as creating heightened burdens.

15:14. Section 5 cases—In the Matter of Microsoft Corporation

Microsoft[29] was the second case that dealt with heightened privacy burdens created by a privacy policy, and this matter dealt with the issue much more directly than the *Eli Lilly* matter. Microsoft was alleged to have made a number of representations regarding privacy, including that it followed "strict" privacy policies. The FTC alleged that in fact Microsoft did not maintain a high level of security and did not use reasonable and appropriate measures to maintain privacy or security. The FTC also alleged that Microsoft had made misrepresentations regarding the amount of personally identifiable information it collected.

This matter was resolved via a consent decree that did not admit the alleged wrongdoing, but placed Microsoft under enhanced reporting and disclosure obligations. It also required Microsoft to establish and maintain a comprehensive information security program and give certain notices to consumers. While the resolution is of some interest, the real import is the FTC's view that statements in a privacy policy to the effect that a company has implemented heightened privacy and security standards bind the company to burdens that may be in excess of what the law would otherwise require.

15:15. Section 5 cases—In the Matter of The National Research Center For College and University Admissions, Inc.

The *National Research Center*[30] matter arose from the allegation that the company had made misrepresentations regarding how and to whom personally identifiable information would be disclosed, as well as who funded the research that was done on the data that was collected. The FTC alleged that these misrepresentations were deceptive practices. The National Research Center was required to make certain privacy disclosures, give notice of certain practices, and not make certain misrepresentations.

15:16. Section 5 cases—In the Matter of Educational Research Center of America, Inc.

This matter[31] arose from allegations similar to those involving the National Research Center, though here the FTC alleged that the information was sold to marketers that

---

29.   http://www.ftc.gov/opa/2002/08/microsoft.shtm (last visited March 29, 2011).

30.   http://www.ftc.gov/os/caselist/0223005/index.shtm (last visited March 29, 2011).

31.   http://www.ftc.gov/os/caselist/c4079.shtm (last visited March 29, 2011).

targeted children. The case resolved on terms similar to *National Research Center*. Both this case and *National Research Center* demonstrated the FTC's desire to end allegedly deceptive acts related to information gathering in general, particularly where children, even those not within COPPA, are involved.

15:17. Section 5 cases—In the Matter of Guess?, Inc.

The *Guess*[32] matter offers a more traditional FTC enforcement profile. Guess allegedly represented that it had implemented reasonable security measures and stored information in encrypted formats. The FTC alleged that in reality, the Guess.com website was susceptible to a commonly known structured query language (SQL) attack that resulted in customers' credit card numbers being acquired. Based upon the representations by Guess, the FTC alleged that Guess's conduct was a deceptive trade practice, though it also alleged that it was an unfair practice. Guess entered a consent order with the FTC that placed security, disclosure, notice, and privacy restrictions on it. The case is one in a series of cases where representations on websites were used as the basis of an enforcement action; the case did not represent a marked departure from prior cases.

15:18. Section 5 cases—In the Matter of MTS, Inc., d/b/a Tower Records/Books/Video

The FTC enforcement action against Tower Records[33] presents an almost identical profile to *Guess*. Tower allegedly made representations on its website regarding information security. The FTC alleged that these representations were not true and that in fact the Tower Records website was susceptible to a commonly known security exploit that resulted in the disclosure of customer's personally identifiable information, including name, address, e-mail address, and order history, to other users of the website. As with the other FTC matters, this resolved via consent decree, with Tower Records pledging to increase security (including implementing appropriate physical, technological, and administrative safeguards), give certain information to the FTC, and not engage in deceptive actions related to privacy and information security. The FTC also required that Tower Records have security assessments done by a Certified Information System Security Professional (CISSP) or similarly-qualified individual.

15:19. Section 5 cases—In the Matter of Gateway Learning

The FTC has also challenged changes to a company's privacy policy that the FTC believed were "material changes." In *In the Matter of Gateway Learning Corp*,[34] the FTC alleged that Gateway Learning had agreed in its privacy policy not to share personally identifiable information with third parties unless the consumer provided express consent. Moreover, the privacy policy also purportedly extended to consumers the right to opt out of the sharing of information if the policy changed in the future. The FTC alleged that personally identifiable information was shared with third parties and that a revised

---

32. http://www.ftc.gov/os/caselist/0223260/ (last visited March 29, 2011).

33. http://www.ftc.gov/os/caselist/0323209/0323209.shtm (last visited March 29, 2011).

34. http://www.ftc.gov/os/caselist/0423047/0423047.shtm (last visited March 29, 2011).

privacy policy was applied retroactively without affording customers the opt-out rights that they were allegedly promised.

This matter also resolved via a consent order that made no admission of the facts or of any liability, but Gateway is now subject to heightened reporting requirements and also has restrictions upon its ability to retroactively apply changes to its privacy policy without consumer's consent.

15:20. Section 5 cases—In the Matter of Petco Animal Supplies

In the case of *In the Matter of Petco Animal Supplies*,[35] the FTC prepared a complaint against Petco Animal Supplies, Inc. arising out of statements it had made on Petco's website regarding Web security.[36] While there is no specific federal law mandating data security for all websites, the FTC alleged that Petco had engaged in deceptive trade practices due to the representations made on its website regarding the security of customers' data. The FTC alleged that Petco made express or implied representations to its customers that certain forms of data were stored in encrypted format. The FTC also alleged that the website was susceptible to certain cyber-attacks that permitted individuals to access credit card data and that this data was not stored in encrypted format. While there was no admission of any of these facts or violations by Petco, a consent order was entered by Petco and the FTC that placed heightened reporting and security burdens upon Petco for an extended period of time.

15:21. Section 5 cases—In the Matter of Vision I Properties, LLC

In the case of *In the Matter of Vision I Properties, LLC, d/b/a CartManager International*,[37] the FTC started an investigation of a company that provided a shopping cart service for other e-commerce websites. These websites made specific representations regarding privacy, including that personal information was not sent, sold, or leased to third parties. The FTC alleged that CartManager, a company that provided shopping cart services for these websites, violated the FTC Act.[38] In most cases, the portions of the websites that gathered the information were CartManager's, but CartManager did not disclose that the information practices on these pages were different from those used on the other pages, even though all pages appeared to be part of the same website. The FTC claimed that CartManager also began renting information to third parties, despite the privacy statements made by the retailers. CartManager also allegedly failed to disclose its information practices to its clients. The FTC considered these acts to be violations of the FTC Act. The consent order that was entered by CartManager restricted its ability to disclose personally identifiable information, required it to pay certain costs, required

---

35. http://www.ftc.gov/os/caselist/0323221/0323221.shtm (last visited March 29, 2011).

36. The FTC prepared a complaint against Petco, but did not ultimately file the complaint as the matter resolved via consent order.

37. http://www.ftc.gov/os/caselist/0423068/0423068.shtm (last visited March 29, 2011).

38. This matter also involved a draft complaint that was not filed because the matter was resolved via consent order.

additional disclosures regarding CartManager's privacy practices, and placed it under reporting obligations to the FTC.

15:22. Section 5 cases—In the Matter of BJ's Wholesale Club, Inc.

In the Matter of BJ's Wholesale Club, Inc.[39] represents a marked departure from prior FTC actions because it is the first time the FTC used its unfairness authority and did not also allege deceptive practices for privacy and security misrepresentation. BJ's Wholesale Club operates a number of membership warehouse stores. As part of its normal business, BJ's accepted credit cards as a form of payment from its members. BJ's collected personally identifiable information from its customers to authorize their credit cards. It also used wireless technology, including WAPs (wireless access points) and scanners to monitor inventory. The FTC filed a complaint against BJ's, alleging that it had

(1) failed to encrypt information while it was in transit or stored on the network;

(2) stored personally identifiable information in a file format that permitted anonymous access;

(3) did not use readily accessible security measures to limit access;

(4) failed to employ sufficient measures to detect unauthorized access or conduct security investigations; and

(5) created unnecessary business risks by storing information after it had any use for the information, in violation of bank rules.

The FTC alleged that as a result of this conduct millions of dollars in fraudulent purchases had been made. Though there was no federal statute that BJ's conduct directly violated, the FTC concluded that these acts constituted an unfair business practice under the FTC Act and brought an enforcement action against BJ's. This matter also resolved via consent order, and the FTC required BJ's to implement a comprehensive information security plan, obtain a security assessment, and report twice a year for the next 20 years, as well as other administrative requirements.

This case is notable because it represents a different enforcement pattern from prior FTC actions. In the past, the FTC had only acted in the security arena when a company was subject to heightened security burdens (under statutes such as HIPAA, COPPA, or GLB), or the company had made specific security promises. Here, the FTC has shown that even in the absence of a specific representation or a statutory burden, companies can face enforcement action for a lack of information security based upon the FTC's unfairness authority, and not based upon deception.

The import of the case is that it represents the first occasion where the FTC brought an enforcement action based upon an information security issue where there was not an alleged misrepresentation to consumers regarding information security. Indeed, it is notable that the allegations by the FTC in this matter rely exclusively on the unfairness prong of the act, not the deceptive prong. Thus, the unanswered question with *CartManager* was answered by the FTC, and it is clear that the FTC views the

---

39. http://www.ftc.gov/os/caselist/0423160/0423160.shtm (last visited March 29, 2011).

lack of information security, whether there is a deceptive statement to consumers or not, as an unfair business practice.

15:23. Section 5 cases—USA v. ChoicePoint Inc.

There was a significant amount of press coverage of the allegations involving ChoicePoint[40] and the alleged issues with security and privacy, including the alleged sale of information on 163,000 individuals to a crime ring. The FTC claimed that ChoicePoint had violated FCRA and the FTC Act due to its alleged conduct that led to the sale of consumers' information. Ultimately ChoicePoint resolved the matter by agreeing to a consent order, which included an FTC-mandated information security program, and paying $10 million in fines and $5 million to set up a fund to assist the consumers that were potential victims of identity theft.

This case is particularly notable due to the monetary penalties. It is also a good example of the benefit of committing to a privacy and information security plan: ChoicePoint is now one of the most trusted names in consumer privacy.

15:24. Section 5 cases—In the Matter of CardSystems Solutions, Inc.

CardSystems[41] represents the FTC's first foray into the information security arena where the alleged violation was not based upon a misrepresentation to consumers. CardSystems processed credit card data for merchants and gathered personally identifiable information regarding consumers as part of that process, including information contained on credit cards' magnetic strips. The FTC alleged that CardSystems failed to implement reasonable security measures, including storing the information for up to 30 days and having a system that permitted a hacker to use simple techniques to steal credit card information and authorization information that was used in a number of fraudulent transactions. CardSystems, in the consent decree that resolved the matter, agreed to implement reasonable information security processes and report to the FTC, as well as meet other requirements.

15:25. Section 5 cases—In the Matter of DSW, Inc.

While initially a case brought by the FTC, this matter[42] has given rise to a number of privacy and security issues. The case arises out of the allegation that DSW, Inc., a shoe retailer, failed to have adequate data security, which resulted in consumers' personal information being acquired in more than 108 stores over a three-month period. While DSW was alleged to have provided notice to some of the affected consumers, despite no statutory obligation at the time to do so, the Ohio attorney general sued DSW, claiming that its failure to give notice to all of the consumers was an unfair business practice.

The FTC also investigated DSW's practices and claimed to have found that DSW engaged in a number of improper acts, including that DSW

---

40. http://www.ftc.gov/os/caselist/choicepoint/choicepoint.shtm (last visited March 29, 2011).

41. http://www.ftc.gov/os/caselist/0523148/0523148.shtm (last visited March 29, 2011).

42. http://www.ftc.gov/os/caselist/0523096/0523096.shtm (last visited March 29, 2011).

- created unnecessary risks to sensitive information by storing it in multiple files when it no longer had a business need to keep the information;
- failed to use readily available security measures to limit access to its computer networks through wireless access points on the networks;
- stored the information in unencrypted files that could be easily accessed using a commonly known user ID and password;
- failed to limit sufficiently the ability of computers on one in-store network to connect to computers on other in-store and corporate networks; and
- failed to employ sufficient measures to detect unauthorized access.[43]

The matter resolved via consent order, with DSW being subject to security and privacy compliance requirements and monitoring.

15:26. Section 5 cases—In the Matter of Guidance Software, Inc.

The *Guidance Software*[44] matter presents a set of allegations very similar to that of Tower Records. In this case, the FTC alleged that Guidance Software had made representations to consumers regarding its privacy and security practices, including that it "took every precaution" to protect users' information. In reality, according to the FTC, while SSL was used, the network was susceptible to common attacks, including SQL injection attacks, and the company failed to assess its vulnerabilities and did not use simple, low-cost, and readily available defenses. Moreover, it did not allegedly use sufficient measures to detect unauthorized access to sensitive information. These alleged failures resulted in an alleged hacker obtaining the information, including credit card information. These acts were alleged to be a deceptive, but not an unfair, practice. The matter resolved via order, and as is typical, no admission of the facts was made. Guidance Software was required to implement an information security program, report certain things to the FTC, and meet other requirements.

While the theory of this matter is not notable, one aspect is—unlike *Tower Records* and *Guess*, the FTC alleged that the failure to use sufficient measures to detect unauthorized access was a deceptive practice. Thus, the FTC may be embarking down a new data security path by imposing some form of monitoring obligation, at least where a company has allegedly voluntarily assumed it via statements in a privacy policy.

15:27. Section 5 cases—In the Matter of Life is Good Retail, Inc.

In this case, Life Is Good Retail, Inc.[45] was alleged to have collected personally identifiable information regarding consumers, including name, credit card number, security code, and e-mail address via Internet and telephone sales, but all of the information was stored on a computer network that was accessible via the Internet. Despite allegedly

---

43. *See* http://www.ftc.gov/opa/2005/12/dsw.htm (last visited on March 7, 2011).

44. http://www.ftc.gov/os/caselist/0623057/index.shtm (last visited March 29, 2011).

45. http://www.ftc.gov/os/caselist/0723046/index.shtm (last visited March 29, 2011).

promising security, Life Is Good Retail, Inc., allegedly failed to take steps to protect this information, including that it allegedly

- stored the consumer information in clear, readable text;
- created unnecessary risks to consumer information by storing it indefinitely on their network, without a business need, and by storing credit card security codes;
- did not adequately assess the vulnerability of their web application and network to commonly known or reasonably foreseeable attacks, such as SQL injection attacks;
- did not implement simple, free or low cost, and readily available defenses to such attacks;
- did not use readily available security measures to monitor and control connections from the network to the Internet; and
- failed to employ reasonable measures to detect unauthorized access to consumer information.

This case relied expressly on the false and deceptive prong of the FTC Act, and did not rely upon the FTC's unfairness authority. This matter resolved via consent decree with typical auditing and reporting requirements. The only notable question raised in this matter was whether the FTC was applying the website policy to all forms of information that were stored on a computer network, including information that was collected via telephone sales.

15:28. Section 5 cases—In the Matter of Goal Financial, LLC

The FTC filed an action against Goal Financial, LLC,[46] an entity that markets and originates student loans and provides loan related services. Goal Financial had a privacy policy, which stated that it limited access to nonpublic information about consumers to those employees with a "need to know" and that it maintained physical, electronic, and procedural safeguards to comply with federal requirements. The FTC alleged that Goal Financial failed to do the following:

- to assess adequately risks to the information it collected and stored in its paper files and on its computer network;
- to restrict adequately access to personal information stored in its paper files and on its computer network to authorized employees;
- to implement a comprehensive information security program, including reasonable policies and procedures in key areas such as the collection, handling, and disposal of personal information;
- to provide adequate training to employees about handling and protecting personal information and responding to security incidents; and
- in a number of instances, to require third-party service providers by contract to protect the security and confidentiality of personal information.

---

46.   http://www.ftc.gov/os/caselist/0723013/index.shtm (last visited March 29, 2011).

Goal Financial employees were alleged to have taken over 7,000 consumer files and to have transferred them to third parties. There were also allegations that a Goal employee failed to properly scrub hard drives before selling them, so that information regarding 34,000 consumers was allegedly exposed in clear text.

The FTC alleged that this conduct violated Section 5 of the FTC Act, as well as GLB. This matter resolved via consent decree, in which Goal Financial agreed to not make misrepresentations regarding its privacy policies, to create and maintain a comprehensive information security plan, to identify material internal and external risks, and to conduct assessments at the time of the resolution of the matter, as well as on a biannual basis. Moreover, Goal Financial was required to submit reports for an extended period of time and provide the FTC with significant amounts of information, along with other obligations that were imposed.

15:29. Section 5 cases—United States v. ValueClick, Inc

ValueClick is an Internet marketing company that was alleged to have engaged in materially misleading conduct in relation to e-mail and other forms of marketing.[47] Specifically, ValueClick was alleged to have used materially misleading headers that misrepresented to consumers that services and goods were free, when in fact they were not. In many cases consumers allegedly had to sign up for other services, or qualify in other ways, to receive the "free" goods and services; often these costs exceeded the value of the free merchandise. As an example, the FTC alleged:

> Once the consumer has submitted his or her personal information, the lead generation Defendants lead the consumer through a series of web pages containing advertisements for various goods and services from third parties. Unbeknownst to the consumer, this is only an introductory tier of "optional" advertisements and offers, after which are three additional tiers of offers that the consumer will have to navigate before he or she can qualify for the promised free merchandise. "Optional" offers do not qualify the consumer for the promised free merchandise.

ValueClick was also alleged to have easy-break encryption, rather than industry standard encryption, which was vulnerable to SQL injection attacks, despite its promise that it would encrypt information. Finally, ValueClick was also alleged to have retained security and other related credit card codes when it in fact should not have.

Although ValueClick denied liability, the matter resolved via stipulated final judgment in which ValueClick paid a fine of $2.9 million and agreed to not make misrepresentations regarding encryption, privacy, and security; to implement a comprehensive privacy and information security policy; to designate responsible employees for these matters; to conduct risk assessments and implement reasonable safeguards targeted to these risks; to do an initial and biannual audit of these matters for 20 years; and to report to the FTC on many matters.

---

47.   http://www.ftc.gov/os/caselist/0723111/index.shtm (last visited March 29, 2011).

15:30. Section 5 cases—In the Matter of Reed Elsevier, Inc. and Seisint, Inc.

In this case the respondents owned or managed several databases that contained sensitive personal information regarding consumers, including through their offer of a branded service known as Accurint.[48] The respondents were alleged to engaged in a number of practices that failed to provide reasonable and appropriate security to prevent unauthorized access to the sensitive consumer information stored in databases accessible using Accurint verification products ("Accurint databases"). Specifically, respondents were alleged to have failed to establish or implement reasonable policies and procedures governing the creation and authentication of user credentials for authorized customers accessing Accurint databases. They also were alleged to have

- failed to establish or enforce rules sufficient to make user credentials hard to guess, including because respondents allowed Accurint customers to use the same word, including common dictionary words, as both the password and user ID, or a close variant of the user ID as the password;
- permitted the sharing of user credentials among a customer's multiple users, thus reducing likely detection of, and accountability for, unauthorized searches;
- failed to require periodic changes of user credentials, such as every 90 days, for customers with access to sensitive nonpublic information;
- failed to suspend user credentials after a certain number of unsuccessful log-in attempts;
- allowed customers to store their user credentials in a vulnerable format in cookies on their computers;
- failed to require customers to encrypt or otherwise protect credentials, search queries, and/or search results in transit between customer computers and respondents' websites;
- allowed customers to create new credentials without confirming that the new credentials were created by customers rather than identity thieves;
- failed to adequately assess the vulnerability of the Accurint web application and computer network to commonly known or reasonably foreseeable attacks, such as "Cross-Site Scripting" attacks; and
- failed to implement simple, low-cost, and readily available defenses to such attacks.

These computer security failures allegedly resulted in customers' social security numbers being exposed. This matter resolved via consent order, which required the respondents to take the following measures:

- designate an employee or employees to coordinate and be accountable for the information security program;
- identify material internal and external risks to the security, confidentiality, and integrity of customer information that could result in the unauthorized disclosure,

---

48. http://www.ftc.gov/os/caselist/0523094/index.shtm (last visited March 29, 2011).

misuse, loss, alteration, destruction, or other compromise of such information, and assess the sufficiency of any safeguards in place to control these risks;

- design and implement reasonable safeguards to control the risks identified through risk assessment, and regularly test or monitor the effectiveness of the safeguards' key controls, systems, and procedures;

- develop and use reasonable steps to select and retain service providers capable of appropriately safeguarding personal information they receive from the respondent, and require service providers by contract to implement and maintain appropriate safeguards; and

- evaluate and adjust their information security programs in light of the results of testing and monitoring, any material changes to operations or business arrangements, or any other circumstances that they know or have reason to know may have material impact on its information security program.

Additionally, there are a number of document reporting and audit requirements that were imposed upon the respondents.

15:31. Section 5 cases—In the Matter of The TJX Companies, Inc.

TJX[49] is a retailer that was alleged to have stored authorization requests and personal information obtained to verify checks and process unreceipted returns in clear text on its networks. It was also alleged to have transmitted authorization requests and responses in clear text on its networks. The following was alleged of the information security practices of TJX:

- that they created unnecessary risks to sensitive information by storing it on computer networks without a business need to do so;
- that they stored sensitive information on networks in a vulnerable format;
- that they failed to use readily available security measures to limit access to a computer network through wireless access points on the network;
- that they failed to adequately assess the vulnerability of a web application and computer network to commonly known or reasonably foreseeable attacks;
- that they failed to implement simple, low-cost, and readily available defenses to such attacks;
- that they failed to use readily available security measures to limit access between computers on a network and between computers and the internet; and
- that they failed to use strong passwords to authenticate (or authorize) users to access programs and databases on computer networks or online.

These alleged actions resulted in the compromise of tens of millions of unique payment cards used by consumers in North America, and there were tens of millions of dollars in costs that were allegedly incurred as a result of the breach, and many consumers became potential victims of identity theft as a result of the alleged conduct.

---

49. http://www.ftc.gov/os/caselist/0723055/index.shtm (last visited March 29, 2011).

The matter resolved via consent order and TJX was required to create a comprehensive information security program that included the following:

- designating an employee or employees to coordinate and be accountable for the information security program;
- identifying material internal and external risks to the security, confidentiality, and integrity of personal information that could result in the unauthorized disclosure, misuse, loss, alteration, destruction, or other compromise of such information, and assessing the sufficiency of any safeguards in place to control these risks;
- designing and implementing reasonable safeguards to control the risks identified through risk assessment, and regularly testing or monitoring the effectiveness of the safeguards' key controls, systems, and procedures;
- developing and using reasonable steps to retain service providers capable of appropriately safeguarding personal information they receive from TJX;
- requiring service providers by contract to implement and maintain appropriate safeguards, and monitor their safeguarding of personal information; and
- evaluating and adjusting its information security program in light of the results of the testing and monitoring, any material changes to its operations or business arrangements, or any other circumstances that TJX knows or has reason to know may have a material impact on the effectiveness of the information security program.

There are also assessment and reporting requirements that continue for 20 years.

15:32. Section 5 cases—In the Matter of Sony BMG Music Entertainment

The *Sony*[50] case, discussed in the context of the Children's Online Privacy Protection Act (chapter 3) also contained allegations that Sony violated § 5 of the FTC Act. This case is more fully discussed in the COPPA chapter.

15:33. Section 5 cases—In the Matter of Premier Capital Lending, Inc.

This matter involved alleged violations of Section 5, as well as the safeguards rule, and it is covered below in section 15:43 in the safeguards enforcement section.

15:34. Section 5 cases—In the Matter of Geeks.com

In this matter[51] the respondents were alleged to have operated a website that consumers used to obtain information and purchase computer products. As part of the process of selling computer products, the respondents gathered sensitive personal information from consumers, including information related to obtaining credit card authorizations. The FTC alleged that the respondents made misrepresentations regarding the efforts

---

50. http://www.ftc.gov/os/caselist/0823071/index.shtm (last visited March 29, 2011).
51. http://www.ftc.gov/os/caselist/0823113/index.shtm (last visited March 29, 2011).

they took to protect this information, which included consumers' names, addresses, e-mail addresses, telephone numbers, credit card numbers, credit card expiration dates, and credit card security codes. Specifically, the FTC alleged that the respondents (1) stored personal information in clear, readable text; (2) did not adequately assess the vulnerability of their web application and network to commonly known or reasonably foreseeable attacks, such as SQL injection attacks; (3) did not implement simple, free or low-cost, and readily available defenses to such attacks; (4) did not use readily available security measures to monitor and control connections between computers on the network and from the network to the Internet; and (5) failed to employ reasonable measures to detect and prevent unauthorized access to personal information, such as by logging or employing an intrusion detection system. The FTC also alleged that hackers had exploited these vulnerabilities.

The consent decree required the respondents to make no misrepresentations regarding steps they take to protect the privacy, confidentiality, or integrity of any personal information collected from or about consumers. They were also required to implement an information security program, and the consent order had standard reporting, third-party review, and document retention requirements.

15:35. Section 5 cases—In the Matter of CVS Caremark Corporation

In this matter[52] the respondent was alleged to have failed to implement reasonable and appropriate security to protect the information CVS gathered, which included name, telephone number, address, date of birth, account information, credit card information, and prescription and other related medical information, as well as several other categories of data. The FTC alleged that CVS discarded materials that contained this information in an unsecure way, including in dumpsters.

The matter resolved via consent decree and required CVS to implement a comprehensive data security plan, as well as to not make any misrepresentations regarding security and privacy of information. CVS was also required to engage in standard reporting, third-party review, and document retention requirements. It should be noted that this was the first health care case brought by the FTC and the first one brought in conjunction with the Office of Civil Rights in the Department of Health and Human Services. This is another indication of the FTC's focus on medical identity theft.

15:36. Section 5 cases—In the Matter of Sears Holdings Management Corporation

This matter[53] arose from allegations regarding online tracking by Sears via its "SHC Community" market research program. Sears represented, via a clickwrap agreement, that users who installed a software application would have their "online browsing" tracked. The FTC believed this representation was deceptive because it failed to adequately disclose the true nature of the software in that the software monitored virtually all of

---

52. http://www.ftc.gov/os/caselist/0723119/index.shtm (last visited March 29, 2011).

53. http://www.ftc.gov/os/caselist/0823099/index.shtm (last visited March 29, 2011).

the users' Internet behavior, including conduct that did not occur with Sears (such as shopping history from other websites), as well as information that was sent via secure methods and headers of Web-based mail. Though this was disclosed in a lengthy end-user license agreement, the FTC felt this conduct was deceptive and ultimately the matter resolved via consent decree.

Sears was required to make clear and prominent disclosure of the features of any "tracking software," which the FTC defined as "any software program or application that is capable of being installed on customers' computers and used on or on behalf of respondent to monitor, record, or transmit information about activities occurring on computers on which it is installed, or about data that is stored on, created on, transmitted from, or transmitted to the computers on which it is installed." The disclosures were specifically required to disclose the types of data collected, including whether the data collected was from other websites, other transactions (including other online shopping baskets), or online accounts, and whether this information included financial or health information. There were also website disclosure requirements and document retention requirements, as well as other remedial requirements.

The case is important to note because of its implications for online tracking and behavioral advertising issues. The case seems to be one based upon the FTC's deceptive act or practice authority, but the complaint does reference the FTC's unfairness authority. The focus of the case is on the alleged failure to disclose material terms of the license agreement (specifically those that related to data collection), so the unfairness authority issue may be less of the focus of this case. As noted above, the importance of this distinction is that the FTC has used its unfairness authority in cases where there was no alleged misrepresentation made, which means that companies can find themselves facing an enforcement action even when they have not made a misrepresentation.

15:37. Section 5 cases—In the Matter of Dave & Busters, Inc.

In this matter,[54] Dave & Busters was alleged to have, in connection with collecting and processing sensitive personal information, engaged in a number of practices that, taken together, failed to provide reasonable and appropriate security for personal information on its networks, including that it

- failed to employ sufficient measures to detect and prevent unauthorized access to computer networks or to conduct security investigations, such as by employing an intrusion detection system and monitoring system logs;
- failed to adequately restrict third-party access to its networks, such as by restricting connections to specified IP addresses or granting temporary, limited access;
- failed to monitor and filter outbound traffic from its networks to identify and block export of sensitive personal information without authorization;
- failed to use readily available security measures to limit access between in-store networks, such as by employing firewalls or isolating the payment card system from the rest of the corporate network; and

---

54.   http://www.ftc.gov/os/caselist/0823153/index.shtm (last visited March 29, 2011).

- failed to use readily available security measures to limit access to its computer networks through wireless access points on the networks.

As a result an intruder was allegedly able to connect to the network and intercept information, including approximately 130,000 unique payment cards.

This, like other data security cases, was a case based upon the FTC's unfairness authority under Section 5 due to the alleged failure to have adequate data security. The matter resolved via consent decree that contained reporting requirements, as well as other remedial requirements.

15:38. Section 5 cases—FTC v. Lifelock, Inc., et al.

In this case the FTC brought an enforcement action against LifeLock[55] arising out of alleged marketing misstatements regarding its products, as well as alleged misstatements regarding data security issues. The FTC alleged that the fraud alerts that LifeLock placed on customers' credit files protected only against certain forms of identity theft and gave them no protection against the misuse of existing accounts, and also that, despite alleged representations to the contrary, LifeLock's data was not encrypted and sensitive consumer information was not shared only on a "need to know" basis. In fact, the agency charged, the company's data system was vulnerable and could have been exploited by those seeking access to customer information. The consent decree required LifeLock to not make misrepresentations and also to implement a comprehensive data security program. The settlement was part of a larger set of investigations that implicated a number of state attorneys general.

15:39. Safeguards enforcement cases—In the Matter of Sunbelt Lending Services, Inc.

This case was the first safeguards enforcement action brought by the FTC in 2000. Sunbelt Lending Services[56] was a mortgage broker that qualified as a "financial institution," and was therefore subject to GLB, including the safeguards and privacy rule. The FTC alleged that Sunbelt failed to identify reasonably foreseeable internal and external risks to the security, confidentiality, and integrity of customer information; failed to implement information safeguards to control the risk, to monitor the customer information, and to implement tests to monitor the safeguards; failed to develop, implement, and maintain a comprehensive written information security program; failed to oversee service providers and require them by contract to protect Sunbelt's customer information; and failed to designate one or more employees to coordinate the information security program. The FTC also alleged that Sunbelt failed to provide its online customers with the notice required by the privacy rule.

The consent that served as the settlement for this matter prohibited Sunbelt from committing further violations of the safeguards for privacy rule, had reporting and assessment requirements, and required the implementation of a security plan that assured the security, confidentiality, and integrity of customers' personal information. There

---

55.   http://www.ftc.gov/os/caselist/0723069/index.shtm (last visited March 29, 2011).

56.   http://www.ftc.gov/os/caselist/0423153/04231513.shtm (last visited March 29, 2011).

were also document retention and disclosure obligations, as well as dissemination of information requirements for executives at the company.

15:40. Safeguards enforcement cases—In the Matter of Superior Mortgage Corp.

In this matter, Superior Mortgage,[57] a financial institution specializing in residential mortgage loans, was alleged by the FTC to have violated the GLB safeguards rule. The FTC alleged that Superior Mortgage failed to do the following: assess risks to its customer information until more than a year after the safeguard rule became effective; institute appropriate password policies to control access to company systems and documents containing sensitive customer information; encrypt or otherwise protect sensitive customer information before sending it by e-mail; and take reasonable steps to ensure that its service providers were providing appropriate security for customer information and addressing their own security risks in a timely and appropriate fashion.

In addition to the safeguards rule violations, the FTC alleged that Superior Mortgage also violated Section 5 of the FTC Act by representing that personal information it obtained online from customers was encrypted using SSL at all times by Superior Mortgage when in fact the information was only encrypted while it was being transmitted between the visitor's Web browser and the website server, and that once received by Superior Mortgage, the information was decrypted and e-mailed to a number of offices in clear, readable text. The agreement with Superior Mortgage prohibited it from misrepresenting the nature and extent of its privacy protections, and also prohibited Superior Mortgage from violating the safeguards rule in the future. There were also assessment and certification requirements, including that Superior Mortgage implement a security program that meets or exceeds the protections required by the safeguards rule and that the security program would operate in a way that would provide reasonable assurances that the security confidentiality and integrity of information was protected. There were also document retention and disclosure obligations.

The order is not notable in what it requires for some of the alleged conduct, but it is important to note that the FTC in this case was explicit about the lack of security of e-mail, particularly when it contains a person's identifiable information.

15:41. Safeguards enforcement cases—In the Matter of Nations Title Agency, Inc.

This matter[58] involved a title company that made representations regarding its information security. Specifically, the FTC alleged that Nations Title claimed that it maintained "physical, electronic and procedural" safeguards to protect customers' confidential financial information when in fact consumer home loan applications were placed in a dumpster. Nations Title also claimed that it had placed measures to guard against unauthorized access to nonpublic customer information. The FTC alleged that Nations Title violated the safeguards rule because it allegedly disposed of confidential financial

---

57. http://www.ftc.gov/os/caselist/0523136/0523136.shtm (last visited March 29, 2011).

58. http://www.ftc.gov/os/caselist/0523117/0523117.shtm (last visited March 29, 2011).

information in a non-secure way. The FTC also alleged that, due to the representations of Nations Title, it had violated Section 5 of the FTC Act, as well as the privacy rule of GLB.

The settlement required Nations Title to not make further alleged misrepresentations regarding the privacy, confidentiality, and integrity of personal information collected from or about consumers, and also required Nations Title to implement a comprehensive data security program that was appropriate under the safeguards rule. There were, as is typical in these settlements, an audit requirement, document disclosure and retention requirements, and required certification of the audit. Finally, the settlement agreement required Nations Title not to violate the disposal rule, which came into effect before the settlement.

15:42. Safeguards enforcement cases—In the Matter of American United Mortgage Company

In this matter,[59] the FTC alleged that United Mortgage violated the disposal rule, which, as noted in chapter 10 requires the appropriate disposal of credit reports, as well as the safeguards rule. Additionally, the FTC alleged that the company failed to provide adequate privacy notices as required by GLB. The resolution required American United to commit no further violations of the disposal, safeguards, and privacy rules and to have certified audits from an appropriately qualified third party. The resolution also required document retention and disclosure to the FTC in a manner that is typical in these matters, as well as the payment of $50,000 civil penalty.

This case is notable in that it was the first safeguards case that obtained a civil penalty, but not the first data security case to do so. It also was the FTC's first disposal rule case.

15:43. Safeguards enforcement cases—In the Matter of Premier Capital Lending, Inc.

In this matter,[60] the FTC alleged that Premier Capital Lending violated the safeguards rule because it allowed a number of activities that violated the safeguards rule. These activities included allowing a home seller to use its account for accessing credit reports for certain purposes without taking reasonable steps to verify the home seller's procedures to handle, store, or dispose of sensitive personal information; failing to assess the risks of allowing a third party to access credit reports through its account; failing to take reasonable steps to review the requests that were made through its account; and failing to assess the scope of credit report information that was stored and accessible in its account. This problem was compounded by the fact that a hacker breached the home seller's computer and obtained Premier Capital's user name and password to obtain and access over 400 credit reports through Premier's account.

The FTC alleged that Superior violated Section 5 of the FTC Act, as well as the safeguards rule due to its alleged conduct. The Section 5 claim resulted from the fact

---

59.   http://www.ftc.gov/os/caselist/0623103/index.shtm (last visited March 29, 2011).

60.   http://www.ftc.gov/os/caselist/0723004/index.shtm (last visited March 29, 2011).

that Premier made representations in its privacy policy that the FTC believed were not true in light of the alleged conduct.

The settlement agreement required Premier to commit no further violations of Section 5 of the FTC Act, including making deceptive claims about privacy and security, and required the company to comply with the safeguards rule, including by implementing a comprehensive data information security plan. The settlement also included standard terms regarding auditing and certification, document retention, and disclosure, and other typical terms.

15:44. Safeguards enforcement cases—In the Matter of James B. Nutter & Company

In this matter[61] the respondent was alleged to have violated the safeguards rule of GLB. The respondent was alleged to make and service single-family residential mortgage loans in the United States and, in connection with that business, collect sensitive personal information from or about customers, including name, social security number, date of birth, and many other forms of personal information. The respondent allegedly failed to take certain actions, including that it did not develop, implement, and maintain a comprehensive written information security program; did not implement reasonable policies and procedures in areas such as employee training in safeguarding personal information; stored personal information in clear readable text on its computer network, creating an unnecessary risk to the information; did not employ sufficient measures to prevent or detect unauthorized access to personal information on its computer network or to conduct security investigations, such as monitoring and controlling connections between the network and the internet or regularly reviewing activity on the network; did not assess risks to the personal information it collected and stored on its computer network and in paper files; and provided back-up tapes containing personal information in clear readable text to a third-party service provider but did not require the service provider by contract to protect the security and confidentiality of the information.

The FTC alleged that an intruder was able to directly access the respondent's network and send spam messages out, and the FTC also alleged that the notices the respondent provided failed to make certain necessary disclosures, including the following: failing to set out respondent's security practices; failing to accurately inform customers that respondent disclosed customer information to third parties, such as credit reporting agencies; and informing customers that they had 30 days in which to exercise their opt-out rights, even though the privacy rule provides that they can opt out at any time during the course of their loans. The FTC also alleged that the respondent failed to meet the requirements of the safeguards rule.

The matter was resolved via consent decree, which contained standard requirements and reporting.

---

61. http://www.ftc.gov/os/caselist/0723108/index.shtm (last visited March 29, 2011).

Practice Pointer—Avoiding FTC action

Closely monitoring the types of information collected, as well as the privacy promises that are being made, is key to avoiding FTC enforcement action. Also, if information covered by other federal legislation is being collected, monitoring compliance with these laws is of critical importance. Avoiding deceptive statements in advertising is also important because these deceptive statements can trigger FTC action as well.

15:45. The FTC's new guidelines on protecting personal information

In 2007 the FTC published "Protecting Personal Information: A Guide for Business."[62] There are five key principles in the guide:

- Take stock
- Scale down
- Lock it
- Pitch it
- Plan ahead

15:46. The FTC's new guidelines on protecting personal information—Take stock

This principle is the starting point of the guidance, and it focuses on an important factor—assessing what information your company collects. It also includes analyzing how information flows occur in your company, so that a true assessment of security can occur after this information is gathered. This includes doing an inventory of all hardware systems that store sensitive data, tracking personal information by talking with those that have access to the information, including sales and marketing, IT, HR and accounting, as well as others such as third-parties that access sensitive data.

Taking stock also includes assessing who sends personal information to your business, how your business receives personal information, what kind of information is collected at each collection point, where is the information stored, and who has access or could have access to the information.

Given their value to identity thieves, the FTC recommends paying particular attention to social security numbers, credit card or financial information, or other sensitive information.

15:47. The FTC's new guidelines on protecting personal information—Scale down

This principle focuses on reducing your company's data footprint. The FTC recommends not keeping, or even collecting, data where there is no legitimate business reason to do so. In addition to the reasons identified by the FTC, reducing your company's data

---

62. http://www.ftc.gov/bcp/edu/microsites/infosecurity/ (last visited March 29, 2011).

footprint also in many cases will reduce the number of laws you are subject to, thereby reducing the compliance burdens.

The FTC recommends only collecting social security numbers for lawful purposes, such as paying employee taxes, but not using them as an employee or customer identification number.

15:48. The FTC's new guidelines on protecting personal information—Lock it

The FTC also recommends properly securing sensitive personally identifiable information. Though electronic breaches get significant attention, the FTC correctly notes that many data losses occur with paper records.

Paying attention to physical security can help solve these issues. Locking away media, paper or electronic, that contains personally identifiable information is recommended. Having protocols to ensure that employees put sensitive information away at appropriate times, including at the end of a workday, is also recommended, as is implementing appropriate access controls to your physical environment. Limiting access to offsite storage and encrypting information when it is transported is also recommended.

Electronic, or technical, security is also covered by this guide. Identifying the servers or other areas where sensitive electronic information is stored is recommended, as is doing a vulnerability analysis of systems and connections, particularly against common attacks. If possible, storing sensitive information on a computer that is not connected to the Internet is also identified as a step to take to secure information, as is encrypting information that is sent to a third party over a public network or stored on removable media or a computer network. The FTC also suggests that thought be given to encrypting e-mails where sensitive information is sent. Doing due diligence on your computer systems is also recommended. Scanning for vulnerabilities and closing unnecessary ports are also identified by the FTC, as is using Secure Sockets Layer protocols when transmitting credit card information or other financial information. Having adequate password management is also identified as an important factor, as is providing training to employees regarding potential fraudulent activities and steps they can take to secure information. Due diligence also includes running background checks on employees that will have access to sensitive information and making employees sign a policy stating that they will follow your company's policies. Assessing which employees have access to sensitive data is also recommended.

The FTC also recommends restricting devices with removable media (including limiting the use of laptops) and the types of data stored on such devices.

The FTC also suggests that companies consider using an intrusion detection system and maintain a central log of security-related information so that monitoring and spotting suspicious activities is facilitated.

Investigating the security practices of third parties who receive sensitive information is also recommended by the FTC.

15:49. The FTC's new guidelines on protecting personal information—Pitch it

This principle focuses on data destruction. Not surprisingly, the FTC recommends that reasonable appropriate data destruction programs be put in place, because the failure to destroy data can facilitate identity theft. This may include shredding of paper records, as well as wiping electronic devices. Making sure that employees who work remotely follow these policies is also important. The FTC does note that the type of regime put in place depends upon the type of data, as well as other factors.

15:50. The FTC's new guidelines on protecting personal information—Plan ahead

The FTC suggests that a company have an incident response plan in place before a security breach happens. It also recommends that companies immediately disconnect a compromised computer from the Internet and that investigations into security incidents start immediately. Planning out notification, both from an internal and external perspective, is also suggested.

15:51. The FTC and the U.S. SAFE WEB Act of 2006

The federal government recently enacted the U.S. SAFE WEB Act of 2006, which broadens the FTC's powers to combat international fraud, particularly fraud arising from spam and spyware and other Internet conduct. There are a number of additions and changes to existing law that are discussed below.[63] These are important to note because they all intended to expand the FTC's powers.

The Act also purportedly clarified, and attempted to resolve, disputes about the FTC's jurisdiction to address foreign harms that impact U.S. citizens, as well as foreign frauds committed by U.S. citizens abroad. Section 5 of the Act attempts to make amendments to address these issues and "clarify" the FTC ability to address these harms.[64]

Sections 4 and 6 of the U.S. SAFE WEB Act expand the FTC's ability to share information with foreign law enforcement. The FTC now has greater powers to share confidential information in its possession in order to assist foreign law enforcement agencies in stopping fraud.[65] This was seen by the FTC as an expansion of authority that was similar to expansions already granted to other federal agencies, including the SEC.

The FTC was also given the ability to conduct investigations and discovery in order to assist foreign law enforcement in matters, where appropriate.[66] This power was added to assist the FTC in stopping foreign-based frauds that are aimed at U.S. consumers.

---

63. For further information regarding this law, including a summary of the FTC's position, see, http://www.ftc.gov/reports/ussafeweb/Summary%20of%20US%20SAFE%20WEB%20Act.pdf, last visited March 7, 2011.
64. U.S. SAFE WEB Act § 3.
65. U.S. SAFE WEB Act §§ 4(a), 6(a).
66. U.S. SAFE WEB Act § 4(b).

In addition to clearing the way for information to be shared by the FTC, the Act also sets the stage for increased information flow to the FTC. Now, the FTC can protect information from disclosure if the foreign law enforcement agency insists on confidentiality as a condition to disclosure.[67]

The FTC also has been granted the ability to have increased confidentiality regarding investigations, in order to prevent the destruction of evidence or targets' moving money offshore.[68]

Like CAN-SPAM, the FTC is required to report to Congress within three years of the Act's passing regarding the FTC's use of its new authority, the number of law enforcement requests, statistics regarding the involvement of foreign law enforcement, as well as recommended reports regarding any new legislation that would assist the FTC.[69]

15:52. Advertising guidelines—The FTC's dot com disclosures

The FTC has provided specific guidance regarding how disclosures should be made on the Internet, particularly in the context of Internet advertising, and these are located on the FTC website.[70] The FTC offered several comments at the outset of these guidelines. First, it noted that the same consumer protection laws that apply to commercial activities in other media apply online. Second, it noted that the FTC Act's prohibition on "unfair or deceptive acts or practices" encompasses Internet advertising, marketing, and sales. In addition, the disclosure stated that many Commission rules and guides are not limited to any particular medium used to disseminate claims or advertising and therefore apply to online activities, and disclosures that are required to prevent an ad from being misleading, to ensure that consumers receive material information about the terms of a transaction or to further public policy goals, must be clear and conspicuous.

In evaluating whether disclosures are likely to be clear and conspicuous in online ads, advertisers should consider the placement of the disclosure in an ad and its proximity to the relevant claim. Additional considerations include the prominence of the disclosure; whether items in other parts of the ad distract attention from the disclosure; whether the ad is so lengthy that the disclosure needs to be repeated; whether disclosures in audio messages are presented in an adequate volume and cadence and visual disclosures appear for a sufficient duration; and whether the language of the disclosure is understandable to the intended audience.[71]

The FTC also offered guidance on how to make advertisements clear and conspicuous on the Internet, including that advertisers should do the following:

- place disclosures near, and when possible, on the same screen as the triggering claim;
- use text or visual cues to encourage consumers to scroll down a Web page when it is necessary to view a disclosure;

---

67. U.S. SAFE WEB Act § 6(b).

68. U.S. SAFE WEB Act § 7.

69. U.S. SAFE WEB Act § 13.

70. *See*, http://www.ftc.gov/bcp/edu/pubs/business/ecommerce/bus41.pdf, last visited March 7, 2011.

71. *Id.*

- when using hyperlinks to lead to disclosures
  - make the link obvious,
  - label the hyperlink appropriately to convey the importance, nature and relevance of the information it leads to,
  - use hyperlink styles consistently so that consumers know when a link is available,
  - place the hyperlink near relevant information and make it noticeable,
  - take consumers directly to the disclosure on the click-through page, and
  - assess the effectiveness of the hyperlink by monitoring click-through rates and make changes accordingly;
- recognize and respond to any technological limitations or unique characteristics of high tech methods of making disclosures, such as frames or pop-ups;
- display disclosures prior to purchase, but recognize that placement limited only to the order page may not always work;
- creatively incorporate disclosures in banner ads or disclose them clearly and conspicuously on the page the banner ad links to;
- prominently display disclosures so they are noticeable to consumers, and evaluate the size, color, and graphic treatment of the disclosure in relation to other parts of the Web page;
- review the entire ad to ensure that other elements—text, graphics, hyperlinks or sound—do not distract consumers' attention from the disclosure;
- repeat disclosures, as needed, on lengthy websites and in connection with repeated claims;
- use audio disclosures when making audio claims, and present them in a volume and cadence so that consumers can hear and understand them;
- display visual disclosures for a duration sufficient for consumers to notice, read, and understand them; and
- use clear language and syntax so that consumers understand the disclosures.[72]

The FTC also noted, not surprisingly, that the rules and guidance regarding the use of terms, though not specifically developed for the Internet, apply to Internet advertising.[73] This obviously also includes the FTC Act.[74]

There are also three key guidelines that the FTC has identified for advertisers, whether or not they advertise in cyberspace: (1) the advertising must be truthful and not mislead consumers; (2) advertisers must have evidence to substantiate their claims; and (3) advertisements cannot be unfair.[75] The FTC also suggests that advertisements be "clear and conspicuous." Consumers must be able to notice, read or hear, and understand the advertisement, including any disclaimers and disclosures.

There are also recommendations specific to online advertising on the FTC website, located at http://www.ftc.gov/bcp/guides/guides.htm. Those advertising in cyberspace

72. *Id.*
73. *Id.*
74. *Id.*
75. *Id.*

should consider a number of issues relative to advertising that include the placement of the disclosure in an ad and its proximity to the relevant claim, as well as the following: the prominence of the disclosure; whether items in other parts of the ad distract attention from the disclosure; whether the ad is so lengthy that the disclosure needs to be repeated; whether disclosures in audio messages are presented in an adequate volume and cadence and visual disclosures appear for a sufficient duration; and whether the language of the disclosure is understandable to the intended audience.

In addition, the FTC provided guidance on all of three of these requirements, but the clear and conspicuous requirement is notable. The FTC recommends reviewing the disclosures from the perspective of the reasonable consumer and determining how the disclosure is perceived in the overall context of the advertisement.[76]

Disclosures that are required to prevent deception—or to provide consumers material information about a transaction—must be presented "clearly and conspicuously" according to the guidance. Whether a disclosure meets this standard is measured by its performance—that is, how consumers actually perceive and understand the disclosure within the context of the entire ad. The key is the overall net impression of the ad—that is, whether the claims consumers take from the ad are truthful and substantiated.

The FTC suggests that advertisers, in reviewing their online ads, should adopt the perspective of a reasonable consumer. They also should assume that consumers do not read an entire website, just as they don't read every word on a printed page. In addition, it is important for advertisers to draw attention to the disclosure. Making the disclosure available somewhere in the ad so that consumers who are looking for the information might find it does not meet the clear and conspicuous standard, according to the FTC.

Even though consumers have control over what and how much information they view on websites, they may not be looking for—or expecting to find—disclosures as stated by the FTC. Advertisers, under the guidance, are responsible for ensuring that their messages are truthful and not deceptive. Accordingly, disclosures must be communicated effectively so that consumers are likely to notice and understand them.

The FTC noted that there is no set formula for determining whether an ad is clear and conspicuous, but that certain factors should be considered, including the following:

- the placement of the disclosure in an advertisement and its proximity to the claim it is qualifying;
- the prominence of the disclosure;
- whether items in other parts of the advertisement distract attention from the disclosure;
- whether the advertisement is so lengthy that the disclosure needs to be repeated;
- whether disclosures in audio messages are presented in an adequate volume and cadence and visual disclosures appear for a sufficient duration; and
- whether the language of the disclosure is understandable to the intended audience.[77]

---

76. *Id.*
77. *Id.*

In addition, the FTC has provided guidance regarding how requiring consumers to scroll through portions of a website impacts the assessment of a disclosure as truthful and not misleading.[78] Particularly for hyperlinking, the FTC recommends reviewing the labeling or description of the hyperlink; the consistency in the use of hyperlink styles; the hyperlink's placement and prominence on the Web page; and the handling of the disclosure on the click-through page.[79]

In light of some of the clickwrap cases, it is no surprise that the FTC recommends displaying disclosures to a consumer prior to purchase or a consumer's incurring a financial obligation.[80] This includes disclosure before a consumer clicks an "order now" or "add to shopping cart" button or link.[81]

There are also a number of other recommendations made by the FTC, including regarding banner advertisement disclosures that should be reviewed in order to understand the FTC's view of Internet advertising.[82]

15:53. Online behavioral advertising guidance

The FTC recently issued guidance regarding online behavior advertising, the *Online Behavioral Advertising: Moving the Discussion Forward to Possible Self-Regulatory Principles*. The FTC both defined what the practice is and identified five key principles regarding the practice.[83] According to the FTC online "behavioral advertising" means the tracking of a consumer's activities online including the searches the consumer has conducted, the web pages visited, and the content viewed in order to deliver advertising targeted to the individual consumer's interests.[84] The five key principles identified by the FTC are the following:

- transparency and consumer control;
- reasonable security, and limited retention for consumer data;
- affirmative express consent for material changes to existing privacy promises;
- affirmative express consent to (or prohibition against) using sensitive data for behavioral advertising; and
- using tracking data for purposes other than behavioral advertising (though this is a call for additional information).[85]

The FTC did not simply prohibit behavioral advertising because the FTC is seeking to balance support for such innovation with the need to protect against harms to consumers' privacy. Indeed, the FTC specifically noted that while behavioral advertising provides benefits to consumers, including in the form of free web content and

---

78. *Id.*

79. *Id.*

80. *Id.*

81. *Id.*

82. *Id.*

83. *See Online Behavioral Advertising: Moving the Discussion Forward to Possible Self-Regulatory Principles,* www.ftc.gov/os/2007/12/P859900stmt.pdf, last visited June 1, 2009.

84. *Id.*

85. *Id.*

personalized advertisements that consumers value, behavioral marketing is considered by some to be largely invisible and unknown to consumers.[86] The FTC noted other issues with consumers, including a lack of understanding of this type of marketing, as well as information security concerns related to harm to consumers if the data fell into the wrong hands. As a result, the FTC proposed the 5 principles noted above, and provided some guidance for businesses as they attempt to implement these principles via self-regulation.

15:54. Online behavioral advertising guidance— Principle 1—Transparency and consumer control

The FTC believes that every website that collects data for behavioral advertising should provide a clear, concise, consumer-friendly, and prominent statement that data about consumers' activities online is being collected at the site for use in providing advertising about products and services tailored to individual consumers' interests and that consumers can choose whether or not to have their information collected for this purpose.[87] One of the challenges noted by the FTC was the need to balance adequate disclosures with the need to make the disclosures easier for consumers to read. Also, the FTC noted that many consumers do not always read privacy policies, particularly if they are long and technical.

15:55. Online behavioral advertising guidance— Principle 2—Reasonable security, and limited data retention, for consumer data

The FTC proposed that companies that collect or store consumer data for behavioral advertising also provide reasonable security for that data. These protections should be based on the sensitivity of the data, the nature of a company's business operations, the types of risks a company faces, and the reasonable protections available to a company.[88] Additionally, as part of the data security issue, the FTC also recommended that companies make some effort to reduce the time period of data retention.

15:56. Online behavioral advertising guidance— Principle 3—Affirmative express consent for material changes to existing privacy promises

The retroactive modification principle has been a difficult one for companies to address. The FTC has stated that before a company can use data in a manner materially different from promises the company made when it collected the data, it should obtain affirmative express consent from affected consumers. The FTC specifically stated that this principle

---

86. *Id.*
87. *Id.*
88. *Id.*

would apply in a corporate merger situation to the extent that the merger creates material changes in the way the companies collect, use, and share data.[89]

While this provides some guidance, it would not completely appear to prohibit retroactive changes if notice is provided and it was made clear at the time of data collection that the company may materially change its data practices in the future, though it provides some support for the argument that companies cannot make material and retroactive changes to their privacy policies, even if the prior policy was based upon opt-out consent.

15:57. Online behavioral advertising guidance—Principle 4—Affirmative express consent to (or prohibition against) using sensitive data for behavioral advertising

While there may be people who desire to have behavioral advertising occur without affirmative express consent, there are issues, including the disclosure of sensitive information, that might make this not an attractive option for many consumers. The FTC has called for additional input on this issue.

15:58. Online behavioral advertising guidance—Principle 5—Using tracking data for purposes other than behavioral advertising

As with principle 4, the FTC called for additional information from groups and individuals on this issue. Among the particular concerns of the FTC was that secondary uses of this type of information are particularly invisible to consumers, and may be inconsistent with the consumers' reasonable expectations on the Internet.

On February 12, 2009 the FTC issued additional guidance, largely reaffirming its prior guidance, regarding behavioral advertising.[90]

---

89. *Id.*
90. *See* http://www.ftc.gov/os/2009/02/P085400behavadreport.pdf, last visited on April 7, 2009.

About the Authors

Andrew B. Serwin is the founding chair of Foley's Privacy, Security, and Information Management Practice and the Consumer Protection Practice and is a partner in the San Diego and Washington, D.C., offices of Foley & Lardner LLP. He also is the Executive Director of the Lares Institute, a think tank that focuses on emerging technology and information governance issues. Mr. Serwin recently ranked second on *Computerworld's* list of "Best Individual Privacy Advisers," and was named to Security Magazine's "25 Most Influential Industry Thought Leaders" for 2009, where he is the only law firm lawyer to receive this award. He is also ranked by Chambers USA – 2009–2011 in the area of National: Privacy & Data Security. He is the author of "Information Security and Privacy: A Guide to Federal and State Law and Compliance", which has been called *"the best privacy sourcebook*," and *"an indispensible resource for privacy professionals at all levels*."

Mr. Serwin previously served on the Publications Board for the American Bar Association's Business Law Section. He is a graduate of the University of San Diego School of Law (J.D., *cum laude*, 1995), where he was a member of the Order of the Coif. He earned his B.A. in political science, *cum laude*, from the University of California, San Diego in 1992.

Peter F. McLaughlin is senior counsel with Foley & Lardner LLP and a member of the firm's Privacy, Security & Information Management and Information Technology & Outsourcing Practices. He is also a member of the Health Care Industry Team and Privacy Litigation Task Force. As the former global privacy director and assistant general counsel of a Fortune 20 health care company, Mr. McLaughlin has specific experience in data privacy and security issues relevant to the health care sector as well as international privacy compliance.

In 2010, the *Legal 500* recognized Mr. McLaughlin's technology work in the area of data protection and privacy. Mr. McLaughlin received his J.D. from Georgetown Law Center in 1993 and was the senior articles editor for the journal, *Law & Policy in International Business*. He earned his B.A. from Columbia University in 1986.

Mr. McLaughlin is admitted to practice in Massachusetts and New York. He is a member of the American Bar Association (ABA) and is vice chair of the ABA Section of Science and Technology Law's Information Security Committee. For four years he was co-chair of the Privacy Security & Data Management subcommittee for the Business Law Section. He is also a member of the International Association of Privacy Professionals, the American Health Lawyers Association and its Health Information Technology Committee.

John Tomaszewski is TRUSTe's General Counsel and Corporate Secretary and is responsible for all of TRUSTe's legal affairs and for providing legal and business counsel to the Chief Executive Officer and the Board of Directors. He also ensures that the organization's online safety programs are built on a strong legal framework, and that TRUSTe's enforcement and compliance efforts are thorough, transparent, and defensible.

Prior to joining TRUSTe, Mr. Tomaszewski served as Chief Privacy Officer of CheckFree Corporation (now Fiserv) and has provided advice to companies on secure eCommerce while in private practice. He frequently lectures on secure e-commerce and public key infrastructure (PKI). He graduated from St. Mary's University School of Law in San Antonio, Texas, where he was the solicitations editor of the Law Journal. He completed his undergraduate work at the University of Texas at Austin.